Family Violence

by

Mildred Daley Pagelow

Department of Sociology
California State University

With the assistance of
Lloyd W. Pagelow

PRAEGER SPECIAL STUDIES • PRAEGER SCIENTIFIC

New York • Philadelphia • Eastbourne, UK
Toronto • Hong Kong • Tokyo • Sydney

Library of Congress Cataloging in Publication Data

Pagelow, Mildred Daley.
 Family violence.

 Bibliography: p.
 Includes index.
 1. Family violence. 2. Family violence — Prevention.
3. Child abuse. 4. Wife abuse. 5. Sex crimes. I. Title.
HQ809.P34 1984   362.8′2   84-8244
ISBN 0-275-91239-6 (alk. paper)
ISBN 0-275-91623-5 (pbk. : alk. paper)

Library of Congress Catalog Card Number: 84-8244
ISBN: 0-275-91623-5

First published in 1984

Praeger Publishers, 521 Fifth Avenue, New York, NY 10175
A division of Greenwood Press, Inc.

Printed in the United States of America

∞

The paper used in this book complies with the Permanent
Paper Standard issued by the National Information Standards
Organization (Z39.48-1984).

10 9 8 7 6 5 4

Preface

Family Violence brings together into one source many theoretical viewpoints and empirical findings from years of scientific research on all types of violent acts, actors, and victims. It was written for students, service providers, persons in law and criminal justice, and concerned members of the general public. It takes a cross-disciplinary approach to complex problems that have been investigated by professionals in a variety of fields. For the first time, people wanting to learn about family violence have a complete text available. There is a vast proliferation of written materials on this subject, but each one addresses a particular type of family violence such as child abuse and/or neglect, incest, wife beating, parent abuse, marital rape, and so forth. The task of gathering together the best of this literature is tremendous and time consuming. With this book, educators no longer have to independently research and analyze the literature, because *Family Violence* provides a realistic analysis of this body of work.

Further, the book's potential is not confined to the classroom. Professionals and paraprofessionals will find this a most useful source of reliable information which will help them grasp an overall picture. With this added insight, they should be better qualified to help their clients by comparing and contrasting issues they are most familiar with to other types of intrafamily violence. They will be better informed by seeing the total spectrum, less susceptible to accepting common myths and stereotypes about victims and abusers, and more able to effect knowledgeable identification, intervention, and prevention of the types of family violence with which they deal in their working lives. The current economic-political climate causes many of us to predict that violence, both in the home and in the streets, is going to greatly increase in the near future. This will result in demands from professionals and trainees in the human services fields for a better understanding of family violence, how to deal with it, and how to prevent it. As social programs are being cut back, people working in social service agencies will be required to develop greater expertise in human problems as they handle larger caseloads. With fewer workers and more clients, there will be less opportunity for specialization and more demand for the broader-based knowledge of generalists. This book helps fill that need: Problem families have multiple problems.

Family Violence is not a "how-to" book of handy techniques for one-to-one service providers, counselors, or field workers, nor is it intended as a self-help manual. Yet it is possible that some readers, through better understanding of family and interpersonal relations, will generate new ideas that are helpful in their own lives. This book is intended to help readers gain some understanding of intrafamily violence, while recognizing that *understanding* is not synonymous with *approval*. My purpose is to stimulate independent thinking so that on the basis of often conflicting evidence, the reader can draw his or her own conclusions while taking into account the influence of social, cultural, historical, economic, and political factors involved in individual behavior. In addition, this work should help the reader move beyond stereotypes, prejudices, "common sense" assumptions, judgmental reactions (those gut-level and subjective feelings based upon personal experiences), toward an ability to reach objective and logical conclusions based on knowledge. Lastly, this book should encourage the reader to put aside emotion as much as possible, recognizing that we cannot play God for others, because no one knows what each of us would do in someone else's situation—we can only speculate.

In researching and writing this book, great care was taken to avoid the narrow focus that can result from disciplinary chauvinism. Due to my professional training, I tend to approach all social problems from a sociological perspective, but a constant struggle was waged to maintain an eclectic, cross-disciplinary approach. If there is an occasional lapse, or an overemphasis on sociological research and theory in some places, I ask readers who do not share this background to be tolerant of the unintended bias.

The book is divided into seven parts containing 13 chapters in a logical sequence for the study of family violence. There is some overlap and repetition because there are so many interrelationships between types of violence. Many homes are battlegrounds where more than one war is waged.

Part I provides an overview. Chapter 1 explains the issue of family privacy and the unique problems of family violence research, definitions, and measurements. Frequency estimates are the focus of Chapter 2. Issues discussed in these first two chapters are raised again in later examinations of each category of family violence.

Part II introduces theories of family violence and explorations of causes. Chapter 3 examines commonalities among various types of family violence and factors frequently found associated with them, such as effects on victims as well as alcohol dependency. It includes proposals for building bridges between theory, research, and intervention. Chapter 4 offers more theories and exposes the prevalence and acceptance of violence in our society, which contributes to violence in intimate and familial relationships.

Part III focuses on physical abuse and neglect of children and psychological abuse and neglect. Chapter 5 gives a historical overview of attitudes and treatment of children by parents and society, the movement to protect children, and the "discovery" of child abuse. It introduces factors associated with maltreatment and other issues, such as violent methods of childrearing. Chapter 6 continues with child maltreatment, building from what research has discovered about abusers and victims, to some societal responses, and a few ideas about identification and intervention techniques. Chapters 5 and 6 concentrate on the more traditional focus of child abuse specialists and researchers: child maltreatment by commission and omission. Chapter 7 critically examines one of the most frequently mentioned ideas in the family violence literature: the "cycle of violence." Many have claimed that abused children become abusing parents, that child abuse leads youngsters into delinquency, and that spouse abuse and spouse victimization are long-term effects of child abuse. Empirical research is explored for evidence of a cycle.

Spouse abuse is the focus of Part IV. Chapter 8 begins with the growth of the battered women's movement, examines the question of battered husbands, and provides a historical overview of marriage. It looks at violence between dating and cohabiting couples and poses questions about why increased intimacy is associated with increased violence. In Chapter 9 the major research on woman battering is introduced and appraised. Some ways to identify women who are being abused by spouses are presented, along with assistance that may be offered, and features commonly found among abusers. Reeducation programs for violence men are also discussed.

Part V deals with seldom discussed topics: violence by children, abuse of adolescents, and parent abuse. A look at the other side of the coin reveals that some children are violent to family members. Beyond the range of child abuse committed during the "tender years"—the focus of most child abuse research and advocacy—is the abuse of somewhat older children by their families and nonrelatives. Finally, abuse of elderly parents by their adult children/caretakers is a newly emerging social problem. The kinds of abuse that occur are discussed and some ideas for their prevention are offered.

Sexual abuse in the family is the focus of Part VI. Incest is addressed first in Chapter 11; detection, intervention, and attitudes toward offenders are discussed. A growing movement demanding "children's sexual liberation" is described as a "pro-incest lobby." Chapter 12 addresses marital rape, an issue studied by only a few scientists because until very recently, there was no such thing as marital rape under the law. The chapter concludes with an examination of pornography and its relationship to incest and marital rape.

The final section of this work looks at the present and future states of family violence. Chapter 13 summarizes the serious problems facing families today, and what may (or must) be done to alleviate some of them. It includes intervention strategies and long-range prevention strategies. The subject of family violence would certainly be depressing unless some vision is to be developed for nonviolent families. Social scientists maintain that since societies are created by people, societies can also be changed by people. Violence in the family is not inevitable, but it can only be prevented through concerted efforts by large segments of the population, individually and collectively. Therefore, some suggestions on what individuals can do are offered. It is hoped that *Family Violence* will in some small way act as a catalyst for others to begin working toward the creation of nonviolent families in a nonviolent society.

Sincere thanks are due to many people who assisted in various ways in the struggle to research and write this book, but to name a few might appear that I am ungrateful to many others who are not named individually. To all of you, please understand that I am grateful for your support and encouragement, scholarly suggestions, and criticisms. For example, librarians are the backbone of all archival research, and I owe many of the staff at California State University, Fullerton and Long Beach, a debt of gratitude for their dedication and tenacity in tracking down books, articles, and government publications. Special thanks must go to Brooke Allison, whose request for a "state of the art" of theory, research, and findings in family violence for the California Commission on Crime Control and Violence Prevention provided the germinal idea for this work.

Heartfelt appreciation must be expressed for the loving assistance and support given by my partner, Lloyd W. Pagelow, who maintained calm strength during trying times, and steadfastly labored over the references and authors' index, letting his cherished garden grow over in weeds. A husband who gives so much time, energy, and skill toward reaching goals not his own deserves public recognition and special tribute. Thank you, Lloyd.

Table of Contents

List of Tables

PART I

Overview

1

The Study of Family Violence

INTRODUCTION

Most Americans cling to an image of the family that includes tranquillity, happiness, love between members bound together by blood and/or legal ties, certainty of behavior, shared norms and values, rituals, and, above all else, *safety*. Even if our own family experiences do not match up to the idealistic images of the family, most of us are inclined to believe that we are the exceptions to the rule and that our closest relatives marched to a different drummer than all our neighbors. Even if we have a family that is less than the cultural ideal, we continue to view the world beyond the family unit as having far more negative features and certainly more danger. Until recently, when people thought of crime, they visualized crime in the streets, in the marketplace, or in politics. The term "violent crime" stirred thoughts of muggings, robberies, rape, and assaults—in other words, crime in the streets—violent acts performed by strangers.

Most people continue to embrace the notion that the nuclear family unit represents love, mutual protection, and security, despite the fact that the media has increasingly shown the "underside" (Adler 1981) of family life. Writers are increasingly stressing the fact that the home is a dangerous place: More violent crimes occur in the home than outside its doors, and more violence occurs between family members than among strangers (Borland 1976; Dobash and Dobash 1978, 1979; Freeman 1979; Martin 1976; Walker 1979). The family is a basic institution of society, which has existed in its present form for several centuries, with a few voices heard now and then decrying the violence within (Cobbe 1878; Mill 1971). However, violence between family members has only recently become recognized as a serious social problem by scientists, legislators, educators, medical practitioners, and some of the general public; and this recognition has largely been due to the writings of a few concerned individuals (Fontana 1964; Goode 1969; Helfer and Kempe 1968; Kempe et al. 1962;

Marriages begin with vows to love and honor "until death us do part," and most couples cannot even imagine that their new lives together will bring anything other than continued love and happiness. Some will reach their goals of living together peacefully, producing children, and growing older with their children in an intact family. Most do not realize that conflict is inevitable between family members, and few have learned effective methods of conflict resolution. Unfortunately, many families that begin with romantic notions become embroiled in conflicts and abuses of power, and the home becomes a private arena of violence.

Source: Roland Hiltscher Photography, Fullerton, California.

Straus 1973). Some others have looked closely at the history of the family and found that the very structure of the family is conducive to violence (Davidson 1978; Dobash and Dobash 1979; Gelles 1979; Pleck 1979). It is important to question why it has taken so long for us to acknowledge this problem.

Living in the privacy of our own homes tends to restrict our vision of others' lives. How can children know how they should be raised? By what standards do we judge our own parents, our siblings, or our closest relatives? Do we know whether we are "spoiled" or "deprived" children when we are growing up in our unique environment? When we visit the homes of our peers, we think we gain some insight into our friends' families, but how can we be sure that what we experience is indicative of every day reality or a facade created for company? Many people reading this book formed their own ideas of family life from media images of families, which they saw as the ideal against which to compare their own realities. Adults who grew up with massive doses of "The Waltons," "Eight is Enough," repeats of "The Brady Bunch," and reruns of the "Andy Hardy" movie series formed their earliest impressions of what families are, or should be, based on these programs or similar media presentations. Even if real life experiences compared unfavorably with media images, it was difficult not to cling to the notions of wise and loving wives and husbands; mothers and fathers who are always available to lovingly assist children in their problems; and attractive, courteous, obedient, and charming children who made mistakes but always came out "winners" by the conclusion of the program or movie. Well-fed, well-clothed, well-housed people, surrounded by loving family members of no more than two generations—that is the ideal type image we maintain of the family—despite personal and scientific evidence that this may well be a rarity, rather than the norm. We cling tenaciously to this image, a "myth of the idealized family," because it offers comfort.

Some readers will insist that their own families are more like the ideal type than some of the troubled families that are revealed in the pages of this book. Families can be either loving or cruel, and sometimes the same families are both, alternating between caring and supportive, or mean and vindictive relationships. There are certain unique features of family life that can add to the quality and intimacy of relationships, or can produce or stimulate conflict between members. Some of these features include (1) time at risk; (2) broad range of activities and interests; (3) intensity of involvement; (4) impinging activities; (5) right to influence; (6) age and sex discrepancies; (7) ascribed roles; (8) family privacy; (9) involuntary membership; and (10) high level of stress. These features have been noted by family sociologists Murray Straus and Richard Gelles in separate and coauthored articles (Gelles 1979; Gelles and Straus 1979; Straus 1978). Gelles (1979, 14) added an eleventh factor: extensive knowledge of social biographies.

Examination of these unique characteristics of the family shows that they can have positive or negative effects on relationships between members. The first, time at risk, means that the ratio of time spent with family members is usually greater than with others beyond the home. The time parents spend with children and encouraging their development can produce strong, loving bonds, but if the time spent is viewed as an infringement on personal rights or unwelcome duty, the level of conflict can grow to the point of hostility or violence. The second characteristic, range of activities and interests, can include family events that vary from informal picnics or outings at the beach, to formal weddings or home dinner parties for important guests. The same behavior by a spouse or child that creates laughter and family harmony at the beach may easily be viewed negatively in another setting. For example, a spouse's clowning or joking, or a child's clumsiness in an informal setting can produce very different reactions on a formal occasion. The third characteristic, intensity of involvement, can produce both positive and negative results. When a newlywed couple visits one set of in-laws or attends a business affair, the appearance each makes can evoke feelings of pride or shame for the other.[1] The idea of "the other half" is a close approximation of how many people view their spouses—as reflections on themselves.

The fourth characteristic, impinging activities, can lead to harmony when couples share the same musical tastes and liking for cultural activities (Straus 1978). But if one person enjoys cocktail parties while the other hates them but likes soccer games and each insists upon the other's company, someone wins and someone loses or they both end up disgruntled and possibly hostile. A family sitting around the living room, enjoying a television program together, can provide amiable feelings of closeness and comfort. However, witness the bitter feuds that can erupt when someone walks in and changes channels. When enough of these win/lose situations occur, even a trivial disagreement can flare into violence in some families.

The right to influence, the fifth characteristic, can be seen in the pride some parents take in their children's behavior or achievements, which fosters bonds of closeness. But when children do not fulfill parental expectations (or one spouse's expectations of the other spouse's behavior), the result can be intense hostility and resentment over such matters as the choice of associates, academic achievement, career choices, or religious beliefs and attendance. Seeing objectionable table manners of someone sitting nearby in a restaurant can be dealt with by ignoring it or by avoiding it by leaving, but if offensive manners are displayed by a family member, scolding, yelling, or slapping may result. The sixth feature of family life, age and sex differences, refers to the comingling of younger and older, and people of both sexes, in the same households, which can provide a rich and full mixture of people with broadly different experiences, tastes, and lifestyles. On the other hand, these same differences can lead to conflict, particularly when they involve abuses of power differentials, since the family traditionally allocates power in a hierarchical structure in which older members (parents) generally have more power than younger members, and males have more power than females.

The seventh characteristic, ascribed roles, refers to the fact that family members are expected to perform certain tasks and behave in certain ways, whether or not they have the desire or ability to do so. If each person fits the role that is arbitrarily assigned him or her, there is a certain comfort in conforming, but if not, there may be resistance and resentment, possibly leading to conflict. Family privacy, the eighth factor, allows loving family members to demonstrate affection physically and verbally, yet disagreements that might be controlled or arbitrated outside the family can flare up and intensify into violence inside the home. Involuntary membership, the ninth feature of family life, is more difficult to define as a positive feature of the family, yet there are some examples, such as when a child is born who does not meet expectations of parents (lacking the desired physical appearance or condition, sex, or creative talents), but the child is lovingly accepted anyhow. On the other hand, if there is incompatibility, it is usually impossible for children to divorce their parents or parents to divorce their children, and sometimes it is perceived as impossible for spouses to even consider divorcing each other. Even after a divorce, parents may continue to have contacts and conflicts with each other because of their bonds to their children.

Stress in the family, the tenth feature, has both positive and negative aspects. For example, stress from economic strain can provide strong motivation for academic or career success, or stress from a child's school underachievement can draw parents together to resolve the problem. If one works in a high-productivity setting, the illness of a coworker can cause extra stress and work, but at the end of the day, this burden can be tabled until the next work day. On the other hand, if a family member is ill, this can cause 24-hour-a-day stress and extra work until recovery is complete. Unemployment, accidents, and death cause unique stresses in families, as well as transitions throughout the life cycle, such as the birth of a child, the last leaving home, and retirement.

The factor noted by Gelles (1979), extensive knowledge of social biographies, can be one of the most positive features of intimate relationships: being open and honest with loved ones, dropping pretense, and revealing ourselves to them as we dare not do with anyone else. Dating relationships usually involve a process of self-revelation and sharing secrets as intimacy grows: letting the other know our likes, dislikes, fears, successes, and failures. However, during an argument each party knows exactly where the "Achilles heel" of the other lies, and unfortunately, many times that is exactly where they strike.

This book deals with the negative side of these unique features of the family. Some students have reacted with anger and defensiveness at exposing the darker side of intimate relationships, saying they do not even know of families where violence occurs. Why not concentrate on the strengths of the family and the beauties of loving relationships? Others even see such exposure as being an attack on the family. Why should we concentrate on such a depressing subject? There are two reasons for doing so.

First, learning about both sides of family relations is helpful in specific ways. It helps us to understand how loving ties can disintegrate into violence; how others interact in ways that are dysfunctional for themselves, their families, and all of society; and through that understanding, learn how to protect ourselves from violence in our intimate relationships. All persons growing up in this society are inundated with positive messages about the family; what a source of joy and contentment it is. Those who live in strong families already know what support, comfort, and affection relatives can offer each other. But we now know that untold millions of people, who are not so lucky, live lives of violence and horror behind closed doors. Nevertheless, many people react adversely to this new but extremely uncomfortable knowledge by trying to deny it, or by insisting that the facts and figures that fill the pages of this book are exaggerations. Some simply are not able to address the issues squarely and opt to avoid them. One writer has eloquently dealt with the human tendency to respond in certain ways to suffering, pain, misery, and obvious injustice (Lerner 1980). Social psychologist Melvin Lerner calls it a *Belief in a Just World,* and says that this belief is inextricably bound up with a person's motives and goals; therefore:

> People want to and have to believe they live in a just world so that they can go about their daily lives with a sense of trust, hope, and confidence in their future. If it is true that people want or need to believe that they live in a world where people get what they deserve, then it is not surprising that they will find ways, other things being equal, to interpret events to fit this belief. (Lerner 1980, 14)

Based on studies of human behavior, Lerner points out that people get sad, unhappy, angry, and upset when they see others' suffering, and because they develop a *sense of injustice,* they create defensive strategies to deal with perceived injustice to reduce their own pain. These include denial/withdrawal, or they may reinterpret the event, the outcome, the cause, or finally, the character of the victim (Lerner 1980, 14–21).

If denial/withdrawal is the chosen tactic, we can turn away in disgust, refusing to look inside those doors, and the human misery will continue and flourish in isolation. We can insist that the problem is not our own, but the fact is that private misery has a way of slipping out the front door: into the school yards, streets, hospitals, workplaces, courts, morgues, and prisons. It can affect our private lives and associations; we can become victims of violence or violent persons ourselves; people we care about can become victims or abusers; and even if we manage to insulate ourselves from all else, nevertheless, we must pay for its costs through our taxes.

The second reason for tackling such a depressing topic and avoiding a head-in-the-sand attitude is that family violence can be reduced or prevented, and the problems of victims ameliorated. Becoming experts on the subject of family violence requires certain characteristics of individuals: A most important one is an underlying faith in the basic goodness of people. It is easier if one has a personal philosophy that insists that the vast majority of humans are born with wide-ranging capacities for love and hate, goodness and evil, selfishness and selflessness. It is easier to maintain this philosophy if we do *not* believe we come into this world already stamped with immutable personality traits, or that the bestial nature of humanity must be constantly repressed in order to maintain the facade of civilization we have attained. Rather, we can cling to the notion that learning is a lifelong process, and what we learn and unlearn is controlled to a great extent by our environment, including the people around us. Even though some people learn to be violent, or a society condones or rewards violence, there will always be a majority of people who struggle against violence. It may be a long and difficult task, but only by direct examination of violence in intimate familial relationships can we learn something about its causes, effects, and possible cures.

This work is developed out of a concern to gather together the research, theories, and reports on all forms of family violence so that readers can gauge the "state of the art" of our knowledge. However, the task does not stop there because there is so little agreement among professionals about family violence, because approaches to research are vastly different, and because many reports are distinctly contradictory in their theoretical assumptions and findings. Scientific analysis of the various works in the literature is extremely important. Such works must be carefully scrutinized and if they contain shortcomings, these must be pointed out so that readers can bear them in mind when the authors present their findings and conclusions. Research reports must be examined for their theoretical assumptions, research design, methods employed, and generalizability and validity of findings. In other words, were rigorous scientific methods used so that findings are believable, or are they little more than hunches or educated guesses? As for *generalizability,* it depends on sample selection whether findings can be true for the population as a whole (such as all American families or all battered children), or limited to only the group studied (a psychiatrist's patients or a volunteer group of battered women staying at shelters). *Validity* refers to whether or not researchers measured the concept they thought they were measuring. For example in studying "abuse," are the injuries accidental or intentional, and in studying "aggression," are the behaviors meant to inflict harm or are they forceful but without malice?

In the social sciences, there are no laws. Scholars can propose theories, and these theories may be tested, but we cannot prove a theory. Research can only offer support. If repeated testing offers strong support to a theory, we can conclude that the evidence is sound and the explanation is useful. If empirical tests offer no support, we may reject the theory and begin looking for other explanations. But sometimes the tests themselves are problematic. Tests may be inadequate for the task; they may not measure what they are designed to measure, or sample selection may introduce biases.

To serve its purpose this book required careful analysis of the material presented. Sometimes this study may seem to deal more critically than usual with issues. Some of this comes from the writer's sociological background and may be explained by introducing some words written by sociologist Peter Berger in his brief but insightful *Invitation to Sociology: A Humanistic Perspective* (1963). Berger, explaining why we teach sociology to college students, says:

> There is . . . a peculiar problem for the sociologist that is directly related to the debunking, disenchanting character of sociology. . . . What right does any man [professor] have to shake the taken-for-granted beliefs of others? Why educate young people to see the precariousness of things they had assumed to be absolutely solid? Why introduce them to the subtle erosion of critical thought? Why, in sum, not leave them alone? (1963, 174)

Berger later provides the answer to his own questions when he says: ". . . sociology is justified by the belief that *it is better to be conscious than unconscious and that consciousness is a condition of freedom.* To attain a greater measure of awareness, and with it of freedom, entails a certain amount of suffering and even risk" (1963, 175, emphasis added). It is Berger's contention that exposure to the form of critical thought called sociology helps people become a bit less content with prejudices, a little more skeptical, and perhaps more compassionate.

If some readers find that taken-for-granted ideas are challenged, research and theories are critiqued, findings are viewed skeptically, much of what the experts say is debunked, and questions are posed without answers but only lead to more questions—all of this is done without apology. If people want uncritical acceptance of common ideas about family violence, they are advised to turn elsewhere: to newspapers, magazine racks, popular fiction, and the television screen. This book promises to challenge more than one firmly held belief because its purpose, like education, is to examine "common sense" ideas and stimulate independent thought. Readers are invited to read it as critically as it is written, to examine issues and ideas from different sides, and then come to their own conclusions. *That* is true scholarship!

PROBLEMS IN STUDYING FAMILY VIOLENCE

Family violence is one area of family living that has not only remained in the shadows; it has actually stayed behind locked doors until very recently. In one of the early articles about family violence, social scientist John E. O'Brien (1971) notes that little scientific research appeared to have concentrated on this issue, saying:

> [I]n the *Index* for all editions of the *Journal of Marriage and the Family,* from its inception in 1939 through 1969, not a single article can be found which contains the word "violence" in the title. During that same period, discussions and studies of "conflict" in the family were quite common. But apparently violence, as such, was either assumed to be too touchy an issue for research or else thought to be so idiosyncratic as to be unimportant as a feature in "normal" families. (O'Brien 1971, 692)

O'Brien touched on two reasons for the avoidance of discussing or researching family violence by the professional community; it appears that it was both "too touchy an issue" and that there was an assumption that it was relatively rare, occurring only in "abnormal" families. But there are other reasons, some of which are discussed by sociologists Suzanne Steinmetz and Murray Straus in the introduction to their 1974 reader. They point out that violence is an everyday occurrence in the family, yet:

> To describe the family in this way is jarring for most of us, since our view and hopes for the family define it as an arena for love and gentleness rather than as a place for violence. As a result,

> it is extremely difficult to see what is actually going on in the
> family. We tend to overlook the violence which occurs there.
> Or, if it cannot be ignored, we tend to repress the memory of
> it. (Steinmetz and Straus 1974, 3)

These writers note several myths about the family, one of which is the "psychopathology myth" that O'Brien refers to above. *Psychopathology* refers to abnormal behavior engaged in by people who are mentally deranged. Another, termed "the myth of the idealized family," was referred to earlier. Steinmetz and Straus (1974, 7) point out the necessity of maintaining such a social myth, saying that it is strengthened and supported to preserve the important social institution of the family. They note that, "This ideology helps encourage people to marry and to stay married. [But] . . . at the same time, the semisacred nature of the family has prevented an objective analysis of the exact nature of intra-familial violence" (Steinmetz and Straus 1974, 7).

Every other institution of our society helps to support the family by associating it with the ideals of love, gentleness, consensus, and harmony. For example, the unmarried political office seeker is disadvantaged compared to the candidate (usually male) who distributes campaign photographs showing himself surrounded by a smiling and an obviously happy and loving wife and children. The clergyman who advertises that "the family that prays together stays together" and churches that give God's blessings to marriages and children, all represent religion's interest in maintaining the idealized family image. Business constantly reinforces the image in advertising and products. Children learn to read from books showing the adventures of nuclear families almost totally devoid of problems that beset most families at some point in time: the harsh realities of family living such as illness, death and dying, quarrels within and outside the home, and so forth. Each institution, politics, religion, economics, and education, does its share to promote the myth.

Regardless of how these common ideas have been maintained, the question remains: Why has it taken so long for scholars to recognize and investigate the terror and pain of so many people suffering within this "near sacred" institution? Even a brief reading of the literature of the family in history clearly shows that violence and brutality are not space age inventions, but have been a part of the family's fabric from the very beginning (Dobash and Dobash 1979; Radbill 1974). Steinmetz and Straus (1974, 17) called violence a "tabooed aspect" of the family, and were in the forefront of the new scholarship that determined to look at violence in a realistic way. They felt that the popularized myths about the family had prevented people from looking closely at the family and taking steps to change it and correct some of its problems.

It is difficult to relinquish old, cherished ideal images. It is probably due more to the human tendency to cling to the myth of the idealized family rather than from any deliberate effort to pretend or cover-up that the myth remained unchallenged as long as it has. However, even when we determine that we will look with objective, scientific eyes for the truth, there are unique problems associated with the study of family violence. Clearly the issue of family privacy is foremost.

Family Privacy

Some people believe that the institution of the family must resist the intrusion of outside forces to protect its members, while others believe that family members need outside forces to protect them. Part of the reason for "selective inattention" (Dexter 1958) by researchers and the public to family violence is the concept of family privacy. This is exemplified in the inscription over the doors of the New York City Family Court, "The Sanctity of the Home and Integrity of the Family" (Kremen 1976, 4). Many writers have addressed the serious question of constitutional rights of individual families and family members from two opposite viewpoints. On the one side are those who insist that the state has no right to interfere in the private lives of its citizens; that anyone who would violate the sanctity of the home is antifamily. Extremists in this position infer that advocates of public concern for, and possible control of, behaviors within the family unit are bent on destroying our most sacred institution. They insist that no one should "invade the domestic forum or go behind the curtain" (a judicial decision quoted by Eisenberg and Micklow 1977). A North Carolina court decided in 1874 that it is better to "draw the curtain and shut out the public gaze" (Davidson 1977a, 19), an idea that many people still accept.

Some of the insistence on maintaining family privacy is based on the historical establishment of patriarchal marriage and common law rights and privileges. Patriarchy is the system of family relations where men are the undisputed heads of a household and other family members are subordinate to them and must defer to their wishes and commands. The patriarch has absolute rights and power over wife and children, who are to serve and obey without question. Describing the position early British law took toward the autocratic patriarchal family structure, Margaret May (1978, 138) says: "The child's duty was that of 'unquestioning obedience,' the wife's to 'submit' and 'defer' to her husband's rule." When we speak of common law, we refer to decisions based on customs of the people, or what judges believe their communities feel is correct (Davidson 1977a). Both the patriarchal family structure and common law are part of the English heritage adopted in America (Davidson 1977a, 18; Dobash and Do-bash 1979, 60).

A sociologist who has done extensive research on marriage and sex roles, Lenore Weitzman, begins her book on marriage contracts by stating: "Blackstone, the renowned English legal scholar, described marriage under the common law of England as the merger of husband and wife into a single legal identity" (1981, 1)—and, as many writers and lawyers have quipped since—"that *one* is the husband!" In fact, both British and American law refused to acknowledge that women were even persons (Sachs and Wilson 1978; Schulder 1970). Blackstone had decreed that the "very being" of a woman was suspended during marriage, with the result that there remained only the husband (Kanowitz 1969). Under common law, wives had no right to sell, sue, or contract without their husbands' approval (Sachs and Wilson 1978). As recently as 1966, the Supreme Court upheld the common law regarding a wife's unpaid debt and a bank lost its suit to collect; dissenting Justice Black stated, "This rule [coventure] has worked out in reality to mean that though the husband and wife are one, the one is the husband. This fiction rested on [the] . . . notion that a married woman, being a female, is without capacity to make her own contracts and do her own business" (cited in Schulder 1970, 165).

This merger of two persons into one has long been defended as the rationale for immunity from testifying against a spouse in court, suing a spouse in court, or why there could be no legal recognition of spousal rape. After all, how, if the two are one, can a person be forced to testify against him or her self in violation of the Fifth Amendment? Or sue one's own self? Or rape one's own body? The idea is explained in these words: "The reasoning followed that since the husband and wife were legally one, the law would not allow one person to sue himself. This view of the merging of the spouses was primarily a political move to settle property claims . . ." (Calvert 1974, 90).

While the purpose for these laws of spousal immunity may have been based on financial and property benefits for husbands, they also protected husbands from suits for battery. Even when wives began to gain some property rights with the passage of the *Married Women's Property Acts* before and after the American Civil War, they were still excluded from suing husbands for abuse. As Leo Kanowitz notes in his textbook on *Women and The Law:*

> [T]he new reason for denying them [spouses] the right to sue one another for personal injuries was allegedly to prevent damage to domestic tranquility. . . . A husband could beat his wife mercilessly, . . . but the law in its rectitude denied her the

right to sue her husband because such a suit, it claimed, could destroy the peace of the home. (1969, 77–78)

In the face of such reasoning, it is no wonder that what occurred in the family has historically been shielded from public and legal scrutiny. How all this applies to parent/child relations and child abuse will be made abundantly clear in Chapter 3, but it should be noted that under the hierarchical, patriarchal family, children and wives were considered property of the head of the family. They were, in fact, chattels of their masters (Dobash and Dobash 1979).

One of the strongest statements defending family privacy against state intrusion, written by law professor Hugo E. Martz (1979) was titled "Indiana's Approach to Child Abuse and Neglect: A Frustration of Family Integrity." Martz's lengthy argument includes a reiteration of the idea that "Legally parents were thought to have a natural or inalienable right to raise their children as they saw fit" (1979, 70), and then he lists the many ways that the state has assumed socialization and control of children previously left to parents. Martz is concerned with the "crucial aspects of coercive state intervention, such as investigation into the family and removal of children . . ." (1979, 74). The author says:

> The family offers an open and intimate environment for working out conflicts between love and duty, and reason and passion, thereby serving as a microcosm for the development of socially satisfying and productive human relationships. Due to its fundamentality as a social unit, the family must be protected from governmental intervention in all but the most compelling of circumstances. . . . Family integrity means simply a wholeness or completeness of the family in an unbroken condition; living together as a family. (Martz 1979, 75–76)

Professionals who frequently encounter, at close range, the terrible injuries, maimings, and even killings in families that are unable to work out "conflicts between love and duty, and reason and passion" are likely to discount Martz's thesis. However, his well-articulated argument documents how abuses to individuals and family units have occurred through improper and misguided outside intervention.

There are some who take the other side of the family privacy argument and believe that the evidence leans in the other direction. Professors of law Alan Eisenberg and Earl Seymour note that while the state is reluctant to interfere with the right to privacy of some citizens, others may need the state's protection from abuses by other family members, saying:

> Our Bill of Rights implies that society protects people from pain at the hands of others, and [protects] their right to pursue

> happiness. In reality, the law becomes ambiguous when the parties involved are living as man and wife. The sanctity of the family home pervades the world of law enforcement. A man's home is his castle, and police, district attorneys, and judges hesitate to interfere with what goes on behind that tightly closed door (Eisenberg and Seymour 1978, 35)

The authors proceed to spell out what occurs behind the door. Some of it consists of assault and/or battery, aggravated assault, sexual assault, assault with intent to commit murder, rape, and murder. These ideas are in close agreement to a statement made by Steinmetz and Straus (1974, 3) in one of the first books published on family violence in the United States: ". . . it would be hard to find a group or institution in American society in which violence is more of an everyday occurrence than it is within the family."

A publication prepared by the now-defunct Office on Domestic Violence with the Child Welfare Resource Information Exchange indicates a cause and effect relationship in these terms:

> Because societal attitudes reinforce the belief that family problems should be resolved in the privacy of the home, a family which has reached a point of tension may see physical force as the primary way to resolve the tension. The reluctance of all social institutions to intervene in family matters encourages and perpetuates spouse abuse. (National Center on Child Abuse 1980a, 5)

Writing about incest and the national "conspiracy of silence," social psychologist Sandra Butler (1979) refers to social isolation, which is commonly found in abusive families, and lack of community assistance for families with problems. She states:

> A factor further discouraging aid to troubled families is that we tend to consider the nuclear family's isolation and self-imposed privacy to be a valuable source of strength. We believe that the family needs to be shielded and protected from the prying eyes of the larger community. Keeping family secrets from outsiders, teaching our children that "blood is thicker than water" and that outsiders are not to be trusted, we reinforce an unhealthy isolation of the nuclear family unit. (Butler 1979, 128–29)

In earlier times when transportation was more primitive, members of the extended family network lived in close proximity to each other, and while they presented a closed door to others in the community, they had some access to each other's lives. Aunts and uncles might live down the street or around the corner; grandmothers and grandfathers were likely to keep in close contact with their children and grandchildren. Now nuclear families still maintain a sense of family loyalty, but there is generally less interference from relatives. Kee MacFarlane, a social worker by training and national expert on child abuse with particular expertise on incest, has this to say:

> The sanctity of the home is such an established aspect of our society, traditionally and legally, that it is not difficult for a family to isolate itself from public view and public censure. Moreover, despite increased public awareness of the issue of children's rights and protection, children are still largely regarded as the property of their parents, whose right and privilege is to raise their children as they see fit. It is therefore extremely difficult for agents of society outside the family structure to act to deter or prevent the occurrence of intrafamily sexual abuse. (MacFarlane 1978, 88)

Family privacy is also invoked in legal arguments concerning marital rape because until very recently the common law influence in all state laws decreed that there was no such thing as rape in marriage. Changes have been occurring slowly, and are discussed in a later chapter, but the majority of states still carry a *spousal immunity clause* that defines rape as nonconsensual sexual intercourse by a man with a female *not his wife*. In an article outlining reasons for striking the marital exemption clause in Texas rape laws, attorney Michael R. Klatt (1980, 121) states that opposition to modification is related to "a policy of judicial nonintervention in family matters," and police nonintervention in domestic disputes.

The issue of family privacy is frequently raised by agents of law enforcement as well as the judiciary because of their hesitancy to intrude or intervene when called upon to do so, which has generated severe criticism. Much has been written on the unwillingness or inability of law enforcement officers, and others in the criminal justice system, to respond appropriately to acts that are dismissed as "family squabbles" when performed in the home although these same acts would clearly be crimes if performed outside of it. This growing body of literature criticizes the failure of the legal system—from police response, through adjudication, to sentencing—to operate on behalf of women battered by their spouses.[2]

Complaints generally center on failures to protect the rights of adult females in the home; there is far less hesitancy by the legal system to operate on behalf of child victims. In recent years, at least, there has been a response to protect the smallest and most powerless members of the family and, according to one study cited by Gelles (1979, 62), the professional group *most* likely to take official action on child abuse are the police.

Changes are also occurring in law enforcement and legal attitudes toward family privacy and wife beating, but there remain competing viewpoints on whether the state has perhaps gone too far by intruding into family privacy and family life (Martz 1979; Thomas 1974; Zuckerman 1976), or has not gone far enough (Bannon 1977; Dobash and Dobash 1980; Fields 1977). It is a sensitive issue and one that needs to be kept in mind by social workers, policy makers, service providers, and the entire legal system. Psychologists Seymour Feshbach and Norma Deitch Feshbach (1978) take into consideration both the privacy issue and the need for intervention to protect individual members. In their article, "Child Advocacy and Family Privacy," they cite another writer concerned with privacy and freedom who stated:

> A liberal democratic system maintains a strong commitment to the family as a basic and autonomous unit responsible for important educational, religious and moral roles, and therefore the family is allowed to assert claims to physical and legal privacy against both society and the state. (Westin 1970, 24)

Following a discussion of the pros and the cons of the privacy issue, the Feshbachs (1978, 174) admit, "Anxieties, anger, and guilt that remain locked behind the family wall fester, intensify, and sometimes disrupt and damage the family." For these reasons and others, the Feshbachs declare that the state and society have a significant interest in what occurs "behind the curtain." Change has been occurring for the past two decades and is likely to continue.

The balancing of civil and human rights of women, men, and children in the family is the major issue. It appears that when persons larger and more powerful abuse the rights of others in their families, then the state has no choice except to intervene on behalf of those unable to protect themselves. In a humane society that constitutionally guarantees certain rights to all citizens, the state cannot do otherwise. When the victims are children, there is no debate about intervention: In all 50 states there are laws regarding the mandatory reporting of child abuse or suspected abuse, including neglect. In California, for example, certain professionals and laypersons who have special working relationships or contact with children are required by law to report to the authorities within 36 hours of receiving or noting information concerning "reasonable suspicion" of abuse (California Department of Justice 1982). The mandate of state intervention on behalf of adults, including the elderly, is not nearly as clear but there is a growing trend moving in the direction of intervention for those who are unable to help themselves. The questions that remain are: What kinds of intervention are most effective and how can they be implemented without causing even more harm? Some possible answers will be explored throughout the book.

Difficulties and Differences in the Study of Private Behavior

The usual problems and limitations of scientific research are even more difficult to resolve when the family is the subject, both because of the private nature of family living and because violence between intimates is normatively considered deviant behavior and thus a taboo subject to outsiders. Access to data on sensitive topics and illicit behavior has been obtained in a variety of ways that satisfy the requirements of scientific research (Straus et al. 1980, 22–23), but the process is slow and there are still many unanswered questions. In addition, no single study, regardless of how well designed or rigorously conducted, can possibly produce *the* answer, the absolute truth. Rather, by taking different approaches and by replication of some studies where possible, each sound investigation adds a unique contribution to a growing body of knowledge.

What is readily apparent is that violence in the family is an historical fact and a serious and pervasive problem. Also clear is that there exist a variety of victim/aggressor types. In addition, intrafamily violence crosses all ethnic, socioeconomic, religious, cultural, and age lines and it occurs in an alarmingly high proportion of American families. Just as there are multiple forms of family violence, the causes and consequences appear to be multidimensional.

Because they are so different, most researchers have focused on one particular type of abuse, usually with the approach taken and the findings reported largely predetermined by the professional backgrounds of the researchers. In other words, depending on the professional training of the observer, the same phenomena can be described in very different ways; that is, a doctor is likely to see child abuse as a medical problem, a lawyer as a legal problem, a psychiatrist as a form of mental disturbance, a social worker in terms of a disturbed family system, and a sociologist as a social problem. This idea is cogently expressed by child abuse researcher David Gil, who says:

> Since the design and the findings of social and behavioral research tend to depend on the questions and hypotheses investigated, and since these questions and hypotheses in turn tend to be generated within the framework of the general assumptions of a scientific discipline and its societal context, it is not

surprising that most investigations of child abuse in the United
States were clinically oriented, and found this phenomenon to
be the result of psychological disorders of the perpetrators or,
at times, of the abused children themselves, and/or certain
pathological aspects of family relationships. (1971, 638)

The theory of child abuse as psychopathology is addressed in a later
chapter in detail, but for now the issue is researcher bias. It is important
to note that there is an inherent disciplinary bias in almost all social, psychological, medical, or other types of research. Professionals view the
world through the frames of reference they develop in their training, and
they adopt the basic assumptions of their discipline as the intellectual
tools used in problem solving (Mercer 1972). This bias can be seen in the
research and findings, as well as in the methods of intervention and prevention that are proposed. Usually clinicians call for "cure," treatment, or
counseling, whereas those in law enforcement are likely to demand deter-
rence or punishment. Pediatrician Eli Newberger and his associate, social
scientist and attorney Richard Bourne (1978) write about the "medicalization" and "legalization" of child abuse, showing how two disciplines have
defined symptoms of family crisis and childhood injuries as specifically
requiring the expertise of physicians and lawyers, although both medical
practitioners and lawyers endorse the therapeutic approach. One method
designed to help overcome conceptual narrowness is an interdisciplinary
child abuse consultation team such as at the Boston Children's Hospital
Medical Center (Newberger and Bourne 1978, 605), in which social workers and nurses join a nonhierarchical team on an equal footing, as much
as possible, with other team members from medicine, law, and psychiatry. The idea of interdisciplinary teams in training, research, and treatment
was lauded by the U.S. Surgeon General, C. Everett Koop, when he addressed the American Academy of Pediatrics in 1982 (1982).

Concepts and Definitions

What is included in the concept *family violence?* A glance at the outline of
this book shows topics such as child abuse, spouse abuse, or abuse of
parents. These topics are usually perceived as violent behavior, which
commonly refers to the use of force that causes injury or damage to a
person or persons. The Straus, Gelles, and Steinmetz research team,
whose study of family violence did not include neglect or incest, bifur-
cates their definition into *normal violence* and *severe violence,* in these
terms:

Normal violence was defined as an "act carried out with the
intention, or perceived intention, of causing physical pain or

injury to another person." The "physical pain" can range from slight pain, as in a slap, to murder (1980, 20). . . . We defined this type of violence [severe violence] as "an act which has the high potential for injuring the person being hit." (1980, 22)

Abuses that refer to acts of commission are easily conceptualized as types of violence. But this book includes other behaviors, such as neglect (acts of omission) and incest, that do not as clearly fit the common definition of violence. However, there is an additional meaning to the term *violence,* which includes the unjust use of force or power, as in deprivation of rights. It is in the broader use of the term that *violence* herein refers to the abuse or misuse of *force* or *power* by some family members against others who are thereby denied their individual and civil rights. Conceptualized this way, incest is a type of family violence. Even though incest does not usually involve violence in the form of physical attack, it always involves an abuse of power. Children who are physically or emotionally neglected, or sexually molested, are denied their individual rights to develop their human potential to the fullest. Gil's definition (1975, 347) of *child abuse* is similar to the author's conceptualization of violence. Therefore, using Gil's definition as a basis and with some modification, the definition of *family violence* as used in this book is:

> Family violence includes any act of commission or omission by family members, and any conditions resulting from such acts or inaction, which deprive other family members of equal rights and liberties, and/or interfere with their optimal development and freedom of choice.

Some may disagree with this interpretation and choice of the term, but it helps add emphasis to the idea that when rights of some are violated by others in the same family, they are *doing violence* to the rights and freedom of choice of those people, whether they are children or adults.

Under the rubric *family violence* lies a number of distinct types of abuse of family members. Sometimes a single type of abuse occurs in a family unit, at other times there are multiple forms occurring in the same families between a single aggressor/victim, or one aggressor with more than one victim, or any combination thereof. Generally, there are three basic types of abuse as distinguished by victims—*child, spouse,* and *parent*—but there are major differences based on who the abuser/s are. For example, children are abused by one or both parents or by other children; spouse abuse includes man to woman or woman to man; parent abuse includes abuse by adolescent or teen-aged children, or abuse of elderly parents by their adult offspring (called "granny-bashing" by the British).

The concept most commonly used in reference to *child maltreatment* is child abuse, in accordance with the dictionary meaning of "to use wrongly, to hurt by treating badly, mistreat, to use insulting, coarse, or bad language about or to." The writer conceptualizes *abuse* and *neglect* as distinct entities. Abuse includes physical and psychological acts of *commission*, whereas neglect involves physical and psychological *omission*. The position taken here is that when both abuse and neglect are present, they are subsumed in the concept *maltreatment*. Many writers do not make this distinction and frequently conceptualize abuse as a global term referring to both abuse and neglect.

By now some of the difficulties of studying family violence may have become more apparent. The various acts and actors multiply into a great many phenomena, sometimes distinct and sometimes overlapping. For example, some children are both physically abused and physically neglected (such as beaten and starved); while others may be physically and emotionally abused, but not neglected (beaten and called names). Other children may fall victim to neglect of both types, physical and psychological, (no attention paid to any of their needs). The combinations of types of acts of violence in the family are almost limitless, so it should come as no surprise that researchers have tended to specialize in certain types of abuse, usually reflecting their professional expertise and sometimes their personal interests.

In addition to the multiple acts and actors on the family violence stage, there are serious problems of definition. What is abuse? What is neglect? Is spanking a child violence? If a man slaps his wife, is that battering? As far as researchers, theorists, and professionals in the field are concerned, the answers are as diversified as the people who propose them. Even in the problem of child maltreatment, the most studied type of family violence, there is no uniform, clear, and concise definition that has been accepted by all. Under the 1974 Federal Child Abuse Prevention and Treatment Act, amended in 1978, Congress has provided this legal definition:

> Child abuse and neglect means the physical or mental injury, sexual abuse, negligent treatment, or maltreatment of a child under the age of eighteen, or the age specified by the child protection law of the State in question, by a person who is responsible for the child's welfare under circumstances which indicate that the child's health or welfare is harmed or threatened thereby. . . .

At first reading, that may seem concise enough, but as sociologist Richard Gelles (1979, 45) queries, "what constitutes 'mental injury,' 'negligent treatment,' 'maltreatment,' 'harm,' or 'threatened harm'"? Many definitions are circular: The phenomenon being defined is explained by words having the same commonly accepted meaning, such as abuse and neglect meaning maltreatment (or vice versa). The *Child Abuse Prevention Handbook* published by the California Department of Justice (1982, 6) asks "What is Child Abuse?" and begins its answer in the following words:

> To many, child abuse is narrowly defined as having only physical implications. In reality, child abuse is any act of omission or commission that endangers or impairs a child's physical or emotional health and development. This includes:
>
> —Physical abuse and corporal punishment.
> —Emotional abuse.
> —Emotional deprivation.
> —Physical neglect and/or inadequate supervision.
> —Sexual abuse and exploitation.
>
> The *act* of inflicting injury or allowing injury to result, *rather than the degree* of injury, is the determinant for intervention.

Again, it can be seen that "abuse" is defined by "abuse," and further that, "child abuse" is an all-inclusive phrase for both physical and emotional abuse as well as physical and emotional neglect. Neither of these two definitions uses the terms "deliberate" or "intent." Does this mean that all poor parents who live in inner-city slums are guilty of impairing their children's health and development by allowing them to breathe massive doses of pollutants? If parents are ignorant of balanced nutritional diets, are they guilty of abuse? If a single mother spends most of her daylight hours employed away from home, is she emotionally depriving her child? And what about accidents? One of the groups mandated by most state laws to report suspected cases of child abuse is the medical profession, but workers face the vexing problem of trying to distinguish between accidental and nonaccidental injuries found on child patients (McNeese and Hebeler 1977). The responsibility for deciding between child abuse or accidental injury is largely in the hands of doctors who, seeing multiple bruises, may diagnose them as resulting from abuse, although this is based on "a presumption, but rather rarely in practice *knowledge* of parental fault" (Newberger et al. 1977, 178). Injuries without witnesses to the acts, then, can result in accusations of abuse.

On the other hand, following the California definition, the presence of bruises is not even necessary, because it says that it is the *act* rather than the *degree of injury* that is the determinant of whether abuse has occurred or not. Following that line of reasoning, parents who slap or spank their children without leaving bruises may be guilty of child abuse. As Newberger and Bourne (1978, 597) note, it is difficult to distinguish between "corporal punishment that is 'acceptable' from that which is 'illegitimate.'" It should be noted that the California Department of Justice handbook (1982) includes "corporal punishment" with physical abuse, yet corporal punishment is not against the law in the public school system in California. Perhaps it is becoming clearer how serious definitional problems are in the study of just one type of family violence, child maltreatment. For the record the writer believes that *no* corporal punishment is "acceptable," agreeing with researchers Straus, Gelles, and Steinmetz (1980, 53) that "slaps and spankings are simply one end of a continuum of violent acts."

As noted earlier, there is no uniform definition of child abuse or clear, objective criteria upon which experts have reached common agreement. Except for the most obvious life-threatening and cruel acts which are undeniably vicious, but which constitute the smallest fraction of all identified child abuse cases, most definitions depend on subjective professional evaluation (Newberger and Bourne 1978). As Gelles notes, "[T]here is no objective behavior we can automatically recognize as child abuse" (1979, 45). The same problems exist for child neglect. Only when it occurs in its most extreme forms is there consensus about neglect.

The author and some others conceptualize abuse and neglect as distinct phenomena, but the definitions are even more vague and ambiguous. Most of the literature on child abuse focuses on physical abuse of children. Neglect is peripheral. Other forms of maltreatment, such as physical neglect and emotional abuse and neglect are usually subsumed under abuse, such as in the California definition cited above. Some people feel that the differences between physical abuse and neglect are only theoretical burdens since they frequently overlap. It is true that sometimes physically abused children are also victims of neglect, but this is not true in all cases. In fact, it appears far more common for physically abused children to also suffer from psychological abuse, for example, name calling (old-timers call this "tongue lashing"), than to suffer neglect.

One phenomenon that has puzzled many professionals who deal with battered children is their intense loyalty and love for their abusers. A review of the literature shows the opposite of neglect in many cases. Parents are often intensely involved with their children and have, usually unrealistic, expectations for their children. According to parents in Parents Anonymous, a self-help group for parents with coping problems, abusive parents truly love the children they beat. According to one abusive mother, the scenario goes like this:

> Sometimes he just drives me crazy with his disobedience—I tell him over and over not to do something, and he waits until I go away and then just does it. So one day I come into the

room and he has this mess all over him and the floor, and I really got mad and grabbed him and started swatting. The more he screamed the madder I got, till finally I hit him a good one and he smashed up against the wall and fell down there. He looked so little there, like a little rag doll, all crumpled up and I thought, "My God! what have I done to my baby?" I grabbed him in my arms and hugged him and petted him till he calmed down and finally went to sleep in my arms. He looked like a little angel sleeping in my arms.

The pattern of intermittent reinforcement of tender caring and closeness before and after beatings is probably one of the important factors that keeps victims emotionally bound to their abusers. Some parents physically abuse their children yet they are also strongly attached and sometimes "fiercely overprotective" of them (Brandon 1976, 7). Physical wounds heal in time. Terror may be forgotten, particularly when abusers are otherwise loving; and children who are beaten get attention, even if it is frequently the wrong kind. Most abused children are not simultaneously neglected.

There are far more neglected children in this country than physically abused, whether by intention, ignorance, or because of poverty, but many children defined as physically neglected are labeled as such due to subjective biases of social agents who impose their own norms and values on persons different than themselves or who cannot comprehend the sometimes paralyzing effects of poverty (Chase 1976; Piven and Cloward 1971; Richette 1969; Thomas 1974). Children are resilient and can usually survive somewhat unsanitary conditions and lack of good medical care (note our country's low sanitation standards only 100 years ago or those in primitive countries today).

Because he saw physical abuse and neglect as conceptually different phenomena, David Gil (1970) attempted to screen out cases of neglect from his large study, but child abuse pioneer Vincent Fontana (1973) disagrees with the necessity of making clear distinctions, saying:

Although we realized that it was useful, from the point of view of diagnosis and treatment, to be able to categorize the physical abuse as one thing and neglect as another, we felt that such a distinction was really of little value to the child in need of help. . . . Any treatment by which a child's potential development is retarded or completely suppressed, by mental, emotional or physical suffering is maltreatment, whether it is negative (as in deprivation of emotional or material needs) or positive (as in verbal abuse or battering). (Fontana 1973, 24)

Opposing viewpoints find sharp distinctions. As expressed in 1952 by one writer: "There is a radical difference in character between cases of neglect and cases of cruelty to children. . . . While neglect may be a form of cruelty, it is more often caused by or exaggerated by extreme poverty or ignorance" (Chesser cited by Zalba 1966, 5). A few other writers agree with this perception, and the National Center on Child Abuse and Neglect (1980b) gathered several articles together for a publication specifically focusing on child neglect.

On the other hand, of all forms of child maltreatment, the types that probably perpetrate the greatest and longest-lasting harm to victims are emotional abuse and neglect, although these are almost totally ignored by writers and researchers. There are no common definitions, and when mentioned, emotional abuse and neglect are usually defined by their results or long-term effects. Emotionally neglected or abused children suffer from lack of attention, or when they receive attention it takes the form of tearing down the child's self-image. The damages from the denigration of self, lack of care and affection, the "nothingness" of growing up in a world where no one transmits the message that the child is *someone,* a unique, special individual, are likely to remain for a lifetime. Except for the most extreme types, physical abuse of children does not usually represent life-threatening behavior (Chase 1976; Gil 1970). Most child specialists recognize that children want and demand attention. If that attention is not forthcoming, they will do something to get it. To some children, it does not matter if the attention their behavior elicits is positive or negative. How many children have been noted at parks, beaches, or supermarkets being totally ignored by parents until they do something "wrong," at which point the parents yell, scold, scream, or spank? They were "rewarded" for their behavior and got the attention they wanted (Dinkmeyer and McKay 1976). In an article written almost 20 years ago, a similar observation about parent-child interactions in public was made by psychiatrists B. F. Steele and C. B. Pollock (1968, 104).

In comparison to emotionally neglected children, these children may be more fortunate: At least they were in their caretakers' presence on an outing and they were not totally ignored. Psychologically or *emotionally neglected children* are those whose parents avoid affectionate contact, withdraw from them, or ignore them. As a 1978 California Department of Justice booklet states:

> When parents ignore their children, whether because of drugs or use of alcohol, personal problems, or other preoccupying situations, such as outside community affairs, serious consequences may occur. . . . [L]ack of attention and affection at

home has led many children into more serious situations outside the home. (1978, 9)

When parents *emotionally abuse* their children, they lean in the other
direction. They do notice their children, but it is critically. Emotional
abuse takes the form of degradation, humiliation, and destruction of the
victim's sense of self so that:

> Just as physical injuries can scar and incapacitate a child, emo-
> tional cruelty can similarly cripple and handicap a child emo-
> tionally, behaviorally and intellectually. Severe psychological
> disorders have been traced to excessively distorted parental at-
> titudes. . . . Emotional abuse has been characterized as a self-
> fulfilling prophecy. If a child is degraded enough, the child will
> begin to live up to the image held by the abusing parent or
> guardian. (California Department of Justice 1978, 7–8)

It is unfortunate that relatively little theory and research has concentrated on neglect and emotional abuse, since it seems obvious that the
problems are serious, widespread, and result in long-term damages to
victims.

These conceptual and definitional problems in family violence have
been introduced here to alert the unwary of the fundamental lack of consensus among professionals in the family violence field. There is widespread disagreement on what constitutes violence, abuse, neglect, sexual
abuse, and so forth, and therefore, decisions as to who is or is not an
abuser or victim depend largely upon subjective criteria (Gelles 1979;
Newberger and Bourne 1978). Medical practitioners, social workers, lawyers, police officers, psychologists, and sociologists may all look at the
same case history and define it differently. Professionals within the same
discipline may disagree, and frequently do. These basic differences influence research findings, estimates made on the extent of each type of violence, and the techniques advocated for intervention and prevention. Definitions proposed by various writers on specific types of family violence
are introduced where appropriate throughout the following chapters.

Methods Used in the Study of Family Violence

Some methodological problems in studying family violence may be obvious. Acts that are considered deviant (at least on the surface) by the population, are difficult to measure with any degree of accuracy, especially
considering the privacy of the arena where they occur. Some research is
done by studying the victims of abuse or their abusers, such as in child
maltreatment. Acts of commission are far easier to measure than acts of

omission. For example, bruises, broken bones, or welts are visible and measurable, but obviously, it is difficult to measure the number of baths or bottles that a baby did *not* receive, except by estimation through viewing the effects. On the other hand, measurable injuries alone on a child are not absolute indicators of abuse because it is frequently difficult to clinically diagnose child abuse (Newberger and Bourne 1978, 597). Someone must make a decision as to whether measurable trauma are accidental or nonaccidental, and even if there are bruises in various stages of healing, other factors besides the bruises themselves must be taken into consideration before diagnosis is made. Neglect is even more difficult to diagnose. Failure to thrive (FTT) in an infant is one type of "pediatric social illness." It is difficult to determine whether FTT occurs because of deliberate withholding of nourishment or individual attributes of the child (Newberger et al. 1977).

For a number of reasons, "medical research has almost exclusively focused on physical child abuse" (Finkelhor 1981a, 18), which has a longer tradition due to the "discovery" of child abuse by medical practitioners. Sociologist David Finkelhor, a researcher of sexual victimization of children, notes that prospective longitudinal studies (tracking events as they occur) and direct observation of family interaction have only been conducted on physical child abuse and that, "Child abuse researchers have also been able to do more detailed and quantitative studies of abusers" (1981a, 19). The reasons for this are that they benefit from being part of a large network of professionals involved in identification and treatment and thus, "This has facilitated such things as access to subjects and follow-ups for longitudinal research" (Finkelhor 1981a, 19).

There are limitations to nonrandom "opportunity" samples that are composed of patients who happen to come to the attention of counselors or physicians, such as the 60 families that were studied in depth by Steele and Pollock (1974). Because opportunity samples come to the researchers' attention through child protective agencies and circumstances beyond their control, or because they brought children for medical attention that aroused suspicions of child abuse, there is the question of *representativeness*. Are they representative of all child abusers, or different from those who do not get discovered, or do not bring their children for help, even when badly hurt? The individual case histories that come from small, focused samples or from volunteer samples help to provide insight into family dynamics, but they cannot be generalized to the public at large because we do not know if or how they are different from other families.

There are almost no clear measures of psychological abuse and/or neglect since they can be restricted by the abuser to occur only in complete privacy. Effects may not be visible until many years after they occur or even remain carefully maintained secrets for the victims' lifetimes. Chil-

dren may grow up in terribly abusive homes and yet never
realization that they were abused. They may not have like
pened to them, but since they had no scale against which
they conclude their childhood experiences were normal. O
hand, using the myth of the idealized family as their scale fo ....maicy,
others may come to the incorrect conclusion in adulthood that they were
physically or psychologically abused and/or neglected.

This points to another problem in research: Most of the studies using
adult respondents have relied heavily on retrospective data. Memory abilities are probably as varied among people as are fingerprints. Some people have razor-sharp memories, while others have only blurred images
and can recall just a few distinct images taken out of context. Questioned
years later about their childhoods, some people will focus on the happy
or humorous highlights while others will focus on the pain and misery;
yet the focus may vary depending upon the environment and their particular mood or circumstances at the time of the interview. An additional
problem or asking people about sensitive or stigmatized behavior is the
tendency of respondents to attempt to please interviewers by giving them
socially desirable answers, which may not be the exact truth.

While retrospective studies have their limitations and problems, so
does the use of official statistics for all the reasons listed above on defining various types of family violence. In official reports there is no way to
accurately identify which cases are accidental or unintentional and which
are deliberate maltreatment of children or adult family members. Because
of nonintervention policies regarding adult victims of family violence, records used are almost always those maintained by child protective agencies
and the juvenile justice system (Alfaro 1978; Smith et al. 1980). When official records of publicly identified cases are used as the data base, such as
in David Gil's (1970) study of child abuse, there is always some question of
bias because of the labeling process by which some cases come to be
officially designated while others drop out of the system (Becker 1966;
Goffman 1963; Kitsuse 1967). This means that some people are much
more likely to have a label attached to them than others, for example,
socially marginal groups such as minorities and the poor (Newberger and
Bourne 1978).

There is little doubt that most acts of violence in the home do not come
to public attention, and that when they do, only a relatively few of them
become part of the official record through the application of the label
"abused child" or "child abuser" (Newberger et al. 1977). Gelles (1979)
writes about the "social construction of child abuse" in which he discusses the individuals or agencies who operate as "gatekeepers" and selectively attach labels. When official records are used as a data base for
research on any kind of deviant behavior, there are always unanswered

questions of how these labeled cases are different, and in what ways are they different, from those that did not come to public attention. Again, this is the question of representativeness.

Since there is no ethical way we can violate the privacy of the home to observe violent behavior, it might be better to design laboratory experiments to watch spouses perform frustrating tasks, and so forth. This is another method that has been used, with varying degrees of success, to study spouse interaction and parent/child behavior (usually mother/child). There are a number of limitations to laboratory experiments or observations, one of which is generalizability of data beyond the artificial setting into real life settings.

The multiple types of violence in the family and the problems unique to family research both contribute to the fact that researchers and theorists have tended to focus on one particular form of abuse and exclude other forms with differing characteristics. While most professionals recognize that there are some commonalities, they have not assumed that there are common causes, cures, or that all types of abuse will yield to the same or similar prevention techniques. Psychologist Alfred Bandura's aggression research findings (1973, 11) support the idea that although different types of violence share some common ingredients, they cannot be assumed to have the same causal factors.

There are different approaches taken to various types of family violence, and like most researchers who study one particular type, sociologists R. Emerson Dobash and Russell Dobash designed their study to focus specifically on one topic, wife beating (1979). This research team insists that the issue of woman battering by husbands should not be subsumed in the more general topic of family violence because they feel it is false to assume that the dynamics, causes, or consequences are the same, stating:

> [W]e must be more concrete about our conceptions of violence, partialling out various types and forms of violence, not assuming a necessary interrelatedness between these forms and types and seeking explanations and understanding of these concrete forms in the wider society, as well as within family interaction. (Dobash and Dobash 1978, 435)

The Dobashes are the leading critics of studying the family system and considering wife abuse as just one manifestation out of many dysfunctions in family interrelationships. Because they find that wife beating is the most prevalent form of abuse in the family, they object to including it under the popularized terms "marital violence" or "spousal violence" (1978, 435). These researchers provide a sociohistorical analysis of the hierarchical structure of the patriarchal family and study wife beating in the context in which it occurs. They believe that understanding why husbands beat their wives cannot be accomplished simply by tabulating the numbers and kinds of violent acts, but rather what is needed is to examine how wives became the "appropriate" victims of husband abuse (1978). The methods used by Dobash and Dobash include historical analysis, records analysis, participant observation, and in-depth, unstructured interviews with 109 self-identified battered wives from which they gathered both quantitative and qualitative data (1979).

The research team of Straus, Gelles, and Steinmetz (1980, 12), took a different viewpoint, insisting that the problem is one of *family* violence. These sociologists obtained the largest survey sample to date, asking for self-reports on a wide range of aggressive acts between family members. Their approach is explained in the statement:

> [T]he whole system must be considered. If one wants to change the occurrence of violence in the family, it is not sufficient to deal directly with such aspects of intra-familial violence as child abuse and fights between husband and wife. To confine attention to such events and their immediate antecedents is analogous to treating the symptoms of a disease. (Steinmetz and Straus 1974, 20)

In the Straus et al. study, a nationally representative sample of 2,143 persons living in intact marital relationships were administered the Conflict Tactics (CT) Scales (1980, 24–26), formerly called the Conflict Resolution Technique (CRT) Scales (Straus 1976a). The survey instrument asked about conflicts between family members in the previous year, 1975. Conflict resolution was measured on a continuum from nonviolent tactics (calm discussion) to the most violent (use of a knife or gun). The Straus et al. research team categorized a range of eight acts along the continuum as "violent," and five of these acts were categorized as "severe violence." Thus it was the researchers' judgment, not their respondents, that defined what was violent and what was not (Ferraro 1979).

It is important to detail the Straus (1980) study here, because it makes an important contribution to our understanding of family violence. This study is unique in several ways. It is the first major study that attempted to measure all reported acts defined as violent which occurred in intact families. It enjoys several advantages over other studies by its use of a large, nationally representative sample, rather than a small, select sample, and it did not rely on official reports of families known or suspected of being violent. Further, the study elicited sensitive data from respondents by asking about conflict resolution with a scale that was developed over a period of years.

Using the CT scale, several types of intrafamily violence reported by one adult member of each family were recorded, including husband to wife, wife to husband, parents to children, children to parents, and between siblings (Straus et al. 1980). This study obtained a numerical count of the frequency of violent acts in one year as noted by Safilios-Rothschild (1978), but there was no substantive measure of events preceding or following each act. The intensity of the blows or the severity of injuries sustained, if any, and the meanings attached to these acts by both the aggressors and victims[3] were not measured either. The scale's structured categories are not mutually exclusive (Dobash and Dobash 1979), which means that several different acts are included in one response category. For example, "Threw or smashed or hit or kicked something," "Kicked, bit, or hit with a fist," or "Hit or tried to hit with something" (Straus et al. 1980, 254).

A limitation to the Straus et al. (1980) survey is its primary focus on acts committed only in the previous year. Straus (1978) admits that violence occurring at any time previous to that one year received very slight attention in his study, yet prior acts may have great significance for the duration of a couple's relationship. Straus explains:

> Unfortunately, our data for events before the year of the survey do not distinguish between who was the assailant and who was the victim. . . . In some cases it was a single slap or a single beating. However, there are several reasons why even a single beating is important. . . . It often takes only one such event to fix the balance of power in a family for many years—perhaps for a lifetime (1978, 446).

There are a number of drawbacks to the questionnaire used in this large survey, some of which the principal investigator pointed out (Straus 1978, 447), and which the research team notes in their book (Straus et al. 1980, 27–28). Critiques of the study acknowledge some serious methodological problems of survey research in general as well as limitations inherent in any forced-choice scale. However, the critics' major complaint seems to center on theoretical assumptions and some conclusions drawn by the research team based on the data their questionnaire gathered (Dobash and Dobash 1979; Fleming 1979; Pagelow 1981a; Pleck et al. 1978; Russell 1982; Walker 1979). One study used the CTS to measure couple violence and found clear evidence that "aggregate husband-wife comparisons are inadequate for concurrent validity estimates and that only couple comparisons . . . ought to be used for this purpose" (Szinovacz 1983, 642).[4] Limitations and acknowledged shortcomings as well as the advantages of the Straus et al. (1980) survey should be kept in mind when its findings, and the estimates of the incidence of various forms of family violence derived from it, are introduced here and elsewhere. Despite these problems, the study served to document conclusively the fact that there is an extreme amount of "everyday violence" in American families.

SUMMARY

This chapter began with the myth of the idealized family, showing why the topic of family violence has been avoided for so long by the public and social science professionals. There are unique characteristics of the family and family living that make it particularly violence-prone. There can be no change unless people become interested in learning as much as they can about family violence. Better understanding will show us how to devise methods to reduce or prevent violence in intimate relationships and in society, as well as the most effective techniques for assisting victims.

There are major problems inherent in studying family violence, some of which are common to any study of private behavior, particularly when the behavior under investigation is socially undesirable. Not only is there the desire to maintain the idealized image of family love and mutual concern, but there is the issue of family privacy. Our cultural attitudes toward the family set it apart as semisacred. What occurs between family members is not generally accessible to outside scrutiny, and some believe that impregnability is necessary for the preservation of the family and, therefore, it must be protected against outside intrusion. Conversely, others believe that persons within the family need assistance and need the protection of forces outside the family from abuses that occur within. At least as far as children are concerned, the state's mandate is clear: They are to be protected from harm, even against parents, and it is the duty of anyone who suspects child maltreatment to report it to the authorities. But for those of us who want to learn more about family violence, the issue of family privacy is a serious consideration.

Most researchers tend to concentrate on one or another type of family violence. While researchers attempt to be objective, individual biases influence studies from start to finish. The types of behavior selected for study, the design of the studies, the questions asked, and how they are asked, as well as the findings are all determined in large part by the professional disciplines of the researchers. This in turn affects the types of intervention and/or prevention techniques that are developed.

Next there is the question of concepts and definitions. Are we all talking the same language? It appears that we are not, because of the wide variation in conceptualization of family violence in all its forms, and because the definitions proposed are frequently vague and ambiguous. Since violence usually occurs in privacy, determinations are made by others who have not witnessed the acts, but must speculate about what occurred. This is particularly troublesome in determining whether or not child abuse and/or neglect occurred, and requires physical evidence as well as subjective interpretation of a variety of sociocultural and economic factors. It is apparent that there is no simple checklist of objective facts that can be tallied to determine if maltreatment occurred or not, except in the most extreme forms of life-threatening and brutal behavior.

The various methods used to study family violence point out some of the problems researchers encounter and some limitations or disadvantages of the different methods. Victims and abusers have been studied in focused samples, obtaining retrospective data. Other methods employed include analysis of official statistics, in-depth study of opportunity samples, and laboratory experiments and observations. As examples of different approaches, one team studied the single issue of wife beating and employed a variety of research methods (Dobash and Dobash 1979), whereas another team used the large-scale survey method to study many forms of family violence using a national sample of intact families (Straus et al. 1980).

Each of the approaches and methods used in the study of family violence contributes in unique ways to our knowledge, but their limitations and shortcomings have been pointed out so that these factors can be kept in mind when drawing conclusions.

NOTES

1. One example of how intensity of involvement can affect a couple can be seen in how some couples change in attitudes from the dating period and after marriage. Bernard (1982, 40–42) talks about changes that occur in marriages, noting that wives make more adjustments and the subtle changes she dubs "female into neuter." During dating, some men approve of their women wearing provocative and "sexy" clothes, but after marriage they disapprove. The color red comes to mind here: Many men find brilliant red a very attractive color and approve of it only on women *other* than their own wives.

2. There have been many writers who have accused the police, prosecutors, and the courts for taking a "head-in-the-sand" approach to family violence; others have noted the lack of training or kinds of training police receive; and some have pointed out personal biases of many professionals in the criminal justice system that have denied equal protection under the law to helpless victims of violence in the home (Bannon 1975; Bates 1980; Bowker 1978; Dobash and Dobash 1979; Eisenberg and Micklow 1977; Field and Field 1973; Fields 1977; Fleming 1979; Hampton 1979; Jensen 1978; Marquardt and Cox 1979; Martin 1976; Pagelow 1980, 1981a; Parnas 1967; Truninger 1971; Walker 1979; Woods 1978).

3. There is an important difference between hitting and trying to hit, yet these acts receive the same numerical count and weight in the CT scale. The intensity of the acts and their meanings are unmeasured, for example: a kick with an open-toes sandal under

a bridge table and an angry kick from a pointed western boot are vastly different in both the aggressors' intent to cause injury (the social meaning behind the act) and possible injury sustained. For example, according to Middleton (1977), a man in Belfast, Ireland, who kicked his wife to death was tried on charges of manslaughter rather than murder because, according to the North Ireland courts, there was no weapon employed in the homicide.

4. Maximiliane Szinovacz's study adds further evidence to the methodological inadequacy of the Straus et al. (1980) study, and support to the Dobash and Dobash (1979) contention that there are ambiguities in the forced-choice responses of the CT scale and that the scale items should be mutually exclusive. Szinovacz found that no husband admitted to "kicking, biting, or hitting" his wife, but that some wives reported their husbands engaged in these acts; the researcher assumes that husbands may be unwilling to admit "feminine" behavior such as kicking and biting, even if they had hit their wives. Also, in the Szinovacz test for scale item reliability and concurrent validity, aggregate data were compared with couple data, and both response inconsistency and biases were discovered. Szinovacz (1983, 631) says: "*Aggregate data* (i.e., data based on husbands and wives from *different* marriages) may eliminate distortions in the data that are due to the reliance on one selected group of respondents, but they cannot replace or serve as a substitute for *couple data* (i.e., data based on husbands and wives from the *same* marriage)."

2

Estimates on the Extent of the Problem

The preceding chapter detailed some of the problems in the study of family violence; the common acceptance of the myth of the idealized family and institutional support for maintaining it, the issue of family privacy, the lack of commonly accepted concepts and definitions, and the limitations to various types of research. All of those factors have an important bearing on estimates. If there is no consensus on what constitutes violence, abuse, or neglect, and there is no objective checklist of symptoms, then there can hardly be agreement on how much violence occurs in American families. Therefore, just as we build knowledge from the contribution made by each study, assessment of the problem comes from a variety of sources.

The only source for an overall appraisal of violence in the family comes from the national survey conducted by sociologists Straus, Gelles, and Steinmetz (1980). Even though they studied many forms of violence in American families, reports from the Straus et al. study unfortunately do not combine them together into a "family violence index," for a cumulative total. Their book begins by explaining that spouse abuse occurs in more than one in six households, that parents hit children in three out of five homes, and that siblings hit each other in the same ratio (Straus et al. 1980, 1). However, there are several tables or charts on specific types of aggressor/victim acts located in different sections of their book. Whenever available, the findings from the national study are included with the findings or estimates supplied by other researchers and sources on the various types or categories of violence.

SPOUSE ABUSE

> Peter, Peter, Pumpkin Eater,
>   had a wife and couldn't keep her;
> He put her in a pumpkin shell,
>   and there he kept her very well.
>
> —Mother Goose Nursery Rhyme

> Next time you are angry with your husband, why not try some
> child-like mannerisms: Stomp your foot, lift your chin high
> and square your shoulders. Then, if the situation merits it, turn
> and walk briskly to the door, pause and look back over your
> shoulder. Or you can put both hands on your hips and open
> your eyes wide. Or beat your fists on your husband's chest.
> Men love this!
>
> —Helen Andelin, *Fascinating Womanhood*, 1975

What is spouse abuse? What is a battered wife? Are husbands beaten? If a
woman slaps a man and he slaps her back, is that battering? Does one slap
count, or must there be more? Should we tabulate the number of slaps,
kicks, punches, or do we count instead the black eyes, bruises, or broken
bones? And what about psychological abuse, intimidation, and coercion
when no physical blows are struck? Does it count as violence if someone
is locked in a room, or locked outside a house at night in the winter without keys, wallet, or transportation? Consider the following scenarios and
determine if you consider them *abuse, violence,* or *battering.*

1. John and Jan, married for two years, are expecting their first
   child. They have had very few arguments, and no violence.
   John's job in construction is almost at an end, and they have
   no savings. After work, John stops off for a "few drinks with
   the guys" and arrives home at midnight. Jan is upset, she
   scolds, he swears, she slaps, he punches her in the belly.
   The next day she has a miscarriage.
2. Rita and Ron have not gotten along since they got married
   six months ago. This evening they went to a company party,
   where Rita spent time talking with the new salesman, and
   eventually the couple returns home. As soon as they get inside, Ron begins to accuse Rita of unfaithfulness, and
   punches his fist through the wall, telling her the next time it
   will be her face. Rita wants to leave but Ron blocks the door

saying, "Try to leave and I'll kill you." Rita believes he means it, and stays.

3. One couple has been married for 20 years and they get along very well, except that Herb has sexual problems: The only way he can get an erection is when one is induced by pain. Whenever they want to engage in sex, Helen gets out the "alligator clips" (spring clips with toothed jaws) and snaps them on his chest, including his nipples, until he is hurt sufficiently to maintain an erection. Sometimes he prefers to be beaten with wet towels.

4. During a dinner party with the boss, Mark begins to talk about a topic that Mary wants him to avoid, so she gives him a kick under the table and he changes the subject. A week later, Mark comes home angry at his boss and accuses Mary of spending money foolishly; she laughs it off and starts to walk away. Like he has done before when angry, Mark grabs her, pushes her up against the wall, shakes her, and shoves her; she loses her balance and falls down the stairs, sustaining a broken leg.

Depending on the researchers and the design of their studies, the scenarios above[1] would serve as measures in different ways, and some would be included in totals for abuse, violence, or battering while others would not. To explain, let us examine the definitions offered in three different studies.

In the fist one, Straus, Gelles, and Steinmetz (1980) separate the concept *violence* into two types. The first one, called *normal violence*, "was defined as an 'act carried out with the intention, or perceived intention, of causing physical pain or injury to another person'" (1980, 20). The second type was called *abusive violence*, about which the authors say, "We defined this type of violence as 'an act which has the high potential for injuring the person being hit'" (1980, 22). The violent acts ranged on a continuum theoretically advancing from least violent to most violent: Eight categories were established as an "over-all violence index." The "severe violence index" was reduced to five categories by excluding "threw something at the other one," "pushed, grabbed, or shoved the other one," and "slapped the other one" (Straus et al. 1980, 253–59).

The national study defined *family* as any couple living together who indicated they were married to each other (Straus et al. 1980, 24). The study uses the term "spouse," "husband," and "wife" when referring to respondents. Most researchers of wife beating or woman battering use the terms wife/woman and husband/man interchangeably, because the women in these studies were involved in intimate conjugal relationships with the men who beat them. The researcher did not ask to see evidence of legal marriages.

The second study we will examine is psychologist Lenore Walker's research on battered wives, which employed the following definition:

> A battered woman is a woman who is repeatedly subjected to any forceful physical or psychological behavior by a man in order to coerce her to do something he wants her to do without any concern for her rights. (1979, xv)

Walker qualifies the term "battered woman" to include only women who were abused more than once by saying, "Any woman may find herself in an abusive relationship with a man once. If it occurs a second time, and she remains in the situation, she is defined as a battered woman" (1979, xv).

The Pagelow study (1981a, 33) of woman battering adopted the following definition:

> In this investigation, *battered women* refers to adult women who were intentionally physically abused in ways that caused pain or injury, or who were forced into involuntary action or restrained by force from voluntary action by adult men with whom they have or had established relationships, usually involving sexual intimacy, whether or not within a legally married state. *Battering* is generally one-way violence . . . that may or may not be accompanied by victims' attempts to defend themselves. . . . Battering is here defined as physical assault which ranges from painful slaps at one end and homicide at the other end of a continuum.

With these definitions in mind, turn back to the four scenarios to see how (or if) they might have been included in these three research projects. In scenario number one, Jan would have been a battered woman in Pagelow study; if strictly following Walker's definition, Jan would not have qualified in her study since it was the first abusive event; and if this incident was reported to the Straus et al. interviewers, Jan's slap would count as an overall violent act and John's punch would count as a severe violent act. Scenario number two would not count in the Straus et al. survey because Ron's wall-punch and threats do not fit any of the violence categories, and neither one made physical contact with a person (victim). What if Rita had tried to leave and Ron began choking her? Choking was not included in any category. If Ron had been psychologically abusive to Rita before, this would count as a battering case for Walker, because this clearly involves intimidation, threats, and coercion, whether or not there was physical contact. Ron's blocking the door would have been defined as restraint by force from voluntary action, so Rita could have been included in the Pagelow study.

As for scenario number three, this would not have constituted a case for either the Walker study or the Pagelow study (in which sadomasochistic sexual practices by mutual consent were excluded), but if either of this couple had been interviewed for the Straus et al. study and admitted that Helen hit Herb, this could be tabulated in the severe violence category, and thus be included in the husband-beating index. Scenario number four would have been included in both the Walker and Pagelow studies as cases of wife beating. Mark's acts (push, grab, or shove) fit the overall violence categories, not the severe violence category in the Straus et al. study, but Mary's kick qualifies for the severe violence category and inclusion in the husband-beating index.

This exercise may help show the variations in definitions and approaches taken in different studies from which estimates are drawn. Compared to child abuse and neglect, it seems at first glance that it should be relatively easy to determine what constitutes adult violence, battering, or abuse, because victims can define it for themselves, as did the victims in most studies of battered wives. About this Walker (1979, xiv) says, "Battered women themselves are the best judges of whether or not they are being battered."[2] But obtaining in-depth data from respondents, such as the context in which events occur, the meanings attached to them, and the results of specific acts, requires lengthy semistructured interviews, which limits the sample size. On the other hand, a large-scale survey like the Straus et al. sample of over 2,000 people, investigating multiple sets of actors (husband-wife, parent-child, and between siblings), necessarily demands some limitations on depth in order to obtain breadth.

Psychologist Walker's research (1979), as well as social psychologist Irene Frieze's study (1979), both included measures of psychological abuse and psychological perceptions of victims of woman battering. Most research on spouse abuse or wife beating has concentrated on measuring physical abuse in marital or quasi-marital relationships, although psychological abuse is not dismissed or ignored as insignificant (Bowker and MacCallum 1981; Dobash and Dobash 1979; Pagelow 1981a; Straus et al. 1980). Almost all writers note the prevalence and seriousness of verbal and emotional abuse and threats, yet problems associated with researching physical abuse in adult intimate relationships is compounded by broadening the research focus and attempting to measure psychological abuse. It is extremely difficult to obtain adequate measures of physical acts of violence committed in privacy, but at least they are measurable, quantifiable, and visible, and so are the results of the acts, in many cases. The focus of the Pagelow study (1981a, 269) is explained in these words:

Battering is clearly distinguished from noninjurious acts such as pushing and shoving where the act is clearly not intended to inflict pain. Battering does not include nonphysical types of abuse such as intimidation, harassment, threats, or other forms of psychological force or coercion, unless they occur in conjunction with physical force or injury. Although such non-physical abuse is undeniably damaging, painful, and injurious, the scope of the phenomenon addressed herein has been restricted to bodily injury.

In a similar vein, Steinmetz and Straus set the parameters for their research interests by saying: "Our choice of physical violence as the central focus does not mean that destructiveness, aggression, cruelty, and nonphysical coercion are omitted from consideration altogether. Rather, it means that we will consider them only insofar as they are related to physical violence" (1974, 4).

Spouse abuse rates then, as discussed here, mainly refer to violent physical acts, whether or not psychological abuse precedes or accompanies the acts reported to researchers. About 28 percent of the couples interviewed in the Straus et al. study (1980, 35) admitted physically violent acts had occurred in their relationships. But for a number of reasons that the authors outline, they believe the actual incidence is much higher, for they say: "[I]t seems likely that *the true rate is closer to 50 or 60 percent of all couples than it is to the 28 percent who were willing to describe violent acts to our interviewers*" (Straus et al. 1980, 36).

This estimate refers to both husband and wife violence, which they say is almost equal. They find little difference among violent couples: 27 percent violent husbands and 24 percent violent wives (1980, 37), and both were violent in the balance (Pagelow 1981a, 270 calls this "mutual combat").[3] A number of other researchers contend that this study overestimates the extent of wives' physical violence compared to husbands, based on limitations inherent in the survey instrument and other factors (Dobash and Dobash 1978; Fields and Kirchner 1978; Pagelow 1978a; Pleck et al. 1978; Russell 1982). Some limitations were discussed earlier. Although wife versus husband abuse is discussed in detail in a later chapter, here the focus is on estimates of husband abuse as well as wife abuse.

The main source of estimations of husband beating to date come from the Straus et al. study, where the violence rates of the two sexes were almost equal: 12.1 percent of the husbands attacked their wives and 11.6 percent of the wives attacked their husbands during the year covered by the survey (Straus et al. 1980, 36). Their report states that 4.6 percent of the acts by wives were included in the husband-beating index, therefore "That is over 2 million very violent wives" (Straus et al. 1980, 41). They cite three other studies done by each investigator separately (Gelles 1974; Steinmetz 1977a; Straus 1974) that "also found high rates of husband-beating" (Straus et al. 1980, 41).

Other researchers who have concentrated on wife abuse insist that wives are victims in the vast majority of cases. For example, Lenore Walker (1979) estimates that one out of every two women is beaten at some point in her life by a man within the context of an intimate relationship. However, this estimate is based on her experience as a counselor and observations from her studies on woman battering, not from a representative sample of wives. On the other hand, sociologist Diana E. H. Russell (1982) obtained a representative random sample of women in San Francisco and out of the 644 ever-married women in her sample, 21 percent reported that they had been beaten by husbands at least once. Interestingly, it was the women themselves who defined violence in response to the question, "*Was your husband (or ex-husband) ever physically violent with you?*" (1982, 89). Their definitions of violence were restricted to the more severe levels (slapping, hitting, beating). The minimal levels of force (being pushed, pinned, held down or struggled with) were not defined by these respondents as violence. Russell (1982, 96–97) notes that the violence rates would have been higher for her sample if techniques similar to the Straus et al. study had been employed.

In social psychologist Irene Frieze's attempt to obtain a control group for her sample of battered women, she sampled women living in the same neighborhoods as each of the battered women matching them in terms of socioeconomic status, ethnicity, and age. After the interviews were completed, she found that 34 percent of the control sample had been physically assaulted by their husbands (Frieze 1980, 10).

There is also some evidence that, just as the violence within marriages tends to escalate over time in intensity and frequency (Dobash and Dobash 1979; Pagelow 1981a; Straus et al. 1980), sometimes this escalation continues on after the relationship has been severed (Fields 1978; Fiora-Gormally 1978; Lewin 1979; Pagelow 1980, 1981a). There is also substantial evidence that some spouses become violent only *after* wives declare their intentions of severing the relationships, which can be a very crucial and even dangerous time. Some men become literally obsessed with the idea that "if I can't have her, nobody can!" and become extremely violent, even to the point of murder (Gepfert 1979; *Los Angeles Times* 1979). The Straus et al. study did not measure violence during or after the severance of relationships because it was limited to couples cohabiting at the time of the interview (1980, 35). In addition, the refusal rate for that study was 35 percent (1980, 25), which could have eliminated the most violent families.

The research team of Dobash and Dobash (1978, 1979) conducted a large study, gathering data from police and court records for one year in Edinburgh and Glasgow, Scotland. All 33,724 police charges were studied carefully to determine the nature of the charges. Cases involving violence were thoroughly scrutinized and categorized by type of crime, location, offenders, victims, and the relationships between offenders and victims. Their table showing sex of victims and offenders in 2,872 cases where these data were available reveals that 91 percent of the offenders were male and 45 percent of the victims were female (1978, 436). Since these data came from Scottish jurisdictions, the author wondered if they were similar to American violence statistics and, therefore, constructed a similar table based on violent crimes in 17 American cities, obtained by National Commission on the Causes and Prevention of Violence (Mulvihill and Tumin 1969).

Table 2–1 shows that of 2,424 violent crimes categorized by sex of victim and offender in the United States, 91 percent of the offenders were male and 39 percent of the victims were female (Pagelow 1978a, 36). This is a remarkably close comparison to the table provided by Dobash and Dobash (1978, 436), which satisfactorily shows that male/female violence and victimization are not very different between the two countries.[4] The percentages from the Dobash and Dobash table are enclosed in parentheses in Table 2–1 for ease of comparing the American and Scottish crime data.

When Dobash and Dobash looked further at assaults between family members, they found 1,044 cases. Table 2–2 shows the types of assaults and percentages. The table supports the contention of the Dobashes that: "Husbands are only rarely assaulted by their wives (1.1 percent) whereas attacks on wives represent over 75 percent of all violence in the family setting" (1978, 437). The Dobashes further state:

> Females, whether they be sisters, mothers, wives or daughters, are more likely to be subject to control through the use of

Table 2–1. Sex of Victim and Offender in All Cases of Violent Crime (percentages)

Offender	Victim					
	Male		Female		Total	
Male	54.5	(51.8)	36.2	(39.5)	90.6	(91.4)
Female	6.4	(3.5)	2.9	(5.1)	9.4	(8.6)
Total	60.9	(55.3)	39.1	(44.6)	100.0	(100.0)*

*Percentages may not add up to 100 due to rounding.
Sources: Mulvihill and Tumin 1969, 210–15 (lefthand figures); Dobash and Dobash 1978, 436 (right-hand figures in parentheses).

physical force than are their male counterparts—and it is in their capacity as wives that the risk is the highest and the danger the greatest. (Dobash and Dobash 1978, 437)

It is important to note that use of official records from the criminal justice system always involves certain limitations, possible cultural biases, and other problems such as underreporting. There is reason to believe that there is considerable underreporting of wife beating, because data from the women interviewed in depth by the Dobashes show that only 2 out of every 98 assaults were reported to the police (1978, 437). However, Table 2–2 gives a clear idea of the proportion of assaults among family members from official records. Victimization percentages show that wives are most likely to be abused, followed by children abused by adult caretakers, parents, followed by children abused by siblings, and finally, husbands.

If Straus (1978, 447) is accurate when he estimates that violence occurs in 50 to 60 percent of all couples, and that 49 percent of *reported* acts involved both parties (Straus et al. 1980, 37), then based on 48 million couples in the United States, there could be roughly about 12 million mutually abusive husbands and wives. On the other hand, if we choose to assume that the vast majority of victims are wives, and if Walker (1979) is correct when she estimates that 50 percent of all adult women are beaten at least once by men they live with in legal or quasi-legal marriages, then there could be over 20 million married women "at risk" for abuse in this country.

The true rate of wife battering is probably more conservative, if we hold our definition to mostly one-directional, repeated beatings. A more accurate estimate probably lies somewhere between Russell's (1982) underreported 21 percent and Frieze's (1980) 35 percent. Bearing in mind definitional problems and differences in research approaches, it is likely that between 25 and 30 percent of all American women are beaten at least

Table 2–2.   Type of Assaults Occurring between Family Members

	N	Percent
Wife assault	791	75.8
Husband assault	12	1.1
Child assault	112	10.7
Parent assault	73	7.0
Sibling assault	50	4.8
Mutual assault	6	0.6
Total	1,044	100.0

Source: Dobash and Dobash 1978, 437.

once during the course of intimate relationships. This estimate would be higher if ex-husbands and ex-lovers are included. If correct, the lower estimation means that one woman out of every three or four may be beaten at least once, and for an unknown number, the *beatings* will continue into *batterings* (theoretical distinctions between "primary" and "secondary" battering were made clear in the author's study [Pagelow 1981a, 41–46]). Thus, at 25 percent of married couples, it translates to about 12 million women beaten or battered in this country alone. One thing is certain: The extent and prevalence of the crime of woman battering is of extreme magnitude. The author is unwilling, however, to speculate about how many battered husbands there may be in this country until there is more precision in definitions of "battering," and in-depth studies of samples of battered husbands are done as have been done on battered wives.

PHYSICAL ABUSE OF CHILDREN

> There was an old woman who lived in a shoe.
> She had so many children she didn't know what to do.
> She gave them some broth without any bread;
> She whipped them all soundly and put them to bed.
>
> —Mother Goose Nursery Rhyme

What is child abuse? Do all people who abuse children also neglect them? Is it abusive to children to spank them, or even to slap them? Is it the kinds of acts, or how many, that constitute child abuse, or does it depend on the consequences of the acts involved? How can parents properly raise their children without discipline? What is the difference between discipline and violence?

The answers to these questions are almost as varied as the people who ask them and the people who attempt to answer them. It is relatively easy to define abuse when we think of burns, bite and lash marks, ruptures, broken bones, and fractured skulls. Injuries that leave permanent damages, life-threatening wounds, or any trauma that results in death—these are clearly the effects of abusive behavior. Abuse then can be defined by its *consequences*. But what about slaps? Slapping a child who is "naughty" is viewed as an appropriate form of parental discipline in this country. What about too many slaps or ones that hit unintended places? What of slaps that cause bruises to tender skin; or the wiggling child who receives a hard slap on the ear causing serious damage; or the child who happens to stumble and fall on a hard, sharp object and sustains a fractured skull? Those are indeed accidental traumata. However, parents who use physical punishment on their children are often separated from "child abusers" only by luck. Even if injuries are determined by authorities to be unintentional, there remains the question of responsibility. Is the injured or dead child *not* a victim of abuse?

As social scientists and professionals think of physical force used on children as different behaviors on a continuum from the least to the most violent, then the question arises as to where "appropriate" force leaves off and "abuse" begins. It is in the gray area between nonviolent parenting and extreme violence where the vast majority of child abuse occurs. This is most troublesome to define and the cause of the greatest amount of arguing among professionals. If abuse is determined by acts, then most people would probably not hesitate to say that it is abusive to kick, beat with leather belts, or punch a child. At the lower end of the violence continuum are slapping and spanking which some believe are abusive and argue strongly against. In this line of reasoning, it is not a question of bruises, broken bones, or measurable injury, it is the *act itself* that constitutes abuse. *Intentions* are also largely irrelevant, because the effects of acts are seen as circumstantial. Two of the questions posed can be answered here: It is not possible to raise a child properly without discipline, but discipline is not synonymous with physical force or violence. There are better ways to discipline children. These questions, however, are what make it so difficult to gauge with accuracy how many children are being abused or have been abused by their parents.

Estimating the incidence of child abuse is problematic in several ways. First and foremost is the lack of consensus in a clear and concise definition (Friedman and Morse 1974, 405; Milner 1981, 876; Shwed and Straus 1979, 6; ten Bensel and Berdie 1976, 455). Second, many estimates are based on studies that focus on publicly identified victims and abusers who very probably represent only a minuscule percentage of the many actual occurrences of child abuse. These studies employ samples of children some professionals defined as abused, and whose parent/s were defined as abusers. The samples were obtained through public social services, patients in treatment, law enforcement or medical agencies, or official records.

Finally, to compound the problem, most estimates include both child *abuse* and *neglect*. This did not occur in the Straus et al. (1980) projected rates, which are discussed below, since that study did not attempt to measure any acts of *omission*, either physical or emotional. Nevertheless, the general lack of distinction between abuse and neglect in estimates of the incidence of child abuse should be kept in mind when reviewing the following material. As noted in the first chapter, the Child Abuse Prevention and Treatment Act of 1973 subsumes neglect in its definition, as well as emotional and sexual abuse, together with the most frequently identified form of physical abuse. Definitions included in the act are also vague and ambiguous, such as: "Child abuse is any act of omission or commission that endangers or impairs a child's physical or emotional health and development" (California Department of Justice 1978, 1). David Gil (1970, 1971, 1974, 1975), who conducted the first nationwide study that included all reported cases of child abuse in 1967 and 1968 (13,000 cases), offers a more specific definition:

> Physical abuse of children is the intentional, nonaccidental, use of physical force, or intentional, nonaccidental acts of omission, on the part of a parent or other caretaker interacting with a child in his care, aimed at hurting, injuring, or destroying that child. (Gil 1970, 6)

Another problem is the issue of "selective labeling" (Gelles 1979, 46), a phenomenon that persists despite laws mandating reporting of suspected cases of abuse, and the "Good Samaritan" laws that followed, which protect persons who report suspected abuse cases to authorities from subsequent law suits. Certain professionals are subject to legal penalties for failure to report, yet there are many physical abuse cases coming to the attention of outsiders that never become part of public record. For example, family doctors are more likely than clinicians to accept parents' explanations and record suspicious injuries and evidence of trauma as accidental (Newberger and Bourne 1978, 595; Sussman 1974, 245). In fact, the largest percentage of reported cases of child abuse and neglect come from persons who are not mandated by law to report suspected cases. The American Humane Association (AHA) reports that for 1978: "Nonprofessionals, which includes friends, neighbors, relatives and other family members, was the largest group of reporters (38.4 percent). Medical personnel, school personnel, and law enforcement personnel each accounted for approximately 11 to 12 percent" (AHA 1980, 19). However, their reports had a lower substantiation rate than reports from professionals, and reports from law enforcement personnel far surpassed all other groups with a 60 percent substantiation rate. *Substantiation* means that investigation was completed, there was evidence to support the report, and the report was submitted within the appropriate time period.

There is one category of abused children that has been almost totally ignored by researchers; adolescents and young teenagers (some exceptions are Amsterdam et al. 1979; Garbarino 1980; Garbarino and Jacobson 1978; Libbey and Bybee 1979; Lourie 1977). When the subject of child abuse is raised, many professionals as well as the general public think of victims only as infants or as very young children. Of over 120,000 substantiated reports on abuse and neglect, the distribution between ages 0 and 17 is almost equally divided in four age categories, and the 8–12-year-old

category is slightly higher than the others (AHA 1980, 28).
lescents complain of abuse by their parents they are frequer
the abuse is determined to be their own fault. People who ar
to help them frequently define them in the parents' own te
incorrigible, truant, disobedient, and so forth. This is an area
more attention from the scientific community, especially since a growing
number of professionals who work with status offenders or delinquents
are recognizing that many runaway children are not running *toward* something, but rather are running *away* from something—a home life in which
they were subjected to abuse, particularly sexual abuse.

For all these reasons, estimates of physical child abuse vary widely,
ranging from 60,000 (Helfer and Kempe 1968), 250,000 (Nagi 1975), 500,000
(Light 1974), to 1.5 million children abused in families each year (Fontana
1973; Gelles 1979). Sometimes documents distributed to the public contain claims that are not substantiated by official records or research. For
example, the California Department of Justice (1982, 4) begins its handbook with the following statement:

> According to the National Center on Child Abuse and Neglect,
> over 1,000,000 children are abused or neglected each year. Of
> these, 100,000–200,000 are physically abused, 60,000–100,000
> are sexually abused and the remainder are neglected. Over
> 2,000 children die each year because of abuse or neglect by the
> adult caretakers.

These kinds of broad estimates are accepted and repeated by the media, the general public, politicians, and some professionals. But they are
not conclusively substantiated by empirical data. The 1980 report from the
American Humane Association documents that the 1978 national study
data base contains 614,291 reports from 53 states and territories, but only
191,739 were in the form of individual data. Of these, only 13.4 percent,
or 25,656, were substantiated cases of abuse (AHA 1980, 18). However, the
report cautions that these statistics do not accurately portray the extent of
abuse, as follows: "It can be conclusively stated that *these reporting statistics underrepresent the actual incidence of maltreatment on a national basis*" (AHA 1980, 4).

Even in so seemingly obvious and indisputable a matter as homicide (or
infanticide), there is no way to obtain reliable figures, and the experts
must rely on estimates. Again, the reason for this is reporting problems.
Gelles lists a variety of sources that estimate between 365 to 5,000 children
die each year in the United States from abuse by parents (1979, 75). The
California Department of Justice booklet suggests one reason: "For example, a child whose death is officially recorded as pneumonia may, in
fact, have contacted the illness as a result of being poorly clothed, fed,

bedded and medically neglected" (1978, 16). In addition, there are various other ways in which deaths of children due to abuse and/or neglect do not become listed in official statistics. As Freeman (1979, 17–19) explains, "The statistics in question are part of a social process in which doctors, courts and coroners participate. Coroners reach a large number of 'open' verdicts and these cases would not . . . [appear in figures as] 'homicide and fatal injury purposely inflicted.'" Many cases of homicide are mistakenly officially recorded as accidents or deaths due to natural causes.

There is one study that does not rely on official statistics of child abuse, nor is it restricted to a focused sample of abused children and their parents, or families suspected of abuse (Straus et al. 1980). The national survey by Straus and his colleagues obtained data on violent acts parents admitted they committed on their children (1980, 51–75), which they projected to national statistics to derive estimates of national incidence. There was a subsample of 1,146 parents who had at least one child aged 3 to 17 living at home. A mother or father in each of these families was asked about a randomly selected referent child (Straus et al. 1980, 60), which, according to the research team, means "Thus, our examination of parental violence is not a study of all the violence each parent engaged in, but rather, all the violence a selected child in each family experienced from *one parent*." These researchers see "ordinary" physical punishment and child abuse as ". . . but two ends of a single continuum of violence toward children" (Straus et al. 1980, 59). When these parents were asked if they had ever used some form of violence on the referent child, 73 percent admitted to at least one violent occurrence in the course of raising a child who was between the ages of 3 and 17 (Straus et al. 1980, 60).

However, when it came to the more dangerous types of violence in the year prior to the interview, 3.6 percent of these parents reported one or more occurrence of at least one of the acts the researchers defined as "severe violence." As Gelles explains:

> We chose to compile an "at-risk" index which combined the items we felt produced the highest probability of injuring or damaging the child (kicked, bit, or hit with a fist; hit with something; beat up; threatened with a knife or a gun; used a knife or gun). (1979, 83)

Based on the parents' reports of acts that fell within these particular categories and extrapolating them to the population of children between 3 and 17 in the United States, Gelles estimates that "between 1.4 million and 1.9 million children were vulnerable to physical injury from violence in 1975" (1979, 83).

Some problems in the instrument used to obtain these data were outlined earlier. Gelles admits (1979, 83) that the researchers do not know *what* objects were used to hit these children (in some cases it could have been fly swatters, pillows, or potentially lethal objects).[5] Straus et al. note these limitations saying:

> We do not know exactly what respondents meant when they admitted that they "beat up" their child, we do not know what objects they used when they hit a child (a pipe or a paddle?), and we do not know whether children who had guns and knives used on them were wounded. (1980, 63–64)

However, no mention is made that the words used in the questionnaire are not exactly the same as those used in subsequent reports (cf. Gelles 1979; Steinmetz 1978a; Straus et al. 1980). For example, one category on the questionnaire is phrased, "Hit or tried to hit with something" (Straus et al. 1980, 255) but subsequent reports subsume reported efforts to hit with completed hits and they are listed as "hit with objects" (Straus et al. 1980, 62), or "hit with something" (Gelles 1979, 83). There is no explanation offered for the translation of attempts into completed acts, except possibly there is an oblique reference to it when the authors discuss the lack of data on consequences of the violent acts, saying, "the things . . . which influence whether someone who is punched is injured or not, are typically random phenomena such as aim or luck" (Straus et al. 1980, 22). Depending on how one chooses to weigh these issues, it is possible these are overestimations of physical abuse of children in the United States.

But there are other reasons why they may be underestimations, as the authors suggest (Gelles 1979, 83–84; Straus et al. 1980, 63–65). Reasons for underestimations include the fact that these were self-reports of socially unacceptable behavior, that they were retrospective reports and that these were two-parent families; thus, there were two parents available to abuse, but only one person in each couple was interviewed. In addition, no children under the vulnerable age of three were used as the referent child; no single-parent families, which have higher rates of reported violence were used; and finally, some extremely violent families may have refused to answer their questionnaires.

Straus, Gelles, and Steinmetz believe that their estimates of violence are conservative for the reasons listed above. In addition, these may be low estimates because their study concentrated solely on acts that occurred during conflicts, which might have screened out premeditated, deliberate, one-directional acts of violence. (This could also explain a loss of many cases of wife beating, as discussed earlier.) There was no measure of violent acts termed *expressive*, in which the major goal was to hurt the victim without apparent reason. Only *instrumental* aggressive acts were counted, that is, acts carried out as part of a conflict or disagreement (Straus et al. 1980, 27). Straus recently (1981a, 2) addressed this issue by saying: "To the extent that respondents followed the literal instructions of Form A, acts of expressive aggression are not reported, producing an underestimate of the violence rate."

Another reason to suspect underestimations is because the research design excluded referent children under three years of age, yet some experts believe that the most dangerous time period for child abuse is from three months to three years; therefore this is the highest group at risk for abuse. Gelles finds three reasons why children in this age span are particularly vulnerable to abuse: their lack of physical durability to withstand punishment, their lack of capacity to understand parental demands, and the structural stress new babies create in their parents' lives (1979, 35). On the other hand as noted earlier, substantiated reports show no remarkable differences between age groups (AHA 1980, 28), but these are *reported* cases. Perhaps *actual* instances are excessive, but little children can more easily be confined to the privacy of the home than older children, and it is possible that for some, public disclosure comes only after death; thus, they are recorded as infanticide rather than child abuse.

It may be apparent that there are limitations to relying on any one study to provide the answers about how much violence occurs in American families or how many children are abused. On the other hand, using most other sources for estimates of violence involves the problems of reporting, "gatekeeping" (the screening process whereby cases are selected or dismissed), and confirmation. Some cases of physical child abuse are never detected by others; some are incorrectly diagnosed as "accidents"; and others are ignored, largely because the observers do not want to become personally involved. Undoubtedly, many cases of true abuse "drop through the cracks" in the system.

In summary, we have estimates but no real consensus on the actual number of children who are abused every year in the United States. From the material discussed it may be obvious that a great many people have dealt with this vexing question and have made estimates based on available studies. There can be little question that abuse of children by their parents and other caretakers is a serious social problem of immense proportions. Limitations in estimates and research must be noted, especially when writers speculate about intervention techniques and the effects on victims of child abuse. The cases that come to public attention are undoubtedly only the tip of the iceberg. We have no idea how many children are seriously and repeatedly abused in the privacy of their parents' homes. In addition, if one conceptualizes abuse as falling on a continuum of violent acts, what one parent defines as normal discipline may very well be defined as abuse by another parent.

PHYSICAL NEGLECT AND EMOTIONAL
ABUSE AND NEGLECT OF CHILDREN

What do we know about the extent of physical neglect and emotional abuse and neglect of children? Actually, very little, compared to other types of maltreatment in the family. There are a number of actors that mitigate against gathering reliable estimates. Definitions are almost entirely lacking; the few that are proposed mostly consist of the short- and long-term *consequences* of these phenomena. When estimates are offered, they frequently include *both* abuse and neglect. Also, there is a paucity of research focusing specifically on neglect, both physical and emotional, as well as emotional abuse. Let us begin by examining a few vignettes that help illustrate some reasons why these issues are difficult to define and thus to measure.

> Martin is an only child of 13 who has spent the majority of his life at the best boarding academies, but when he is at the major family residence, he is attended by paid caretakers. His parents have mutual social and business interests and frequently travel together for long time periods. When all three are at the same residence, the parents' time is spent organizing, planning, and entertaining. Martin is quiet and withdrawn, and his parents totally ignore his presence, except when important guests are nearby.

By comparison to many children, Martin would probably be considered an extremely fortunate boy to have so many material advantages. It is almost impossible to conceive of Martin's case being included in any study of emotional neglect of children; in the first place, who would be likely to make such a distinction? If anyone is ever going to decide that Martin suffered from parental maltreatment, it will probably be Martin himself, during a psychotherapy session. His type of neglect will only be defined retrospectively in terms of its consequences. The second vignette is much more common.

> The Hunters are the prototype of an upwardly mobile middle-class family with two children, aged 2 and 4. Neither child was planned, but Judy quit college at the first pregnancy so they are dependent on Ted's income. They live far beyond their present

financial means, and are constantly confronted with money problems and efforts to maintain their status in the community. They fight often, and Judy is a secret alcoholic. Neither one has patience or time for the children, whom they both resent. They ridicule and scold the children in private but act loving in public.

These children may be victims of both emotional abuse and neglect that will cause them problems all their lives, but it is highly unlikely that they would be included in any estimates or research, at least not until their emotional damages manifest themselves in antisocial behavioral or personality patterns. As in Martin's case, the maltreatment they experience is invisible outside their home and may only be detected by its consequences, if ever. Unknown numbers of children in each generation suffer from being ignored, and when they are finally noticed, it is with derision, ridicule, and contempt. People who grow up to physically abuse their children are more likely to come from these kinds of childhoods than to have suffered physical abuse as children. The third vignette is the situation most people identify as neglect, and is the one most likely to come to public attention or become part of research statistics.

Rose is 21 years old and the mother of 3 children; the first one was conceived when she was 15 and the father refused to marry her. She dropped out of school and went on welfare until she met and married Pete, who is unemployed most of the time. He left after the latest birth. Rose and her children live in an inner-city tenement with rats, roaches, no hot water, an overflowing toilet, a broken refrigerator, and no beds. The baby's toe was chewed off by a rat, and after Rose took the infant to the clinic, a social worker visited her apartment.

Now this is a *typical* case of neglect. The social worker sees the unsanitary conditions, the lack of food (or rotting food) in the refrigerator and cupboards, the filthy, undernourished children who probably have headlice, have never been to a dentist nor been seen by a physician since they were born. Ultimately, Rose is declared to be an unfit mother who neglected the children, the children are taken from her and placed in protective custody, and Rose and her children become part of the official record. Statistics bearing out these statements will be presented shortly, but first let us see how professionals define neglect.

In contrast to most of the literature, where neglect is defined largely in terms of identification factors (for example, what is *not* present) or their consequences, an article by professor of social work Norman Polansky and his colleagues provides a fairly concise definition of neglect as follows:

> Child neglect may be defined as a condition in which a caretaker responsible for the child either deliberately or by extraordinary inattentiveness permits the child to experience avoidable present suffering and/or fails to provide one or more of the ingredients generally deemed essential for developing a person's physical, intellectual and emotional capacities. (Polansky et al. 1977, 5)

This is one of the few articles that focuses specifically on child neglect; it is the lead article in a later publication by the National Center on Child Abuse and Neglect (NCCAN) (1980b) called *Selected Readings on Child Neglect*. This booklet contains five other articles that deal mostly with standards, treatment, and legal issues, and only touch on definitions.

Other scholars have attempted to deal with the problem of defining child neglect but most simply offer examples of consequences for clarification (McNeese and Hebeler 1977, 3; ten Bensel and Berdie 1976, 454). One article provides no definition of neglect, yet it sets out standards of child neglect for professionals to use for identifying cases and is composed entirely of descriptions (Cantwell 1980). By contrast, a follow-up study of hospital patients offers the following brief definition with no further elaboration or description: "'Gross neglect' was defined as omission on the part of the parent(s) or designated caretaker to take minimal precautions for the proper supervision of the child's health and/or welfare" (Friedman and Morse 1974, 405). Whatever "minimal precautions" may be, they remain unstated, and that is generally the way it is in the study of neglect: *It is largely determined to have occurred by its consequences.* The other problem in obtaining estimates of the incidence of child neglect is the lack of conceptual distinction between neglect and abuse. However, one booklet (NCCAN 1979) that focuses on child abuse and developmental disabilities notes important differences. One of the authors of the booklet attempts an explanation in these terms:

> *The Majority of Abuse Cases Do Not Involve Battering but Neglect and/or Emotional Abuse.* The so-called battered child syndrome is only the very final expression of child rejection. It is not necessary to beat or physically injure a child to abuse him, nor is physical abuse the sole or only form of rejection from the family unit that can be practiced. In battering, we are looking at the most extreme and to society most violent (but by no means the only) form of abuse. (Briggs 1979, 4)

Other experts believe there are enough differences to merit separate study, while at the same time they recognize considerable overlap (Gil 1970; Giovannoni and Becerra 1979; Kadushin 1974; Kent 1973; Steele and Pollack 1968; Young 1964). Some strongly object to the lack of distinction between child abuse and neglect, in both public and professional thinking, saying:

> A tenet of this report is that neglect and abuse are probably related but by no means identical. Unless we approach them as separate entities, there will be no way to determine whether they represent "a difference that makes a difference" for identification, treatment, and programmatic policy. Commonalities between the two should be empirically demonstrated rather than presumed. (Polansky et al. 1977, 3)

In their review of the literature on child abuse, Marc Maden and David Wrench (1977, 197) present a list of authorities who believe that child abuse and neglect are sufficiently "symptomatically, if not etiologically, distinguishable." They agree that the pattern appears to be discrete and therefore their review ". . . excludes neglect from the child abuse definition. Additionally, maternal deprivation, failure to thrive, and all forms of emotional injury are excluded on the basis that their relationship to child abuse has not been clearly established" (Maden and Wrench 1977, 197).

Despite some apparent distinctions, most writers use the terms *abuse* or *maltreatment* as global concepts that include neglect; they place child neglect on the same continuum with physical abuse because they do not perceive these phenomena as being mutually exclusive (Fontana 1964, 1973; O'Neill et al. 1973; Silver et al. 1969a; Smith 1975).

Part of the explanation of why physical neglect and emotional abuse and neglect have been subsumed under the more general term abuse is because these forms of maltreatment are much more difficult to detect and measure. Polansky et al. (1977, 3) note that abuse permits a more concise definition than neglect and further that, "The traditional preference of investigators for readily manageable problems may well be a major reason why abuse has been the more popular area of study." Of these other three types of child maltreatment, physical neglect is easier than emotional abuse or emotional neglect to identify and measure, once victims have come to the attention of medical or educational personnel; but again, those that do are usually only the extreme cases.

Since physical neglect of children is so difficult to define and is seldom researched as a distinct entity, few experts have proposed estimates of it except in the broadest terms. The best way remaining to try to gauge incidence is to examine officially reported cases of neglect, bearing in mind that these are extreme underestimations of the problem.

Data collected by the American Humane Association for 1978 show that only 40 percent of reported cases were substantiated as cited in the *Sourcebook of Criminal Justice Statistics—1980* (Hindelang et al. 1981). Of the 76,804 substantiated cases, 61 percent were charges of neglect; another 6 percent were both abuse and neglect; and 33 percent of these substantiated cases were instances of abuse (Hindelang et al. 1981, 274). In other words, there were 46,494 substantiated reports of neglect compared to 25,656 cases of abuse, and 4,654 substantiated cases of both abuse and neglect (American Humane Association 1980, 18).

This evidence shows that child neglect is reported and is substantiated when reported, at a higher rate than child abuse. Cantwell (1980, 1), referring to earlier American Humane Association statistics, says that of almost 100,000 cases reported, 58 percent involved neglect alone while 15 percent included both abuse and neglect. Gil (1970, 103) screened out 3,570 cases from his analysis because they did not fit his criteria of intentional and nonaccidental acts, and he says that almost half (about 1,700) of these were cases of neglect. However, Gil did find in his physical abuse sample that about one-third of the cases also included child neglect (1970, 128–29). Another investigation that separated out acts of omission from the study sample found that 40 percent of reported child abuse cases among air force families were cases of child neglect (Shwed and Straus 1979, 6). The national incidence study of family violence (Straus et al. 1980) did not attempt to measure any acts of omission, concentrating instead on acts committed for purposes of conflict resolution; so there are no data to be obtained from that study.

Since there are very few studies that focus specifically on neglect, and since almost no writers dare to hazzard even an educated guess on the incidence in this country, we are left with the grossly underreported cases that were substantiated in the American Humane Association (1980) statistics. Of the almost 18,000 cases of neglect in 1978, the single most stressful factor in these families was insufficient income (44.1 percent), and more than one-third (38 percent) reported stress from family discord. The American Human Association report (1980, 33) states: "Insufficient income, inadequate housing and social isolation were more prevalent among families reported for neglect than for abuse." Of all maltreatment reports combined, the most common type was deprivation of necessities (86.4 percent), and the least common type was major physical injury, about which the report notes: "These data reconfirm the knowledge that most maltreatment does not involve major physical trauma. In fact, only 1.9 percent of involved children suffered injuries such as fractures or brain damage" (American Humane Association 1980, 34).

Of 66,121 substantiated reported cases of maltreatment, the vast majority (96 percent) of almost 43,000 neglect cases indicated either no treatment or moderate treatment was required, although neglect *can* lead to death: "It is important to note that 105 children died as a result of neglect, and 28 more died as a result of neglect in combination with abuse" (American Humane Association 1980, 35). Earlier in this section, a vignette of the "typical abuse" situation was presented; to demonstrate how Rose's case matches available statistics, here is what the American Humane Association found. Neglectors include overrepresentation of mothers or mother substitutes (about half are families headed solely by women); young parents (most between 20 and 29 years); minorities; lower educational levels (almost half are high school drop-outs); low income (77 percent had incomes under $9,000 in 1978). Comparing features of families in which maltreatment occurs, the report states:

> When families involved in abuse and those involved in neglect are viewed separately, two distinct profiles emerge. The overriding characteristic of neglectful families is lack of sufficient income. Further, almost half of these families are headed by a mother figure only, and they tend to have more children than families involved in abuse. (American Humane Association 1980, 38)

In summary, it should be apparent that there are even more difficulties in establishing baselines on incidence of child physical neglect than child physical abuse. As mentioned earlier, while some children are the victims of parental/caretaker acts of commission and omission, other children suffer one or the other, but not both. There is no reason to throw all cases into one category and then search for a common etiology, prevention, and cure. These problems might be closer to resolution if professionals from various disciplines could reach a consensus on an unambiguous definition of child neglect and then conduct rigorous research on this specific issue. Most of the "gatekeepers" (Gelles 1979) who make determination of neglect must rely on subjective criteria by which they apply their own (usually white, middle-class) personal standards of cleanliness, child care, diet, and housing (Thomas 1974). Some of the problems of cultural, racial, or other personal biases of gatekeepers are examined by Frank Schneiger, director of the Protective Services Resource Institute, and several other authors in a National Center on Child Abuse and Neglect (1978a) publication. This booklet contains reprints of 11 articles, each of which addresses cultural and economic variations among families that illustrate the complexities of reaching consensus on the issue of neglect.

We can use various measures to estimate the extent of physical and emotional neglect and emotional abuse of children in the home, and produce a wide range of rates. All estimates are subject to some shortcomings, biases, and errors, but there is strong and sufficient evidence to show that these forms of abuse are so prevalent that at least one out of every three children is victimized in one or more of these ways. It is doubtful if everyone would agree that any of these three types of maltreatment except physical neglect should be of concern to researchers and policy makers because of the issue of family privacy. Child psychiatrist Albert Solnit (1980, 140–41) believes that society should provide "attractive, accessible voluntary services," but otherwise he states, "Since there is little or no agreement on what constitutes emotional and psychological neglect, the dividing line between respecting and intruding into family privacy should be physical abuse of the child or neglect that represents the imminent risk of serious bodily injury to the child."

INCEST AND SEXUAL ABUSE OF CHILDREN

What is sexual abuse? How does it differ from incest? Are both of them always violent? Is it incest only when it includes sexual intercourse between blood relatives? Does it always involve at least touching? How can anyone tell the difference between close, warm physical contact and sexual abuse? When a father undresses his five-year-old daughter for bed, fondling her chest and examining her body before dressing her in pajamas, is that abuse? When a little girl sexually arouses her father by crawling up on his lap, snuggling, blowing in his ear, and kissing his neck, is that incest? What about a father who secretly spies on his pubescent daughter when she is in her bedroom or the bathroom, but does not make sexual physical contact?

At first glance, the answers to some of these questions may appear to be obvious, but child psychiatrist Alvin Rosenfeld (1977, 231) points out that there is a continuum of sexuality in the family saying, "Incest and the sexual misuse of children seemed to be the extreme and very abhorrent ends of a spectrum that included an implicit notion of normality." The unanswered question is: What is normal sexual family interaction? Sociologist David Finkelhor writes about *Sexually Victimized Children* (1979a) and makes a distinction between sexual abuse (which he also refers to as victimization) and incest. Finkelhor (1979a, 83–84) explains in these words:

> Incest and sexual abuse are sometimes confused, but they are
> not the same. Sexual abuse normally refers to sexual relations
> between an adult and a child. Incest refers to sexual relations
> between two family members whose marriage would be pro-
> scribed by law or custom. . . . For our purposes, we will use
> incest to mean sexual contact between family members, in-

cluding not just intercourse but also mutual masturbation, hand-genital or oral-genital contact, sexual fondling, exhibition, and even sexual propositioning.

This definition offers explicit examples of sexual contact, but it makes no mention of nonphysical sexual contact, such as voyeurism, through which an adult gets sexual satisfaction, as by covertly watching a young girl's naked body. In one clinical case study of victims of father/daughter incest, Judith Herman and Lisa Hirschman (1980) excluded seductive behaviors such as when fathers display intense interest in their children's bodies, but it seems that Rosenfeld (1977, 233) takes a more accurate view of acceptable boundaries of sexual behavior when he lists, "No attempt by the parents to satisfy their adult, genital-sexual needs through their children," as well as, "adequate privacy for both parents and children in overt sexual matters." Two questions that parents can ask themselves to determine whether or not what they are doing to or with their children is appropriate are: "Am I doing this for my own sexual satisfaction?" and "Is this something I would not want anyone else to know about?"

The topic of incest or other forms of sexual abuse of children in the home has recently attracted the attention of social and behavioral scientists to a far greater degree than ever before (Burgess and Holmstrom 1975; Finkelhor 1979a, 1980, 1981b; Giarretto 1976; Meiselman 1978).[6] The Straus et al. study (1980) did not attempt to measure sexual abuse of children or incest, so there are not data or estimates from that source.

The fact that some states require reporting of child abuse in distinct categories including sexual assault, along with more liberalized attitudes toward discussing sexual behavior, may partially explain the recent wave of research interest. However, there are no reliable base lines of incidence, and most estimates appear to be little more than educated guesses. Jerome Kroth, of the California Department of Health, evaluated the Child Sexual Abuse Treatment Program in San Jose, and his report states: "The upswing in interest in child abuse and child sexual abuse in particular must be tempered by the fact that the state of the art in information collection on the topic is backward, scattered and in desperate need of development" (Kroth 1978, 29).

Most of the early studies or reports were based on a few case histories that were taken from patients or from medical records. Sociologist S. K. Weinberg's (1955) sample of 203 cases of incest, mostly father/daughter incest, was large for its time and, compared to most reports, still is larger than most. Commenting on the lack of scientific literature, Carolyn Swift (1977) explains the problem in these words:

The scant data available—mostly surveys and anecdotal accounts—are open to the criticisms of memory deficit and subjective distortion inherent in retrospective studies. Disagreement over the definition of sexual abuse, methodological problems involved in observing and measuring private events and societal taboos complicate scientific attempts to explore the subject. . . . No national statistics documenting the sexual abuse of children exist. (Swift 1977, 322–23)

Other writers tend to agree. Kroth (1978, 122–26) described a review of the literature on incest as a "Rorschach blot" because he found, like David Gil, that this research reveals much subjective bias and a strong tendency for professionals to "use ambiguous, contradictory and paradoxical data to weave a tale which corresponds with how the observer wishes to see the information" (1978, 122). In addition, most writers have implicit or sometimes explicit assumptions that abusers are male (usually fathers or father-figures) and victims are female. It is important to know whether the data support these ideas, but sometimes that is difficult to learn from reports. For example, Kroth's 336-page report fails to reveal the sex ratios of victims and offenders of the incestuous families in the data he analyzes, despite the fact that he presents 72 figures displaying data on demographic features including age, income, and ethnic background of perpetrators (1978, 41–118).

This lack is noted by Swift (1977, 323) who says: "Available data are usually based on samples of female children—or are not retrievable by sex. Female children undisputedly constitute a major population at risk for sexual exploitation." Henry Giarretto (1976), director of the California Sexual Abuse Treatment Program (CSATP), addresses only father/daughter incest in his article. He uses the same explanation for focusing on this one type of victim-offender relationship as Raylene DeVine (1980a, 26), who says: "Father/daughter incest is the type most commonly reported to authorities. Perhaps for this reason, it also is the type most commonly studied and about which most is known."

Another report does not state the number of children treated, but it does make the sex ration of victims and offenders clear. Lucy Berliner, at the Sexual Assault Center of Seattle's Harborview Medical Center, says that of incest victims, 95 percent are female and 99 percent of the offenders are male; 82 percent of these are fathers or surrogate fathers (1977, 331). The interdisciplinary team of Burgess, Holmstrom, and McCausland (1977) studied a sample of 44 intrafamily sexual assault victims, and only two (5 percent) were boys; this percentage is compatible with Berliner's data.

However, there is reason to believe that sexual abuse of boys in families occurs at a higher rate than most reports indicate (Swift 1977). In a survey of students at eight northeast colleges and universities, Finkelhor obtained a sample of 796 respondents: 530 females and 266 males (1979a, 42). From this all-white, predominantly middle-class college sample, Finkelhor found that 19.2 percent (N 102) of the women and 8.6 percent (N 23) of the men had been sexually victimized (1979a, 53). As this researcher notes, the ratio of boy/girl victims is unlike most other reports which found girl victims outnumbered boys ten to one (cf. DeFrancis 1969). Still, there are important differences between the males and females in Finkelhor's sample. Boys are generally somewhat older when abuse occurs; their victimization occurs significantly less frequently with older family members (only 17 percent of the males were abused by relatives older than themselves, compared to 44 percent for females); when their sexual partner is also adolescent, sexual encounters are seldom coercive; and finally, the males' experiences, according to Finkelhor, "are evaluated fairly positively" (1979a, 81).

Concentrating strictly on incest, as compared to victimization, Finkelhor found that "there were more incidents of incest than of sexual abuse" (1979a, 83). Twenty-eight percent of the women (N 148) and 23 percent of the men (N 61) admitted sexual experiences with a member of the family. The only blood relatives that were not named as sexual partners were grandmothers, but there was one mother partnered with a girl and one aunt with a boy, which supports other estimates of the relative rarity of female incest offenders. Father and stepfather incest constituted just over 1 percent of the Finkelhor sample which, extrapolating to the population "means that approximately three-quarters of a million women eighteen and over in the general population have had such an experience, and that another 16,000 cases are added each year from among the group of girls aged five to seventeen" (1979a, 88). As Finkelhor notes, 1 percent is in keeping with previous surveys (cf. Gagnon 1965; Hunt 1974).

One of the latest studies, and one of the very few to employ a representative sampling technique, was conducted by sociologist Diana E. H. Russell in San Francisco (1980a, 1981, 1982). In her sample of 930 women, Russell found that 172 women (18 percent) reported at least one experience of incestuous sexual contact (1981, 5).

As for other estimates of the incidence of child sexual abuse, one source estimates that there are between 80,000 to 100,000 children who are sexually molested each year, about 25 percent of them by relatives (De Francis 1969). Sarafino (1979) extrapolated reported cases from four locales to the 1970 census population and estimated 74,225 reported cases nationwide in one year. Then, using projections of unreported crimes to reported assaults, Sarafino estimates that about 336,200 sexual assaults against children occur each year (1979, 130). This is in the same general range as an earlier study reported by Greenberg (1979, 289), who notes: "These figures are many times greater than for the battered-child syndrome." Yet attorneys Josephine Bulkley and Howard Davidson state: "The true incidence of child sexual abuse is difficult to measure, since it is the most underreported form of child abuse" (1980, 2).[7]

However, our interest here concerns sexual abuse of children within the family unit, whereas these estimates refer to all cases, inter- or intra-family. As Finkelhor's study showed, more of his respondents reported sexual experience with family members. In another report (1981b), Finkelhor estimates that as many as 15 to 30 percent of all American women and 5 to 10 percent of all American men have been sexually victimized as children. The Berliner report states that 75 percent of all the sexual abuse cases at the Harborview Sexual Assault Center involved a known offender (1977, 331). Most of these known assailants are family members, since other reports indicate that parents or guardians are implicated in between 72 and 80 percent of sexual abuse cases (Nakashima and Zakus 1979, 301). If that is the case, then using Sarafino's estimate (1979), based on the 1970 child population in the United States, there are more than 250,000 children sexually abused by family members each year.

Officially reported and substantiated cases of sexual maltreatment are of little assistance in trying to determine the extent of sexual abuse of children in the family because of the private nature of family life and the greater unwillingness of people to report on other family members. Of over 82,000 substantiated cases of child maltreatment in 1978, only about 7 percent, or just over 6,000 children were identified as victims of sexual maltreatment (American Humane Association 1980, 34).

Based mostly on research evidence and estimates from the experts cited above, it is reasonable to say that more than a quarter million children are victims of incest each year in the United States. Put another way, about one out of every five females and one out of every eleven males are sexually victimized during childhood, usually by family members or trusted friends of the family. People tend to react initially by disbelieving these kinds of statement, but slowly and often painfully, long-forgotten (or repressed) memories return for many: unwanted touching, strange feelings when left alone with certain adults, trying to wiggle away from the caresses and kisses of older relatives, not being able (or allowed) to say "no, don't" to disliked looks, uncomfortable pats, or being undressed by some adults. Confronting and dealing with resurfacing memories may be made easier by learning that the "awful secret" never told to anyone is actually shared by many others. Later sections of the book tell what we have learned about sexual abusers of children and their victims, and some proposals are offered to help them as well as some preventative ideas.

This section on incidence of sexual abuse in the family did not include two issues that will be discussed in detail in a later chapter: One is the emerging controversy over what has been euphemistically termed "children's rights" to sexual activity with adults. The other is also a newly emerging issue: marital rape. Few scientists have addressed marital rape, in large part because until very recently laws excluded husbands from prosecution for raping their wives. The study by Diana Russell (1982) is the only one that obtained a representative sample of women who were asked about rape and attempted rape from which statistics can be extrapolated to the population of women at risk for rape by husbands. Out of the 644 women who had ever been married, 87 women (14 percent) said they were the victims of at least one completed or attempted rape by their husbands or ex-husbands (Russell 1982, 57). For a number of reasons, Russell believes these data provide a very low estimate of wife rape. One reason is that many of the respondents did not define forced, unwanted sex as rape because they saw it as their "duty" (1982, 58). Even if this is a very conservative estimate of the true prevalence of wife rape, 14 percent applied to the American population of 48 million married women means that one out of seven, or almost 8 million wives are at risk of marital rape at least once during or after their marriages.

OTHER TYPES OF FAMILY VIOLENCE

Sibling Violence

There has been a notable lack of interest about most other types of family violence, particularly sibling violence, although lately there has been some attention paid to parent abuse, which will be addressed later. Most professionals exert little or no effort to theorize about or research violent children, except when their violent behavior goes beyond "normal" violence or is directed at persons in schools or on the streets. There is no lack of interest when children are publicly labeled delinquents, but until that time, their violent behavior is overlooked.

Why is it that Americans pay little or no attention to fights between siblings that sometimes end in cut lips, bruises, and occasionally even black eyes? Conflicts between toddlers over toys often result in one child knocking over the other, pushing, shoving, or cracking the other one over the head with the desired toy. Parents are much more likely to intervene and get upset over the consequences of the fights rather than at the fights themselves. Why is this? It seems that in our competitive, violent culture, most of us see this kind of behavior as normal. We only frown on violence when it goes *too far* (Lubenow 1983). Members of the scientific community, like their neighbors, have tended to ignore violence by children except when it takes extreme forms and is then labeled pathological. Most of the studies of violence by children are done with small, select samples of children who have committed homicide (Adelson 1973). Children's "middle-range" violence is overlooked.

Fortunately, despite its problems and limitations, the Conflict Tactics (CT) Scale used in the Straus et al. (1980) study included a schedule asking about child versus child, or sibling violence. The same factors—under- or overreporting, no measure of the context in which the acts occur, injuries (if any) sustained, and associated problems in using retrospective data—all must be kept in mind when reviewing these data. However, the CT Scale does provide us with a numerical tabulation of the acts and their frequency reported by one parent of one child in 733 families from a national probability sample (Straus et al. 1980, 80–90). The subsample was drawn from the 1,146 intact couples who were parents: 733 had two or more children between the ages of 3 and 17 living at home. It should be remembered that the person interviewed was one particular child's parent, not the child.

According to these researchers (Straus et al. 1980, 81), sibling violence is the most frequent type of family violence; four out of five of these children reportedly carried out at least one violent act each year. Extrapolating from their data to the population of children in that age range translates to: "Over 29 million American children engage in one or more acts of physical violence toward a sibling in a single year" (Straus et al. 1980, 81).

Table 2–3 shows the percentages of the various acts measured on the CT Scale. We may assume that some of the acts such as slapping, pushing, shoving, or even throwing things by youngsters, especially, are unlikely to do any serious damage. And Straus et al. admit that the percentage for hitting is highest for the very youngest children, but they say the rates are still high at older ages, particularly for boys (1980, 81,89). Using data on "beating up" a spouse or child, they make this comparison: "Although 1

Table 2–3. Percent of Children Who Were Violent to a Sibling in the Previous Year

Violent Act	Percent
Any violence	82.0
Pushed or shoved	74.0
Slapped	48.0
Threw things	43.0
Kicked, bit, punched	42.0
Hit with an object	40.0
Beat up	16.0
Threatened with a knife or gun	0.8
Used a knife or gun	0.3

Source: Straus et al. 1980, 81.

percent of the children were 'beaten up' by their parents and 1 percent of their parents 'beat up' each other, 16 percent of the children 'beat up' a brother or sister" (Straus et al. 1980, 83).

It should be remembered at this point that it was a parent, not a child, who defined certain behavior as "beat up," which was vaguely defined as something more than one blow (Straus et al. 1980, 245), regardless of whatever the particular circumstances may have been surrounding these reported events. Still, these data certainly make average American homes look like training grounds for adult combat troops. There will be further discussion about the Straus et al. (1980, 87) data on sibling violence in a later chapter, which will include the higher rates in families with boys, as well as the overall decrease in rates of violence as the children get older. Why there may be so much violence in families, particularly among the males of the families—adults or children—will also be further explored.

Parent Abuse

Sometimes violence is turned against parents, either by adolescents (Warren 1979), or when the parents are in their "golden years" by their middle-aged children. However, the subject of parent abuse has so recently been approached by professionals and researchers that there are almost no social scientists who are ready to venture a guess about the extensiveness of parent abuse. When researchers do discuss parent abuse, it concerns abuse of elderly parents by their adult offspring. There are no national incidence rates available yet, but with a growing proportion of Americans living longer lives, and with the vigorous political lobbying of aging Americans, some studies are certain to be conducted on this subject in the near future. Those studies will face the same types of problems that all other family violence research has had to deal with; family privacy, lack of consensus in conceptualization and definitions, and methodological problems. Some additional problems will arise in identifying victims. Nancy King (1983, 2), director of a senior services project, explains: "Unlike children who are in regular contact with teachers, doctors, and other adults, infirm elders are often isolated and, therefore, their mistreatment is less likely to be noticed by those who might be alert to symptoms of abuse."

Despite the lack of extensive research data, some estimates have been offered. When researcher Suzanne Steinmetz testified before a congressional committee in 1980, she estimated that at least 500,000 elderly citizens are abused each year (King 1983). One report edited by Marilyn R. Block and Jan D. Sinnott (1979) contains the results of a study that contacted agencies, individual professionals, and elders who lived in the communities. Their findings reveal:

Slightly more than 4 percent of elder respondents reported cases. If this incidence holds nationally, nearly a million cases would be expected nation-wide. Wide variations are found in estimates of child and spouse abuse. Elder abuse appears less frequent than spouse abuse (20% incidence rate) but as high as child abuse. . . . The elders surveyed were fairly representative of elders nationwide. (Block and Sinnott 1979, 80)

This finding concurs with the United States House Committee on Aging's 1981 report estimating that 4 percent of the elderly in this country are abused each year. Indeed, if these sources are accurate, their 4 percent finding translates to between 900,000 and 1 million abused elders in this country. Since the over-65 age group is growing at a fast rate, perhaps aged victims of family violence will soon outnumber child victims. These may or may not be accurate estimates, considering that they are based on very few, and largely exploratory studies, but they do point to the fact that the elderly in this country can no longer be ignored when we consider family violence.

SUMMARY

This chapter looked at the estimates made by a wide variety of experts on the extent of family violence. Since most researchers focus on a specific type of violence rather than a violence index, that was the approach taken here. Estimates vary widely, largely due to the way researchers and agencies conceptualize the various issues, the definitions they employ, and the methods used to study them. Consequently, the same behaviors may be interpreted differently from one study to the next.

Based on analysis of the evidence, it appears that wife abuse yields the highest incidence rates of severe violence and the largest population of victims, at a conservative estimate of 12 million beaten wives per year in the United States. If the reader chooses to use the Straus et al. (1980) estimates, there could be about 12 million wives and husbands physically beaten each year. In any case, spouse abuse affects all family members, whether they are direct targets of violence or not (Pagelow 1981b). Spouse abuse has been researched much less than child maltreatment, and perhaps new research findings will help answer many important questions.

Estimates on the extent of physical child abuse range roughly from less than 1 million to almost 2 million children abused or "vulnerable to physical injury from violence" (Gelles 1979) in a given year. Few researchers have studied physical neglect and emotional neglect and abuse, and even fewer have tried to estimate their incidence apart from physical abuse. But if we use officially reported cases of child abuse and neglect as a starting point (recognizing that the statistics are grossly underrepresentative of true incidence), and examine the ratio of abuse to neglect, we can see that there are approximately twice as many substantiated cases of neglect reported each year as abuse cases. On that basis then, compared to physical abuse, there may be between 2 and 4 million children physically neglected each year. There are no figures available from which to project emotional abuse and neglect, but there certainly must be millions of children who suffer these forms of maltreatment.

When it comes to sexual abuse in the family, estimates of sexual abuse of children range from 80,000 to 250,000 each year, and unestimated numbers of wives are subjected to rape or attempted rape in any given year. The only study to measure incidences of sibling violence (Straus et al. 1980) found that 16 percent of children aged 3 to 17 beat up siblings. Extrapolating that rate to the population of American children in the same age range (about 36 million during the year when the beatings occurred), infers that about 11.5 million children may either beat or be beaten by a sibling at least once every year. As for abuse of elderly parents, at the 4 percent estimate, it seems possible that 1 million elderly persons are now victims of abuse by relatives in their homes, but that figure promises to increase sharply in the coming years as their numbers increase.

The one firm conclusion that can be drawn from all these estimates and projections is that the family is hardly the idealized image that most of us harbored—that it is literally a battleground for many types of abusive behavior. What can be done about it remains to be discussed. The next chapter looks at similarities and common features found in various types of family violence. There are not many, but it is important to recognize the few threads that seem to run between otherwise vastly different phenomena because many homes contain multiple types of violence.

NOTES

1. All of these composite cases come from the writer's study of woman battering, but number 3 was excluded for the reasons given. As long as sadomasochistic acts for the purpose of sexual arousal and enjoyment were mutually agreed upon, they were not considered as spouse abuse (Pagelow 1981a, 269–70). However, when one person did not voluntarily participate and was forced into violent activities, that was identified as abusive. Several such cases did surface during interviews, but in each of them, the women unwillingly "played" the victim-role.

2. Some may insist that victims are likely to exaggerate or deny their own contributions to the violence. About the former, Walker has this to say: "If a woman has reason to suspect she is being battered, she probably is. If she errs in her judgment at all, it is in denying or minimizing the battering relationship. Battered women rarely exaggerate" (1979, xiv). As for "one-sided views," Dobash and Dobash state: "The women we inter-

viewed were willing to explore their own actions related to the violent episode and indeed we would have been surprised if they failed to do so given the widespread tendency to blame women in such situations" (1979, 259–60).

3. Also excluded from the writer's study were cases dubbed "mutual combat," in which couples are equally determined to do battle with one another, usually within certain implicit limitations (1981a, 270). An earlier study of couples married at least ten years typed those who regularly engaged in this type of activity as "conflict habituated" couples (Cuber and Harroff 1965). This form of mutual violence occurs between people fairly matched in aggressiveness and hostility that differ from the writer's use of the concept "woman battering," referring to generally one-way attacks from which a woman may or may not defend herself.

4. The largest difference in the data provided by Dobash and Dobash (1978, 436) and the data from Mulvihill and Tumin (1969) concerns the target of women offenders: Scottish women aggressed against other females more than males, whereas when American females were the aggressors, their targets were more likely to be males. In fact, they aggressed against males at about twice the rate for Scottish females. An earlier paper (Pagelow 1978a) suggested some reasons for the differences, one of which is the easier accessibility of firearms for women in the United States. Guns have been called the "great equalizer"; regardless of size of muscular power, the aggressor having a weapon, particularly a loaded gun, shifts the balance of power in his or her own direction.

5. There is some ambiguity about the response category labeled "hit with something" or "hit with an object." On page 261 of appendix B in the Straus et al. book (1980), the authors report that they yielded to objections to including hitting a child with an object as an indicator of child abuse, and therefore computed Child Abuse Index B to omit that item. Severe violence indexes show two titles listed for child abuse: Index A includes "hitting with an object," and index B excludes "hitting with an object" (1980, 260). In the text of the book, however, there are three separate references to parents who hit their children with objects without any indication of exclusion (Straus et al. 1980, 61–63), and Gelles (1979) makes no mention of excluding it in a separate index.

6. There has been a great proliferation of articles and books on the topic of sexual abuse of children and incest in just the past few years, and new reports are being published at an astounding rate, now that the cloak of secrecy has been lifted from discussing this taboo (Brongersma 1980; Bulkley and Davidson 1980; Doron 1981; Gomes-Schwartz 1981; Greenberg 1979; Greenwood 1980; Groth 1979; Herman 1981; Julian and Mohr 1979; Kiersh 1980; MacFarlane 1978; MacFarlane et al. 1980; Middleton 1978; Mrazek 1980; Nakashima and Zakus 1979; Pascoe 1979; Quirk-Haas 1980; Russell 1981; Sanford 1980; Sarafino 1979; Schwartz and Fitzgerald 1980; Shamroy 1980; Sink 1981; Spencer 1978; Summit and Kryso 1978; Tierney and Corwin 1981; Tsai and Wagner 1977).

7. It should be noted that many statements about underreporting are unscientifically based on pure conjecture or unsubstantiated impressions. Exceptions to this are statements derived from victimization studies such as the National Crime Surveys wherein respondents report personal victimization not reported to police (Hindelang et al. 1981, 227–90). Claims of underreporting have considerable reliability when they are derived from studies in which samples report their victimization to researchers, and disclose whether or not they also reported to authorities (see Finkelhor 1979a). For example, the Dobash and Dobash (1978, 1979) study found that only two out of ninety-eight assaults by husbands were reported to police (1978, 437). The author's own survey sample reported that the police were called in more than 50 percent of the cases (N 200) on at least one occasion (Pagelow 1981a, 81), but underreporting cannot be determined because there was no measure of the total number of assaults on these women.

PART II

Theoretical Viewpoints

3

Similarities in Various Types of Family Violence

Most of the writers whose works are cited in this book are specialists who concentrate on one type of family violence or another: child maltreatment, spouse abuse (usually wife beating), incest, sexual abuse of wives, sibling violence, parent abuse by adolescents and teens, abuse of elderly parents by their adult children, spouse homicide, infanticide, filicide, patricide, and so forth. For example, child maltreatment can be and frequently is divided into several specialties: physical abuse and neglect, physical abuse, physical neglect, psychological abuse and neglect, adolescent abuse and neglect, infanticide, and filicide. This specialization makes intuitive good sense, because the victims and victimizers may be vastly different, so that theories proposing identifying features or treatment protocols are necessarily narrow in focus. An explanation for one kind of family violence may be very inappropriate for another. Nevertheless, there are some similarities and features commonly found in many types of family violence, and it is important to recognize these.

Sociologist David Finkelhor (1981a) is one of the few researchers and authors who has made an attempt to examine the various types of family violence and search for similarities between them. Many other writers either accept the idea that the differences are so great that they choose to concentrate on one specific kind of abuse to the exclusion of the others, or they assume that they are all "pieces of the same pie" and that answers to one sort of abuse will lead semi-automatically to answers to all. Few writers have attempted to systematically examine the wide variety of behaviors, the aggressors, and the victims for similarities and commonalities. But as Finkelhor (1981, 1) notes, there are separate groups of professionals around the country talking and writing about, lobbying for, and intervening in spouse abuse, child abuse, and child sexual abuse as separate areas. Further, he explains:

> Each problem has its separate set of agencies, separate set of theories, and separate history of how it became "discovered." Perhaps most serious, in this day of waning public policy interest and waning public resources for social problems, there are some bitter rivalries and political infighting among the proponents of these separate problems, as each tries to get policy makers to give priority to their particular kind of family abuse. (Finkelhor 1981a, 1)

These are some of the reasons why it has been difficult to study family violence. It involves the monumental task of gathering together the vast array of theoretical and research literature into one concise and unambiguous format. Practitioners in the social service and criminal justice fields frequently deal with multiproblem families in which they discover there are several types of abuse occurring simultaneously. To be fully trained and equipped to handle these cases efficiently, they must become cognizant of both the similarities and the differences among types of abuse. There are some common features and these should not be overlooked. As Finkelhor (1981a, 2) says, finding commonalities may help offset some factionalizing tendencies and benefit research and theory, as well as help reduce some of the political adversity and competition among professionals in specialized fields. Each of these similarities or features commonly found in violent families suggest ideas about how this knowledge can be applied to reduce violence.

POWER DIFFERENTIALS

In one of the earliest articles on family violence, family sociologist William Goode (1971) wrote about "Force and Violence in the Family." Goode began his article by explaining that, for a number of reasons, he was substituting "force and its threat" for the term he preferred to us, "power." In the context in which it is used here, *power* means the ability to impose one's will upon another with or without consent or resistance, and therefore, force or its threat is merely one method out of many to obtain compliance. Power has a broader meaning and is clearly more appropriate to use, for example, when speaking of incest. Incest is an abuse of power by an adult that seldom involves violent physical force, although it is more likely to involve a threat of force. Incest is more likely to involve, at least in the beginning, seduction and the implied promise of rewards instead of force.

Family violence has one underlying feature common to all types: It involves power differentials—the bigger or the stronger or the ones with the greater access to valued resources—these are the ones who impose their wills on others who are smaller, weaker, or without resources. Finkelhor (1981a, 3) goes one step farther when he notes: "The most common patterns are not merely for the more powerful to abuse the less powerful but for the most powerful to abuse the least. This is an interesting commonality: Abuse tends to gravitate to the relationships of *greatest power differential.*"

Finkelhor then goes on to use sexual abuse as an example: The most commonly reported form of sexual abuse involves adult males in authority positions victimizing girls in subordinate positions (1981a, 3). Family members have unequal statuses based on sex, age, and roles, as well as physical strength and access to resources. Compared to persons outside the family, some adult males may be in subordinate, powerless positions, but within the family unit, they may have extreme power which they exploit. Finkelhor also compares the extreme power differentials that are common to another type of family violence, saying:

> In physical child abuse a similar principle of the strongest victimizing the weakest operates. First, statistics seem to show that the greatest volume of abuse is directed against the most powerless children, those under the age of six. And I believe the statistics should also be interpreted to show the more common vulnerability to be at the hands of the more powerful parent—the father.[1] (1981a, 4)

The Straus et al. (1980) study, which included children only between the ages of 3 and 17, found that among parents' acts toward children, "The rates for violent acts peaked at two ages: The youngest in our sample (3 and 4 year olds) and the oldest (15 to 17 year olds)" (Gelles and Straus 1979, 25). It would seem that these data on violence against the youngest age group support Finkelhor's contention of greatest power differential, but what about the peak rates at the older age group? The fact is, the data show an overall decrease from the younger ages until age 10 to 14, with a slight increase at the next age level, 15 to 17. However, within the behavior categories the most frequently reported violent acts for the young are still lower for the oldest age group. In other words, most of the violent acts parents reported they engaged in were in the categories: "pushed/grabbed/shoved," and "slapped or spanked" (Gelles 1979, 87). Both of these types of parental acts declined over all age groups: Pushed, grabbed, or shoved went from a rate of 39 percent for the 3 to 4 year age group to 20.8 percent for the 15 to 17 age group. Slapped or spanked markedly decreased from 84.1 percent for the toddlers to 23 percent for the older teenagers. In only one category was there an increase in the rate from the younger to the older, and that rate went from 1.1 percent to 1.7 percent of the parents who admitted they "beat up" their child in the past year.

Research shows that parents use less physical punishment on their children as they become older (Steinmetz 1977), but there is a corresponding crossover of the children most likely to be punished at adolescence. Child abuse reports show that boys are slightly more likely to be victims until around age 12, and then girls become the primary victims (American Humane Association 1980, 28). Little boys may be treated physically rougher due to cultural ideas of promoting masculine stereotypes of the "little tough guy," and overall, this rougher treatment leads to more abuse. Then at adolescence, attention turns from sons to daughters because parents are concerned about their budding sexuality. As girls begin to want and demand more freedom from parental scrutiny, parents simultaneously begin to set restrictive rules that are enforced by physical punishment and restraint.

These ideas probably provide partial answers, but there is another corresponding change that is generally ignored: While the girls are developing sexually, the boys are also developing in physical stature and prowess. From a social learning or exchange perspective, it may become less attractive for a parent who is somewhat past his physical peak to continue hitting or punching a boy who now stands eye-to-eye with him. A man who has terrorized his son for years may begin to realize that some day he might get punched back! Certainly by the adolescent years, the power differential between parents and sons has decreased, but there is still a great power differential between parents and daughters. Unfortunately, the table Gelles (1979, 86) provides for parent-to-child violence is not broken down by both age as well as sex, but it does show that sons were slightly more likely to be victims than daughters. There is one notable exception: The rates for acts ever committed against children show that girls were more likely to have experienced the two most severe types of violence—being threatened with a knife or gun, or to have had a knife or gun used against them.

In sum, the evidence lends its weight to support the idea of the greatest power differential. Parents' power diminishes relative to boys' increasing power, but remain substantial relative to girls. It is likely that some parents who focused most of their abuse on their sons turn their aggression on their previously unabused daughters once the boys grow to a size sufficient to strike back. Frequently, this is what happens when fathers have been sexually abusing their eldest daughters; when the girls get old enough to seriously resist and demand freedom, the fathers then turn to younger, and more powerless, victims in the family (Middleton 1978).

Finkelhor (1981a) also notes the disparity in power in the case of spouse abuse, citing the Straus et al. study (1980) where wives were found more likely to be abused when they were not in the paid labor market, excluded from family decision making, and having less education than their husbands. In other words, the less power the wife has relative to her husband, the more likely she is to be physically abused. As Finkelhor (1981a, 5) states, "Once. again abuse gravitates to the greatest power differential." These findings argue against the ideas of some people who believe and claim that women are most likely to be beaten when there is fierce competition for domination and control between husband and wife. In other words, the "uppity" wife is more likely to be put back in her (subservient) place than the quiet, obedient wife who has little or no power in the relationship. To the contrary, the Straus et al. (1980) findings show that the less power the wife has, the more likely the husband is to abuse his greater power; conversely, the more egalitarian the relationship, the less likely spouse abuse will occur.

Application: Reducing Power Differentials

Almost all writers and researchers of spouse abuse have called for an end to unequal power relationships between men and women, both in the home and in society, and for the replacement of this norm with egalitarian relationships (Dobash and Dobash 1979; Gelles 1979; Pagelow 1981; Steinmetz and Straus 1974; Straus 1978; Walker 1979). In addition, if "abuse tends to gravitate to the relationships of greatest power differential" as Finkelhor claims, the same reduction of power differentials should also work to reduce physical and sexual abuse of children. To that end, many people are engaged in a struggle for children's rights both at home and in society. As a result, children in some jurisdictions are given advocates in court, juvenile justice laws are being revised to give children power to defend themselves that they formerly lacked, and there is a strong and growing movement in this country trying to prevent sexual molestation of children by teaching them that they have a right to say no to unwanted touching by adults.

But what about other types of abuse in the family? Is the same imbalance of power present in sibling violence and abuse of parents by their children? So little research has been done into sibling violence, it is difficult to provide strong empirical evidence to support the idea but casual observation in the neighborhood and playgrounds indicate that much of the violence occurs when children bigger and stronger act forcefully against smaller and weaker children. Learning theory would support this idea, because if the behavior emitted is not rewarded but is punished, that behavior is unlikely to recur. Children who attempt aggression against other children with whom they are fairly evenly matched in terms of physical strength are less likely to perceive aggression as rewarding than are children where there is a considerable imbalance in their favor. As for abuse of parents, particularly frail elderly parents, there is hardly any doubt about there being an important power differential, despite the paucity of empirical research. Regardless of age, the more self-sufficient and mobile the older parent is, the less likely that parent is to be victimized by his or her caretakers. On the other hand, the elderly may be bedridden and greatly demanding but have the power of accumulated financial resources that they use as a power leverage to take advantage of their caretakers or keep them in check. Some abuse of the elderly occurs when their children take control of their finances, and thus the power differential swings in the other direction, after which other abuses may occur.

SOCIAL ISOLATION

Regardless of which type of abuse is being studied, another important commonality is social isolation of the family, which is frequently noted in the literature (Pagelow 1981a; Steele and Pollack 1974; Walker 1979). The list of unique characteristics of the family devised by Gelles and Straus that contribute to making it a violence-prone institution contains the factor they categorized "privacy" (Gelles 1979, 14). By this they are referring to the insulation of the family from the eyes, ears, and the rules of the larger society. They note that as privacy increases, the level of social control decreases. Interestingly, two studies have found that there is a greater likelihood of child abuse in families without telephones (Gaines et al. 1978; Newberger et al. 1977).

Perhaps the embeddedness of a family in kinship or friendship networks serves to prevent family violence by the members' reluctance to violate norms of behavior, or it might serve also to defuse petty irritations from developing into inflammable situations by having others around to talk with or intervene when necessary. The isolation does not have to be geographic; families are found to have high levels of violence when they live in high density living areas as well as in rural areas (until the recent wave of research on incest, many people assumed that most sexual abuse occurred among rural families). Judith Herman and Lisa Hirschman (1980) find that most father/daughter incest occurs in families that are notable for their extreme paternal domination and isolation. Also writing on sexual abuse, Kee MacFarlane (1978, 88) finds that family isolation, plus parents' attitudes of ownership of their children both make it difficult for persons outside the family to deter or prevent this crime from occurring.

Lack of family or community ties serves to release the family from obligations of explaining their behavior inside and outside of the home or their reasons for moving from one location to another. Gelles and Straus (1979, 33) report that their large study found higher rates of abusive violence toward children among parents who had lived in the same neighborhood less than three years. Many parents of abused children are noted for frequent household moves (Smith et al. 1982), and one of the reasons it is so difficult to gain evidence of abuse is that the victims are often taken to different places for medical treatment (McNeese and Hebeler 1977). Families that repeatedly move from one residence to another are unlikely to become embedded into the community by joining organizations, and it is not just the geographic mobility of violent families that distinguishes them from others, but rather their isolation from the communities they live within. Gelles and Straus say that "Participation in organizations outside the home made an even greater difference [than moving patterns]" (1979, 33). In their study, families that did not belong to or attend meetings of any community or neighborhood organization had much higher rates of child-directed violence than did "joiners."

Studies of wife abuse show that whereas the husbands may have friendship networks and social contacts most often outside the home, the victims are most frequently isolated in the home (Dobash and Dobash 1979). On the other hand, there is one study of formerly battered wives that found little evidence of wives' social isolation; on several measures the wives were significantly less isolated than their husbands (Bowker 1983a, 43). Perhaps the difference is that the 136 women in social scientist Lee Bowker's study were all women who had *beaten wife beating* (1983). The author's own study showed that many women who were beaten had been gradually isolated from outside contacts. The process by which this occurred varied: Sometimes it was because of frequent family moves (such as in the military), or because the abuser behaved so ungraciously when the wives' friends were in their home that they gradually ceased their visits, or because the husbands accused their wives' families or friends of being "troublemakers" and refused to let them have contact any longer. However the isolation occurred, it became a fact of their lives for many formerly very sociable women to find themselves cut off from anyone who knew them or cared about them. In many cases, it was not until this process was completed that the physical violence began, but it is not clear whether this gradual isolation of victims was a deliberate maneuver on the part of the abusers, or if the abuse could only occur when the husbands realized that their wives were now totally dependent upon them for the "looking-glass" upon which they based their self-image. In either case, most of the women who arrive at shelters have had no close personal friends for years and have had very little contact with their own families.

Abused elderly, especially when they are nonambulatory, are likely to have severely restricted contacts outside the places where they reside. As long as they are able to leave home alone, they may develop and maintain friendship and community networks, but as their dependence increases their worlds shrink. If they are unable to attend community events and maintain friendship networks, they increasingly come under the control of their caretakers. When they move into the residences of their children they are strangers to the neighborhood, or when their children move into the parents' residences, they (the parents) may become the "invisible inhabitants" of a neighborhood. Especially if they are confined to home or to a bed, no one outside realizes they even exist, so that what happens to them in the privacy of the home is protected by an invisible wall of isolation. If the family they live with is involved in community organizations, they usually are known to the community; if not, they are "nonexistent." As Gelles notes, "Where privacy is high, the degree of social control will be low" (1979, 14).

Application: Reducing Social Isolation

If social isolation is a common feature to all forms of family violence, then this suggests that we must begin to think of ways to decrease isolation and begin to involve all families into community networks where no family or individual is "invisible." It would be extremely difficult to beat your children or your wife one night, and then step out the door the next day to water the lawn in front of your neighbors or attend church services with your community. When your next-door neighbors do not even know your face, or if you belong to no community organization, wife beating may be possible, because you are nameless and anonymous. Therefore, one method to break down the walls of privacy or social isolation is to involve *all* families in the social fabric of the neighborhood.

There are many methods to accomplish this, but one that comes to mind is an increasingly popular program that is being promulgated by police departments across the country to prevent household burglaries, called *Neighborhood Watch*. Through this program even the infirm elderly and physically handicapped become known to their neighbors, at least by name and telephone number, and some innovative program planners are inviting them to use their talents, along with those of their more able-bodied neighbors, in the common protection of their neighborhoods. Just imagine the changes that occur when the family that previously resisted all attempts at friendly contact finds out it is the only one not attending a neighborhood meeting. Abusers want anonymity, but instead of a low profile, they become highly visible to people up and down the block by their refusal to join in a common endeavor. Suddenly, they find that they are more than a street number to the mail carrier—they have been noticed by their neighbors. If they yield to social pressures and join, it can be the first big step toward decreasing the isolation within which so much family violence thrives.

Hopefully, it is becoming evident why theory building is so important in the social sciences and why research and theory go hand in hand. Exploratory research tries to uncover commonalities and patterns found in human behavior, theorists propose *why* and *how* events occur as they do. When theories are tested and receive support, findings suggest solutions to problems. If these features of unequal power and isolation are common to all types of family violence, then they may serve as signals to professionals seeking prevention or trying to identify dysfunctional families. They also suggest methods of amelioration.

EFFECTS ON VICTIMS

Low Self-Esteem

Victims of all types of family violence share a common experience of denigration of self that results in diminished self-esteem. The shame and feelings of worthlessness so often expressed by battered wives is shared by maltreated children as well as maltreated elderly parents. Sexually abused children feel "different" and ugly, and often reveal that they fear that others may be able to look at them and see their awful "secret." These common feelings of worthlessness are the product of the psychological abuse that coincides with the sexual abuse.

Wives who are battered by their husbands frequently report that the psychological abuse began first, followed by and then accompanying physical abuse (Pagelow 1981a). When a woman has been told often enough that she is worthless, ugly, stupid, and sexually unsatisfactory by the man she married and loved, she begins to give the demeaning words credibility, and when she is isolated from others whose care might counterbalance this negative portrait, she comes to accept it as her self-image.

The child who is physically abused is almost always likewise psychologically abused before or during the violent attacks. Told that they are stupid, clumsy, unwanted, and hopeless, they begin to believe that this is what they *are*. Many times they defend their parents' abusiveness by claiming that they were "always getting into trouble." Similarly, the neglected child—when he or she is not being totally ignored (which is another form of psychological abuse)—will often be berated for wanting attention. When a hungry child wants something to eat but mother is too drunk to make the attempt to prepare a meal, the child is likely to be told that he or she is a nuisance, a "brat," or a "pain in the neck."

The incest victim is told that she better not complain because, after all, she was "the one who started it." In the beginning, the child's psychological abuse consists of attempts to convince her that she really *wants* father's sexual attention. Later, when she tries to break away, accusations begin that she is "trash" or a "whore" because she wants to go out with boys her own age.

When aged parents require more and more attention and care, the abusive caretaker scolds them for the problems they create and even plays on their fears that they will be abandoned if they do not "behave." Much like hostages in desperate situations, they become very grateful to their custodians for any little thing that is done for them because they feel so worthless and dependent.

How these unrealistic and negative self-images develop and come to be accepted by victims of family violence is explained by important social-psychological and sociological principles, such as the *looking-glass self* proposed by Charles Horton Cooley (1902). The looking-glass is our society, which acts as a mirror in which we observe the reactions of others to us and to our behavior. We form our beliefs about ourselves by the images we see reflected. The attitudes of others show us whether we are intelligent or stupid, attractive or repulsive, interesting or boring. If we receive positive impressions, or at least believe they are positive, we form positive self-images and continue to act in ways that bring approval. If we receive negative impressions, our self image diminishes. Subsequently we are likely to try to change, but if we fail to see an improved image, our self-esteem drops even more.

Within the confines of the home, family members have fewer "mirrors" to produce alternative images, thus negative images are much more likely to impress themselves upon family members whose mobility is restricted: the very young, the aged, and wives whose husbands control their outside contacts (Pagelow 1978a). Cooley (1902) believed that self-images developed in childhood are more stable and long-lasting, and therefore are crucial to behavior and personality development, although self-images and self-evaluation change throughout life as we and our environment change.

Another sociological theory explains not only how negative self-evaluations are accepted, but how people tend to adopt the characteristics others attribute to them. This is the principle proposed by Merton (1968) of the *self-fulfilling prophesy*, which explains how ideas that are untrue in the beginning tend to produce behavior that matches the originally false ideas. This is a key proposition adopted by labeling theorists who explain deviant behavior as being a response to and acceptance of labels that are attached to some people (Becker 1966; Lemert 1972). Sociologist Erving Goffman (1963, 30) writes that a response to being labeled deviant is to embrace the label; in other words, persons become what they are accused of being.

It is easy to see how children who are constantly ridiculed and demeaned by parents (and teachers) form a negative self-image and begin to act as they are expected to act: clumsy, stupid, ugly, mean, and so forth. Children are very impressionable and have no (or few) memories of success. How can the self-fulfilling prophesy apply to adults? The attacks may have to be more vicious or longer-lasting for a formerly competent person to begin to adopt negative attributes, but on the other hand it may be more difficult for them to reject false ideas as nonsense because in the case of spouses and aged parents, their self-images have an investment in the abuser. The spouse chose the abuser as her or his lover and the parent produced and raised the abuser as her or his child. In order to reject what the abuser says about one's self, it is necessary to reject the abuser as a worthwhile and important person; simultaneously, this means that the victims must admit to themselves that they made serious mistakes in their choices or "failed" in one of life's most important tasks. Whichever they do, they will suffer from greatly diminished self-esteem. Finkelhor has this to say about psychological abuse and its effects on victims:

> All forms of family abuse seems [sic] to occur in the context of psychological abuse and exploitation, a process victims sometimes describe as "brainwashing." Victims are not just exploited or physically injured, but their abusers use their power and family connection to control and manipulate victims' perceptions of reality as well. . . . This "brainwashing" that occurs along with family abuse is potent because families are the primary group where most individuals construct reality. Family members often do not have enough contact with other people who can give them countervailing perceptions about themselves. (1981a, 7–8)

Understanding the development of low self-esteem and how it affects the behavior of victims of family violence is very important for professionals who want to help them. Combining the first factor, isolation, with psychological abuse increases the possibility that victims suffer from low self-esteem, and thus this could be one of the first indicators for effective intervention.

Shame and Helplessness

There are other effects that victims of family violence share in common: One of the most commonly noted is the sense of shame and humiliation they feel. The wife feels that she is the only one whose husband beats her; therefore it must be her fault somehow. The child feels that if he or she was nicer, daddy or mommy would not act that way. The incest victim feels that her body has betrayed her. The elderly parent wonders "where did I go wrong?" Self-blame is common to all victims of family violence. Many crime victims have similar feelings, for example, the rape victim who feels at fault for not locking the windows or not starting home earlier, or the burglarized person who feels violated and believes the crime would not have occurred "if only I had (or had not). . . ." However, according to Finkelhor, "Although victims of violence and exploitation in other settings also blame themselves, it is particularly severe for victims in families, where the abuser is a powerful person who has had a powerful effect on shaping victim's perceptions" (1981a, 8).

Unlike victims of crimes perpetrated by strangers, victims of family violence are much more likely to experience feelings of helplessness and entrapment (Walker 1979). Burglary victims are likely to move into a period of anger and resolution that they will never again be violated by intruders and assuage their grief over lost possessions by taking greater preventative measures to secure their homes. Rape victims are likely to learn methods of self-defense and prevention after they pass the crisis period. But victims of family violence know their abusers, live with them, fear retribution if they disclose the crimes, most frequently are dependent upon them, and either love or have loved them. Finkelhor explains in these terms:

> [T]here is a kind of entrapment that stymies the victims of all kinds of family abuse. The abuse often goes on over an extended period of time and the victims have difficulty either stopping it, avoiding it, or leaving entirely. . . . [V]ictims of spouse abuse, child abuse and sexual abuse often do not try to escape their abusers, in fact, in many instances, they want to go back and go to great lengths to protect their abusers from outside intervention. (1981a, 10)

Another feature that is commonly, but not always, found as an effect of family violence—extreme loyalty to the abusers—is addressed shortly. At this point the issue is the perceived helplessness of victims of family violence. Psychologist Lenore Walker (1979, 42–54) stresses the *learned helplessness* theory to explain why battered wives seem unable to do anything to stop the abuse or to escape from it. This theory builds upon the work of experimental psychologist Martin Seligman (1975) who confined dogs and other animals to cages and administered electrical shocks to them so that no matter what they did there was no escape. Eventually, they became paralyzed by fear and helplessness so that even when the shocks ceased, they made no attempt to escape; the dogs had to be literally dragged from their cages.

Although many of us are reluctant to generalize findings from laboratory experiments on animals to explain human behavior, there is also a sociological theorum, the *definition of the situation.* Offered long ago by William I. Thomas, it states: "If men define situations as real, they are real in their consequences" (Thomas and Thomas 1928, 572). If a spouse is psychologically and physically abused and believes that she is hopelessly trapped in her situation, she *is* trapped. When a child is convinced that nobody in the world would want to have anything to do with him or her, that child will not turn to neighbors or school officials and ask for help. When infirm parents believe they are totally dependent upon cruel caretakers, even though they have economic means to buy better care elsewhere, they *are* dependent. Reality is socially constructed and when victims of family violence perceive themselves to be trapped and helpless, they are.

When professionals attempt to intervene on behalf of victims of family violence, they are frequently frustrated by their clients' inability to take charge of their own lives and function independently. From the perspective of the helper, the client has every opportunity to begin again without fear and pain, but from the perspective of the client, the burden of shame and helplessness remains. Patience and supportive encouragement are essential so that in time, the client can gain (or regain) a sense of wellness and strength.

Effects Shared by Some Victims: Loyalty and Behavioral Patterns

There are certain effects of family violence that are found among some, but not all, victims. David Finkelhor makes reference (1981a, 10), to the fact that victims of family violence frequently want to go back to these situations and even try to protect their abusers from outside intervention. This is particularly noted among child victims of physical abuse, who sometimes seem to prefer the parents that abuse them over the nonabusive parents. It is not as often noted among children who are neglected, since they may cling to the parent (or anyone) who notices them and provides services for them. It is, however, also found in children who are being sexually abused, especially in the early stages, for they have been convinced that they are special, "daddy's princess" (Herman and Hirschman 1980). Later, even though they may have spent years trying to avoid their fathers' touch, they are more defensive of him and more angry at their mothers for having failed to protect them (Finkelhor 1981a, 9). Many adults who were victims of paternal incest admit they never told anyone about the abuse because they feared their fathers would be sent to prison; they did not want to punish their abusers—they just wanted them to stop (Armstrong 1979).

This extreme loyalty among victims is not confined to child victims. Many aged parents insist to police that their children did not mean to harm them, despite severe injuries or deprivations. This is extremely vexing to police officers called by concerned neighbors (Wellins 1980). Abused wives, discussing their problems in shelters, are frequently lured back to their abusers because they are concerned about the welfare and well-being of the men who beat them and caused them to leave for their own safety. Finkelhor sums it up in these words: "One additional result of abuse in the family context is that many of the victims often maintain a rather incredible allegiance to their abusers in spite of all the damage that he does" (1981a, 9).

There is another set of responses that occurs frequently, but again not always, among persons identified as victims of family violence. This is a constellation of long-term behavioral characteristics that appear among victims of different kinds of abuse. Finkelhor says they report "surprisingly similar long-term patterns: depression, suicidal feelings, self-contempt and an inability to trust and to develop intimate relationships in their later lives" (1981a, 10). These characteristics may not hold for all victims, but there are some that seem to be frequently evident. One pattern is an apparent lack of self-confidence and the other, as noted by Finkelhor, is an inability to trust others in intimate, meaningful relationships. For example, one adult female victim of incest confided that her lover notes her moods and wants her to "open up," but she resists because she is convinced he could never understand. An adult male victim of incest desperately wants to marry and begin a family, but he finds that when intimacy reaches a certain point, he involuntarily begins to back away. Another male adult who was physically and psychologically abused by his father and stepmother admits that even though he wants to marry and is heterosexual he cannot maintain intimate relationships with females.

Application: Understanding and Helping Victims

These commonalities noted among victims of family violence must be viewed with some caution. They cannot be generalized to all victims since there is no way to identify all victims. The observations noted above are

based only on those victims who have come to the attention of researchers by one means or another. Greater confidence can be placed in those
similarities found in almost all victims suffering psychological abuse: the
low self-esteem, the shame and humiliation, and the feelings of helplessness. These features are commonly evident, regardless of the type of victimization suffered. On the other hand, we do not know if the people
studied differ in significant or important ways from victims who never
come to the attention of professionals. Nor do we know much about how
long these feelings last, since most of these people and their problems
are observed shortly after they are discovered by outsiders. Observations
and research show that many victims make remarkable recoveries beginning as soon as they are removed from their previous lives of pain, fear,
and humiliation. Most children undergo swift changes in behavior and
personality almost as soon as they arrive at shelters with their mothers
(Pagelow 1982a), but some must receive professional help to begin the
process of recovery. Battered women have shown speedy recovery, once
they find they are safe and that there are viable alternatives to the kinds of
lives they had been leading. Some previously battered women move away
from the "victim status" and begin professional lives or assume leadership
positions. On the other hand, some do not recover quickly, and neglected children and children who were sexually abused may have a lifelong struggle to gain feelings of competence, self-worth, and the ability to
trust.

The last two effects on victims of abuse—loyalty toward abusers and the
long-term effects such as depression and suicidal feelings—have been
noted in some, but not all, victims of all types of abuse. Instead, some
victims harbor deep-rooted anger and resentment at the way their parent/
s treated them, turning the pain outward. Since there are differing reactions by victims, caution must be employed when generalizing about reaction to abuse. Observations raise interesting questions but they do not
provide definitive answers, although they may serve to point the way toward needed future research.

ALCOHOL ABUSE AND CHEMICAL DEPENDENCY

The question is frequently raised among nonprofessionals about whether
or not family violence is caused by drinking or drug use. Dating back to
the temperance movement, the specter of the "devil rum," which caused
men to beat their wives and drunken parents to beat their helpless infants, has been popularized. However, despite the fact that there is a
strong correlation between alcohol use and violence, social scientists are
unwilling to propose a *causal relationship*. As Irene Freize and Jaime Kno-

ble (1980) note, the main supporters for the view that alcohol consumption has a direct causal relationship are battered women and public opinion. Diana Russell's book on marital rape (1982) contains a chapter about abusive husbands who also use mood-altering chemicals, and she notes the frequency with which female victims of rape and other violence attribute alcohol as *the* reason for the behavior, saying:

> The relationship between the consumption of alcohol and wife abuse is a controversial one. Although the victims of wife abuse, along with the general public, believe there is a causal relationship between the consumption of alcohol and violent behavior by husbands, researchers do not necessarily agree. (Russell 1982, 156)

Theorists also do not necessarily agree because, as Frieze and Knoble (1980) explain: "Relatively few actually propose a direct causal relationship between alcohol and marital violence." There is, however, widespread agreement among researchers that there is an association between alcohol use and various types of family violence. In contrast, even though there is growing evidence of a strong correlation between drug use and family violence, mood-altering drugs have largely been ignored by victims, social scientists, and the general public. This is not to suggest that the use or misuse of alcohol and other drugs *causes* violence, but rather, it is to ensure that they are not overlooked. Any factor that repeatedly appears in research findings should be closely examined to see what part it plays. Chemical ingestion is one such factor, particularly in the case of alcoholic beverages. Other drugs have largely been ignored by researchers.[2] Chemical dependency or misuse may be considered an important contributing factor to family violence. This section examines research findings to see what has been learned on this subject.

Research efforts in this country on these two major social problems—family violence and alcohol abuse—have focused exclusively on one or the other. Separate bodies of research have clearly documented that these problems take a large toll of American resources in the workforce and productivity, human lives and health, social and medical services, the criminal justice system, and the family system (Hafen and Brog 1983). Psychiatrist Peter Steinglass (1976, 97) estimates that between 9 and 15 million adults in the United States abuse or are addicted to alcohol. In 1980 self-reports of excessive use of alcohol showed that 46 percent of the men and 33 percent of the women said they sometimes drink more than they should. In 1978 West Virginia led the nation at 58 percent of all arrests being made for alcohol or other drug-related offenses, followed by South

Carolina at 56 percent (Flanagan et al. 1982, 281, 372).

Approximately 10,000 suicides, or more than one-third of the suicides in this country in 1981, were estimated to be alcohol-related (Hafen and Brog 1983). A report from a U.S. Senate subcommittee hearing in 1977 estimates there are more than 28 million children of alcoholic parents. Alcohol abuse is reported to occur in 40 to 60 percent of all cases of spouse abuse, whereas only about 15 percent of child maltreatment cases reported that alcohol dependence was one of the stress factors present (American Humane Association 1980). Why there may be a wide disparity in abuse of spouses versus abuse of children will be commented on later in this chapter. In discussing all types of family violence, Finkelhor (1981a, 6) has this to say: "The statistics are remarkably consistent, showing over half of abuse incidents, either physical or sexual, as being related to the use of alcohol. The figure is probably even higher since the presence of drinking is not always easy to determine."

Despite the estimates above, the information we have is fragmentary and largely inconclusive. Looking first at research in the chemical dependence field, even when there is recognition that alcohol abuse, physical aggression, and/or neglect occur within families, there seems to be a general assumption that recovery from alcohol abuse leads to termination of intrafamily violence (Behling 1979; Wilson and Orford 1978). Some writers suggest a system theory of family interaction/substance abuse (Klagsbrun and David 1977), or devise and test theraputic treatment modalities for couples where one has a drinking problem (Steinglass 1976), but seem to overlook aggression or violent behavior. One clinical experiment focused specifically on conflict resolution between nonalcoholic and alcoholic spouses, but while some behaviors were categorized as "coercion-attack," "hostile-dominant" and "hostile-submissive," no mention is made of aggression or the use of force (Billings et al. 1979).

To summarize, when research from the substance abuse field looks at the family, violence is peripheral to the line of inquiry (Byles 1978; Kellermann 1974), and when it looks at aggression and violence, the family is peripheral (Lang et al. 1975; Mayfield 1976; Wolfgang and Strohm 1957). Even though "marked aggression" is listed as a symptom on most progression charts for chemical dependence, an underlying assumption seems to be that aggressive behavior is most likely to occur in the public, rather than the private arena of the drinkers' lives. Researchers study criminal homicide and note that about one-third to 64 percent involve the presence of alcohol in one or both parties (Wolfgang and Ferracuti 1982, 190) and find that when women are murdered they stand an almost equal chance of being killed by their husbands than by anybody else (Wolfgang 1967a, 23). Yet associations between alcohol use and wife murder are treated as separate and distinct phenomena.

Research in the family violence field again tends to fall into categories of different types of violence, primarily spouse abuse, child abuse, and sexual abuse. Beginning with child abuse, out of the more than 600,000 cases of child maltreatment reported to the American Humane Association (AHA) in 1978, there was only enough additional information on almost 33,000 substantiated reports to be able to screen for stress factors. Alcohol dependency was listed as one of the stress factors present in the home for 14.6 percent of the cases, which indicates that at least 5,000 children are known to have suffered alcohol-related maltreatment in one year (AHA 1980, 32). Drug dependency was present in only 4 percent of the cases.

Around 1,000 children are estimated to die each year from parental abuse or neglect (Fontana 1973; Gelles 1979; Gil 1970), but attorney Douglas Besharov (1978) says that abuse or neglect is suspected in 2,000 cases per year. How many of these children's deaths are related to parental alcohol abuse is unknown, but a number of researchers have noted associations between child maltreatment and alcohol abuse (Mayer and Black 1977; Wilson et al. 1977; Wilson and Orford 1978), although it should be noted that some samples were obtained through institutions funded in part or whole by alcohol prevention or treatment programs which introduces bias to those respective studies (Spieker 1978; Star 1978). There is also strong evidence that there is a link between alcohol abuse and incest (Hindman 1979). Alcohol abuse may have a stronger association with physical and emotional neglect of children than outright physical attacks (Hindman 1977, 1979).

If experts are correct about a greater tendency toward child neglect, this may account for the lower association of alcohol abuse with child maltreatment than spouse abuse as noted earlier, since it is more difficult for outsiders to detect neglect (Mayer and Black 1977). Margaret Hindman (1977) notes that most alcoholics have difficulties in child rearing, although not all of them seriously abuse or neglect their children. Drawing on research reports, Hindman (1977, 4) explains that many alcoholic fathers realize the potential danger of physically abusing their children when drunk, so they deliberately refrain from disciplining during those periods. Hindman says, "these fathers, while drinking, are considerably more likely to abuse their wives than their children" (1977, 4). This could help explain the disparity in associations between alcohol abuse and violence against wives or children: Children are more likely to be neglected, which is less visible to outsiders and thus less likely to be reported. Alcoholic husbands may be inclined when drinking to deflect their violence from their children to their wives.

From his position in a naval alcohol rehabilitation center, Daniel Behling (1979) found a highly significant relationship between family conflict, child abuse, and alcohol abuse. Behling's study found that 69 percent of the child abuse cases in the navy personnel families involved one or both parents being either alcoholics or alcohol abusers. Interestingly, the 51 cases studied did not originate as child maltreatment cases, but were referred by physicians for other family problems. These cases included physical abuse (51 percent), neglect (39 percent), and sexual abuse (10 percent). In addition to the high association of parental alcohol-related problems, the Behling (1979, 90) report states that 63 percent of the abused children had at least one grandparent who was either alcoholic or abused alcohol.[3]

Another study in the alcohol prevention field looked at 29 children of 11 families with one parent in treatment at a London hospital alcohol treatment center (Wilson and Orford 1978). Marital "conflict" was reported in nine of these families, which appears to refer mainly to physical violence. In some of these families the alcoholism was viewed by the children as a lesser problem than the violence. Except for one case, the alcoholic parent was the source of violence (Wilson and Orford 1978, 127), which extended to property, the wives, and sometimes the children (in four cases, which is 44 percent). In one of the most serious cases, a man attacked both his wife and two stepdaughters. The authors of the study say: "The elder daughter would be attacked when she tried to protect her mother from beatings, and both children had been hit while their mother was absent. These children lived in an almost constant state of terror" (Wilson and Orford 1978, 127). It should be noted that this is the exceptional case where the nonalcoholic parent was violent. The children felt the mother was justified in her drinking as a response to the violence, but wanted her to stay sober because they felt her drinking provoked their stepfather's violence.

Children in violent families are victims, whether they are the *direct* targets of abuse or *indirectly* involved by witnessing parental violence (Pagelow 1982a). Clare Wilson and Jim Orford (1978, 127) have come to similar conclusions, for they say:

> We felt that many children we interviewed were affected by violence whether or not they had been beaten themselves. Some were involved in separating and pacifying their parents, attending to their injuries and tidying up after fights. Others experienced fear and worry because of violence, and one or two would stay away from school or friends to try to prevent a parental quarrel or to protect a parent.

Children living with alcohol-abusing parents are affected in many ways, frequently reporting to researchers that they feel neglected and rejected, often by the nonalcoholic as well as the alcoholic parent, and older children sometimes are forced into becoming pseudoparents to younger siblings and also to the adults (Cork 1969; Fox 1968; Hindman 1977).

Most of the research on spouse abuse tends to note a high level of drinking among the violent men, much more than among the abused women, but alcohol abuse was not a major focus of the studies.[4] A few researchers nevertheless have directed considerable attention in their reports to the relationships between alcohol abuse and spouse abuse (Frieze and Knoble 1980; Gelles 1974; Richardson and Campbell 1980). The report by Irene Frieze and Jamie Knoble (1980) indicates that substance abuse and violence patterns fall into five basic categories including one in which some wives become violent when they drink or take drugs, although these researchers comment, "little physical damage occurred in these marriages. The severe violence was nearly always associated with male violence" (1980, 21). Frieze and Knoble believe that, for men, alcohol and violence are related saying, "men who drank more tended to be generally violent inside and outside the home. These men were the most violent to their wives" (1980, 17). Wilson and Orford (1978, 123) also found marked differences in male and female drinking patterns.[5] Gelles (1974, 111) found that drinking accompanied violence against spouses or children in 48 percent of the 44 violent families in his study. Gelles (1974, 77) reports that alcohol-related violence in his sample was "almost exclusively male violence."

The battered wives Gelles interviewed (1974) tended to blame the alcohol for the violence, as other researchers have noted (Bowker 1983a; Frieze and Knoble 1980; Morgan 1981; Pagelow 1981a; Roy 1977; Russell 1982). Battered wives subscribe to popular notions that drunken husbands lose all inhibitions and beat wives and children *because* they are drunk; that is, the "nice guy" turns from Dr. Jekyl to Mr. Hyde because of booze. Gelles (1974) rejects this notion, referring to evidence that drinking behavior patterns are socially learned.

The idea that drinking behavior is learned, rather than being due to involuntary responses to chemical reactions of the body when alcohol is ingested, is accepted by many. Craig MacAndrew and Robert Edgerton (1969) give cross-cultural examples showing that drunken comportment is situationally variable: In some cultures people engage in excessive drinking but never become aggressive while in other cultures people ritualistically drink heavily before becoming violent. There are some sections of the country, as well as some occupational and ethnic groups, that consume more alcohol than others, yet drinking behavior within these groups varies widely. Behavior patterns associated with drinking even change over time. For example, in the 1940s and 1950s, a teen-aged boy's idea of "masculine" drinking was to drink as much as possible without getting drunk—the goal was to "drink everyone else under the table." The youth who remained standing while all the others passed out or got sick was a "real man." Contemporary standards of drinking demand that teens drink to get drunk quickly and then perform the most outrageous or dangerous acts possible in order to win admiration from peers.

Another rebuttal to the notion that alcohol itself lowers inhibitions is that some people drink excessively but never get aggressive or violent (depending on the individuals, they may get sick, pass out, or fall asleep) (Schuckit 1980). Others do not drink, or drink sparingly, but engage in violence. There are also drinkers who are violent on some occasions and nonviolent during other drinking episodes, and some who are violent when both drunk and sober. Therefore, Gelles (1974) and others (Bard and Zacker 1974, 1976) believe that alcohol is used as an excuse for violent behavior.

Some explanations for uncharacteristic behavior after consuming alcohol are the *disavowal* theory (McCaghy 1968), which is used to neutralize the deviant behavior by positing that " I didn't know what I was doing—I was too drunk to know!" In essence, "I'm still the nice guy you always knew but the liquor did it to me." The second explanation is the idea of *time out* proposed by MacAndrew and Edgerton (1969), which means that some people drink in order to do what they want to do but cannot do while sober because they need an excuse (the alcohol) to show that they are not responsible for what happens. This is the *bottle courage* of men who plan to beat their wives (or rape a neighbor, or mug a stranger) but drink first so that later, when accused, they can try to escape responsibility by saying they cannot remember what they did. As Gelles explains, "Thus, individuals who wish to carry out a violent act become intoxicated *in order to carry out the violent act*" (1974, 117). Many family violence researchers subscribe to the disinhibitory theory or the time out idea that alcohol consumption is used to shift the blame from the aggressor to the effects of the alcohol (Bowker 1983; McClelland et al. 1972; Pagelow 1981a; Roy 1977).

One sample of battered women reported that alcohol use by their assailants was involved in half of the first violent incidents, and the use of intoxicants increased until it peaked at 63 percent in the worst incidents (Bowker 1983). Sometimes researchers make mention of violence against wives associated with drinking, but concentrate on other features of the conflicts in the relationships. For example, the Dobash and Dobash (1979) sample was mostly obtained from shelters for battered women in Edinburgh and Glasgow, Scotland, and although there are frequent references throughout the book about husbands drinking at the pub, there is no major focus on an association between alcohol abuse and the violence. The quotation from one wife begins, "He had come home from work and he'd been drinking . . ." (Dobash and Dobash 1979, 101). When discussing the

time that assaults usually occurred (between 10 P.M. and midnight), Dobash and Dobash state, "In Britain it is also not unusual for men to be
away from the home between approximately 7:00 and 11:00 P.M. drinking
at the pub" (1979, 121).

The Pagelow study (1981a) obtained data that are not published elsewhere on alcohol abuse and wife beating. A questionnaire asked women
who had been beaten by spouses several questions about the involvement of alcohol in the violence; 50 percent of the survey sample, or 119
women, said they felt there was a connection. This is close to the Frieze
and Knoble sample, where 52 percent of the battered women said there
was "some" or a "definite" problem in their husbands' drinking. One item
in the Pagelow scale asked the women if their abusers were under the
influence of alcohol during the time of the beatings; 319 women responded and 65 percent of them said that alcohol was involved to some
extent. Only 24 percent indicated that neither alcohol nor drugs was involved in the violent events. Frieze and Knoble also asked if alcohol was
involved in specific violent events; their sample reported that husbands'
use of alcohol was involved in 49 percent of the first beatings, and 57 percent in the worst violent incidents (1980, 13).

Another question in the Pagelow scale asked about frequency of drinking. Of the 314 women who responded, 36 percent said their spouses
drank alcoholic beverages "to the point where he may be an alcoholic,"
and 26 percent said the men drank "very often." The women were also
asked directly if they drank alcoholic beverages: only 4 percent chose the
response "very often" and 1 percent (three women) indicated they felt
they might be alcoholics. A large difference in the women's reports of
their own and their spouses' usage is between the 28 percent of the
women who never drink alcoholic beverages versus the 8 percent of nondrinking violent husband. By comparison, Frieze and Knoble (1980, 10)
report that 38 percent of the violent husbands drank daily or went on
binges, and 12 percent of the wives versus 4 percent of the husbands
never drank.

The Pagelow scale contained another item asking women about mood-
altering drug use by themselves or by the men who beat them. These respondents reported low rates of use of either drugs or alcohol for themselves, but of the 172 women who reported the kinds of drugs the men
used, 8 percent indicated alcohol and 26 percent indicated that a combination of drugs and alcohol were used. Frieze and Knoble (1980, 21) found
a correlation between husbands' use of drugs and their violence, but did
not elaborate on it, merely noting that the issue merits research.

In-depth interviews with battered women in the Pagelow study revealed that many of them believed that alcohol abuse was the cause of

their spouses' violent behavior, and that if the men's excessive drinking would stop, the violence would also cease. Some women commented that their husbands beat them when they were sober as well as when they were drunk, but still insisted that alcoholism was the basic cause for the violence.

Application: Intervention
in Alcohol-Abusing Families

Evidence has been provided throughout this section from research focusing on alcohol abuse, child maltreatment, or spouse abuse, showing that there are associations between these behaviors, but there has been very little effort to tie these problems together for theory building and further research. Alcohol abuse plays an important role in spouse abuse and other forms of family violence. Such violence may not be limited to only one type of abuse; several types of victimization may occur in the same families, including sexual abuse (Hamlin et al. 1979; Sanchez-Dirks 1979). Although a strong correlation does not indicate causality, it does indicate that intervention or prevention techniques must address *both* problems—alcohol abuse and family violence—in order to be effective for dual-problem families. Professionals dealing with dysfunctional families must become aware of the possibility that by focusing too narrowly on the presenting problem, they may be missing interrelated problems.

Traditionally, prevention and treatment programs have focused specifically on alcohol abuse, or child maltreatment, or wife beating. Even when one or more of the associated problems surface during treatment, protocols are not developed to deal with them. Just as researchers tend to approach problems with a specific focus determined by their own area of professional training and expertise, professionals in the helping services tend to give highest priority to the presenting problem and may even ignore the presence of associated problems with which they are less familiar. A number of writers have complained about the compartmentalization of treatment programs, differing functions and philosophies in agencies, and "bifurcation in responding to abused children and battered spouses" (Hamlin et al. 1979, 21). For example, Hamlin, Hurwitz, and Spieker (1979, 19) say:

> Alcohol and other counselors not specifically trained to deal with family violence may be not only unaware of resources but also uncomfortable in bringing these problems out into the open. Conversely, knowledge about alcohol abuse and its treatability is often minimal among those who intervene in family abuse situations.

Margaret Hindman concurs, saying, "Surprisingly, although alcoholism has been singled out as a factor in child abuse, parents are rarely questioned directly about drinking practices in investigations of child abuse cases" (1977, 3). Psychiatrist Steinglass complains that family therapists lack interest in alcoholic families and are reluctant to deal with it in their practice saying, "Since family therapists prefer to work with directly observable behavior, retrospective reports of intoxicated behavior are often overlooked or not solicited, and abusive drinking rarely becomes a focus for therapeutic interest" (1976, 120). From the battered women's shelter movement's perspective, Janet Wright and Judy Popham (1982, 53) have this to say:

> Crisis-oriented services for abused women and children often do not recognize or pursue treatment for alcohol and other drug abuse. . . . Very little cooperation occurs between chemical abuse and woman abuse programs. In some communities there is outright hostility between the workers in these two fields.

However, as Hindman (1977) observes, changes are occurring, but slowly. In the alcohol-abuse field, prevention and intervention services are geared toward helping the individual with alcohol dependence (Orford 1975), but today they are moving steadily in the direction of including the drinker's family into programs. In programs for battered wives and the few that have been established for adult abusers, awareness is growing that attention needs to be directed towards the role of alcohol in violence. Service providers to adult victims of family violence insist that it is essential that alcohol-abusing aggressors need to break their chemical dependence, but do not accept it as the primary cause of wife beating and feel that alcohol prevention alone will not prevent violence towards spouses. To help bridge the knowledge gap, Janet Wright (1982) produced a manual designed as a cross-training program for counselors working in the fields of wife abuse and chemical dependency.[6]

Given that there are ideological, professional, training, and political differences between people who come in contact with alcohol abusers, child abusers, and wife abusers and their victims, what can be done to address interrelationships? A special assistant to the National Institute on Alcohol Abuse and Alcoholism, Ruth Sanchez-Dirks, offers the following suggestions:[7]

1. Training curricula should be developed to teach alcoholism workers to identify and handle the potential for family violence.
2. Training curricula should be developed to train health and

social service professionals in the identification and handling of alcoholism.

3. Research should continue into the relationship of alcohol to child abuse and wife battering.
4. Treatment and prevention programs need to be developed that aim to break that [intergenerational] cycle.
5. Treatment and protective personnel [for battered wives and children] need to deal with the violence from a total family perspective.
6. All members of the alcoholic family need help in dealing with themselves and the alcoholism as a family and as individuals.
7. Research further the personality characteristics and the role of social and environmental circumstances, in order to differentiate between these troubled persons for purposes of diagnosis and prevention.
8. It is necessary for programs to develop cooperative agreements to treat each other's clients and to determine which agency will have the ultimate responsibility to coordinate treatment. (Sanchez-Dirks 1979, 16)

All these recommendations should be followed, because better understanding of both family violence and alcohol abuse will point the way to more effective intervention techniques.

POWER AND POWERLESSNESS

The issue of power and powerlessness is a probable cause or at least a contributing factor to violence in the family yet almost no writers have made direct reference to it, although many of the books and articles on the subject reveal the presence of this phenomenon in violent relationships. It is a pattern that emerges in so many types of family violence, but it largely goes unacknowledged. If there is to be a global explanation of family violence it can begin with *power/powerlessness,* in which one actor or unit (such as a group) perceives itself to be lacking power in its environment, but as powerful in relationship to other actors or units. This is *relative power,* not *absolute power,* meaning that there is power only in relationship to less powerful others.

Power here is defined as the capability of carrying out one's own will and assuming control over others, with or without legitimacy, based on having a larger share of physical, psychological, and/or material resources. Pioneer sociologist Max Weber (1964, 152) defined power as the ability to control the behavior of others, with or without their consent. Powerful persons are those who are able to realize their will, even if others resist it (Mills 1956, 9). When applied to the family, it is easy to see that there is a hierarchy of power, traditionally based on sex, age, and the distribution of material and personal resources. Usually the person who has the major share of these attributes and resources is an adult male, and in most types of family violence, it is men who constitute a majority of the perpetrators. The power position of men as heads of the family has been legitimized down through the centuries by the traditional patriarchal family, and all social institutions have supported and recognized that power. Men have the position with the greatest power *within* the family unit, but relative to the environment *beyond* the family home, *some men perceive themselves as extremely powerless.*

This may help explain why not only some poor men but also some men high in socioeconomic status abuse wives and children in the home. No matter how high a man goes in the economic, political, or educational world, there are always other persons who either have more power or who are capable of stripping him of his power. Even dictators cannot dominate forever by force alone! When some men feel powerless in relationship to others in their social circle, they find compensation by knowing that in relationship to members of their families, they are powerful. When they exert power to compensate for powerlessness elsewhere, they are *scapegoating,* a concept introduced by Georg Simmel (1904). Briefly, this occurs when goal-directed persons become angry and hostile when their desires are frustrated. They are stymied and they do not know who or what is blocking them from their goals. Sometimes they do know, but the obstacle is too powerful or fearsome to fight directly, so they find weaker targets who cannot retaliate to use as scapegoats against which to displace their hostilities. We see examples of this every day (people driving rudely in heavy traffic, slamming down telephones, being nasty to service workers, and so forth).

After scapegoating, the person or groups of people justify their actions by convincing themselves that the targets deserved what was done to them. Insecurity about one's own self-worth makes an individual especially prone to denigrate others. It should be noted that professionals who have worked with wife beaters find that these men show signs of low self-esteem and insecurity, and these same characteristics are noted in parents who abuse their children (Ganley and Harris 1978; Pagelow 1981a; Steele and Pollock 1974).

Writing on the functions of conflict, Coser (1964, 41) suggests three possible ways of expressing hostile feelings: direct expression of hostility against the person or group that is the source of frustration; displacement of such hostile behavior onto substitute objects; and tension-releasing activity which provides satisfaction in itself without need for object or object substitutes. This may help explain differences in response by people who become angry or frustrated; some choose the first way and directly confront the people who offend them, probably nonviolently in the vast majority of cases; others choose the third way and find socially acceptable tension outlets, such as strenuous physical exercise or sports. Family violence can be the result of persons who try the first way when the sources of their hostility are family members, but who do so by using violent methods, as well as those who displace their hostility from outside sources onto less powerful family members, which is scapegoating.

Power/powerlessness and scapegoating are not complete answers to family violence since they can only tell us why some people turn their frustrations into aggression against others, but cannot explain why others do not. The answer to why some people lash out violently in response to feelings of powerlessness, while others just as disadvantaged (or even more so) do not, may lie in the actors' sense of control over their situations. Most researchers who have written about wife beating, for example, believe that abusive men exert force and violence in order to dominate and control their wives. If they cannot change their own sense of powerlessness by taking charge of the situation that frustrates them, they can at least still exercise control over the family unit, thus temporarily exchanging feelings of powerlessness for feelings of power. As explained by social learning theory, if the aggressor gains a sense of enhanced power through scapegoating family members, then that behavior is likely to be repeated. Some who attempt to control others through coercion or violence do not find their behavior gives them a sense of power, so they discontinue these methods. The factors suggested here apply to all types of family violence, not only to wife abuse.

David Finkelhor (1981a) looked for common features of family violence and saw power as a connecting thread. He determined that family abuse is the abuse of power, and that in the family it is not merely a situation where the more powerful abuse the less powerful, but where the *most* powerful abuse the *least* powerful. As noted earlier, Finkelhor states, "This is an interesting commonality: abuse tends to gravitate to the relationships of *greatest power differential*" (1981a, 3). Building on this theme, Finkelhor shows how several types of family abuse involve the greatest power differentials (he omits sibling and parent abuse, but the same principle applies there, particularly for aged or handicapped parents). Closely aligned with the author's own ideas on the subject, Finkelhor (1981a, 5) talks about "abuse as response to perceived powerlessness," stating:

> This is another commonality among the different kinds of abuse that involves power: Although they are acts of the strong

against the weak, they seem to be acts carried out by abusers in part, to compensate for their perceived lack of or loss of power. In the case of spouse abuse and in the sexual abuse of children, this attempt to compensate is often bound up in a sense of powerlessness particularly with regard to the masculine ideals in our society.

These ideas of power/powerlessness can be easily demonstrated, as in the case of wife beating: A husband feels powerless to control his employment, coworkers, economic status, and other elements of his environment, but when it comes to the family unit, *here* he has power. He may feel anger or frustration at his boss, a clerk at the unemployment office, the chairman of the board, a judge, or a patient who just died, but he is unable to lash out at the source of his anger and frustration. When he feels powerless elsewhere and if he feels his power within the home threatened, or even if he just needs to reestablish to himself that he does have control somewhere, he may demonstrate it by using violence against his wife, or his children, or both. Or he may sexually abuse his daughter, stepdaughter, or son. The incest perpetrator is not driven by "lust" or by deprived sexual needs but rather by a desire for power; after all, sexual fulfillment can be obtained easily and cheaply outside the family in our society.

When a mother lashes out at her screaming child, it can be that the child is the real object of her hostility because she cannot stand the noise any longer and feels powerless to stop it (Coser's first method of expressing hostility), or it can be that she feels unfairly treated by her husband, the welfare board, or her boss, so she scapegoats her child. In either case, power/powerlessness explains her actions. The woman who neglects a child or children is most frequently young, uneducated, poor, and a single parent; the stage is set for powerlessness. Regardless, she can refuse to diaper, bathe, or feed her children, no matter how much they fuss or cry. Thus, at least in reference to her even more powerless children, she can say "No! I won't do it, and you can't make me! I don't know what to do for myself, so I won't do anything for you, either."

Power/powerlessness is also a factor in abuse of elderly parents, particularly when the parents are frail, physically restricted, or disoriented mentally. They can be a tremendous financial and emotional burden on their middle-aged children who may have planned for years for the day when their parenting burden would be lifted and they would finally be able to do the many things they had dreamed of, but postponed. Untrained and unprepared for the total responsibility of dependent parents, their children may feel totally powerless in this situation. However, they do have power over the helpless one who is the cause of their misery, and they can exert this power by withholding services, medicine, or attention. They can, in effect, *punish* their parents, scapegoating those who are even more powerless than they and who cannot retaliate.

Children are at the bottom of the ladder in the pecking order, and thus they are the most powerless in the family unit, compared to all the adults with whom they reside. But a child's power, relative to another child, can be great. When a child has been unfairly (or even fairly) punished by adults, that child may be fiercely angry and hostile but feels powerless to strike back at them. If there is a smaller sibling or neighbor playmate, they may scapegoat the other child or children. If the punishment received was in the form of valued possessions removed, he or she is likely to take something from the other; if the punishment was physical, that is likely to be the form that the displaced anger and hostility will take. Thus, we can see the creation and development of the neighborhood (or schoolyard) bully.

Finkelhor (1981a) appears to have arrived at conclusions similar to these ideas. He gives a series of examples of the various forms of abuse of power in the family and states:

> These are all examples of the uses of abuse to compensate for a perceived loss of power. The abuse may not always be instrumental, it may be expressive. Abuse can be a way of retaliating against another family member who is seen in some way as responsible for that loss of power. Or it can be a way of trying to regain control by using coercion or exploitation as the resource for getting one's will carried out. But in either case, the abuse is a response to perceived power deficit. (Finkelhor 1981a, 6)

Closely related to these ideas of power/powerlessness is a sociological concept called anomie. *Anomie,* as introduced by pioneer sociologist Emile Durkheim (1966) and expanded upon later by Robert Merton (1968), refers to feelings of normlessness and of being somehow detached from the rest of society. As noted earlier, one of the common features of violent families is their isolation, being cut off from relatives, friends, or support systems. Abuse occurs in privacy. Some examples are the higher rates of violence in military families, the social isolation of sexually abusive families, child neglecting parents, and battered wives (Dobash and Dobash 1979; Pagelow 1981a; Walker 1979). It is easy to see how children who are educationally handicapped, especially in terms of communication, suffer from anomie. These children cannot feel they are part of the larger society so they cope in the only ways they know (King 1975).

As swift changes occur in society, in norms of behavior, and in roles within the family, all of these lead to a blurring of expectations and definitions of what is right or wrong in the family. The absolute power of the rigid hierarchical structure of the patriarchal family has been slowly weakening since the industrial revolution, especially in recent decades when increasing numbers of wives and mothers have become part of the paid labor force. Contributing part of the family income has given increased power to many women who are thus more likely to challenge traditional notions of subservience. A man who spent his youth in a traditional family where his father's desires were paramount and whose father's decisions were "law," often finds the newer norms of family living, where not only the wife's wishes are expected to receive consideration, but also the children's, vexing and confusing. A woman who expected to be a full-time wife and mother, devoting herself to her family as her mother did before her, may find that she has no (or not sufficient) money from a husband's paycheck to support the family. She may not even have the father of her children living at home.

There are couples who adhered to the "American Dream" of hard work and sacrifice in order to be able to enjoy security and comfort in their later years. Then through no fault of their own but through economic recession, they lose their businesses, jobs, savings, or homes, and are full of confusion and feelings of powerlessness. Many couples sacrificed through years of child-rearing, looking forward to the "empty nest," only to find themselves burdened with aging parents. To further complicate matters, there have been swift changes in recent years in sexual norms, which create confusion for many parents who grew up in a sexually repressive society. What are the rules? What are the new roles, rights, and responsibilities of family members.

Application: Redistributing Power to Reduce Family Violence

If power/powerlessness and anomie are contributing factors to family violence, then this may help explain how and why some people feel that their lives and futures are totally out of their own control. Some changes would have to be initiated in order to bring some sense of power and control into the lives of people and thus to reduce violence. In the next chapter, we examine the issue of structural inequality that gives disproportionate shares of resources and thus power, to some people at the expense of others. For now, we can consider one area of life in which people could have enhanced feelings of power and control: the workplace. Employers have found that giving workers more autonomy, flexible rules, and greater control over their work through collective decision making (rather than imposing rigid hierarchies) increases motivation, productivity, and job satisfaction. There is no reason to believe that this reaction is unique to the place of employment.

In view of the social expenses incurred by family violence, perhaps it is about time that we apply some of the principles suggested by organizational research that have been used by profit-seeking large corporations to the benefit of stockholders and workers alike. David Gil (1974) adds to the many voices that speak of stress in families, pointing to frustration and alienation in the workplace, exploitative human relations, and competition, all of which lead to a variety of deviant behaviors. He suggests that, "Perhaps the most frequent locus for discharging feelings of stress and frustration originating in the formal world of work is the informal world of primary relations, the home and the family" (1974, 121).

SUMMARY

Because most research and theories of family violence tend to take diverse approaches to the topic, concentrating on one or another type of violence which tends to emphasize differences, this chapter set out to highlight similarities and common threads that connect one type to another. If these features hold true for most types of family violence, then they provide clues suggesting approaches for effective intervention and how violence may be reduced or prevented.

The first common feature is power differentials, whereby people with the most power in families tend to abuse others with the least power. Consequently, ways must be found to reallocate power in the family to protect the rights of the least powerful. There are movements now working for the rights of children, women, and seniors, trying to gain some degree of power for these categories who lack power in society in general and in the family in particular. Social isolation is another feature common to violent families, but ways can be found to integrate them into communities and provide services that offer support, rather than interference, in private lives. Effects on victims include some that are extremely common, such as low self-esteem and a sense of shame and helplessness. Other effects, such as loyalty to the abusers and certain behavioral characteristics, are frequently noted but are not present in all cases.

Alcohol abuse is found in a high percentage of cases of all types of family violence, and we need to create and implement intervention methods that can help dually afflicted families. So far there have been no major studies that measure the interaction between both behaviors. We do not know enough about: patterns of alcohol use; time ordering—if alcohol consumption occurs closely or immediately preceding, during, or after violence; or the way alcohol interacts with personality or stress factors, or both, to increase the likelihood or violent behavior. We need research to fill gaps in scientific knowledge about these important issues and help service providers in these currently antagonistic fields to understand common issues and concerns in order to "build bridges so that the needs of dually affected families can be sensitively and effectively met" (Wright and Popham 1982, 59). Once that is accomplished, intervention and prevention protocols can be employed more efficiently and effectively to reduce both alcohol abuse and family violence.

We have come full circle when we again address power/powerlessness at the conclusion of this chapter. The earlier section talked about power differentials, wherein the victims are powerless relative to the abusers. In this final section, power is again the issue, but it now refers to the sense of powerlessness the abuser feels relative to the social environment and his or her attempts to gain control and enhancement of power within the family. The first section suggests that a way to reduce violence is to enhance the power of the most powerless family members; the final section suggests that if abusers gain a greater sense of control and power in their own lives, they will be less likely to scapegoat less powerful others in the family.

NOTES

1. The question of which parent is more likely to physically abuse children is discussed in detail in a later chapter where examination of the evidence shows that fathers are more likely to abuse children whereas mothers are more likely to neglect them.

2. Very few writers make note of associations between violence and any mood-altering drug usage except alcohol. Apparently popular ideas about violent drug addicts stem largely from media impressions such as news coverage of police struggles with people on "bad trips" with PCP and earlier, LSD. Testifying at hearings in San Diego, before the California Commission on Crime Control and Violence Prevention in 1980, psychiatrist Sidney Cohen of UCLA Medical School said that effects of drugs are largely determined by the environment of the user and social expectations. Cohen (1980, 41) reported that if violence is expected, it will occur, whether the drug is alcohol or another chemical. He said that reaction depends on the expectations of the user, his mood, the setting, and the people around him. Not minimizing the fact that violence does occur with some drug taking, particularly for brain-damaged people, Cohen still pointed out: "Most drug taking is not associated with violence; even the most violence producing drug [sic] are taken by most people and no violence results" (1980, 41).

3. Many writers in the alcohol-abuse field note that there seems to be an intergenerational transmission of the problem, possibly through a "predisposition" from the emotional trauma children suffered from growing up with alcohol-abusing parents (Black 1979). Due to a complex set of factors, including the fact that children of alcoholics are less likely to receive treatment than their alcoholic parents (Chafetz 1979), between 30 and 50 percent of children of alcoholics grow up to abuse alcohol themselves (Bosma 1975; Cork 1969; Fox 1968), as do their children after them.

4. Researchers who have concentrated on wife beating have frequently noted the high percentage of cases where alcohol consumption was involved to some degree in the violence, but it was one of many variables noted and not the major thrust of research interest (Bowker 1983a; Dobash and Dobash 1979; Frieze 1980; Walker 1979).

5. The report by Clare Wilson and Jim Orford (1978, 122–23) notes that there are distinct differences in behavior patterns of male and female drinking that most researchers ignore. In their study, the majority of the men drank almost entirely away from home, arriving home drunk every night; by contrast, the women did most of their drinking at home and showed much more variability in their drinking behavior, with two female heavy drinkers drinking all day but still maintaining their ability to do their work (inside or outside the home).

6. The book, *Chemical Dependency and Violence: Working With Dually Affected Families,* by Janet M. Wright (1982), costs $11.50 prepaid. It can be ordered from the Wisconsin Clearinghouse, University of Wisconsin Hospital and Clinics, 1954 East Washington Avenue, Madison, WI 53704. This 134-page book is divided into two sections; the first includes information and exercises for trainees during a nine-week period; section two includes exercises for ten sessions and focuses on intervention techniques for working with the entire family.

7. These suggestions are greatly abbreviated from the original recommendations made by Ruth Sanchez-Dirks in her article, "Reflections on Family Violence" (1979, 16).

4

Alternative Views on Family Violence

There are a multitude of theories on the causes, identifying features, and ameliorative and preventative measures of family violence. Generally, these theories are applicable to specific aggressor/victim acts of commission or omission, in keeping with the parameters of the research designs of the studies. Sometimes there is an overlap, as in child abuse and neglect, but most theories are introduced and tested on a sample selected to investigate one particular set of behaviors. Not infrequently, while concentrating on one type of family violence, researchers discover other forms of violence occurring in the sample families, and the theories are modified *ex post facto* to explain the other phenomenon.

As noted in the previous chapter, an explanation for one type of family violence may be very inappropriate for another. For example, the ages at which children are abused or neglected may lead to very different results even though the children are subjected to the same behavior. Leaving a four-week-old baby alone in a house for four or five days is likely to have disastrous results that could result in death, but leaving a child of 12 to fend for himself or herself for the same length of time might go totally unnoticed by anyone except the abandoned child. Whipping a ten year old with a belt might leave bruises but no permanent damages, but the same instrument used with the same force on a baby might result in infanticide. Even the same act involving children of the same ages may be defined differently by the parents, based on cultural beliefs and customs.[1]

Victims and victimizers may also be vastly different in another type of family violence, parent abuse, depending on the ages of child and parent. The dynamics surrounding an attack by a 15-year-old son using a lead pipe on his 35-year-old father may have little in common with a 50-year-old waitress who ties her 80-year-old mother who suffers from Altzheimer's disease (an increasingly common type of senility), to the bed when she (the daughter) goes out at night; yet both are cases of parents abused by their children. Can the same theory have equal predictive power for three different types of wife abusers: men who both beat their wives and rape them, men who beat their wives but never force sex on them, and men who rape their wives but never use any other kind of physical violence on them?

For many people, the importance of theory is unclear, but basically it is necessary in order to gain understanding of phenomena by putting them into perspective; to explain events, and whenever possible, to be able to predict events. Theorizing is an attempt to gain a sense of understanding of why and how events occur (Turner 1974).

Since it appears, at least at the present time, that no single theory can adequately explain and predict the wide variety of behaviors, actors, and situations involved in all types of family violence, this chapter will introduce some of the most popular theories that have been offered thus far, as they offer explanations usually pertaining to one or another type of abuse. Very few theorists have attempted to include all types of family violence into a global paradigm.

A GLOBAL THEORY OF FAMILY VIOLENCE

The major exception is the theory proposed by sociologists Murray Straus, Richard Gelles, and Suzanne Steinmetz (1980). Called the *System Model of Intra-Family Violence,* it is illustrated by a flow chart that includes multiple bidirectional variables (Steinmetz and Straus 1974, 18–19), and is explained in these terms:

> We have tried to suggest some of the social forces which act as antecedents and consequences of familial violence in Figure 4–1. This figure is intended to show that we are dealing not with one-directional influences but with a whole *system* of mutually influencing and interacting forces, with each part of the system providing feedback to the others. That is, societal violence is in a two-way interaction with familial variables. (Steinmetz and Straus 1974, 17)

The major problem with the proposed system theory is that it is so extensive and multidimensional that it cannot be tested. Among critics of the system approach are sociologists R. Emerson Dobash and Russell Dobash (1976, 1979), who feel it is essential to progress from concrete, middle-range theories, building toward more general, abstract theories. They note that theorist Robert Merton (1968) also advocated theory building in this manner. The Dobashes argue that broad generalizations are untestable unless they are based on the empirical context in which they are meant to apply, and state:

> When general, abstract propositions such as these are applied to differing social contexts they either become transformed beyond recognition, and as such are no longer general propositions, or they become meaningless and inapplicable. We maintain that the most fruitful procedure for the sociological analysis of violence . . . is the development of theoretical or conceptual schemes which are meant to apply to clearly delimited empirical contexts. (Dobash and Dobash 1976, 2–3)

However, the approach taken by Straus et al. (1980) toward a more general theory of family violence insists that the entire system must be considered with variables interacting as parts of the whole. Steinmetz and Straus (1974, 20) explain in these words:

> If one wants to change the occurrence of violence in the family, it is not sufficient to deal directly with such aspects of intrafamilial violence as child abuse and fights between husband and wife. To confine attention to such events and their immediate antecedents is analogous to treating the symptoms of a disease.

On the other side of the argument, Dobash and Dobash (1979) believe that it is essential to understand events surrounding violent episodes and the environment in which they occur before any real understanding can be reached. Professor of social work Eloise Rathbone-McCuan (1980, 297) states other concerns: She worries that searching for theoretical frameworks "can lead to serious conceptual pitfalls." On the one hand, there is a temptation to take a theory constructed to explain one type of family violence and try to apply it to another type in which the dynamics are dissimilar. Rathbone-McCuan warns, "Drawing too many theoretical parallels prematurely may distort initial conceptualizations of the problem" (1980, 297). In addition, there are serious problems in trying to construct a global theory now, because there is no widespread theoretical agreement yet. Rathbone-McCuan notes:

> These researchers [Gelles and Straus] stress the need for such a theory of intrafamily violence because of the extent to which

this kind of family violence occurs. They cluster a number of
theories into three general categories: intra-individual, socio-
psychological, and sociocultural. (1980, 297)

At this point in time we have barely begun to amass necessary and sufficient knowledge of all the types of violence against family members. Sociologist David Finkelhor has intensely studied sexual victimization of
children, and he concludes that perhaps there can be no all-encompass-
ing explanation for even that one type of abuse, because there is so much
variation within it (1979a, 147). Research has shown clearly that there are
important differences between types of abuse, so how can we possibly
assume that they can be lumped together for one explanation equally applicable to all? Besides, is this necessary? When more ideas are proposed
and tested, we are accumulating valuable knowledge during the process.
Then, when similarities and differences become clear, these serve as clues
suggesting methods of identification, intervention, and prevention. The
"state of the art" of family violence theory construction is summarized by
psychiatric social worker Joan Scratton (1976, 28–29) in these terms:

> The dynamics of violence are sufficiently complex to preclude
> any definitive conclusion with respect to which of many theo-
> retical positions approximates the seminal truth. . . . What
> emerges from empirical findings is that intrafamilial violence
> cannot be encompassed within any one dimensional perspec-
> tive. Genetic, biopsychological and social factors interact with
> intrafamilial variables to produce the phenomenon under re-
> view. At this point in our knowledge it is clear that no one sin-
> gle explanation will suffice. . . . Further research is needed to
> differentiate between types of violent acts and those who com-
> mit them and the circumstances conducive to their
> occurrence.

It may be too soon to attempt to construct a theory that covers such a
wide divergence of behavior, regardless of its sophistication, as long as it
remains untestable. The one that has been proposed includes every element of individual, sociological, psychological, economic, and environmental factors so that it appears that any possible contingency that could
relate to violent behavior is covered somewhere in it. Almost everyone
agrees that no single factor can explain family violence, or explain even
one type of family violence, so there must be multivariate models to be
tested. Yet in his small primer on theory construction Blalock (1969, 2)
comments, "One can readily point to the possibility of assembling so
many miscellaneous facts on a subject that it becomes virtually impossible
to make any sense out of them." The systems model proposed by Straus

et al. (1980) is complex, multivariate, and shows intuitive insight, but at the present time, the methodology of operationalizing and scientifically measuring each of many variables and their multidirectional feedbacks appears to be an overwhelming task.

Some other explanations for family violence are presented next, and it will become clear how each one contributes to better understanding and theory building.

INDIVIDUAL PSYCHOPATHOLOGY

> "They must be sick! only a crazy person would beat a kid like that!" "Sure, I get mad at my wife (or kids) but I'm not loonie enough to do what he did—he must be insane." "Only a man with a perverted mind would have sex with his own kid." "These people are mad dogs—they should be shot."

These are the comments one hears from neighbors, friends at the club, or patrons at the tavern, but they were not very uncommon among professionals until recently. When they first came to public attention, all types of family violence, beginning with child abuse in the 1960s, were initially viewed as rare occurrences engaged in by psychopathological individuals, the most depraved persons who suffered from some sort of "mental illness." As David Finkelhor says,

> [I]n all cases they were analyzed as extremely pathological behaviors. Incest offenders were seen as backwoods degenerates and feebleminded freaks. Child beaters were seen as depraved. Wife beaters were seen as alcoholic rogues and psychopaths and were considered to come from only extremely lower class and disorganized families. (1981a, 12)

It should not be surprising that the first theories on each type of family violence came from clinicians, psychiatrists, and psychologists, because of their close associations within the medical field.[2] When radiologists, using newly developing techniques with X-rays, first began systematically noting long-bone fractures and multiple fractures at different stages of healing on the same child, they were most likely to engage in consultation with pediatricians, who in turn were likely to call in professionals in the mental health field. Even before the grass roots movement in the 1970s that disclosed wife beating as a social problem of major proportions, there were some in the medical and psychiatric professions who had battered wives and their abusers as patients. A few batterers were convicted of their crimes and sent to prison, where they were examined by psychiatrists (Schultz 1960). Sometimes convicted wife beaters were court-ordered into psychiatric examination (Snell et al. 1964).

Since people in related fields in medicine were most likely to come in close contact with victims and their abusers sooner and with easier accessibility than any others in the social and behavioral sciences, it should be expected that the first reports and the first theories would expound the *medical model*. That is, these practitioners are most likely to view family violence as a sickness, postulating that people who harm others in the kin network are deviant individuals who behave as they do because of some mental aberration. Researcher David Gil (1971) clearly saw the tendency of social and behavioral scientists to harbor certain preconceptions and basic assumptions, derived from their professional training, and thus to ask questions likely to elicit the answers they expect. In other words, there is not only researcher bias, but there is professional bias, that determines in large part what we see.

Psychopathology theories propose that certain kinds of people are child abusers or neglectors; that they are different enough from other people in skills, temperament, personality, life histories, or even physiologically, that they may be identified by some combination of special characteristics. If such identification could occur, theoretically at least, these criteria could be applied to prevent child abuse and neglect. The original ideas were that parents who abuse are immature, impulsive, dependent, narcissistic, egocentric, demanding, and sadomasochistic. They were assumed to manifest these personality characteristics because they suffered some form of "mental illness," or pathology. Although at one point Steele and Pollock (1974, 92) state that their 60 patients would not seem much different than people randomly selected from a crowd on city streets, their diagnosis of *Pathology of the Attackers* (1974, 94) gives the following general characteristics:

> [T]hey present the wide spread of emotional disorders seen in any clinic population—hysteria, hysterical psychosis, obsessive-compulsive neurosis, anxiety states, depression, schizoid personality traits, schizophrenia, character neurosis, and so on. . . . They presented mixed pictures such as "obsessive-phobic neurosis with marked masochistic features and mild depression."

In other words, although clinicians wanted to classify abusers into an *abuser profile*, the ones they studied did not clearly fall into one consistent category of psychosis or neurosis. After the initial furor, it became apparent that child abusers were no more likely to be psychotic than the general public, and that the types of neuroses they displayed were so varied and dissimilar that "It was not possible to make a simple diagnosis in most patients" (Steele and Pollock 1974, 95). Nevertheless, despite lack of strong empirical support, this theory remains one of the most popular and widely accepted, and researchers continue to search for specific psychological characteristics of individuals and pathological mental states of abusive parents.[3]

Even if researchers do not necessarily agree with its tenets, many of them design their studies to test the psychopathology model (Ellis 1981). Rizley and Cicchetti (1981a) largely discount earlier research findings as being of limited value because of questionable reliability and validity,[4] yet their clinical observations had convinced them "that there is a substantial psychopathology in maltreating or violent adults," so they have undertaken a three-year longitudinal study at Harvard University using improved diagnostic methods.

Some researchers decided to examine child victims for special characteristics that invite parents to abuse them. It was not long after the "battered baby syndrome" surfaced and the psychopathology model was introduced that researchers began searching for specific characteristics of victims, trying to identify which babies are high risk for abuse (Haggerty 1964; Milowe and Laurie 1964). The *role of the child in abuse* was examined by William Friedrich and Jerry Boriskin (1976, 581), and these authors note that the earlier theory by Milowe and Laurie suggested two out of four possible causal factors in child abuse dealing specifically with characteristics of the child victim: "Defects" in the child that precipitate abuse and a personality that "served to invite others to hurt him."

Most writers were careful to point out that some "defects" in the child might be present only from the viewpoint of the abusive parent/s, but sometimes it appeared that the victims were blamed, as happened to a much greater extent in all other forms of family violence. Finkelhor notes that difference, but he also claims:

> It was harder to blame a one, two or three year old child than an adolescent or adult woman. But even in this case one can find evidence of a belief that abused children were, in fact, extremely aggressive and provoking and if it had not been for their waywardness, they would not have been abused. (1981a, 13)

Research testing the medical model on victims included studies of "failure to bond," failure to thrive, prematurity, various types of differentness, physical and mental handicaps, listlessness, and fussiness. After reviewing the literature on the role of the child in abuse, Friedrich and Boriskin (1976, 588) modified and enlarged previous theories and suggested that different combinations of four factors cause abuse: "special child," "special parent," "crisis," and "cultural tolerance [for severe corporal punishment]."

Nevertheless, like an evolutionary growth process the narrowness of the original individual psychopathology theory of child abuse and neglect has been modified, expanded, and improved. From their initial concentration on abusers, then child victims, the theory and research expanded to include *both* abusers' and victims' characteristics, searching for interactive effects or psychodynamics, and finally moved to include environmental stress factors. As evidence accumulated that psychological or personality problems *alone* cannot explain the cause of child abuse, the model expanded to include situational, environmental, and social factors in addition to individual characteristics. Now when scales are being devised to try to identify abusing from nonabusing parents, a variety of sociocultural and economic factors are included along with a battery of attitude and psychological tests. Similarly, when other social scientists construct theories, they begin from a sociocultural framework but include some individual psychological traits into their models (Gelles 1979, 38; Steinmetz and Straus 1974, 18–19). In recent years the trend has been from micro to macro theories of child abuse and neglect.

The earliest theory on the phenomenon of violence between married or cohabiting couples, or spouse abuse, was also the psychopathology model: The batterers, their wives, or both, were defined as psychopaths.[5] Victims were described as masochistic, frigid, castrating, sadistic, and so forth. Wife beating was considered to occur rarely, and then only among deviant individuals with severe emotional problems or alcohol addiction. First addressed by clinicians, this theoretical framework reflects the professional training of the researchers, as may be expected (Gil 1971). Their initial response was to study individual characteristics of victims, rather than abusers, a practice that brought sharp criticism from some writers (Stark and Flitcraft 1981; Wardell et al. 1981). There were some practical reasons for taking this approach, one of the most important of which was that it was almost impossible to obtain and study a sample of men who beat their wives. If approached, most denied the violent behavior or minimized it, denied responsibility, and refused to cooperate (Ganley and Harris 1978).

The early reports on wife beating were generated from a few case histories of beaten wives, while only two focus specifically on the batterers (Faulk 1974; Schultz 1960). The latter is an analysis of ten prisoners convicted of wife assault. From England, sociologists Dennis Marsden and David Owens (1975) wrote an article, "Jekyll and Hyde Marriages," and in the United States, psychiatrists Snell, Rosenwald, and Robey (1964) wrote about "The Wifebeater's Wife." The team of Snell et al. was assigned 37 accused wife beaters for analysis by the court, but when the men refused or resisted attempts at interviews, the doctors focused in on 12 of the men and their wives who cooperated. Despite the high refusal rate and the court's interest in the men, their article focuses on the women. Their descriptions of these few wives is contradictory; they say the women are domineering, masochistic, frigid, aggressive, indecisive, masculine, passive, overprotective of their sons, and emotionally deprived. According to these male psychiatrists, the wives *needed* periodic punishment for their "castrating activity" (Snell et at. 1964, 111). This article was severely criticized by a number of writers, including other psychiatrists such as Elaine Hilberman (1980), but at the time it was published there was very little else in the literature on wife beating, so it has been quoted many times in the intervening years as "scientific findings" on battered wives. In the more recent past, some wife beaters have been studied directly as participants in research (Coleman 1980; Ganley and Harris 1978), but largely because of their refusal to cooperate, data on most abusers come from researchers who study their victims.

The medical model tends to view wife beating as an individual, rather than a social problem and looks for personality characteristics of the abuser and abused in violent relationships (Elbow 1977; Star 1978). Some of these writers let the "mask of scientific neutrality" (Wilson 1976) slip aside and reveal personal prejudices in their writings. British professor of social work Elizabeth Wilson (1976) sharply criticized a British psychiatrist, Jasper Gayford, who wrote some of the earliest articles on battered wives. In a later article, Gayford categorized the victims into stereotypes such as "Tortured Tina," "Fanny the Flirt," and "Go-Go Gloria" (1976), hardly the kind of writing expected in scientific journals. Another article revealing personal bias was written by clinical psychologist and family counselor James Kleckner (1978), in which he calls battered wives and their abusers "co-conspirators" and throws most of the blame for abuse onto the victims. For example, he states that abused wives do not really object to being beaten because, "The chronically abused wife is one who permits her husband to beat her, refuses to take punitive action afterward, and remains in the same situation so that she may be beaten again" (Kleckner 1978, 54).

Despite the early acceptance of the individual psychopathology model, later trends have been to discount or disconfirm many of its explanatory factors, and to propose wider models that include sociocultural and situational factors. For example, psychiatrist Elaine Hilberman and psychiatric nurse consultant Kit Munson (1978), wrote an article in which they reviewed the cases of 60 battered women involved in ongoing treatment at a mental health clinic, whose abuse was unknown to the referring clinicians except in four cases. These writers reveal that the women were being treated for a variety of physical and mental symptoms over the years, but the attending doctors were not told of the violence at home, nor did they ask (Hilberman and Munson 1978, 464). Later, Hilberman wrote an article claiming that mental health professionals generally ignored wife beating, but when it was identified, assumed it represented "some intrapsychic liability on the part of the victim," and further, that it was assumed to occur infrequently; thus it was defined as an individual problem (1980, 1336).

Hilberman, Munson, and others have done much to revise the earlier psychopathologic model. Supporting their contentions, recent research has clearly shown that the extent of the problem is far greater than previously estimated. The pervasiveness of spouse abuse in this society is now estimated to occur between one out of every two couples, so it is clearly a social problem of immense proportions, not one of just a few maladjusted individuals. The response to the medical model of individual psychopathology is best expressed by two researchers who state:

> Within this pattern of nonrecognition, the view that battering is a "private event" which arises from individual or familial peculiarities (pathologies) plays a distinctly ideological role. In straightforward terms, the ways in which clinicians and social scientists see "the battered woman," the ways in which she is "known," partially determine the help she is given. But the help she is given is part of her problem, not of its solution. (Stark and Flitcraft 1981, 1)

It should be obvious by now how important theory is, and how important are the connections between theory and research. The only other theoretical framework that was proposed as soon as the "discovery" of child maltreatment occurred in the 1960s and the disclosure of wife beating in the 1970s, and that still permeates the literature is the *cycle of violence*. The idea of an intergenerational transmission of violence was introduced by Henry Kempe and his colleagues, Silverman, Steele, Droegemueller and Silver (1962) regarding child abusers, and was introduced later pertaining to wife beaters by Jasper Gayford (1975a, 1975b, 1975c). In their seminal article, although Kempe et al. warned that their knowledge of factors involved in child abuse was limited, they did suggest that "often parents may be repeating the type of child care practiced on them in their childhood" (1962, 24). The "commonsense logic" of this statement was immediately accepted by almost all persons subsequently writing on the topic, although it still has not received strong empirical support based on rigorous, scientific research. Because this idea has been advanced so frequently by scientists, service providers, and the mass media, it is the major focus of Chapter 7 and is discussed in detail there, rather than attempting to examine it fully here.

SOCIAL LEARNING THEORY

"My old man hit me all the time, and I turned out OK, didn't I?" "I tried to hit him back once, and then he really beat the hell out of me. He said he'd kill me if I ever did that again, and boy, I never did!" "Whatever my pa said in our family was the law! He got the best of everything, and my ma and sisters waited on him hand and foot. That's how it is in my house—I yell, they jump." "I been doing this all my life—I don't take no sass from nobody."

These statements are not unusual; most of us have heard expressions similar to them sometime in our lives. Each one represents at least one principle derived from social learning theory.[6] The first is an example of *modeling*. The second is from a battered wife; in this case the violence had *functional value* for her abuser but had none for her. The third statement includes both imitating a *high status role model* (his father) and *reinforcement* for his bullying. The last principle illustrated is that behavior which receives reinforcement is most likely to be *repeated*. These principles are discussed in detail shortly. *Social learning theory* is defined as an integration of differential association with differential reinforcement, so that people with whom one interacts are the reinforcers that result in learning of deviant and nondeviant behavior (Akers 1973). According to sociologist Ronald Akers, the type of behavior that is consistently and most frequently reinforced by others is the one most often exhibited.

Social learning theory has been widely proposed as an explanation for spouse abuse[7] but to a much lesser degree for other types of family violence, although its tenets can provide understanding of intrafamily dynamics. This framework also provides insight into parent abuse, sibling violence, and physical and sexual abuse of children, but it has been proposed less frequently (Barnett et al. 1980). Anthropologists Margaret Mead (1973) and Ashley Montagu (1973, 1976) both provide strong evidence that culture has a more important role in developing personalities and behavior than inborn characteristics. Some people still cling to the innate aggression notions of Konrad Lorenz (1966) and Robert Ardrey (1966) and Sigmund Freud's "instinctual inclination," but Albert Bandura (1973, 13–14) says that these are ideas, not theories, because they can neither be verified nor disproved through empirical research.

Never do this to a child! Children are not toys! Tossing a child into the air may be fun for Dad, but this can result in permanent injury to a child or even death through a subdural hematoma, a blood clot on the brain. Parents generally approach the important task of parenting without any formal training, often imitating the way they think their parents treated them, or the way they see other parents interact with their children. They are unaware of how easily a child can be injured. For example, under extreme stress and frustration, parents may take children and shake them severely, because they fear that if they slap the child, they may cause injuries and therefore become child abusers. There are no visible signs when subdural hematoma has occurred, but a child can become permanently brain-damaged or die, and the injury is discovered only during the autopsy.

For some time, a popular theory was that humans are instinctively aggressive because of genetic transmittal; then a shift came about and the prevailing viewpoint was that people were products of their culture or environment—the old "nature vs. nurture" argument. Now most social scientists reject a dichotomy between heredity and environmental influences and believe that there is an interactive effect. Biology and genetics determine a person's physical build and sex, which influence personality and behavior in combination with the external environment into which that person is born. The person is neither a victim of his/her genetic makeup nor a helpless pawn of his/her environment, as experimental psychologist Albert Bandura explains:

> [B]oth sets of factors interact in subtle ways in determining behavior. Where certain biological equipment is needed to perform manual aggressive acts, structural factors, which have a genetic basis, may partly determine whether initial aggressiveness proves successful and is further developed, or whether it fails and is discarded. Possession of a brawny physique . . . increases the probability that physically aggressive modes of behavior will prove effective. (1973, 26)

This may help explain why some family members are more likely to be abusive than others. Men are generally taller, heavier, and physically stronger than women (even though very few men may possess a "brawny physique" compared to other men); adults are bigger and stronger than children; and adult children are stronger than aged parents. Bandura does not say that *all* persons who are advantaged by "certain biological equipment" are going to aggress against disadvantaged others, but he does say that if initial aggressiveness is successful or fails, the outcome will determine future behavior. For example, if a husband does not want any more argument about the way he spends money, therefore slaps his wife and gets her to stop talking about it and then she is afraid to bring it up later, then his action was "successful." If a man is feeling impotent in his social or economic relationships and makes a sexual move toward his daughter that she cannot repel, by which he gains a sense of potency and power, then his action was "successful." If a caretaker is feeling overworked and frustrated by an aged parent and threatens to withhold food and medicine, whereupon the parent is contrite and begs for forgiveness, that caretaker was "successful." In all the above examples, according to social learning theory, behavior bringing success is most likely to be repeated.

One of the basic propositions of social learning theory is that reinforcement following behavior increases the probability that the behavior will be repeated, and another is that intermittently reinforced behavior is the most difficult to extinguish (Hilgard and Bower 1966). Akers points out that two major parts of the learning process are reinforcement and punishment (1973, 49). Emphasis is placed on *reinforcement* rather than punishment, because punishment has been shown to have relatively short-term effects on extinguishing behavior and because immediate reinforcement outweighs effects of delayed punishment in controlling behavior (Bandura 1973; Hill 1971). In other words, punishment is not as successful in changing behavior because it is only effective for a short time, especially if it occurs after a delay. On the other hand, reinforcing (rewarding) desirable behavior immediately after it occurs, especially on an occasional basis, rather than after every incidence, is most likely to cause that behavior to be repeated. For example, to slap a child for taking candy is likely to be forgotten quickly, but to reward a child after she hangs up her coat increases the probability that she will do it again. Unfortunately, too few parents know these simple facts, and continue to slap their children for breaking rules and ignore the times they obey the rules or do something well. This basic idea of social learning theory is the foundation of most courses on effective parenting.

In addition to reinforcement, *modeling* is another important factor for learning, especially for children. In a variety of social psychological tests, children observing aggressive behavior not only showed they remembered aggressive acts, but they closely imitated them, particularly when the acts were performed by a male adult model (Bandura 1973). The boys were more likely to imitate aggression spontaneously, but when they were rewarded for imitation, children of both sexes increased their performance until they were almost equally aggressive (Bandura 1973, 72–85). As Bandura (1973, 80) stresses, "people learn more than they usually perform, unless given positive incentives to do so," and the girls revealed they had learned but were unwilling to demonstrate it until they were sure their behavior would be rewarded.

Earliest socialization occurs in the home, thus children receive reinforcement and/or punishment from their adult models, and while they later learn sex-appropriate behavior from many other social sources, studies have shown that "Children were much more inclined to imitate a familiar aggressive model than an unfamiliar one. This was especially true of boys, who performed approximately three times as many matching responses as the girls . . ." (Bandura 1973, 80). According to Bandura's test findings, it made no difference to either boys or girls if they had a nurturant relationship with the model or not. In other words, children, especially boys, are likely to imitate behavior of a male model they know but do not necessarily like.

Other research findings that support social learning theory are that if a model's behavior appears to have *functional value*—if it achieves desired results—observers have strong incentives to practice these behavior patterns; and the more opportunity for practice, whether physically or mentally rehearsed, the more permanent the behavior patterns become (Bandura 1973, 78). If a young boy sees his father demand, and receive, choice foods and personal service from others in the family by force or threat of force, that kind of behavior is likely to be perceived as functional. Then the boy practices his father's behavior with his younger sibling or other children in the school yard. If that behavior is reinforced, it proves functional for him, so he is very likely to practice that behavior until it becomes a permanent pattern. On the other hand, if his sibling is bigger than he is, or he is smaller than his target in the school yard, his behavior is unlikely to be rewarded and is much less likely to be repeated. There is one other possibility; the child may only mentally rehearse, saying to himself, "When I get big like Dad, people will give me what I want, or else!" This child may grow up to be a man who never hits anyone until he beats his wife or child.

Tests have also shown that people do not necessarily have to personally witness aggressive behavior: They learn equally well from "pictorial representation" and verbal description, provided that they are old enough to understand, and that it commands their attention (Bandura 1973, 73). This helps explain why some people become aggressive adults although their homes of orientation were nonviolent; ours is an extremely violent society and messages accepting or even approving of violence are all around us. Constantly hearing people tell of the benefits of violent behavior, or seeing aggressive behavior being rewarded in the media, can convince some people that such behavior is necessary and appropriate.

Another important factor should be noted: *attention* in the learning process. The first formulation of ideas about appropriate or inappropriate behavior patterns is established in the parental home while a young child is in a relatively closed social system with fewer distractions that impede learning, so that reinforcement and models receive a major share of a child's attention. Bandura has this to say:

> The people with whom a person regularly associates delimit the types of behavior that he will repeatedly observe and hence learn most thoroughly. . . . The behavior of models who possess high status in prestige, power, and competence hierarchies is more likely to be successful and therefore to command greater attention from others than the behavior of models who are socially, occupationally, and intellectually inept. (1973 69–70)

As mentioned above, children can mature in nonviolent homes but become violent adults, and this frequently occurs when their reference groups approve of or use violence to achieve their goals: Their peers are *high status models* in their eyes. This was the basic idea of the differential-association theory to explain juvenile delinquency (Sutherland 1939). But it also explains why children are more likely to model their behavior after their fathers than their mothers: In the hierarchical structure of the patriarchal family, the husband/father position carries highest status in prestige and power (Dobash and Dobash 1976, 1978). Both boys and girls are more likely to imitate a violent father than a nonviolent mother, especially if she is a victim of abuse, but the behavior is less likely to be reinforced for girls when they practice behavior that is considered sex-inappropriate. Boys who are aggressive are much more likely to be rewarded for such behavior, especially when they live in an environment where traditional ideas of masculinity include the "tough guy" or macho stereotype (Bandura and Walters 1970a).

It is true that socialization of boys and girls into adulthood contains many messages of sex-appropriate behavior and that it is not rewarding, and sometimes painful, to deviate from cultural norms (David and Brannon 1976; Grossman 1977; Pleck and Sawyer 1974). Little girls (and women) often witness modeled aggression that is rewarding for others, but it takes special inducements for them to act contrary to sex role expectations. Bandura reports the results of his experiments where children watched aggressive adult models, and the different responses of boys and girls in these tests:

> [B]oys, who are generally encouraged to emulate feats of physical prowess, spontaneously performed all they had learned when they saw aggression well received. When models were punished for their aggressive actions, boys performed less than they had learned, but they later readily exhibited additional imitative responses when they produced rewarding results. By contrast, girls, for whom physical aggression is traditionally regarded as sex-inappropriate and hence negatively sanctioned kept much of what they had learned to themselves, regardless of how the male model's behavior was treated. Their learning was not manifested in action until they received direct assurance that it was acceptable. In predicting the occurrence of aggression, one should be more concerned with predisposing conditions than with predisposed individuals. Given that aggressive modes of conduct have been learned, social circumstances largely determined whether and when they will be performed. (Bandura 1973, 67)

When girls and boys become adults, they have internalized culturally approved sex-role expectations that largely relegate girls to "feminine" characteristics of timidity and dependence, and boys to "masculine" characteristics of aggressiveness and independence. To overcome strong social and cultural pressures to conform and rewards for conforming, deviation must be accomplished by reinforcements sufficiently powerful, plus punishments for conformist behavior (Pagelow 1978a, 28–30). Females do not generally receive powerful reinforcement for aggressive behavior, particularly when they direct it against adult males. On the other hand, they may be rewarded but are seldom punished for behavior "appropriately" feminine, at least not directly.

Many authors propose that stereotypic gender role socialization along extremes of "masculinity" and "femininity" is an important contributing factor in family violence, particularly in wife beating.[8] Straus (1976b) writes about cultural norms that legitimize marital violence and discusses "compulsive masculinity" which refers to the requirement that boys and men prove to others that they are "real men" by their disdain for any attributes considered feminine. The author's own study found that strict interpretation of dichotomized sex roles literally set up men to be aggressive (and if necessary, violent), and women to be passive, dependent, and frequently, victimized by men (Pagelow 1978a). But not all men or women follow sharply antithetical gender roles, nor accept them as their definitions of manliness or womanliness, so how can social learning theory explain the behavior of people who reject them? Despite learning and social pressures that promote stereotypic sex-role behavior, some men and women obviously see these roles as dysfunctional. Some may have tried these behavior patterns but found they were not rewarded or that the behavior was not personally rewarding.

This is the power of social learning theory: It clarifies why some people behave in both conforming and deviant ways. It shows how children establish personalities and behavior patterns, but it is not confined only to children because learning is a lifelong process. Socialization experiences change throughout the life cycle, and people modify their personalities and behavior accordingly. Childhood socialization is important but people can and do reject certain behavior when it is not rewarded and adopt different patterns that seem to bring greater success. An aggressive child can become a nonviolent adult; a passive woman can become a husband beater; a "good child" can become a parent abuser; and a wife beater can learn to express himself in ways that do not involve the use of physical force.

The single most serious criticism of social learning theory is that one of its basic assumptions depends on the human cognitive processes, on the idea that people usually act in ways that they perceive to serve their own best interests. Social learning theory assumes rationality and some degree of thinking concerning the costs/benefits ratio involved in action. It does not fully account for some types of spontaneous, nonpremeditated behavior that is unrewarded and even self-punishing. For example, there is the "tough little guy" who likes to pick fights with big men to show his masculinity and who often pays dearly, yet does not seem to get the message. Or there is the frustrated parent who wants a child to stop crying, and slaps the child to get him or her to stop: This is a *shining example of illogical behavior* performed by millions of parents each year.

The next theoretical framework expands from the social psychological level of social learning theory into a broader, social structural viewpoint.

THE SOCIAL SYSTEM

> "This is a man's world, and don't you forget it, baby!" "People who are poor in this country are only lazy, they don't want to work and better themselves." "A man's home is his castle." "Mother who abandoned baby at church arrested; prosecutor promises maximum sentence." "Why don't these people take care of their children?"

Many writers believe it is the way our social system is structured and the institutions within it cause family violence. For example, Eli Newberger scoffs at a government agency report that (as usual) "pins the blame on the parents" for child abuse and neglect, whereas he says: "One could also do no better to design a system to make parents fail" (1973, 18). David Gil (1974) presents a long list of the causes of family violence that include: the dominant social philosophy and value premises; the social, economic, and political institutions; the quality of human relations that are created by this system; our views on children's rights and our treatment of them; and employment-related stress and frustration. Writing for the Carnegie Council on Children, Kenneth Keniston (1977) and Richard de Lone (1979) show how the social system has taken away a number of controls from family members, but has still left parents with the responsibilities for meeting demands from society. When they fail to meet these demands because of structural inequality, discrimination, stigmatization, and so forth, the parents (not the society) suffer the burden of guilt and blame.

Structural Inequality

Inequality in our society is mentioned frequently in the literature on violence, but it consists of different categories such as economic, educational, sexual, racial and ethnic inequality, and inequality in availability of health and social services. All of these are strongly related. Official statistics on child maltreatment reveal that *reported* parents are more likely to be poor, young, educationally deprived, and that members of minority groups are overrepresented as well as female single parents. Even though reported cases may not be representative of the total population that maltreat children, they do show that many children suffer abuse and neglect fostered at least in part by structural inequality. Institutional barriers to some people for equality of education, employment, and opportunity have little to do with individual characteristics but with discrimination on the basis of sex and race or ethnicity. Long-standing inequalities affect the behavior of persons within the family unit, not only regarding children, but also regarding battered women. One of the reasons frequently given by wives for staying with abusive husbands is their lack of opportunities for financial independence to provide for themselves and their children (Dobash and Dobash 1979; Pagelow 1981a; Straus 1978).

Stress

Closely related to structural inequality is stress, another commonly mentioned factor associated with family violence. Most recent articles and books refer to the fact that stress frequently triggers violent behavior (Helfer and Kempe 1974, 1976; Madden and Lion 1976; Martin 1976; Straus et al. 1980). By itself, stress is not a necessary or sufficient factor to explain violence, but when it occurs in addition to a number of other factors, violence is likely to occur. Many people live extremely stressful lives but never resort to violence as a solution, so it must require certain other conditions.

Writers tend to associate stress mainly with poverty, but many poor people lead nonviolent lives that contain a large share of stressful factors. Stress can easily cross socioeconomic lines, as many persons in the middle and upper classes can testify. Decisions must be made daily by corporation executives, surgeons, attorneys, bankers, and stock brokers that are very stressful, considering social pressures for individual financial success in this country. Evidence of our stressful culture lies in the high rate of stress-related diseases: heart disease, ulcers, hypertension, and so forth. One crisis counselor in an affluent area mentioned that many troubled families he meets have large incomes but their standard of living is so expensive they believe they cannot afford needed professional help. A poor mother worrying about food and clothing for her children might not agree, but the stress for a rising executive worrying about paying the harbor lease for his boat or tuition for his children at the best academy may be comparable to her own. In our competitive, materialistic society, there is extreme stress in "climbing the ladder of success," and then struggling to stay there.

Patriarchy

Researchers Dobash and Dobash (1979) see the cause of wife beating and other abuses of the powerless in the family as the hierarchical, patriarchal structure of the family in the social system. Their theory on wife beating borrows from social learning theory, especially in terms of the learning of traditional gender roles: the patriarchal structure of the family. This theoretical model gains strength by borrowing also from conflict theory which postulates that when there are unequal distributions of scarce and valued resources, conflict is inevitable. Patriarchy demands that power be vested in men, and that women are to serve in subordinate positions to men. The very foundations of the patriarchal family promote violence against females, particularly wives, according to Dobash and Dobash (1978, 1979, 1980) as well as others. Research by the Dobashes showed that in almost 900 cases of violence in families where the sex of offenders and victims was known, females were the victims in 94 percent of the cases and were offenders in only 3 percent (Dobash and Dobash 1978, 436).

Historical research shows that the hierarchical structure of the family vests power in men to dominate and control others, and to use whatever means are viewed as required to maintain their authority. Further, the unequal relations between men, women, and children in the family are supported by all social institutions (Barnett et al. 1980; Jaffe 1980). Professor of social work Ellen Barnett and her colleagues, Pittman, Ragan, and Salus state:

> In American society the traditional structure of the family has been patriarchal. . . . Frustrations for both partners occur as a result of rigid and idealized role expectations. The reluctance of all social institutions to intervene in family matters encourages and perpetuates spousal abuse. (Barnett et al. 1980, 6)

Like the Dobashes, another research team, Stark, Flitcraft, and Frazier (Stark et al. 1979; Stark and Flitcraft 1981) agrees that the root cause of wife beating is patriarchal relations in the family, and also that the development, maintenance, and continuance of the patriarchal family is a political issue that many researchers and service providers try to avoid by reducing it to "private troubles" (Stark and Flitcraft 1981, 12).

The next theoretical framework to be discussed also moves beyond the individual level and involves the social structural acceptance and approval of violence, which may not singularly *cause* family violence, but certainly contributes to its occurrence.

CULTURAL APPROVAL OF VIOLENCE

"Be a man! fight for your rights!" "Are you gonna take that sitting down?" "What a hero! that guy killed 23 Japs in WW II." "Kill the ump!" "Protect you home and loved ones—buy a gun."

Many writers constantly insist that our culture promotes, stimulates, and even encourages and rewards violent behavior, and that this cultural approval of violence is an important factor in family violence (Finkelhor 1979a; Gelles 1979; Straus et al. 1980). However, this is almost entirely approval of *male* violence: It is masculine to be macho (Pagelow 1978a). Females are expected to be nonviolent, but to admire and respect male violence, or at least to view men's violence as "natural" and inevitable.

Sports

After awareness has been raised regarding the pervasiveness of cultural approval of violence, it seems almost unnecessary to even discuss that which is so obvious, the popular obsession with unnecessarily violent sports such as hockey and boxing. Civilization has not progressed very far from the days when Christians were thrown to the lions to entertain the masses. Today's audiences pay millions of dollars to watch two men beating each other into bloody masses until one falls unconscious. A race that involves a spectacular accident is preferred to one that does not. One lesson in the glorification of violence in this culture comes from observing audiences at boxing matches, or automobile or speedboat races. Some men die as a result of their "entertainment" careers; many more suffer permanent physical damages.

Toys

Children learn early that violence is *fun*. Toy stores contain playthings for children to enjoy pretending to kill, destroy, and explode other people and things. Weapons of all sorts abound: bazookas, machine guns, rifles, handguns, missiles, tanks, fighter planes, and so forth, and all the sundry play-war-people to go with them. Sweden recognized the dangers of training children in violence and has banned all weapons and war toys, while the United States, with the highest rates of violent crime in the world, continually ignores the training-in-violence such toys promote. It has always seemed ironic to the author that Christians in the United States celebrate the birth of Christ by turning their homes into virtual arsenals of imitation death and destruction, providing weapons to little children.

Amid strains of "Peace on Earth," children entertain themselves by playing war. More will be said later about giving children precise imitations of weapons for killing.

Movies

The mass media constantly transmit messages of violence: Consider movies in theaters and on television. Newspaper entertainment pages are filled with advertisements for horror or "action" films, sometimes suggesting dismemberment with dripping daggers and women's bodies—dead, dying, or preparing to die (Ebert 1981; Elias 1979; S. Feshbach 1980;

Nine guns are shown here—can you identify which ones are toys and which are real guns? Shown in this photograph are some of the "Saturday Night Specials," guns that are cheap and easily concealable. The toy gun is designed so closely matching the real guns that even experts are unable to tell the difference at a distance of ten feet. The toy gun in this photo is Number 1, but it closely resembles actual weapons. It is a copy of a Colt pistol; it is 4.5 inches long, 3.5 inches high, and only 1.75 inches thick. This toy gun is similar to the one held by a five-year-old boy, pointed at a police officer, that resulted in a fatal shooting.

Ryan 1981). There has been a noticeable increase in movies featuring torture and killing of females, for example, the infamous *Snuff,* which was purported to be the filming of the actual torture of a woman, concluding with her mutilation murder.[9]

Movie critic Desmond Ryan's (1981) reaction to *Mania,* which he termed a "vile, bloody movie" depicting "festering hatred for women," was so bad that he walked out after "40 blood-drenched minutes," wanting to "throw up." Chicago film critic Robert Ebert (1981) reviewed *I Spit on Your Grave* and said, "The film itself was garbage—reprehensible, vile." What disturbed Ebert most was that this and other recent movies take the audience to the violence from the vantage point of the rapists/butchers/killers and that the recent trend of horror films has been to encourage audience identification with the killer, not with the victim as earlier films did. Ebert not only believed that this film directed the audience to "stand in the shoes of the killer," but that the audience around him did exactly that: cheering on the killer, shouting and laughing loudly at the climax of each violent episode, yelling support for the rape and violence on the screen.

Advertisements

We do not have to patronize these films, but we are involuntarily exposed to their messages of violence through billboards, posters, television ads, and newspaper ads. The movie *Tattoo* was promoted with a picture of a woman's nude body (not showing her head) with ankles bound, tattooed the entire length. There was an advertising blitz featuring this image on home television screens, billboards, magazines, and newspapers across this nation. People had no choice about seeing this image—it was there. In response to those who disagree that tattooing mutilates a body, it is a painful process by which scarification is performed with needles, thus it *is* violence: Further, the binding of the ankles indicated nonconsent by the woman, which indicates that she was a victim. Perhaps the most odious part of this advertisement was the slogan imprinted just under the model's legs: "Every Great Love Leaves Its Mark," which associated love with violence. It also associated sex with violence, which psychologist Seymour Feshbach (1980) calls "a dangerous alchemy."

Protest groups meet stiff resistance. One of the first groups organized to eliminate media violence, Women Against Violence in Pornography and Media (WAVPM), reports that an underground feminist group in New York defaced over 200 subway posters advertising *Tattoo* (News Page 1981, 4), after unsuccessful attempts to get the producer to listen to their protests. WAVPM protested an ad promoting *For Your Eyes Only;* they received a phone call from the vice president in charge of advertising at United Artists, who explained that:

[T]he purpose of the ad was to sell tickets, and images of violent sex sell better than most other images. The violence in the ad, he explained, "had nothing to do with violence against women," but rather was in keeping with the genre of James Bond films (which of course are quite violent and sexist). (New Page 1981, 5)

In sum, *violent sex sells best.*

Printed Materials

Outside the home, magazine and newspaper racks are everywhere: on the sidewalks and in the stores and supermarkets, featuring bold, shocking headlines and photographs designed to catch the eye and entice potential purchasers to search for more inside the pages. This includes newspapers that contain much violence in their news reports (Shaw 1982). Take one issue of a regional newspaper, for example. The first three pages contained nine accounts of violent acts including: the headline article about the kidnapping, beating, torture, and rape of a 15-year-old girl; a convicted rapist freed pending appeal; a man who killed his wife, three children, the family dog, and himself; another man whose wife left after an argument in a cocktail lounge whereupon he followed her, hit her with his car, and then ran over her body; a teenage boy who brought a rifle to school and killed his teacher; and a father who killed his six children. The last article begins with these words:

The estranged wife of a man accused of murdering their six children has testified that he drove to her motel in Milwaukee to see the expression on her face when he told her, "They're all dead. How do you feel?"

Newspapers carry other violence into our homes. News pictures feature violent scenes whenever available (recall some of the prize-winning photos from Vietnam). Televised news programs feature large doses of violence. Note how the cameras focus in on dead bodies whenever possible: on the blood seeping out from a covered body, or on the gurney carrying the covered body of John Belushi after his sudden death.

Before giving a talk on violence at a university, the author stopped at a nearby corner "Mom and Pop" grocery store, to check the availability of magazines featuring violence. From the 20-foot display rack of magazines, three were brought to the cashier, who was a boy of about 14, the son of the store owners. One magazine was a "detective" type, another a "romance" type, and the third was an issue of *Hustler* (June 1978) with a cover showing a meat grinder with an inverted nude figure of a female protruding from it. What was most disconcerting was the youthful age of the other customers at the magazine racks as well as of the boy through whose hands these materials passed at the cash register. The contents of the magazines were in keeping with their covers: torture, sadism, castration, dismemberment, incest, bestiality, and rape.

Fashion Advertisements

The selection of these particular magazines from the store rack was done purposely to illustrate the violent contents, but the glorification of violence is found not only in "cheap" magazines, it is also found in high-fashion magazines which feature either overtly violent or symbolically violent advertisements. The most violent of all are ads for shoes, usually featuring women as victims, being stepped on, kicked, or straddled by men, but there was one set of advertisements in which the roles were reversed. Just after it was published, a student brought to class an ad series showing women (displaying the latest fashions) in various scenes strangling, slapping, gouging, and assaulting men in one issue of *Vogue* (1981, 253–61). The most shocking was a shoe ad: a close-up photograph of a woman's leg wearing a shoe being violently pushed into a man's face.[10] The same magazine featured another full-page shoe ad: a black and white drawing of a woman's clothes closet, with a woman's leg in the foreground striding away. Barely visible in the middle of the closet, from behind the dresses, appeared just the bottom of a man standing there (trousers and a man's shoes). The only reference to the illustration was in small type at the bottom of the ad: the word "surprise."

Violence is almost inescapable in our culture: Billboards, movie theatre displays, and record covers all flash scenes of torture, sadism, or mayhem to our eyes, whether we want to see them or not (Lederer 1980; Liddick 1978; Prelgovisk et al. 1977; Zuckerman 1979). Young people are bombarded with scenes of violence; for example, a fashion magazine sent to a teenage girl that was intercepted—and strongly protested—by the girl's mother which contained:

> [P]hoto after photo of adolescent girls being sexually exploited. One image showed a teen . . . standing with her hands in her pockets while a man fondled her breasts. Another photo showed a young model's dress being pulled off her body, while in another a fan blew the model's skirt above her waist while a photographer shot pictures of her crotch. (*News Page* 1981, 5)

Unlike many other cases of offensive advertisements that remain unchallenged, the clothing manufacturer received over a hundred phone calls and letters within a week of the ad's distribution, and he promised that in the future his company's ads would not feature the sexualization of teens.

Television

Even if we could avoid public displays and glorification of violence, almost all of us have television sets in our homes. The Cooperative Extension of the University of California (Human Relations 1981), published a four-part series called *TV and Families: The Plug-In Drug?* Citing many excellent sources, the report states that families are adversely affected by too much TV and by the wrong kind of TV viewing. In particular, overexposure causes children to suffer in many ways, including exposure to racist and sexist stereotypes, an increase in learning difficulties, and, of course, reactions to very heavy doses of violence.

> By the end of high school the average young person has seen 20,000 murders on television. Violence has been consistently emphasized in prime time and Saturday morning broadcasts, the very programs to which children have easy access. Prime time drama averages about eight acts of violence per program hour; there is a violent act every two minutes of children's Saturday morning cartoons. (Human Relations 1981, Part III, 2)

Although long-term effects are not clearly established, the report suggests that extensive exposure to TV violence has at least the following three effects on children: (1) increased aggressive behavior including hyperactivity, aggression, disturbed sleep, and nightmares; (2) passive desensitization to violence (bystander apathy) and immunity to reaction to violence when it occurs; and (3) exaggerated sense of danger and mistrust creating fearfulness and difficulty in distinguishing between fact and fantasy. Inability to distinguish fact from fantasy can victimize children, but it can also promote their victimizing others by acting out the violent behavior they see examples of so frequently. Thus children overexposed to violence on television may become more aggressive, and at the same time they have become desensitized to pain and have a confused sense of reality while they mimic their role models performing violent acts. These are the necessary ingredients of learning behavior: modeling and imitation, and, if the behavior is rewarding, it is likely to be repeated (Bandura and Walters 1970a, 1970b).

In his speech on violence in the family and society at the 1982 meeting of the American Academy of Pediatrics, C. Everett Koop, the surgeon general of the United States, noted these facts: children spend at least two and a half hours before a TV set each day; many of today's high school graduates will have spent more time before TV than in classrooms; and adults spend about 40 percent of their leisure time watching television, the third largest use of time, only surpassed by sleep and employment (Koop 1982, 5).

Not only can massive doses of televised violence have very damaging effects on children, but there is also evidence that it effects adults adversely as well. Koop (1982, 5) noted this in his speech and said: "There *is* a relationship between violence that is televised and the violence that takes place in the 'real world.'" Television screens provide a great amount of violence in entertainment programs, sometimes making even murder and other violent crimes the basis for comedy (Rosenberg 1982). News presentations are, of course, full of violence, as mentioned earlier. Seymour Feshbach (1980), whose research has been on television and aggression, says, "perception of the same violent event has been shown to be more likely to evoke aggression in both children and adults when the violence is seen as real, as in a newscast, than when seen as a fantasy, as part of a dramatic presentation." However, after recounting the different responses to watching violence and sex on the screen, Feshbach comes to the conclusion that the greatest stimulus to violence is "when the exposure consists of the joining of sex and aggression, as in the presentation of a rape sequence." In the case of "mixing sex with violence," which Feshbach calls a "dangerous alchemy," the evidence is strong that viewing these scenes causes sexual arousal in males and a conditioning for violent responses.

Video Games

Another feature of our rapidly changing society is the availability and popularity of video games. Unfortunately, most of them deal with violence: blasting, destroying, or obliterating the "enemy" one way or the other, such as *Pac-Man*, which swallows the opponent. So far, the violence inherent in these games has been overlooked by most people in this country, although they were commented on by the surgeon general in his address mentioned earlier (Koop 1982). Koop noted the correlation between the increasing popularity of violent video games and violent behavior by youngsters, saying:

> [W]e are just beginning to assess the data. But I do know these games are not constructive. Whether they show soldiers or spacecraft or men from Mars or just from "the other side," we *zap* them—and that means annihilation. . . . [P]hysicians ought to recognize that a diet of violent entertainment for the

violence-prone individual is as unhealthy as a diet of sugar and starch is for the obesity-prone individual. (Koop 1982, 6)

Some television advertisements for video games feature simulated war rooms where there is an impending nuclear attack to lure viewers into the excitement of playing a thermonuclear war (and coming out of it as the "winner"). Another game features players as being vehicle drivers whose aim is to kill as many pedestrians as possible; after they "hit" each figure, a skeleton appears on the screen. Boys have enthusiastically become "hooked" on video games, whereas girls have tended to lag behind. Some believe it is "only natural," that violence is an integral facet of video games, but that is not true. There are games available that allow players to demonstrate skill and speed that do not involve destruction; unfortunately, these are fewer in number and not as widely advertised as destructive games. Games involving violence are much easier to sell to a market already predisposed towards violence.

Children are a large part of the market for violent video games, but there are other games designed specifically for adults, the so-called "X-Rated" games produced initially by a California firm. The greatest furor erupted over the release of one game *Custer's Revenge,* which resulted in legal action by several outraged groups, trying to get it removed from the market. The court agreed that the game was in bad taste but it ruled that the company has a constitutional right to produce and sell it. The game is described in these words:

> *Custer's Revenge* . . . depicts a nude Anglo man raping an Indian woman who is tied to a stake. The object of the "game" is for "Custer" to move through a hail of arrows to the woman. If he is hit by an arrow, he loses his erection; if not, he rapes the woman. As he thrusts into her, her legs fly up and she has what Mr. Kesten [the company's president] calls "a smile" on her face. (Childers 1982, 1)

The *Custer* video game received the greatest amount of publicity and negative public reaction, but there are two other games produced by the same company. One is *Beat'Em and Eat'em,* which features a man masturbating from a rooftop into the mouths of two women on the street below; the other is *Bachelor Party,* in which a nude man attempts to have intercourse with as many of the eight women on the screen as he can (Jordon 1983). Pornography, sadomasochistic devices, X-rated videotaped movies, and now video games are all part of a multibillion dollar industry that has a large and ready market among American buyers (almost all of whom are male) who enjoy mixing sex and violence. These materials are not only available in shops, but there is a large and growing mail order industry and the products are being brought into ordinary family homes where children can gain access to them.

Role Models

Another sign of our changing times is a growing trend among school children[11] to replace John Wayne with Bruce Lee as their hero. Wayne and other cowboy heroes were hardly strangers to violence in their screen roles, but now as boys wait in lines on school yards, they practice their form of "martial arts" on each other. They try to imitate Lee and Kung Fu by hitting each other with homemade versions of nunchakus or throwing weapons called "stars." Imitation nunchaku are easily made by cutting a broom handle into two pieces, approximately 12 inches long, and fastening them together at one end with a short piece of chain. These "toys" are deadly weapons that require a license in some states. Stars are thin pieces of metal cut into a variety of star shapes that have been sharpened at all the tips. The object of this weapon is to throw it accurately so that it penetrates and lodges in the flesh of the enemy. Boys as young as junior high age use clandestine techniques to make these weapons using schools' shop equipment. Children can buy all these weapons from mail order catalogues; companies do not screen potential buyers or their ages.

Children, almost exclusively boys, have always been fascinated with weapons, so this is nothing new. Parents have placed imitation weapons in their hands as early as two years of age, and when they get a little older, they frequently try to build their own "real" ones, such as the zip-guns that were so popular a generation ago among adolescents and young teens. A Boys and Girls Club's shop manager said that when children come into the shop, the boys' choice for their first project is to make a weapon—any weapon—but preferably a gun. These children are simply reflecting the American "love affair" with guns; the odds are about even that their parents have at least one firearm in their homes, and the majority of gun owners have more than one firearm (Block 1976).

Firearms

It is impossible to write about our violent culture and its effects on families without addressing the part that firearms play in making ours the most violent nation in the industrialized world. The United States has the highest rates of homicides and accidental deaths by firearms. The homicide rate in 1973 for the United States was 130 times the rate in England and Wales. British police do not even carry guns except on special assignment (Block 1976, 19).[12] Add to the homicides (22,000 in 1975); the accidental deaths (3,000 are killed and 20,000 persons are injured each year); and then the suicides (in 1978 there were 15,397 suicides committed with fire-arms, 12,830 males and 2,567 females), and the role that guns play in American violence becomes clearer. There were 57,939 Americans killed in combat during the entire course of our military involvement in Viet-nam, but more than two times that many Americans were murdered with guns in their own country during the same time period (Block 1976, 1).

In his carefully reasoned presentation of arguments for and against gun control, Irvin Block (1976, 4) notes the "gun mystique" of many Americans who feel they share a cultural continuity with pioneers and a traditional link with the Minutemen who helped win the American Revolution. Sixty million American families own guns, and half the people who own guns own a handgun. Between 1962 and 1968, "the annual number of rifles and shotguns manufactured and imported doubled, while the number of handguns *more than quadrupled*" (Block 1976, 8). In just one year, hand-guns produced and imported jumped from 1.7 million in 1967 to 2.5 mil-lion in 1968. It is difficult to know exactly how many firearms there are in American homes, therefore estimates range from 90 to 200 million. Why are there so many guns, and why do so many Americans feel as strongly as they do about gun ownership, that they get emotional as soon as the issue of gun control is introduced?

In actuality, the majority of Americans *do* favor at least some form of gun control. According to a number of polls, between 67 and 78 percent of all Americans favor gun registration, while 51 percent favor an outright ban on handguns. Even when polls are taken of only the people who ad-mit to gun ownership, 55 percent of them favor gun registration. Most of the legislation that has been introduced (and much of it struck down after intensive lobbying by the powerful National Rifle Association) has focused only on handguns, for good reason. Whereas 70 percent of gun-owning families have rifles, only 6 percent of murders in 1975 were committed with rifles; 9 percent were committed with shotguns, but handguns were the weapons used in 51 percent of the murders (Uniform Crime Reports 1976, 17). All told, that totals 66 percent, or about two out of three murders that were committed with firearms.

These statistics seem to support gun owners' claims that they need guns for protection from potential killers. Being law-abiding citizens them-selves, they reason that they need their own gun for self-protection from armed burglars or deranged strangers who enter their homes at night. However, the statistics do not support these notions. Only 21.6 percent of all murders in 1973 were committed in connection with a felony such as a robbery, burglary, gang war, or sexual attack; a few were suspected to be felonious but not proved; the balance then show that almost three out of four of the murders in 1973 were spontaneous, unpremeditated acts, as Block (1976, 14) notes:

All the rest, 71 percent, were "crimes of passion" committed against husbands, wives, children, lovers, love rivals, friends, and argumentative acquaintances. Most killings were the result of quarrels between people who knew each other. . . . Murder is usually a spontaneous outburst of unreasoning rage in which the murderer goes for the most easily available weapon. Given a choice, the potential murderer is likely to reach for a pistol or revolver. Though the handgun is inefficient for hunting and sport, it is the most efficient weapon for murder at close range between people who know one another. It is convenient, concealable, and can be used with surprise.

Well then, some might argue, how about all the murders of innocent family members by burglars who broke in at night that were prevented by householders who had a gun handy for protection? These number very few, actually. The vast majority of assaults on property are committed by burglars who rely on stealth; they do their work when nobody is home. The majority of residential burglaries are committed during daylight hours (Flanagan et al. 1982, 320), and only after the culprits have used a variety of techniques to ensure an empty residence. As Block explains:

They are after your jewels, your cameras, your television set, not your life. If cornered or surprised, they can be dangerous and have the advantage in nearly every case. A burglar is delighted when you own a gun. A gun is a good thing to steal— and that's how many guns in criminal hands have been acquired. . . . The robber and the rapist also have the advantage. They depend on speed and surprise and by the time you realize what they are up to, it is too late to find your gun or use it. Should you try anyway, or should you have a gun on you, your chances of getting killed are vastly increased. Instead of protecting you, the gun may cost you your life. (1976, 11)

The best way to keep guns out of criminal hands is to not provide easy access to them in the homes of law-abiding citizens. Block notes that at least 100,000 weapons are stolen from individuals each year. To make handguns efficient weapons for self-defense, the owner must be trained in their use and practice marksmanship, and they must be kept *loaded*. Is a loaded handgun protection? Whose hands are likely to get to it first?

One argument for legal control of handguns is the number of accidental shootings that result in death or injury; the number of children who die each year after playing with the guns they found concealed in their parents' possessions (there were three such deaths in a two-week period in Orange County, California, as of this writing). If one has ever known the parents of children who die like this, they are difficult to forget. In addition, think of the suicides that occur during deep depression that might have been avoided if there had not been a gun "conveniently" close by. The suicide rate for white males ages 15 through 24 rose from 8.6 in 1960 to 20.8 in 1978, and the vast majority of these suicides were accomplished with guns (Koop 1982, 2).

One of the most compelling arguments Block (1976, 15) presents for some form of gun control is the strong correlation between gun ownership and crimes carried out with guns. Regions of the country where statistics show the highest gun ownership also show the highest gun murder rates and the highest percentages of aggravated assaults committed with firearms. And while far more men are killed with guns in homicides, accidents, and suicides than women, women are most likely to be killed by husbands, parents, or their children; so homes that contain guns are dangerous places for women. The problem with all the campaigns for gun control is that they have used a less than honest approach: They emphasize "crime in the streets"—getting guns out of the hands of the criminals—whereas the real purpose should be to get guns out of the homes and hands of (usually) law-abiding citizens who do not have the self-control and good sense to keep guns dismantled and out of reach so they cannot be easily reached and used, most frequently against themselves. Surely America's "love affair" with guns needs rational reconsideration rather than raw emotion; it is a love affair with a very high price that all of use pay, even if we do not own guns.

A Case History

One tragic incident illustrates most clearly the association between family violence and our violent culture. In March 1983, in Southern California, a lone white police officer responded to a neighbor's report that a little boy and his mother had not been seen for about two weeks. The officer went to the apartment in a racially mixed neighborhood, and when he received no answer at the door, the manager gave him the key. Inside the darkened interior, he saw it was so sparsely furnished that he believed it may have been burglarized. Approaching another room, he found the door locked from the outside by a rope around the door knob. His knocks went unanswered, and he called out twice, "Policeman!" but there was no response. As he admitted later, he suddenly felt that he might have walked into a trap, but be decided against calling for backup help and kicked in the door. There, in a dark room with its only light coming from a 12-inch black and white television set, he saw a figure holding a gun, pointed at him. He shot, and killed a 5-year-old boy who had been left alone while his mother worked for their support. The child had pointed a toy gun that was a close imitation of a real gun, and in the dim light from the small television screen, the officer had mistaken both the size of the child and the "weapon" he thought was intended for him.

Some other items in this sad case include the fact that the 29-year-old black mother was the sole wage-earner for herself and her son (his father was in prison). On her low income job she had been unable to find reliable childcare. Being very concerned about protecting the boy from harm, she had secured the door to keep him "safely" inside the room where he had his toys and the television set to entertain him. Was this mother guilty of neglect?

The young officer had been on the force for about five years, and part of his fearfulness, which he admitted, had racial undertones: There had been some minor disturbances in the same area previously. After the incident, the officer suffered an extreme emotional reaction and has since obtained therapy. Was this officer "trigger-happy" when he mistook a small child for a would-be attacker? Was he guilty of negligent manslaughter?

Both cases went before the grand jury and after deliberation, the finding was that neither one was guilty of a crime. A little boy died, and two lives will never be the same, but there was no crime. Wasn't there though? Why would an experienced police officer shoot so quickly? Perhaps because so many American homes contain firearms and because so many police officers are killed and wounded each year in ambushes. Why did the little boy have a toy gun in his hand that is such a close imitation to the real model that even experts have difficulty distinguishing between them at a distance of ten feet? Perhaps because our gun-crazy culture insists on admiring weapons of death and because manufacturers want profits. Why did a loving mother provide her son with an imitation gun and a television set for his entertainment? Perhaps because "all the other kids have them," and because even if there is no money for other furniture, a TV set is mandatory in an American home. Why did the child point his toy gun at the officer? Perhaps because he had seen so many "shootouts" on television that he could not distinguish reality from fantasy. Why was this woman working at a job that paid so poorly she could barely exist? Perhaps because she wanted to avoid the shame of taking welfare payments (or maybe she could not get them even if she wanted them), or was it perhaps because she is a black woman who was "lucky" to get a job at all? Why was the child home alone instead of in a child care center? Perhaps it was because the United States provides less child care services than any other industrial nation in the world, and because we give no subsidies as many other nations provide for each child. A crime was committed—but the *officer*, the *mother*, and the *little boy* were all victims—of our society.

Strangely, many police officers are opposed to gun control, even though so many of them are killed and wounded by firearms in the wrong hands, but many others realize their own jobs are made much more dangerous by armed civilians. Many people including the author insist that the war on crime should be waged by those best equipped and trained for the job, the police. Block (1976, 18) agrees, saying:

> A more important war on crime—the unarmed war—must still be waged by citizens in the improvement of the nation's economy and in the strengthening of its social and political institutions. An important part of that process is turning back from cultural attitudes that advocate and romanticize violence. The willing surrender of "self-protective" firearms would be a giant step in this direction. It would be a commitment to the rule of law and a denial of the medieval notion that every home is an arsenal, every house an armed fortress. We cannot live safely or happily with that notion.

Obviously, if we want to prevent family violence we must give serious consideration to the part that firearms play in family violence in the United States.

SUMMARY

In the previous chapter, we looked at similarities and common features found in all types of family violence, as a starting point for constructing a global theory of family violence. This chapter continued in the search for understanding, beginning by looking at the major proposal for a general theory of family violence. To understand a problem of so many variations, a multidimensional model is a necessity. There can be no single factor as the underlying cause. Straus and his colleagues (1980) have been working in that direction, as well as some others.

This was followed by examination of some alternative theories of family violence, usually proposed to explain one particular type of violence or another. The individual psychopathology model was the first framework suggested to explain child maltreatment, and later, spouse abuse. Research findings soon showed that parents who maltreat children, and the children themselves, are not psychologically distinguishable from the general public, and therefore the model was expanded in recent years to include socioenvironmental factors, although the original model still remains popular among many professionals.

The prevailing social psychological theory that has strong explanatory powers is social learning theory. It was first offered to explain wife beating, but it is just as useful a framework for studying other types of violent behavior. Social learning theory states that people learn aggressive behavior by observing models, and that if these are high status models who command attention and repeatedly use aggressive behavior that appears to be functional and rewarded, observers are likely to imitate them. If the observers' subsequent aggression is reinforced, it is likely to be repeated and become part of their behavioral patterns.

As research has progressed from examining individual factors on a micro level, expanding and improving by adding social, economic, and political factors on a macro level, we next looked at a number of viewpoints clustered in a social-structural framework, under the heading *the social system*, briefly summarized here. Some experts believe that family violence is endemic to our economic-political system, and that little will change until massive structural changes are made (Gil 1971, 1974). Social inequality, through out institutions, denies some segments of the population equality of opportunity and freedom of choice. Stressful family life is common to disenfranchised groups, but is also common in our competitive, materialistic culture among all classes of people. Stress has been found by many researchers and professionals to be ubiquitous in dysfunctional and violent families. Another feature of our social system and institutions, strongly reinforced in the family, is the system of patriarchy, the vesting of power and prestige in males, regardless of individual capabilities. Patriarchy justifies the unequal distribution of resources and power in the family, and when this power is abused, there is violence. Patriarchal men believe that they have the right and even the duty to maintain control over wives and children, and they will enforce their dominance by physical means when they believe it is necessary.

The chapter concluded with a broad overview of our cultural approval and acceptance of male violence, which helps to promote violence between intimates. Violence is almost inescapable for most Americans: in sports and other entertainment, the media, and printed material. Finally, the distinctly American proclivity to own and keep firearms in their homes was discussed, illustrated by one tragic incident that included many of the unique features of our violent culture and how they each contribute to family violence.

The theories reviewed here are suggestions of ways to understand why and how family violence occurs. They can be used as "building blocks" for a testable theory of family violence and for further research. Workable and efficient intervention techniques depend heavily on sound theory supported by rigorous empirical research.

Next we begin an in-depth discussion of child maltreatment, which covers two chapters. The following chapter examines historical attitudes toward children, and the growth of the movement to protect children from parental abuse.

NOTES

1. Some social workers may disagree, but motivation is an important legal element in determining guilt, punishment, and even the seriousness of the crime (such as between first degree murder and accidental manslaughter). Consider the difference in motivation in these two cases, both of which involve the belt whipping of a 10-year-old child because of low grades on a school report card: In one case, the father is an unemployed alcoholic who is searching the household for money to buy another bottle when he comes across the report card. The other case involves a refugee Vietnamese family where all the children are expected to bring home report cards containing only high grades to maintain family "honor"; the child is forced to lay face down on the floor while both parents participate in administering punishment. The acts, the force, the weapons, the children's ages, and the results are the same, but the motivations are different. Should the abusers receive the same sanctions? Or the same treatment modalities?

2. Some of the earlier writers using the psychopathology framework include Bennie and Sclare (1969); Court and Kerr (1971); Fontana (1964); Helfer and Kempe (1968); Jacobucci (1965); Kempe et al. (1962); and Steele and Pollock (1968).

3. Writers who concentrate on abusive parents for individual pathologies include Bakan (1971); Court and Kerr (1971); Fontana and Robison (1976); Gaines et al. (1978); R. Rohner (1981); Smith and Hanson (1974, 1975); Smith et al. (1973); Weston (1974); and Wolfe et al. (1981).

4. Detailed critiques of the psychopathology model have been written by a number of researchers including Gelles (1979); Gil (1971, 1974); and Pfohl (1977).

5. Individual psychopathology is the theoretical approach applied to wife beating by Dewsbury (1975), Lion (1977); Saul (1972); Scott (1974); and Shainess (1977).

6. Much of the information in the following section on social learning theory is taken from an earlier paper (Pagelow 1978a).

7. Even when social learning theory is not proposed as a major theoretical framework guiding research designs, its propositions are found as underlying assumptions in much of the literature on spouse abuse (Barnett et al. 1980; Dobash and Dobash 1979; Pagelow 1978a, 1981a, 1982a; Walker 1979, 1981).

8. The topic of stereotypic gender role ideas of men and women in violent families has been noted by many writers and is considered to be an important contributing factor to family violence (Coleman 1980; Dobash and Dobash 1979; Libby and Straus 1980; Pagelow 1978a, 1981a; Star 1980; Straus 1978; Walker 1979, 1981).

9. There are even reports that the film *Snuff,* which was banned in many communities after protests by thousands of citizens, is being sold and rented on videotape for home viewing by stores on the East coast and in British Columbia (News Page 1983), and at least one retail chain with nine stores in California carries this film in its catalogue (Mar 1983, 3). A few examples of other movies featuring torture and killing of females include: *Prom Night, Friday the 13th,* (and its later editions), *Terror Train, He Knows You're Alone, Halloween, Dressed to Kill,* and *The Texas Chain Saw Massacres.*

10. Students noted a difference between the ads showing men being assaulted and kicked by women and ads showing women as victims: When the victims are female, they

are usually depicted as finding the abuse pleasurable or at least they are passive victims; the men in the Vogue series are shown grimacing or as if in pain. The conclusion drawn can be that these ads play on the stereotypes of women as "willing victims" or masochistic.

11. These comments about the popularity of Kung Fu and Bruce Lee hero-worship, and the manufacture of these types of weapons by school children apply to the recent phenomena common among Southern California youngsters, which may or may not spread to other parts of the nation yet.

12. The information contained in this section on firearms and gun control is largely derived from the Public Affairs Pamphlet No. 536 (Block 1976), unless otherwise indicated. This and other brief, concise pamphlets on a wide range of social issues may be purchased from Public Affairs Pamphlets, 381 Park Avenue South, New York, NY 10016.

PART III

Child Abuse and Neglect

5

Beginning at the Beginning: Child Maltreatment

Ours has been called a "child-centered" society. Americans spend fortunes on furniture especially designed for children, buy billions of dollars worth of baby food, and spend additional billions on toys for children. Books and magazines tell us how to please our children and promote their growth, we spend our precious tax dollars on their education and demand the best, and the media provide them with entertainment. Most Americans believe this is only natural. Childhood is a very special stage in life and all parents want only the best for their children—these are ideas that few people want to challenge.

Actually, the idea of *childhood* is a relatively recent invention (Aries 1962). Historically, children have been treated as nonpersons, yet they have been expected to carry their own weight in the family, even as recently as the industrial revolution. The notion of childhood varies according to time, class, and culture. The status, roles, and responsibilities of children have changed over time and cross-culturally (Takanishi 1978, 9). When the industrial revolution began, children worked on the farm and in the cottage industries, and later went to work with their mothers or both parents in the factories. To this day, children are expected to carry their burden of support in underdeveloped countries. As late as the nineteenth century, children in industrializing nations were contracted into the labor force with their parents or guardians. Cecelia Sudia (1978, 50) produced records from an American mill showing an 1815 labor contract for a man, his sons of 10, 13, and 16 years of age, his 12-year-old daughter, his sister, and her 8- and 13-year-old daughter and son. The *weekly* wages listed for the Dennis Rier family ranged from $5.00 for the father to 75 cents for the 8-year-old girl, adding up to a grand total of $15.16! Mills continued to operate on a family basis, although a hundred years later, records show that the age of working children was a least 16, and whole families were not under a single contract (Sudia 1978, 50–51).

Today, acts that are considered by many to be child abuse were commonly done by parents in earlier years without arousing public outrage or legal censure. To put current attitudes about children into proper perspective, it is important to look at the historical status of children, their rights and duties, and adult perceptions of and behavior towards children. What was formerly viewed as appropriate treatment of children is now considered deviant. In other words, the acts have not changed, but the norms, or common definitions of right and wrong, have changed. Sociology pioneer Emile Durkheim pointed out long ago that it is not an intrinsic quality of the act itself, but the way society collectively views it that defines deviance (1964, 70). Durkheim said, "it is no longer possible today to dispute the fact that law and morality vary from one social type to the next, nor that they change within the same type if the conditions of life are modified" (1964, 70). Labeling theorist Howard Becker later stressed that deviance is created by society because it establishes the rules (1966, 8), and the rules pertaining to children have changed drastically over time. It may surprise some that children have not always been viewed as "bundles from heaven"; on the contrary, for many centuries children were viewed as inherently evil little creatures who were possibly possessed by devils or other evil spirits. The first section of this chapter gives a detailed overview of childhood prior to modern times, which may provide a shocking contrast to present day ideas about children and childhood.

The next section tells about the development of the movement to protect children, the "child-saving" period, which progressed into the "discovery" of child abuse, the topic of the section that follows. Next we look at research on four types of child maltreatment: physical and emotional abuse and physical and emotional neglect. This section shows how theory, research, and findings are closely tied to the professional backgrounds and training of the individuals who propose and test the theories (Gil 1971; Takanishi 1978). We focus on some of the most frequently advanced ideas about perpetrators of physical and emotional abuse and neglect, as well as their victims. One of the questions most commonly asked by professionals and nonprofessionals alike has to do with *profiles,* or individual characteristics of victims or perpetrators, but most social scientists are turning more and more toward including a multitude of sociological, political, economic, and environmental factors when attempting to answer questions about persons most likely to maltreat children and the children most likely to become victims.

THE CHILD AND CHILDHOOD IN HISTORY

Probably most contemporary Americans have heard the Biblical dictum, "spare the rod and spoil the child." Almost every source that discusses child-rearing from antiquity to the eighteenth century recommends the beating of children (deMause 1975), and even modern day parents insist that child discipline properly includes beating, when "necessary" (Stark and McEvoy 1970). The difference between past and present views seems to be only in the norms guiding "necessity," acceptable levels of violence, and degree of injury inflicted. Historian and psychoanalyst Lloyd de-Mause wrote a chilling article in which he states:

> A child's life prior to modern times was uniformly bleak. . . . A search of historial sources shows that until the last century children were . . . offered beatings and whippings, with instruments usually associated with torture chambers. In fact, the history of childhood is a nightmare from which we have only recently begun to awaken. . . . The further back in history we went, the lower the level of childcare we found, and the more likely children were to have been killed, abandoned, whipped, sexually abused and terrorized by their caretakers. (1975, 85)

Children were not considered in terms dealing with a specific age range of human life. There was no special word to apply to males between 7 and 16 years of age; there were only infants and adults (Plumb 1972). The transition from infancy to adulthood appears to have been between the ages of 5 and 7; that was about the age of legal responsibility for crime under common law, although during the Middle Ages, most ideas of age were vague and imprecise. According to J. H. Plumb (1972, 206), "a child of 'about seven' could be any age from five to nine."

Language provides clues to cultures, and Plumb (1972, 205) notes that until the seventeenth century the word "child" did not refer to an age state but expressed kinship, and the word "boy" referred to a male of any age who was in a dependent position. Noted historian Phillippe Aries (1962, 27) writes that at the beginning of the eighteenth century the word "child" was a term of friendship, used to greet or flatter someone or induce another to do something; for example, "A captain will say to his soldiers: 'Courage, children, stand fast.'" Unlike these other writers, Aries does not refer to brutality toward children in his history of childhood; instead, he makes the following points:

> In medieval society the idea of childhood did not exist; this is not to suggest that children were neglected, forsaken or de-

> spised. . . . [I]t corresponds to an awareness of the particular
> nature of childhood, that particular nature which distinguishes
> the child from the adult, even the young adult. . . . [A]s soon
> as a child could live without the constant solicitude of his
> mother, his nanny or his cradle-rocker, he belonged to adult
> society. (1962, 128)

Perhaps the difference between the history of childhood that Aries provides and the histories produced by many other writers is based not so much on personal biases, but rather on the viewpoint taken in the approach of each to their studies. Aries concentrates on historical works of art, education (which, of course, was available only to the upper classes), and the nobility. Aries seems to accept history uncritically, as he found it recorded (by the affluent literate); other writers may have taken a more skeptical and investigative approach. Aries's ideas of parental "benign indifference" have been criticized by others who believe parents were destructive and irrational toward children (Hunt 1970).

Works of art also provide clues about the status of youngsters. In pictorial records of history, children are represented as miniature adults, sharing in all aspects of adult life: social, economic, and sexual (Aries 1962; deMause 1975; Plumb 1972; Takanishi 1978). Plumb explains:

> [It] is very rare to find children depicted as children before the
> beginnings of the modern world, at the time of the Renaissance. In Chinese paintings, as in medieval manuscripts, they
> are usually shown as small adults, wearing the clothes, often
> having the expressions, of men and women. . . . One has only
> to look at the church monuments of Elizabethan England to see
> how distant the concept was of childhood as a separate state.
> There lined up behind the father are three or four little men, all
> dressed like himself in the formal clothes of the age, and behind his wife kneels a group of little girls wearing the habits of
> women. Only infants are clothed differently. (1972, 206–7)

Once having been sensitized to the idea of children as miniature adults, a trip to a fine art museum would probably convince most skeptical persons that children were indeed portrayed as miniature adults, although some may still not accept the idea that pictorial representation reflects social attitudes toward youngsters.

Most writers of the history of childhood note that there were fluctuations in cultural ideas about children, which caused them to be treated cruelly and inhumanely in one era, and then swinging toward a more romantic notion, treating them more kindly (Plumb 1972; Radbill 1974; Takanishi 1978). The beginning of the sixteenth century reflects one of the latter periods when the notion of the child as an "innocent" emerged, at least among the middle and upper classes, stemming largely from the teachings of the Jesuits and other educators. Religious works of art, depicting Jesus as a graceful, affectionate, realistic baby or child, began the transition (Aries 1962).

In the same manner, ideas about childhood ranged from evil to holy. In early American history from the seventeenth until the nineteenth century, children were regarded as innately sinful, after which time they were categorized as redeemers in the late nineteenth century ("A little child shall lead them" from Breckinridge, cited in Takanishi 1978). But despite these swings toward moderate treatment and concern for childish innocence, the bulk of historical evidence shows what deMause (1975) declares to be a track record on child-raising that is "bloody, dirty, and mean." Aries suggests that attitudes toward children were casual and at times indifferent (rather than cruel), because until about age seven, mortality rates were extremely high. The reasoning was that if one cannot be sure a child will survive, why bother to lavish love and attention on something that *does not count?* This was the prevailing attitude toward children, expressed by a quotation from the seventeenth century that, after all, "The little one did not count because she could disappear" (Aries 1962, 128). Parents may have avoided attachment to their children until they survived the dangerous early years to protect themselves from the pain of loss.

Some wholesale abuse of children may have occurred because they were seen as the *property* of their fathers and as such could be used or misused as economic assets among the poor, or as objects for adults' amusement among the middle and upper classes and royalty. According to Michael Freeman, an attorney and lecturer in law at London University:

> We have spoken of parental rights but in law until 1886 it would be more accurate to speak of paternal rights. The legal and social structure of the family in England until late in the 19th century stressed the principle of paternal domination which was thought to be the will of God. (1979, 43)

Samuel Radbill, a lecturer in the history of pediatrics, states the situation in these words: "A child was once virtually its father's chatel. The *Patria Postestas* of the Romans endowed the father with the privilege to sell, abandon, offer in sacrifice, devour, kill, or otherwise dispose of his offspring" (1974, 6). Although Radbill comments that this right was "practically never invoked," (1974, 6), he later refers to cannibalism of infants for purposes of health, vigor, and youthfulness (obviously for the benefit of the diner, not the slain infant) and notes references to cannibalism in the Bible and Greek mythology (1974, 9). Along these lines, deMause (1975, 86) says that "In every age, the deliberate mutilation of children's bones and faces prepared them for a lifetime of begging." Children were mutilated by their parents so that when they were sent into the streets to beg, they could attract sympathy and consequently more money for the family, or they might be sold to speculators who trafficked in children to set them up as professional beggars (Radbill 1974, 6). To make them successful beggars, children frequently suffered "gouged eyes, amputated or twisted arms and legs, and broken and deformed feet" (Radbill 1974, 6). Paradoxically, if children were *born* with deformities or any unusual features, they might suffer the ultimate child abuse, infanticide. Infanticide was also widely practiced as a form of population control in societies lacking contraceptives, and it was encouraged by Plato, Aristotle, and others in order to rid society of diseased, deformed, or excess babies (Langer 1972). In fact, historian William Langer (1972, 96) says:

> In England as late as 1878 about 6 percent of all violent deaths could be classified as infanticides. . . . In the 18th century it was not an uncommon spectacle to see the corpses of infants lying in the streets or in the dunghills of London and other large cities.

Along the same lines, but without referring to the particular epoch in which it occurred, Radbill (1974, 8) makes the following statements:

> Superstition can lead to infanticide. Man fears the unusual, so that twins, monstrous births, or congenital defects frequently bode evil. . . . In China, India, and throughout the Orient deformed children were usually destroyed at birth; and in sixteenth-century Europe, Martin Luther ordered mentally defective children drowned because he was convinced they were instruments of the devil. . . . The Roman Law of the Twelve Tables forbade rearing deformed children.

Abuse of children crossed class lines, occurring among both rich and poor. One writer (deMause 1975, 86), goes into detail about the sexual abuses of children among the upper classes and royalty for the amusement of adults, describing unweaned infants subjected to fellatio, "infants castrated in the cradle for use in brothels," and servants who molested their young charges. He says, "Little Louis XIII was often hauled into bed by his parents and others and included in their sexual acts" (deMause 1975, 87). Based on writings in the diary kept by the physician assigned to Louis XIII, Plumb (1972, 208) describes in detail the young dauphin's life, saying:

> The dauphin and his sister were stripped and placed naked in the king's bed and when the children played sexually with each

other, Henry IV and the court were hugely amused. The queen, a pious and rather austere woman, thought nothing of seizing his genitals in the presence of the court, and the dauphin often displayed himself, to the amusement of his staid middle-aged governess.

It should be noted that this journal describes the life of the most important child in France. David Hunt (1970) also had access to the diary when he attempted a psychological analysis of family life in history, and he agrees that children in seventeenth century-France were seen as not quite human. Hunt studies families of the upper class and nobility and found that nursing babies were regarded as "gluttonous little animals," and that mothers preferred to turn their infants over to *wet nurses* (women hired to breast feed babies), because a nursing baby was thought to be "sucking away the mother's blood" (1970, 121).

Sometimes during the course of being used for the pleasure of adults, children were subjected to practices that were physically dangerous, abusive, and potentially lethal. Infants tied up tightly in swaddling bands were often thrown around like a ball for amusement, and according to deMause (1975, 85), a brother of Henry IV was being tossed from one window to another when he was dropped and killed.

Despite these examples of child maltreatment among royalty, undoubtedly much more abuse of children occurred among people of all classes based upon religious beliefs concerning redemption and sin, and culturally accepted practices of "discipline" for the child's supposed own good. Stephen Pfohl explains in these terms:

> The purposeful beating of the young has for centuries found legitimacy in beliefs of its necessity for achieving disciplinary, educational or religious obedience. Both the Roman legal code of "Patria Patistas," and the English common law, gave guardians limitless power over their children who, with chattel-like status, had no legal rights to protection. The common law heritage of America similarly gave rise to a tradition of legitimized violence toward children. Legal guardians had the right to impose any punishment deemed necessary for the child's upbringing. In the seventeenth century, a period dominated by religious values and institutions, severe punishments were considered essential to the "sacred" trust of child-rearing. (Pfohl 1977, 310–11)

Samuel Radbill (1974) writes about the same sort of parental justification for severe physical punishment, tying this in with religious beliefs and practices. Most of us have heard some parent, at some time, furiously threaten a misbehaving child that, "I'm going to beat the devil out of you!" That was no idle threat by parents of even the recent past (up to the beginning of this century, and perhaps still flourishing in some families) who believed that children are "innately sinful" (Takanishi 1978, 11) and have to be severely beaten by parents or caretakers in order to "drive out the devil" (Radbill 1974, 3).

These, then, are the most frequent reasons given in history for beating children: discipline, religious beliefs, and in order to force education on them. It should not come as a great surprise that when many abusive parents are confronted with the evidence of their crimes, they attempt to explain and justify their behavior by using these same reasons. Radbill begins his essay on the history of child abuse and infanticide with the statement:

> Maltreatment of children has been justified for many centuries by the belief that severe physical punishment was necessary either to maintain discipline, to transmit educational ideas, to please certain gods, or to expel evil spirits. Whipping children has always been the prerogative of teachers, as well as of parents. (1974, 3)

It was commonly assumed that parents, particularly fathers, had the right to do almost anything they wished with their children, but as Freeman (1979, 42) notes, "[the law] may have turned a blind eye towards infanticide but the killing of a child was murder." A newborn infant could be disposed of without punishment. Caretakers would beat and otherwise abuse children grown beyond infancy with immunity from the law. However, it was better to avoid killing them, unless they were prepared to claim that the children were possessed by evil, demonic spirits. The laws regarding caretakers' rights and obligations were adopted in the colonies, and as Pfohl (1977, 311) explains:

> Even in the late eighteenth and early nineteenth centuries, a period marked by the decline of religious domination and the rise of rationalism and a proliferation of statutes aimed at codifying unacceptable human behavior, there were no attempts to prevent caretaker abuse of children.

Pfohl goes on to tell about an American court decision in a child abuse case in favor of parental judgment as to the appropriateness of punishment, which found that there can be no criminal liability, except when the punishment results in permanent injury to the child (1977, 311). *Parens patriae* is the legal doctrine that specifies power of the state to assume parental authority when parents have failed to fulfill their responsibility toward their children. Courts were generally reluctant to intervene in family matters, a tradition that still has great influence. Up until the nineteenth century when *parens patriae* was invoked, it was almost always only in matters pertaining to wealth and property disputes. In 1817 the poet Shelley lost custody of his children "on the grounds of his behavior and atheistic beliefs" (Rosenheim 1978, 429–30). A decade later another father lost custody of his children to his deceased wife's parents because of "scandalous conduct" (Rosenheim 1978, 430). However, poor children were unlikely to receive court protection from parental abuse in any form.

Family poverty was frequently associated with parental and institutional abuse of children, such as when children were put to work in factories, at the very beginning of the industrial revolution. Even if families did not send their children out to work, pauper children from the poorhouses worked in the mills in England, as Radbill explains: "Children from five years of age upward were worked sixteen hours at a time, sometimes with irons riveted around their ankles to keep them from running away. They were starved, beaten, and in many other ways maltreated" (1974, 12). The first child labor laws were passed by Parliament in 1802, but this only succeeded in breaking up the pauper apprentice system. The law did not apply to children sent to work in the mills by their parents. These children still had a twelve-hour work day and could be beaten with leather thongs by their supervisors. "Sometimes they were dipped head first into cisterns of cold water to keep them awake" (Radbill 1974, 12).

Industrialization and child labor flourished at the same time in America, where children from four to ten years of age were employed in cotton mills or were bound out to servitude under the early colonial apprenticeship system while as young as four years of age (Radbill 1974, 11). The first child labor law in the United States was passed in 1887 in Alabama, which limited children under fourteen to an eight-hour work day, but the law was repealed in 1894 (Takanishi 1978, 21).

The beginnings of modern attitudes toward children and childhood began developing in the nineteenth century, which marked the premeditated intrusion of government into child rearing (Rosenheim 1978, 431). The *Progressive Era,* which saw the outpouring of reforms and child protective legislation, was a period in which many other changes were simultaneously occurring. The interactive effects are explained in these words:

> Industrialization and urbanization, the rise in political consciousness of the masses and the extension of suffrage to women, the growth of large-scale organization in business, labor, and government—these were among the phenomena with which nineteenth century society sought to contend. They colored social perception of and response to the needs

of children. A disparate array of youth—from foundlings to street Arabs, immigrant illiterates to native-born thieves—claimed the attention of reformers. Their conceptions of the problems to be solved and the solutions to be sought are, in many instances, alive to this day. (Rosenheim 1978, 432)

Regardless of the complex way it happened—ethnocentrism, elitism, or a burning social conscience—whether these phenomena led into the broad political, social, and economic changes is open to speculation, but it is clear that they led into the Progressive Era.

THE MOVEMENT TO PROTECT CHILDREN AND THE "DISCOVERY" OF CHILD ABUSE

The earliest effort to protect children, specifically from infanticide, was in the establishment of foundling homes, but as soon as one of these homes opened its doors, it was swamped by more babies than it could handle, and thus the mortality rate in such homes was 80 to 90 percent (Langer 1972). In his discussion of foundling hospitals, William Langer (1972, 96) tells of one in London that admitted 15,000 children in the first four years, but only 4,400 of these babies survived to adolescence. This situation was not unique to England. Justine Wise Polier, a Children's Court judge in New York City, quotes Professor Amos G. Warner describing the situation in American foundling hospitals in the 1890s in these words:

> "In a great majority of cases, it can matter but little to the individual infant whether it is murdered outright or is placed in a foundling hospital—death comes only a little sooner in one case than in the other. This fact, that foundling hospitals are, for the most part, places where infants die, is not sufficiently appreciated by the public. A death-rate of 97 per cent per annum for children under three years of age is not uncommon." (Warner, quoted in Polier 1941, 34)

The American system, patterned after the British, also took care of homeless, neglected, or unwanted children by establishing a system of indenture, out-of-door relief, and almshouses, but the mood of a growing country began to disapprove of these methods. Orphan asylums had operated since early in the eighteenth century—the first one opened in 1727 in New Orleans—established by a private religious group (Polier 1941, 14). The first public orphanage opened in 1794. Most children however, were housed in private orphanages, which was politically expedient but which gave no entry to inspection, regulation, or even financial accountability to outside forces (Polier 1941, 17). While the public had no knowledge of what occurred within those private institutions where children were warehoused until they were old enough to be put out to work, citizens *were* aware of the terrible conditions in almshouses, and finally a law was passed in 1875 to remove all destitute children from almshouses. However, there were not enough public orphan asylums, so the children were frequently discharged into private orphanages, thus making a transfer from one oppressive institution into another.

The modern-day foster home system began from the practice orphan asylums followed in placing the children into "adoption" or indenture. It did not begin from benevolent ideas of finding good homes for unfortunate children; rather it was a way of discharging older wards into what could be construed as a form of slavery. There was no investigation of families willing to take charges, and "adoption" did *not* signify the "creation of a new, permanent parent-child relationship" (Polier 1941, 23). Generally, the children worked for a specific number of years for only their food and lodging, and if they were lucky, they were treated reasonably well.

Later an experiment began that involved gathering up destitute, homeless children in eastern cities and sending groups of 20 to 40 children to western states to be placed in any homes where citizens were willing to accept them. Philanthropic organizations around the country organized to send children from the slums out into the countryside (Platt 1969, 40). From 1854 to 1875, approximately 20,000 children were "dumped" in this manner, with no further concern or follow-up to see what happened to them (Polier 1941, 24). The practice continued. One agency out of many, the Children's Aid Society, sent 31,000 children into homes in the west from 1853 to 1929. The agencies gradually began setting standards for placement and supervision (Polier 1941, 24).

The idea of foster homes came from the need for placement of destitute and homeless children, but eventually some others began to seek homes for "wayward children"—children accused of status offenses—incorrigibility, vagrancy, and truancy, and even some convicted of actual crimes. One of the first to suggest using foster homes in this manner was the superintendent of the Children's Aid Society of Philadelphia in 1893 (Polier 1941, 39–40). The idea met much resistance apparently, because Polier reports that only small numbers of these children, who received little public sympathy, had been placed into foster homes at the time she wrote her book (1941).

In actuality, there was little distinction made in the public's mind about homeless, destitute children, and "delinquents." As Smith, Berkman, and Fraser (1980) note, the link between child abuse, child neglect, and the juvenile justice system started being forged in the 1820s, and continued strengthening with urban industrial growth and massive immigration, bringing people with:

> . . . lifestyles that were offensive to predominantly Protestant aristocracy. A new class of persons appeared in American society—the urban poor. These people came to be called the "dangerous classes" because they threatened the traditional American institutions of the church and family. Family life in the "dangerous classes" was thought to be lax and undisciplined. Their parents were supposedly either unwilling or unable to rear and discipline their children in conformance with colonial childrearing techniques [i.e., harshly]. Their children, wandering aimlessly on city streets, came to be a common sight. Concern grew over the plight of these neglected children and the inability of their families to rear them properly. (Smith et al. 1980, 26–27)

The state first devised legislation giving itself authority to intervene in homes defined as neglectful and abusive, removing the children and transplanting them into institutions for "proper upbringing," at the same time that orphan asylums or houses of refuge for homeless children became public institutions. As Smith et al. (1980, 27) say, "the States made little or no distinction between neglected and delinquent children. Both were confined in houses of refuge. . . ." It should be obvious that motivations for this reform movement had their basis in ethnocentrism and chauvinism to a greater extent than in unprecedented concern over helpless children. There was also a certain amount of self-interest for economic benefits by the upper and middle class people who waged campaigns to conserve children and train them as workers for the new industrial society. Professor of education Ruth Takanishi (1978, 13) explains that battle cries like "the right to childhood" had a special purpose:

> While all children shared this focus of these polemical, fervent statements, the reformers had a specific group of children in mind—the handicapped, abused, neglected, delinquent, and dependent child, most typically from the poor and/or immigrant strata of the urban centers.

Righteous citizens demanded laws and institutions that swept up homeless children from the streets, took other children out of their homes, put thousands of them into houses of refuge, sent thousands more across the land to be put into strangers' homes, indentured others at back-breaking labor, all for the purpose of "child saving." Anthony Platt (1969), who writes about *The Child Savers*, (reformers who saw their role as serving morality and saw themselves as altruists and humanitarians rescuing the less fortunate), says that even kindergartens were established in order to prevent crime by getting children off the city streets.

Other writers criticize the motives of these "concerned citizens" who wanted to snatch children out of their parents' homes and the alley-ways. For example, Stephen Pfohl (1977, 312) says:

> The underlying purpose of the House of Refuge Movement was that of preventive penology, not child protection. This crusade registered no real reaction against child beating. The virtue of removing children from their homes was not to point up abuse or neglect and protect its victims, it was to decrease the likelihood that parental inadequacies, the "cause of poverty," would transfer themselves to the child and hence to the next generation of society. . . . Thus . . . the whole nineteenth century movement toward institutionalization actually failed to differentiate between abuse and poverty and therefore registered no social reaction against beating as a form of deviance.

The first recorded hint of concern by the public for an individual case of child abuse occurred in or about 1871 or 1875, when a little maltreated girl named Mary Ellen was discovered and her plight generated front-page newspaper headlines. When would-be rescuers discovered there was no established agency that could wage a legal battle to protect the child and remove her from her legal custodians, the Society for the Prevention of Cruelty to Animals took up her case on the basis that Mary Ellen, being human, was a member of the animal kingdom and therefore entitled to protection under the laws protecting animals (Armstrong 1983, 117).[1] Accounts differ widely on dates and specifics, but public uproar over this well-publicized case led to the establishment of the Society for the Prevention of Cruelty to Children (SPCC) in 1874, ten years after the founding of the society to protect animals (Takanishi 1978, 21).

This new institution, dedicated to the purpose of protecting children from abuse in their homes, was given police functions through legislation requiring law enforcement and court assistance (Pfohl 1977, 312). Apparently though the society concerned itself more with garnering increasing public support for the institutions already established for poor and destitute children than attempting to protect children from abusive caretakers in their homes or institutions. As a result, the number of children placed in institutions increased, and the society withheld a fixed label of deviancy from the perpetrators of abuse. Pfohl (1977, 312) says: "Natural parents were not classified as abusers of the great majority of the so-called 'rescued children.'" The society focused, instead, on cruel employers and foster or adoptive parents; "Rarely did the SPCC intervene against the 'natural' balance of power between parents and children" (Pfohl 1977, 312).

Gradually, the power of the refuge movement and the SPCC declined, as simultaneously the newly emerging professions of social work and child psychology began growing.

Illinois passed the first Juvenile Court Act in 1899, although even before that, in 1874, Massachusetts passed a law providing for trials for juveniles apart from adults, and New York did so in 1892 (Platt 1969; Smith et al. 1980). Establishment of the juvenile court system was heralded as a major breakthrough for "children's rights" to special treatment, and reformers insisted that judges would act as kindly father figures who would act "in the best interests of the child." As Takanishi (1978, 14–15) says, "Hence, judges had unlimited discretion in the handling of cases, and the children were bereft of any rights under the law." Theoretically, the act's purpose was to *protect* juveniles from standing trials like adults and being sentenced to adult prisons, but the results were a *stripping away* of constitutional *rights* from youngsters and a blurring of the line between children who were to be protected and those who were to be punished. The importance of this turn of events is expressed in these words:

> The juvenile court institutionalized the concept of legal immaturity of children and the weakness of the family to function adequately in this area. For the first time, a special court was created to process not only delinquent youth, but neglected and dependent children as well. These children could be referred to the court by "any reputable person."
>
> The [court] represented an extension of the power of the State to intervene into situations of family breakdown and to take neglected and dependent children out of these disorganized families and place them into well-regulated institutional setting. On at least one very significant level, there is this significant link between the juvenile justice system and abused and neglected children. It is a link that was created by the State itself. (Smith et al. 1980, 27–28)

The juvenile court system is but one example of many showing how the work of many people, some of whom sincerely try to help or protect others, turns out differently than expected. Two of the less savory results of the juvenile justice system, as it has operated over the years are the commingling of children who have done no wrong with children who are accused of wrongdoing, and the taking away of children from some parents who through no fault of their own are too poor to meet the minimum standards demanded of them by others (Thomas 1974).

The "discovery" of child abuse came about in the 1960s after more than a decade of growing interest by physicians, particularly some in the relatively new discipline of pediatric radiology. It began however with an article published in 1946 by a researcher of children's X-rays, John Caffey, who observed the frequent association between subdural hematoma and long-bone fractures in children. Caffey and others who noted these phenomena first looked for internal medical explanations until, some 11 years later, Caffey (1957) specified "misconduct and deliberate injury" as primary factors. As Pfohl (1977, 315) notes: "The discovery of abuse was on its way." Somewhat more systematic observations were made over the next four years and then the "discovery" was announced as a major social problem. Radbill (1974, 19) describes the events in these terms:

> In 1961, the American Academy of Pediatrics conducted a symposium on the problem of child abuse under Dr. Kempe's direction. To direct attention to the seriousness of the problem, he proposed the term "the battered child syndrome." This symposium, which attracted a large number of people, was the stimulus for the beginning of present-day interest.

The following year, C. Henry Kempe and his colleagues published their seminal article, "The Battered-Child Syndrome" (Kempe et al. 1962), and suddenly, after centuries of indifference and/or cruelty, a new social movement was born in which thousands of people would become engaged and billions of dollars would be spent. The first state to pass a child abuse law requiring physicians to report suspected cases of child abuse was Colorado in 1963 (Takanishi 1978, 24). By the end of the 1960s, legislation was passed mandating child abuse and neglect reporting in every state of the Union. In 1974 Congress finally passed the Child Abuse and Prevention Act and established the National Center on Child Abuse and Neglect. Very quickly, the literature on child maltreatment proliferated, whether journalistic, speculative, or scientific. Gelles (1975a, 363–64) notes the progression of events:

> The Department of Health, Education and Welfare published the *Bibliography on the Battered Child in 1969*. Since this bibliography was printed, the number of published articles, research reports, and books on child abuse has multiplied tenfold. . . . In June 1973, the Department of Health, Education and Welfare authorized three million dollars for research on child abuse, and the National Institute for Child Development spent an additional $200,000 in 1974.

Gelles (1975a, 364) further explained that $60 million was authorized to be spent over a three-year period for developing programs to prevent and treat cases of child abuse. Since then, on a continuing basis, money is spent, research is conducted, treatment and intervention programs are created and expanded, and the media arouse and maintain public interest in the topic, sometimes on an educational level but often on a sensationalistic level.

Child maltreatment, having surfaced first from one branch within the medical community, remained a "medical problem" for years, rather than being considered "social deviance" (Pfohl 1977). In his critique of "The Discovery of Child Abuse," Pfohl (1977, 318) says:

> The opportunity of generating a medical, rather than socio-legal label for abuse provided the radiologists and their allies with a situation in which they could both reap the rewards associated with the diagnosis and avoid the infringement of extra-medical controls. What was discovered was no ordinary behavior form but a "syndrome."

Pfohl notes that the Kempe et al. report represented the efforts of a coalition of radiologic, pediatric, and psychiatric specialists who called abuse a "clinical condition" (1962, 17). In addition, these writers state:

> Psychiatric factors are probably of prime importance in the pathogenesis of the disorder, but our knowledge of these factors is limited. Parents who inflict abuse on their children do not necessarily have psychopathic or sociopathic personalities or come from borderline socioeconomic groups, although most published cases have been in these categories. In most cases some defect in character structure is probably present; often parents may be repeating the type of child care practiced on them in their childhood. (Kempe et al. 1962, 24)

David Gil (1970) was one of the first social scientists to study child abuse outside the medical model. Gelles (1973) criticized the "psychopathological model," but until recently the problem of child abuse and neglect remained largely within the "professional turf" of psychiatry, psychology, pediatrics, and radiology. This can be partly explained by the fact that people in these fields had greater availability of research subjects and data; as Finfelhor (1981a, 19) explains: "In addition to their longer tradition of research, child abuse researchers have also benefited from the fact of having a large network of professionals involved in the identification and treatment of the problems. This has facilitated such things as access to subjects and follow-ups for longitudinal research." Only recently have professionals from other disciplines conducted child maltreatment research, called some of the earlier "findings" into question, and developed some of the multidimensional theoretical models that are currently receiving more popular support. For a long time, the medical model held sway and provided explanations upon which intervention and prevention services were designed, and which still are unquestioningly accepted by many service providers as well as others.

WHAT HAVE WE LEARNED ABOUT CHILD MALTREATMENT?

It is obvious that the scientific community remains keenly interested in finding answers to puzzling questions about child abuse and neglect. However, the problems in theory and research on child abuse and neglect remain much the same as when Gelles (1973) wrote his critique.

Individual/Psychological Factors

When radiologists "discovered" child abuse and the phenomenon became labeled a "syndrome," clinicians moved in quickly to search for pathology among caretakers, seeking a cure for this "disease." For example, two battered-child specialists with backgrounds in nursing and social work, Joan Court and Anna Kerr, wrote an article titled, "The Battered Child Syndrome—A Preventable Disease?" (1971). Some of the personality characteristics named in the literature were of persons having emotional problems, being impulsive, immature, depressed, lacking self-control, inadequate, hypersensitive, dependent, egocentric, narcissistic, demanding, and insecure (Bennie and Sclare 1969; Kempe et al. 1962; Steele and Pollock 1968). Later, searches began for specific characteristics of victims, trying to identify which babies are at high risk for abuse. These included studies of failure to bond, failure to thrive, prematurity, differentness, physical and mental handicaps, listlessness, and fussiness (Ainsworth 1980; Gaines et al. 1978; NCCAN 1979).

Despite much attention to individual psychological features, test results have been largely inconclusive or contradictory. There has not been an "abuser profile" developed that contains sufficiently distinct characteristics to enable professionals to distinguish between abusers, potential abusers, and nonabusers, or victim-prone children. Psychodynamic theories abound, but empirical evidence supporting them is lacking. Clinical psychologists Jerry Sweet and Patricia Resnick (1979, 54) note *ex post facto* studies using the Minnesota Multiphasic Personality Inventory (MMPI) scores of maltreating and nonmaltreating parents, and warn that "there is a danger of interpreting differences in profiles between groups to imply that maltreating parents are 'sick' and that this sickness 'causes' them to maltreat. The logic is circular."

One of the reasons these studies of individual characteristics have been so popular, in addition to the factor of subject availability, is because of the underlying hope that if abusers could be distinguished in certain ways from nonabusers, abuse could be prevented by screening parents and intervening before it occurs. However, even if prediction had a high degree of accuracy, implementation of prevention protocols would present serious moral and legal questions (Alvy 1975). As Sweet and Resick (1979, 46) warn, "the obvious infringement of civil liberties in requiring parents of newborns to complete personality tests, along with the possible high incidence of false positives, would make such an undertaking unacceptable."

The "state of the art" in child maltreatment research is rudimentary and inconclusive. Part of the problem lies in the methodologies employed: small "opportunity" samples, biased samples, lack of control groups, and so forth. Researcher F. G. Bolton and his colleagues used the content analysis method on almost 3,000 abstracts listed in a National Center on Child Abuse and Neglect research bibliography (Bolton et al. 1981). Only about 20 percent of all published works listed fell into a research category, and 84 percent of these were *ex post facto* examinations of case records or aggregated statistics. These researchers state: "There is a realistic reluctance to consider this body of literature 'empirical' in nature" (Bolton et al. 1981, 536). Also, research samples were small: The first two quartiles contained samples of fewer than 60 subjects.

Clinicians still study cases that come their way as patients or are identified by others in the system as "abused." They continue to search for personal characteristics of abusers and/or victims. Small samples are common. For example, Fontana and Robison (1976) studied a sample of only 62 mothers, but unfortunately this does not prevent some from generalizing their findings. Wolfe et al. (1981) studied five abusive mothers and compared them to a control sample of five nonabusive mothers. Others obtain larger samples with controls (Smith and Hanson 1974, 1975; Smith et al. 1973), but their reports do not disclose how well they are matched. For example, Robert Ellis (1981) had 43 cases at risk and 35 controls "not at risk," but how they were selected is not revealed. The child psychiatrist research team of Richard Gaines and colleagues (1978) had a large sample (N 240) of low socioeconomic status mothers, but the controls were not matched.

Since almost all studies are speculative or retrospective, it is tautological to identify abusers as having "low self-control" or "low coping skills" (Bennie and Sclare 1969; Kempe et al. 1962). As Gelles explains: "This type of analysis does not distinguish the behavior in question from the explanation. . . . The types of after-the-fact explanations offered by the psychopathologic model offer little predictive power in the study of child abuse" (1973, 614). Circular reasoning is abundantly clear in a statement such as: "The person who just committed suicide was suicidal."

The trend in recent years has been to expand and modify the individual psychological model to include other variables, such as stress in the lives of people who maltreat children.

Social Psychological/Stress Factors

Social psychological and stress theories are closely related, and many researchers include both in their search for understanding of child abuse and neglect. These researchers use a multivariate model that takes into account the social system in which abuse occurs as well as the particular circumstances surrounding abuse and neglect. At the same time, it acknowledges some effect of personal characteristics of abusers and their victims. Obviously it is a more sophisticated paradigm than the earlier individual/psychopathological model.

Stress is frequently mentioned as a *triggering mechanism* that when combined with existing factors associated with battering or neglect, serves to set the process in motion (Gaines et al. 1978; Garbarino 1976; Herrenkohl and Herrenkohl 1981; McNeese and Hebeler 1977; Straus 1980a; White and Newberger 1981; Wolfe et al. 1981). A number of scales to measure stress factors along with a wide range of other variables have been constructed and applied in tests of this model (Gaines et al. 1978; Herrenkohl and Herrenkohl 1981; E. Rohner 1981; R. Rohner 1981). However, the same definitional and methodological problems plague this research as other research projects on child abuse and neglect. There is also lack of replication or longitudinal studies (Miller and Challas [1981] is one of the rare exceptions).

Findings from these studies are frequently at variance with each other and many times, when an association is identified, it is so weak that it has limited explanatory power. One study compared hospital-identified abuse and neglect cases with nonmatched controls, arriving at a total sample of 240 (Gaines et al. 1978). After measuring stress, personality factors, emotional needs, and coping skills, the researchers found that only 6 of the original 12 variables discriminated between groups, but "only 12% of the discriminant space was accounted for" (Gaines et al. 1978, 537). Further, they found no support for the hypothesized relationship between mother-neonate bonding or children with physical or mental impairments. Neglectful mothers (the sampling technique excluded all fathers or other abusers or neglectors) had the highest levels of poverty-related stress factors (unemployment, illness, eviction, and arrest). Gaines et al. state:

> Stress although relatively ubiquitous, was highest in the neglect group, distinguishing these women from abusers or con-

trols. . . . It may be concluded that although stress and personality variables are indeed relevant to the maltreatment
syndrome, they leave 88% of the phenomenon unexplained,
and predict parent category only 15% better than chance.
(1978, 538)

The study by Gaines et al. (1978) is probably one of the most carefully
designed and rigorously conducted investigations of child abuse and neglect. Definitions are clear and concise, and cases that involved both
abuse and neglect or sexual abuse were screened out. All cases assigned
to their abuse and neglect samples were confirmed by public agencies.
But for reasons not explained, the researchers also screened out father
perpetrators and failed to match the control sample closely on important
demographic variables such as income and education. The authors did
note significant differences between maltreating and nonmaltreating
mothers in race, religion, number of children, and whether or not there
was a telephone in the home (Gaines et al. 1978, 533–34).

Eli Newberger and his colleagues (1977) at a children's hospital tested
associations between child maltreatment and stress, using medical records and maternal interviews, and found that there were associations with
more extreme stresses. However, when they examined histories between
maltreating families with the control sample, they found there were few
characteristics that distinguished between them (Newberger et al. 1977,
183). They then devised a test comparing abusers with controls on the discriminant characteristics and found that some abusers would have received a *false negative* (cases labeled nonabusive which really are abusive)
misclassification, and some of the nonabusive controls would have received a *false positive* (cases labeled abuse that are not) misclassification.
Because most protective service institutions are always poorly funded and
understaffed, these researchers strongly warn against rapid clinical
screening methods. Despite the fact that they found associations between
certain stresses and different types of child maltreatment, they say, "caution is urged in interpreting these findings to support the value of predictive screening for child abuse" (Newberger et al. 1977, 184). Until there is
further intense study, Newberger et al. (1977, 184) caution that, "the extent and nature of what we already know about misclassification should
incline us away from child abuse screening."

Finally, some who work within the framework of social psychological or
stress explanations look at a violent culture for answers to child abuse, as
in spouse abuse (Gelles 1979; Libby and Straus 1980; Shwed and Straus
1979; Straus et al. 1980). David Gil (1975) goes beyond other writers in locating the causes, consequences, and prevention of child abuse in the
entire social structure. Gil outlines different levels of the social system

that abuse children: caretakers who abuse in homes, abusive institutions, and a society that places the lives, health, and welfare of children at the bottom of the list of public concerns. In his strong indictment, Gil states:

> Of the three levels of child abuse sketched here, the societal level is certainly the most severe. For what happens at this level determines not only how children fare on the institutional level, but also, by way of complex interactions, how they fare in their own homes. (1975, 349)

In the course of about ten years, the study of child maltreatment moved from the individual psychopathological level into the social-psychological level, and as social scientists outside of medicine began to study the problem, the focus broadened to the macro level of the social system. Since early studies involved small opportunity samples of patients and officially reported cases of child maltreatment, the suspicion that poor parents are more likely to mistreat their children was raised almost immediately. Evidence on whether or not violence and socioeconomic status are significantly related is presented next.

Poverty Factors

Is violence more common among poor people, and are poor parents more likely to abuse and neglect their children? Two facts are quite clear: Many of our children and their families live in poverty, and many of our children and their families are violent. How poor and how violent? Using a scale set at official poverty lines, Richard de Lone states that children constitute over 40 percent of all poor persons. By using a relative definition of poverty set at half the American median income, de Lone finds that: *"more than a quarter of all American children live in poverty"* (1979, 7). If, as so many writers insist, poverty causes stress and stress triggers violence, then one out of every four children in the United States has a possibility of living in a violent family milieu. What do various researchers have to say about socioeconomic status? Is it true that violence is mainly a poverty-related problem?

Whether one is reading reports on child abuse and neglect or on wife beating, when the writer addresses social class of families in which violence occurs, there is usually a *disclaimer* inserted somewhere. To explain, some writers claim there is an association between low socioeconomic status and violent behavior, but the majority insist that violence crosses all socioeconomic, cultural, racial or ethnic, and religious lines. The writers who fall into the latter category then must explain why official statistics reflect an overrepresentation of poor families. Frank Schneiger, the executive director of the Protective Services Resource Institute, has this to say about experts on child abuse and neglect:

> First, there is the standard disclaimer to the effect that ". . . we all know that problems of abuse and neglect are spread throughout the socioeconomic spectrum.". . . [T]hese remarks imply that the socioeconomic distribution is at least relatively random and that families at various levels of society are, in general terms, equally affected. . . . On the part of majority culture members, statements of universal incidence reflect a desire to avoid being considered racist or culturally biased, labels which are likely to follow the presentation of a contrary view, i.e., one who asserts a higher incidence of abuse and neglect at lower socioeconomic levels and among minorities. (Schneiger 1978, 2)

Schneiger suggests that if the claims of relative random incidence are accurate, then child protective agencies are neglecting the needs of the nonpoor because their caseloads are heavily weighted with poor children and their families. Or, on the other hand, he says:

> [I]f such agencies engage in unwarranted intrusions into family life, this pattern of intervention indicates that the poor are once again being doubly victimized. In addition, given a national social structure which finds a disproportionate segment of the nation's minority groups at the lower end of the scale, an assertion of even relatively equal incidence among all socioeconomic groups must raise real questions about the impact on family life of poverty, discrimination, and insensitive or socially destructive government policies, each of which are used to explain a variety of other social ills. (Schneiger 1978, 2)

The point that Schneiger makes is that child abuse and neglect may be expected products of impoverished families in an affluent society, but he also points to the value judgements and class-related personal biases of child protective workers who come in contact with poor families.

The disclaimer that Schneiger refers to is usually followed by statements that suggest reasons why the poor are overrepresented in caseloads, client sample, and official statistics. This example is from a California Department of Justice booklet, *Child Abuse: The Problem of the Abused and Neglected Child:*

> Child abuse, contrary to popular beliefs, occurs in all cultural, ethnic, occupational and socio-economic groups. There is a proportionately higher incidence of abuse *reported* in minority

and low-income families, but it is also true that these families have more contact with agencies who have legal reporting responsibilities (welfare, public health clinics, etc.). In addition, the stress factors in these families tend to be higher. (1978, 18–19)

Another government publication repeats the above statement almost verbatim, but adds reasons why persons of higher socioeconomic status (SES) are less visible than the poor: because they have other avenues for help, because money can buy housing or escape, or because they are reluctant to seek help for fear of possible social, career, and economic losses (Barnett et al. 1980, 3).[2] One follow-up study of abused children selected 563 children, all of whom were under the jurisdiction of the Los Angeles Juvenile Court and all of whom were from families of low SES (Kent 1976). The report acknowledges that there are "probably significant biases in the known incidence of child abuse," lists reasons for greater visibility of abusive families that are also poor and then states the assumption that poverty-related deprivation and stress aggravate tensions and increase possibilities of abusive behavior on the part of parents. One footnote has significant explanatory power regarding protection from scrutiny of nonpoor parents; it reads:

> The percentage of cases of child abuse reported here from the private medical sector is extremely low, averaging about 1% nationally and in Los Angeles County, the site of the present study. This may be due in part to a reluctance of the private physician to become involved in a painful social and legal process which has questionable benefits to his patients, but it may also reflect a "low index of suspicion" for child abuse when the physician has known the family as patients for several years. Whatever the cause, it is clear that the more impersonal circumstances of a hospital's emergency and ambulatory services are more conducive to reporting. (Kent 1976, 31)

Interestingly, this study of abused, neglected, and protective service children, all of them from low SES families, found that the neglected children were the *poorest of the poor,* coming from the most impoverished homes: young parents with lower education and employment and more children.

As for the low reporting rates of private physicians, which may eliminate many middle- and upper-class families from identification, other writers also note the reluctance of physicians in private practice to make "damning value judgements about parents," but there is a selection bias favoring minority and poor children for child abuse diagnosis because they are more often seen in public clinical settings (Newberger et al. 1977, 184).

Another researcher, Elizabeth Elmer (1977), using a low SES sample for a follow-up study found, when comparing abused with nonabused children, that there were few differences between the groups—the vast majority of the children had developmental problems. The author states: "The surprising finding was the extent of various problems across the entire sample. Seventy percent of the children had speech problems; over 50% showed some degree of disturbance; and 39% were achieving poorly in school" (Elmer 1977, 273). The disabilities were randomly distributed among the study and control groups, leading the researcher to conclude that "the effects on child development of lower-class membership may be as powerful as abuse."

Elmer's findings appear to lend support to the claims of other writers who say that the primary abusers of children are the economic/political system and social institutions that literally condemn millions of children and their families to lives of deprivation socially, materially, intellectually, and physically (Chase 1976; de Lone 1979; Gil 1971; Keniston 1977). Gil's own study of abused children found an overrepresentation of low SES families, but his analysis did not lead him to conclude that poor people are more violent than the more affluent or that there is a causal relationship between poverty and violence. Gil did not assume that the reported cases he studied accurately reflected the true incidence of child abuse in the United States.

Some writers insist that there is too much evidence of violence in upper SES families to assume that more violence occurs in poor families.[3] Finkelhor's study (1979a) of childhood sexual abuse found that a high proportion of university students had been victimized in this way. Other studies using university students (some at highly prestigious campuses) show that rape and battering commonly occur among the more affluent (Cate et al. 1982; Laner and Thompson 1982; Parcell and Kanin 1976). Richard O'Toole and colleagues (1981) conducted an experiment using doctors and nurses as subjects to identify which cases were or were not child abuse and these researchers report:

> There is the commonly held view that lower class persons are more violent. . . . One respondent [doctor] stated that he had seen abuse while a resident but that "it doesn't occur in the suburbs" where he now practices. . . . The physicians we interviewed about cause cited a number of signs of abuse but the largest single cause was poverty. . . . [I]t may be easier to apply the label when the deviant is socially distant from the labeler and powerless. Thus the physicians in the experimental vi-

gnette study judged lower class persons as child abusers more often than middle-class persons when all other variables describing the case were held constant. However, the nurses did not. (1981, 13)

The authors note that nurses asked for additional "clues" before reaching diagnosis, and were not as influenced as the doctors were by socioeconomic status and race in their judgements. O'Toole et al. (1981, 13) believe (1) that nursing theory is more eclectic, (2) that there is less social distance between the labeler and the powerless since nurses come from more varied socioeconomic backgrounds, and (3) that there is the influence of nurses' sex role socialization (most nurses were female, most doctors were male).

In his analysis of "The 'Discovery' of Child Abuse," Pfohl (1977) critically examines the personal, political, and organizational interests involved in promoting public interest in the newly found problem, and the attaching of a deviant label to a large segment of the public, *poor parents*. Pfohl also points to social distance between accusers and accused; he notes that there was no resistance by the poor to the stigma of yet another sign of "social pathology"; and he says this (1977, 320–21) about the accusers:

> They either have a professional stake in the problem or represent the civic concerns of certain upper-middle class factions. In either case the labelers were socially and politically removed from the abusers, who in all but one early study (Steele and Pollock), were characterized as lower class and minority group members. The existence of a wide social distance between those who abuse and those who label, facilitates not only the likelihood of labeling but nullifies any organized resistance to the label by the "deviant" group itself. . . . Labelling was generated by powerful medical interests and perpetuated by organized media, professional and upper-middle class concerns. Its success was enlarged by the relative powerlessness and isolation of abusers, which prevented the possibility of organized resistance to the labelling.

It seems obvious that Pfohl believes, like Becker (1966, 8), that deviance is created by society and defined by those who have the power to apply labels to others. After centuries of cruelty towards children by people at all levels of the social strata, suddenly certain acts were defined by one group as deviant, and punitive measures were devised and imposed against a class of people who had no power to resist or fight back. Becker expresses his ideas in these words:

> I mean . . . that *social groups create deviance by making the rules whose infraction constitutes deviance,* and by applying those rules to particular people and labeling them as outsiders. From this point of view, deviance is *not* a quality of the act the person commits, but rather a consequence of the application by others of rules and sanctions to an "offender." The deviant is one to whom that label has successfully been applied; deviant behavior is behavior that people so label. (1966, 9)

Becker's analysis of what constitutes deviance explains why the *same acts* committed by parents in earlier centuries without stigma are now defined as cruel and criminal, i.e., deviant.

Poor families are simply more visible to public scrutiny and censure than affluent families. On the other hand, many writers take it as a "given" that, despite biases in reporting, there is more violence in poor families than in more affluent ones.[4] Among these are Harold Martin and his colleagues (1974), who believe there is a predominance of low SES families, not only among reported, but among abusive families. They point to various socioeconomic factors that undeniably impinge on the lives and welfare of poor children that put them automatically into the higher risk group, such as:

> Minimal prenatal care, crowding, poor medical care, marginal nutrition and a bad physical environment are all prevalent in the lowest SES families. Illness is more common among the poor, and medical care is worse. Prematurity and low birth weight are related to SES. Even more discouraging are the *combined* effects of medical high risk factors and low social class. (Martin et al. 1974, 42)

Still, these authors say that family dysfunction cannot be explained on the basis of SES *alone,* even when they use an example of abusive military families who lived in a civilian neighborhood where "housing and physical environment were markedly inferior" (Martin et al. 1974, 43). Another example comes from a pediatrician who warns against the "class theory of violence," yet he writes that "the incidence of subsequent battering and physical abuse in low birth weight infants is approximately three times" what would be expected (Stern 1979, 21), and then points out that low birth weight is also associated with lower SES. In other words, poor mothers are likely to have little or no prenatal care, inadequate diets, and so forth, and then to produce low birth weight babies that are at risk for abuse.

But renowned expert Brandt Steele (1976) reminds readers that despite physical, intellectual, and environmental deprivation, most poor people are not violent, in the family or on the streets. He says:

> Too often one hears or reads about the experience of "growing up in a ghetto" or of being a member of a lower socioeconomic class or a minority group as if these were constants, as if ghettos and lower socioeconomic groups were homogeneous masses, all of whose members had identical experience and ended up living the same way. This, of course, is far from true. The majority of people, probably three-fourths, who grow up in poverty in an inner city environment do not become violent or involved in criminal behavior, and probably even a higher percentage of them do not abuse and neglect their children. (Steele 1976, 11)

After reviewing many documents of opposing viewpoints, readers are offered the following conclusions. First, evidence of higher incidence of violence among lower SES families is highly questionable, although poverty and its effects on poor families is certainly conducive to violence. Second, of all the crimes in the family, the one most clearly associated with poverty is physical neglect of children. It is unclear how many cases of neglect are the result of *deliberate* withholding of care and comfort, and how many are the results of absolute deprivation in the environment and of ignorance. Sixty percent of all substantiated cases of child abuse reported to the American Humane Association (1980, 18) are neglect cases. One must wonder: How many of these cases appeared on the records in the first place because social agents of higher socioeconomic status, belonging to the dominant ethnic and cultural background, were unable to understand the limitations and constraints in their clients' care of their children? How many reports are moral judgments by personally offended caseworkers?

To illustrate, a student brought to class a newspaper clipping with a Miami dateline and a headline that states, "Mother allegedly starved baby." The article quotes a police homicide sergeant who said: "The case is without question the most outrageous death I have ever investigated. It's incredible that anyone could watch their own flesh and blood waste away like this." The officer is also quoted as saying that the baby "died with the most incredible diaper rash you've ever seen." These are descriptive phrases capable of inciting emotional response from readers. The clipping was read aloud and students were asked to comment. The response was mixed: Some cast total blame on the child's mother, while others were more reserved in judging the mother's guilt. Interestingly, the students who were less condemning of the mother were generally older females and minorities.

The article reveals the following facts: The mother, charged with third-degree murder and manslaughter, was a 34-year-old woman with six other children, existing on welfare, living in a house "filled with flies and broken windows," according to the police sergeant. The 19-month-old baby had been born prematurely and with Down's Syndrome, and the medical examiner found the baby had recently suffered from bronchial pneumonia. Her death was listed as "protein and caloric malnutrition." The child's grandmother said her daughter "did the best she could on welfare," but police said the child was fed "cold, canned evaporated milk mixed with water." There was no mention of the child's father or if there was a father-figure in the home.

This case is strikingly similar to the horror stories cited by Philadelphia Judge Lisa Richette when she wrote about *Throwaway Children* (1969). It is surprising that the baby survived as long as she did, under the circumstances. If there is a *killer* of this baby in Miami, it must be a composite of many professionals in the social system who looked the other way when they might have offered help. At about age 32, a welfare mother gave premature birth to her seventh child, who suffered the handicap of physical and mental retardation. Was the mother given the option of institutionalizing the baby instead of taking it to her impoverished home where she would have to care for it and six other little ones alone? Was she given necessary instructions in the care and feeding of a handicapped baby? Was she offered a support system of visiting nurses and social workers to look in from time to time? Was the baby's pneumonia medically treated or did it go unattended because of a punative medical system that subjects indigents to long delays in the crowded waiting rooms of clinics, only to be shuttled impersonally in and out because of understaffing? Was there a stove for heating the childrens' food? What will it cost Dade County and the State of Florida for a trial to incarcerate this woman and how much taxpayers' money will be spent to provide for the other six children until they reach maturity? Finally, in a city that has experienced intense racial tension related to police practices—was this mother a member of a minority group?

One compelling argument for increasing our concern for troubled families comes from a letter to the editor written by David Epstein (1981), an attorney involved in child abuse and neglect cases. Captioned, "False Economy in Child-Abuse Cases," Epstein writes of Los Angeles County's large-scale transfers or demotions of trained, experienced children's workers out of these specialized services, and putting them into doing eligibility work for welfare, in order to save money. The remaining child services workers are inexperienced and struggling under "mountainous caseloads," Epstein writes. "In short, children and their parents can often be *saved* and the county saved thousands of dollars in expenses for long-term care," but because of these cutbacks Epstein says:

> The economic stupidity of this move alone boggles the mind. . . . [I]t is a grave injustice to children and parents. . . . The quality of a civilization can be judged by only a few standards. One of them, I believe, is how children are regarded and treated. By that standard, the County of Los Angeles has taken a long step backwards into barbarism. (1981, 2)

Until we actually know the extent of family violence in our society—until we have a *reliable base rate* of all types of family violence—a decision as to whether there is more or the same violence in families across social class is largely a matter of believing what one *wants* to believe. Regardless of the stance, one can always find empirical and theoretical support for it.

Too Many or Unwanted Children

Another factor frequently mentioned in the literature concerns the idea of "too many" children, or unwanted children, in abusive families (Gaines et al. 1978; Gelles 1979; Gil 1970; Kent 1976). Some writers propose that children are more likely to be abused and neglected when they live in large families (Goode 1971; Kinard 1979), but official statistics fail to give this much support. Of almost 71,000 substantiated reports, only about 30 percent had more than two children in the household (AHA 1980, 30). Cases of neglect, which is strongly associated with financial stress, more frequently came from households with more than two children (36 percent). Gelles and Straus (1979, 33) report that the national survey found more violence in families with two children than with only one, but that the rate did not increase with additional children.

The author's study (Pagelow 1981a) found that battered women in the sample had fewer children than national averages: 306 women had given birth to an average of 2.4 children; the average number of children for couples up to 25 years of age in 1977 was 3.4 (Rawlings 1978, 19–20). However, there were 125 children by other men that were brought with their mothers into the relationships that became violent (Pagelow 1981a, 141–42). Although 36 percent (N 127) of the mothers reported previous marriages, an even higher percentage of their spouses had a prior marriage (44 percent, N 153), and 42 children were brought by their fathers into the violent relationships. These "reconstituted" families may introduce stress factors that trigger violence, but it is possible that the percentage of reconstituted families found in this sample is approximately the same as in the general population.

There is considerably more evidence that *unwanted* children are in danger of violence (Berger 1978; Calef 1972; Guttmacher 1979; Prescott 1975; Weinstock et al. 1976). Professor of social work Mildred Beck (1970) gathers together evidence that mothers who unwillingly gave birth produced babies with physical or mental impairments at a higher rate than would be expected, and the few longitudinal studies available show severe behavioral problems of children born to women unable to obtain abortions. Beck talks about "compulsory pregnancy" and asks, "What kind of a mother can a woman make if the *rejection of the pregnancy is stable over time?"* (1970, 270).

Since there are more reports of maltreatment in poor households, the matter of unwanted pregnancies and the availability of abortion for poor women is a very serious consideration, according to physician Lawrence Berger (1978) and the Guttmacher Institute (1979). Women who have not completed high school are 45 percent more likely to have contraceptive failure (Guttmacher 1979, 20). About one out of every four women gets pregnant before the age of 19 (more than a million every year), and 80 percent of these pregnancies are premarital (Dickman 1981; Henshaw and O'Reilly 1983; Zelnick et al. 1979). Only about 35 percent of these are legitimated by marriage. Nearly two-thirds of sexually active teenage women never practice contraception, or practice it inconsistently (Guttmacher 1981, 14). Approximately half of all girls who marry at ages 14 to 19 were either pregnant with their first child or had given birth to their first child when they married. They may soon enter public welfare rolls, because one out of every two teenage marriages ends in divorce within five years (Dickman 1981).

In 1977, 26 percent of all illegitimate births were to teenaged mothers (age 15 to 19). Unlike girls 20 years ago, when 90 percent gave their children up for adoption, 96 percent of unmarried mothers are now keeping their babies (Guttmacher 1981). In 1976, there were approximately 1.3 million teenage pregnancies, with 570,000 ending in live births (44 percent of these were illegitimate); 380,000 were terminated by abortion and 152,000 by miscarriages (Tietze 1978). About 30 percent of the slightly under 1.6 million abortions performed in the United States in 1980 were on teenagers (Henshaw and O'Reilly 1983).

However, many more unwanted children will be born in the United States, now that the Hyde Amendment[5] denies funds to pay for abortions for poor women, which includes many teen-aged women. In addition, abortion laws may again become restrictive to all women. About one-third of these forced births will be to young women, who have the lowest rate for mortality through legal abortion, but a mortality rate from pregnancy and childbirth approximately six times higher (Berger 1978, 1475). There is also a strong association between young maternal age and low birth weight infants, and each succeeding birth increases risk to either infant or mother along with possibilities of intellectual and behavioral deficits in the children. Berger has these strong words to say:

> Carrying an unwanted pregnancy to term has the potential for disrupting a teen-ager's schoolwork, personal relations and parenting ability. Young parental age has been associated with decreased educational attainment, martial instability, and child abuse. . . . The costs of pregnancy and childbirth, hospitalization of low-birth-weight infants and women with complications from illegal abortions, and support for additional and larger families by AFDC and foster care may far exceed previous expenditures for abortion. (1978, 1476–77)

According to the Guttmacher Institute (1979, 32), one-half of the welfare program, Aid to Families with Dependent Children (AFDC), payments ($4.7 billion) goes to households in which the mother gave birth as a teenager. Irving Dickman (1981, 4) concurs with this but says that AFDC outlays in 1979 amounted to $9.4 billion. If only one-third of the 205,000 women who got Medicaid abortions in 1977 in states that are no longer paying for them had been forced to carry their pregnancies to term, conservative estimates of the *first-year* cost would be about $75.2 million (Guttmacher 1979). The reports also cite physical and economic dangers including abuse, neglect, mental retardation, and birth defects for the babies, as well as lifelong poverty for the babies and their young mothers. Over 1.3 million children are being raised by 1.1 million teen-aged mothers (Dickman 1981), half of whom are unmarried (Guttmacher 1981); and about one-half of all families below the poverty level in 1981 were female-headed with no husband present (U.S. Bureau of the Census 1983, 2). Of the maltreating families reported to the American Humane Association in 1981, 43 percent were receiving public assistance compared to 11 percent of all U.S. households, and 43 percent of these families were headed solely by females (1983, 10). Some demographers estimate that about half of all children will spend some time in a single-parent family in the future (Sawhill 1979).

Other cuts in Medicaid have forced pregnant women to take risks with their own and with their babies' health. One report states that out of about 1,500 pregnant women in Oregon, 10 percent received no prenatal care, 13 percent did not know where they would deliver their babies, and 90 percent planned to go to a hospital only after beginning advanced labor so they would not be refused admittance (Coalition on Women and the Budget 1983). The death rate for babies born to mothers under 15 is twice that of babies born to mothers between 20 and 30 years old. Nine percent of teenage mothers attempt suicide, which is seven times the average for teenage girls without children who attempt suicide (Dickman 1981, 3).

Some of the stress factors found in the American Humane Association (1980, 32) analysis of 32,842 child abusing families were "New Baby/Pregnancy" and "Continuous Child Care." Gelles (1975b) found that wife battering occurred frequently during pregnancy, and so did the Pagelow study (1981a). The issue of unwanted children has serious implications for prospects of a nonviolent society, and the author agrees with Beck who suggests that there are serious questions about its effects on the mentally ill and retarded, the physically handicapped, and delinquents. Beck summarizes by stating, "there are few who would contest the premise that *all* children have the right to come into the world wanted and loved" (1970, 272).

SUMMARY

This is the first of two chapters that focus on child abuse and neglect. It is designed from the standpoint that it is difficult to understand a phenomenon like child maltreatment, which today is defined as a major social problem, without learning something about its historical background. Children in earlier centuries were subjected to behaviors that today are considered deviant and are legally prohibited. A relatively short time ago, parents who whipped their children were applauded for dutifully handling their responsibilities by chastising a wayward minor; a similar whipping today could result in forfeiture of parental rights and other legal sanctions. As society changed, social standards or norms, changed along with it. The state limited powers of parents relative to their children, and simultaneously legislated increasing powers for itself to intervene in previously private relationships.

Even though the evidence is strong that many of the moralistic childsavers were motivated more by ethnocentric, racist, and economic motives than by loving concern for helpless children, they forged a new concept of children's rights. We now recognize children as members of a distinct age group entitled to special rights and privileges, as well as to protection from harm. All these social changes, as well as technologic ones, had to occur in order to set the stage for the profound impact that the announcement of the "battered child syndrome" had on the population.

The issue of child maltreatment was initially introduced by members of the medical community; thus the first theory was a "medical model," proposing that abusers and/or victims have unique psychological characteristics that set them apart from ordinary or "normal" people. Attempts to find distinguishing characteristics have largely failed: the evidence is weak, inconclusive, and frequently contradictory. It was a temptation to present here some screening scales, but their introduction might be construed as giving them validity. It is better to gain fuller understanding of the complexity of abusive families than to try "quick and dirty" screening techniques (Newberger et al. 1977) in order to point the finger of blame at some people. Theories and research have expanded to include numerous other social, economic, and cultural variables in the search for causes of child maltreatment, and stress factors are important triggering mechanisms in violent families. In our competitive and materialistic society, stress is frequently associated with financial problems, and since economically marginal people are overrepresented in reported cases of maltreatment, many people assume that more violence occurs in these families. Although all SES levels encounter financial stress, violence occurring in higher status families is less likely to be reported.

Our review of research findings shows that conclusions are mixed. However, while there may not be sufficient evidence that there is more family violence within families of low SES, we do have overwhelming evidence that _poverty itself_ damages, maims, injures, and kills millions of people. A striking example of this is the follow-up study of abused and nonabused children by Elizabeth Elmer, who found high levels of language difficulties, sadness, and fearfulness among both the abused and control groups. Elmer therefore concluded that "the effects on child development of lower-class membership may be as powerful as abuse" (1977, 273). As long as we tolerate a society in which some persons have barely enough resources to survive while others have far in excess of needs and enjoy extravagant consumption, we are _all_ guilty of violence. If we condone poverty, we condone violence.

Closely related to stress and poverty is the question of too many or unwanted children. While there is little evidence that large families are more violent, there is some growing support for the notion that "unwantedness" is an important consideration. What can be done about these issues that impact on family relationships so heavily? Setting aside stress and poverty until the next chapter, let us consider briefly the question of unplanned and unwanted pregnancies, which result in unwanted babies who are in great danger of being maltreated. If enough citizens became concerned about this issue, they could organize a nationwide educational campaign to help parents learn how to deal with the issue with their own youngsters _before_ they become sexually active. Almost everyone agrees that children should be discouraged from engaging in sexual activity until they are older and that they should receive sex education from their parents, but many parents are unable to discuss sexual matters openly with their children. In the meantime sex education—including instruction in birth control methods—is now woefully lacking in the United States (Orr 1982). Sex education could be introduced into the regular school curriculum, before young people become sexually active, so that they would be able to make informed choices about pregnancy. Parenting classes could also be included in this educational process.

For young women who become pregnant and elect to carry to term and keep their babies, there could also be nurseries and child care centers at schools. Even though most administrators realize that child care facilities are important in order to keep teenage mothers in school, they explain that there is "strong community opposition to school involvement in child care" (Zellman 1982). In order to qualify for federal funds under Title IX of the 1972 Education Amendments,[6] schools cannot discriminate against pregnant students regardless of marital status—they are entitled to the same rights as other students. At present, most schools provide only minimal provision for pregnant students or student-mothers. According to a study by Gail Zellman, *"The schools neither seek nor want an active role in dealing with student pregnancy or parenthood"* (1982, 20). Still, young mothers *could* be encouraged to remain in school and complete their educations.

Finally, pressure could be put on government leaders to protect women's rights to abortion and to restore payment for abortions for poor women. Until there are 100 percent safe, effective, and freely available[7] contraceptive methods, freedom of choice must be available for all women, not just for the wealthy. Proponents of the Hyde Amendment argued that the government must remain neutral on divisive moral issues, but as long as the government is providing money for birthing but not for abortion, it is *not* neutral. Michigan's governor, William Milliken, said, "Once the government decides to pay for medically necessary health services for the needy, it departs from its position of neutrality by deciding to fund or not to fund a particular health service" (Guttmacher 1979, 40). Just as society has changed in its regard of children and their human rights, we can move forward in preventing "mandatory motherhood" and help insure that infants are born to parents ready, willing, and able to care for them.

NOTES

1. The details change slightly concerning the case of Mary Ellen, depending on the source one uses. Pfohl (1977, 312), for example, says "In 1875, the Society for the Prevention of Cruelty to Animals intervened in the abuse case of a nine-year-old girl named Mary Ellen who had been treated viciously by foster parents." Radbill (1974, 12) gives no date for Mary Ellen's discovery, but he notes that she was maltreated by her adoptive parents, the SPCA intervened on her behalf, and as a result, the Society for the Prevention of Cru-

elty to Children was founded in 1871. Writer Louise Armstrong (1983, 117–18) notes these discrepancies and presents two different vignettes from history in the year 1874: In one, Mary Ellen was eight years old, abused by her stepparents, and discovered by a church worker. The second involves a nine-year-old, beaten brutally by her parents, and discovered by a nurse.

2. Some years ago, the writer worked at a mental health clinic in a community with a large population of military families. Whenever one of these families came for mental health guidance, the case was almost always listed under the wife's name as primary patient, even when it was her husband who was seeking assistance. The explanation given was that the men, afraid their military commanders might learn of their problems and deny them promotion as a result, would have refused treatment without this subterfuge.

3. Many writers insist that violence is found at all levels of the socioeconomic structure, but that it is more visible to outside agents of social control at the lower levels than among the more affluent; therefore they do no accept the idea that poor people are actually more violent (Allen et al. 1969; Armstrong 1978; Brown 1981; Butler 1979; Davidson 1978; Dobash and Dobash 1979; Levine 1976; O'Toole et al. 1981; Pagelow 1981a; Pfohl 1977; Steele 1974, 1976; Steele and Pollock 1974).

4. Other writers admit that while violence crosses class lines, conditions of poverty and living in lower class neighborhoods are conducive to violence, and that more violence occurs among poor families than among the more affluent (Alfaro 1978; Bolton 1981; Gelles 1979, 1981; Martin et al. 1974; Miller and Challas 1981; Pfouts et al. 1981; Straus 1979; Straus et al. 1980).

5. In 1976, the Hyde Amendment was passed by Congress, which prohibited the use of federal funds to pay for abortions except to save a pregnant woman's life, and in 1977 the Supreme Court ruled that states and localities need not pay for "nontheraputic" abortions for indigent women. This is despite the fact that federal funds pay for childbirth and other pregnancy-related health expenses and that public hospitals do not need to perform abortions (Guttmacher 1979, 6). The Hyde Amendment's impact is felt heavily by poor young women; as Irving Dickman (1981, 18) says, "Under the Hyde Amendment, the number of Medicaid-funded abortions using federal funds dropped from 250,000 in 1977 to almost zero in 1979."

6. Title IX of the 1972 Education Amendments specifies that pregnant students must be treated the same as other students with regard to enrollment, reentry, and assignment to classes. It provides that pregnant or parent-teenagers, regardless of marital status, have the same rights as other students, cannot be expelled from school or barred from any program, course or extracurricular activity. Despite school administrators' unwillingness to recognize special needs of these students, research psychologist Gail Zellman states, "With the passage of Title IX, student pregnancy and parenthood became, legally, school matters" (1982, 15).

7. The United States has one of the highest teenage birthrates of the developed nations in the world (Guttmacher 1981), and at the same time, the contraceptives available are among the most expensive. Further, the more effective methods are also the most expensive (Torres and Forrest 1983). The first time unmarried teen-age women engage in sex, if any contraceptives at all are used, they are most likely to be the condom, and the next method is likely to be withdrawal (Guttmacher 1981).

6

Children Abused by Parents and Society

That tiny little creature, welcomed with squeals of delight by parents, relatives, siblings, and all their friends, changes forever the lives of the persons entrusted with its care, nurturance, and welfare. A baby is a special, delightful creature that naturally deserves and receives all possible attention. As the baby grows and develops into a bubbling, curious child, the special favors and privileges of infancy take new form, but they are there, nevertheless. Children deserve, and get, *love!*

How can anyone feel anything but love toward a child? More to the point, how can people love children, but still lash out and hurt, even kill, little, defenseless children? When we think about parenthood, we tend to overlook the times when plans of adults are spoiled because of a sudden fever or the nights when nobody gets sleep because of a baby's screams for which frantic parents cannot find the cause nor the cure, yet one or both have to go to work as usual the next day. We do not consider the temper tantrums that have no solution, the frustrations over the seeming impossibility of toilet training, the sudden vomiting on good clothes, or the tossing of food that is suppose to be swallowed! People who have never had the responsibility of caring for young children are seldom prepared for the sights, sounds, and especially the *smells* unavoidably associated with them.

This chapter looks first at some of the things we have learned about parents who maltreat children, then at our parenting practices, and then at some of society's responses to children who are victims of parents and society. A few ideas are pondered about what kind of changes could be made, individually and collectively, to prevent child maltreatment.

PARENTS WHO ABUSE
AND NEGLECT CHILDREN

What have we learned about parents who abuse and neglect their children? Are fathers more likely to strike out and injure children, or are mothers more frequently abusive parents? Since mothers are assigned the largest share of the childrearing task, when we think of a parent becoming enraged at a child that cries, refuses to potty train, or has trouble taking food, the parent may be automatically assumed to be a mother. Mothers also have the major responsibility for tending children, so when a child suffers from malnutrition, diaper rash, lack of proper clothing and health care, the parent who neglects is also most frequently assumed to be the mother. The general public and many professionals make the assumption that mothers are the *primary* abusers and neglectors of children, that is, the parent who most frequently maltreats the children. Is this a correct assumption and, if so, why?

A child abuse conference speaker described her reactions toward mothers who had abused and/or neglected their children when she first joined child protective services. Her deep feelings of revulsion and shock at these women caused her to lose objectivity and professionalism when dealing with them. Finally, she realized that her intense reactions occurred because these were *mothers* who were the perpetrators of crimes against their own children. "Mothers," she said, "are the people we expect to be always endowed with love, warmth, and kindness—always there when we want or need them." Even when the crime was sexual abuse committed by a male, she had often agreed with fellow officers that the mother was equally guilty because she did not *protect* her child, as mothers are supposed to do.

The speaker confessed that she had fallen sway to the stereotype of "holy motherhood," and when women did not fit that image, her response was an extreme, emotional, and punitive one. This reaction to "unfit mothers" (Mahan 1982) is not unusual; as professor of social work Judith Martin (1981, 3) notes (without agreement), "No matter who actually harms the child, mother has failed in her duty to create a safe environment for her young."

To understand this, think of the image the word *mother* evokes. The role prescribed for mothers that has been commonly accepted by many Americans for generations as ideal, is quoted by Bernard in her book on motherhood:

> "A mother's calm strength, her sense of humor in the small
> tragedies, her courage, her justice, her loving service to each
> family member—these are the things that build a home, these

are the things that make the mother the center—the heart—of the home. [She] . . . has achieved that selflessness which enables her to rise to the need of each member of the family. . . . The wise mother will concern herself with all the varied interests of the family outside the home. . . ." (1975, 5)

The frustration and helplessness of parents who have no escape from the seemingly incessant crying of infants are hard to understand except by parents who have had the same experiences. Added to the inability to understand what the baby is crying for, is the finding that the sound can render a parent temporarily deaf. Scientists have recently found that the decibel level of a baby's screams can reach between 100 and 117 decibels—a sound level that surpasses the normal talking level by 30 times. The level of sound emitted by a screaming infant is higher than that of a car horn and almost as great as a jackhammer; it is also higher than pile drivers, downtown city traffic, compressors, most rock music, motorcycles, subways, and power mowers.

These words illustrate the traditional norms and values of American society regarding woman's position in the family. This is the way millions of persons, both female and male, regard the institutions of the family and motherhood, and such ideas affect the approaches social and behavioral scientists take toward the study of the family.[1]

Child abuse bibliographies easily promote the idea that mothers are the primary abusers of children: Fathers are all but invisible except when the topic is sexual abuse. Many researchers collect samples only of mothers. For example, Richard Gaines and his colleagues (1978) studied 240 poor mothers and a control sample of "normal" mothers. One study concentrated on 60 women with children under five years of age (Rosen 1979); another purportedly concerned with *parents* concentrated on mothers' stress (Garbarino 1976). The concepts of motherliness (Steele and Pollock 1974); mother-child bonding (Stix 1981); maternal attachment and failed attachment (ten Bensel 1978; Bolton 1981); and intervention programs for mothers (Conger et al. 1981), all receive considerable attention in the literature. Samples are frequently small. One study included five abusing mothers and five controls (Wolfe et al. 1981) while another concerns only two young mothers (Flynn 1970). One article focuses on a mother of three sons who was a battered wife (one pregnancy ended in "spontaneous" abortion). The woman had a skin problem that appeared on two of her sons, therefore both pediatricians and surgeons agreed that the children's lesions resulted from maternal child abuse (Stankler 1977).

The titles of some studies refer to parents' or victims' characteristics, but their samples consist only of mothers (Calef 1972; de Lissovoy 1979; Green 1976). One investigation is unusual because it included both mothers and fathers as research subjects. This report describes 125 mothers and 89 fathers of 134 battered children, finding a high percentage of intrapsychic problems among the parents (Smith et al. 1973). However, the following year another article by two of the same authors, describing the 134 children, makes no mention of fathers but includes descriptions of the mothers, their pregnancies, deliveries, and postpartum adjustment (Smith and Hanson 1974). Strangely, the fathers who had been diagnosed earlier as having "abnormal personalities" (64 percent of them) had disappeared from further discussion.

Martin (1981, 1) notes that the structuring of treatment programs insures overrepresentation of abusive mothers, being designed for mothers and operating during daylight hours only or for inpatient therapy, precluding attendance by employed fathers. Some articles describe treatment programs of small therapy groups of ten mothers (Bellucci 1972), and inpatient therapy including behavior and personality modification for 62 mothers (Fontana and Robison 1976).

The high visibility of mothers in the literature seems to indicate that mothers are not only the primary abusers of children, but probably constitute the vast majority of abusers. That assumption does not appear to be supported after a careful inspection of the statistics. However, a cautionary note: Two factors must be kept in mind when discussing child maltreatment. One is the lack of agreement on clear and concise definitions of child abuse and neglect. The other is that most estimates are based on official statistics of child abuse or neglect with inherent biases, or on studies that have serious methodological problems.

The American Humane Association report (1980, 22) shows that of 106,611 substantiated cases of child abuse and neglect in one year, the vast majority of perpetrators were natural parents, and when broken down by abuse or neglect, fathers were the primary *abusers* in 55 percent of the cases, while mothers were the primary *neglectors* in 68 percent of the cases.[2] Focusing strictly on child abuse (deferring the subject of neglect until later), and looking closer at the substantiated cases of child abuse, the family composition shows that fathers were present in only 76 percent of maltreating families (American Humane Association 1980, 29). Thus, if we calculate on the basis of fathers present, that is, "at risk" to abuse, then the percentage of abusive fathers or father-substitutes jumps to 72 percent. If we calculate only on families where both parents are present and thus both are available to abuse, 76 percent of the abusers are fathers.[3]

A recent report on 830 reported abuse cases in Wisconsin (Kadushin and Martin 1981, 106) states that fathers were abusers in 59 percent of the cases, but it is not possible to calculate the percent of abusers by their being present as done above because detailed family composition is not shown.[4] In a large study utilizing nationally reported abuse statistics, Gil (1970) found that almost 48 percent of the abusers were mothers or mother-substitutes, but there were no fathers present in almost 30 percent of the families, therefore the fathers, compared to mothers, had a higher involvement rate (Chase 1976, 106). Gil explains:

> Though in absolute numbers slightly more children in the sample were abused by mothers than by fathers, one must remember that 29.5% of the children were living in fatherless homes. Fathers or substitutes were involved as perpetrators in nearly two-thirds of the incidents occurring in homes that did have fathers or father substitutes. . . . Thus, the involvement rate of fathers was actually higher than of mothers. (1970, 116)

David Finkelhor (1981a) believes that "men and fathers are more likely to abuse" if the time at risk factor is taken into consideration. Finkelhor

(1981a, 4) comments that there are "roughly equivalent numbers of pure incidents of physical child abuse committed by men and women, . . ." but he also notes the greater amount of time mothers spend with children than fathers.

Judith Martin (1981) attempted to determine the ratio of maternal versus paternal child abuse patterns in written reports, but found that this distinction was difficult and sometimes impossible to find in many reports. Martin analyzed 76 recent publications on abusing parents and found that only two dealt exclusively with males, whereas 41 percent focused exclusively on mothers (1981, 4). She says that a number of reports systematically excluded fathers without explanation, and when it came to identifying abusers or establishing intervention programs for child abusers, the authors made a simple assumption that only mothers need be studied (1981, 4). When she reviewed other research, Martin found:

> [I]t frequently proved difficult to determine whether they had actually studied both parent types. Discovering the sex of the sample subjects sometimes became a lesson in detection. In one work this information remained unclarified until page 51. (1981, 5)

This researcher found that the role of the female is clearly considered to be primary, and notes the numerous references to *mothering,* an overemphasis, and the absence of *fathering,* a deemphasis (Martin 1981, 5). Other writers continue to refer to small opportunity samples with high proportions of females studied by medical professionals, such as the Bennie and Sclare (1969) report of ten cases, as cited in Gelles (1973, 616). Without comment, Gelles also cites the classic report by Steele and Pollock (1974) on 60 abusing parents in which "the mother was the abuser 50 times" (Gelles 1973, 616). Many writers who cite this case study do not mention the sample selection process of the psychiatric patients, but Brandt Steele and Carl Pollock caution readers against generalizing from their statements, saying:

> Our study group of parents is not to be thought of as useful for statistical proof of any concepts. It was not picked by a valid sampling technique nor is it a "total population." It is representative only of a group of parents who had attacked children and who came by rather "accidental" means under our care because we were interested in the problem. (1974, 90)

Steele and Pollock had some difficulty trying to identify which parent was the abuser (they never could determine the perpetrator in two cases), and they often identified the guilty party only after obtaining corroboration from parents and other relatives. One mother was declared the abuser only after she was observed in a joint interview with her own mother (Steele and Pollock 1974, 91). Martin (1981, 2) notes the tendency of researchers to *assume* that mothers are the guilty party because of powerful cultural expectations and social attitudes about the role of each parent in child rearing. She cites one study of 25 abusive families in which, despite intensive treatment, the therapists were able to clearly identify the abuser in only 12 instances. Martin (1981, 2) speculates: "It is possible that the lack of definitive information available to most investigators in the field leads them to guess that the mother's role in the incident is more significant. Her activities as a parent, therefore, tended to get studied." In sum, there are many problems in research reports as noted by F. G. Bolton and his colleagues (1981) in an article that critically analyzes the child maltreatment literature and asks "when is research . . . research?" Others have noted similar complaints (Gerbner et al. 1980; Polansky et al. 1977).

The national study of family violence (Straus et al. 1980) does not rely on official records and since the sample consists of intact couples, it avoids the bias introduced by single-parent families. There was at least one child between the ages of 3 and 17 living with 1,146 of these couples, and the Conflict Tactics Scales (CTS) were administered to one or the other parent-figure regarding a referent child (Gelles 1979, 78). Reports say that 68 percent of the mothers and 58 percent of the fathers admitted to "at least one violent episode during the survey year (1975)" (Gelles 1979, 80). The ratio of mother versus father violent acts narrowed to 76 and 71 percent respectively when respondents admitted *ever* having performed certain acts. However, the most dangerous and potentially injurious acts were performed more by men than women, such as "threatening with a knife or gun," or actually using a knife or gun (Gelles 1979, 84).

Data from this study pertain to violence in the course of conflict resolution only, not to neglect. Because of problems inherent in studies using official statistics, this study could not yield an accurate measure of child abuse, but the limitations to the instrument used in the Straus et al. (1980) study of family violence, as noted in earlier chapters, are also applicable here.

There are some important gaps in the data obtained by the CTS. First, as mentioned earlier, the scale contains a question, "Did you hit or try to hit [spouse, child, etc] with something?" But the phrase *or try to hit* was deleted in subsequent research reports, so that attempts, as well as hits, were counted as hits. Second, there is a problem in not knowing what the *something* was that was used to hit, as there is in another question that asks respondents if they "threw something at the other one" (Straus et al. 1980, 255). There can be a life or death difference between a pillow or another soft, light object and a pipe, belt, or potentially lethal weapon. Gelles (1979, 83) notes that "we do not know what objects were used to hit the child (a pipe or a paddle?). . . ." Third, there is no information on whether the object thrown actually hit the target or not, and fourth, what were the injuries (if any) sustained by the children? What were the parents admitting to, when they said they had "beat up" their child in the previous year? Could they have been referring to spankings?[5] The authors say they "assume that beating up a child implies more than a single blow" (Straus et al. 1980, 61). Regardless of whether we approve of it or not, the vast majority, 84 to 97 percent, of Americans approve of spanking children as a form of discipline (Stark and McEvoy 1970).

These limitations should be kept in mind when reading reports about findings from the survey (Gelles 1979; Steinmetz 1980; Straus 1980a). Suzanne Steinmetz acknowledges that mothers being more violent "is understandable" because they spend more time with children and they have greater responsibility for child care (1980, 340). On the other hand, Gelles notes a "small but significant difference" (1979, 84) between mothers' and fathers' use of violence, but he disagrees on the time factor explanation, saying:

> It has been frequently argued that mothers are more prone to use violence because they spend more time with their children. We hypothesize that the explanation for mothers' greater likelihood of using violence goes beyond the *simple justification* that *they spend more time* with the children. Our future analyses of the information gathered in our survey of violence in the family will examine this relationship from a number of points of view, including family power, *coping ability,* resources, and *personality traits.* (Gelles 1979, 84, emphasis added)

Here Gelles is suggesting that possible explanations for maternal violence can be found in factors such as "coping ability" and "personality traits." Remarkably, this is written by the same author of the now-classic article originally published in 1973, and republished in the same volume as the quote above: "Child Abuse as Psychopathology: A Sociological Critique and Reformulation" (1979, 27–41). The earlier article had demanded less concentration on individual characteristics and more emphasis on sociological factors; Gelles had strongly denounced the literature's overemphasis on "sick" parents, "mental illness," emotional problems, "defects of the character structure" including personality traits, and so forth. In the introduction to the same book, Gelles (1979, 13) lists 11 features of the family that make it a violence-prone setting—and the very first factor is: *time at risk.*

Nevertheless, the less time spent in taking care of children, the less possibility of lashing out at them. Fathers who are unemployed are much more likely to abuse their children than employed fathers (Dumont 1977; Light 1973), and while their striking out may be triggered in large part by stress and feelings of impotence and frustration, an attendant feature of fathers' unemployment is that these men are likely to spend much more time than usual at home with their children, thus they have more time at risk.

The Role of Mothers

Undoubtedly, many mothers abuse their children. Women are the largest category at risk of perpetrating child abuse. Reasons for this include the isolation of the modern nuclear family, the much greater responsibility assigned to mothers for the care, nourishment, and behavior of children, and the greater percentage of time they spend with children. It seems that we should *expect* mothers to be the primary abusers of children. Despite all that, for various reasons noted above, the literature does not provide strong and conclusive evidence that this is so. Even though many writers overemphasize maternal child abuse and deemphasize or totally ignore paternal child abuse (and when the abuser is unquestionably a male, cast a net of blame onto the mothers, as in incest), a careful reading of the available literature reveals that men are the primary abusers of children (Kadushin and Martin 1981; Martin 1981).

Nevertheless, many women do abuse their children. Forty-five percent of substantiated reports of child abuse were committed by mothers or mother-substitutes in 1978 (AHA 1980, 22), and the majority (68 percent) of neglectors of children were mothers.[6] If we are concerned about reduction of violence in society, then it is important to ask *who* are these maltreating mothers, *why* do they do it, and what can be done to *prevent* women's violence against children? These questions are not independent of each other; finding answers to the first question suggests answers to the others. Again, readers must be cautioned to note the biases inherent in most statistics and findings from samples of abusing mothers. Social and legal agencies have greater and easier entree into poor and minority families, particularly poor families headed by single mothers. The arm of the state reaches into these families and can point a finger of blame at women unable to defend themselves or counterattack the state's claims (Schneiger 1978).

The poor and minorities are overrepresented in caseloads, client samples, and official statistics, although most writers insist that violence crosses all socioeconomic, cultural, racial or ethnic, and religious lines (California Department of Justice 1978). There are ways that families with financial resources can escape scrutiny, for example, the Smith et al. (1982) follow-up of abused children found that higher SES families tended to move away and become unavailable for study.

Among the families in the American Humane Association report (1980, 29), *female* single-parent families are greatly overrepresented, constituting 24 percent of the abusive families and 46 percent of the neglecting families. For comparison, only 14 percent of all families in the United States in 1980 were headed by a single female caretaker (AHA 1983, 9). Also in 1980, 10 percent of all families lived in poverty, but 50 percent of all families below the poverty level in 1981 were maintained by women with no husband present (U.S. Bureau of the Census 1983, 2–3). Families headed by black women fared the worst: 70 percent of these families were poor, compared to 39 percent of white female-headed families. Only about 11 percent of U.S. households received public assistance in 1981, but out of the maltreating families reported in 1981, 43 percent were receiving some form of public assistance (AHA 1983, 10). Eighty percent of welfare (AFDC) homes are headed by women and one-half of all AFDC payments go to households in which the mother had given birth as a teenager (Guttmacher 1979, 10, 32). Just being poor, or being a single parent, makes a mother much more likely to suspected of abuse or neglect (O'Toole et al. 1981).

Once the stigma of the label *abuser* is attached, it is difficult to erase (Newberger and Bourne 1978). A single parent of two boys aged 11 and 13, who was employed full-time and attended classes at night, shared her personal experiences with classmates at a state university, by saying:

> About two years ago, someone reported me to CPS [Child Protective Services], saying that I abuse my sons. People came to my home and asked all kinds of questions, and I know they didn't believe anything I told them. The boys were called from their classes at school and asked lots of personal questions—at first they were scared—and none of us knew what it was all about. They didn't find anything to "hang" me for, but ever since then, they keep watching us to see what's going on. My sons get called to the principal's office every so often, and once in awhile, they're stopped out on the streets by people asking how I treat them. By now the kids think it's funny, and they feel real important, too. Now and then, when I'm going to punish them or "ground" them, they'll get smart-alecky and tell me I'd better watch out and not get mean, or they'll tell CPS that I'm abusing them. I feel like I'm being harassed by the authorities, and I've been found guilty without a trial. They won't tell me who reported me, but I wish they would, so I could face my accuser and tell her (I think it's a neighbor who doesn't like me) flat out how much I care for my boys and how tough it is trying to be both mother and father to the kids. I think it's

spoiling my relationship with my boys, 'cause I always feel like
I'm on the defensive and they know it.

The most common characteristics of *reported* cases of child abuse and
neglect reveal certain patterns: the parent/s are young; the first child was
born to a teen-aged mother (frequently an unwanted or premarital pregnancy), babies are also more likely to be low birth weight and premature;
and the parental educational level is low. All these characteristics appear
more frequently among poor persons than among others, and have a particular relevance for women, especially minority women and single
mothers.

These features are also conducive to definitions of *neglect* labels attached to poor mothers. It is difficult to write about neglectful mothers
without including poverty in the discussion, although the association between poverty and maltreatment was discussed earlier. James Kent's
(1976) study of abused and neglected children found that the neglected
children were the "poorest of the poor," coming from the most impoverished homes having young parents with lower education and employment, and more children. Children born to young mothers or poor mothers who have inadequate diets and health care are much more likely to
deliver low birth weight babies, and the probability that these babies will
be maltreated is greater than in normal weight babies. As Leo Stern (1979,
21) writes, "the incidence of subsequent battering and physical abuse in
low birth weight infants is approximately three times" that which would
be expected. Despite the lack of a concise definition of neglect (Giovannoni and Becerra 1979; Kent 1976; Polansky et al. 1977), the "gatekeepers"
who make such determinations rely on subjective criteria by which they
apply their own (usually white, middle class) personal standards of cleanliness, child care, diet, and housing (Thomas 1974). It should be asked
how much of what is officially defined as neglect is the *willful* denial of
good sanitation, feeding, and care of children, and how much of it is due
to *ignorance* or simply due to lack of money?

Journalist Harriet Stix (1981) presents a case where a baby's "failure to
thrive," usually diagnosed as neglect, was due solely to a mother's ignorance of how to properly feed her infant. A home visitor watched as the
mother attempted to spoon feed the baby, but when the baby spit some
of the food back out, the mother began putting away the food, thinking
the baby's appetite was satiated. She did not understand that this is a normal pattern of children just learning to eat solid food. Many other children
are labeled as neglected because of subjective biases of social agents who
impose their own norms and values on persons different than themselves, or who cannot comprehend the sometimes paralyzing effects of

poverty (Chase 1976; Piven and Cloward 1971; Richette 1969; Thomas 1974).

But for single parents and minorities, it is difficult to avoid poverty, and the proportion of single parents among the poor is growing. Between 1970 and 1979, the total number of families in the United States increased by 12 percent, but the number of householders who were mothers with children present in the home increased by 81 percent (Rawlings 1980). There were approximately 15 million mothers and children under the age of 18 living in families with no husband/father present in 1979 (Rawlings 1980). As noted earlier, 50 percent of these fatherless homes are likely to have incomes below the poverty level (U.S. Bureau of the Census 1983).

Some fathers continue to contribute to family support after separation or divorce, which helps maintain their families above the poverty level. However, of the 7.1 million women with one or more children under 21 years of age in 1979, 41 percent of these mothers were never awarded payments and had to depend on other sources for support of their children. And of those who were awarded child support, many received less than the full amount or nothing.

As Table 6–1 shows, out of 7.1 million families with children under 21, only 1.7 million mothers had a dependable source of income from child support payments, but the overall average payment in 1978 was $1,800, about 20 percent of their mean total money income (U.S. Bureau of the Census 1981). The more children there are, the less likely the mother will receive child support payments. Whether or not a mother is awarded and receives child support payments, as well as the amount of such payments, is strongly correlated with socioeconomic characteristics. In other words, a white woman with four or more years of college, who is employed at white-collar work, and has unearned income (such as money from trust funds) is in the most favorable position. The least favorable position for

Table 6–1. Number of Women in 1980 with Children under 21 Years of Age Who Were Members of the Household but Whose Father Was Not; the Number Awarded and Supposed to Receive Child Support; and the Percentages of Payment in 1978

Number of women with one or more children under 21 years of age living in their household:		7.1 million
Number of women awarded child support and supposed to receive payments in 1978:		3.4 million
Of the 3.4 million:	Received full support	49%
	Received less than full support	23%
	Received nothing	28%

Source: U.S. Bureau of the Census Current Population Reports, Special Studies, 1981, Series P-23, No. 112.

being awarded or receiving child support is occupied by women who never completed high school and never married.

If single-parent mothers are employed full time and have less than 12 years of schooling, their wages will be approximately 56 percent of male workers with the same amount of education (U.S. Bureau of the Census 1980). Even if the mothers are well educated (graduated from college and have postgraduate education), they can expect to earn almost $2,000 *less* than male high school drop-outs, or $8,360 less per year than a man with similar education (U.S. Bureau of the Census 1980, 19). If these are young mothers, their chances of even obtaining full-time employment are considerably restricted, since unemployment rates for persons 16 to 19 years old consistently average about three times the rates for adult white women and four times the rates for adult black women. Many persons under 19 years of age are already parents and/or married, especially among the poor population.

Being a young, black female creates *triple* jeopardy for a mother and subsequently, her children. In December 1981 the rate of unemployment of black teen-agers was 41 percent (U.S. Department of Labor 1982), but according to news sources, that rate has risen to 49 percent while the national unemployment rate is around 10 percent.[7] Blacks are overrepresented in reports of child abuse (American Humane Association 1981, 17), as well as in poverty. The average black family income in 1976 was only 59 percent of that of white family income, which is exactly the same ratio of female to male median earnings for full-time employment.

The continuing disparity between men's and women's wages, and minorities' and whites' wages, plus unemployment patterns, are not based on individual characteristics but reflect structural inequality, which affects the behavior of persons within the family unit. It would be extremely difficult to be an exemplary parent when one is exploited on the job with substandard wages and lack of opportunity for advancement, or when one is abused by the welfare system. It must be doubly difficult for a single parent in those situations.

Although minority, poor, and single-parent families are overrepresented in reports of child abuse and neglect, children also suffer in more affluent, two-parent homes, so the factors above do not alone explain maternal abuse. The process of becoming a parent is normally a difficult one. Sometimes it is called a *crisis* or a *transition* to parenthood, but studies find that the transition is easier if: the couple has been married for some time, the child was wanted and planned, and there is an uncomplicated pregnancy and delivery. Conversely, the transition is more difficult if: it was a premarital pregnancy, the mother is in poor health, the father does not value fatherhood, or the baby is fussy or nonresponsive. Most studies show that marital satisfaction drops after parenthood, especially for mothers, even among mothers who say their "ideal family" consists of four or more children (Glenn and McLanahan 1982). Following the birth of the first child, even the most egalitarian couples become more traditional in the roles they perform, with mothers assuming the major responsibility for child care (Miller 1974). When a child in a two-parent family is sick at night, it is usually the mother who is expected to render care. If both parents are employed, it is almost always the mother who is called at work by schools when a child is ill or in trouble.

The direct and indirect costs of having children are substantial; so what are the perceived advantages of having them? The most frequently chosen reasons for having children given to researchers Hoffman and Manis (1979, 586) were that children bring "love and companionship," and that children provide "stimulation, fun, and activity." These choices indicate expectations of what children will provide parents, rather than what parents will do for the children. If parents are struggling to pay the rent, will they be able to enjoy much *companionship?* If they are trying desperately to hold their relationship together, will the noises and demands of children provide much *fun* for them? These responses from married adults clearly show unrealistic (and uninformed) expectations of the "joys of parenthood." In addition, once the children arrive, who will take care of them?

Sociologist Jessie Bernard documents the harmful effects of motherhood as it is currently structured in this country, saying: "The way we institutionalize motherhood, giving mothers the exclusive responsibility for the care of children and making this care their exclusive activity, has destructive effects on women as well as on children" (1975, 67). Bernard shows that we know what is necessary for healthiest childhood development, but then we "make it as hard as possible to supply these essentials by making one person alone responsible for supplying them all by herself in an isolated household" (1975, 72). The isolation of a mother/child household, she says, is related to lack of physical affection and also to the "infliction of pain" (Bernard 1975, 73).

Addressing the issue of maternal child abuse, Bernard quotes Margaret Mead who "knows more about child rearing than perhaps anyone else in the world" (1975, 84). Mead described her own "blind responsive rage" at her inability to deal effectively with her screaming infant daughter; she then better understood the desperation of young, inexperienced mothers. Bernard goes on to show that the role of mother is structured as an ideal that is almost impossible to maintain on a constant basis, explaining:

> Mothers may from time to time laughingly refer to their small children as little monsters. . . . For mothers must fool themselves as well as others. They are not allowed to express any-

thing but love for their children, certainly not complaints. . . .
Still they cannot always experience the prescribed emotions
twenty-four hours a day. Patience is limited. They cannot by
themselves, alone, absorb all the aggression from their children. (Bernard 1975, 85)

Even the best of babies can be difficult sometimes, and many babies
and young children are unresponsive, unaffectionate, very demanding,
and difficult to the point where they can try the patience to the limit of
almost anyone entrusted with their care. There is some evidence that
there is an interactive effect between especially difficult children and child
abuse (Kadushin and Martin 1981). This has been shown to some extent in
developmentally disabled and handicapped children.

To summarize, mothers can and do neglect and abuse their children,
but certain factors in combination, seem to be mentioned repeatedly in
the literature. There is an association between the factors listed below and
a greater probability of child abuse or neglect.

Factors that Increase the Probability
of Maternal Child Maltreatment

1. young mother
2. single mother
3. unwanted pregnancy
4. difficult birth
5. other young children at home
6. low birth weight infant
7. low education level of parent/s
8. mother's health problems
9. child's health problems
10. lack of respite from child care
11. social isolation
12. irritable or unresponsive infant
13. poverty (substandard environment; poor medical care;
    malnutrition, and so forth)

Child abuse and neglect has been viewed as an individual problem, but
there are many contributing factors that could be eliminated by a caring,
concerned society. The literature shows that mothers can and do react to
frustration, desperation, and lack of adequate preparation for the almost
impossible total responsibility assigned to them for child care by lashing
out (or ignoring) their charges. Some children simply do not match the
smiling, pink, gurgling image of the Gerber Baby! Most women receive no

training to prepare them for the realities of the full-time burden of child care. When there is an unexplained fever, teething and feeding problems, diarrhea, toilet training, mischief, self-endangering, temper tantrums, and nonstop screaming, almost any mother can lose control, even it only momentarily. Still, these features of childrearing do not take into account other stressful factors that may exist independently of the child such as illness in the immediate or extended family, financial, housing, employment, or spouse problems. Yet all of these environmental stresses act to compound the mother/child problems. When looked at from this point of view, it seems like the system is already set up for child abuse and neglect, and the wonder of it is that *more* mothers are not charged with these failures!

Identifying Maltreating Parents

People concerned with child maltreatment need to become sensitized to some of the characteristics of parents or their attitudes and behavior toward their children that may indicate potential maltreatment or its occurrence. For that purpose, indicators have been gathered together from a number of sources (Eskin and Kravitz 1980; McNeese and Hebeler 1977; NCCAN 1975a, 1975b), but most of these sources originated with Kempe and Helfer (1972). The presence of one or two indicators may be merely circumstantial, but if several of them are present, they may warrant closer consideration and serve as clues to the possibility of maltreatment by a parent or parents. They are as follows:

**Factors Associated with
Parental Child Maltreatment**

1. *Isolation:* there is a lack of social support from spouse, friends, relatives, neighbors, and community groups. Fail to keep appointments, discourage social contacts, and never participate in school activities.
2. *Unrealistic expectations of child:* expecting or demanding behavior that is beyond the child's years or ability.
3. *Overly critical:* seldom discuss the child in positive terms or may compare one child unfavorably to a sibling. Disappointed in the child's sex.
4. *Harsh disciplinarians:* rigid, authoritarian, and demanding. Stringent standards and expectations; firmly believe in physical punishment.
5. *Negative parent-child interactions:* seldom look at the

child and fail to make direct eye contact. Avoid talking to the child but when they do, it takes the form of demands or criticism; ignore crying or become extremely bothered by the crying. Seldom touch the child; ignore demands for feedings or feel the child is too demanding during feedings; react with excessive disgust to diaper changes or spitting up.

6. *Child's name:* reason for choice and when. If there was a long delay in choosing name, this can indicate the child was viewed as an "it" rather than a person; if named after a parent who has since disappointed caretaker spouse, the child may become a symbol of pain/hate/rage of his/her namesake.

7. *Unwanted child:* one or both parents desired abortion; "one too many" children in family; mother denied pregnancy or was frightened, depressed, or suffered repeated illnesses during pregnancy, or if the child was born during a "grief period" (a death in the family, a divorce, or separation).

8. *Child confinement:* child is not seen outside the home or at school for extended periods of time.

9. *Medical care for injury or illness:* delay in seeking treatment; refuse consent for diagnostic studies; reluctant to give information; unable to explain injuries, offer farfetched or contradictory explanations; project cause of injuries onto sibling or third-party; history of child's repeated injuries; hospital "shops"—take child to different doctor, hospital, or clinic each time medical care is needed.

10. *Inappropriate behavior when seeking medical care for child:* overreacting and seeming hostile or antagonistic when questioned, or underreacting by showing little concern or awareness, act detached, or more preoccupied with personal problems unrelated to the child's injury or condition.

11. *Unhappy with parental responsibilities:* lack parenting skills and are discouraged, depressed, and frustrated with the role.

12. *Own childhood histories:* complain of being unwanted, unloved, unappreciated, neglected, beaten, or psychologically abused or neglected, or subjected to excessive parental demands.

13. *Dysfunctional family history:* unusual stress factors present, for example, unemployment, divorce, separation, or death in the family; appear to be misusing alcohol or other drugs.

Caution should be taken to prevent false accusation of parents; none of these characteristics individually are sufficient to *prove* child maltreatment. They are offered here only to sensitize readers so that if several or many symptoms occur in some families, there is the possibility that maltreatment has or will occur. Appropriate intervention in families with a number of these characteristics may serve to prevent violence from occurring, or assist them in getting the kind of help needed to prevent it from happening again.

On the other hand, sometimes families are so well isolated and invisible to scrutiny, that the only evidence of maltreatment is shown by the victims, so some characteristics and behavior patterns of victims is presented next.

Identifying Child Victims of Maltreatment

Victims of child maltreatment frequently give signs to outsiders that are subtle and may not be noted by anyone except the most perceptive observers. Drawing from a number of sources, below are some characteristics and behaviors of child victims that, in combination, may indicate victimization (NCCAN 1975a, 1975b; Eskin and Kravitz 1980; Kempe and Helfer 1972a; McNeese and Hebeler 1977; Pagelow 1982a). Of course, indicators vary according to the child's age.

Factors Indicating that a Child
May Be the Victim of Maltreatment

1. *Inappropriate clothing:* always wears long sleeves or high necklines regardless of the weather or refuses to undress for gym class.
2. *School attendance:* habitually truant or late for school, or arrives at school early and remains late. Often tired and may fall asleep in class.
3. *Physical contact:* being hungry for affection but unable to use appropriate methods of obtaining it, or being apprehensive and fearful of affection or physical contact, especially with an adult.
4. *Extremes in behavior:* cries often or cries very little; excessively fearful or fearless of adult authority; extremely ag-

gressive and destructive or unusually passive and with-drawn; hyperactive, being very disruptive and demanding attention or being withdrawn and shy; some may act like "parents" to their parents, catering to their needs or those of other adults.

5. *Sudden changes in conduct:* regressive behavior such as pants-wetting, thumb-sucking, disruptiveness or passivity, or personality changes when they know their parents are not nearby.

6. *Physical condition:* dirty, unclean, hair lice, skin sores; often hungry and may hoard food or take food or lunch money from other children; show signs of malnutrition, for example, paleness, underweight, unable to participate in physical activities with others, or lack normal strength and endurance. Show obvious need for dental care, eyeglasses, or immunization.

7. *Physical trauma:* bruises in various stages of healing, recur-ring over a long time-period; frequent burns, welts, bruises or broken bones from improbable "accidents;" limping or obviously painful movements that have no apparent causes.

8. *Learning disabilities or developmental delays:* when testing indicates no physical or psychological abnormalities.

Caution must be exercised in deciding whether or not to report suspi-cions of neglect and/or abuse to the authorities. A child who is suffering should *never* be ignored, but some children are exceedingly clumsy or move quickly and have frequent accidents. Experts warn that particular bruises on a child less than one year of age represent abuse (McNeese and Hebeler 1977). However, some infants are born with certain bone dis-ease such as *osteogenesis imperfecta,* a chalklike condition of the bone, or *Mongolian spots.* This is a discoloration (which looks like bruises) of the skin of non-Caucasian children; they usually appear on the back but may be on other parts of the body. They disappear as the child grows older. It is difficult for anyone except an expert to differentiate these con-ditions from abuse. For an example of self-inflicted injuries, one of the author's own sons managed, when he was a toddler, to stand up on and rock a straight-backed chair until it fell, causing a severe black eye. The next day he followed the same routine and blackened the other eye! At that time, the sight of a two year old with both eyes swollen shut and discolored brought stares of disapproval, but today the same sight might bring false charges of child abuse.

One of the best sources regarding visual identification of injuries and physical trauma inflicted on children is a booklet written by Margaret

McNeese and Joan Hebeler (1977). Although this is a journal that was published by CIBA Pharmaceutical Company for medical professionals, it contains excellent illustrations by John Craig and a clearly understandable descriptive text that makes it useful for persons outside the medical profession.[8]

Reporting Suspected Cases of Child Maltreatment

Certain people are required by law to report certain types of child maltreatment, but this varies by the 50 states or jurisdictions which include American Samoa, Guam, Puerto Rico, and the Virgin Islands. For example, *any person* must report in 19 jurisdictions, while in others only certain professionals must report (NCCAN 1980c, 6). Professionals required to report usually include medical, social work, and educational personnel and sometimes child care workers and members of the clergy. Failure to report in 45 jurisdictions includes criminal liability (generally a misdemeanor), punishable by from 5 days in jail and/or a $10 fine up to a year in jail and/or a $1,000 fine; and/or civil liability. This last might include medical malpractice suits against doctors who fail to report (NCCAN 1980c, 16). "Good Samaritan" laws protect nonmalicious reporters from retaliatory suit by guardians. Age of the child is set at 18 by all jurisdictions except Wyoming, which sets it at 16 years; but some states extend protection to physically or mentally disabled persons, and two states restrict protection to include only never-married persons (NCCAN 1980c, 6).

What must be reported also varies. Only 48 states specifically include neglect as a reportable condition, and less than half of the jurisdictions include mental or emotional injury in their definitions of child abuse (NCCAN 1980c). Religious immunity is allowed in 44 jurisdictions, which means that withholding certain medical treatment because of parents' religious beliefs is permitted by law. Reporting requirements vary from "immediately" to "as soon as possible" for oral reports, and from 24 hours to 7 days for written reports (NCCAN 1980c, 14,17). There are legal restrictions in many relationships, such as psychotherapist/patient, attorney/client, and minister/confessor, that have specific privileges of confidentiality, but these are sometimes inapplicable in child maltreatment cases. Physician/patient and husband/wife is specifically abrogated in most, but not all jurisdictions, which means that in a few jurisdictions, the law cannot force inquiry into confidential communications (NCCAN 1980c, 13–14).

There are so many variations by jurisdictions that cannot be detailed here, therefore readers who are concerned with the laws are strongly advised to obtain state-specific requirements from their own states, such as the *Child Abuse Prevention Handbook* (California Department of Justice 1982) cited earlier, or for an excellent national overview, the *Child Abuse and Neglect: State Reporting Laws* complied by the National Center on Child Abuse and Neglect (NCCAN 1980c).

There are still other issues frequently mentioned in the literature concerning child abuse and neglect that need to be considered, such as the violent ways in which parents respond to their children's behavior.

VIOLENT METHODS OF CHILD REARING

One factor frequently mentioned in the child abuse literature is the violent method of child discipline commonly used in the United States, corporal punishment. Many writers agree that it may be one of the causes of violence, not only in families but in society as a whole (N. Feshbach 1976, 1980a; Fontana 1976). Some call for a reexamination of our standards for parental control over children that give awesome powers to (usually untrained) parents in the privacy of the home. Some call for a Bill of Rights for children and for legal protection which they are now denied under existing juvenile court and institutional practices (Bakan 1971; Gil 1970;

The training we give little children often has unintended consequences. Children hit other children—parents hit children for hitting others—and children get the message that hitting is "OK." Physical punishment teaches children that love and violence are associated, that this is what big people use to get what they want, and that violence is an appropriate response to frustration and stress.

Source: Hicks Marlowe.

Holt 1974). For example, Adah Maurer (1981) attacks corporal punishment in schools by exposing far-ranging and even sadistic abuses of children, and calls for educators to "put paddles away." Maurer quotes a resolution adopted by the Council of Representatives of the American Psychological Association in 1975 as follows:

> Research has shown that the effective use of punishment in [sic] eliminating undesirable behavior requires precision in timing, duration, intensity and specificity, as well as considerable sophistication in controlling a variety of relevant environmental and cognitive factors, such that punishment administered in institutional settings, without attention to all these variables, is likely to instill hostility, rage and a sense of powerlessness without reducing the undesirable behavior." (1981, 28)

If professionally trained educators are not expected by the APA authors of this resolution to have at their disposal enough "precision" or the needed "considerable sophistication" to produce positive results from corporal punishment of school children, what does this imply about physical punishment of children by their untrained parents in the privacy of their homes? In addition, parents may be expected to have less objectivity and more emotional reactions to their children's misbehavior than professional educators. Many other professionals from a variety of fields insist that the culturally accepted practices of physical punishment of children in their homes and institutions must be abandoned if we want nonviolent adults (Elmer 1979). Some writers have suggested that adult sexuality can become disordered as a result of spankings on the buttocks—the favorite locus for physical assault recommended by almost everyone of the "spare the rod, spoil the child" lobby (Alexander and Ross 1961; Bakan 1971).

The law does not forbid corporal punishment either in schools or by parents, although sometimes beatings given to school children in one state would constitute child abuse in another (Newberger and Bourne 1978). Corporal punishment could fall within statutory definitions of child abuse, since it may constitute infliction of nonaccidental physical injury, nevertheless:

> No state, however, prohibits parents from using reasonable corporal punishment in the upbringing of their children. Five states expressly permit the use of reasonable corporal punishment and note that it is not child abuse. In addition, 26 jurisdictions have enacted laws that justify the use of physical force upon a minor by a person responsible for his care and supervision to the extent reasonably necessary to maintain discipline or to promote the welfare of the minor. (NCCAN 1980c, 5–6)

The problem of course, comes in the interpretation of terms like "reasonable," "discipline," and "welfare of the minor." As the NCCAN report notes, these *justification statutes* may be (and are) used by parents, guardians, and teachers as a defense in civil or criminal proceedings for child abuse. There is sufficient and reliable evidence that multitudes of children are abused in their homes, schools, and institutions, and almost all of it is defended on the grounds that it was reasonable and necessary to maintain discipline, for "the child's own good" (Bakan 1971; Gil 1971; NCCAN 1978b).

In her treatise against corporal punishment in schools, Maurer provides findings from many studies showing the negative effects of physical punishment on children, and says:

> The English team of Bowlby and Burbin studied and wrote about "Personal Aggressiveness and War" in 1950. Their conclusion: "Corporal punishment escalates; discipline becomes harder to enforce. More energy is spent policing as children develop deviousness. The 'bad boy' becomes the 'hero'; gangs form to defeat the teacher." Later investigators repeated the work and came to the same conclusion. . . . (Maurer 1981, 25)

Maurer cites other research findings showing that developmental psychologists "have been unanimous in their findings that punitive parents produce poorly adjusted children" (1981, 25). Some writers point out that these children will obey parental demands only as long as they are watched, but will not obey when they think they can "get away with it" (Maurer 1981, 25). This results in rebellious children and parents who must constantly be on guard, watching and ready to repeat the punishment. Other researchers cited by Maurer expected that punishment for aggression would lead to inhibition of aggression, but instead found a positive correlation: The more punishment, the more the child's aggression grew (1981, 26).

Not only has it been clearly shown by behaviorists that punishment is the *least* effective means of controlling behavior, but belief is growing that *physical punishment teaches children that: love and violence is associated; that this is what adults use to get what they want; and that violence is an appropriate response to frustration and stress* (N. Feshbach 1980a; Gelles 1979; Pagelow 1982a; Straus 1979; Straus et al. 1980).

The author has long been opposed to the use of physical punishment on children for these same reasons, although many people incorrectly associate this idea with a disapproval of discipline. Children require discipline, but we now have developed far better methods than slapping, spanking, or beating children. Because their memories are short, children quickly forget what they were slapped for the last time, thus physical punishment must be repeated, and it frequently is repeated with increasing force "so you won't forget *this* time!" Violence tends to escalate in incidence and intensity over time until it becomes, in some cases, child abuse or even homicide, by sheer accident. The author's viewpoint is summarized in the statement: *"Child abuse begins with the first slap."*

Gelles and his colleagues have insisted for some time that slapping or spanking children constitutes violence against children, despite cultural norms supporting the use of physical force for disciplinary purposes. American parents not only *approve* of physical punishment for children, but between 84 percent and 97 percent of all parents *use* some form of physical force on their children (Blumberg 1964; Erlanger 1974; Stark and McEvoy 1970). Gelles explains his position thus:

> [O]ur previous research indicated that almost all acts, from spankings to murder, could somehow be justified and neutralized by someone as being in the best interests of the victim. . . . [A]cts [that] parents carry out on their children in the name of corporal punishment or acceptable force, could, if done to strangers or adults, be considered criminal assault. (1979, 79)

Nevertheless, Gelles (1979, 80–81) reports that 73 percent of the parents in the Straus et al. (1980) study admitted to at least one violent occurrence in the course of raising a child who was between the ages of 3 and 17, which these researchers believe are underestimates.

Richard Welsh (1976) describes himself as an "avid anti-corporal punishment advocate" and states that using a belt or a stick on a child has long-term (negative) effects on behavior; he makes a distinction between such practices and hitting a child's bottom with an open hand. Welsh gives a number of reasons for this distinction and explains his own feelings thus: "I believe a child should *never* be hit, but I offer my colleagues a note of caution. Very few people will listen to an extremist. Let's stop the belts and sticks now; we'll get to the hands later" (Welsh 1977, 55). One ten year follow-up study of school children and their families found that the *most powerful* factor in predicting long-term aggressive behavior was the use of a belt or stick on children in their developmental years (Langer et al. 1976).

Current child-rearing practices in the United States are heavily laden with violent behavior that has the latent effect of teaching children how to become violent adults. When a child first learns impressions of social interaction in a violent environment, it is only natural that the behavior is imitated beyond the family unit (Goode 1969). If that behavior is rewarded and not negatively sanctioned, it is likely to be repeated (Bandura 1973; Bandura and Ross 1961; Bandura and Walter 1970a). Children do not have to be the direct targets of physical abuse, they can also be abused by witnessing violence against others in the home (Lewis et al. 1979b; Pagelow 1982a; Steele 1974). However, evidence is growing that witnessing violence against others may have an even stronger effect on children than being targets of abuse, *particularly* when they are boys (Bach-y-rita and Veno 1974; Burt 1978; Button 1973; King 1975; Owens and Straus 1975; Pfouts et al. 1981).

There are a host of other factors that contribute to child abuse and neglect. These include, but are not limited to, such factors as: structural inequality, cultural approval of violence, and stressful living in our fast-changing, competitive, and anomic society. What can be done to improve the quality of life enough to prevent child abuse and neglect, and violence in general? Changes have been made in the past, not always to the benefit of large segments of society; frequently reforms that are theoretically designed to help have far-reaching consequences not always intended or anticipated by the reformers.

SOCIETY'S RESPONSE
TO CHILD MALTREATMENT

One writer, Richard de Lone (1979), tells how public and professional response to hunger and poverty led to the development of social policy that turned very quickly into a repressive system of social control. Giving the title "Help That Hurts" to one chapter in his book, de Lone (1979, 79) states:

> But there are . . . limits to social programs that have attempted to create a more egalitarian society through assistance to individuals. . . . The ironic result is that programs designed to assist individuals often end up offering help that hurts.

> Examples of this structural irony are provided by three programs aimed specifically at helping children: Aid to Families with Dependent Children (AFDC); the so-called child welfare system, which includes foster care, institutional care of children outside their homes, and the family court system that helps steer both; and the juvenile justice system.

As Ruby Takanishi (1978, 9) says, the child welfare movement produced a "problematic legacy." Takanishi attempts to show that many of the child welfare movements of the "child-saving era" (Platt 1969) were theoretically concerned with children's rights and welfare yet, "The reforms became our problems, problems which are themselves subjects of contemporary reform efforts" (Takanishi 1978, 9). Some of the examples she provides to support this contention include the development of the intelligence test by Binet, who wanted an objective procedure to replace the previously unjust subjective methods used to define children as mentally retarded and place them in institutions (Takanishi 1978, 9). The "labeling" and tracking of children on the basis of tests has come under considerable dispute among scientists and educators, and now many are demanding that they be eliminated.

Another example provided by Takanishi (1978, 10) is the establishment of special classes for blind, deaf, and "mentally defective" children in public school, a practice that has come under attack for further handicapping children. Parents and others are now struggling in a movement to "mainstream" these children. Child labor laws resulted after bitter battles to protect children from long hours and cruel working conditions, but this movement was generated during a period when men were leaving rapidly depleting farm lands and joining the growing industrialized labor force (Blau 1979; Wertheimer 1979). In other words, children (and women) were being "protected" out of jobs in factories to make room for men workers, and children were thus forced into prolonged childhood and public education. The movement gained impetus at a convention in 1887 of the all-male American Federation of Labor when their leader, Samuel Gompers, condemned child labor (Takanishi 1978, 22). Now, according to Takanishi (1978, 10), "Present day reformers propose strategies by which adolescents can gain access to occupational sites of activity from which they have been effectively banished by child labor laws."

In Chapter 5, we saw how humanistic efforts to save infants led to the establishment of foundling hospitals, and these in turn led to the delayed deaths of thousands of children. Orphan asylums and houses of refuge led to taking children from poor homes and off the streets into private charitable institutions that were subject to no outside inspection, regulation, or control (although the public ones that came later where hardly ideal arrangements for young children). The children who were most likely to be picked up to be "saved" were usually the little ones of the "dangerous classes" (de Lone 1979, 55). Using the slogan "It is easier to form than reform," the targets were "a specific group of children . . . the handicapped, abused, neglected, delinquent, and dependent child, most typically from the poor and/or immigrant strata of the urban centers" (Takanishi 1978, 13). As soon as these unfortunate children were old enough to work, they were indentured out to work in a form of (at least, temporary) slavery. Some were "adopted" out to any families willing to take them, which began the present-day foster home system.

Foster Homes for Maltreated Children

Originally, there was no screening of families willing to take children to be "saved," no requirements were placed on them to ensure the well-being of the children, nor was there any follow-up on these placements. In the case of foster homes, the practice came first, and social policy developed later as the practice became institutionalized. The foster home system has become depended upon as an alternative to protect children from parental abuse and neglect. One writer comments on child abuse and social policy:

> The strategy of removing children from their parents stems from the illness conception of abuse. . . . If this is an accurate appraisal, then separation is necessary for the protection of the children. Much of the child abuse research supports this conception, indicating to child welfare policy-makers that removal is a necessary and appropriated form of intervention. Yet the research which supports this view is unreliable and should not be used to legitimate policy. If this conception is *incorrect*—and no one can determine that at this point—removal may be an undesirable method of intervention for several reasons. (Turbett 1979, 207)

J. Patrick Turbett (1979, 207) continues by pointing out the negative consequences to abused children who are involuntarily removed from their parents: the trauma of separation, adjustment to parent surrogates and new surroundings, and a set of factors that are emotionally and sociologically harmful to the children. He states: "In many cases, the negative effects of the solution outweigh the negative effects of the abuse. This is especially true when one notes that less than 1% of all abuse results in serious or permanent injury to the child" (Turbett 1979, 207, citing Gil 1970).[9]

Temporary placement in foster homes may be a valuable mode of intervention, removing children from their parents to protect them from abuse (Lipner 1979, 37). Meanwhile, many researchers (usually working within the medical model) are developing tests and measures to apply to parents to *predict* "abuse-proneness." The far-reaching implications of adopting screening techniques to test parents who have *not* abused their children should be obvious and sobering. But Inga-Britt Stibner concludes that it would be much better "if authorities work in a predictive and preventive way instead of not interfering until child abuse already is a reality" (1981, 3).

Most of the writers who are concerned about too much or the wrong kind of intervention are involved with the issue of child neglect, which constitutes the majority of all reported cases (AHA 1981). Studies of child neglect find substantial evidence of a relationship with poverty (AHA 1981; Giovannoni and Billingsley 1970; Kent 1976; Thomas 1974). From the vantage point of those who write about inappropriate intervention in child neglect cases, they see removal of children as a punitive social response to poor or ignorant parents. This is a much more expensive alternative than providing assistance such as financial aid, education, counseling, and support services (Thomas 1974). Professor of law Ellen Thomas begins an article with a 1966 quotation from Judge Justine Polier (Polier was a New York City Children's Court judge who wrote a book on institutional abuses of underprivileged children) that reads as follows:

> [M]others in the aid to families with dependent children (AFDC) program receive on the average less than $1 a day for each child. If we find that the home is inadequate . . . we remove the child to the home of a stranger . . . paying from public funds up to $7 a day. . . . If the child is removed to an institution, the institutions is paid up to $14 a day. Finally, if the child becomes emotionally disturbed, payments from public funds may range from $10 to $25 a day. Thus, the further the child is removed from his family, the more we are ready to pay for his support. (quoted in Thomas 1974, 60)

Although these figures are considerably less than they would be today (in 1979, average monthly AFDC payments for a family of three was $241, according to the Guttmacher Institute [1979, 27], which computes to approximately $2.66 per person per day), nevertheless they allow us to make a comparison of the relative costs for child maintenance in his or her own home and the escalating costs of alternatives. Thomas (1974, 47) tells about some welfare mothers who went to court in 1971 to try to obtain the same amount to care for their children at home as that paid to foster parents for childcare. One of the plaintiffs was receiving $48 a month for one child, whereas foster care payment would have been $105 a month. The case was dismissed, and the court's decision reads as follows:

> Some children must of necessity be placed in foster homes due to the financial inability of the parents to provide a suitable home. If such parents were to receive the same aid per child as foster parents receive there is no doubt that they could do a better job in supporting their children. Nevertheless, to give them that additional aid . . . would result in an overall reduction in money available for foster home care. (Thomas 1974, 61)

Despite this, no state legally permits children to be removed from parents on the basis of poverty alone but, "Nevertheless, children doubtless are, in practice, removed from their homes because the parents are poor" (Thomas 1974, 61). In his stinging indictment of involuntary removal, professor of law Hugo Martz argues against the practice, stating:

> Removal has been described as the coarsest implement used by the state on the family. Involuntary separation of the family is probably the most drastic disruption to family stability. It has been portrayed as a terrifying and painful experience which damages the child's personality and normal growth. The impact of removal is particularly traumatic for the child when it occurs precipitously and without preparation, which is often the case. In fact caseworkers and police officers often prefer surprise removal because the task is much easier. (Martz 1979, 91)

Documenting his comments throughout, Martz points to the effects on the children and their parents who are publicly stigmatized before friends, neighbors, and relatives. Poor parents are severely impacted; involuntary removal causes them "to feel as if they have been stripped of the last thing of value in their lives" (1979, 92). Finally, Martz concludes that the overall harm may exceed the damage the intervention sought to avoid and that, "clearly a child should not be removed except as a last alternative in extreme cases" (1979, 92). Other law experts agree with Martz (Thomas 1974, 17–73), although most of them admit that some circumstances warrant removal, but Martz advises ways in which to minimize the harm to parents and children should removal occur.

Once children have been removed from their homes, is the placement usually temporary, and do the parents receive help in the meantime to be able to take proper care of their children after their return? The answer to both questions is no, according to some writers (Chase 1976; Gil 1971, 1975; Thomas 1974). In the first place, foster home placement is *not temporary* for the children, because they tend to remain wards of the courts for years. They do however seem to be moved frequently from one family to another, so these *are* temporary families in that sense. Writer Naomi Chase (1976, 116–17) cites one study of 6,000 children in foster care and says that only one-fourth of these children were returned to their homes. James Kent (1976) studied children under court dependency for abuse (N 219) or neglect (N 159) in Los Angeles during November 1971. In his study, Kent found that 90 percent of the children had been under court jurisdiction for at least a year and 40 percent had been there for three or more years. Further: "About 80% of the children were still placed out of home at the time of follow-up, most of them in foster care (65%), some to relatives (28%), and the rest in institutions" (Kent 1976, 28).

Besides not being the short-term measure foster home care is usually expected to be, nor always being "in the best interests of the child" (Thomas 1974, 72), sometimes it hardly represents an environment superior to the one the child was removed from. Gil's study found that 2 percent of the abused children were living in foster homes, but in addition, 13 percent of them had been in foster homes or institutions at some point in their lives (1971, 640–41). Abuse does occur in replacement homes and if the removed children are later returned to parents, there can be additional abuse, particularly if the parents have received no assistance in the interim, which they usually do not. Within a two-month period in southern California, three children died from abuse in their foster homes, including one infant who died after being sodomized by her foster father.

These points are not intended to condemn foster home care; good foster homes are scarce, which makes it difficult for placement workers to effect a "perfect match." Many foster parents are kind, loving, and generous people, but in numerous ways they are abused by the "system." They are frequently not informed about special problems the children have in their backgrounds, and support services to guide and assist foster parents are often minimal or nonexistent. Generally, foster parents can obtain medical, dental, and optimetric care for the children at no cost, unlike the children's natural parents (except those natural parents who happen to be on welfare). However, payments for board and care are never generous and if the children have special needs or problems, it may be up to the foster parents' own resources to provide for them. The following case history is an example of how the system sometimes works.

> One woman became a foster mother to a beautiful girl of 14 when the woman was hardly old enough to be the child's natural mother. The girl came from an extremely deprived childhood, but she was assigned without any instructions or guidance about her special needs. The girl was described as "low normal intelligence," but because of frequent family relocations and lack of parental concern, she was only in the sixth grade, so she attended class with children much younger and smaller, setting her apart and making it difficult for her to develop friendships.
>
> After a time of loving care, the girl revealed that she had been sexually abused by several of her mother's boyfriends and raped by her older sister's husband some years earlier. Her mood swings were particularly difficult to deal with: she could

be laughing, warm, and responsive one minute and suddenly go into a sullen withdrawal and a refusal to speak to, or even acknowledge the presence of, any family member. Despite more than a year of pleading with the child welfare agency to arrange for professional therapy, the bureaucracy was unresponsive. A few days after her 17th birthday, she went for an intake screening to see a psychiatrist, but a week later she "eloped" at night with a 31-year-old man who had been meeting her at the school she attended. Since the welfare department did not seem to be actively seeking her return, the foster mother tried to investigate where she might have gone. The school's vice-principal admitted that school officials knew of the clandestine meetings at the school yard, skipping classes, and so forth, but they never reported these happenings because they assumed that since she was "only" a foster child, she was merely an "unpaid mother's helper." The vice-principal acted surprised that there could be an emotional or affectionate attachment between a foster parent and child. The caseworker at the child welfare department, confronted by the fact that the young girl never received the professional help she so obviously needed, shrugged off official responsibility by saying, "Unfortunately, our hindsight is better than our foresight."

It took more than a year before the case was closed. The man who had won the trust and affection of this child returned with her to the state, whereupon they were promptly stopped by the police. They had been under surveillance by the FBI because the child was a juvenile ward of the state; the man had violated the Mann Act, a federal statute; and he did not report his change of address to the draft board. Both were immediately taken into custody; the man was tried on charges of kidnapping and statutory rape with strong evidence provided by the FBI. The judge sentenced him the six months he had spent waiting for trial and put him on parole; the girl was institutionalized for three years, until she reached the age of 21.

The foster mother recalled later that when the caseworker first asked her to take the child, she protested that she was too young and inexperienced to mother a 14-year-old, but the worker said that at least this way the girl had a chance at a good life. Unfortunately, the odds were slim.

Some Innovative Responses

Parents Anonymous (PA), one of the most promising types of intervention for abusive families, was originated by an abusive mother and has been maintained ever since by abusive parents, with or without community social services support. Marcia Seal explains:

> P.A. was founded five years ago by a parent with an abuse problem. She had gone to some ten different social service agencies looking for help, but the only "help" available was the removal of her children. From her perception, such "help" was not helping her; professionals were avoiding dealing with her problem. Since then, chapters have developed throughout this country, and in other nations as well. (1980, 40)

Parents Anonymous is a free, self-help, nonprofit group. It offers real, practical help to parents who have abused their children in the past or fear they will do so in the future (Bacon 1977). In 1974 PA received a grant from the federal government. At that time it consisted of 60 loosely knit chapters, mostly in California, but by 1978 there were 800 chapters, at least one in every state, helping over 8,000 parents deal with their problems (MacFarlane and Lieber 1978). In one year alone, 200 new chapters were established, and the PA toll-free hot-line received over 11,000 calls in 1977. As a condition of continuing federal funds, PA members cooperated in an outside evaluation, and they rated it highly as a means of dealing with their abuse problems (MacFarlane and Lieber 1978). PA is a grass roots self-help program that works.

Unfortunately, it appears that the official, bureaucratic system is not as responsive and helpful to troubled families as one might expect, given the years of professional training received by personnel. Sometimes the best help comes from concerned and dedicated people, such as those in PA, who may or may not have professional training, who work outside the "establishment."

One very active PA group in north Orange County, California, is sponsored by an organization called *For Kids Sake*, founded by former law enforcement officer Jim Mead. Mead began fighting bureaucratic red tape when he physically removed an extremely abused little girl from an abusing foster home to his own home, with the approval and support of his wife, Pat Mead. Later, he found the girl's year-older brother in a mental institution, and took the boy to his home for a "visit" that became permanent, reuniting the siblings. Since then, their home has consistently had six children in residence.

For Kids Sake exists on a slim budget obtained from public donations and speaking engagements, assisted by a few professionals and many volunteers. For Kids Sake conducts parent groups at low cost, runs a 24-hour hotline, counsels abusive and neglectful parents, educates professionals in the criminal justice system and medicine as well as the general public, and maintains an extensive library for public, student, and professional use. Working outside the paid professional system, Mead has developed methods to help prosecutors build strong child sexual abuse cases that simultaneously protect victims from additional trauma.

The effective work performed by For Kids Sake is outside the mainstream of the helping professions. One problem of official agencies and their agents is discussed by John Holt (1974) when he discusses "help" and "helpers." He talks about the Good Samaritan who makes himself a permanent protector, something that can befall any service providers who feel that their superior knowledge and advanced training qualify them to know what is best for their clients, and as a result, they begin to *play God* with others' lives. These people begin to believe that their clients cannot get along without their help, and since they depend on helplessness, they create the helplessness they need. Holt (1974, 51) expresses his ideas in these words:

> The trouble with the helping professions—teaching, psychiatry, psychology, social work—is that they tend to attract people who want to play God. Some of them, perhaps most of them, want to play a kindly and benevolent God; others, and perhaps without knowing it, may want to play a harsh and cruel God, to take out of the hides of others what some earlier God took out of theirs. In either case the effect is much the same. For a person can only play God if he can make other people into his puppets. And, as the early Christians knew, it does not take much frustration to turn God into a Devil.

Holt gives several examples of workers and institutions that *play God* with the lives of helpless others, such as elderly people being forced to survive in worlds of pain and agony, and residents of a state "home" for retarded children (1974, 52–56). He cites an article about a child at one such institution for retarded children:

> A year ago on Christmas David . . . was burned on his face, ear, chest, and wrist. This Christmas he could look back on a year in which he had a fractured nose (which wasn't x-rayed until two days after the fracture), a fractured finger, and gashes requiring stitches on his head at least six times. When he was 10 years old, David, who is mentally retarded, was toilet-trained, ate politely, and talked happily with his parents. Now, after two years at Willowbrook, he "soils his bed," said his mother, "I

can't describe how he eats, I hate to sit next to him," and "he carries on conversations only with himself." (Holt 1974, 52)

Holt continues with examples of inhumane treatment of children in "protective" institutions, the victims of which he says, "No one is more truly helpless, more completely a victim, than he who can neither choose nor change nor escape his protectors" (1974, 52). Unfortunately, what Holt describes is all too true, as the following case illustrates.

> A soft-spoken, sad-eyed old lady brought her grandson, a child who was obviously severly developmentally handicapped, to a portrait studio for a Christmas photograph. The child ignored everything around him, seeming to be in a world of his own, never looking up at the adults around him. About eight years old, he muttered sounds to himself, but did not speak words, and nothing seemed to get his attention until his grandmother mentioned that he like singing commercials from television advertisements. The photographer and grandmother began singing some of the most common ones, and very quickly, the child's head raised and he began smiling and trying to repeat the sounds although the words were not intelligible: a happy child's face was successfully recorded on film. Once the singing stopped, his head fell down and he resumed his detached muttering.

> It was difficult to produce a pleasing portrait of this young child, because he had a number of bruises on his face, a clump of hair was missing from his head, and he had jagged, broken front teeth. The grandmother explained that his parents had placed him in a state institution for the retarded, where he was frequently beaten by unknown assailants, and "for his own protection" he was often put into a padded isolation cell. The staff had explained to the grandmother that the child was constantly being victimized by the other children, but she was convinced that his wounds were as likely to come from the staff as the other children. The grandmother described the padded cell in which the boy was locked, and how frantically he screamed at being "locked up like an animal." She cried as she explained that he had "gotten worse" since he was institutionalized, but there was no way she could prove her suspicions nor remove him from this dangerous place, since she was unable to care for him in her own home. While the adults talked, the child crawled around on his hands and knees, inspecting the floor, making sing-song sounds in a world all of his own.

It is hard to imagine that this child would not have fared better in a home setting, especially if parents or caring relatives were given support systems, home visits by social workers, financial assistance, and specialized training. And it would probably cost taxpayers much less for much more. Fortunately, citizens and public officials are trying desperately to right some of the wrongs of institutions for children (NCCAN 1978b).

SUMMARY

This chapter and the previous one looked at ideas proposed by professionals to explain maltreatment of children, and the evidence suggests that there is no single-factor explanation, nor a specific type of person most likely to be a child abuser or neglector. Carefully designed studies show very few differences between abusing and nonabusing families, when controlling for socioeconomic status. Abusing families are just like everyone else in many ways. Child maltreatment is an extremely complex problem that does not yield to simple solutions. This chapter looked at parents who maltreat children, particularly mothers, and the stresses that occur in single-parent, poor, and even two-parent nonpoor families. Then some clues were presented that in combination may help identify maltreating parents and their victims, followed by a short overview of reporting regulations. In some states, anyone must report suspicions, but in most states, certain professionals who work in close contact with children are required by law to report. Caution must be observed to avoid false reports, but to neglect reporting in the face of evidence is inhumanitarian. A child's life could hang in the balance. Factors must be carefully weighed, but the ultimate decision rests with the observers.

Next the debate on violent childrearing methods was presented. The evidence clearly shows that physical punishment does not correct behavior in the intended direction, but that it does teach unintended lessons. An informed and concerned public could begin by demanding that corporal punishment be banned in institutions such as schools, and also by parents, as has been done in Sweden (N. Feshbach 1980b).

Finally some "solutions" that society has offered to the problem of child maltreatment were discussed. In the past, people intervened to impose different types of social control, and sometimes their "cures" resulted in wholesale cruelty to others. People in the helping professions must be constantly on guard against the urge to "play God" with other people's lives, and to question their own motives when they tell other people what they *must* do. People from higher classes need to be careful to see that their class or cultural biases do not cloud their personal judgement of others. It is imperative to gain rapport with other people so that even if we do not *approve* of their behavior, at least we can try to *understand* it (which does not mean to condone it). Like children, many adults are anxious to please and to do right, but they should be *taught* what to do, rather than *forced* to do as others dictate.

Many parents who maltreat their children are ignorant: They are people who believe that since it is only "natural" to have children, they will naturally know how to raise their children. Some even believe that good parenting is "instinctive." They often have unrealistic expectations of their children's capacity to respond to them or to their wishes. To them, the baby who refuses to stop crying on command is "disobedient" or "hateful"; the infant who soaks a diaper just after being changed is "spiteful"; or the child slow to potty train is "stubborn"; and the child who spits food back at the parent is "mean and nasty." So many times an abusing parent complains, "S/he doesn't love me or s/he wouldn't do those things!"

Good parenting is *not* instinctive or even easy—it must be learned. Effective parenting courses should be taught in all schools beginning very early, but at the present time, good courses must be searched out at some churches or organizations, like For Kids Sake. Also, having others around to help explain and instruct helps immensely, but in our isolated nuclear family system, few young parents have older, experienced relatives available. Hot-lines for crisis calls and "warm-lines" for consultation can help overcome isolation. We do not have home visitors or visiting social workers on a large scale as they have in other countries in Europe and Scandinavia. On the other hand, there are some good parenting books available now (a list of them is found in the Appendix). However, when caretakers are misusing drugs, particularly alcohol, neglect is likely to occur. In those cases, the drug-dependency problem must be addressed first, and when that is under control, the parent/child problems can be approached.

Depending on one's definition of abuse or neglect, ample evidence is available that *most* parents abuse or neglect their children physically and/ or phychologically. What is needed is greater sensitivity to the issue and watching parent-child interactions in any public place. Observe children ignored at beaches or public swimming pools, at picnics were little arms are yanked, bodies pushed and spanked, and loud demands and insults hurled as children spill, fall, or refuse to respond quickly enough—all this constitutes *middle-range* abuse or neglect. See what happens to children on the streets, in supermarkets or stores, or even after church services, noting that this occurs in public, and imagine what happens in the privacy of the home.

This kind of parent-child interaction is viewed by most people as "normal," and they conceptually distinguish between what the writer calls "middle-range" and "severe-range" maltreatment: the kind that results in parents becoming publicly labeled and stigmatized as abusers and/or neglectors. Almost *anyone* who uses physical punishment can become a se-vere-range abuser—it is largely a matter of circumstance and perhaps even "luck"—one hard slap can result in a red-faced youngster, but the same intensity slap could result in serious injury or the child's death if the child falls onto a sharp object. If the child is injured from the slap, whether the parent is defined as a child abuser or merely the parent of a clumsy child subject to "accidental injury" may depend on whether the con-cerned parent takes the child to a private physician or to a public health facility.

Most people cling to the notion that child abusers/neglectors are differ-ent from themselves in very basic ways and that *they* could never, under any circumstances, do as *those* people have done! As an exercise in em-pathy, readers are invited to scan the following vignettes, to imagine themselves as the adults in the scenarios and to guess what they would do in these situations.

> You are isolated from friends and family, totally responsible for care of a teething baby who refuses to sleep at night, cries fre-quently and for long time periods at a pitch that grates your nerves and can be heard for long distances, and who rejects cuddling or being held. Add to that the recent death of a loved one (or current illness of one), and job frustrations or insecur-ity. You have not had a solid night's sleep in three days and you must get to work early in the morning for a meeting with your supervisor.

The stage is set here for child abuse or neglect. Lack of sleep can easily lead to heightened impatience (abuse) or depression (neglect). What would *you* do?

> You are a young welfare mother with three children whose husband left home after you became pregnant with the young-est child, now 14 months old, who has asthma. You could not afford the white dress and veil for your oldest child's First Holy Communion, but you wanted her to look as nice as the other children and not feel ashamed, so you made the sacrifice. She did not want to take off her pretty new clothes when she got home, and when you were trying to get her to do so, she ran past the kitchen stove, knocked the family's stew off the stove to the floor, and ran into the baby's highchair, knocking him over. In the ensuing mess, her new dress was torn.

What would *you* do? Would you be a "supermom," who would be able to cope with multiple disasters, or would you give in to your rage, frustration, and disappointment by lashing out at a young child who cannot (and who should not have to) understand your family's financial situation?

> You are a father of two young children who has been desperately searching for a job during three months of unemployment. Your wife has taken an all-night job, and you finally got an 8 o'clock appointment for a promising interview with a very good company. You must leave home by 7:30 at the latest, and although you wife usually arrives home by 7:00, today she is late. You are dressed in your only good suit and waiting by the door at 7:35.

What would *you* do? Would you give up the job interview good-naturedly, or would you leave the children home alone, assuming she will return soon? If you do, remember you could be subject to charges of neglect, and even worse, what if the children decided to play with matches? Would you take them along and leave them locked up in the car (assuming that you even have a car)? If you want to add to this scenario, imagine that your wife arrived home at 7:40, just after the baby threw up his breakfast all over your only good suit!

> You are a middle-class woman who married a man against your parents' approval and they have cut you out of their lives. Your husband has worked his way into corporate middle-management, but he keeps total control of the money. Last night he came home late and drunk, and beat you up again. This morning your 12-year-old raised a terrible scene because she can't have new designer jeans, and the 6-year-old screamed because dad ran over his bike in the driveway last night. They left for school and you just discovered that the 3-year-old painted the new wallpaper with vaseline.

What would *you* do? The point is that most of us *cannot* know what we would do unless we *are* in those particular situations—we can only guess. However, if we accept the idea that slapping and hitting are appropriate responses to stress and frustration, we *may* use physical force in moments of crisis. The best idea is to remember that *child abuse begins with the first slap.*

One of the most popular explanations found in the mass media and scientific writings is that violence is *bequeathed* from one generation to the next. The idea of the *cycle of violence* is explored in depth in the next chapter.

NOTES

1. The idea of "maternal instincts" was not even called into question by the writer of a recent textbook on marriage and family when he instructed college students that "certain fundamental sex-differentiated behaviors are androgen-programmed," for example: "Females have a greater predisposition to care for infants" (Udry 1974, 48).

2. Neglect is discussed in greater detail later. Likewise, sexual abuse of children—perpetrators of which are overwhelmingly male—is excluded here, because that topic is reserved for a later chapter. With the exception of the American Humane Association report (1980), all the studies reviewed in the following section excluded sexual abuse cases from their samples.

3. The differences came from computing families where fathers were present (in the 72 percent two-parent and 4 percent father-only families), and fathers "at risk" were 72 percent of the abusers. The 76 percent ratio came from eliminating the father-only families, and using the two-parent families only, where mothers and fathers were equally at risk.

4. However, Alfred Kadushin and Judith Martin comment that 40 percent of the families were single-parent, and 60 percent of the abusive mothers and 25 percent of the abusive fathers were raising their children as single parents (1981, 106).

5. Straus and his colleagues note that they "do not know exactly what respondents meant when they admitted that they 'beat up' their child, we do not know what objects they used when they hit a child (a pipe or a paddle?) . . ." (1980, 63).

6. Although fathers constituted only 22 percent of the neglectors, if we calculate their involvement on the basis of families in which they were present, which in that report was only 54 percent (50 percent two-parent and 4 percent father-only families), then fathers were 71 percent of the neglectors in the families in which they were "at risk."

7. Unemployment rates are traditionally underestimates, particularly for minorities and women, since they do not include never-employed people seeking employment, persons who have despaired and dropped out of the job-market, persons holding part-time employment who wish to work full-time, and underemployed persons.

8. "The Abused Child: A Clinical Approach to Identification and Management," written by Margaret C. McNeese, M.D. and Joan R. Hebeler, M.D.; illustrated by John A. Craig, M.D. *Clinical Symposia*, Volume 29, Number 5, 1977 can be purchased for $2.50 from CIBA Pharmaceutical Company, Medical Education Division, P.O. Box 12832, Newark, New Jersey 07101.

9. Severe injuries constituted one percent of the cases Gil (1970) studied, but of reported cases in two recent years, major physical injury to victims constitutes four percent (American Humane Association 1981, 1983).

7

Exploring the Popular Idea of a "Cycle of Violence"

Reviewing the literature on any type of family violence, whether it be child abuse and neglect, wife abuse, incest, or abuse of elderly parents, reveals an idea that is frequently advanced. Sometimes writers refer to a "cycle of violence," others use the phrase "intergenerational transmission of violence," still others adopt the slogan, "violence begets violence." The *cycle of violence* specifies a process whereby violent behavior is *bequeathed* from one generation to the next. It is undoubtedly the most frequently mentioned theoretical framework in the literature on family violence. Many writers make a blanket assumption that children who were abused in their homes of orientation or were witness to parental violence grow up to become juvenile delinquents/criminals and/or abusers/victims of violence in their homes of procreation (Barnett et al. 1980, 9, 29–31; Gelles 1974, 169–70, 1979, 95–119; Hunner and Walker 1981; Owens and Straus 1975, 193–211; Straus 1978, 453–54; Straus et al. 1980, 75, 97–122).

The popularity with which the notion of a cycle of violence has been accepted by many is expressed by sociologist Murray Straus, who writes: "The idea that child abusing parents were themselves victims of abuse, and that wife beating husbands come from violent families, is now widely accepted" (1981b, 5). The transmission of violent behaviors is generalized to explain all forms of family violence, including child, spouse, and parent abuse. In their insistence that being abused as a child leads to juvenile delinquency or adult criminality, some apply an *ex post facto* 'abused child' label onto samples obtained in prisons, detention centers, and hospitals (Bender and Curran 1974; Button 1973; Sendi and Blomgren 1975), while others trace reported cases of abused children through the juvenile justice system to see how many later end up charged with crimes (Alfaro 1978).

Moving beyond the writings of social and behavioral scientists and into the community where victims and abusers come into contact with persons in the legal and helping professions, there is an unquestioning acceptance of the existence of a cycle of violence. Child-abuse programs and intervention modalities adopt the position that parents who were abused as children are high-risk parents. Whenever there is a media presentation on child abuse, whether it be fiction or documentary, references are made repeatedly that child abusers were themselves victims of parental abuse. Even though some social scientists are still debating the question, most persons outside academia seem to view the matter as absolute fact: Children who live in violent homes are going to be juvenile delinquents as adolescents, or else perpetrators/victims of violence as adults!

It is possible that many professionals working with victims and perpetrators of family violence are so unquestioning about the validity of the cycle of violence because of their keen desire to "do something" about it, and there *is* some common sense appeal to the slogan. It is an attention-getter that the media employ, like "Smokey the Bear." It *sounds* intuitively reasonable, and if it transmits an emotional appeal to masses of people, even if not factually accurate, what can be the harm? If the phrase "cycle of violence" raises money for child-abuse organizations or other humanitarian causes—why not use it—whether or not it has been substantiated?

THE IMPORTANCE OF THE QUESTION: FACT OR FICTION?

In the current state of the art in family violence research, there is no way that a cycle of violence can be proved or disproved; therefore, it is a supposition but not a theory. As explained earlier, we do not have reliable base rates of how many adults in the population were abused as children; in fact, there is no consensus on a precise definition of abuse and/or neglect. We cannot learn with certainty how many of the present category of parents were themselves abused, or lived in violent households, and who are now nonviolent, law-abiding adults. Conversely, we do not have reliable statistics on the proportion of adults who matured in nonviolent homes, but who got into trouble with the law as juveniles, or who now terrorize their spouses and/or children.

Almost any research report on child abuse and neglect contains at least one reference to a cycle of violence. Like the theory of individual psychopathology, it has endured over the years and only a few writers have seriously explored its validity or offered any kind of challenge to it. The popularity of the "cycle" has reached all levels of our society, professionals and nonprofessionals alike, and there are many people who live with the fear that they are *predestined* to become violent with people they love. In the course of the writer's study of woman battering, many people were encountered who were fearful of enjoying intimate relationships with others because they had grown up in violent homes. These people had not behaved violently yet, but they were holding themselves back from enjoying life in certain ways, because they feared their own capabilities for violence, which they abhorred.

Some findings of family violence research that explore the issue of a possible cycle of violence are reviewed next, divided into the claims made about the effects of child abuse on victims. This review will show that a simple, nondiscretionary *cycle* is very doubtful, but there is greater evidence of bequeathing violence in some families when a more focused model is employed.

"ABUSED CHILDREN BECOME ABUSERS," OR DO THEY?

Some people whose lives have been directly influenced by the idea of a cycle of violence have been described in detail earlier (Pagelow 1981a, 1982a). People who recall pain and the terror of abuse from their own childhoods are likely to postpone parenthood, or fear becoming parents because they do not want to inflict suffering on their own children. In one case, a young woman fearing motherhood, pregnant with her first child, had been beaten by her husband and fled to a shelter. She expressed great fear and concern that she was certain to become an abuser of her child, since she had been abused as a child. She said she had seriously considered putting her child up for adoption so she could never do it harm, until she found that there was a home nearby where she could go to await the birth of their child and continue residency for six months to learn parenting skills and to adjust to motherhood. She asked, "What exactly are the chances that I'll become an abuser? How many abusers were abused when they were children?"

This is a reasonable question to ask. A search of the literature reveals that many writers repeat the claim, but few produce any sound empirical evidence to support it (Chambers 1980; Chase 1976; Gelles 1979; NCCAN 1975a). Most writers have done no original research but have gathered reports in the field and repeated findings and assumptions from these secondary sources. Michael Freeman (1979, 21–32) presents a detailed critique of the literature in which he objects to a lack of a common definition and scientifically sound research methods, small and nonrepresentative samples, biased data, unsupported generalizations of findings, researcher bias, and studies that begin and end with "relatively untested commonsense assumptions." In essence, many writers report impressions, informal observations, opinions, and ideas as *fact* without strong empirical evidence to support them, which F. G. Bolton and his colleagues (1981) call "think pieces."

Examining the Evidence

An early article asking "does violence breed violence?" in its title (Silver et al. 1969b), looked at the hospital records of 34 abused children and found evidence that four (12 percent) of the abusers had been abused as children. The article by Silver, Dublin, and Lourie will be discussed in greater detail in the section about child abuse and delinquency, but it must be noted here that these authors gave a "yes" answer to their question, despite the fact that 88 percent of these abused children had parents for whom no evidence could be found that they had been abused in their own childhoods. Their 12 percent finding is close to David Gil's (1970, 1971) finding that 11 percent of the abusers in his study were abused in their own childhoods.

The Brandt Steele and Carl Pollock article (1974) that was originally published in 1968 is frequently cited by writers as evidence of a *legacy of violence,* but the authors recognized limitations in their work and warned against generalizing their findings. These two psychiatrists said that their study group of parents was "representative only of a group of parents who had attacked children and who came by rather 'accidental' means under our care because we were interested in the problem" (Steele and Pollock 1974, 90).

There is not sufficiently strong evidence in the Steele and Pollock report to justify the prevailing belief in what Straus (1981b, 5) calls the "violence begets violence theory." Steele and Pollock found that abusive parents came from families that could be described as authoritarian, demanding, unrewarding, and from homes where they were deprived of warm, loving, supportive relationships (1974, 97–98). The only statement referring to actual abuse of these parents as children is: "Several had experienced severe abuse in the form of physical beatings from either mother or father; a few reported '*never having had a hand laid on them*'" (1974, 97, emphasis added). "Several" out of 60 hardly seems conclusive evidence to support such widespread insistence that one need only look at the abused child's parent to see another abused child. Yet most writers who offer the Steele and Pollock work as support for the cycle of violence theme ignore the fact that *a few* parents in the study had never experienced even the "normal" physical punishment from parents most American children receive. Further, they take terms such as "authoritarian" and "criticism" and make assumptions not supported by Steele and Pollock's words that these are synonymous with abusive.

Vincent Fontana and Esther Robison (1976) studied 62 mothers who came to an outpatient clinic and they repeat the "abused-abusers" theme, but they present no data to support it. They only note that the "majority of the mothers reported being severely abused and neglected during their early childhood" and that all came from homes "involving violence" (1976, 763). Many writers accept the idea to the point that it appears to be taken as a given, whether or not they can offer empirical evidence to support it (Crozier and Katz 1979, 213; NCCAN 1979, 5; O'Toole et al. 1981, 10; Steele 1974; ten Bensel and Berdie 1976, 456).

Not all writers are totally unquestioning; a few check their data to see if they offer support. The Child Welfare League study of 171 abusive and/or neglectful parents found that the primary complaint of their own childhoods was "excessive restrictions" (Shapiro 1979, 34). The report states: "Descriptions of their childhood experiences varied from the relatively comfortable to the severely traumatic, but histories of child abuse were not frequently reported" (Shapiro 1979, 38). Although they criticize previous reports, Ross Rizley and Dante Cicchetti appear to believe that there is a "transmission of different types of child maltreatment" (1981b, 7), and they set up a model to explain how this transmission can be broken. Roy Herrenkohl and his colleagues designed a study to test the intergenerational transmission of abuse theory and their findings offer some support, but the strongest support comes from respondents in their sample who had *multiple* abusive caretakers (Herrenkohl et al. 1981, 5). Their tables show that 62 percent of the parents who admitted using severe or abusive measures with their own children had *not* been abused as children by any caretaker, but at the same time, they comprised 44 percent of the abusive parents (Herrenkohl et al. 1981, 5). In other words, the majority of abusive parents had not been abused in their childhoods, while the majority of parents who had been abused did not abuse their own children (although a large percentage of them did).

A recent report on a longitudinal study of abuse victims documents the difficulties involved in locating only 313 victims out of an early sample of 2,400 victims (Smith et al. 1982). Carefully pointing out potential bias in their statistics, these researchers found that only 10 of the formerly abused children out of the 313 had become suspects of abusing their own children, as compared to none of the control subjects (Smith et al. 1982, 29). The suspected victimizers were young, predominantly female, poor, and minority members; all these characteristics are likely to subject them to easier scrutiny and reporting by social service agencies (Pagelow 1982b). However, since the study's sample was drawn from abuse victims of 10 to 25 years earlier, some of them may not yet have reached parenthood, and therefore were not "at risk" at the time of the study. Smith, Bohnstedt, and Grove (1982, 31) say:

> We had hypothesized more adult suspects among early victims. However age was undoubtedly a factor affecting our inter-generational repeat victimization analysis. The current data files include many early victims just now approaching adulthood and we are arranging for further longitudinal tracking. (Smith et al. 1982, 31)

In what may be one of the best tests of this model so far, Dorothy Miller and George Challas (1981) conducted a longitudinal study of parents who had been abused, comparing them to a control group of parents who were not abused when young. Measuring their 118 respondents on numerous dimensions, they found that abusers in their sample come from multiproblem families, suffered trauma in childhood, have poor socialization, financial dependency, and emotional instability. Using scales designed to predict which parents were most likely to abuse their children, they found that 24 percent of the abused persons were ranked as highly potential abusive parents compared to 6 percent of the nonabused group. Their findings are summarized in these words:

> Persons who were abused as children tended to fall more heavily into these categories—but being abused as a child is not the *only* predictor of a parents' potential for child abuse. A life of social and psychological disorder must accompany this parental outcome. In conclusion, we must recall that 45 percent of the persons abused as children were rated as not abusive to their own children, while 47 percent of persons who were *not* abused as children do have some potential for child abuse. . . . While child abuse casts a long shadow, it does not determine the next generations' fate, but poverty, ignorance, and unstable parental careers may. (Miller and Challas 1981, 8)

This seems to be the latest trend among researchers who adopt the theoretical viewpoint of a cycle of violence. They now study multiple factors in families of origin besides parental violence (Ellis 1981; Gelles 1981). However, to summarize the current state of the art, most reports on child abuse and neglect are about relatively small, focused samples; a few studies are retrospective; and only two have been located thus far that are longitudinal. Only one early study with a large sample reported the percentage of abusers who had been abused as children, and that was a mere 11 percent (Gil 1970, 1971), which means that no evidence of a cycle of violence was found for 89 percent of the parents who abused their children. Reasons why the idea of a cycle is so popular among service providers, academics, and government leaders, despite lack of strong empirical evidence, will be suggested in the summary section of this chapter.

"ABUSED CHILDREN BECOME DELINQUENTS," AND, IF THEY DO, WHY?

Many of us want to predict human behavior, particularly when it comes to deviance. Social and behavioral scientists study culturally defined "deviants" with the hope of isolating facts about these people, and with the hope that their individual and collective histories that can explain their behavior. The state and its agents of social control have a vested interest in obtaining answers that may be used in designing social policy. Since the "discovery" of child abuse in the United States in the 1960s (Pfohl 1977), reasons for its causes have been demanded by policy makers for purposes of control and prevention, and searched for by scientists. When prisoners and violent persons began claiming that they had been abused as children, policy makers became keenly interested in long-range effects of child abuse.

The claim very frequently encountered in both popular and scientific literature on child maltreatment is that abused and neglected children are expected to become delinquents at adolescence and/or become criminal adults. These ideas have been accepted almost without question by the general public, as well as by many practitioners in the helping professions and some persons in the criminal justice system. If they are found to have strong empirical support, the mandate seems clear for agents of social control to take swift and decisive action to prevent child maltreatment and later deviant behavior, then the model tested by social scientists should be expanded to include other variables, and social control agents should rethink methods currently in vogue for prediction and prevention. There is a real need to examine the present state of knowledge so that intervention and prevention policies can be appropriate and effective.

However, even if a strong relationship is established as existing between childhood violence and later deviant behavior, this cannot be interpreted to mean there is necessarily a *causal* relationship. Such a blanket assumption would be hazardous because there are too many possible intervening variables that can influence outcomes not included in simple "cause and effect" models. Most responsible writers have called for multivariate models, which offer the greatest promise for understanding such complex issues (Martin 1981).

Nevertheless, some reports have lent support to "reform programs" that turned out to be another form of punitive social control specifically aimed at the most powerless segment of society: minorities and the poor.

Child abuse and neglect charges are more easily lodged against poor parents who disproportionately appear on official records, and it is children from poor families who can most easily be traced through agency records to adolescence (Pagelow 1982b). For example, Peggy Smith and her fellow researchers (1982) found they were unable to locate and follow up on a higher percentage of abuse victims from middle-class families than those from lower SES families. It is also clear that the juvenile justice system employs the same screening system as the adult criminal system whereby persons of higher social class are much more likely to "drop through the cracks," so that minority and poor children are also overrepresented in official delinquency records.

This section focuses on possible relationships between child maltreatment (abuse and neglect) and delinquency. It would be interesting, particularly for social learning theorists, to narrow delinquency to violent behavior only, but it is difficult to differentiate from reports the proportion of offenders who are adjudicated on violent crimes as compared to property crimes and status offenses. The majority of children who are labeled delinquent are charged with status offenses (acts that would not be criminal if committed by adults); and of the crimes committed by juveniles, the majority are property crimes, rather than violent crimes. Violent juveniles comprise the very smallest proportion of incarcerated delinquents.

Examining the Evidence

A review of the literature reveals many conflicting theoretical viewpoints and research reports that contain the problems mentioned earlier. In addition to the shortcomings in the professional literature, an important factor is the lack of accurate baseline data on abuse/neglect/delinquency. We do not know how much of each actually occurs that is never reported and never comes to the attention of officials and researchers. The cases that come to our attention and scrutiny are very likely only the "tip of the iceberg," and we have no way of knowing in what ways known cases differ from the unreported, unsuspected cases. These points should be kept in mind before drawing inferences from the "findings" reported here.

Some writers take a theoretical leap from childhood violence experience to adult violence (Burt 1978; Owens and Straus 1975; Swartz 1981), whether to violence against others or violence against one's self as in self-mutilation (Bach-y-rita and Veno 1974; Ross 1980). Some propose that neglect, rather than overt aggression against children, leads them into criminal acts, whereas abuse is more likely to lead to rebellion, and thus to status offenses (Glasser and Garvin 1981).

One group of researchers suggest that victims of child abuse are less likely than their nonabused siblings to commit aggressive acts, and their data support this hypothesis (Bolton et al. 1977). Bolton, Reich, and Gutierres postulated that abuse victims would be less likely to imitate aggressive parental behavior because they would not perceive it as rewarding behavior; conversely, their siblings who only witnessed it but were not targets would perceive aggression in a more favorable light and thus imitate it. Their data appear to offer support, because only 7.8 percent of the victims were reported for aggressive crimes whereas their siblings had a much higher rate of 17.2 percent (Bolton et al. 1977). *Aggressive crimes* refer to such acts as fighting, vandalizing, breaking and entering, and purse snatching. In addition, by comparing delinquents from abusive and nonabusive families, they found that the victims of abuse were extremely likely to be reported for escapist crimes (92 percent), and their siblings less likely (83 percent). *Escapist crimes* refer to behavior such as runaway, truancy, keeping late hours, and so forth. The control delinquents who came from nonabusive homes were even less likely to be reported for escapist crimes (77 percent for the delinquents and 69 percent for their siblings). Looked at in another way, these data argue against the cycle theory, because nonabused delinquents were reported for aggressive crimes more than the abused.

Conversely, another research team studied 73 violent families and found that children who are targets of abuse, especially when the aggressors are *both* mother and father, are much more likely to engage in deviant behavior than their siblings (Pfouts et al. 1981). Pfouts, Schopler, and Henley define deviant behavior on two scales: social and emotional behavior, and "other" (undefined). Most of the social behaviors are nonaggressive, but 30 percent of 106 children were reported to have engaged in assault (compared to 40 percent for truancy). On the emotional behavior scale, the highest percentages were in depression (64 percent) and anxiety (66 percent). In reality, it seems perfectly normal that abused children would be depressed and anxious; in fact, to *not be* depressed and anxious would be far more deviant (these children were residing in their abusive homes when the scales were administered). Incidentally, all of these 73 families were economically deprived and had a multitude of problems. This is compatible with Elizabeth Elmer's (1977) findings of "sadness and anxiety" common to both abused and nonabused children. These children had another commonality: they all lived in poor families.

Another study obtained a sample of 105 children referred to juvenile court. Investigating the backgrounds of these "delinquents," researchers found that 20 children had parents with criminal records while the parents of the other 85 had no criminal records (Lewis et al. 1979a). Next, researchers Lewis, Shanok, and Balla examined the children's medical histories and found significant differences between the groups. They "found a strong association between paternal criminality and serious medical problems in these delinquent children" (Lewis et al. 1979a, 288). The differences were most striking before the age of four, and they state that injuries at this stage are most likely to have lasting effects on children's adaptation to school, peers, and society in general (1979a, 291). Further, Lewis et al. state that they knew that some of these children of criminal fathers had been severely beaten and/or tortured, and that the fathers had engaged in reckless and dangerous behavior, so their children may have modeled this type of behavior, causing even further injury to themselves (1979a, 291). In a similar study, Dorothy Lewis and Shelley Shanok compared delinquent and matched nondelinquent children and found more evidence of medical trauma among the delinquent sample (1979, 214). Unfortunately, neither of these studies with the same principal author tells the sex ratio of the children under investigation.

As noted by critics of the child abuse and deviancy literature, many writers generalize from very small samples. The Bolton et al. (1977) study mentioned earlier is one of the very few exceptions; theirs was a relatively large sample of 774 abused children. On the other hand, J. W. Reich (1978) searched through official records to locate 20 sexually abused children to see if they committed escapist or aggressive crimes. By comparing them to some nonsexually abused delinquents, it was found that the victims had been charged with escapist crimes more often than the nonabused. Lewis et al. (1979a, 1979b) studied 97 juveniles charged with serious offenses; Goodwin, Simms, and Bergman (1979) studied six female adolescents; and M. Gross (1979) studied four young females. These last two studies looked for a relationship between incest and "hysterical seizures."

Studying homicidal youth, Charles King (1975) had only nine persons in his sample; S. H. Frazier (1974), studied 31 convicted murderers for a "premurder personality." Following this trend, Ismail Sendi and Paul Blomgren (1975) obtained ten adolescent murderers, ten who had threatened or attempted homicide, and ten hospitalized "controls." This study found eight environmental factors in the homicidal youths' backgrounds that "predisposed" them to violence. Still others conclude from studies of very small samples of persons convicted of violent crimes that they frequently had been abused as children (Bender and Curran 1974; Duncan et al. 1958; Easson and Steinhilber 1961). William Easson and Richard Steinhilber (1961), for example, made clinical examinations of seven boys who attempted murder and one murderer. They found clear evidence that two of the eight boys had been abused by a parent, and they "suspected" abuse in the histories of three others. Other writers take a look at people who commit crimes and search for factors in childhood to account for their deviance. One such study is that of 29 fathers convicted of filicide; 12 (41 percent) "remembered parental violence (two from their mothers)" (Scott 1973, 203). Another study of six male adults convicted of murder found that four had been abused by one parent with noninterference by the other (Duncan et al. 1958).

One of the earliest articles on child abuse is titled "Violence Breeds Violence—Perhaps?" (Curtis 1963. The title of a later article begins with the question "Does Violence Breed Violence?" (Silver et al. 1969b). Both articles base their affirmative answer to their title questions on very shaky evidence: The few isolated clinical case reports from various sources cited above. Interestingly, the small sample of convicted murderers cited in the George Curtis article (also in Silver et al. and many others) is a reference to the 1958 article by Glen Duncan and his colleagues, which was the basis for Vincent Fontana's seminal and very influential statement:

> Studies by these physicians [Duncan et al.] lead to the conclusion that among murderers, remorseless physical brutality at the hands of the parent had been a constant experience. . . . It would seem that imitation and identification with violent parents can lead to the adult abnormal behavior beginning with the physical abuse of individuals and leading to ultimate [sic] murder. Dr. Carl Menninger believes that every criminal was an unloved and maltreated child. (Fontana 1964, 19)

It is ironic that a report published in 1958, based on a sample of only six convicted male adult murderers, was used to provide "hard evidence" that abused children later commit crimes of violence. Yet that claim was repeated in 1963 and in 1969, although by 1964 Fontana had already generalized four out of six murderers to "every criminal" believed to be a maltreated child!

One of the two articles to answer "yes" to its title question, "Does Violence Breed Violence?" written by Larry Silver and his colleagues (1969b), is cited above and earlier in this chapter. These writers did a follow-up study on victims identified through hospital records four years after the initial report of abuse, and found evidence of continuing abuse of the children (1969b, 405–6). As support for their conclusion that violence breeds violence, these authors state that 7 of the 34 abused children "had already come to the attention of the court because of delinquency" (Silver et al. 1969b, 406). As evidence, the authors sketch six of the "delinquent" cases, all of which were status offenses except for one 13-year-old violent offender. Based on this flimsy evidence, the article concludes: "Violence does appear to breed violence. A longitudinal study and review of family backgrounds over three generations shows that some abused children become the abusive parents of tomorrow" (Silver et al. 1969b, 407).

In investigations of self-mutilation, criminologist Robert Ross (1980) studied 120 girls incarcerated in a Canadian "training school," most of whom were admitted as "unmanageable," and he found 96 (80 percent) had *carved* themselves.[1] *Unmanageable* means that these young women were "status" offenders. In essence, the majority of the girls, 12 to 17 years of age, had been found guilty and given indeterminate sentences for such acts as "habitual truancy, alcohol and/or drug abuse, running away from home, and unacceptable sexual behavior" (Ross 1980, 34). The report indicates that there was a highly significant relationship between histories of child abuse and self-inflicted "carving," since 67 percent had been victims of violence by parents or parent figures (Ross 1980, 35). However, these findings should be viewed with caution because the 120 girls were not randomly selected; they were chosen for study because they were members of a behavioral modification project. Ross properly warns readers of these limitations, by saying:

> It must be emphasized that this is a highly selected group of subjects. They constituted the most severe behavior problem cases in the training school system. They are *not* representative of the larger population of delinquent girls, and one *cannot* assume that the incidence of childhood violence in these cases indicates the incidence of child abuse in female adolescent offenders. (1980, 35)

In another article, Alan Button (1973) describes an experimental clinical study of 90 incarcerated boys and 90 controls, initiated with the theoretical assumption that "violence begets violence." He reports that the convicted youngsters came from extremely violent homes and that "They have become, in their teens, dehumanized" (Button 1973, 37). However, he does not provide any statistical data; Button uses only descriptive terms to illustrate his conclusions plus a few quotations from the boys.

Brandt Steele, a pioneer in the study of child abuse, writes that "almost without exception" (1974, 3) abusing parents were themselves abused as children, yet he admits that our knowledge of how many abused children become juvenile delinquents is very scanty. Steele notes that we are limited to retrospective histories and that "nobody has ever followed abused, neglected children on into adult life in a longitudinal study." The situation described by Steele in 1974 has hardly changed. A recent book looks for associations between child abuse and juvenile delinquency, but not one of its 19 articles reports on a longitudinal study (Hunner and Walker 1981). In a few follow-up studies, researchers tried to locate as many children as possible who had been reported earlier as abused, but there were many lost cases, and the sample sizes all tended to be small. Elmer (1977) obtained 17 children eight years later; Friedman and Morse (1974) located 41 cases five years later; and Martin and Beezley (1977) studied 50 cases four and a half years later. However, the sample selection process is not reported, so it is unknown what percent of the abused population they drew. These were efforts in the right direction, but they still do not provide a follow-up to adulthood as suggested by Steele (1974).

On the other hand, a report to the New York Assembly from the Select Committee on Child Abuse (Alfaro 1978) describes a large data base of two samples retrospectively studied. The first sample includes 5,136 children whose families were reported in 1952 or 1953 for suspected child abuse or neglect; the children were tracked through state agencies to see if they had subsequent court contact. The second sample includes 1,963 children officially reported as delinquent or ungovernable in the early 1970s whose histories were traced backward for any *prior* records of their being abused or neglected (Alfaro 1978, 5–6).

One of the findings about the second group states: "Delinquent children who were reported as abused or neglected tend to be more violent than other delinquents" (Alfaro 1978, 16). However, the next finding seems to contradict this when it states: "Child maltreatment cannot be used as an indicator or predictor of a particular type of juvenile misbehavior" (1978, 16–17). The latter statement is based on the fact that out of the first sample of more than 5,000 reportedly abused or neglected children, only 16 percent had later been referred to juvenile court (Smith et al. 1980, 30). The slim differences in violence between maltreated and nonmaltreated juveniles are discussed below. Alfaro is extremely cautious about interpreting his data to mean a cause-and-effect relationship. He expresses the idea that childhood maltreatment may "predispose" some children toward later "delinquency or ungovernability" more than others, but he also recognizes other factors that intervene. Despite this, a report from the California Commission on Crime Control and Violence Prevention (1982, 20) states that Alfaro's findings "indicate a strong association between being abused and neglected as a child and subsequent criminal and violent behavior."

Another team (Smith et al. 1980) studied the Alfaro report and notes that the data show there was only a 4.5 percent greater likelihood that maltreated children were violent than their nonmaltreated peers, hardly a major difference in outcomes. However, Charles Smith and his associates comment: "Although Alfaro did not determine the statistical significance, it is likely that the difference between the two groups is significant because of the large number of cases involved in his sample" (Smith et al. 1980, 136). Despite such small differences, they conclude: "While the evidence is by no means conclusive, it again adds weight to the evidence of a link between abuse, neglect, and juvenile delinquency" (Smith et al. 1980, 136). This statement summarizes the way many writers approach the complicated issue of child abuse/neglect/delinquency: They tend to look for whatever evidence can be found and start accumulating it, bit by bit, until finally it sums to a total that supports preconceived notions. Some do not introduce any empirical findings that argue against their theoretical assumptions.

There is one recent study, however, that seems to have overcome most of the limitations and methodological deficiencies of many of the others mentioned above. Although its major drawback is heavy reliance on official data, the longitudinal study by Peggy Smith and her colleagues (1982) of neglected, physically abused, and sexually molested children is rigorously designed and employs control samples. In addition, the authors readily point out limitations and potentials for bias that are introduced because of cases lost. Out of 2,400 victimization cases reported in San Diego between 1955 and 1975, only 313 cases were selected for study (Smith et al. 1982, 11). Cases lost to the sample consisted of victims who left the community; some could not be tracked; some cases had been purged from police files in 1962; and classification problems prevented retrieval of others.

Nevertheless, using records from a number of cooperating community agencies and a variety of screening and analysis techniques, these researchers checked demographic features, recidivism rates, recidivism by type of injury, family mobility, and so forth. When they looked at arrest records of victims and controls, they found that more of the victims (34 percent) than controls (23 percent) had been arrested, but arrests were associated with poverty since "among low SES victims and comparisons the arrest rates are not significantly different" (Smith et al. 1982, 29). On the other hand, arrest rates for medium SES victims were higher than their matched controls. Unfortunately, it cannot be determined at this time whether these arrests were for violent crimes or property crimes. As the authors say:

> The above figures do not differentiate juvenile delinquency records from adult arrests, number of arrest, and type of offenses although that data has been collected and computerized and awaits analysis. It is our subjective impression that victims were more often involved in repeat arrests for more serious offenses. (Smith et al. 1982, 29)

It will be interesting to learn what further analysis shows on type of offenses and ages at arrests.

A higher percentage of abuse victims still attending public school were found to have behavioral problems, but the sample of these victims was reduced to 76 children (Smith et al. 1982, 31–32). Of all the problems noted, only one category indicated violent behavior, and there, 9 percent of the victims, compared to 1 percent of the controls, were located in school guidance files. "Blind" ratings[2] by school nurses and counselors indicated victims fell below controls in academic achievement, emotional stability, peer/social adjustment, and health (Smith et al. 1982, 33–36). Since these children were victims of different kinds of maltreatment, it would be helpful to learn which type of victimization was represented at higher levels in these categories of maladjustment, but that information is not presented. Overall, there was an approximately equal percentage of victims rated on school achievement as being high achievers (21 percent) or low achievers (22 percent); the balance of 58 percent received mixed ratings (Smith et al. 1982, 35–36).

In summary, what this investigation pointed out was that the most "problematic" children came from the most problematic families: families suffering from "a variety of physical, social, financial, and emotional problems" (Smith et al. 1982, 39). The multiproblem families of the victimized children showed a clear relationship with socioeconomic status, family structure, social deviance, and social stress, and the authors see subsequent maladjustment of children "as products of the entire family disorganization, not just as consequences of the victimization incidents, per se" (Smith et al. 1982, 43). This report offers empirical support for theoretical assumptions expressed in an earlier article (Pagelow 1982a), suggesting that victims' own behavior in response to public disclosure and stigmatization may generate a self-fulfilling prophesy, at least as much as the victimization itself.

The researchers offer suggestions that chronic, multiple problem families cannot respond to short-term efforts, but require long-term intervention strategies aimed at both the victimized children and at "strengthening the family unit" (Smith et al. 1982, 44). Throughout their report, the relationship between social adjustment and socioeconomic status seems to be of vital importance. Along those same lines, some important factors noted in the Alfaro (1978) report include the following: "Apparently, the socio-economic status of children and families is not considered important enough to be recorded in these records, and, one must assume, to be considered in devising treatment plans" (1978, 28). As for the "treatment" these New York families received, it was "either placement or casework supervision, and for most cases, nothing else." Most child protective services are directed at the parents to get them to stop maltreatment, but "Little is done to help the child overcome the experience . . ." (1978, 30). Alfaro talks about the label assigned to the children that may well affect their later lives, the "hodge-podge" of uncoordinated programs, and the lack of intensive, long-term help given these families. He concludes: ". . . there was no long-term commitment to supporting families with an organized array of services to help them overcome their problems" (Alfaro 1978, 33). It will be interesting to learn what the Smith et al. (1982) research team discovered regarding the types and extent of intervention services received by victims and their families in San Diego between 1955 and 1975.

As is noted below, even when "help" is given, sometimes parents and children are even worse off than others who receive no services (de Lone 1979, 96).

What Kinds of "Help" Do Maltreated Children Receive?

As Alfaro (1978) notes, the usual response to disclosure of child maltreatment is casework supervision[3] or placement in foster homes in cases where officials believe children are in serious danger (Thomas 1974). Because there is usually a shortage of good foster homes, especially for minority children, many are placed instead into group homes. If the children have special problems or do not adapt well to their new environments, they may be rejected by their new caretakers or run away, which frequently results in their being transferred to institutions. There can be little doubt that this is the worst form of caretaking possible. So-called "training schools" do little more than train youngsters into deviant behavior. The majority of adolescents sentenced to detention halls or camps are *status offenders*. In other words, the behavior for which they are being punished would not be considered a crime under laws for adults.

Jane Latina and Jeffrey Schembera (1976) estimate that there were 100,000 youngsters held in correctional institutions in 1975, at a cost of $30 per day or more. They point out that 23 percent of the boys and 70 percent of the girls are guilty of such "crimes" as running away, truancy, "incorrigibility," or they simply must be temporarily removed from their homes (1976, 45). These writers describe a system of volunteer homes on a short-term basis, devised to keep status offenders from incarceration in security facilities. This program included screening, training, and considerable support services for the caretakers, plus community support. In four and a half months, over 1,000 children were temporarily lodged in homes instead of being sent to detention; and at the same time, the State of Florida saved at least $60,000 (for foster care at $8 per day) or about $250,000 if the same number of days were charged for secure detention (Latina and Schembera 1976, 48).

Another innovative program, a kind of "halfway" effort for boys already held in an institution, is described by Starr Huffman (1975). This system allowed boys to spend weekends in foster homes as a "step out of the institution" and to gain confidence in establishing close relationships since, "Many boys had been through a long and damaging series of foster homes . . ." (1975, 351). Unlike most foster parents, the ones in this program received close support from caseworkers on an individualized basis.

These unusual programs called for approaches that benefited a few out of the many children shuffled about in the system. What is the process whereby maltreated children enter the "system" that is supposed to protect them? Their cases are brought before juvenile court, which was established to protect children from adult criminal courts and jails. As Ruby Takanishi says, "The juvenile court system was created to separate children from adult institutions to create more humane and corrective procedures" (1978, 10). The other side of the coin of this benevolent act is that, in the process, children lost basic rights guaranteed to adults under the constitution and were subjected to "unbridled discretion," "arbitrariness," and the "absence of procedural rules" (Takanishi 1978, 10).

The Juvenile Justice System

The first juvenile court was established in 1899 in Chicago after almost 30 years of reform efforts by child-saving organizations (Platt 1969, 134), but 83 years later, a census of local jails on June 30, 1982, shows that almost 2,000 juveniles were in custody (U.S. Department of Justice 1983). That some juveniles could still be incarcerated in adult jails would shock the warden of Joliet State Penitentiary in Illinois, who called for the removal of children from jails in 1899, saying: "You can not take a boy of tender years and lock him up with thieves, drunkards and half-crazy men of all classes and nationalities without teaching him lessons in crime" (cited in Platt 1969, 132).

A contemporary judge, John C. Collins, who served in juvenile court for six years, writes about the history of failure of the American juvenile justice system, but notes its benevolent beginnings from the Illinois court that assumed jurisdiction over children who were neglected and dependent, children described as incorrigible, truant, or engaging in "immoral behavior," and, finally, youths who had committed criminal acts (1981, 109). However, there were shortcomings that began to receive increasing scrutiny. For example, "Assuming the role of benevolent parent, the juvenile court provided neither the formal procedures nor the Constitutional protections available in adult court. Children had no right to either a public trial or attorney, and there were virtually no standards of proof established" (Collins 1981, 109). Still, it took from 1899 until 1967 for the Supreme Court to consider the constitutional rights of a child when it reached the Gault decision (Takanishi 1978, 10). When the Supreme Court reached its landmark decision, a lower court's decision was overturned, and procedures for juvenile courts were established on the principle of due process of law. The Gault case involved a 15-year-old boy, accused of making an objectionable phone call, who was sentenced in a "kangaroo court" to a state institution for six years.

The Gault decision was a step in the right direction, but what about the children already in custody? Collins has this to say:

> If the philosophy of the Juvenile Court has been that children should be protected and rehabilitated, we have failed miserably. If the philosophy of the Juvenile Court has been to protect society, the picture is equally dismal. An estimated 75% of adults now serving time have been involved in the juvenile court. At best, the juvenile system doesn't prevent crime—at worst it fosters it. (Collins 1981, 111)

Judge Collins tells how 900 children were released from detention by the Texas Youth Council only after three years of litigation showing violations of the children's civil rights, widespread beatings and physical abuse, and "Solitary confinement for weeks at a time was prevalent, as was the administration of heavy doses of tranquilizers" (1981, 111). Only 5 percent of 2,442 youngsters, many under the age of 13, incarcerated in 1973 were committed for violent acts, and 24 percent were committed for "disobedience." Widespread maltreatment of youngsters in institutions has been well documented over the years (James 1969; NCCAN 1978b). The magnitude of the problem may be greater than the maltreatment of children by their parents (Gil 1971). The foreword of a National Center on Child Abuse and Neglect publication (1978b) begins by stating:

> Over 400,000 children live in residential institutions such as treatment centers, temporary and long-term shelters, detention homes, centers for the mentally retarded and developmentally disabled and group homes; an additional 400,000 live in foster homes. . . . [A]ll too often children are victims of maltreatment in the very institutions which are operated to care for and serve their needs. These children are largely voiceless and at the mercy of adults who operate the institutions or agencies.

Detention centers housed almost 77,000 juveniles at any point during 1975, but there were almost three-quarters of a million admissions and releases during that same year (Rhoades and Parker 1981, 17). Many of these are the children that Fabricant (1981) writes about in *Juvenile Injustice*. Because the system focuses in on the hard-core troublemakers, many troubled children "drop through the cracks" without receiving the help they so badly need. Yet the juvenile justice system's guiding philosophy, according to Philip Rhoades and Sharon Parker (1981, 18), "has been a paternal rehabilitative one under the concept of *parens patriae*. The state is to deal with juveniles in a protective and rehabilitative manner while providing the community with protection from juvenile crime."

Charles Smith and his associates trace the linkage historically between juvenile delinquency and child neglect statutes, where there was "little or no distinction made between neglected and delinquent children. Both were confined in houses of refuge, and behavior patterns of neglected children were seen as a prelude to juvenile delinquency" (Smith et al. 1980, 27). From the beginning of public acknowledgment of child abuse and neglect as a social problem, victims were *expected* to become juvenile delinquents. This court was established not only to process delinquent youths, but neglected and dependent children as well—there is no clear line of demarcation between victims and accused offenders. This shows at least a symbolic relatedness. The *Child Savers* (Platt 1969) had helped bring about changes that extended powers of the state to intervene in families, to take children away from their homes, and to put them into foster homes and institutions. The link was forged. Smith et al. state:

> The most important aspect of this link is the labeling and adjudication of abused and neglected children and adolescents as status offenders. Although they are referred to the juvenile court because they are victims, they often leave the system being defined as offenders. (1980, 33)

These writers offer overwhelming evidence that abused or neglected children are more likely to come into the juvenile justice system for status offenses, usually for avoidance or escapist "crimes," such as running away from home. They are also more likely to be confined in detention facilities until hearings, adjudicated as status offenders, and sent to institutions for longer time periods (almost *twice* as long) as children from nonabusive homes. Finally, they are more likely to suffer from abuse in these institutions (Smith et al. 1980, 33–36, 144)

As offensive and as unfair as all this sounds, there is considerable empirical evidence that this is what happens when some abused and neglected children get old enough to resist oppression in the home or try to avoid or escape it. Charges are brought against youngsters for keeping late hours, having an objectionable boyfriend, associating with companions objectionable to their parents, avoiding their homes until late hours, and many other behaviors that indicate resistance to adult authority (Smith et al. 1980, 140). For merely staying out late, a child who spent earlier years alone and neglected, now having reached adolescence, may be stigmatized by a label, incarcerated with other young people who committed *criminal* acts, and finally released as a "juvenile delinquent" with a record—which proves what many professionals expected to find all along. The "self-fulfilling prophecy" is realized by many children whose parents, neighbors, social workers, and teachers have repeatedly told them they are worthless, misfits, hostile, lazy, underachievers, and bad (see Button 1973). Richard de Lone bitterly attacks social program bureaucracies that categorize children by labels which include, "the 'predelinquent' (an absurd term that is a stunning example of the self-fulfilling logic of stigma)" (1975, 95).

Females in the Juvenile Justice System

When addressing the issue of the juvenile justice system (and the adult criminal justice system), most writers tend to ignore the position females hold in it and concentrate on males only, possibly because males constitute a statistically much larger proportion than females in both systems (Bowker 1978; Simon 1981). Only recently has that oversight begun to be corrected, and evidence is fast accumulating that girls and women share some problems in common with their male counterparts, but frequently fare worse in both systems because of gender-specific discrimination (Chesney-Lind 1978; Crow and McCarthy 1981; Davidson 1982; Feinman 1980; Smart 1977). Young females were included in the early reformers' ideals, viewing them as future citizens to be "saved," but as Meda Chesney-Lind notes (1982, 12), standards of behavior are set higher for females than males so that "While officials speak endlessly about protecting women, in practice young women offenders, most of whom come before the court for status offenses, are punished more harshly than their male counterparts, even those males charged with criminal acts."

The double standard and the virgin/whore dichotomy have a powerful impact on treatment of girls, and much of their behavior is judged in sexual terms. Females are expected to be pure and chaste, while the opposite is expected of boys. Ruth Crow and Ginny McCarthy begin their book with the statement: "'Equal justice under the law' is not the same for young females as it is for young males" (1981, xi). Judge Lisa Richette (1981, 104) notes that females suffer a double burden in the legal system: being female and being considered a child. Richette refers to the *perpetual infantilism* of women in the juvenile justice system. Girls are often incarcerated for the same acts that are considered lauditory for boys, but Richette insists that "the juvenile court should no longer act as a 'legal chastity belt' in its dealings with young women" (1981, 105). Chesney-Lind claims that women's status as property leads to denial of their private rights and thus, "In Napolean's immortal words, a woman is little more than a 'womb with legs'" (1982, 11). Although more forthright than most of the early reformers would perhaps have stated it, that seems to have been their attitude toward "wayward girls" when the first reform school for girls was established in 1857, where "Saving the erring mothers of the next generation became vital" (Brenzel 1982, 28). The Lancaster School in Massachusetts began with the intention of providing a "loving family circle" for poor girls, but the girls persisted in being "stubborn," "wayward," and "immoral"; in other words, they were the status offenders of that era

(Chesney-Lind 1982, 11).

A former chief attorney of the Juvenile Legal Aid Society in Chicago, Patrick T. Murphy, wrote a scathing critique of the juvenile justice system that begins with: "From what I have seen, the child welfare and juvenile justice systems do much more harm than good" (1977, vii). Murphy recounts cases where children are denied adults' constitutional rights, charged with noncrimes, and convicted because parents and public defenders agree to admissions of guilt for the children. He describes the process in these terms:

> Children sent to correctional institutions as "minors in need of supervision" generally fell into two sometimes overlapping categories. The larger group consisted of adolescents, mostly girls, who could not get along with their parents and left home overnight or for several days. . . . [W]ell over half of those who left home under such conditions were not at fault. The parents made unreasonable demands on their daughters, who responded not irrationally by leaving a sick situation. The parents called the police, who eventually arrested the girls. Normally, they were pleaded guilty by a court-appointed lawyer who conferred not so much with the client as with her parents. The child was then placed on probation. (Murphy 1977, 18)

Violation of probation, usually through committing acts similar to the initial charges, can result in incarceration in a "correctional" facility. For example, sexual activity by girls (but not by boys) can result in violation of probation and institutionalization (Murphy 1977). What is wrong with a system that was originally set up ostensibly to help children and secondarily their families, but that apparently does so much harm to so many people? Judge Collins (1981) believes that removing status offenders from juvenile court jurisdiction would be a step in the right direction, but he feels that the juvenile justice system is as destructive to at least as many children as it helps and therefore that the best way to deal with juvenile crime is by prevention. Collins (1981, 112) also says, "There is no need to point out that there is poverty in America, high unemployment among youth, and serious problems of discrimination based on ethnicity, sex, and race."

Once more, the issues of poverty and discrimination are raised in the relationship between maltreatment of children and juvenile delinquency. There does not appear to be conclusive evidence that child maltreatment itself propels children into delinquency, but poor children who receive public attention as suffering abuse or neglect are more easily traced through the system to adolescence. Further, their appearance again in statistics is likely to be due as much, if not more, to their underprivileged circumstances than to any long-term effects of maltreatment. The next section examines the "cycle of violence" in reference to spouse abuse.

"ABUSED CHILDREN BECOME SPOUSE ABUSERS OR VICTIMS," OR DO THEY?

Although research on child abuse and neglect has been conducted on a larger scale and for a longer time period than on wife abuse, the assumptions of a "cycle of violence" have also frequently appeared in the literature. Writers who mention a spouse-abuse cycle usually are referring to an assumption that men who batter their wives grew up in violent homes, and the women who become victims of spouse abuse grew up in violent homes. These ideas are widespread throughout the literature, as are the other ideas about abused children in adulthood discussed earlier. Ideas about a cycle of violence can do serious harm to individuals who accept them unquestioningly. For example, a young male medical student described the pain of living his entire youth in a home where his father beat his mother. Unable to get his mother to leave or to prevent his father from beating her, he eventually learned to hate both his parents because of the pain they inflicted on him. At the time of the interview, the young man said he did not date women seriously saying, "I don't ever want to marry because I'm afraid I'd be like my father. I can't take that chance." Perhaps he did marry at a later date, but there is a lingering question of how much unnecessary pain his earlier fears caused him. Another man *did* erupt into violence one night, after nine years of nonviolent marriage, beating not only his wife but also his daughter who attempted to protect her mother. Apparently he could not forgive himself for this behavior, because the following day he killed himself. It may have been only circumstantial, but this man had also been the victim of child abuse.

The time to examine the so-called "theory" of the cycle of violence is somewhat overdue, particularly as it applies to women who are battered by their husbands or lovers. A very compelling reason for doing so is because of the implications it holds for these women. If there is no substance to it, then it may be just one more, but a very subtle method of victim blaming. This should come as no surprise to most feminists, since women have frequently been blamed for their own victimization by men, such as in rape (Brownmiller 1976; Griffin 1975; Pagelow 1978a; Russell 1975). Women have even been accused of making men violent in the first place (Pogrebin 1974). Child victims of incest have been accused of "seducing" fathers and stepfathers, and both they and their mothers have been declared as consciously or *unconsciously* assisting or colluding in incest (Lukianowicz 1972). Meiselman (1978, 162) cites a 1975 textbook for psychiatrists from which she provides quotations and concludes: "From statements such as this, a naive reader could easily get the impression that the incestuous father is the helpless victim of his wife and daughter!" Little girls have been accused of inciting men into pedophilia (Virkkunen 1975), and battered women have been found guilty of "provoking" men into the violence (Gelles 1974; Snell et al. 1964). One writer throws the total responsibility for abuse onto the victims by saying:

> I have never seen a chronically abused wife who truly objected to being abused. The chronically abused wife is one who permits her husband to beat her, refuses to take punitive action afterward, and remains in the same situation so that she may be beaten again. (Kleckner 1978, 54)

Whether they have any empirical support for their suppositions or not, many writers appear eager to throw blame for their victimization onto the victims.

On the other hand, *if* it is true that living in a violent home as a girl puts one into a cycle whereby she is victimized as an adult, then there must be something about that person that brings about the violence, or she may be attracted to violent people, or violence itself is attractive—each of these positions has been advanced by some professionals and nonprofessionals. For example, Erin Pizzey, one of the early leaders in the shelter movement for battered women, whose book was first published in England in 1974 and later in an American edition (1977), called worldwide attention to the plight of women battered by the men they lived with. Pizzey has notions about women who live surrounded by violence or the threat of it, so that they have "adrenaline highs" on violence from which they must be gradually deprogrammed. Speaking in the United States, Pizzey told audiences that women with extremely violent experiences are likely to leave one batterer in exchange for another, unless they are reprogrammed for less "exciting" relationships. Pizzey's ideas of the effects of violence on children are, not surprisingly, very similar to those she holds about adult female victims. One writer repeats them, saying:

> [S]urvival would dictate that one must become innured [*sic*] to much of the pain. Erin Pizzey, in a description of abused children noted the presence of such an increased tolerance for pain and named consequences with which I concur: "Children from violent families are so used to being beaten, uncomfortable, ill and cold, that they don't even feel it. When pain thresholds [*sic*] get that high in a child, sometimes the only way they feel anything is in the middle of a violent act. Children can become addicted to violent relationships. . . ." I believe that sim-

ilar consequences accrue to women who remain in intimate relationships in which they are raped and battered. (Doron 1981,
3)

It is easy to understand where Pizzey gets such ideas; Pizzey's acknowledgments page in the 1974 publication commends psychiatrist Jasper Gayford, who was then conducting research at Chiswick, the London shelter
she helped establish. Gayford's work has been severely criticized for its
lack of scientific rigor and objectivity (Wilson 1976). Gayford's published
articles contain statements that Pizzey apparently accepts unquestioningly
such as when he says: "Often they [battered women] need protection
against their own stimulus-seeking activities. Though they flinch from violence like other people they have the ability to seek violent men or by
their behavior to provoke attack from the opposite sex" (1975a, 197). In
another article Gayford says, "It is easy to see how this violence can pass
on to even another generation" (1975b, 290). It should be noted that in
this, one of the earliest reports on woman battering, already the suggestion of a "cycle" of violence is raised. Another article that same year by
Gayford concludes with the statement: "Children of battered wives present the most challenging problem: unless something is done these children will become the battered wives and the battering husbands of the
next generation" (1975c, 244).

The ideas expressed by Gayford in 1975 about a cycle of violence specify
a differential effect, based on sex, on children who experience paternal
battering of mothers. Despite a paucity of sound empirical evidence and
no longitudinal studies to support the cycle of violence ideas that "abused
children become abusing parents," and almost no research on wife beating, suddenly a writer applies this "common sense assumption" to children who live in households where fathers beat their mothers. However,
Gayford's ideas are specific: He proposes that little girls whose mothers
are beaten grow up to be beaten wives and little boys whose fathers beat
their mothers grow up to be wife beaters.

Examining the Evidence

Suggesting that little girls whose mothers are beaten grow up to be battered wives implies a cause and effect relationship that runs counter to
the claims by researchers of wife abuse. Several recent studies have focused specifically on wife abuse (as compared to other studies of "family
violence" that include a multitude of types of behaviors, perpetrators, and
victims), and they generally avoided basic assumptions that some women
have particular characteristics that lead to their victimization (Bowker
1983a; Bowker and MacCallum 1981). The major studies of wife abuse all

take the stance that in a culture such as ours, where male violence is largely approved and condoned, and "masculine" ideals include aggressiveness, almost any woman can become a victim and almost any man can become an abuser. Walker (1979) contends that male violence against females is so common in this country that about one out of every two women is likely to be beaten in at least one intimate relationship. Other researchers believe that violence against wives is historically structured into marriage under patriarchy (Dobash and Dobash 1979).

The author's study (Pagelow 1981a), guided by social learning theory, supports the idea that men, more than women, are influenced by and likely to imitate violent role models, encountered during childhood, particularly if they witnessed their fathers beating their mothers. Professionals who developed a program for male batterers reveal that the men had been violent in more than one relationship (Ganley and Harris 1978). Out of 21 long-term intimate relationships, men in a treatment program admitted that they had been physically abusive in all but three; from this the writers deduce that the violence has much more to do with the way the men express and resolve stress than it has to do with individual women. Psychologists Anne Ganley and Lance Harris say:

> It is our assumption that battering men will continue to be violent even if they change partners, unless a major change occurs within the individual men. It is not a matter of his finding the right partner who will solve his problem of assaulting others. (1978, 6)

Nevertheless, some proponents of the "cycle of violence" believe that children living in violent families where either they were abused as children or witnessed intraparental violence are likely to grow up to be either perpetrators or victims of violence in their families of procreation (Gelles 1974; Owens and Straus 1975; Steinmetz 1977b; Straus 1978, 1981b). In this broad model, there is little to suggest that there may be different effects of observation and/or victimization experiences, and it does not discriminate between effects on boys and effects on girls.

Most speculations infer that the cyclical effect is as strong on women as men. Gelles's article (1976) on why abused wives stay with battering men is an excellent example of obfuscation of concepts and variables in the broad, nondiscriminatory model. For example, Gelles says, "The more an individual is exposed to violence as a child (both as an observer and a victim), the more he or she is violent as an adult" (1976, 662). According to this statement, both boys and girls are expected to become violent adults, and violence "exposure" includes both being direct victims of violence (as in child abuse), and observing others' violence, which could include all forms of family violence but which presumably means parental violence:

fathers who beat mothers or the reverse, or "mutual combat" between them. The most common form of abuse being wife beating, the writers cited here usually are referring to children who do or do not observe their mothers being beaten by their fathers. Combining a wide range of actors, victims, and observers into a simplistic assumption that A leads to B throws such a wide net that it cannot be tested. An article on this issue suggests that readers:

> . . . should be cautioned immediately to note the frequent tendency to combine two distinct phenomena regarding child-hood exposure to violence: *observing* parental violence and being *victims* of parental violence. . . . The reader would do well to separate these phenomena conceptually, where possi-ble. While observation and victimization are both elements of childhood experience in violence, they cannot be assumed to have the same impact and effect in adulthood and may also be reacted to differently on the basis of the sex of the child and the sex of the abusing parent. (Pagelow 1981b, 411)

Conversely, when Gelles was trying to explain why abused wives stay with their abusers, he hypothesized that the more that women are ex-posed to violence as children, the more they are "prone to be the victims" or "approve the use of violence in the family" as adults (1979, 101). Gelles's data do not appear to give strong and conclusive support to his assump-tions. The author tested his hypothesis with data from her survey sample, and they offered no support (Pagelow 1981b). That test conceptually dis-tinguished between observation of and victimization by violence in child-hood. Contrary to Gelles's assumptions, women in the Pagelow study who had been abused as children were likely to leave violent relationships somewhat sooner than women who were inexperienced in violence. The majority of the inexperienced women described their parental homes as being authoritarian but nonviolent; many felt they had been "overpro-tected," which handicapped them in dealing with violent men.

There were some interesting differences in homes of orientation of the 350 sample women and their spouses. The data these women provided on their spouses show a large and statistically significant difference between the men and women on measures of being observers and/or victims of abuse. Almost three-fourths of them said they had never seen their moth-ers beaten by their fathers, but of those who knew about their spouses' childhoods, more than half said their husbands' fathers beat their mothers (Pagelow 1981b, 402). The survey showed that 43 percent of the women had never or very seldom been physically punished, compared to 47 per-cent of their spouses who had been physically punished often or very often (Pagelow 1981b, 404).

In addition, there was a statistically significant difference between the persons who administered the punishment these people received. The women's punishers were equally likely to be either parent or parent-figure; the men's punishers were far more likely to be fathers or father-figures than mothers or mother-figures (Pagelow 1981b). According to many women interviewed in this study, their husbands had been disciplined extremely harshly, some suffering broken bones, being tied to chairs, thrown down stairs, and so forth, and in the vast majority of cases, the abusers had been male parent-figures.

Even Stark and Anne Flitcraft (1981) found no support for the idea that women abused as children are most likely to be abused as wives, but instead, they suggest that these ideas of "multiple pathologies" of "violent families" serve to blame victims and produce images of the "inevitability" of abuse that conjure up the "battered woman syndrome." Lee Bowker's study (1983a, 52) found no relationship between wives' previous experiences with violence and their marital victimization. Dobash and Dobash (1979) also argue strongly against the idea of women learning to be victims of husbands' beatings though childhood violence, and unlike some other researchers, they looked at siblings of abusers and their victims. They have this to say:

> Little attention has been paid to the siblings of the individuals studied and little effort has been made to specify what a violent background is. We can see at least two very serious flaws in such research. First, we can say that almost everyone comes from a violent household if our definition of violence is sufficiently vague. . . . To discover that a murderer was sometimes slapped by his mother or father may superficially confirm the cycle of violence theory, but such confirmation is suspect indeed. . . . If we discover that a man who beats his wife comes from a home in which his father beat his mother but that his three brothers do not beat their wives, then we have one case that appears to confirm the cycle of violence thesis and three that refute it. (1979, 155)

These points by the Dobashes are valid. In the Pagelow study there was an extreme case of brutality inflicted by a father on his son and the boy's mother. In adulthood the son beat two wives and his own mother after the father died. This appears to confirm a cycle of violence, but the man in this case was the eldest of five children all of whom were abused, although not as severely. Despite similar histories, *none* of his siblings are violent with their spouses or children. (Pagelow 1982b)

BOYS AND VIOLENT FATHERS

There are major differences in explanatory power of the intergenerational transmission of violence theory, based on the sex of the "teacher" and the child who learns this behavior and acts upon it as an adult. Murray Straus, one of the earliest proponents of a nondiscriminant model of the cycle of violence, indicates in one article that his data vary according to sex of adult abuser and child observer (1979, 222). Straus states:

> The effects of observing one's father hit one's mother are greater than effects of observing one's mother hit one's father. Being the child of a *father who hit his wife* is associated with a 39% greater rate of child abuse compared to *men* whose fathers did not hit their wives (13.3 versus 9.7). . . . The greater effect of father's violence to his wife on sons, and of mother's violence to her husband on daughters, suggests that violence by a parent of the same sex as the child provides the strongest role-model. (1979, 222)

By this statement, Straus acknowledges a same-sex role model effect on children who observe parental violence and its relationship to later child abuse. Since evidence strongly indicates that the most frequent and most severe type of spousal violence is that of wives beaten by husbands, the type of interparental violence children are most likely to witness is their fathers beating their mothers. Many studies show that battering husbands (but not their wives) frequently grew up in violent homes where their fathers beat their mothers and/or their children, such as Bowker's study (1983a, 53), where the men experienced much higher frequencies of childhood violence.

Other writers have taken a closer look at differential effects of violent childhood experience; for example, Natalie Jaffe (1980, 20) writes: "Research shows that abusive men are more likely to come from a home with parental violence than are their victims." Walker's study showed that men, but not women, in violent couples are very likely to have come from a violent home which included "witnessing, receiving, and committing violent acts in the childhood home" (1981, 7). Another study that tested the theory similarly found that there were no significant differences between battered and nonbattered women in regard to family backgrounds, but there were statistically significant differences between men who were violent and nonviolent, based on being victims of child abuse and/or witnessing parental spouse abuse (Rosenbaum and O'Leary 1981, 68). Finally, an investigation of wife beating that gathered a control sample of nonbattered women tested the theory of intergenerational violence and found:

Another common stereotype of battered women is that they come from families where their parents were also violent towards one another. . . . The majority of battered women in both groups *did not* come from violent families. The battered group women's husbands were the most likely to have come from a violent household while the nonviolent husbands were least likely to have had this family background. (Washburn and Frieze 1980, 3–4)

One report on 110 men who sought treatment for their violent behavior (wife abuse) states: "Being abused as children or witnessing violence between their parents appears to contribute to being violent as an adult" (Kuhl 1981, 10). A similar study with a smaller sample reported that 63 percent of the violent men had either been "battered as children or to have witnessed physical abuse in their families" (Ganley and Harris 1978, 3). Researchers who compared childhood experiences of their victims have almost always found violence in batterers' backgrounds, but even when they found that victims' homes of origin were violent, there was a still higher level of violence in the men's backgrounds (Gayford 1975a; Hilberman 1980; Scott 1974).

Some tests have found little support for the cycle of violence. For example, one study tried to differentiate between men who are violent with immediate family members or others outside the home, but the researchers found that "exposure to family violence as a child did not discriminate between [them] . . ." (Hanneke and Shields 1981, 5). Unfortunately, they did not have a control group of nonviolent men for a more informative test. Another researcher strongly questions this perspective by saying:

[W]e must remember that the cross-generational transmission of abuse accounts for a small proportion of the abuse cases. . . . Given that many factors are probably responsible for the cross-generational tendency, we would thus expect to observe any given factor's influence only in an extremely small percentage of the cases. (Herzberger 1981, 6)

Without a doubt, more writers have argued for or against the "cycle of violence" or "intergenerational theory of violence," regarding both child abuse and spouse abuse (and some have given it more than passing notice regarding sexual abuse of children and parent abuse). In addition to the writers noted earlier who theorized about and tested the cycle of violence theory, other reports constantly appear. As a blanket assumption, it has received popular acceptance, but little scientifically sound support (Martin 1981). Perhaps it will have greater explanatory power when it is modified to a more specific model.

CYCLE OF VIOLENCE

Boys who witness paternal violence and who also are targets of physical punishment by their fathers may be more likely to follow their same-sex role model's behavior in adulthood. But there is stronger empirical evidence that boys who grow up to become wife-abusers more frequently came from homes where their fathers beat their mothers than boys who were abused by their fathers.

Source: Hicks Marlowe.

SUGGESTIONS FOR MODIFYING
THE "CYCLE OF VIOLENCE" THEORY

The major problem with the popular cycle of violence theory is that it is usually indiscriminately applied to males and females in spite of the fact that, whenever reports are categorized by sex, they show that there is a much stronger and consistent association between boys who witness or are subjected to violence and later adult violent behavior than is true for girls. Improvements could be made by focusing on a specific target category by controlling for gender of violent actors and victims, and controlling for witnessing adult violence or being victims of violence as a child. When the research focus has been thus narrowed, it appears that boys who *witnessed* paternal violence are more likely to become violent than boys who were *targets* of paternal violence, but boys who were targets of *paternal* violence are more likely to become violent adults than boys who were targets of *maternal* violence. However, some data indicate a stronger association between marital violence and boy-victims than boy-witnesses (Bowker 1983a). Anna Kuhl's (1981) study of wife abusers found that 68 percent had been spanked with an object, whereas 37 percent reported violence between parents. Many reports do not distinguish between boys witnessing or being targets of violence as when Karen Coleman says, "Thirty-nine percent of the sample were abused as children or had witnessed conjugal violence. . ." (1980, 210). Obviously, much more research testing these associations is needed.

How can it be that boys and girls reared in violent homes learn lessons on violence differently? As detailed in Chapter 4, some suggestions come from learning theory, the differential responses to modeled aggressive behavior of boys and girls, and the cultural approval of "masculine" violence. This suggests why boys are more likely to imitate the violent behavior of same-sex role models than girls are to imitate violence from either parent. On the other hand, if their mothers are violent and are rewarded for it, girls are more likely to view violence as appropriate behavior for females, as Straus et al. (1980) found. Yet there is a greater probability that boys have fathers or father-figures who approve of and use violence in the home because of cultural approval of male aggression (McCord et al. 1970) and their greater potential for being rewarded due to males' greater muscular power and size.

At this point, the evidence is not overwhelmingly supportive of a cycle of violence theory for males, but there are sufficient indicators that more research may show a strong association. If so, this would certainly have implications for future social policy. The broader model that implies a pattern of "monkey see—monkey do" is too simplistic to be useful, since not all children who grow up in violent homes become violent adults. More needs to be learned about the quality of the relationships of boys with violent fathers to discover why some boys model their adult behavior after fathers while others do not.

SUMMARY

At this point, there is no scientifically sound empirical evidence that there is a *causal* relationship between being an abused child and becoming an adult child abuser. There is evidence of a weak association, but when up to 90 percent of child abusers cannot be shown to have been abused in their own childhoods, the association can be considered hardly greater than chance. There are too many other factors involved in the learning process and a wide variety of environmental stresses and triggering mechanisms that may be present when behavior erupts into violence. Most researchers are now testing multivariate models in their studies of family violence, and this approach offers greater promise of finding the set of personal and environmental factors most likely to produce child abuse.

Since the "abused become abusers" theme has little empirical support, why do so many service providers and agency workers insist on using it? There are four possible reasons: One, they believe it because it has a ring of common-sense logic to it. This seems to be the best explanation for why so many people interpreted abusers' descriptions of their childhoods to mean abuse, when *most* people, if pressed to explain failure, could describe their own childhoods in the same terms. For example, how many nonabusers grew up with parents who were critical, authoritarian, demanding, wanting prompt obedience, or even unloving? (Probably many of our most successful citizens could describe their parents in these same terms!) Two, because they take it as a "given"—people tend to find what they expect to find—thus they know the questions to ask. Three, accused abusers are aware of popular assumptions of a child-abuse cycle and may provide social agents with the explanation they expect to find, in the hope of using it to lessen personal responsibility. It is not unusual for persons accused of committing offenses against society to deny responsibility (Matza 1969) and to blame their behavior on circumstances in their past over which they had no control. When faced with the facts of their crimes, abusive parents may use the "I was an unloved, abused child" slogan as an effort to discount responsibility and to appeal for sympathy and understanding from their accusers. Four, to minimize the seriousness of their acts and to show they used "normal discipline," they may claim, "This is the way I was raised—my old man beat the hell out of me, and I turned out OK!"

Finally, the simplicity of the emotion-evoking theme is very useful and effective for fund-raising purposes for agencies. It provides a way for concerned citizens to act upon their sympathy for helpless child-victims: By donating money to this or that worthy organization caring for abused children, they can prevent child abuse in the future! Legislators use the slogan effectively too, when they want to secure passage of new child protective legislation or for other political purposes. It seems doubtful that people who use the slogan of a cycle of violence for child abuse, considering the advantages it brings them and the causes they espouse, would abandon its use, even if it was shown conclusively to have no substance at all.

As for the second theme that child abuse produces delinquents and even criminals, what can be said about the frequent claims that prisoners convicted of violent crimes were victims of parental abuse in their youth? As shown, the few studies that began with this assumption used small, purposeful samples of prisoner populations from youth correctional facilities and adult prisons, and even then they were unable to produce overwhelming evidence. In fact, many reports did not even distinguish subjects by type of crime for which they were convicted: status offenses, property offenses, or violent crimes. As Smith et al. (1982) found, getting in trouble with the law can be as much related to socioeconomic status as to childhood experiences in violence. In addition, just as parents accused of child abuse may try to minimize personal responsibility for their crimes, convicted delinquents and criminals may claim that they too are victims of circumstances beyond their control.

On the other hand, there is some empirical evidence that the formerly abused and neglected have a slightly greater chance of ending up in official statistics than persons never officially reported for childhood victimization. (At this point, it would be well to remember that nonabused samples used as controls to compare with abused may in fact have been victims, but never publicly identified as such.) Connections between child protection agencies and the juvenile justice system are clear. Entering the first, by becoming an identified case, can serve to increase an abused child's chances of entering the second. Once having been labeled and stigmatized as a "juvenile delinquent," a child has an even greater chance of becoming an adult criminal. As discussed elsewhere (Pagelow 1982a, 1982b), becoming accused of crimes may be more a result of the system than of the previously suffered abuse.

Research has provided some support for the claim that abused children become spouse abusers, but none of the studies show strong associations with becoming victims. Evidence that victimization is unlikely to be "bequeathed" from battered mother to daughter will relieve victims from the onus of guilt implied in earlier suggestions. Little girls who live in violent homes may or may not grow up to become battered wives, but they will not have to fear that there is some hidden personality trait that *inevitably* attracts them to violent men. As Ganley and Harris discovered from their sample of batterers, "Usually the target of [their] anger becomes someone or something in the batterer's immediate environment (such as a spouse) and yet that person may have nothing to do with the distress" (1978, 4).

If further research focusing on a more refined model produces strong support for a father/son cycle of violence, such findings would have important implications for social policy and helping professionals. Attention of researchers and therapists involved in spouse abuse may then become more intensely focused on the men who beat their wives, and their sons. Programs in the community and at shelters may be expected to pay special attention to boys with violent fathers, reeducating them in nonviolent methods of stress and problem resolution, providing them with nonviolent same-sex role models and teaching them different ideals of masculine behavior. If the boys are direct targets of paternal abuse, this factor would be an important consideration for intervention in the family unit, possibly leading to a more concerted effort by social agents to stop further violence by restraining the fathers, taking a more active stance by child protective workers, or in instances unamenable to change, placing the children in protective custody.

At the same time, helping professionals would be able to develop protocols based on this added knowledge for programs for adult male batterers of wives or children. If violent fathers refuse to acknowledge their destructive behavior or to take responsibility for it and therefore do not seek ways to become nonviolent, these factors could be taken into consideration by professionals who might otherwise be inclined to urge the family unit to remain intact. It may become desirable to avoid prolonged contact between violent fathers and their sons until the men assume control over their own behavior and the examples of "manhood" they are showing to boys who love them. Lawyers and judges involved in child custody suits and visitation rights need to become informed about the possibilities of boys' modeling fathers' violent behavior.

In sum, slogans such as the "cycle of violence" may be detrimental to some people (such as those abused in childhood who fear such a cycle), but very useful to others. Persistence of the claim inspired research efforts to test it, leading to some suggestions of a more refined model and further testing. The basic purpose of social science research is to build a body of knowledge by accumulating bits of information through testing theories.

The next two chapters examine the most common form of family violence: wife beating. Chapter 8 introduces the battered women's movement, and then the issue of a "battered husband syndrome" is addressed; the basis for claims that husband beating is the "most underreported" crime of family violence is also examined. Next there is an historical overview of marriage and the rights and duties of husbands and wives. Finally, we examine dating violence. Recent research shows that violence begins early among dating couples, and that as intimacy grows in some relationships, so does the potential for violence.

NOTES

1. The form of self-mutilation described as "carving" by inmates at the Ontario, Canada, correctional institution for girls included cutting various parts of their own bodies that ensured permanent scars, performed with any sharp object they could find. Ross (1980, 34) says that self-mutilatory behavior was a perennial problem at the institution and the majority of inmates engaged in it.

2. "Blind" ratings means that the school nurses and counselors rated the performance of the students without knowing in advance which ones had been abused and which ones were the controls.

3. Readers should not conclude that casework supervision is considered unimportant in the issue of child maltreatment because it is not discussed in detail here. On the contrary, it seems better to avoid the topic because that is fairer than to merely introduce it and move on without full discussion, which would require more space than available. Social workers and other professionals who deal with dysfunctional families are the most important link between the larger community and individuals who need their help so desperately. While the *official* policy of most communities is to keep families intact whenever possible, the funds necessary for good social service systems are never enough. At the same time that cases of child maltreatment are rapidly increasing, budgets are being slashed, and the few remaining case workers are frequently inexperienced and badly overworked (Epstein 1981). Los Angeles no longer has preventative intervention services because 150 caseworkers were eliminated, and workers can accept only cases severe enough to remove the child from the home. Caseloads of children's service workers have recently been cut in Los Angeles County from about 150 to 80, whereas some other states limit workers to 20 to 25 per worker (Edelman 1983). This reduction to a still-staggering load was accomplished by screening cases to eliminate all except children under 12 who are in "immediate mortal danger," and by employing "exit criteria" through which workers are to close cases as quickly as possible "unless the child is bleeding in the street" (Edelman 1983). Yet every time a child is killed by parents or foster parents, the media demand "reform" and the public looks for some individual caseworker/s to blame!

PART IV

Spouse Abuse

8

Lovers, Spouses, and Violence

Popular songs reflect the ideas, customs, or ideals of a culture or a particular time period, as reflected in the multitude of Christmas carols and seasonal musical compositions, wartime tunes, and romantic love songs. A few years ago, dating couples were likely to have strolled along in the park, holding hands and singing songs about people only hurting the people they love. "Hurt," in this case, implied that lovers hurt each others' *feelings,* not the body or the mind. Modern Americans strongly endorse romantic love and almost all believe that love and marriage are inseparable. That romantic love leads to couples sharing their lives, and that tender concern for each other is made permanent by marriage are notions that have been supported for years by our culture, Madison Avenue advertising firms, and the mass media. It is no wonder then that the disclosure in the early 1970s of extreme violence in many marriages initially led to disbelief and denial by the general public and by most politicians.

DEVELOPMENT OF THE
BATTERED WOMEN'S MOVEMENT

Wife beating turned out to be one of the "best kept secrets" of family life, only exposed after feminist groups around the world demanded safehouses and assistance for battered women and their children. The issue of woman battering was first raised and commanded widespread attention in Europe. It was not until late 1975 and early 1976 that U.S. women and their supporters began to demand help and protection for women beaten by their husbands. When the feminist movement was rekindled in the United States at the end of a decade of turbulent social protests in the 1960s, one of the first issues that American feminists addressed was rape. They organized rape crisis centers and advocated sociolegal changes to protect victims' rights.

The battered women's movement began in a London neighborhood when a group of women organized to protest high food costs. Later the women rented from the local council a small, dilapidated, old house where they could meet to gather and share information on legal and welfare rights, and so forth (Sutton 1978). Chiswick's Women's Aid opened its doors in November 1971 (Dobash and Dobash 1979). Very quickly, neighborhood wives who had no other place to go began coming with their children, begging to be allowed to stay at least overnight to escape violent husbands. Social worker Jo Sutton, a pioneer in the battered women's movement, says, "Between 1966 and 1971 the only major safe places for battered women were with friends or relatives or in a prison, a hospital, or a mortuary" (1978, 577).[1] Although the house was rented for daytime use only, "their need was so obvious and so great that the group broke the terms of their lease and the first refuge was in operation" (Sutton 1978, 577). Word spread after the first few refugees were allowed to stay, until the place became extremely overcrowded, and it has remained that way ever since. Other women's rights groups responded to the newly surfacing problem. Some obtained government housing, others located unoccupied places owned by the government, and battered women and their children *squatted*, that is, set up residence. The National Women's Aid Federation (NWAF) was established as a clearinghouse and resource for women's groups in the United Kingdom, helping new units organize and network as well as exerting political pressure for legal changes to assist victims of husbands' violence.

One of the women who helped found Chiswick's Women's Aid, Erin Pizzey, used her considerable skills to obtain widespread publicity through coverage on radio, television, newspapers, and speaking tours (Sutton 1978; Tierney 1982). Pizzey wrote a book, *Scream Quietly or the Neighbours Will Hear* (1977), first published in Britain in 1974, describing in detail the horrors faced by battered women in their daily lives. The battered women's movement gained initial impetus from Pizzey's contributions, and one of the first studies of battered women was conducted at Chiswick (Gayford 1975a). Feminist groups from other countries that wanted to help battered women sent visitors to Chiswick to learn methods of dealing with politicians and about the operation of safe-houses. The first shelter on the continent opened in 1974 in Amsterdam, Holland, and the battered women's movement spread worldwide. In March 1976 the International Tribunal on Crimes Against Women in Brussels, Belgium, was attended by more than 2,000 women from 33 countries. Women from Australia, the United Kingdom, France, Germany, the Netherlands, Ireland, Japan, and the United States endorsed a resolution calling for action on the rights of battered women and their children throughout the world (Russell and Van de Ven 1976). By the end of the 1970s, there were approximately 150 shelters in England and Wales and 20 in Scotland (Dobash and Dobash 1979; Tierney 1982).

The battered women's movement dawned upon the scene in the United States somewhat later than other Western industrialized nations, but its beginnings are similar to the grass roots movement in other countries. *Grass roots* means that these were people who joined together in a common cause not necessarily related to establishment professions or political parties. The originators were avowed feminists; some sympathizers who joined later did not share feminist ideology but saw woman battering as a social problem needing their professional expertise or worthy of humanitarian advocacy (Tierney 1982).

The U.S. movement began with a small study conducted in an affluent county in Maryland and reported to the National Organization for Women (NOW), showing that the prevalence and severity of wife abuse was far greater than expected. The March 1976 NOW newsletter, *Do It Now*, announced the establishment of a task force co-chaired by activist Del Martin to deal with the Problem from coast to coast, and called for scientific research and for shelters to protect victims from further abuse. Martin (1976) wrote the first book published in the United States that focused specifically on wife beating. Probably the first U.S. shelter for battered women was initiated by a feminist organization called Women's Advocates in St. Paul, Minnesota. Women's Advocates began with a phone service in 1972 and, after a long struggle, finally opened Women's House in 1974 (Martin 1976, 197–98). Two earlier programs restricted their help to women beaten by alcoholic husbands, but they later opened their doors to victims of spousal violence whether or not the violence was related to alcohol consumption (Tierney 1982). These were Rainbow Retreat, opened in 1973 in Phoenix, Arizona, and Haven House in Pasadena, California, which reopened in 1974.[2]

Feminist and grass roots groups began the struggle to provide safety for battered women, but success did not come easily. Politicians and people in decision-making positions usually reacted with skepticism and demands for evidence that this was a social, rather than an individual, problem. Most community bodies denied that violence occurred in *nice* families; they maintained that violence rarely occurred but, when it did, it was only between "sick" individuals, mostly people of the lower classes (Pagelow 1981a). Therefore, wife beating was not a social problem but an individual, psychological problem. Feminist groups refused to accept these ideas and accumulated evidence from diverse sources to show decision makers that woman battering was a serious and widespread problem that required immediate public concern. Gathering statistics was difficult because social service agencies did not keep the kinds of records necessary to show severity or frequency of wife abuse. Hospitals kept no records, and even when law enforcement was involved, their records usually did not make retrieval of these calls direct and error-free. The FBI gathers crime statistics and releases them annually in the *Uniform Crime Reports,* but wife abuse is included in a catch-all category called "disturbance call (family quarrels, man with gun, etc.)." This category includes brawls between adult relatives, fights between drunks at social gatherings, or, for example, a man waving a gun at neighbors for walking on his lawn (Pagelow 1981a, 211). Feminist writer Del Martin (1976, 11) states the problem this way:

> Obvious sources of information are police reports, court rosters, and emergency hospital admittance files, but wife-abuse is not an official category on such records. Information on the subject gets buried in other, more general categories. Calls to the police for help in marital violence, for instance, are usually reported as "domestic disturbance calls," or DDs.

Martin explains that under certain circumstances, officers may not file reports, or if severe injuries occur or the wife dies, the incident is reported as assault and battery, aggravated assault, or homicide. Martin's book, *Battered Wives* (1976), had the same impact on the American social consciousness as Pizzey's earlier book had in Europe. Martin (1976) provides the kinds of evidence most of the victim advocate groups used to document the extent and severity of wife beating: Gathering together whatever statistics were available from a number of different sources. One by one, shelters opened their doors to victims and their children, and the movement gained momentum until, by 1980, there were estimated to be about 150 shelters and 300 "shelters, hotlines, and groups acting as advocates for battered women" in the United States (Tierney 1982, 208). The exact number is not known because some groups manage to open up a new shelter at the same time as others are closing due to lack of funds. An Office on Domestic Violence (ODV) in the Department of Health, Education, and Welfare was established during President Carter's administration to serve as a clearinghouse and information exchange, but it was disbanded almost immediately when the new administration took over after the 1980 elections. Had the ODV survived, it would be possible to closely monitor the growth or changes in the battered women's movement.[3] Most shelters are struggling for survival, and many had to be closed due to cutbacks in funding for social services affecting women and children, legal aid, and the CETA program from which many shelter staff were obtained. Even some funding sources have been eliminated, such as the Law Enforcement Assistance Administration (LEAA).

Despite these setbacks, between 1976 and 1980 the movement in the United States led to a great many changes. Some states have legislated funds to help establish shelters, and a few have attached an additional sum to the marriage license fee as a sort of "battery insurance." The extra revenues are mandated to be spent on shelters or other services for battering victims. All told, 49 states and the District of Columbia passed laws to help protect the civil and personal rights of battered women (Lerman 1981a). For example, among the laws passed in California, temporary restraining orders (TROs) were modified so that a person could obtain one without having to first file for divorce; TROs were expanded to include cohabitees, and once obtained, a violation could result in immediate police enforcement. *Restraining orders* or *temporary injunctions* are types of *protection orders* that are injunctions designed to prevent violence by one member of a household against another. They usually consist of court orders that forbid a certain person or persons to make personal contact with another party; sometimes they stipulate the distance a specified person must maintain from the person who obtained the order. Attorney Lisa Lerman (1981, 1) explains that, depending on state law, a court may "order an abuser to move out of a residence shared with a victim, to refrain from abuse of or contact with the victim, to enter a counseling program, or to pay support, restitution, or attorney's fees." In most states a battered woman obtains an order by going before a judge and, either directly or through her attorney, explaining why her husband is a threat to her safety and must be prevented from making personal contact or harassment at her home or elsewhere, such as at work. Some states have simplified filing for a protection order so that women who cannot afford attorneys can go to courthouses and file the necessary papers themselves.

A TRO carried little weight before the new California law, because when police were called to evict a violator, the responding officer could only recommend that the victim go back to court to complain to a judge, since the officer had no sure knowledge that the TRO was valid.[4] Now, as soon as a TRO is issued, a notification is placed on file in the district in which the complainant lives so that all an officer has to do is call headquarters to get confirmation. If the violator refuses to leave, he may be arrested.

Another example is a Pennsylvania law, the Protection from Abuse Act that was passed in December 1976. It requires police to act on the complainant's request to evict her assaulter. Officers may no longer use discretion to "cool things down" by persuasion or by telling the husband to take a walk until he is calmer. An assault by a husband usually must be more severe and the evidence stronger before an arrest may be made than if the assault was on a stranger, and almost all assaults on a wife, even if resulting in bodily injury, are classified as *misdemeanors*. Police do not normally make arrests for misdemeanors except when committed in their presence; responsibility for the decision to arrest or not is placed on the victims. Officers must arrest whether or not they witness the crime when they determine it is a *felony,* such as an aggravated assault, a deadly weapon was used in the perpetration, kidnapping was included, or there are life-threatening injuries indicating an attempted homicide. Under the Pennsylvania law, when a woman states she has been beaten and asks the police to remove her husband from the premises, he must leave. Soon afterward, the wife must go to court to *show cause,* that is, to convince a judge that she was beaten and that she fears for her safety if her husband is allowed to return home. The judge may decide to order the husband to stay out of the family residence for a time period of up to a year.

Many police units across the country have been sensitized to the issues by new training programs and have learned more appropriate intervention techniques than those used in the past (Bard 1969, 1970; Bard and Zacker 1971, 1976; Frederick 1979; Parnas 1967; Wellins 1980). In addition to passing new laws, existing laws have been examined and in some cases modified, and pressure has been applied demanding stricter enforcement (Eisenberg 1979; Eisenberg and Seymour 1979). By 1981, 28 states had passed laws requiring more specific record keeping for data collection from agencies that assist violent families (Lerman 1981a). The Police Executive Research Forum commissioned a study of police policies and procedures for handling these cases and produced a report of the findings and recommendations for improvements, including officer training or retraining (Loving 1980). Despite all these efforts, getting strict law enforcement in wife beating cases is still slow (Bowker 1983a). During an interview, activist and researcher Kathleen Fojtik (1982, 7) described a homicide case in which a wife was shot and killed by her husband after she had filed 18 assault cases with the local police and had told friends and witnesses that "the police did nothing."

Other responses to the problem of wife abuse are some books designed to educate both the victims of spouse abuse and concerned citizens who come in contact with them (Bowker 1983a; Davidson 1978; Fleming 1979; NiCarthy 1982; Walker 1979; Watkins 1982). In California two pamphlets are specifically directed toward assisting and informing victims (Voluntary Legal Services Program 1980; Younger 1978). The National Institute of Mental Health not only has funded research on family violence, but very quickly produced an annotated bibliography on *Violence at Home* (Lystad 1974). The U.S. Commission on Civil Rights published a number of books and articles (1982a, 1982b), and as early as January 1978, held a Washington, D.C., consultation on battered women which gathered together leading experts and hundreds of service providers from around the country, later publishing the entire proceedings (1978). A bill was introduced in Congress in three consecutive years, called the Domestic Violence Prevention Act, which would have allocated only $55 million over a five-year period for shelters, research, networking, and a clearinghouse, but it never managed to pass before the end of each session of Congress. The effects of these efforts and a synopsis of the gains and failures of the battered women's movement are presented in the final section of Chapter 9, at the conclusion of this two-chapter part on spouse abuse.

It was not long after the American public became aware of the fact that many women are repeatedly beaten by their husbands before some voices raised the issue of "husband battering." This was now proclaimed to be the "most underreported" type of family violence. The next section looks closely at the issue and examines the evidence that was produced to support it.

THE QUESTION OF A
"BATTERED HUSBAND SYNDROME"

When the problem of violence between spouses first caught the attention of social scientists and began to be researched, the primary focus of concern was centered on battered women because of their overrepresentation in the victim category, plus special factors that tended to keep them there (Dobash and Dobash 1976; Eisenberg and Micklow 1977; Flynn et al. 1975; Martin 1976; Pagelow 1976; Straus 1976b, 1978). While some writers were describing wife beating as the most unreported crime in the nation, a few other voices began to be heard making counter claims. Two sources quote sociologist Suzanne Steinmetz as saying: "The most unreported crime is not wife beating—it's husband beating" (Langley and Levy 1977, 187; Time 1978, 69). Thus, the newly emerging social problem of woman battering became clouded by confusion over the introduction of the notion of "husband battering" by a few individuals. Steinmetz, a member of the Straus et al. (1980) research team, wrote a number of articles about a "battered husband syndrome" that received worldwide media publicity (1977b, 1978a, 1980).

It began in 1977 when, during a scholarly meeting, Steinmetz presented a paper entitled "The Battered Husband Syndrome," a title she later used for an article (1978a). She proposed looking at "the other side of the coin" (1977b, 64; 1978a, 499) and apparently claimed that her research findings indicate that 250,000 American husbands are battered by their wives each year. The very idea of husband battering seemed to titillate the collective imagination of the mass media. *Time* magazine, which never devoted more than a few inches of column space to battered wives, published a full page on "The Battered Husbands" (1978, 69). They refer to Steinmetz's book and state: "Extrapolating from her studies of domestic quarreling in Delaware's New Castle County, she estimates that each year at least 250,000 American husbands are severly thrashed by their wives" (1978, 69).

Large and small newspapers across the country ran articles on battered husbands (*San Gabriel Valley Tribune*, 1978, 5), using headlines such as, "Who Struck Jane . . . or John?" (*Los Angeles Times*, 1978, VIII28). *The Chicago Sun-Times* ran an article that states: "Husbands are victims of physical assaults as often as wives, according to a study funded by the National Institute for Mental Health" (1978, N3), but the *Chicago Daily News* had earlier declared that the "Husband is [the] more battered spouse" (1977, 3). Fascinated reporters and national television talk show hosts latched onto the topic and telecast interviews from coast to coast. Eventually the claim of 250,000 battered husbands exploded into 12 million battered husbands (Storch 1978) and spread internationally. Headlines in a Norwegian newspaper article referred to Steinmetz's research and told readers about "12 Million Battered American Husbands."[5] Government officials in Finland were concerned about what provisions should be made to accommodate male victims of spouse abuse in proposed shelters for battered wives.[6] The media continued to show great interest in the "other side of the coin," and the topic of husband battering was paraded before the public, just as Steinmetz averred that "the horrors of wife-beating are paraded before the public" (1978a, 499).

News of the battered husband "syndrome" penetrated policy-making circles, and at the U.S. Commission on Civil Rights consultation on "Battered Women: Issues of Public Policy," the idea was both publicly and privately denounced by many participants as a divisive and destructive tactic (cf. Leghorn 1978). At congressional hearings on proposed domestic violence legislation, witnesses carefully chose words describing battered women as "battered spouses" (Pagelow 1978b), and substituted the term "domestic violence" for wife beating, because political acumen indicated that identifying a social problem as a *women's issue* meant sure defeat for their goals. As sociologist Kathleen Tierney noted in her analysis of the development of the battered women's movement, "Until the mid-1970s, 'domestic violence' meant riots and terrorism . . ." (1982, 213). The Sociologist for Women in Society unanimously adopted a resolution calling it a "pseudo issue of battered husbands," yet the image of thousands, perhaps millions, of husbands suffering as much as wives appeared to trivialize the issue and minimize the needs of battered wives, sometimes resulting in withdrawal of funding. One participant at a White House meeting on family violence in 1978 reported that her group was refused funding for a shelter for battered women and their children on the basis of *discrimination against men* because the group was unprepared and unequipped to offer identical shelter and services to battered husbands. Specialists in family and divorce law, Marjorie Fields and Rioghan Kirchner (1978, 216) contend:

> Steinmetz's essay on violence against husbands is filled with baseless conjecture which gives substance to what had been a latent backlash against the movement to aid battered wives. The press has made much of her inaccurate conclusion that wives are "slightly higher in almost all categories" of violence than husbands. In Chicago this incorrect statement was used to defeat efforts to obtain funding for a shelter for battered women and their children.

Examining the Evidence

It is unclear how Steinmetz arrived at the estimation of 250,000 battered husbands that has been quoted so frequently, but it seems to have occurred in the following manner. From her Delaware sample of 57 intact couples with two children, Steinmetz identified four wives as victims of serious assault (1977a). Based on an estimated county population of 94,000 couples, and converting to rates per 100,000, she calculated that this represented 7,016 female victims per 100,000 population. Then comparing her own data against police reports of 26 cases of spouse assault (24 women victims and 2 men victims), and calculating that "only about 1 out of 270 incidents of wife-beating are ever reported to the authorities" (1977b, 65), she concludes:

> Although there were no husbands as victims of serious assault among the study population, in two of the cases reported to the police, the victim was the husband. If the same degree of underreporting was present for husbands, then one could suspect that 540 incidents (574/100,000) occurred in New Castle County during 1975.

This may be how Steinmetz generalized *unreported* cases of husband battering in one county to 47 million couples nationwide, arriving at an estimated figure of 250,000 battered husbands in the United States.[7] This figure was adopted despite the fact that Steinmetz failed to find even *one* battered husband in her own "stratified quota sample of normal American families" (Steinmetz 1977a, 7).[8]

The table provided by Steinmetz (1978a, 502) to support her argument is both incomplete and inaccurate. Three categories of the most potentially dangerous types of violence, all of which were engaged in more by men than by women, were omitted. These were: *beat up spouse, push down,* and *choke* (Pagelow 1978a). Fields and Kirchner (1978, 216) note these discrepancies and strongly object, saying:

> Steinmetz indulges in a little flim-flam when she presents her version of "Table 1". . . . The Straus et al. data even as set forth on Steinmetz's "Table 1" do not, as she asserts, show wives to be higher in "almost all" of the seven categories of violence she presents. . . . When the omitted category, "beat up spouse" is included, the figures show that husbands exceed wives in the most serious types of violence, "beat up spouse" and "used knife or gun."

In addition, one category was added to Steinmetz's own study, which only husbands engaged in—the potentially very dangerous act of *used knife or gun*—but this item was not in her original reference source (1977a, 89). Figures from the reference sources also differed from the table Steinmetz constructed: The sample size of her New Castle County study changed from 49 (1977a, 89) to 54 in the article (1978a, 502), a 10 percent increase in sample size. However, there was an almost 50 percent increase in the rate of wives *pushing, shoving,* and *grabbing,* since Steinmetz's original report (1977a, 89) shows that 22 percent, compared to the table constructed later (1978a, 502), which indicates that 32 percent of the wives engaged in this behavior. Notably, this category, by virtue of the increase to 32 percent, is the *only category* in which her own sample wives exceeded husbands in violence—by 1 percent. Finally, the data from two other studies included in the table came from Steinmetz's secondary analysis of a small sample of Canadian college students and a "broad-based non-representative group" (Steinmetz 1978a, 501).

In sum, the data provided on the table Steinmetz used to support her claim that "not only the percentage of wives having used physical violence often exceeds that of the husbands, but that wives also exceed husbands in the frequency with which these acts occur" (Steinmetz 1978a, 503) simply do not agree. Conversely, they argue against these claims, even with the removal of some figures, the addition of others, and the changing of still others (Pagelow 1978a). There were still other kinds of "evidence" used by Steinmetz to support the notion of a battered husband syndrome, such as a reference to comic strip characters like *Maggie and Jiggs* and the *Katzenjammer Kids,* as reflecting "common family situations" (Steinmetz 1978b, 2).

Another repeatedly used bit of evidence was a single case taken from a newspaper article about a man severly beaten by his wife (Steinmetz 1977a, 90; 1977b, 69; 1978a, 505). The victim in this instance was a "wealthy, elderly New York banker" who won a separation from his younger wife by producing evidence of extreme cruelty. Historian Elizabeth Pleck and her colleagues note that economic incentives of divorcing men may lead some to falsely report victimization or to "overcome their reasons not to report . . ." (Pleck et al. 1978, 681). Attorneys Fields and Kirchner (1978) also point out that there may be economic motives for publicly disclosing private shame and embarrassment (which Steinmetz claims keeps battered husbands from reporting). They explain that New York law requires that "a person must have certain specified complaints about his or her spouse"—which includes cruelty—and so:

> It is in the husband's pecuniary interest to show his wife is guilty of marital fault so that he will not have to pay alimony or give her a share of the property. Even if husbands are shy about voicing complaints as Steinmetz suggests, their lawyer's prodding and their financial self-interest overcome any tendency toward reticence when the husband has a complaint to use in the economic struggle. (Fields and Kirchner 1978, 221)

Finally, Steinmetz points to the work by criminologist Marvin Wolfgang (1958), who conducted the classic study on criminal homicide. In various terms, Steinmetz claims that wives are as violent as husbands because there was "virtually no difference between the percent of husbands or wives who were offenders" in the Wolfgang study (1977a, 90; 1977b, 69; 1978a, 505). Pleck et al. (1978, 682) respond to this by noting that Steinmetz neglects to mention that wives are "seven times more likely to have murdered in self-defense," and that she does not mention the association between excessive violence and spouse slayings. Wolfgang (1958, 214) points out: "Husbands killed their wives violently in *significantly* greater proportion than did wives who killed their husbands." Wolfgang defines violent homicide as "severe degrees of violence in which more than five acts are involved . . ." (1958, 214).

Probably the most important, and most publicized, contribution Wolfgang's famous study made to our understanding of patterns of homicide was his introduction of the concept *victim precipitation* (1958, 252). Victim precipitation refers to self-defense murders; in other words, the murder victims begin the abuse, but their victims strike back and kill the original attacker. In their critique of Steinmetz's claims, Fields and Kirchner state: "Analysis of spouse murders show . . . that wives kill husbands who have a history of beating them, although husbands kill wives without provocation" (1978, 219). More will be said in the next chapter about spouse homicide, but for now it should be noted that Steinmetz's claims rest in large part on the study in which she was co-investigator with Richard Gelles under principal investigator Murray Straus, who has this to say about the national study: "These data do not tell us what proportion of the violent acts by wives were in response to blows initiated by husbands. Wolfgang's data on husband/wife homicide suggests that this is an important factor" (Straus et al. 1980, 449).

There was a prompt and forceful response to the notion of a battered husband "syndrome" by a number of other researchers who largely denounced it as "much ado about little" (Dobash and Dobash 1978; Fields and Kirchner 1978; Pagelow 1978a; Pleck et al. 1978). Many others have addressed the question of whether or not there is such a thing as a "battered husband syndrome" (Abrams 1978; Adler 1977; Barnett et al. 1980; Berk et al. 1981; Frieze 1979; Jaffee 1980; Marquardt and Cox 1979; Star 1980; and others). Almost all writers who discuss the question of wife abuse versus husband abuse come to the conclusion that the proportions of male victims are minuscule compared to female victims. Even when men stay in violent relationships, they have a wider range of alternatives available than women. There is no way to determine how many wives' attacks are self-defense or victim precipitated. It is known that when battered women do strike back, they tend to use objects or potentially lethal weapons as "equalizers" (Dobash n.d.; Fiora-Gormally 1978; Fromson 1977; Lewin 1979; Martin 1976; Mitchell 1978; Wolfe 1979).

In 1977 Minnesota was one of the first states to require data collection relating to battered women from every medical profession and law enforcement agency in the state, and the following year the law was amended, requiring data analysis and a report on the feasibility of creating shelters and social service programs for men, similar to the ones provided for women (Minnesota Department of Corrections 1979). Over 4,000 reports were received in an 8.5-month period, but a data collection form to obtain background information on *abused men* and on the services needed by them was utilized throughout the state only during a brief reporting period ending November 15, 1978. During that time, there were 966 reports, 95 percent of which were incidents of assault on women by men with whom they were or had been residing (Minnesota Department of Corrections 1979, 58). The other 5 percent consisted of male assault victims who ranged in age from 11 to 87 years old; 50 percent were 29 years or younger. Minnesota Department of Corrections personnel continued to collect data, and they estimated 86,945 assaults by males on their female partners during 1980 and 1981; out of 3,900 reports in 1981, 3,737 were reports of males battering females, and 163 (4 percent) were reports of females battering males (Watkins 1982, 38).

Dobash and Dobash (1978) provide solid evidence on the relative violence of women and men in society and in the family. Gathering data from police and court records in one year, they found 3,020 cases involving violence of which males were the offenders in 91.4 percent of the cases (1978, 435–36). Percentages of victims and offenders by sex were shown earlier in Table 2–1, as they were compared to data from a similar study in the United States (Mulvihill and Tumin 1969). The data obtained by the Dobashes in Scotland and the data from the United States are strikingly similar. Women in both countries were offenders less than 10 percent of the time, and they were victims in 39 to 45 percent of the cases in the two studies. The only remarkable difference is in the percentage of American women arrested for violence against a male victim, which is almost twice the Scotland charges (6.4 percent compared to 3.5), and female to female violence is less in the United States sample than the Scotland sample.[9]

Moreover, when the Dobashes narrowed their inquiry into all cases of violence between family members, they found an even larger differential between males as offenders and females as victims. There were 898 cases involving violence between family members (all assaults on spouses, children, siblings, and parents), and Dobash and Dobash (1978, 436) say: "These data reveal that violence occurring between family members almost always involved male offenders and female victims, a pattern which prevailed in almost 94 percent of the cases." Males comprised 97.4 percent of the offenders, compared to 2.6 percent female offenders.

Analysis of the "Battered Husband Syndrome"

Almost all studies of marital violence involved interviews with one or the other spouse, but not with couples. Maximiliane Szinovacz's rare study included *both* husband and wife using a modified CTS and found *response inconsistency,* which means that spouses tended to disagree considerably on the occurrence and frequency of violent behaviors (Szinovacz 1983, 641). Response inconsistency in couple data is very common (Bokemeier and Monroe 1983), but couple data provide more accurate and complete information, and Szinovacz shows that aggregate data (such as used in the Straus et al. study, 1980) cannot substitute for couple data. Using couple data and comparing them to aggregate data, Szinovacz (1983, 643) found 50 percent more violence by husbands and 20 percent more violence by wives. Men and women obviously view violent behavior differently; as Szinovacz (1983, 642) notes:

> [T]hey may very well differ in their definition of violence and accordingly report or fail to report especially minor forms of

violence. Thus, husbands may not report or even recall some violent acts by their wives because they did not take these behaviors seriously.

Sociologist Emily Stier Adler (1981) also interviewed couples and found approximately equal acts of violence reported by husbands and wives, but while the wives tended to take their husbands' (or their own) violence seriously, many of the husbands saw their wives' violence as ineffective and/or nonthreatening. These men perceived their wives' serious attempts to hurt them as amusing or, at most, annoying. One husband is quoted as saying, "she can beat me all over my head and it won't hurt me" (Adler 1981, 313). A quotation from the same man's wife follows: "I hit him a couple of times in the arm. And as he stood there laughing at me I belted him a couple of times; I belted him again. I felt better after. He laughed. He thought it was hilarious" (1981, 313). Adler notes that the husband added that the episode did not bother him, but his wife hurt her hand, and she was so upset that she cried.

Undoubtedly, many women are violent, and some of them are extremely violent and can create an environment of real fear and danger for their husbands. There is not sufficient scientific evidence of a large-scale *syndrome* that compares to the evidence of a widespread and serious battered wife problem, yet there must be many husbands who have been beaten severly by their wives more than once, but who remain for various reasons. Proportionately, only a few men are the vulnerable elderly, frail, physically handicapped,[10] or are muscularly weaker than their wives. If these men have the misfortune of having violent wives, they may be unable to defend themselves or prevent the violence. Although the idea was bandied about that old men are frequently beaten by their much younger and stronger wives, statistics show that it is relatively rare for husbands and wives to have great age differentials. As Stephen Rawlings writes in his population report, "among married men age 45 and over, only about 1 in 900 had a wife under age 25" (1978, 4). As mentioned earlier, data on battered husbands collected in one state found that half of the men who complained of abuse by wives were under 30 years old, and only three of the men were 65 or older (Minnesota Department of Corrections 1979, 58).

The vast majority of men are not *physically* or *economically* restrained from walking out the front door and never returning if and when their wives become violent. Men are, on the average, larger and muscularly stronger than women, so if they choose to strike back they can do greater physical harm than is done to them, they can nonviolently protect themselves from physical harm, or they can leave the premises without being forcibly restrained.

There are other factors besides the average man's superior size, weight, and muscular strength that mitigate against his being a helpless victim of a violent wife. Due to the design of men's clothing, they are more likely than women to carry their wallets containing cash, identification, and credit cards on their person for a hasty exit. A woman may have to search around for her purse, or have it snatched away when she attempts to flee. If there is even one operable motor vehicle, a man is more likely to have the keys in his possession, or to be physically capable of taking them despite resistance. Even in the case of a vengeful wife who disables the family car to prevent her husband's quick departure, a man is often more likely to know how to replace battery cables or distributor wires than a woman in a similar position.

Why then would the average man remain with a violent wife after being subjected to physical abuse? There are a number of reasons that a man may stay after one violent episode, but there are few reasons that can adequately explain why he would stay until he was subjected to the same kind of repeated episodes of increasing violence that many battered wives are unable to prevent or to leave. Some men may remain beyond the first episode of violence for the same reasons most women do not leave after the first assault: the spouse is truly contrite and loving afterward; the victim loves the abuser; the behavior is excused by circumstances, for example, stress, alcohol, and so forth; the abuser has many other positive features; the victim is unwilling to expose private embarrassment to family and friends; there is great investment in the relationship; and/or there are children. Among men who remain after an initial attack (primary battering) and stay after the violence has been repeated (secondary battering) (Pagelow 1981a), the reasons seem to center on issues such as material and economic concerns, psychological dependency, and fear for safety of the children. Factors such as these indicate the need battered husbands have for legal and psychological counseling, rather than the varied needs of battered wives, the most important of which is usually safety for themselves and often for their children. Indeed, data obtained from abused husbands confirm that the primary service needs of assaulted men are support groups, counseling, and legal services (Minnesota Department of Corrections 1979, 60). One battered husband expressed his situation in these terms:

> She was the first woman I loved, and I did love her! There were many nice things about her: she was smart, she was fun to be with, and she was a wonderful mother to our two little girls. But she could be mean as hell, and she'd hit me with anything she got her hands on. I just tried to protect myself—I never could really let her have it—no matter what. But finally, I had

enough, and I just took a walk and never went back, except to see my girls. (Weren't you afraid she would hurt them? Is that why you stayed?) No, I knew she'd never touch them, she was always good to them; I didn't have to worry about them. But then she got married again, and they were both into drugs, and one night she killed him. I tell you, she was *mean!*

This man was undeniably a victim of abuse by a very violent woman, but his case differs in important ways from the experiences of many battered wives who are unable to walk out and never go back. In the first place, they may be physically restrained from leaving or have to leave when the abuser is not around; they usually take their children with them; they may not have transportation, employment or other source of income; and they usually fear that their abusers will find them and either harm them more or force them to return. This battered husband knew that he *could* strike back or leave whenever he was ready: he had a job, a car, money of his own, and no fear of being followed and forcibly returned; *the decision was his to make.* His psychological and physical scars remain, but he is totally free from his abusive spouse.

There is little doubt that many men suffer abuse from their wives, although social learning theory leads to the conclusion that the abuse is mainly psychological rather than physical, because physical abuse by wives is much less likely to be rewarded, given the usual differential in physical prowess plus the cultural approval of male violence. Nevertheless, when abuse by wives is physical, the kinds of assistance battered husbands need are more limited than the needs of battered wives, but they *are* available and the men must take the initiative and search out the kinds of help they need. The preponderance of scientific evidence leads to the conclusion that the vast majority of victims of spousal violence are females, whether wives or lovers (Eisenberg and Micklow 1974; Fields and Kirchner 1978; Flynn et al. 1975; Hilberman and Munson 1978; Lynch 1977; Martin 1976; Pleck 1977; Walker 1978, 1979). Statistics show that for *all* crimes of violence, violence against women by men is approximately six times greater than that of women against men (Mulvihill and Tumin 1969, 210–15). As an assistant district attorney, Charles Schudson (1978) handled hundreds of spouse abuse cases and only one of these included a battered man. In the years since 1977 when the image of the "battered husband syndrome" was publicized, there has not been a single report of scientific research on a sample of battered husbands.

Although a recent article in *Time* magazine (O'Reilly 1983, 23) credits Murray Straus with saying that he estimates 282,000 men are beaten by their wives each year, Straus had written several articles earlier, warning about the likelihood of bias in the data of his national study resulting from over- and underreporting by respondents, and pointing out the differences (not measured by the CT Scale) in severity of injury and lack of alternatives of wives (1976b; 1978; 1980b; 1981b). In writing about the study upon which Steinmetz (1977b) based many of her claims, Straus states:

> Although these findings show high rates of violence *by wives,* this should not divert attention from the need to give primary attention to wives *as victims* as the immediate focus of social policy. There are a number of reasons for this. . . . In short wives are victimized by violence in the family to a much greater extent than are husbands and should therefore be the focus of the most immediate remedial steps. (1978, 448–49).

In sum, there undoubtedly are many violent wives and some battered husbands, but the proportion of systematically abused husbands to abused wives is relatively small, and certainly the phenomenon does not amount to a *syndrome* as popularized. Paradoxically, when Steinmetz was presenting the idea of a syndrome, besides talking about comic strip characters and newspaper items about a rich old man, she also drew on accounts of the punishment historically meted out to "a husband who allowed his wife to beat him" (1978, 499). The fact is a husband beaten by his wife was (and still is) an anomaly, and it was precisely because such events were departures from the general rule that they were noted in the book she cited. Historian Elizabeth Pleck and her colleagues (1978, 682) comment that Steinmetz neglected to mention that the examples she used were presented by the author as "conspicuous exceptions to the far more prevalent pattern of wife-beating." However, history does help us better understand the present, and the history of marriage and husband/wife relations reveals much that explains contemporary violence against wives.[11]

MARRIAGE AND THE FAMILY IN HISTORY

Sociologist R. Emerson Dobash and Russell Dobash are the leading proponents of studying wife beating in a wider sociohistorical context, and their book, *Violence Against Wives: A Case Against the Patriarcy* (1979), provides several chapters that trace women's position in society and the family through recorded history. These authors maintain that violence against wives is "normal" behavior that has been accepted and promoted down through the ages; violence against women in the home is not abnormal or deviant but:

> Rather, it is a form of behavior which has existed for centuries as an acceptable, and, indeed, a desirable part of a patriarchical family system within a patriarchical society, and much of the ideology and many of the institutional arrangements which supported the patriarchy through the subordination, domination and control of women are still reflected in our culture and our social institutions. (Dobash and Dobash 1978, 427)

History is replete with laws, customs, and legends that show that women have been beaten, tortured, and killed by their spouses to such an extent that when these acts became public knowledge, if the abusers were not commended for their actions, their acts were at the least ignored. Terry Davidson (1977b) gathers together historical evidence of men "castigating" their wives and even being *urged* to do so for moral reasons. Coincidentally, she uses the same historical evidence of the punishment meted out to men who "allowed" their wives to beat them in the sixteenth century that Steinmetz (1978, 499) uses to support her idea of husband battering, but Davidson presents it as an example of the *rarity* of husband beating, compared to the *norm* of wife beating (1977b, 12). Davidson writes that the man's punishment took the form of an "extended practical joke" and was the occasion for ribaldry and festivity, saying, "In a French marriage, the norm, where beating was concerned, was husband-beats-wife, not vice versa" (1977b, 13).

Marriage and husband/wife relations cannot be discussed without reference to more general man/woman relations, and regardless of the historical or anthropological source used, there is substantial evidence that women have been dominated, controlled, feared, hated, loved, and admired by men over the centuries. In fact, the word woman derives from the Anglo-Saxon *wifman,* which literally means "wife-man." As historian Vern L. Bullough (1974, 3) explains, "the implication seems to be that there is no such thing as a woman separate from wifehood. As individuals, with few exceptions, women did not count. They were mothers, wives, daughters, sisters, proper and forgotten." While most agree that women have historically been assigned a position inferior to men, their status and influence have waxed and waned in different cultures during different periods.

Ancient Greece is portrayed as an era in which women's status and influence reached an apex, although most of our knowledge of this period is derived from mythology, plays, and legends, and the women who did manage to achieve some recognition and freedom were extremely rare (Bullough 1974). Julia O'Faolain and Lauro Martines (1973) surmise that women in preclassical Greece enjoyed a far superior status to that of their successors, but they also note that in Athens, women fell into three categories: mistresses for pleasure, concubines to attend to their masters' physical needs, and wives to bear children and be faithful housekeepers. Sparta had a more rigid caste system comprised of slaves, noncitizens, and citizens. The authors explain, "A woman was never a citizen. She had neither political rights nor legal capacity and, being subject to a guardian, was unable to dispose of her own person" (O'Faolain and Martines 1973, 9). Laws were written clearly defining when, and how, daughters could inherit from their fathers. For example, if an heiress had a son, he would possess the estate two years after puberty and thereafter pay "alimony" to his mother (O'Faolain and Martines 1973, 13). There was no alternative to marriage for a respectable Greek woman; it was arranged by her guardian, and her consent was not required. O'Faolain and Martines (1973, 15) provide a quotation of Euripides on marriage from the *Medea*, written about 400 B.C.:

> Surely, of all creatures that have life and will,
>   we women
> Are the most wretched. When for an extravagant sum,
> We have bought a husband, we must then accept him as
> Possessor of our body. This is to aggravate
> Wrong with worse wrong. Then the great question:
>   will the man
> We get be bad or good? For women, divorce is not
> Respectable; to repel the man, not possible.
> . . . And if in this exacting toil
> We are successful and our husband does not struggle
> Under the marriage yoke, our life is enviable.
> Otherwise death is better. If a man grows tired
> Of the company at home, he can go out, and find
> A cure for tediousness. We wives are forced to look
> To one man only.

Some historians account for the origin of patriarchy and the inferior position of women relative to men as dating back into prehistoric time when men discovered that they, and not vague ancestral spirits, played a part in paternity. As Bullough (1974, 11) states, though, there is no consensus about when such a momentous discovery took place. Maternity was never in doubt, but once men discovered the connecting link between semen and subsequent birth of a child, the role of the mother became considered inferior to that of the father. Bullough notes (1974, 12): "Since, moreover, the semen is visible while the ovum is not, it is easy to understand why throughout recorded history man has assumed that he was primarily responsible for procreation." The woman's role could not be entirely dismissed, but even when a connection was made between two "seeds," the seed of the female was considered inferior, passive, and weak, while the seed of the male was viewed as active, strong, and most important.

Many writers have examined evidence of connecting links between demands of men for domination and control of women and their own fears, antagonisms, and even hatred of women through the centuries, largely associated with sexual and reproductive matters (Delaney et al. 1976; Dworkin 1974; Hays 1964; Masters and Lea 1964, Montagu 1968; Pagelow 1981c, and others).[12] Anthropologists have shown that in various cultures males have imitated female menstruation, pregnancy, and childbirth, even to the point of isolating the new mother in the hut and the father emerging with the infant that he had "delivered" from his own body. There are a wide variety of rites, rituals, and punishments administered to women that are associated with menstruation and childbirth that reveal both fear and envy (Delaney et al. 1976; Frazer 1958; Hogbin 1970). H. R. Hays (1964) believes that male attitudes and images of females were influenced by deep, almost universal anxieties about sexuality. Bullough (1974, 16) explains:

> [I]nevitably the male has tended to project his fears and antagonisms in terms of derogatory attitudes toward the female by insisting that women are evil, inferior, and valueless. Thus women should be made to obey, be kept in their place, or assigned to some unreal role which neutralizes them and removes them from the sphere of competition. Emerging from such attitudes are traditions and stereotypes which are used to justify male domination of the female.

Male anxieties about females' sexual abilities and capacities gave rise to the sexual double standard, restrictions on women's freedom, and the virgin/whore dichotomy that denigrates sexual activity by females and at the same time venerates sexual prowess among males (Bullough 1974; Hays 1964; Pagelow 1981c). These primitive fears and attitudes have been transmitted cross-culturally and through time via nursery rhymes, fairy tales, mythology, taboos, laws, textbooks, literature, religion, psychotherapy, and the media: films, television, advertising, and pornography (Pagelow 1981c). Most of all, men wanted to insure that their heirs were their own issue, therefore monogamy (at least for women) had to be invented. In ancient Greece, there was a form of "matrimony" without a contract, which was signified by a banquet offered by the bridegroom to prove that the woman was a wife rather than a concubine. However, the bride did not attend the banquet because a woman's place was at home, in the women's quarters or *gynaeceum*, a remote section of the house that was never entered by any man except a close relative (O'Faolain and Martines 1973, 16). The aim of Greek marriage was to produce an heir, but not too many; thus abortion, contraception, and exposure (leaving an infant to die) were methods used to limit the family. Decisions regarding these matters were left entirely to the husband.

The first law of marriage was formalized in Rome by Romulus, who is credited with the founding of Rome in 753 B.C. The law stipulates in part: "This law obliged both the married women, as having no other refuge, to conform themselves entirely to the temper of their husbands and the husbands to rule their wives as necessary and inseparable possessions" (O'Faolain and Martines 1973, 34). There were no alternatives to marriage for women, but the law now spelled out the rights and obligations of husbands and wives, which were heavily weighted to insure husband's *rights* and wives' *obligations*. As Dobash and Dobash (1978, 428) explain:

> The man was the absolute patriarch who owned and controlled all properties and people within the family. A wife was obligated to obey her husband and he was given the legal right and the moral obligation to control and punish here for any 'misbehavior', including adultery, drinking wine, attending public games without his permission or appearing unveiled in public.

Husbands' rights to judge, control, and punish their wives were written into law, legitimating their subjugation through force. Whipping was reserved for minor offenses, but wives could be, and were, put to death for drinking their husbands' wine or for infidelity. On the other hand, wives were forbidden to reprimand or even *touch* their husbands as punishment for the latter's infidelity. The double standard was written into law because: "The husband's authority had to remain inviolate in order that there would be no question about the pedigree of the male children who were to inherit the family name and possessions" (Dobash and Dobash 1978, 428). Changes occurred in the Roman Empire that modified the subordinate position of women (outlawing, for example, the beating of upper class women), but then a new religious group whose members called themselves Christians began to gain converts and power, and they demanded the continuance and maintenance of the control and authority of the patriarchy.

As Dobash and Dobash note (1978, 428): "Christianity embraced the hierarchical family structure and celebrated the subordination of wives to their husbands." Christian scriptures commanded women to be silent, obedient to their husbands, and to accept their husbands' authority. In fact, the first Christian Roman emperor, Constantine I the Great (later canonized as a saint), was the first emperor to order the execution of his own wife (Davis 1971). Constantine secured his empire through his marriage by proxy to Maximian's infant daughter Fausta in 298 A.D., but later, when she was of no further use to him, Constantine had his young wife killed. She was scalded to death in a cauldron of water brought to a slow boil over a wood fire, "a protracted and agonizing death indeed," because he suspected her of adultery (Davis 1971, 235–36). Historian Elizabeth Gould Davis says, "this precedent set the pattern for the next fourteen centuries" (1971, 235).[13]

The church and the state joined forces to support husbands' dominance and wives' submission, and the writings of Martin Luther, John Knox, and John Calvin, leaders of Christian splinter groups, strongly reinforce that heritage (Davidson 1977b; Dobash and Dobash 1979). Civil and religious laws continued to spell out the rights of husbands to "chastise" their wives for the most minor offenses to the most serious. One writer describes a sixteenth-century Russian domestic code that demanded absolute obedience from women in these words:

> Disobedient wives were to be soundly thrashed, but "not straight on the face or on the ear," since the husband would be sorely disadvantaged should his spouse become blind or deaf or otherwise incapacitated. "Keep to the whip," enjoined the Code, "and choose carefully where to strike. . . ." (Masters 1964, 19)

Wives could be punished for almost anything that displeased their husbands, whether or not the women had control over or responsibility for the real or imagined violation. For example, wives might be disposed of if they had no children or if they produced girl babies instead of the desired sons. One writer (Hays 1964, 12) describes a Bulgarian folk rhyme as the "ultimate in savagery;" the rhyme expresses sentiments of a man who has nine daughters:

> If the tenth, too, is a girlchild,
> I will cut both of your feet off,
> To the knees I'll cut your feet off,
> Both your arms up to the shoulders,
> Both you eyes, too, I will put out,
> Blind and crippled you will be then,
> Pretty little wife, young woman.

One period in which women gained somewhat higher status was under the French aristocracy, and when the French Revolution occurred at the end of the eighteenth century, women's rights were broadened even more. But when Napoleon Bonaparte came to power, he formalized the Civil Code and "imposed his views that women must be legal minors their entire lives. They were 'owned' by their fathers first, and later, by their husbands" (Davidson 1977b, 15). Napoleon's law demanded that wives should be punished along with their husbands for the husbands' wrong-doings, even to the extent that a wife should also share a prison sentence. According to Napoleon, the wife shared her husband's good fortunes; thus she should also share his misfortunes. Besides, many men became criminals because of their wives (Davidson 1977b, 15–16). Although American law was influenced most strongly by British Common Law, the Napoleonic Civil Code had a far-reaching influence on many European countries and even had its effects on countries as distant as Japan and Bolivia.

Under the Civil Code married women could be beaten, punched, and permanently disfigured for minor disobedience or for "scolding," and under English law they did no better. As Dobash and Dobash (1978, 429) state: "Under English Common Law a married woman lost all of her civil rights, had no separate legal status and became the chattel of her husband. The right of the husband to chastise his wife was considered a natural part of his responsibilities." But while British women had the misogynist Blackstone to explain common law in his *Commentaries,* they also had philosopher John Stewart Mill who petitioned Parliament on behalf of women's rights and wrote a controversial essay, *The Subjection of Women* (1971), resulting in the gathering of statistics and widespread discussion. Eventually, though, the furor waned without instituting reform legislation. Then in 1878 an upper-class British woman, Frances Cobbe, published a paper, "Wife Torture in England," in which she called attention to the notorious beating and kicking of wives with hob-nailed shoes, comparing the fate of wives in Liverpool to slaves in the United States. Her paper states that a wife in England is "liable to capital punishment without judge and jury for transgressions which in the case of a man would never be punished at all, or be expiated by a fine of five shillings" (Cobbe 1878).

The few voices that were raised calling for mercy and justice for wives remained unheard, and jurists and legislators continued to listen to the voice of Blackstone who explained that husbands had the right and duty to "chastise" their wives, like their apprentices or children, for "correction" purposes (Davidson 1977b; Dobash and Dobash 1979). Both wives and children were property of the husband and father under English Common Law, and, if parents separated, the father had the primary and "natural" right to the custody of his children. Fathers were presumed to have superior skills and knowledge to train children (especially sons), and Blackstone stated that mothers were entitled only to their children's "reverence and respect" but no power over them (Weitzman 1981, 100).

Women in the American colonies had fared somewhat better under the law, although there was no place for unmarried women in Puritan society; the few that resisted marriage had to reside in family households and assist with chores and children. Some English Common Laws were gradually modified to fit new world conditions, allowing women more freedom in commercial areas, such as conducting business or entering contracts, but ironically they lost many of these rights during a wave of legal conservatism after 1776 and the American Revolution (Sachs and Wilson 1978, 70). As Terry Davidson explains, "With Blackstone as a guide, America's first states formed their wifebeating laws" (1977b, 19). The first wife-beating case in the United States came to the supreme court of Mississippi in 1824; the court unheld the husband's right of chastisement in cases of "great emergency," saying that husbands should not be subjected to "vexatious" prosecutions for assault and battery (Davidson 1977b, 19; Dobash and Dobash 1979, 62). Other states followed. The first states to rescind the "ancient privilege" of wife beating were Alabama and Massachusetts in 1871. Now it was no longer legal to beat a wife with a stick, pull her hair, choke her, spit in her face, or kick her on the floor. It took Mississippi 50 years to repudiate its earlier decision and to call it a "revolting precedent" (Dobash and Dobash 1979, 63).

Laws have changed slowly over time, but some individuals' ideas of marriage remain firmly entrenched in the tradition of patriarchal power, rights, and duties. This overview focused on marital violence, showing that much of the history of marriage has been bloody and mean. One writer notes:

> Husbands have, in many times and places, been able to beat, mutilate, and even murder their wives with impunity. Fathers have been accorded the right to determine whether a female child should be killed or permitted to live. Widows have been compelled to destroy themselves upon the death of the husband. (Masters 1964, 44)

However, the question remains: Is it the institution of marriage itself that leads to the battering of women by men, calling some writers to equate the marriage license with a "hitting license" (Straus 1976b), or does the problem go deeper, back into male/female relations themselves? One way to find answers to this question is to examine male/female intimate relationships outside of marriage, such as cohabiting couples and dating couples. Reports from research on violence between unmarried couples are now beginning to appear, and these findings are addressed in the next section.

INTIMACY AND VIOLENCE:
THE "DATING GAME"

One of the first writers to note that violence occurs between unmarried as well as married couples was Del Martin (1976, 18), when she questioned Richard Gelles's often quoted assumption that "a marriage license also functions as a hitting license" (1974, 153). In her book she mentions that Gelles suggests that violence between couples is considered acceptable within marriage, but not outside of it, and comments:

> Unmarried women who have been beaten by their mates undoubtedly would take exception to Gelles's interpretation. It may well be that the shared home, not the marriage vow, is the key element here. Some men may feel that they have the right to exercise power over the women they live with whether or not they are legally married to them. (Martin 1976, 18)

Traditional ideas of male/female relations can and do exist in nontraditional quasi-marital relationships, which involved the sharing of residence and intimate sexuality and all the other activities associated with marriage, with the exception of marriage ceremonies. Martin (1976) explains that patriarchy gives the man rights over the property and the individuals that comprise his household; so when a man who subscribes to traditional ideas engages in a live-in situation without marriage, those beliefs are likely to have a strong influence on his expectations of male/female rights and obligations. Many couples set up joint residency as a kind of "trial marriage," before entering into legal marriage. The author's study of woman battering attempted to see which of these ideas is correct: Is it marriage or the shared home that encourages violence? This section adds another question and explores these three assumptions:

> *The marriage license is a hitting license:* being married leads some people to assume rights, privileges, and control over their spouses.

> *Cohabiting violence:* a shared residence and sexual intimacy is just as likely to result in some people assuming the same "rights" over cohabitees as though they were legally married.

> *Dating violence:* male/female relations themselves are structured such that intimacy between couples, living together or not, results in some people assuming rights to control and dominate others.

The Marriage License Is a Hitting License

Carol R. Watkins (1982, 3) notes that many battered women say they did not know their husbands were violent before marriage, and that the violence often starts after the wedding, sometimes on the honeymoon, regardless of the length of the courtship. Lenore Walker (1979, xv) begins her book by stating that although battering relationships also exist outside of marriage, "it is important to note that battering relationships are more frequent among married couples. The marriage license in our society also seems to serve as a license to violence."

R. Emerson Dobash and Russell Dobash (1978, 437) clearly state their assumptions that marriage itself, based as it is on a hierarchy of power vested in the patriarchy that legitimizes wife beating, sets the stage for violence: "it is in their capacity as wives that the risk is the highest and the danger the greatest." Dobash and Dobash (1979, 81–86) describe dating relationships as relatively idealized performances wherein each person tries to "put his/her best foot forward" to impress and please the other. Both of them have distinct expectations of what marriage holds in store. Frequently these notions are based on sex-role stereotypes and ideals they learned from parents, friends, school, and the media (Dobash and Dobash 1979, 86). Jessie Bernard (1982) aptly describes the destruction of preconceived notions after marriage in what she terms the "shock theory of marriage." Dobash and Dobash (1979, 86) says:

> Since the period before marriage is rarely preparatory for marriage but is quite distinct in character, involving different goals and activities, it is to be expected that considerable changes in the lives of the couple will occur with marriage, when questions of financial support, domestic work, reproduction, and child care must be resolved.

In their interviews with 109 battered women, Dobash and Dobash found that violence usually did not occur until after marriage but began soon afterward. By the end of their first year, 59 percent had experienced violence, and 92 percent had been beaten within the first five years (1978, 438). However, violence occurred in many relationships during the courtship. Twenty-three percent of their sample reported being physically abused before marriage, usually because of unfounded sexual jealousy, or in retaliation for the women's attempts to establish a single standard for sexual behavior, and their subsequent efforts to terminate the relationships (Dobash and Dobash 1978, 1979). Most of the women battered during courtship believed that the violence would disappear once they were married.

A large majority (94 percent) of Lee H. Bowker's sample of 136 battered women were married to the men who assaulted them, but premarital violence occurred in 27 percent of the cases (1983a, 40). For most of these 39 women, violence occurred only once or twice, but it occurred at least 14 times in five cases. Like the Dobashes' study, the primary cause was attributed to jealousy. As Bowker explains, "Many of the suitors assumed that their future wives were personal property and became violent whenever the women showed any independence, particularly where that involved contact with other males" (1983a, 40). Interestingly, Bowker (1983a, 29–35) provides three composite case histories, and the first one details the first beating, which occurred on the couple's wedding day. The second vignette involves a marriage that took place when the woman became pregnant; the first beating occurred three months after the wedding. The third

Is the marriage license a hitting license? Some researchers believe it is, and whether or not some legislators believe it serves symbolically as a hitting license, they have instituted laws in some states, attaching a surtax to the marriage license fees. The additional funds raised in this manner have been allocated to shelters for battered women and other services for victims of marital violence.

Source: Roland Hiltscher Photography, Fullerton, California.

case was that of a teen-age bride who married to escape an unhappy home situation; the husband was known to have a fierce temper and had been in a juvenile institution because of his violent behavior. Bowker states: "During the seven-month courtship, he slapped her a number of times, either after an argument in which he expressed extreme jealousy or when he had been drinking" (1983a, 34). The violence consisted mostly of slapping and yelling, but on one occasion he hit her with his fists, and a beating a month before the wedding almost caused the woman to cancel her plans, but her mother prompted her to overlook the incident as something unlikely to be repeated. As Bowker says, "The first incident of marital abuse occurred during their honeymoon" (1983a, 34).

A personal friend of the author married an air force officer only after living with him for two years; she had had a disastrous first marriage and wanted to ensure that her second marriage would be a good one and that she would have a happy home for her young daughter. Satisfied that her lover would be a good husband and father, she married him and was beaten for the first time on their wedding day. His comment was: "I bought you; now you're mine, and you'll do what I say!"

This last case and the three vignettes above from the Bowker study all seem to support the idea of the marriage license as a "hitting license," and the majority of women in most studies report that they had not been beaten before their weddings (77 percent in the Dobash and Dobash study). Strangely, some men become even more possessive of their women as the wedding approaches or just after it occurs. One of these was a wealthy man of 48 who had been living with a 25-year-old woman for four years without violence; two days before their elaborate wedding, he beat her with a whip; the day before the wedding he took her to his attorney's office for her to sign a prepared prenuptial agreement disclaiming any rights to his property or gifts in the event of a divorce. This woman said later she was in a state of shock at the bizarre turn of events and she could not imagine canceling the wedding, because it would have meant disclosure of her intense humiliation to close relatives and friends. After two years of beatings, she finally left him.

Violence also occurs among the affluent when a couple is only dating, and yet they marry. An example of this is detailed in *Woman-Battering: Victims and Their Experiences* (Pagelow 1981a, 189–98). In that case, the woman was literally kidnapped and forced into marrying her husband because of threats to herself, her son, and her parents. At the other end of the socioeconomic strata, there was a very young woman who resisted her father's attempts to get her to marry a man he had chosen for her; the father beat her and threatened to throw her out of his house. She acquiesced and married her very violent suitor. This case is very similar to the third vignette presented by Bowker (1983a, 33–35), where the woman is pressured by a parent to marry someone she fears. A few women initially were somewhat flattered that their lovers were so possessive of them and believed that only love could produce such strong emotional reactions (see NiCarthy 1983a, on "addictive love and abuse").

The shortest marriage in the Pagelow survey (1981a) was three weeks. In that case, the bride was also beaten on the wedding day. However, the average length of marriage of the 281 legally married women was six years. The range of time spent living together for the entire sample of 350 women surveyed was from less than a year to 42 years (1981a, 112). The questionnaire asked the women about the first time they saw their abusers become violent (to themselves, others, pets, or objects). On the average, the violence began about one year after the couple began living together, but for 28 of the married women the violence began sooner: on their wedding day, the day before, or within the first month of the wedding. A few women were never struck until seven to ten years later. Threats had preceded many of these attacks, but in some rare cases, the men had never previously displayed violent behavior. One women wrote: "I was completely shocked. We had been in school together, I had known him for 11 years before we began living together—and he had never, ever been violent before!" The first attack in this case occurred three months after the wedding.

Cohabiting Violence

The survey part of the Pagelow study showed about 18 percent of the women had *not* been married to the men who abused them (Pagelow 1981a, 99), and that is far higher than estimates of the proportion of non-married, cohabiting couples in this country, which range around 2 percent (Bird 1979, 12; Glick and Spanier 1980, 21). Another survey of 120 battered women, conducted for the Department of Health, Education, and Welfare, discloses that 12 percent of the respondents were not married to the men who abused them (Service Delivery Assessment 1980, ix). If only about 2 percent of all cohabiting couples in the United States are unmarried, then samples of battered women that contain 12 to 18 percent unmarried women might lead to the conclusion that there is an even greater probability of being beaten when cohabiting than when married. On the other hand, due to sample selection techniques used in these studies, it is possible that a greater proportion of unmarried women show up in these samples because they have fewer support systems available, such as sympathetic families that might have provided them shelter, and thus anonymity.

On the other hand, the national probability sample of intact couples gathered by Straus et al. (1980) is expected to be a representative subsample of unmarried cohabitees. Kirsti Yllo and Murray Straus found that out of the 2,143 men and women, 40 cohabitors (1.9 percent of the sample) were not legally married to their partners (1981, 342). This is close to the 2 percent estimate mentioned earlier, but Yllo and Straus believe that the census estimate and their subsample are probably underestimates of the actual rate of cohabitation in the United States. Data from the cohabitors reveal a much higher rate of violence among them than among married respondents, and Yllo and Straus state: "cohabiting women are almost four times more likely to suffer severe violence as married women" (1981, 343). While rates of violence are high in the first two years for their married sample and steadily decline to a low rate for those married over ten years, the rate for cohabitors is almost double during the first two years and increases until the tenth year, and they are nonviolent after that. Yllo and Straus (1981, 345) explain:

> [T]he violence rate goes up to a full 50% for those who have been living together for three to ten years. The rate then drops to zero for those couples who have been living together for over ten years. The barriers to dissolving a marriage may explain why longer established marriages are more violent than cohabiting arrangements of similar duration. However, it does not explain why the rate of violence is appreciably higher for cohabiting couples who have lived together from one to ten years.

These researchers also found that while these arrangements overall are more violent than marriages, there are certain cohabitors who are less violent than their married counterparts. In addition to those who lived together for over ten years, they found much lower rates of violence among people over 30, divorced women, and persons with high incomes (Yllo and Straus 1981, 345).

It is apparent that many women are battered by men they live with, whether they are married to them or not, so the idea that the marriage license is a "hitting license" (Straus 1976b, 543) may be an exaggeration. But even without a marriage license or a shared domicile, many women are beaten while dating or during the courtship stage.

Dating Violence

Some recent studies have found an astonishingly high rate of violence between dating couples (Cate et al. 1982; Henton et al. 1983; Laner 1982; Laner and Thompson 1982; Makepeace 1981, 1982). Stanley Parcell and Eugene Kanin (1976) were among the first to look at the violence that occurs among dating couples on college campuses. Parcell and Kanin (1976,

8–9) found that 83 percent of their sample of 282 women at a prestigious university experienced episodes of male sex aggression, stating:

> The 234 victimized respondents reported a total of 5,135 episodes of male sex aggression. Well over half (64 percent) of the respondents reported being offended at some level of erotic intimacy during their high school years, and 60 percent of the respondents reported being offended by aggressive males since entering college.

About one-half the sample reported having been victims of sex aggression during a single academic year (Parcell and Kanin 1976, 9). To be included in the category "sex aggression" required the following critera: the episodes had to be offensive and displeasing to the respondents, and reacted to with resistance by them. Resistance consisted of one or more of the following acts by the offended female: arguing, fighting, pleading,

Researchers have only recently begun to look at violence between dating couples and have found high rates of violence, even among high school dating couples. Overall, they find that the frequency of violence increases as intimacy grows.

Source: Family Docudrama Series by Eileen Cowin, photographer. © Eileen Cowin. Reprinted with permission.

screaming, crying, or other behaviors such as maneuvering and flight. Respondents reported that "40 percent of all sex aggressions resulted in the male obtaining sexual intimacy against the female's will;" 29 percent of attempted rapes resulted in rape, and 100 percent of those who attempted rape with violence were "successful" (Parcell and Kanin 1976, 13). Yet, "the offended female resorted to parents, college deans, or the police in less than 2 percent of all episodes" (Parcell and Kanin 1976, 13–14).

Some might argue that this study looks only at sex aggression in dating typical of "one-night stands" on college campuses without taking into account longer-term intimate relationships of women and men in the premarital (or pre-cohabiting) stage. Roger Libby and Murray Straus (1980) investigated the relationship between sex and violence by gathering a sample of 190 unmarried male and female students at three New England universities in 1975. Libby and Straus looked for sexual meanings behind the acts, and found that: "For men who follow the traditional male stereotype of sex as a dominant and exploitative act, higher levels of sexual activity are associated with the aggression and violence typically associated with attempts to dominate" (1980, 133). This study adds more evidence to the author's contention that men who are physically violent with women are traditionalists—those who subscribe to notions of male domination and control—in other words, *the patriarchy*. Libby and Straus confirmed their hypothesis that when sex connoted an act of warmth and human bonding, sexual activity was associated with nonviolence (1980, 144).

In the spring of 1979, sociologist James M. Makepeace (1981) conducted a study of 202 female freshmen and sophomores from rural and small towns who attended a midwest college, asking about various types of courtship violence that they had either experienced themselves or courtship violence of people they personally knew. The study showed that 62 percent of the respondents knew someone who had been involved in such violence, and 21 percent had at least one direct personal experience in courtship violence (Makepeace 1981, 98). Makepeace also conducted a study to compare courtship violence experienced by males and females at three campuses: two private religious colleges for women or men, and a coeducational state university (1982). Self-administered questionnaires collected data from 150 single students, 50 from each campus, asking about acts of courtship violence done to them and by them. Makepeace found that 21 percent of the seniors and 25 percent of the freshmen had been involved in courtship violence (1982, 25). The data did not support several of the researcher's hypotheses. He did not find higher rates of courtship violence at the public institution, and senior women at the private campus reported much higher rates of courtship violence, especially their own violent acts, than their counterparts at the public university. However, the survey instrument was a modified CT Scale, which can only quantify acts that are reported to occur, and Makepeace notes it cannot reveal "their meaning or the definition of the situation in which they occurred." For a number of reasons, he believes that the violent acts by the private school women were "predominantly self-defensive" (Makepeace 1982, 27).

A research team headed by Rodney Cate at Oregon State University also used a modified CT Scale in a study of violence among dating students. The Cate et al. sample consisted of 355 college student volunteers; 22 percent reported they had either been a victim or aggressor toward a premarital partner, and in over half of the violent cases, the abuse was reciprocal (1982, 83). For 72 percent, violence first occurred during "serious" dating or after engagement or cohabitation. Obviously, some of these relationships were severed, but the authors note: "Of the 53 percent of the respondents who were still dating partners with whom they had experienced violence, 83 percent (38 respondents) specified that the abuse had first occurred after the relationship became intimate" (Cate et al. 1982, 83). This seems to indicate that if violence occurs early in a relationship before intimacy is established, it is likely to lead to its termination, but the longer a relationship lasts and the more intimate the couple becomes, the less likely it is to be terminated after violence occurs. If that is the case, it lends support to William Goode's (1971) idea of an *investment factor* in intimate relationships and also helps explain why so many married women remain in their relationships when abuse occurs, usually soon or just after they have invested in a marriage.

When Mary Riege Laner and Jeanine Thompson (1982) designed their study of abuse and aggression in courting couples, they hypothesized that they would find more of these behaviors in relationships defined as "serious and meaningful." Also using a modified version of the CT Scales, they obtained 371 responses from college students and found that more than 68 percent of the women and 64 percent of the men had had at least one violent courtship experience (Laner and Thompson 1982, 239). The data supported their hypothesis, because they found that "violence is more likely to occur in more involved than in less involved relationships" (1982, 242).

However, this study revealed a much higher level of dating violence than other studies. In another article, Mary Riege Laner (1982, 6) suggests reasons why higher rates of violence were found in this sample: the survey instrument included more of the conflict tactic items than used in the other studies, and the questionnaire was distributed following classroom lectures on family violence which Laner believes may have helped "prime" students to reveal violence in their own relationships. As in the other studies of dating violence, Laner's study asked if the events were mutual, and 67 percent of the men, compared to 48 percent of the women, said that they were mutual (1982). Laner notes the importance of the differential response by stating:

> If sex of respondent had not been controlled, a small majority of all (combined) respondents would have appeared to report violent premarital events as mutual. Such a finding would have supported Cate et al's (1982) report that 68% of their sample saw such events as "reciprocal." (1982, 6)

There will be some discussion in Chapter 9 about how gathering data from one but not both persons in a couple (aggregating data from females and males), and then comparing them to explain couple relationships, can introduce bias and distort findings. Nevertheless, in this study of 371 single college students, the men in serious premarital relationships not only perceived violent interaction as mutual more often than did the women, but the men also claimed the violence was precipitated by jealousy and rejection, and that they were "goaded into violence" (Laner 1982, 11). Women were more likely to cite "anger and power struggles" as precipitating factors and to say that drinking and/or drug use was involved.

Another investigation of dating violence obtained a sample of 644 high school students (Henton et al. 1983). This is the only study in which the majority of respondents were male (55 percent). In other studies where the sex ratio is noted, female students usually constitute a slim majority, although females constitute 65 percent in the Laner and Thompson study. The students' ages in the Henton et al. (1983) sample ranged from 15 to 19, compared to 18 to 34 years in the Laner and Thompson study (1982) and 18 to 31 in the Cate et al. study (1982). June Henton and her colleagues found that 12 percent of their young volunteer students had experienced some type of physical violence with a dating partner (Henton et al. 1983, 3), but when broken down by sex of respondent, only 8 percent of the males compared to 17 percent of the females reported violent episodes. Like the other reports cited above, abusive behavior began after the couple became seriously involved in a large majority (77 percent) of the cases, but their average age when violence first occurred was only 15.3 years. Henton et al. (1983, 7) note:

> However, in 23.1% of the relationships, violent acts were started during casual dating. This finding indicates that although abuse may be viewed as more acceptable in relationships of increased intimacy, there is a substantial amount occurring even before individuals feel any commitment to the relationship.

Although 59 percent of the respondents reported that they terminated the violent relationships, 36 percent of the high school students who continued their relationships reported that their relationships improved after the violence occurred. Males expressed "significantly more positive attitudes toward premarital violence" than did females, and the same was true when questioned about their attitudes toward marital violence (Henton et al. 1983, 11–12). Paradoxically, about one-third of the young people involved in violent episodes interpreted the violence as *love,* and the ones who stayed in violent relationships reported perceptions of having limited alternatives.

One writer, social worker, and activist, Ginny NiCarthy (1983a), after working for and with abused women, decided that one approach to reducing wife beating is to educate young women *before* or *when* they are involved in abusive relationships. Teacher and counselor Ann Muenchow and NiCarthy offered a course on "Addictive Love and Abuse" to teen-age women in an alternative school program for pregnant teen-agers (a very high risk group for abuse). The self-help course is structured into eight sessions, with exercises for each, and is fully detailed so that others may adopt it or use it as a prototype for their own programs (NiCarthy 1983a). This course description could make a valuable contribution to reduction of interpersonal violence if it stimulates the introduction of same or similar courses for young people. As Henton et al. (1983, 14, 16) say about their sample of high school students:

> This ability to define abuse as love, together with the romantic notion that if problems do arise, they will go away on their own . . . may allow violence to be tolerated without creating undue stress for the couple. . . . Romance and violence in dating relationships appear to be a contemporary, accepted version of love and war for many couples. The threat of physical and psychological injury engendered by abusive partners is oftentimes not perceived as sufficient risk to outweigh the value of these relationships.

The course conducted by NiCarthy and her associate deals pragmatically with feelings of love and distinguishes between *nurturing love* and *romantic love.* It suggests that the romantic variety tends to have unrealistic expectations and can easily become "addictive," depending on how the couple handles the period following the "honeymoon" stage of rose-colored glasses. NiCarthy (1983a, 120) states, "Not every romantic relationship becomes addictive, of course, but a tendency to addictive love will be supported by a persistent blindness to a partner's flaws."

SUMMARY

In this, the first of two chapters in the section on spouse abuse, there was an examination of how the issue called "wife beating," "woman battering," or "wife abuse," which was later changed to "spouse abuse" or "domestic violence," came to the attention of many people around the world. It did not erupt out of the case loads of mental health professionals, the research findings of social scientists, or from criminal justice statistics. The issue was raised by victims themselves and the women and men who became their advocates and "champions" (Hampton 1982). The movement began in England and spread widely before it came to the attention of Americans. Del Martin notes that *Time* magazine ran an article about the London shelter, Chiswick, but only in the 1974 European edition (1976, 15). Kathleen Tierney (1982, 213) searched the *New York Times* Index and found "There was not a single reference to wife beating as a social or community issue from 1970 to 1972" (1982, 213), and that more intense *Times* coverage on the issue did not begin until 1976.

Movement leaders initially met with denial and resistance from decision makers, but dedicated themselves to gathering statistics and other evidence indicating that wife abuse is a large-scale social problem requiring changes in attitudes, shelters where women and children can receive temporary safety and specific social services, and changes in the helping and legal services. Aided by widespread media attention, their efforts met with some success, although never enough to adequately attend victims' needs, which is now apparently dwindling away (Johnson 1981; Tierney 1982). The present status of the battered women's movement is discussed at the conclusion of the next chapter.

The movement to help women beaten by their husbands and lovers was hardly underway when attention was drawn to claims made by a few individuals that "husband battering," not "wife battering," was the most underreported crime in the American family. The mass media were immediately attracted to this provocative idea and exploited it heavily, and very shortly the notion of a "battered husband syndrome" had spread around the world. As Tierney notes, wife beating was a good subject for the media because it was controversial, it mixed elements of violence and social relevance, and provided a topic for serious discussion without requiring a sacrifice of entertainment, action (1982, 213), and, certainly, emotion. If wife beating was good for the media because it engendered controversy, husband beating was even better. Yet an examination of the evidence offered to support claims of a large-scale problem of physical abuse of husbands reveals that it was largely based on statistics that were altered by the addition of some, the elimination of others, and the changing of still others. Some unscientific evidence was also proposed, but most importantly, the context in which violent acts occurred, their meaning to the actors, and the results of the acts were all either ignored or unknown.

As noted in this chapter, husbands are sometimes physically and psychologically abused by their wives, but their alternatives to prevent or escape the violence are greater than those available to most battered wives, and their needs for outside assistance are usually limited to support groups and counseling, or legal services. Analysis of scientific evidence shows that when spouse abuse occurs the victim of the most severe and most frequent physical abuse is much more likely to be a wife rather than a husband. This comes as no surprise to historians or anthropologists who have studied man/woman and husband/wife relations and observed the power vested in the patriarchy that was maintained and supported by cultural institutions.

The third section of this chapter examined the historical foundation of the family, and the explicit rights and obligations of husbands and wives in family law, which made wives and children chattel to their husbands and fathers. Formally through law and informally through legends, myths, and sayings, men have been expected to provide materially for their charges, while wives and children were expected to give obedience, loyalty, and their services in exchange. If a woman failed to please the man upon whom she was dependent, he was expected and instructed to "chastise" her for her failure. Even before the invention of the family in ancient Rome, there is substantial evidence that in many cultures domination and control were assumed by men in order to assure that the children born to their women were truly their biological heirs. The men who *failed* to dominate their subordinates were frequently ridiculed and humiliated in public to show displeasure at their deviance (Davidson 1977b; Dobash and Dobash 1978, 1979). History is replete with examples of men's willingness to use force and violence to maintain superordinate status over their wives and children, particularly their daughters.

Marriage may have institutionalized patriarchal husband/wife relations, but there is considerable documentation that intimate heterosexual relations are often violent *outside* of marriage. The final section of this chapter examined research evidence that shows many wives were beaten just before, just after, or even on their wedding days, which helps support the idea that the "marriage license is a beating license." Researchers have also found that a large minority of their samples were beaten for the first time during their courtships to the men they later married, some during cohabitation prior to marriage; and that the unmarried are overrepresented in samples of battered women. Violence reported by married persons compared to violence reported by unmarried cohabitants shows much higher rates of violence among cohabitors (Yllo and Straus 1981). All this supports the idea that the shared residence may be a more important factor than the institution of marriage.

However, some researchers have begun examining courtship or dating relationships going further back to college and even among high school students. They have found that between 21 and 65 percent of college students and 12 percent of high school students report violence or abusive behavior in their nonmarital relationships (Henton et al. 1983; Laner 1982; Makepeace 1981). Further, whenever these studies inquired about the first instance of violence, they found that the majority occurred during the more serious and intimate stage of the relationships. This seems to indicate that as intimacy grows, so does the possibility of violence between males and females. None of these studies obtained qualitative measures on the context in which the violence occurred, which ones were one-way aggression and which were self-defensive, or what injuries, if any, occurred as a result, but Makepeace (1981, 1982) speculates that a large proportion of the violent acts performed by females in his study were acts of self-defense. Probably what is the most significant finding out of this new body of research is that many of the couples continued their relationships, despite the occurrence of violence. For example, Henton et al. (1983) found that 41 percent of the high school students in violent relationships continued dating, and some participants claimed the violence enhanced their relationships. This surely indicates, for those concerned about the reduction of family violence, that male/female roles and attitudes about love and intimacy need to be restructured in ways that develop less emphasis on possession and domination, and more on empathy, respect, and consideration for their own and others' rights. Ginny NiCarthy's classes (1983a) which teach teen-agers about "addictive love" seem to be a step in the right direction.

NOTES

1. According to activist social worker Jo Sutton (1978), in Great Britain, battered women who could not stay with friends or relatives could take their children and stay safely in temporary accommodations for the homeless. The 1948 National Assistance Act allowed accommodation for homeless women and their children, and since men were not admitted, battered wives were protect from violent husbands. However, in 1966 husbands were also allowed accommodations and fleeing wives were no longer secure in these places.

2. Haven House was originally established in 1965 by Al-Anon women for families of alcoholics (Martin 1976). Alcoholics Anonymous is a self-help group for alcohol abusers and Al-Anon is an auxiliary group for other members of the problem drinkers' family to help them learn how to survive alcohol-related problems and the drinking behavior itself. According to Del Martin (1976, 197), Haven House housed 600 women and 2,000 children before new fire regulations forced it to close in 1972. It reopened in 1974.

3. It is difficult but not impossible to monitor the battered women's movement in the United States. Some organizations that formerly distributed newsletters free of charge are now forced to require subscriptions, due to cutbacks in funds but some others had budgets slashed so badly they ceased to exist. Funded survivors include the Center for Women Policy Studies, producing a bimonthly newsletter, *Response to Violence in the Family,* an excellent source of information. Yearly subscriptions for individuals in the United States can be obtained by sending $25.00 ($10.00 additional for foreign postage) to CWPS, 2000 P Street NW, Suite 508, Washington, DC 10036-5997. A community health center that sent free newsletters for over four years now asks for a $10.00 subscription fee: *SANEnews,* P.O. Box 1076, Middletown, CT 06457. Feminist Betsy Warrior, working with an activist group in Boston, has released the eighth edition of the *Battered Women's Directory* (1983), listing shelters and services for victims in the United States and around the world, resources, research and articles. The 275-page publication is available for $9.50 from Directory, Betsy Warrior, 46 Pleasant Street, Cambridge, MA 02139. Also, a coalition of three feminist groups has a quarterly publication, *Aegis: Magazine on Ending Violence Against Women.* An individual yearly subscription may be obtained by sending $10.50 ($19.50 for two years) to Feminist Alliance Against Rape, Box 21033, Washington, DC 20009.

4. Under the old system, TROs were practically of no value to battered women, since many of the violations occur at night or during the weekends when courts are closed. In most states, the wife had to return to court with her lawyer, the judge might order the violator to come to court on another date, at which time the wife, lawyer/s, and husband would usually gather for the husband to receive only a scolding. It was unusual for a husband to be arrested for violating a TRO unless there were other changes in connection with it, such as destroying property, disturbing the peace, public intoxication, or violent behavior witnessed by a responding officer. If a wife had little or no money to pay a lawyer, or had children or a job she could not leave, the process discouraged further action. In addition, a restraining order or order of protection does nothing to deter some violent men determined to punish their wives for their action; to these men it is simply a piece of paper, nothing more.

5. Newspaper clipping provided and translated by Asta Magni Lykkjen, Oslo, Norway, August 21, 1978.

6. Discussed during a private conversation with Pirkko Lahti, Helsinki, Finland, August 7, 1978.

7. Perhaps another method was employed, but the writer has been unable to deduce it any other way from available printed sources.

8. In summary, the estimation of 250,000 battered husbands may have been arrived at in the following manner: extrapolating results from her own New Castle County study, comparing these figures with police reports of serious family assaults in the same year, obtaining an incidence rate based on county population, estimating the rate of underreporting, and then generalizing this rate to the national population of 47 million couples.

9. Perhaps some of the higher rate of American women's aggression against male victims is a reflection of the easy availability of firearms in this country, which tends to lessen size, weight, and muscle differentials. By contrast, guns are much more difficult to obtain in Scotland and Great Britain, and they are not to be found in approximately one out of every two homes as they are in the United States (note the earlier discussion in Chapter 4 on the prevalence of firearms in the United States).

10. Although some who proposed the idea of widespread husband battering included in their list of potential victims men who are physically handicapped or incapacitated, there were two wives in the writer's study who were beaten and abused by husbands confined to wheelchairs and suffering from degenerative, incurable diseases. To most

people, this may seem preposterous, yet the children who came with their mothers to a shelter provided full verbal accounts of lives of terror and dictatorial domination by two apparent tyrants. The psychological abuse these families suffered apparently made them so fearful of being locked in rooms, whipped with belts, and so forth, that they failed to see the relative physical weakness of their abusers. The notion of helpless old men being battered by much younger wives was also raised and this undoubtedly does occur, but again, in the writer's study there was one 81-year-old man who psychologically terrorized and physically abused his 65-year-old wife. There seem to be unusual cases on both sides of the debate.

11. The following section necessarily is an abbreviated overview of centuries of man/woman, husband/wife relations. For readers who are interested in exploring in greater depth the historical foundations of marriage and the family, there are a number of excellent sources that should be consulted. These include, but are not limited to, the following: Bullough (1974); Davidson (1977b, 1978); Davis (1971); Dobash and Dobash (1978, 1979); O'Faolain and Martines (1973); Russell (1982); Sachs and Wilson (1978); Stannard (1977); and Weitzman (1981).

12. An earlier article by the writer provides an in-depth discussion of male fear and envy of women and their sexual and reproductive capacity, and examination of ideas that may help explain some of men's historical and cross-cultural violence against women (Pagelow 1981c).

13. The importance of this largely ignored fact of history is that the emperor set the pattern for Christian conduct: By this time, Christianity was the state religion of the Roman Empire, and heresy to the church became treason punishable by torture and death. Constantine I not only boiled his wife alive, but he also murdered his son and brother-in-law, and had his nephew whipped to death (Davis 1971, 237).

14. For a revealing commentary on this, see Bernard (1982) on the "shock theory of marriage."

9

Abused Wives and Their Abusers

Who are the women who are abused by their husbands or lovers, and why do they stay after the first beating, only to be beaten again and again? This chapter begins by giving some insight into the lives and experiences of battered women from their perspective, as obtained by researchers and the people who have worked for and with them. Next, we look at abused women who fight back, how some attempt to stop the violence or get out, and the results of these efforts. Identifying behavioral and situational factors of battered women are presented, followed by suggestions on how concerned people can assist a woman living with a violent man. No discussion of wife beating would be complete without taking an in-depth look at the men who abuse their wives or lovers, and what is being done or can be done to curb their violence; so that is the focus of the next section. The chapter concludes with an analysis of the contemporary response to wife beating: shifting societal attitudes and resources and the potential for reducing or eliminating spousal violence.

ABUSED WIVES: WHY DO THEY STAY?

To many people, it seems clear that something must be "wrong" with any woman who would stay in an obviously dangerous situation, and that no man in his right mind would beat, choke, punch, kick, and maim his wife and (frequently) the mother of his children. That is why, when the topic of wife beating first came to the attention of professionals, the common notion was that either the victims, their abusers, or both were psychopathological individuals. Soon after the battered women's movement started, articles began to appear, some speculative and others descriptive, about a few women beaten by their spouses. Once victims or their abusers were identified, interest focused on individuals involved in violent relationships to see how *different* they were from "normal" people. How different are they? Interpersonal dynamics are important in this issue, but the abused and their abusers are discussed separately here for purposes of clarity and for better understanding, because most research focuses on one or the other, but not both persons, in violent couples. An exception

The decision to leave an abuser is one that many women feel they are unable to make, particularly when there are children involved. Due to the psychological abuse that accompanies physical abuse, many women feel helplessly trapped in a situation and fearful of making any decision on their own. Their children may be supportive and desperately want to end the violence between their parents, but some, who spent earlier years agonizing over the violence and finally came to accept it as part of their lives, may resist leaving and the disruption of their own lives and lifestyles. In most cases, ending the abuse begins with the victim leaving home, but unless there is a shelter she can reach that has room for her and her children, there may be no safe place of refuge.

Source: Family Docudrama Series by Eileen Cowin, photographer. © Eileen Cowin. Reprinted with permission.

is one report on 20 abused wives and their violent husbands (Rosenbaum and O'Leary 1981), but discussion of these findings is deferred to the section of this chapter on abusive husbands.

Abused Wives: What Kind of Women Are Battered?

Woman battering has been defined in various ways by different writers; Ginny NiCarthy's definition is expressed in the following terms:

> Battering is physical force used by one person against another, to coerce, demean, humiliate, punish, or simply to release tension or demonstrate power. A battered woman is one who has been subjected to battering by her intimate partner on more than one occasion. An abused woman is one who has been subjected to physical assault, or emotional abuse, or both, by her intimate partner on more than one occasion. (1983a, 116)

Obviously, the topic here is not *mutual combat* (Pagelow 1981a, 270), in which both parties are equally determined to do battle with one another and inflict as much damage as possible on each other, usually within certain implicit limitations. Such couples were identified as *conflict habituated* in a study of long-term marriages (Cuber and Harroff 1965). This type of relationship seems to involve people who have a mutual need to express aggression in order to achieve the rewards that accompany a "truce," but this may be as difficult to understand as sadomasochistic practices engaged in by other couples. Woman battering includes mostly one-way violence that may or may not be accompanied by victims' attempts to defend themselves (Pagelow 1981a, 33).

In her foreword to Jennifer Baker Fleming's book, *Stopping Wife Abuse*, Del Martin asks the following questions; readers are invited to ponder them awhile to see what their own answers might be.

> Did you ever back down from an argument with a man because you felt intimidated? Did you feel that if you said anything more the situation might get out of hand? Have you ever felt threatened by a man's superior physical strength? Were you afraid that if he became any angrier he might strike you? Have you ever stayed in a relationship longer than you should have? Did you stay because you felt responsible for the other person? Were you afraid of loneliness? Did you stay because of the children? Did you have gnawing doubts that you could not make it on your own in the outside world? Were you fearful that you

couldn't earn a decent living and manage the children by yourself? (Martin 1979a, 9)

These questions are addressed to women, but some men living with
women they believe are potentially violent may also try answering them
for themselves. The odds are greater that more female readers than male
readers will, if they are totally honest with themselves, admit that at some
point in at least one intimate relationship, they could respond "yes" to
several of the above questions. Due to socialization into "appropriate"
feminine roles, most females are likely to have relationships where the
threat of force is present. The difference in whether or not they *involve*
force may be determined in large part by their individual sense of self and
their "mission in life" (Martin 1982, xvii). In her introduction to Ginny
NiCarthy's book, Del Martin points out what many researchers have come
to accept: that almost any woman can find herself in an abusive situation.
Martin (9182, viii) states that we have learned that: "The battered women
is no different from the rest of us, that the plight of the battered woman
magnifies what most women have experienced at some point in their
lives." Martin makes these pointed remarks:

> Just because you haven't been physically hurt does not mean
> that you are not in an abusive situation. Women are battered
> and abused in so many ways by the men with whom they relate
> intimately and by the double standards of patriarchal society
> and its institutions. Non-physical abuse may not make the
> headlines, but it is just as real and can produce indelible scars,
> however invisible they may appear to be. Emotional abuse (de-
> meaning verbal assaults, humiliation, isolation, jealousy, eco-
> nomic dependency, ridicule) assaults a woman's self-esteem
> and makes her feel "helpless." In many cases, such psycholog-
> ical abuse is a prelude to physical abuse. If unchecked, vio-
> lence escalates in severity and frequency, and sometimes leads
> to murder. (1982, xviii)

Activists and most researchers of woman battering agree with Martin's
contention that abuse ranges on a continuum from mild insults to homicide, and that battered women are no different from other women; their
abuse is only a matter of degree. There is no estimate for the percentage
of women who terminate destructive relationships early, because all research on wife abuse has concentrated on relationships that reached
physical violence. The turning point frequently comes when emotional
abuse and threats turn to action and the first single incidence of violence
occurs: This is the *primary battering* stage (Pagelow 1981a, 41–45). How

victims respond at that point is crucial in determining whether the violence ceases or continues and develops into the *secondary battering* stage, which is the recurrence of violence that tends to become systematic and increases in frequency and intensity over time (Pagelow 1981a, 45–51). Wives who have reached this stage are the ones most researchers have studied and most activists have encountered. If primary violence occurs and the victim does not take strong and decisive action that may involve disclosing the behavior to outsiders for immediate intervention, or making it absolutely clear that she will never tolerate a second occurrence (and meaning it), then secondary battering is most likely to occur.

Generalizing from volunteer case studies to produce a "profile" presents the possibility of error if the women are not representative of the larger population of battered women, yet samples of battered women gathered by Pagelow and others indicate certain frequently noted features of their relationships that point to "greater risk" of violence and may be considered *danger points* for women to avoid:

Factors that Increase the Probability of Violence in an Intimate Relationship

Dating violence: continuation of intimate relationships in which any degree of courtship violence has occurred.

Youth: marriage or cohabitation at a young age, especially after a brief courtship period.

Premarital pregnancy: dependency is already established; a combination of youth and premarital pregnancy is extremely dangerous.

Stepchildren: entering a new relationship with a dependent child or children by another man.

Isolation: breaking off close contact and relationships with friends and family; lack of support systems.

Unknown history: lack of knowledge about the man's former intimate relationships whether they be with lovers, wives, or parents.

Dependence: lack of ability to function independently because of health, education, or occupational deficits.

Woman battering occurs among all ages and in all ethnic and racial, religious, educational, occupation, and socioeconomic groups. Whether violence occurs once or many times depends on multiple factors; some of which are external and some of which are internal to the victims. According to NiCarthy, "Contrary to popular thinking, there is no such person as *the* battered woman. . . . [M]any different kinds of women become involved with, and remain loyal to, men who beat them, and for a variety of reasons" (1983, 117).

Why an Abused Woman Stays with an Abuser

Reactions to primary battering and action following secondary battering largely depend on factors *external* to the victims: the material and physical resources they have or do not have (money, friends or family, transportation, education, physical health, number of children, their ages and their health, and so forth). These women may seek outside intervention, and the results of their efforts help determine in large part whether the violence continues or is terminated (Pagelow 1981d). There are other factors that are *internal* to victims: whether or not they strongly subscribe to traditional ideology, which is a belief that women are inferior to men and their role as wife or lover is to be subservient, supportive, encouraging, loyal, and self-sacrificing. Victims often have a strong commitment to marriage that is reinforced by cultural institutions, and pressure is exerted on them by family, religion, and community norms (Dobash and Dobash 1979; Pagelow 1981a, Walker 1979).[1]

Victims of battering were asked in the Pagelow survey why they continued to stay with their abusers after the first instance of violence, and almost half (47 percent) said it was because they *hoped for change.* An abuser is most likely to be sincerely contrite and repentant after the first time he lashes out. Because the man is loved and has many other positive features, the couple is likely to "kiss and make up," both believing that the violence was a freak occurrence that will never happen again. The second largest category (29 percent) responded that they *lacked alternatives;* the third category (15 percent) said they wanted to *keep the family together;* and 10 percent said they stayed because of *fear.* There were other questions asked about their reations to being beaten; answers to these and other commonly noted responses from women who remain with men who beat them are listed below.

Fear

Although only 10 percent of the women said they stayed with their abusers beyond primary battering because of fear, by the time it progressed to the secondary stage, the most commonly mentioned reason was fear:

78 percent (273 women out of 350) indicated fear. Del Martin states, "Battered wives give many reasons or rationalizations for staying, but fear is the common denominator. Fear immobilizes them, ruling their actions, their decisions, their very lives" (1976, 76). The fear is not always only for their own safety. Sometimes they also fear for the safety of their abusers; they believe the men will "fall apart or commit suicide" if they leave (NiCarthy 1983, 117). Their fear often extends to their children, whose lives have been threatened by their fathers, or because they believe the abusers' threats to take the children from them. Their terror may extend beyond their homes; in many cases they do not seek help from friends, neighbors, or their families, because they know their mates' explosive anger can endanger others' lives (Martin 1976, 76). It does happen. For example, a young wife fled to her parents' home after a beating; her enraged husband followed and shot his father-in-law to death. One woman received shelter from her brother and his wife; all three were held at knife point by her furious husband. Another case involved a man who beat a woman and her mother in full view of her father and young son, who were unable to stop the violence (Pagelow 1981a, 189–98).

The most dangerous time period is when abused women are attempting to leave the batterer or immediately thereafter, as many case histories show. Unfortunately, persons outside these relationships often do not take seriously enough the woman's concern for her spouse's potential for extreme violence, believing that her fear is merely hysterical exaggeration. Outsiders should understand that if there is anyone who knows the abuser's capability for violence, it is his primary target. Her fears may be shown later to be unrealistic, but it is far better to exert extreme caution unnecessarily than to make false assumptions. The lives of the victims, their children, and persons trying to assist them may be at stake.

Helplessness

The second most frequent response to the Pagelow survey question asking the women's reactions to battering was that they felt *trapped;* 224 women indicated this feeling (64 percent). In addition, 215 women felt *powerless* (61 percent) to do anything to prevent the abuse or escape from it. That is, approximately two out of every three battered women surveyed saw no way out of their situations. Lenore Walker (1979) discovered that many of the women in her sample felt the same, and she related these feelings to the "learned helplessness" of animals in Martin Seligman's (1975) study, when no matter what their response, the animals were punished until they simply became paralyzed by fear. Other psychologists have compared the terror and trauma of victims of battering by husbands to a form of "frozen fright" because the women are "brainwashed by terror" (Symonds 1975).

One topic rarely mentioned in the literature is a phenomenon commonly called the *Stockholm Syndrome* (Hilberman 1980; Ochberg 1980), which is similar to the reactions of captives aboard a train in Holland and to the Patty Hearst case. These cases all involve hostages held in constant fear for their lives and safety, isolated, terribly abused and mistreated, who very quickly begin to develop positive feelings toward their captors. These are totally helpless people, who are confined and realize that everything they need and want depends on the whims of others. Even the slightest favor (or lessening of their pain or punishment) is seen as a "gift" from their captors, to whom they are grateful. Hostages frequently develop negative feelings toward their rescuers; in Holland several former captives gave their lives during demonstrations for their former captors. NiCarthy makes this analogy:

> The occasional indulgences . . . [often unpredictable] provide intermittent reinforcement for staying in the relationships. The hope for change is activated by periodic moments of closeness or other satisfactions, and may be the counterpoint to the longer periods in which the woman feels both hopeless and helpless. These techniques of emotional abuse are similar to those which have been used to control prisoners of war. . . . As stated in a report published by Amnesty International, these techniques induce "dependency, dread and debility." To the extent that a person is victimized by these techniques, she or he tends to become immobilized by the belief that she or he *is* trapped, *cannot* escape. (1983, 117–18)

Terms that battered women in the Pagelow survey used to describe their reactions give some support to these ideas: 203 women selected *confused* and 201 chose *alone* (about 58 percent of the sample), while others indicated depression and humiliation. Until shelters began opening their doors to battered women and their children, victims may well have developed symptoms similar to hostages in life-threatening situations, because most had no safe place to go and when they turned to others for help—whether to police, ministers, medical professionals, traditional therapists, or social workers—their efforts frequently failed. It was not unusual for them to find that appeals to outsiders made their situations even worse; many women told of turning to professionals and being reprimanded or being told that it was their own failure to maintain a "happy home" that caused their husbands' displeasure and, thus, the violence.

Guilt and Feelings of Failure

Del Martin (1976) writes about women's belief that the success of their marriages depends entirely on them, and that it is their duty to "keep the family together." Martin believes sex-role socialization conditions women to:

> take great pride in a good marriage, and often take full responsibility for a bad one. Her sense of responsibility will lead her to feel ashamed if her marriage "fails," and she will try above all else to save face. . . . Women in our culture are encouraged to believe that the failure of a marriage represents their failure as women. . . . [T]hey have no value as individuals apart from their men. (1976, 81)

When these feelings are strengthened and reinforced by pressure from professionals, friends, neighbors, and relatives, battered women are likely to perceive themselves (and be seen by others) as "deviant," rather than the persons who beat them (Pagelow 1981d). Fleming (1979) also documents the feelings of guilt and failure these women suffer, showing that they assume responsibility for the abuse because they have internalized society's edict that wives must meet their husbands' needs. Their guilt is compounded by the many times others ask "What did you do to provoke him?" (Metzger 1976).

Hope for change, fear, helplessness, guilt, and feelings of failure are all internal factors that operate to keep battered women locked into violent relationships, but factors external to victims also exert a powerful force and limit their alternatives. A few of these are examined next.

Lack of Resources

It has been well documented that battered women are frequently isolated: cut off from others who might give assistance if the violence came to their attention. They often lack any *freedom of movement*. They may be left at home without transportation, and when they must shop for groceries or go out for medical attention, their abusers take them where they must go, staying with them all the time (Eisenberg and Micklow 1977; Martin 1976). Ironically, many times others mistake this for "loving concern" and comment: "What an ideal couple—they're always together!" If the women are employed outside the home, they may be driven to and from work by their husbands, or their movements are closely monitored, and they must account for any extra time spent away. They withdraw from any social activities that do not also include their husbands; the wife's visitors are made to feel unwelcome in her home until the only visitors that enter are friends of the husband (Dobash and Dobash 1979).

The resource that battered women lack the most is *economic independence*. Wealthy women may have charge accounts but no cash, checking accounts, or credit cards (Martin 1976, 84). Husbands who beat their wives keep a tight rein on their wives' actions and money: the last thing in the world they want is for the women to leave them. One way to ensure that is to tightly control all the family finances. Even when a wife is gainfully employed, she may have little or nothing to say about how her contribution is spent, and, in some cases, abusive husbands accompany their wives on payday so the checks are turned over to them immediately (Dobash and Dobash 1979; Martin 1976).

As Fleming (1979, 83) explains, "In violent marriages, the husband invariably controls the family finances—usually with an iron hand. It is the rare victim who has more than a few dollars she can call her own." Both Fleming and the Eisenberg/Micklow team (1977) tell about women who saved for two years to accumulate pitifully small sums for bus fare to escape with their children out of town. In another case, one woman hid some of her own earnings in her husband's dirty socks and then deposited the money in a bank; the bank book was hidden in a clothes pin bag until she finally was able to afford tickets to travel a thousand miles away with her two toddlers (Pagelow 1981a, 184). These cases may seem unusual, but they are not rare.

Fleming (1979, 83) asks pointedly, "Why does she stay? The answer is quite simple. If she has children but no money and no place to go, she has no choice." Having *dependent children* is another reason why battered women stay tied to abusive men. Sometimes the men are extremely loving fathers (or at least they provide for the children financially); thus the mothers endure their fear and pain for the sake of the children. Their socialization convinces them that an intact home is better for their children than having no father, and that they should sacrifice their own self-interest for their children. They often do not recognize the harm done to the children who live in a home where one parent they love beats another parent they love (Dobash and Dobash 1979). Mothers frequently do not decide to leave until they realize that their children are also victims of the violence, directly or indirectly (Pagelow 1982a).

If they are lucky, their children are in good health and old enough to attend school, but many children of battered women suffer from chronic illnesses or various handicaps (Pagelow 1981a). Still, if they leave, where will they go, and how will they provide for themselves and their children? Even if they are well educated, they may have been out of the employ· ment market for so long that their skills are outdated, or they may have no marketable skills. If they are gainfully employed, they often have to terminate their jobs to prevent their husbands from finding them to punish them or force them to return home. This can be a serious career setback for middle-class women. Finding new jobs can be difficult, especially when the women are older, not particularly attractive, minority group members, or burdened with preschool youngsters, due to the lack of adequate and inexpensive child care facilities in this country. Regardless of education and job skills, women have higher unemployment and underemployment rates in this country than men.

A battered woman who fears violent retaliation may hesitate to go to court for child support, and even if she does, awards are often less than adequate. In addition, child support orders are most likely to be ignored. Leaving a husband, despite his abuse, is a difficult choice for many women: It almost inevitably means that the woman and her children will suffer a severe decline in their standard of living. Table 9–1 shows the expected family income of all families, white, black, and Spanish, and the income for married couples, male householders with no wife present, and female householders with no husband present.

Table 9–1 shows that intact couple families enjoy a higher standard of living than single-parent families, but when the single parent is a woman, their income is likely to be *half or less* what it is expected to be when both husband and wife are present. In rounded figures, it costs a woman (depending on her skin color) between about $11,000 and $13,000 to live in a household without a husband present, and in all cases, the income lost is more than she can expect to receive at paid employment. On the other hand, a male householder loses approximately 23 percent of the family income, or it costs about $5,000 per year to live without a wife present.

Employed females receive a much smaller income than males, as Table 9–2 shows. In the 26-year period shown on the table, white women employed full-time, year-round in 1981 received proportionately less than they received in 1955, and while black women receive proportionately far more in 1981 compared to black men, they still only receive about 55 percent the median income of white male workers. A black woman may have less economic dependency on a black man, but if she is self-supporting and on her own, she is even more disadvantaged economically than a white woman. Income rates are higher for individuals, but as family members, income rates are lower. While the overall poverty rate for families in the United States in 1978 was 10 percent, among families headed by women, the rate was much higher. In 1978, 24 percent of white, 51 percent of black, and 53 percent of Spanish-origin female householders lived below the official poverty level (Rawlings 1980, 34–37). Those with children under 18 fared even worse; mothers and their children are much more likely to be poor:

Table 9–1. 1981 Median Income of All Families and Families with Householder Working Year-Round Full-Time by Race and Spanish Origin of Householder (in dollars)

	White	Dollar Difference	Percent Difference	Black	Dollar Difference	Percent Difference	Spanish	Dollar Difference	Percent Difference
All families	23,517			13,267			16,402		
Married couples	25,474			19,624			19,329		
Single householders:									
Male householder (no wife present)	20,421	−5,053	−20	14,489	−5,135	−26	14,793	−4,536	−23
Female householder (no husband present)	12,508	−12,966	−51	7,506	−12,118	−62	7,586	−11,743	−61

Source: Current Population Reports, Consumer Income, 1983, Series P-60, No. 137, 33–34.

The poverty rate among children living in families maintained by women was much higher than for children in families overall (51 percent versus 16 percent). Among children in Spanish-origin and Black families maintained by women, the rates were 69 and 66 percent, respectively, compared with 40 percent for their White counterparts. (Rawlings 1980, 34)

When a woman leaves her abuser, her economic standard of living very likely takes a drastic drop. If she has dependent children, she must take into consideration the lives and welfare of her children, who have roughly one chance out of two of dropping below the poverty level (two out of three for minority children). Is it any wonder that many battered women remain with their abusers for many years, sometimes until the children have grown up and left home? However, in some cases abuse begins during pregnancy, even before the first child is born. This is another reason some abused women stay.

Violence during Pregnancy

BABY STILLBORN; FATHER ARRESTED

On Christmas day in 1978, a local newspaper carried a small story with the above headline. Piecing together the case from brief accounts in the news reveals the following: the father reportedly had either kicked or hit his 28 year old wife, who was

Table 9–2. Persons 14 Years Old and Over, by Total Median Money Income for Year-Round Full-Time Workers from 1955 to 1981

	Males			Females			
Year	White	Black	Percent Difference[a]	White	Percent Difference[a]	Black and Other	Percent Difference[b]
1955	4,377	2,665	61	2,858	65	1,468	55
1960	5,572	3,683	66	3,377	61	2,289	62
1965	6,802	4,272	63	3,935	58	2,672	63
1970	9,447	6,638	70	5,536	59	4,664	70
1975	13,233	10,151	77	7,737	58	7,598	75
1980	19,720	14,726	75	11,703	59	10,960	74
1981	21,178	15,771	74	12,665	60	11,604	74

[a]To white males.
[b]To black males.
Source: Current Population Reports, Consumer Income, 1983, Series P-60, No. 137, 120–22.

eight months pregnant with their sixth child. One report said the baby had a heartbeat just before surgery and was still breathing after being taken by caesarean section, but died a short time later. The father was charged with felony wife-beating and the death of an unborn fetus, and four days later was arraigned and released on $50,000 bond posted by his wife.

Why would a woman post bond for the release of a man who attacked her with such force that her baby died? The answer may be deduced from the previous section on economic disadvantages of mothers with dependent children; this woman had five. How could a man beat or kick a pregnant woman, especially one who is eight months pregnant and mother of his children? Finkelhor (1981a, 3) provides an answer when he notes that the most common pattern of family violence is "for the most powerful to abuse the least." When a woman is pregnant, she is particularly vulnerable and may be less able to defend herself or retaliate. For example, one woman's first attack occurred during pregnancy, but she managed to fight back effectively each time it occurred, until she became ill with a degenerative disease. When she was no longer able to protect herself, her beatings increased in frequency and intensity (Pagelow 1981a, 55–56). Writers often fail to note the importance of beatings during pregnancy, even though they offer quotations from battered women who refer to it. Dobash and Dobash (1979, 111) list miscarriages among the severe injuries their sample suffered, and Walker (1979, 104–5) comments on the frequency with which it occurs, but relates it to the husband's jealousy of sharing his wife, calling it "prenatal child abuse." Fleming (1979, 436) does not elaborate on findings that "pregnancy appears to be related to battering."

There does indeed seem to be a correlation between pregnancy and battering. Rioghan Kirchner, legal assistant in the Family Law Unit of the Brooklyn Legal Services, noted an association but also the lack of attention to this factor by writers. Kirchner investigated the cases of 357 women alleging cruelty during their marriages and found that 69 percent of them were pregnant either before or just after their marriages (1977, 12), compared to 49 percent of 243 nonbattered women, which is a statistically significant difference. In-depth analysis of ten cases of beating during pregnancy revealed:

> Nine of the ten women in this sample were beaten for the first time during their first pregnancy. The tenth . . . reported minor slapping and pushing around prior to her first pregnancy with an escalation in frequency and violence as soon as her husband became aware that she was pregnant. Significantly, four

husbands beat their wives only when they were pregnant, and treated them with affection when they were not. (Kirchner 1977, 8)

Although the other six men continued beating their wives after pregnancy, the four who beat only during pregnancy are not unusual. Although contraceptives were illegal in Ireland, one 23-year-old mother of five children obtained pills through the black market, but whenever her husband found them, he would dump them down the toilet. He also beat her only when she was pregnant (Pagelow 1979, 26).

Writing about pregnancy-related violence, Richard Gelles (1975b) found that, out of 44 violent families in his study, ten respondents referred to violent incidents while the wife was pregnant. Gelles (1975b, 82) proposes five factors that contribute to the high rate of violence during pregnancy. Kirchner's (1977) report criticizes some of the assumptions Gelles makes in his 1975 article, compares her data to his, and finds support only for his last two factors: *prenatal child abuse* and *defenselessness*. Kirchner's sharpest criticism is directed at this statement by Gelles (1975b, 83): ". . . we believe that for many families violence which brings about a miscarriage is a more acceptable way of terminating an unwanted pregnancy than is abortion." Although the death and injury rate in Kirchner's sample was very high[2] (three babies died and one was born brain-damaged), she says that there was no evidence that the women preferred being kicked, beaten, or choked as a method of birth control. On the contrary, Kirchner (1977, 14) states: "Some husbands may find this method of birth control more acceptable than abortion, but, I have yet to meet a battered woman who would agree with this premise."

In the Pagelow survey, 306 women had one child or more living with them during their relationships with the men who battered them (1981a, 142), and 69 out of the 281 married women (25 percent) said they were pregnant at the time they married their husbands. Of those who said they were pregnant at some point when they lived with their abusers, 60 percent said they had been beaten during their pregnancies. This is a far higher rate than the 23 percent Gelles (1975b) found in his small sample, but it is probably a more accurate estimate of the occurrence because in-depth interviews with many battered women revealed frequent references to stillbirths, miscarriages, and brain-damaged children, most of which the women attributed to battering during pregnancy. In addition, many of the children had birth defects and chronic illnesses, as well as physical and emotional handicaps. Unfortunately, data on these problems were not systematically gathered.

If it is difficult for healthy women without children to put an end to being physically abused by leaving, it is far more difficult for pregnant women or women with dependent children to leave or stop the abuse in other ways, since they are much more vulnerable. Women *do* try various methods to prevent or stop their husbands from abusing them; some are examined next.

FIGHTING BACK OR GETTING OUT

Some researchers describe battered women in their samples as "passive" individuals, without distinguishing between the aftereffects of sometimes years of physical and psychological abuse, and the persons they were *before* they began their ordeals and the persons they become soon *after* the abuse ceases. Despite their isolation and lack of resources, the victims of spouse abuse try a variety of techniques to stop the abuse, to get help, or to leave (Pagelow 1981d). Before and during the time of an attack, the women respond in different ways. Table 9–3 shows the techniques used by 276 women in the Pagelow survey to try to prevent an attack. One-third of the survey respondents said they did not even try to defend themselves once an attack began, but of those who said they attempted self-defense, many added a statement such as: "I tried to once and he really flipped out and beat me worse than ever. He told me if I ever tried that again he'd kill me. I never tried again. I believe he would." Some did try.

Table 9–4 shows the responses of the women in the Pagelow survey during violent episodes. Lee H. Bowker's book *Beating Wife-Beating* (1983a) is an analysis of the techniques used by 146 formerly battered women, which consist of: talk, promise, threaten (nonviolence), hide, passive defense, aggressive defense, and avoidance. One-third of his respondents

Table 9–3. Survey Women's Responses to Prevent Spousal Abuse

Response Category	N	Percent
Did not know was coming	22	8.0
Tried talking him out of it	67	24.3
No use—too scared	14	5.1
Stood up for own ideas	18	6.5
Tried to pacify him	80	29.0
Tried to prevent—begged him to stop	30	10.9
Got out of his way	45	16.3
Total	276	100.0*

*Percentages may not add up to 100 due to rounding.
Source: Pagelow 1981a, 66.

employed "talk," compared to 24 percent in the Pagelow sample, but only 32 percent of the Bowker sample who tried talking their spouses out of violence felt it was a "fairly successful" method (Bowker 1983a, 64).

Whereas 26 percent of the women in the Pagelow survey reported they fought back, as shown on Table 9–4, 29 percent of the Bowker sample tried "aggressive defense" at least once, and 2 percent rated it as "very successful," while 40 percent rated it as "fairly successful" (Bowker 1983a, 68). The concepts *fighting back* and *aggressive defense* are basically the same behavior, but although the women in Bowker's study who responded this way were inclined to view it favorably, he cautions that, "In many of these cases, their husbands responded with an increase in the severity of the violence" (1983a, 47). Bowker correctly feels it could be a dangerous strategy that might lead to increased injury to the wives, and he adds:

> Threats appeared to work when the husbands were convinced that the women were serious. These threats usually involved pointing out to the husband that he could not be on guard at every moment, particularly when he was sleeping, and that she would kill him at some future time when he was not expecting it if he continued. . . . (1983a, 68)

The same threat was voiced by a respondent in the Pagelow study, who reported that she "waited until her drunken husband fell asleep, later awakening him with a knife held at his throat. She reminded him that if he beat her in the future, he had better kill her then, because he could not stay awake forever" (1981d, 289). This particular woman had endured about 18 years of weekly beatings, and she realized that her action could easily have led to her own death (a distinct possibility), but at that point, she preferred to take the gamble between death and the cessation of beatings. Her husband knew she was telling the truth and never beat her

Table 9–4. Survey Women's Responses to Physical Attack

Response Category	N	Percent
Fought back	68	25.5
Tried (at least once) but it got worse	64	16.5
Self-defense only	78	29.2
Scared of being killed	61	22.8
Used avoidance techniques	16	6.0
Total	267	100.0*

*Percentages may not add up to 100 due to rounding.
Source: Pagelow 1981a, 67.

again. A few others in the author's study traded violence for violence successfully, but most of them had not had very long histories of abuse. It is a dangerous gamble, because many other women who fight back are seriously hurt and some become homicide statistics.[3] This technique seems to be successful only for the most desperate women who also use some object as a weapon to "equalize" the strength differential. However, weapons can be turned back against those who use them.

Many battered women try repeatedly to get assistance from outsiders, but only a few of them are successful (Pagelow 1981a). Failing that, they begin the process of leaving (some with the idea that it is permanent, and others trying this technique as a "scare" tactic to show they will not tolerate any more abuse). In the Pagelow survey, 273 women (78 percent) had left their abusers at least once before the violence stopped (some by going to a shelter, some by divorce, and some by other methods). A few had left only once before, but more had attempted to leave two or more times, only to return. Only 7 percent had stayed away for over a year, although 23 percent had made new homes for themselves in the interim. The majority obtained temporary shelter with parents or relatives. A large majority (84 percent) returned because their spouses found them, threatened them, or convinced them that they were repentant and the women believed their husbands would change (Pagelow 1981d, 288). Out of the entire population of battered women, we cannot estimate how many succeed in breaking off their relationships by leaving, but there is much evidence that although many leave and do not return, others spend years or the rest of their lives trying to avoid men fanatically dedicated to pursuing them, harassing them, or even killing them (Martin 1976; Pagelow 1980, 1981a).

When their escape tactics fail, some try other tactics, but many resign themselves to their "fate" and wait for their own death or that of their abusive spouses. Of those who see death as a release from pain and terror, some will attempt suicide and a few will succeed. Almost half of the Pagelow survey sample contemplated suicide, and 23 percent of them attempted suicide at least once (1981d, 287). Others contemplate killing their spouses, some of these attempt it, and a few succeed (Fiora-Gormally 1978; Fromson 1977; Jones 1980; Lewin 1979; Meyers 1983). Although Wolfgang's study of criminal homicide found that husbands and wives kill their spouses in almost equal proportions, he also found that husbands were significantly more likely to have *precipitated* their own murder than wives (1967b, 82). Wolfgang also says:

> The number of wives killed by their husbands constitutes 41 percent of all women killed, whereas husbands slain by their

wives make up only 11 percent of all men killed. . . . Husbands are often killed by their wives in the kitchen with a butcher knife, but nearly half of the wives are slain in the bedroom. (1967a, 23).

Statistics more recent than Wolfgang's show that out of 1,814 spouse murders in 1980, 1,027 victims, or 57 percent, were wives killed by husbands (Flanagan and McLeod 1983, 368).

Some people express concern that formerly battered wives who strike back with deadly force are not always found guilty of murder (Mitchell 1978). A *Time* magazine article (1977) notes several cases in which battered women who killed their abusers were acquitted of murder on grounds of temporary insanity or self-defense. It mentions the highly publicized case of Francine Hughes who immolated her drunken ex-husband; a Chicago wife who shot her husband when he resumed abusing their child; and an Orange County women who shot her ex-husband who traced her to California from Texas with the avowed purpose of bringing her back or killing her. It neglects to mention the numerous cases in which battered wives are found guilty of manslaughter or murder of abusive spouses, which was not overlooked in a *Washington Post* article a month later (MacPherson 1977). This article cites a number of cases that had caught media attention, such as the wife of a six-foot five-inch, 255-pound Philadelphia Eagles lineman, who had repeatedly called the police for protection from beatings. When police responded, all they did was tell him to walk around the block to cool off, or just discuss football with him (MacPherson 1977), until one night the battered wife stabbed him to death.

The wives who killed their abusers and aroused the interest of the judicial system as well as the media were the particular ones in which the wives claimed *self-defense,* a claim that requires the imminence or immediacy of impending peril, such that a person is permitted to use "commensurate force" to defend one's self (Fiora-Gormally 1978). Several of these cases required a broadening of the traditional viewpoint, because the homicide did not occur during a struggle, but in some cases took place after the husband fell asleep or, as in the Jennifer Patri case, when the man came through the front door. The major defense argument was based on *cumulative terror* (Fiora-Gormally 1978) of impending doom that was the result of years of fear, pain, and helplessness exploding in violent acts. In the unsuccessful Jennifer Patri self-defense plea, both she and her 12-year-old daughter had suffered sexual abuse. The wife bought a 12-gauge shotgun after her husband moved out to live with another woman and threatened to kill her and kidnap the children; she shot him when he returned to pick up the children (Wolfe 1979).[4]

The women in these cases had made numerous complaints to police and public agencies but received little or no assistance (Eisenberg 1979; Eisenberg and Seymour 1978, 1979; Fleming 1979; Marquardt and Cox 1979; Martin 1976). When their wives turned to outsiders for help and received none, it strengthened their abusers' convictions they could do whatever they wished (Fromson 1978). All major institutions prefer nonintervention in "family squabbles" or apply pressure for reconciliation of the couple. Terry Fromson (1977, 1978) claims the state's interest in preserving the family and marriage is unreasonable, arbitrary and not rational. Fromson (1977, 170) says that when women seek protection under the law, there is no privacy, relationship, or family to preserve, and battered women are entitled to the same protective mechanisms and equal administration of the law as any other citizens. However, they frequently do not get equal protection under the law and, in final desperation, take the law in their own hands. Sometimes their abusers are killed, and sometimes they themselves are the ultimate victims.[5]

It is not only the law that turns its back on victims who cry out for help; many agents of social services see or hear evidence and refuse to acknowledge it or advise the women to continue to try to make theirs a "happy home." Almost everyone in this society has known at least one couple in which the wife was the victim of repeated physical abuse, yet we usually do or say nothing. As Laura Meyers (1983, 352) comments:

> We all remember the horrifying instance of Kitty Genovese, the young New York woman killed in the early 1960s as dozens watched and none sprang to her aid. But how many remember that when bystanders were asked later why they did not help, many responded they thought her attacker was her husband?

There are many people who do care and would help if they were sensitized to some of the "hidden messages" given off by abused women. The following is a list of some of the signals that may indicate that a woman is being controlled, dominated, and possibly physically abused by a man with whom she has an intimate relationship.

Factors that May Indicate a Woman Is in an Abusive Relationship

She is not active in social activities or withdraws from them after having been an active participant. She makes excuses for not attending meetings, and so forth, or makes appointments that she fails to keep without adequate explanation. She never engages in any activity at night unaccompanied by her spouse.

She has no close friends of her own. She seldom invites people to her home, or when she does, visitors get subtle cues they must leave before her spouse returns. If her spouse returns home when visitors are present, her demeanor changes and she becomes distraught or nervous; it becomes apparent that visitors are expected to leave quickly. Her spouse may be insulting to guests.

She appears nervous and cannot ever accept an invitation or a responsibility without checking first with her spouse; in a crowd she lacks spontaneity. She may arrive late or leave suddenly without explanation, or make frequent telephone calls. If someone comes up from behind her and puts a hand on her, she will jump away but laugh it off later.

She seldom has any cash and has "forgotten" her checkbook but may have a credit card with her.

She wears heavy makeup or sunglasses, even indoors. Her wardrobe includes scarves, turtleneck sweaters, long sleeves, and/or slacks. She may mention that her spouse exerts an unusual influence on her choice of clothing. She breaks dates to swim but if she goes to health spas, she insists on private dressing rooms.

She has many "accidents," and at her place of employment, she receives and places many phone calls to her spouse. He may deliver her to work and pick her up afterward. She may have a high absenteeism rate and an assortment of physical complaints. She cannot attend company affairs, or if she does, she only attends accompanied by her spouse. He is either at her side all the time, or watches her "adoringly" from across the room. He is the "perfect" spouse and the life of the party.

She and her spouse have frequent changes of residence that seem unrelated to employment requirements.

For those who have at least one close friend who fits several of the above descriptions, the next question is what can an "outsider" do to help a woman who is being beaten but who is neither admitting it nor asking for help? This is where *empathy* is important: having the ability to put one's self into the other's position. To gain insight into your friend's problems, obtain a copy of Ginny NiCarthy's book, *Getting Free* (1982), a very helpful handbook for women in abusive relationships.[6] Then, try to get your friend to read it. There is no "perfect solution" to the problem; solutions vary widely depending on the actors in the scenario. Once alerted, the person who wants to help should find the following points useful.

Helping Someone Who May Be a Battered Woman

Be nonjudgmental: ask a few nonthreatening questions or simply be a good listener; do not force the issue. If no information is offered:

Discuss a hypothetical case: mention a "friend" who is feeling helplessly trapped in a violent situation to show that even a "normal" woman can become involved in a relationship that turns violent.

Listen carefully: if the woman admits to her situation, it is much more helpful to ask questions than to offer advice, and to listen to the answers; steer her to experts for answers, if possible.

Become informed: gather important information about agencies that offer help for abused wives, especially nearby shelters, their restrictions (if any), and their telephone numbers. This and all other information should be transmitted to the victim discreetly. Be very cautious when communicating with her at her home (in person, by mail, or by telephone).

Tell her she needs evidence: if she tells you about a recent beating, convince her to obtain a physical (or dental) examination, even when she believes her injuries are minor (some may not be obvious). Try to get her to tell professionals the true cause of her wounds, have pictures taken of bruises, and so forth, and to gather other evidence, even if she expects to continue living with her abuser.

Offer unconditional friendship: explain your willingness to help if called upon. She needs to know that someone else appreciates the seriousness (and potential danger) of the situation, and that if and when the moment arrives when she must leave suddenly, her friend will be standing by. Tell her to have copies made of house and car keys and to carefully hide them outside the house.

Storage of documents: important papers should be secured outside her residence in the event she must leave quickly (birth certificates of herself and the children, health records, insurance, car registration, bank books, passports, and any other documents she may need later).

Be careful: do not dismiss her fear of potential danger as un-realistic exaggeration, and if personal involvement is included, use extreme caution not to leave a trail of "clues." The police may be helpful, but follow the advice of the staff at the nearest shelter about assisting her to leave. If she leaves home, she should *never* return for belongings without a police escort. If her abuser is a police officer or has close friends on the force, the shelter staff can offer best advice on alternatives.

The best that family members or friends of a battered wife can do is to assure the woman of the constancy of their loyalty and concern in a non-judgmental manner; *she needs to know there is sanity in a world gone insane.* The worst thing they can do is to condemn her for her stupidity for staying in the situation or to condemn her husband for his brutality. Caring friends and relatives must refrain from criticism, while doing all they can to rebuild her diminished self-esteem and, above all, being patient until she makes her own decisions. She may make false starts that are disappointing, but with a dependable support system, she will likely take appropriate action when she realizes that her spouse is the only one who can make him stop his violence.

MEN WHO ABUSE

IF VIOLENCE IS A PART OF HOW YOU FEEL . . . If you sometimes feel violent and you are a man, we would like to hear from you. We all have feelings of anger and there are many ways to let it out. When men's anger is directed against women, the results can be painful, sometimes tragic. If you want to talk to another man we offer a sensitive, non-judgmental atmosphere in which you can discuss your feelings and experiences with violence (from a 1980 poster created by the Eugene, Oregon, Rape Crisis Network Men's Group).

A few programs like the Oregon group have been organized in response to the apparent need to do something for male spouse abusers, because some men know that helping violent men's victims is not enough. Usually they set up their programs in collaboration with women's rape crisis centers and/or shelters. They know that some battered women return from shelters to the men who beat them, and that men whose wives leave them are likely to find other women to beat. This section first introduces some research findings about men who batter and then discusses intervention programs for violent men.

Men Who Batter: What Are They Like?

Very little scientific research has been done on spouse abusers compared to their victims. The reason is not researcher apathy but rather the difficulties encountered in trying to gather nonbiased samples. Most batterers tend to deny their violent acts, minimize their intentions or results, project blame onto victims, or simply refuse to cooperate. When the question of woman battering surfaced, clinicians and researchers responded by studying individual characteristics of victims, rather than abusers, which brought sharp criticism from some writers (Stark and Flitcraft 1981; Wardell et al. 1981). Early reports of abusers were of small, biased samples of convicted violent men (cf. Faulk 1974; Scheirell and Rinder 1973; Snell et al. 1964). Data on wife beaters were later obtained indirectly through information from their victims (Dobash and Dobash 1979; Fagan et al. 1981; Pagelow 1981a; Walker 1979). These studies found that batterers often come from violent childhood homes where they witnessed parental vio-

Feelings of powerlessness and frustration outside the home can result in abuse inside the home. When a man feels angry and is helpless to retaliate against those who anger him and he loses any sense of control, he may try to assert his control by dominating—scapegoating—those who have even less power than he has. Wife beating is one of those ways.

Source: Nancy Dombeck, photographer.

lence, usually their mothers beaten by their fathers (Pagelow 1981a), although some reports do not specify between witnessing and/or experiencing childhood violence (Coleman 1980; Service Delivery Assessment 1980). The Fagan et al. (1981) study of 270 victims reports that 45 percent of their abusers witnessed parental violence and 37 percent had been abused as children. In the Pagelow study (1981a, 168–71), 53 percent of the batterers had mothers who were beaten by fathers; 45 percent were frequently punished, most often by fathers or father-figures, and about half described this punishment as "extremely severe."

Difficulties of obtaining samples of abusers may be overcome by using a variety of methods of case finding, although each one presents certain problems (Rouse and Coulston 1982). One of the earliest reports describing a small sample of men who had abused their wives was written by therapists Anne Ganley and Lance Harris (1978) from their observations of voluntary inpatients at the American Lake Veterans Hospital in Tacoma, Washington. Similarly, Karen Howes Coleman (1980), researcher and family therapist at a clinic in Texas, writes about 33 male volunteers who had been involved in conjugal violence. Another study obtained a larger sample of 85 violent men, but, unfortunately, the report does not specify how the sample was drawn (Hanneke and Shields 1981). Dorie Klein's preliminary report (1982) discusses in-depth interviews with 30 men, either in voluntary counseling or in court-mandated counseling, who used physical violence with spouses.

Only one report discovered thus far utilizes a sample of couples to study differences between abusive and nonabusive husbands (Rosenbaum and O'Leary 1981). The sample of 20 abusive husbands and 53 abused wives was obtained at the Victims Information Bureau of Suffolk County (VIBS) New York (again, a self-selected therapy group). For comparison purposes, they obtained 20 unhappy but nonviolent couples from a marital therapy group, plus a stratified random sample of 20 satisfactorily married couples as a control group.[7] Alan Rosenbaum and Daniel O'Leary (1981, 68) found no significant difference between the wives, but they found that the abusive husbands had witnessed spouse abuse and experienced child abuse more than the other husbands.

In an attempt to obtain a representative sample, sociologist Linda Rouse (1983a) mailed 220 initial contact letters to individuals from a randomly selected list of 300 names and obtained 79 usable completed responses. Although the CTS was sent to only 55 men in that sample, Rouse made some important discoveries regarding the "cycle of violence" discussed in Chapter 7. Rouse says, "The single most important type of childhood exposure was observation of violence, which was associated with greater use of abusive conflict tactics" (1983a, 1). A larger sample of 110 violent men was obtained by Anna Kuhl (1981) through standardized intake forms at 14 programs concerned with spousal abuse in the state of Washington but, again, these were volunteers who were seeking treatment as abusers. These limitations should all be kept in mind throughout this discussion of abusers, because when volunteers are studied, researchers do not know in what ways they may differ from the larger population. It is safe to assume that the relatively few men who are concerned enough about their violent behavior to seek professional assistance or fill in lengthy questionnaires must differ from the vast majority of abusers of the women who call hot lines, fill shelters, and need police assistance. These men never come forward to ask for help. Volunteers must be primary batterers or more sensitive men who are greatly disturbed at their own behavior. Among wife beaters, these men must be the *cream of the crop.*

Most people want to know what wife beaters are like. They want to learn distinguishing characteristics of these men so they can identify abusers from nonabusers. As early as 1977, Margaret Elbow constructed a typology of batterers into four major personality types, but they are broad generalizations based on a review of the sparse literature available at that time. One of the most publicized "profiles" comes from Lenore Walker (1979, 36). James Koval and his colleagues (1982, 147–48) drew together characteristics found in their literature search. Some of these factors are modified and expanded in the following list of features which, in combination, may identify violent spouses. The list includes some of the most commonly noted features of the men and their backgrounds, obtained directly from abusive men and indirectly from their battered wives.

Commonly Noted Features
of Men Who Abuse Their Wives

Low self-esteem: these men feel like "losers" who build dependency relationships with women perceived as "winner"; they gain vicarious satisfaction through their wives' accomplishments, but when they feel they are losing control, they achieve a sense of superiority by dominating "their" women. Low self-esteem is exacerbated by their own violence.

Traditionalists: they believe in the patriarchal family, male supremacy, and the stereotyped masculine sex role in the family.

Emotionally inexpressive: fear, tenderness, and self-doubt are repressed; and the only emotions they can and do express are anger and jealousy.

Lack of assertiveness: people who do not know how to assert themselves are frequently aggressive.

Social isolation: they have difficulty building and maintaining close, personal ties, so their social relationships are cursory and shallow.

Employment problems: unemployment, underemployment, or job dissatisfaction that not only affect self-esteem, but also introduce serious stresses into interpersonal relationships at all socioeconomic levels.

Alcohol dependency: particularly when they were socialized in a milieu where alcohol consumption was associated with aggressive, drunken behavior.

Violence in home of orientation: mainly when fathers or father-substitutes were violent with their mothers, but also if they or their siblings were abused by fathers.

Authoritarian personalities: these people are deferent to higher authorities but frequently scapegoat persons unable to protect or defend themselves; included are some religious fanatics.

Moody: wide variations in mood swings: the charming, loving father and husband who suddenly, sometimes with no apparent provocation, reverts to an angry, hostile, and violent man, and vice versa; a feature that has been referred to as the "Dr. Jekyll and Mr. Hyde syndrome" (Fleming 1979, 90) or a "dual personality" (Walker 1979, 36).

Wall punchers: they demonstrate anger by punching walls or other objects or by hurting animals; these are *danger signals that should not be ignored.*

Obviously, some of these features are interrelated. One or a few of these characteristics may not be sufficient indicators of men who batter; whether a man batters a woman or not depends in large part on the woman, and whether or not his abuse is likely to be rewarded and not punished. Intimate relationships involved self-disclosure, and a man who is tempted to strike out usually has some preconceived ideas about whether his violence is likely to bring about desired or undesirable results. Women should be cautious about establishing intimacy with men who were violent in childhood, are violent with others, or who show contempt for women in their family or in general.

To outsiders, wife beaters are indistinguishable from other men except that they use violence to control and dominate their wives. Most studies find that both victims and their violent spouses are similar to national statistics on most demographic items, crossing socioeconomic strata, religious, ethnic groups, and occupations. Walker says: "They were unrecognizable to the uninformed observers and not distinguished by demographic data" (1979, 36). And Fleming says: "As is usually the case with stereotypes, the stereotype of the abusive man just doesn't fit. . . . He could be anyone . . ." (1979, 287).

What to Do about Wife Abusers?

> I felt I loved my wife and family very much. I kind of wrapped my world around my family, but I wasn't much to express it. I was the kind of person that held everything in. I never told my wife "I love you" much, but in the meantime my anger, my verbal abuse was very evident to everyone (quotation from an EMERGE client used in advertisement, September 10, 1982).

There are approximately 150 U.S. programs that offer services to men who batter, either exclusively or as part of other work, and of these about 10 to 12 are all-male collectives working to end male violence against women (Mettger 1982a). One of the latter is EMERGE, a Boston men's collective, probably the oldest and most active group, initiated in response to requests of area women working at shelters. Other such groups are AMEND (Abusive Men Exploring New Direction) in Denver, and RAVEN (Rape and Violence End Now) in Saint Louis (Most 1981). Of the groups around the nation, some are organized and run by men but maintain close ties to shelters, some operate as adjuncts to shelters, some are communitywide groups, and a few have been started by traditional mental health agencies (Mettger 1982a). Canadians have developed many programs for victims and their abusers and a wide array of services.[8]

EMERGE offers mostly two-man facilitator group counseling, although it also provides individual counseling; equal emphasis is placed on community education and training; and it provides training workshops in cooperation with shelters. EMERGE has coproduced with Mark Lipman an educational film about men who batter women called *To Have and To Hold,* which is available for purchase or rental.[9] RAVEN has produced a quarterly newsletter since 1981 that serves as a forum and a network among programs. Both men and women subscribe to this newsletter to learn about the different programs, issues, books and articles, and resources (Mettger 1982a, 8).[10].

A program directly attached to a shelter began in 1979 at the House of Ruth in Baltimore, Maryland, which offers an ongoing counseling group for both abusers and couples. Women are included in counseling only if they are very clear about wanting it (Mettger 1982a, 2). Other small groups for male abusers initiated by shelters exist around the country, such as one in Long Beach, California, facilitated by a male and female team of counselors.[11]

Community intervention models include two in Minnesota: the Domestic Abuse Project (DAP) in Minneapolis and the Domestic Abuse Intervention Project (DAIP) in Duluth. These two groups work cojointly with established agencies to effect institutional change in the criminal justice and social service systems (Mettger 1982a). Both reject the traditional approach to counseling and agree with the mandatory arrest policy of Minnesota as providing the best incentive for change: The men have a choice between jail or counseling. They insist that "one of the reasons men learn to be violent is because it has no consequences," and that since violence is a learned behavior, it can be unlearned (Mettger 1982a, 7).

That violent behavior is learned is the underlying philosophy of the nation's leading expert on men who batter, Anne L. Ganley, who began her pioneering work with Lance Harris at the American Lake Veterans' Hospital in Tacoma, Washington (Ganley and Harris 1978). Ganley has conducted many workshops for professionals who work with men who batter and has written a manual for participants.[12] Ganley's intervention strategies include the following: (1) a clear and consistent goal—ending the battering; (2) client accountability—the abuser is responsible for his behavior; (3) constructive confrontation—the men are challenged by their peers to avoid minimizing or denial; (4) psychoeducational approaches and rejection of traditional approaches—the emphasis is on teaching and learning new skills; and (5) structured format and directive counselor role—the counselor is an active teacher/role model, sets limits, and facilitates interactions (Ganley 1981).

Ganley (1981, 4) believes that: groups progress faster; peer role models are effective; two leaders are best (both sexes or both men as long as they are knowledgeable), for groups of eight to ten men. Whether or not groups are co-led by a woman and a man as facilitators is one area of disagreement (Mettger 1982a, 8), but some say the initial adjustment happens quickly and men unlearn stereotyped attitudes with a female counselor present. Other arguments deal with court-mandated versus voluntary participation, but the most serious point of contention deals with drawing away badly needed and scarce funds from services for violent men's victims (Mettger 1982a, 23). Still, there is agreement on the necessity of this work because:

> In keeping with their traditional view of masculinity, most abusive men are unable to express their emotions verbally. "I've talked to men who can't ask their wives for a hug," says Tim Peterson, coordinator of the AMEND groups. "They can't identify any emotions except anger." (Most 1981, 8)

Men and women are working out differences in approaches and solutions to spousal violence. In August 1982 about 130 people attended a two-day forum in Milwaukee. They agreed that: sheltering women and children remains paramount in importance; systems advocacy receives precedence over counseling; men's programs are monitored by, accountable to, and allied with women's programs; and men's programs continue to address sexism (Mettger 1982a).

SOCIETY'S CONTEMPORARY
RESPONSE TO WIFE BEATING

Considering the history of marriage, it could be expected that when the issue of wife beating was initially raised, there would be widespread refusal by social institutions to acknowledge the problem, in the United States and other countries. Despite denials or apathy, the battered women's movement grew internationally, and gradually forced changes. The first step was the establishment of temporary safe housing for women and their children, but despite their growth in the 1970s, there were never enough to shelter all the victims who needed them. For example, by 1978 there were seven shelters in the entire state of Minnesota, but between 79 and 85 percent of the women requesting shelter had to be turned away (Minnesota Department of Corrections 1979). The unmet need was great; as the author commented: "[S]uppose a community had only one hospital and it had to turn away 85 percent of all prospective patients, or if 79 percent of all criminals given prison sentences could not be housed in the state prison" (Pagelow 1981a, 213). Decision makers and funding sources never rushed forward to provide sufficient victim services.

Although the grass-roots movement to provide shelters was largely initiated by feminists, surveys show that by the beginning of the 1980s, fewer than half the existing shelters were either founded by or directly related to feminist groups or ideology, while the balance were started by church groups or civic organizations (Johnson 1981). The realities of political and economic life resulted in large-scale "cooptation" by the criminal justice system and establishment institutions (Johnson 1981). Some practiced "moral entrepreneurship," capitalizing on feminist issues, while others sought to advance personal underlying goals of maintaining the family unit (Tierney 1982).

Shelters provide much more than just safe havens for refugees: they provide counseling (for women, children, and sometimes men); educational programs (parenting classes, employment preparation, and so on); advocacy (social services, legal, medical, school systems, and so forth); and community outreach and education. In addition, shelters perform a broad range of services for the public, such as giving information and referrals to many people who call their hotlines. The Minnesota Department of Corrections (1979) publication notes that shelters in that state received almost 8,000 calls and 376 letters requesting information in an 11-month period. One shelter in Kentucky provided housing to 236 women and received 2,709 hotline calls during 1978 (Loseke and Berk 1983). Traditional service providers are often unable or unequipped to render the kinds of services many battered women want and need. Donileen Loseke and Sarah Fenstermaker Berk (1983, 4) say "the lack of other community services may lead many women to make a variety of requests, some having nothing to do with the primary service of shelter provision."

Despite their filling otherwise unmet needs and performing valuable services to entire communities at relatively low costs, shelters have always suffered from short-term and inadequate funding. Since 1980 cutbacks in federal, state, and local expenditures for social service programs have led to drastically reduced budgets for most. The CETA (Comprehensive Employment Training Act) program, which provided many shelters with workers at low cost, and some funding sources such as LEAA (Law Enforcement Assistance Administration), have all been disbanded. Block grants to states have resulted in less money being competed for by many nonprofit organizations, such as those serving victims of family violence, that is, children, wives, the aged, and so forth. Private foundations are swamped with grant proposals, and at the same time that economic recession has caused many unpaid volunteers to seek paid employment, there is a greater than ever demand for the services of the fewer volunteers. As a result, many shelters have had to reduce their services or close their doors (Response 1983, Mettger 1982b).

The battered women's movement attracted activists in the legal and criminal justice fields, and as noted in Chapter 8, many laws have been passed or existing ones modified, and pressure has been exerted on police, prosecutors, and the courts to enforce adequate laws already on the books.[13] State laws to protect or assist battered women are in a constant state of flux (Lerman and Livingston 1983), but legislation at the federal level has not been successful. Bills addressing the need have been offered since 1977, but none have been passed (Tierney 1982, 209). At this writing, the Domestic Violence Prevention and Services Act has been amended into the Child Abuse Reauthorization Bill because its authors hope that this strategy ensures its passage: "A vote against funding for family violence programs is a vote against money for child abuse prevention, a most unpopular stance politically" (Fullwood 1983).

When the issue of child abuse and neglect was first raised, opponents to the passage of federal legislation relied mainly on the issue of family privacy, saying that the government has no business interfering in the personal lives of citizens. The question of family privacy and confidentiality has also arisen regarding battered wives, and some opponents to domestic violence legislation fear that the battered women's movement is "anti-family." Also related to child abuse laws is an idea proposed by some who believe that medical personnel and other professionals should be required to report to authorities when they come in contact with women they suspect have been criminally assaulted. The rationale behind the idea to extend such a law to include adult victims is based on the fact that citizens who do not report crimes are considered culpable and may be charged with obstructing justice. Thus, if a doctor examines an injured child whose injuries indicate nonaccidental injury (the commission of a crime), a report is mandatory. If the proposed changes were enacted, the same would apply to adult victims of battery, which is already required by law in cases of gunshot wounds and certain animal bites. A report must be filed.

Proponents of mandatory reporting feel victims need external assistance in view of their helplessness, fear, and lack of protection from retaliation they must face alone. If such laws were passed, the burden of reporting would be taken away from the victim; thus the attacker cannot hold her responsible. Opponents to this idea generally believe that mandatory reporting violates doctor/patient confidentiality and invites intrusion into private lives, possibly causing greater harm. Moreover, some feel this would be an extension of the "perpetual child" image of women, and that women who are battered should be the only ones who have the right to make the decision whether to report or not. One category of women have limited choice regarding reporting, those who live on military bases, because spouse abuse programs and services are most frequently located in health clinics and medical facilities that have mandated reporting protocols they must follow. One report on violence in military families states:

> Because many family violence programs have been placed in medical settings and involve medical personnel or counselors assigned to medical facilities, spouse abuse cases are subject to non-confidential medical reporting regulations. Reporting requirements often evoke fear in many couples that seeking help will harm service members' careers. (Turner and West 1981, 4)

To ensure confidentiality for battered women in military families, some methods have been devised to provide needed services while circumventing regulations, such as obtaining outside funding and housing their services in nonmedical facilities. The secret is kept, but the victim gets medical care.

A similar split between protection of individual decision-making rights and the need to enforce criminal justice law has arisen regarding prosecution of spouse abusers. Some advocate more frequent police arrests of abusers thereby placing the burden for further action on the prosecutors (Lerman 1981b; Oberg 1982). Many insist that the decision to file charges should be made by prosecutors rather than by victims (Lerman 1981b, 5). Traditionally, the burden of arrest or prosecution has been left to victims, but even though wife beating has been illegal in most states since 1870 (Pleck 1979), very few batterers were prosecuted and even fewer were sentenced. Police have been reluctant to arrest for numerous reasons, but the foremost reason mentioned by law enforcement officers is the victims' tendency to drop charges. Lerman says that research shows that even though only less than one-tenth of all wife-beating cases involve the police, police responding to these calls rarely file reports, and even more rarely make arrests (1981b, 3). She says: "In many cases, abusers are not arrested even where the violence is so serious that a homicide is imminent" (Lerman 1981b, 3). Like Martin (1976), Lerman produces studies that show the large percentage of repeat calls to some homes prior to homicide. Some of the reluctance to intervene in what police and prosecutors view as "family squabbles" or "minor disputes" has to do with family privacy. Lerman says:

> Throughout the legal system, the family is treated as a sacred entity, as a stable social unit which must be preserved or at least left undisturbed. Viewed through this preconception, violence within families is minimized, treated as a minor disruption, a normal part of life. (1981b, 2)

Even when arrests are made, most prosecutors use a screening process whereby the majority of cases are eliminated. Sometimes prosecution depends on victims agreeing to live apart from abusers or filing for separation or divorce. The screening process attempts to determine which victims will make good witnesses, because as Lerman says: "A prosecutor's priorities may be set based not on the seriousness of the injury inflicted or the likelihood of recurrence if no action is taken, but on the likelihood of conviction and the benefit to the prosecutor's career" (1981b, 3).

Those who advocate taking the choice away from victims and demanding that the criminal justice system initiate prosecution have made some headway recently. Prosecutors in Santa Barbara and Los Angeles, California, sign charges themselves rather than asking victims to sign, since they believe this procedure reduces unnecessary pressure on victims.

> If the complainant is given responsibility for the filing of a charge, she is rendered a target for retaliation by the abuser. If

the prosecutor signs the complaint and explains to the victim that it is the state and not she who is filing the charge, she is less vulnerable to intimidation. . . . The Los Angeles City Attorney takes a hard line on withdrawal of charges, and refuses to drop any case based on the victim's request, unless there are "compelling circumstances." (Lerman 1981b, 7)

On the other hand, if victims in Seattle, Washington, ask that charges be dropped, their assigned advocates do all they can to encourage them to appear in court, but if they still insist on dropping charges by the date of the trial, the prosecutor requests the judges to drop the cases. Whether victims should be permitted to make decisions to prosecute or not, or whether agents of social control should have that choice is an issue that is undergoing considerable debate. Some advocates insist that taking the choice out of the hands of victims is further reinforcement of their lowered self-esteem and the feelings of powerlessness that accompany physical abuse. None of these issues lend themselves to clear and simple solutions.

Certainly, it is not easy trying to obtain justice for victims while maintaining vigil over the rights of the accused, but at least now many people are engaged in the struggle. This is far different than the situation that existed before the battered women's movement. Laura Meyers (1983, 351) tells about one of the cases in a lawsuit against the New York Family Court officials and the police department for violation of battered women's rights:

A grim tale of judicial and police non-response to wife-battery unfolds in the cases cited in the New York suit. Carmen Bruno alleges that police ran into her apartment while her husband was still hitting her. The officers had to pry his hands from her neck and her face was bleeding from what have since become permanent scars, and still they refused to arrest him.

SUMMARY

In this, the second of two chapters on spouse abuse, the problem of wife beating was the major focus. Beginning with questions about abused wives and why they stay, it is necessary to understand first that abuse ranges on a continuum from mild insults to homicide, and what happens (or does not happen) the first time a spouse uses physical violence sets the stage for the future. Some danger signals that point to greater risk of an intimate relationship developing into a violent one were presented. A list of features frequently found by researchers indicates that a battered woman is likely to report several of the following: courtship violence, beginning a marital relationship at a young age, especially when she's pregnant or has a child by another man, social isolation, lack of knowledge about her spouse's prior relationships, and dependency. Women stay with men who abuse them because of factors such as: fear; helplessness; guilt and feelings of failure; lack of resources signified by lack of freedom of movement, economic dependence, and dependent children. Some women are battered during pregnancy when they are both dependent and vulnerable.

Common notions prevail that battered women are basically passive, due in part to the fact that some researchers do not distinguish between characteristics of the women *before* the violence began or *after* the violence ceases, most frequently studying them shortly after they have left their violent spouses. However, the women actively try various tactics to prevent or stop the violence. When attempts fail, they try to get help from outsiders and next try leaving the situation. Most of the women who gain entry at shelters have left their homes before, only to have to return, sometimes because they were pursued or convinced that their abusers were "reformed." For some, all their attempts at preventing or avoiding the violence fail, and they resign themselves to violence until death. We do not know how many succeed at their attempts at suicide, but many contemplate it and quite a few attempt it. Some become so desperate they attempt to kill their spouses, and a number do so. This section includes some suggestions on how outsiders may identify a woman who is in an abusive situation, plus some ideas on how they may assist them.

Trying to understand spouse abuse requires looking at the problem from the perspective of victims and abusers, but far more research has been conducted on wives than on husbands. Fortunately, some researchers have managed to gather samples of violent husbands, so we are able to gain some insight into what battering men are like from their findings, although these men are mostly volunteers in therapy groups. Recognizing that they (like the battered wives who have been studied) may not be representative of the population of men who abuse, we are nevertheless able to gather together some characteristics that are most frequently found. The "profile" that emerges is of men who lack self-esteem, are highly traditional, cannot express any emotions except anger and jealousy, lack assertiveness, are social isolates, may have employment problems, may drink too much, had fathers who beat their mothers, fit into the "authoritarian personality" type that scapegoats people unable to retaliate, and have unpredictable mood changes. They give off danger signals by punching holes in walls or displacing aggression onto objects or pets.

Most professionals believe that violence is *learned* behavior and that there are some violent men who can be reeducated into nonviolent responses to anger, stress, and frustration. Men have formed groups in this country and others to deal with men's violence, most of them working closely with women's shelters and rape crisis groups. Therapy models have been developed for men who join voluntarily or through court orders, and they appear to be successful, but no long-term follow-ups have been done on any programs yet. Linda Rouse (1983b, 17), who studied abusers, takes a cautious viewpoint saying, "Some men do change. Most do not. Current estimates are that 9 out of 10 batterers do not believe they need to end their abusive behavior." The first step in the process to change is to take responsibility for their behavior, and stop minimizing, projecting, or denying it. The author and others believe that the best determinant for success is strong motivation and that the violent man has not used this mode of expression for a long time period: The shorter the time violent behavior has been employed, the greater the probability of change with appropriate help. Much of the likelihood of discontinuing violence depends on the sincerity of the abuser in desiring change: As modes of behavior are learned, they can be unlearned and new modes substituted. At last, men and women are working together to help *both* victims of violence: the man and the woman.

Finally, this section concludes with an overview of the latest responses to wife beating. The first and greatest effort of the battered women's movement was to establish and maintain shelters for victims and their children, but money has always been too short, and the scarce resources there had been have even been withdrawn in recent years. Many of the shelters that were hanging on with "shoestring" budgets have folded, and others have had to severely curtail services. However, another branch of the battered women's movement has had lasting effects that are not likely to be withdrawn because of budget cuts. While proposed legislation has failed at the federal level, most states have introduced new laws or have modified old ones, and the woman who is battered is not as likely as in prior years to turn to outsiders for help and find none available. The criminal justice system and the judiciary have been impacted in ways that do not yet guarantee women freedom from violence in their homes, but give them at least more alternatives, greater protection under the law, and hope that their civil rights are not violated without recourse.

NOTES

1. Lenore Walker's (1979) "Cycle Theory of Violence" has been accepted by some service providers and persons in the helping services as a "formula" for understanding

the dynamics of wife beating. The theory suggests three distinct phases: the *tension-building stage,* the *acute battering incident,* and the *kindness and contrite loving behavior state* (1979, 55–70). The third stage has been questioned by a number of researchers (Dobash and Dobash 1979; Pagelow 1981a) who found that either it never occurred, or if it did, it was only after the first few incidents of violence. For abusers who were contrite after the first outbreak of violence, it soon became a matter of "cognitive dissonance" where they must define themselves as justified for their behavior; that is, the victims "provoked" the violence or took some action that deserved the behavior of the aggressor. During Pagelow's numerous interviews with victims, many denied there had been any kind of repentant period or expression of remorse by their assailants; some others mentioned that there was some sort of loving, "honeymoon" period only after the first few outbreaks of violence. After that the verbal and psychological abuse increased in intensity while the "lovingness" decreased. There has also been some criticism of the first phase, the tension-building stage, since many battered women claim that violence could erupt at almost any time without warning, in sudden mood changes, although at other times there could be some noticeable rising tension before an attack. Walker has completed her second, larger study of woman battering, and tested her cycle theory of violence (1983). Her findings confirm that three phases occur in a cycle but she says, "Over time, the first phase of tension building becomes more common and loving contrition, or the third phase, declines" (1983, 43).

2. Out of these ten cases, Kirchner (1977) found that one woman miscarried in her eighth month after a beating, another bore a brain-damaged child and during her next pregnancy she was kicked in the stomach in her ninth month and the child was born dead, while another baby died of "crib death" at the age of two months.

3. As in rape, only the victim can make the choice to fight back or submit; uncompleted rapes usually occur when victims fight back, but if they are unsuccessful, they are more likely to be injured in the struggle (Queen's Bench Foundation 1976). On the other hand, many victims who are mutilated and killed did not resist rape, so nonresistance is not insurance. Each set of circumstances is unique: the environment, the victims, and the aggressors, and unfortunately, there is no way of knowing in advance what the outcome of resistance or submission may be.

4. Jennifer Patri's self-defense plea was unsuccessful; she was found guilty of first degree murder and sentenced to ten years in a Wisconsin prison (Eisenberg 1979).

5. For a brief, insightful review of the question of battered wives who kill their assailants, written in terms understandable to those outside the legal profession, read Meyers (1983, 345–52).

6. To obtain a copy of NiCarthy's book, send $7.95, plus $1.00 for postage and handling (plus Washington State tax when applicable) to The Seal Press, 312 S. Washington Street, Seattle, WA 98104. Another publication due to be released in 1984 is Linda Rouse's booklet, *You Are Not Alone: A Guide to Battered Women,* by Learning Publications.

7. It should be noted that although there were 53 wives willing to enter therapy and be studied by researchers, only 20 husbands joined their wives in the therapy group. This shows that the majority (62 percent) of the abusive husbands refused to participate in therapy and, consequently, were not studied by researchers. Unfortunately, this leaves only speculation as to how the approximately two out of three abusive husbands differed from those studied.

8. Canadians have established a wide variety of programs and services in response to the problem of wife abuse, including shelters for battered women and their children, programs for men who batter, information kits, and educational film libraries. They have also made considerable changes in the criminal justice system, and established a national clearinghouse. Information may be obtained by writing to Dr. Susan Lee Painter, Head,

National Clearinghouse on Family Violence, Social Service Development and Grants Division, Health and Welfare Canada, Ottawa, Ontario K1A 1B5, Canada. Information kits are published in both English and French. The Clearinghouse gathers and distributes information on wife battering, child abuse, incest, and elder abuse. Social workers can obtain a policy statement containing guidelines on identifying battered women, providing services, and educating others about family violence by contacting The Canadian Association of Social Workers, Committee on the Status of Women, 55 Parkdale Avenue, Ottawa, Ontario K1Y 1E5, Canada.

9. For copies of EMERGE's publication list or information on film rental or purchase, write to EMERGE, 25 Huntington Avenue, Room 324, Boston, MA 02116. For information on another film, *The Rites of Violence*, a documentary produced by the Domestic Abuse Intervention Project (DAIP), write to the Minnesota Program Development, 2 East 5th Street, Duluth, MN 55805, or telephone 218/722-2781.

10. Anyone interested in joining the RAVEN network should write to RAVEN, P.O. Box 24159, St. Louis, MO 63130, or telephone 314/725-6137. Another group that offers peer counseling for men who batter is Men Overcoming Violence (MOVE), which may be contacted at 3004 16th Street No. 12, San Francisco, CA 94103, or by calling 415/626-MOVE.

11. Networking with others trying to reeducate violent men can be most helpful because of information exchange and because the task often results in discouragement. Experiences of one man working in a small program in Eugene, Oregon, provides insight into how they operate:

> One project is the Anger Control Group (associated with the local battered women's shelter, WomanSpace). The Anger Control Group is a confidential group for men who have had or are currently experiencing difficulties with physical or emotional abuse of women. There is no fee for the group, which is run on a drop-in basis every Tuesday evening. The ACG has dealt, so far, only with primary batterers . . . though it is open to all. Results have apparently been excellent. The men who come (about 6/week) are quite sincerely seeking to rid themselves of violence. But while battering is stopped through the group therapy, not many men hang on to deal with the roots of violence. The attitude is somewhere around: "give me the tools to keep me from being violent, but don't change anything else." And once the crisis of violence is dealt with, the men don't come back. The notion of "needing to control" which is the basic male dilemma is not perceived as any kind of problem by the men. They see the problem of violence as just an illegitimate method of control, or as a method of control that was not accepted by their mates. (Goldwater 1980)

12. The participant's manual, called *Court-Mandated Counseling for Men Who Batter: A Three-Day Workshop for Mental Health Professionals,* can be obtained for $10.00 at the Center for Women Policy Studies, 2000 P Street NW, Suite 508, Washington, DC 20036. Other information may be obtained from CWPS about training programs by writing or calling 202/872-1770. CWPS also has a number of excellent films available for loan to educators or professionals.

13. The Center for Women Policy Studies regularly provide updates on laws pertaining to woman battering in its bimonthly newsletter, *Response,* that are thorough and comprehensive. One book for professionals, *Prosecution of Spouse Abuse: Innovations in Criminal Justice Response,* by Lisa G. Lerman, 1981, 227 pages, is available for $10.00 from CWPS, 2000 P Street NW, Suite 508, Washington, DC 20036. Ann Marie Boylan and Nadine Taub wrote a comprehensive analysis of domestic violence laws, *Adult Domestic Violence: Constitutional, Legislative, and Equitable Issues,* 1981, 521 pages, for the Legal Services Corporation Research Institute. Written for lawyers, the book is available for $4.00 from the National Clearinghouse for Legal Services, Inc., 500 N. Michigan Avenue, Room 1940, Chicago IL 60611.

PART V

Other Kinds of Abuse and Other Victims

10

Other Forms of Family Violence

This chapter addresses three types of family violence that have received comparatively little attention from the research community, although interest has been growing lately. These three types are: violence by children, abuse of adolescents, and abuse of elderly parents. Descriptive accounts and research findings on these topics are beginning to appear in the literature, and there is promise that more will be known about them in the coming decade.

VIOLENT CHILDREN, OR "KIDS WILL BE KIDS"

Almost everyone in this country has witnessed at least one physical fight between children, for most of us, such events occur innumerable times, to the point that they become commonplace and a part of "normal" childhood behavior. Everyone sees children at parks, beaches, at the school yard, or going to and from school: punching, shoving, and hitting each other. These are taken for granted as just normal, everyday acts of violence that children use to settle their squabbles. *Violence by children is seen, but it is not seen as violence.* This may help explain the lack of scientific inquiry into the phenomenon of childhood violence or sibling violence. Social and behavioral scientists grew up in families and raise families of their own, and like other parents, probably take it for granted that "kids will be kids" or, more frequently, *boys will be boys.* Many parents unwittingly train youngsters in violence and then when they observe their children fighting with siblings, conclude that such behavior is natural, unavoidable, or "instinctive" (Ardrey 1966; Lorenz 1966). Social and behavioral scientists have largely ignored intrafamily violence of children, except when it reaches an extreme level such as homicide (Adelson 1973; Sergent 1972), or when it spills outside the front door of the home to the streets and school yards (David and David 1980; McDermott 1979; Scott 1979).

Seeing little boys fighting on the streets and schoolyards is so common that most Americans pay little or no attention to it. To most, it is "natural" that boys will settle disputes by violence, yet many people would be surprised to know that fighting among children is virtually unknown in some cultures. Children in our culture *learn* that the way to settle disputes is by physical force, and cultural approval of violence surrounds them: in their homes, their communities, and their nation.

Training Children (Boys) into Violence

It is possible that most Americans (including members of the scientific community) fail to see the difference between aggression and assertiveness, and inculcate in our children the idea that it is better to fight than to endure an insult or be defeated by another. Probably still influenced by the Puritan ethic that fostered competition, Americans love "winners" and scorn "losers." Social psychological experiments provide some evidence that people in this country dislike and are willing to (and do) punish losers after they are defeated (Berkowitz 1965; Geen and Berkowitz 1966, 1967). Another factor (probably also related to our Puritan background) is that we tend toward *victim blaming* (Ryan 1971).

Americans not only *approve* of physical punishment for children; they *use* it ("spare the rod and spoil the child"). A serious article with a humorous title, "If you don't stop hitting your sister, I'm going to beat your brains in," notes that parents *tell* children not to use violence, and then *use* violence on them (Bordin-Sandler 1976). A probability sample of 1,176 adult Americans found that over 90 percent had been spanked "sometimes" when they were children, and a third were spanked "frequently" (Stark and McEvoy 1970, 54). Respondents largely believed (86 percent) in "strong discipline" for children by their parents (1970, 54). One question asked if they agree with the statement that "when a boy is growing up, it is very important for him to have a few fistfights." Rodney Stark and James McEvoy report that 70 percent agreed with this philosophy and the researchers state: "This approval reflects and inculcates a concept of masculinity that emphasizes physical aggressiveness" (1970, 110). Thus, it is "normal" for boys to be violent.

One noted researcher, Albert Bandura, and his associates conducted rigorous social-psychological experiments on aggression, testing social learning theory (Bandura 1973; Bandura and Ross 1961; Bandura and Walters 1973, 1970a, 1970b). When Bandura and his colleagues tested parental learning models, they controlled for peer support systems and compared parental attitudes of aggressive boys to parental attitudes of nonaggressive boys. The research team found considerable differences in parental values and attitudes, as Bandura explains:

> The families differed most strikingly in the extent to which they trained their sons, through precept and example, to be aggressors. . . . [P]arents of the aggressive boys displayed little antisocial aggression, but they repeatedly modeled and reinforced combative attitudes and behavior. While intolerant of aggression toward themselves, one or the other of the parents almost invariably encouraged their sons to aggress toward peers,

teachers, and other adults outside the family. During the early childhood years, the instigation often took the form of demands that the boy use his fists in dealing with antagonists. . . . (1973, 94)

The interview quotations from parents are rife with demands for "masculine" aggressiveness from their sons. In this study, Bandura and Richard Walters obtained a sample of 52 adolescent boys and their parents (1970a, 93): 26 who were identified by social agents as repeatedly exhibiting aggressive, antisocial behavior, and a control group of 26 nonaggressive boys, matched on certain criteria for comparison. They say:

The study was confined to boys who were of average or above average intelligence, who came from legally intact homes (i.e., homes that were not broken by separation, divorce, or death of a parent), whose parents were steadily employed, and who did not live in deteriorated or high-delinquency neighborhoods. (Bandura and Walters 1970a, 93)

The mothers, fathers, and sons in each of the 52 middle-class families were interviewed separately (usually simultaneously) by three interviewers, using a semistructured interview schedule (1970a, 94–95). Their findings are of extreme importance in understanding violence, particularly in view of the current popularity of the "cycle of violence" theory, discussed in Chapter 7. By comparing aggressive boys and their parents with the control group, Bandura and Walters found some striking differences (1970a, 96–98). In the aggressive group, not only was there a distinct disruption in affectionate relationships of the parents to each other but of the sons to their parents, particularly to their fathers. The researchers saw evidence that "in the majority of cases a severe break had occurred in the father-son relationship," and "the aggressive boys showed very much less warmth for their fathers than did their controls" (1970a, 96–97). The aggressive boys showed less warmth toward either parent than the controls, but the aggressive boys had something positive to say about their mothers whereas they were "indifferent, critical, or hostile toward their fathers" (1970a, 97).

By comparison, the control's parents indicated much more warmth toward each other, and their sons expressed significantly more warmth toward their fathers. When tested for *identification with* parents, both the aggressive and control groups identified more with fathers than mothers, and some aggressive boys still showed a *preference* for their fathers. The authors summarize:

[T]he parents of the control boys made more use of psychological disciplinary methods. In contrast, the parents of the aggressive boys resorted more freely to such methods as ridicule, physical punishment, and deprivation of privileges. . . . The male child, however, must eventually identify with a male adult in order to fulfill the masculine role that is demanded of him very early in life. . . . It was found that the fathers of the aggressive boys had spent relatively little time in affectionate interaction with their sons in early childhood, were lacking in warmth for them, and were more hostile, rejecting, and punitive than were the control fathers. In turn, the aggressive boys were critical and disparaging of their fathers. (Bandura and Walters 1970a, 100)

Another study of 174 nondelinquent but aggressive boys and their parents involved a longitudinal design from a social learning perspective (McCord et al. 1970). William McCord and his colleagues did not find a direct link between aggressive parents and aggressive boys: 15 percent of the aggressive boys were raised by aggressive fathers, and 10 percent of them were raised by nonaggressive fathers (1970, 56). At the other end of the spectrum, of the nonaggressive boys, 10 percent had aggressive fathers while 18 percent had nonaggressive fathers; as the authors note, the differences were not statistically significant (1970, 55–56). By comparing the boys' family environment over a period of almost six years, the researchers produced a list of characteristics[1] of parental behavior that were strongly associated with aggressive/nonaggressive behavior of the boys. The authors report:

In a general sense, therefore, we can argue that the *aggressive boys* were most likely to have been raised by parents who (a) treated the boy in a rejecting, punitive fashion; (b) failed to impose direct [other times called consistent] controls on his behavior; (c) offered him an example of deviance; and (d) were often involved in intense conflict. (McCord et al. 1970, 62)

The exact opposite of the above factors were descriptive of the family environment of the nonaggressive boys (McCord et al. 1970, 63). The authors say, "Neither social class, immigration patterns, ethnic group, nor paternal occupation was significantly related to the child's aggression" (1970, 43). Later they note: "the antisocial, aggressive boys came from homes in which they were rejected and treated in an inconsistent fashion" (McCord et al. 1970, 64).

The boys in this study were categorized into three different groups: aggressive, nonaggressive, and a middle group, described in these terms:

Ninety-seven boys were, by the norms of American society, normally *assertive*. They participated, at times, in fights, acts of destruction aimed at other children or adults, occasional battles with teachers or other community officials, and bullying of weaker children or adults. They differed from the openly aggressive boys, however, in that their hostile responses were sporadic exceptions to the general pattern of their lives. (1970, 46)

This is a good example of what most Americans would call "normal boyhood behavior," or in the terms of Straus (1981b) or Gelles (1979, 80): "ordinary" violence. One of the few articles that deals with children's violence against other children—not from the viewpoint of juvenile delinquency or criminal violence—but within the range of "normal" childhood behavior, is one by Edward Scott (1979). Scott talks about the "school ground bully," who threatens or uses physical force to control and dominate other children, sometimes using extortion to get money or food from them (1979, 199). Some school halls and yards are literally *armed camps*, where administrators, teachers, and students carry weapons despite guards and patrols (David and David 1980).

How Violent Are American Children?

What do we know about violence by children that spills out beyond the front door? It is clear that many are violent and some are extremely violent. Most figures on violence come from crime statistics which are found in the *Uniform Crime Reports* (UCR). When using these sources, it should be kept in mind that children may be charged with "crimes" for acts that if committed by adults would not be chargeable, that is, status offenses such as runaway, truancy, incorrigibility, curfew violation, and so forth. The majority of young persons (particularly females) arrested are charged with noncrimes and as such, may be considered *deviant* rather than criminal, and when they do commit crimes, not all are violent. Overall, males outnumber females arrested by five to one, and while arrests of young females have increased at a higher rate than boys, their offenses at a young age are largely running away (status), promiscuity (morals), or petty theft (property). These differences by sex are important to remember, because the differences are apparent within the family as well.

Persons under 18 are arrested for crimes at a rate disproportionate to their numbers in the population. Arrest rates of juveniles constituted 29 percent of *all* arrests in 1976, while persons aged 10 to 17 years constituted only about 15 percent of the total United States population (Uniform Crime Reports 1977, 16). But when it comes specifically to *Index crimes* (murder, forcible rape, robbery, aggravated assault, burglary, larceny-theft, and motor vehicle theft), rather than constituting 15 percent, they made up 43 percent of the arrested population (Uniform Crime Reports 1976, 41). Although criminal arrests decrease over age categories, young people are still vastly overrepresented in arrest statistics.

Between 1967 and 1976, there was a 98 percent increase in arrests for violent crimes by persons under 18 years of age (Uniform Crime Reports 1977, 175). Broken down by offenses, the increases are as follows: criminal homicide, 87 percent; forcible rape, 57 percent; aggravated assault, 91 percent; robbery, 111 percent.[2] And young people can be extremely violent. One study of 78 child victims of sexual assault aged from just under two years to twelve-and-a-half, found that 43 percent of the abusers were juvenile males (Shamroy 1980). In the Queen's Bench Foundation study of rape, the largest age category of the assailants was the youngest: 16 to 20 years (38.4 percent) (Queen's Bench 1976, 97). The report does not state how many juveniles are in this category but interestingly, as the ages advance, the percentage of assailants in each category drops. However, as Finkelhor notes, younger offenders are usually not reported, but when they are, they are "disposed of by the juvenile justice system" (1979a, 141).

To summarize, juveniles are arrested at about double their proportion of the population, which may be partially explained by youthful ignorance of how to commit crimes and escape arrest unlike more experienced adult criminals. But what is notable is that while all arrests are increasing, there was an almost one hundred percent increase in violent crimes by juveniles and a lesser increase in property crimes. Adult crimes have increased by about the same percentage in property crime with a smaller increase in violent crime.

These figures, of course, do not reflect the number of cases that "dropped through the cracks" because of differences in police reporting practices and definitions of crime and juvenile laws in different jurisdictions. Crime rates that the FBI draw from local police records constitute less than half of all crimes committed yearly in the U.S., according to victimization reports (Flanagan and McLeod 1983), and of those reported, only 21 percent of the *violent* crimes listed in the UCR Index were cleared by arrest (Uniform Crime Reports 1977, 161). These statistics should leave no doubt that young people can be criminally violent outside the family, and are becoming increasingly violent. Children, like adults, are also violent in the family.

Sibling Violence

What about those "bullies" in their homes with their families? As noted in Chapter 2, the national survey by Straus et al. (1980) found the highest rates of violence between siblings. Some interesting findings are those concerning the effects of the sex ratio composition of families. The authors say that they found girls use less violence than do boys, regardless of whether girls have "only sisters, only brothers, or both brothers and sisters" (Straus et al. 1980, 87). In addition, they found a moderating effect on violence if there is at least one girl in the family (the boys are somewhat less violent) but the girls are somewhat more violent when they have brothers than if they are in all-girl families. At every age level, all-boy families have more violence than all-girl families, and at the 15- to 17-year age level, almost 60 percent of all-boy families still contain sibling violence (1980, 89). The only type of violent act that increased with the age of the children was in the use of a knife or gun; as the researchers say, "This went from 2.6 percent of preschoolers to 6.5 percent of high schoolers" (Straus et al. 1980, 90).

Murray Straus (1981b) provides some interesting comparisons of parent to child and child to child violence. By separating parent to child acts into four categories (from none, to "ordinary" physical punishment, to one or two acts of abuse, to three or more acts of abuse), Straus plots the percentage of children who "repeatedly and severely attacked a sibling" (1981b, 4). The figure shows that among children who received no physical punishment from parents, 13 percent of them repeatedly and severely attacked their siblings in the survey year. Straus (1981b, 5–6) says:

> By contrast . . . 76 percent of the children who were repeatedly abused by their parents repeatedly and severely assaulted a sibling. In general the more violence experienced by the child, the higher the rate at which such children are violent towards a sibling. It does not take being a victim of child abuse to produce an elevated rate of being violent to others. Ordinary physical punishment also "works." In fact children who experienced only culturally permissible physical punishment frequently and severely assaulted a sibling at almost three times the rate of children who were not physically punished during the year (42 versus 15).

Straus found a strong positive correlation between the severity of violence that 100 children received from parents and violent acts by children to their siblings. Straus's report provides data that tentatively support the idea that as physical punishment of children increases, physical violence against siblings also increases. Even among children receiving "ordinary" physical punishment, more than 40 percent repeatedly and severely attacked a sibling, according to reports from one parent (Straus 1981b, Figure 1). Unfortunately, the tables Straus (1981b) provides do not reveal the sex ratio of the children who abused their siblings, which leaves important questions unanswered. As noted earlier, Straus et al. (1980, 89) shows that boys were much more violent with siblings at every age range except among the very youngest: three to four years old. Boys are also the most frequent targets for physical abuse by parent/caretakers until age 11; from age 12 and beyond, girls are the major targets (Gil 1971, 639; Hindelang et al. 1981, 275).

However, Straus (1981b) does not present an analysis on a case-by-case format. In other words, these are correlations of abuse administered and received, which give an overall picture of percentages, but they do not show if the same positive correlation occurs on an individual basis. Does the same association occur in all cases, or are there just enough cases in the sample to show this pattern? In other words, these are aggregate data (Szinovacz 1983), not data comparing individual parents with their children, so they do not reveal whether or not the children who are violent are the same ones whose parents are violent with them.

Boys with Violent Role Models

Children who live in homes where fathers beat their mothers are affected by an environment of violence. Erin Pizzey (1977) noted differences in the behavior of children who came with their mothers to Chiswick. According to Pizzey, the girls tend to be shy, quiet, and cling to their mothers, whereas the boys are frequently destructive and aggressive:

> It's very noticeable that the boys' behaviour differs from the girls'. We've never had a school ask us to remove one of our girls because they were too violent to cope with. All the damage to our house and to the neighbours' houses is done by the boys. They have broken down the walls and keep over-running the neighbouring gardens. Exasperated neighbours ring up to complain when puppies are stoned. (1977, 71)

Pizzey says the response to this type of situation was to set up unique facilities for teen-aged boys with special staff to cope with their "acting-out" behavior.[3] There is a possibility that boys, if they have lived with and observed their same-sex role model beating their mothers, may identify with their fathers, seeing them as powerful winners (Pagelow 1982a, 65). Pizzey (1977, 76) describes one family of boys in these words:

> It turned out that their father, when bored, used to smash up their house and, when really bored, would shoot down all the crockery with his air rifle. These pastimes seemed very exciting to small boys. All the neighbours were terrified of him and if,

as one neighbour did, someone complained about the
screams coming from the house, their windows were smashed
or nasty things happened to their animals. As far as the boys
were concerned, Dad was a sort of superman who could defy
everyone, even the police.

Shelters in the United States may refuse to admit boys above a certain
age, usually 13 to 15 years, but not because of their antisocial behavior, at
least, that is not the stated reason.[4] The problem of boys' violence has
arisen from time to time in various shelters, but one of the "unofficial"
reasons that older adolescent and teen-aged boys are unwelcomed at
most shelters is a matter of security. That is, while youthful sons of violent
men may not be acting aggressively (in fact, many are concerned and caring toward their mothers) there is the ever-present danger that the boys
have identified with their fathers and out of loyalty or other motives, may
disclose the location of the shelter to them. For the safety of the women
and children living together, shelter locations are kept secret to the greatest extent possible.

While most of the evidence points to boys who learn and use violence,
girls also learn it. Girls are more likely to use it when the prospects for
reward are apparent (Bandura 1973); or to use indirect aggression to hurt
others or obtain their goals (Feshbach and Feshbach 1976); or to turn it
inward against themselves (Ross 1980). Occasionally, young people attack
and kill their school teachers (Daily Pilot 1978; Register 1982). Sometimes
violence by adolescents results in homicide of family members, parents,
or friends (Bender and Curran 1974; Easson and Steinhilber 1961; King
1975; Sendi and Blomgren 1975). Of all *reported* cases of family violence,
the majority of victims are female, *except* in the case of abuse from their
own children (U.S. Department of Justice 1980, 28–44). Cases reported in
national crime surveys tend to be attacks on younger parents by their adolescent or teen-aged children who are more likely to strike out at fathers
than mothers. Sociologist Carol A. B. Warren (1979) studied 15 adolescents being treated at a psychiatric hospital who had attacked their parents; 8 of them had attempted to murder a parent. An excerpt from the
records of a 12-year-old boy who once threw a knife at his mother says he
"poured gasoline in the bathroom while his mother was in there, threw in
a match, and shut the door" (Warren 1979, 6).

There also have been several highly publicized cases of *parricide* (killing
one's own parent) in the recent past, such as the case of the Jahnke family
in Wyoming, where a 16-year-old son and 17-year-old daughter plotted to
kill their father (Lubenow 1983). The son shot and killed his father and was
found guilty of voluntary manslaughter, and the daughter was found
guilty of aiding manslaughter, despite evidence that for years, the father

had mentally and physically abused his wife, daughter, and son, and, in addition, sexually abused his daughter (*Los Angeles Times* 1983a, 1983b). One writer says that parricide follows certain patterns:

> Almost all murders of parents are committed by sons, and in the rare cases that involve daughters, they often recruit a male agent. Usually parent killing involves a drunken, physically abusive father killed by a son who sees himself as the protector of not only himself but also of his mother and siblings. (Lubenow 1983, 35)

Like adult violence, even more of children's violence may occur within the family rather than outside the front door. Unfortunately, little attention has been focused on this topic by parents, social scientists, and community leaders. Not all violent children remain violent into adulthood, but one method to prevent this is to insure that rewards do not follow aggressive or violent behavior. We must begin to take violence by children seriously.

ABUSE OF ADOLESCENTS

When the topic of child abuse or neglect is raised, most people focus on totally helpless and dependent infants and children, and strong emotions are generated at their plight. As research has generally avoided examining violent children, it has also tended to ignore child victims over the age of 12 who are still dependent on their caretakers and helpless to survive without the support of their parents. No longer small children, this segment of the maltreated child population arouses much less interest or sentiment from the general public, social services, and academicians. This section examines the problem of the victimization of adolescents within three major categories: adolescents as victims of siblings, as victims of parents, and as victims of others outside the family.

Adolescent Victims of Siblings

Social worker, writer, and specialist educator of teen-agers, Ginny NiCarthy (1983b) made the following comments:

> I'm especially interested in what you have to say about sibling violence, which I think has been grossly overlooked. Perhaps four or five of ten in our group of teens has been assaulted by her older brother. Where's the line between "normal" sibling rivalry-horseplay and teen battering?

Almost nothing has been written about sibling abuse, even in the form of descriptive studies. As noted earlier, Straus et al. (1980, 81) estimates that over 29 million children engage in one or more violent acts toward a sibling every year. These researchers found that 16 percent of the children were reported to have "beat up" a brother or sister, and that girls use less violence than boys (Straus et al. 1980, 83–89). They also found that all-boy families had about twice the rate of violence of all-girl families at the 15- to 17-year age level, but for boys in families with only sisters, the level of violence was less than boys with brothers and sisters. Given the socialization of boys to aggression, if a girl grows up in a home where there is at least one brother, she is more likely to experience violence than if she has sisters only. If her brother is violent, she may be the target because she is accessible and because of family privacy. Sometimes the abuse is sexual; one battered woman answered a question about prior physical abuse in these terms:

> Sure, I got introduced to sex by my brother. I was only about ten years old at the time. My brother was 15 then and he liked to grow things in the garden and he kept his tools and little plants in this old shed down at the edge of our property. One day our folks were gone, and he called me to the shed to look at something he said was strange. I did, and he had this gang of his buddies there, waiting for me. He held me down while each one of his pals raped me. I screamed and kicked and fought, but they just laughed. It hurt so bad I thought I'd die, but they thought is was funny. Afterward, my brother put my pants back on me and told me if I said anything to anybody, he'd bring them back to do it to me again. A gang bang, that's what it was! And after that, he'd fuck me any time he had the chance, 'cause he said the guys had "broken me in" to sex. I knew my folks wouldn't believe me if I told, 'cause he was their pride and joy; besides, I felt like trash . . . rotten.

Louise Armstrong (1978) notes that brother-sister incest is reputed to be the most common and least traumatic, but then provides a case history of a girl, who was raised in a large house mainly by servants. Her brother was nine years her senior. Her abuse by her brother began at the age of three, but while she could not recall the details of the first sexual encounter, she did recall vividly the medical treatment she received for gonorrhea. The woman told Armstrong, "I can remember friends of mine—you know, also from super-rich families—where the mothers would be off. And they'd be raised by help and be sexually abused by their brothers" (1978, 182).

David Finkelhor (1979a, 89–91) shows that the highest rate of reported incestuous relationships are between siblings (39 percent reported by girls and 21 percent reported by boys), but at least 30 percent of the girls' experiences involved threat or force. We do not know how many of all sibling incestuous relationships are accomplished by coercion, threats, or force.

Although the scientific evidence is sparse, there are sufficient indicators to conclude that many adolescents are victims of sibling violence, whether the form the abuse takes is sexual or otherwise. It is obvious that much research needs to be done in this area.

Adolescent Victims of Parents

When parents strike out at children, injuries are likely to be more serious the younger the child's age, due to their relative strength and physical size. Yet reporting statistics show that "major physical injury generally declines with age up until the age of 15, when it increases again" (American Humane Association 1981, 23). Patricia Libbey and Rodger Bybee note that physical abuse of adolescents is widespread, saying that "almost half of the known cases of abuse involved youth between the ages of 12 and 18" (1979, 101). Ira Lourie (1977, 275) believes that "The abuse of adolescents is a problem of epidemic proportions." Unlike abuse of younger children, issues raised in adolescent abuse are the seriousness of the injury, the behavior of the child, and community norms (Libbey and Bybee 1979). Bruce Fisher and Jane Berdie (1978) also note that almost as many cases of maltreatment occur among children age 10 to 18 as among younger children, but they believe major factors are judicial attitudes, seriousness of the injury, and the behavior of the child, because people often look for "provocation" and *justification*.

Following a workshop on youth abuse and neglect in 1975, Jane Berdie and her colleagues (1977) describe the unique problems of adolescents abused by their parents. Young people are not viewed as helpless or as innocent as children under 12, and many people view the effects of parental abuse as evidence that the children "got what they deserve" (Berdie et al. 1977, 8). On the contrary, writers who have studied abused adolescents believe that they should be treated as victims of aggression, and that even though their behavior may evoke or deserve more frequent punishment, "it would be injudicious to maintain that they merited the severe abuse of being burnt, being choked or having had their bones broken" (Amsterdam et al. 1979, 282).[5]

In a nationwide study of 1,000 adolescent girls, Gisela Konopka (1975) found that 12 percent reported having been beaten by adults, 9 percent said they had been raped,[6] and 5 percent reported sexual molestation by adults or much older youths. Berdie et al. (1977, 8) report that a study by Hopkins and Brandt Steele of 100 juveniles in a detention center found that 84 percent of the youth had been abused in early childhood, while 77 percent had been abused by a family member within the six months prior to the interview.

Adolescent abuse sometimes is a continuation of child abuse (Kempe and Kempe 1978). In some cases, it occurs as a result of escalation from preciously used forms of physical punishment, and in other cases, it does not occur until the child reaches adolescence, as in half the cases studied by Libbey and Bybee (1979, 122). Lourie (1977) studied 70 cases of "confirmed" adolescent abuse and found that most begins when the child reaches an age where struggles begin over separation and control. Fisher and Berdie (1978, 173) report the following statements from adolescents they interviewed:

> I'm a 14-year-old girl. My Dad has whipped me and beaten me all my life. It keeps getting worse. Yesterday he punched me hard in the stomach a bunch of times. I'm scared to death. I'm afraid he's going to kill me.

> I'm Jim, I'm 16. I've run away from home 13 times in the last three years. My Dad hates me. He beats me up when I'm home. Last time he hit me in the face with his fist. I'm in a runaway home now. But they say I can't stay here much longer. Sooner or later, they always send me back home.

> My name is Alice. I'm 14. My Dad has sex with me. I'm sure my Mom knows, but she's afraid to do anything about it. Maybe she doesn't care. She's been sick a lot. I love my Daddy, but I don't want to do it with him anymore. I'm scared.

As Gerald Lubenow (1983, 36) comments about the Jahnke parricide mentioned earlier, most social agencies are reluctant (or refuse) to intervene in families before tragedies occur. Lubenow says that when 16-year-old Richard Jahnke approached local authorities for help, they treated him like a "rebellious teen-ager" (1983, 36). Yet research shows that abused adolescents are unlikely to turn to outsiders for help except in emergency situations. In cases of chronic abuse, "the adolescents had been in therapy for months before they spoke of abuse by their parents" (Libbey and Bybee 1977, 123). Statistical data were compiled on the types and degrees of injuries to youth, but nothing documents the "degree of emotional confusion or disturbance reported by the adolescents" (Libbey and Bybee 1977, 123). Sadly, this may be the most devastating and long-lasting injury of all.

Clinical psychologist Beulah Amsterdam and her colleagues (1979) wanted to know how children respond to parental physical punishment. They gathered a sample of 105 adolescents from a diverse population, and found that 96 percent had received some form of physical punishment while growing up. Only 24 percent dealt with their punishment by talking with someone. Eleven percent had been severly abused: they had been burned, choked, bitten, had arms twisted or bones broken. The majority believed that it was a sign of parental caring and half saw it as a parental effort to make them a "good child" (Amsterdam et al. 1979, 279–80). Severity of punishment was correlated with victims' feelings of guilt: "The more severly the subjects were punished, the more they felt they deserved being punished" (Amsterdam et al. 1979, 281). Significantly more females tended to withdraw and saw parental punishment as justified. Victims' coping responses were to become hypervigilant, inhibited, and withdrawn. Abused adolescents' responses were delinquency, running away from home, and thoughts of or attempted suicide (Amsterdam et al. 1979, 282).

James Garbarino (1980, 124) found that 35 percent of the "crimes" committed by youngsters coming from homes in which abuse was present were *escape* offenses, that is, running away, truancy, and so forth. Reportedly, over 1 million juveniles run away from home every year in the United States (Ritter 1979). Even when juvenile service workers come in contact with runaways, they are unlikely to report suspected cases of abuse (Fisher and Birdie 1978). When runaway adolescents fall into the jurisdiction of the juvenile justice system, it frequently means they are stigmatized and introduced to even more deviant behavior (Garbarino 1980). Shelter homes, runaway programs, hotlines,[7] and family intervention on behalf of abused adolescents are badly needed (Fisher and Berdie 1978). The reasons why children run away from home are cited by Frances Koestler (1977, 4–5) in these terms:

> [By parents]: 1) He had an argument with his father and his father told him to get out. 2) It was a mutual agreement. The best thing at the time. 3) We told him when he thought he could make it on his own without our help, he could leave. So he did. 4) He had gone away before, but unfortunately he came back. [From a 12 year old girl]: My stepfather raped me, then said he'd kill me if I ever told. I was afraid to stay there another minute.

So, at the rate of one million a year, adolescents are running away from home, and what do they find when they escape from family tyranny?

Adolescent Victims of Others outside the Family

Not all adolescents run away because of abuse; some are overtly or covertly parental "throwaways" or "pushouts" (Koestler 1977, 3). Some leave because of youthful desires for adventure and independence; many express an inability to communicate with their parents and indirectly reveal dysfunctional families with multiple problems. Others reject parental norms and values and leave to adopt alternative lifestyles. Youth services and shelters are too few and always financially strapped, and conflicting state laws make it extremely difficult to adequately serve the needs of runaway youth (Fisher and Berdie 1978; Koestler 1977; Ritter 1979). Alternative, community-based programs, almost entirely founded and staffed by volunteers, are perhaps the most effective helpers of runaway youth, about half of whom were abused or neglected in their homes (Fisher and Berdie 1978). In the first year of operation, 4,000 children applied for help at Covenant House in New York City: When their needs cannot be solved by public assistance, many of them become victims of the $1.5 million sex industry that feeds on hungry, homeless children in the Times Square area of New York City (Ritter 1979).

Adolescent boys' major problems outside the family that are not self-inflicted (such as gang activity, automobile accidents, alcohol and other drug consumption, and so forth) are mainly sexual. Both boys and girls are more likely to have been subjected to physical and/or sexual abuse at home before they became juvenile prostitutes. Debra Boyer and Jennifer James (1982, 79) report that between 40 and 75 percent of adolescent prostitutes were victims in their homes of orientation. Adolescent involvement in prostitution includes far fewer males than females: There are approximately 600,000 female and 300,000 male juvenile prostitutes in the United States (1982, 77). Noting that adolescent prostitution has increased by 183 percent for females and 245 percent for males in the nine-year period until 1978, Boyer and James say: "Some are as young as eight years old; most are between twelve and sixteen" (1982, 77). These writers say:

> Adolescents in particular are regarded largely as a burdensome charge. Many young people themselves perceive this social reality. Our lack of genuine concern for children is reflected in the 1,000,000 who run away each year, the 2,000,000 who are battered in their homes, the 1 in 10 adolescent girls who become pregnant, the 1 in 5 who are sexually abused before they are eighteen, and the thousands who survive economically and personally through prostitution. (Boyer and James 1982, 83)

Connections between child prostitution and child pornography are strong, and the commercially sexually exploited child is usually a runaway or from a dysfunctional family (Baker 1978). Thousands of children are used in child pornography in Los Angeles, California (Baker 1978). One police official reported that "of the thousand of children . . . involved in the 'kiddie porn' industry, many 'were recruited from a vast army of runaways'" (cited in Koestler 1977, 8). Judianne Densen-Gerber (1980, 79) says, "Los Angeles police estimate that adults in that city alone sexually exploited over 30,000 children under seventeen in 1976 and photographed many of them in the act. Five thousand of these children were under twelve." Organized crime uses children in pornographic films, books, and magazines as well as in prostitution, but many of the victims are provided by their own parents or caretakers, as in the notorious Roman Polanski case (Densen-Gerber 1980). Testimony at congressional subcommittee hearings revealed that, "In some instances, it is the children's own parents who reap the proceeds of this kind of sexual exploitation" (Koestler 1977, 8). Some parents sell their children into pornography and/or prostitution. One case graphically illustrates this:

> The youngest mother I personally delivered during my medical training was nine years, eight months old. She had been prostituted by her own mother from age three. When she delivered a son, she thanked God that it was not a female who would have to experience a life similar to her own. (Densen-Gerber 1980, 78)

There are other ways parents sexually exploit their children. Densen-Gerber (1980, 77) tells of a *Ms. and Mr. Nude Teeny Bopper Contest* held in Naked City, Indiana, where the parents and their children are paid $10 each for the children to enter the contest naked. She also notes that in 1977 when a television crew happened to stop at a Naked City restaurant favored by truckers, they found 11- and 14-year-old girls waiting on tables, stark naked, in 18-hour shifts for $15 a day, and comments: "These circumstances were found to be violations of the minimum wage law, the child labor law, and the liquor licensing regulations. There were no laws to address the matter of their nakedness" (Densen-Gerber 1980, 78).

Legal statutes are inadequate or inappropriate when children are working for a parent, or penalties are so limited they pose no real deterrent. Parental criminal responsibility in child pornography is unclear (Baker 1978), although some new legislation is attempting to control the sexual exploitation of children (Densen-Gerber 1980, 81).

More will be said in Chapter 11 about sexual abuse of children and adults, but at this point associations between child and adolescent abuse and neglect, runaway children, prostitution, and pornography should be noted. When children run away from abuses inside the home, they may be picked up on the streets and at bus terminals by "smooth-talking pimps who woo them with protestations of love and promises of fun and big money" (Densen-Gerber, 1980, 78). Koestler (1977, 15) has this to say:

> That the adolescent in flight may often serve as the unconscious emissary from a troubled family in need of help has been borne out by the experience of the runaway programs. Sister Lorraine Reilly, who is in charge of group homes for urban nomads in the Bronx, New York, says: "The runaway is often the healthiest person in the family. Wait till you meet the families. The child who runs away is saying, 'I'm not going to be part of this.'"

When parents report a runaway child and the child is recovered, the first response of authorities is to return the child to his or her parents. Consider, for example, the following case history:

> Two runaway boys were assigned to a child protective services worker who, after gaining their trust, learned that their father, in addition to brutal beatings forced them to have intercourse with their mother while he watched. Convinced they were telling the truth, the worker recommended the children be removed from their home; he told his supervisor why, but insisted the children's confidentiality be honored. It was not; the supervisor called the parents to his office and related the story they had told. The mother said nothing but cried softly; the father furiously accused his children of being pathological liars. The children were subsequently released to their parents. The following morning, the worker found the boys huddled outside the door to his office building; they ran away during the night after being severely beaten with a bicycle chain; they bore bruises over their entire bodies. Despite his "betrayal" of their trust, he was the only friend they had. This time the children were taken into protective custody.

Children betrayed by parents are betrayed by others outside the family, and by the institutions that are mandated to protect them. Another category of relatively powerless people is the elderly, also subject to abuse in the family and by society. Earlier attention focused on abuse in institutions, although only 5 percent of the aged are institutionalized (Schaie 1982), and very little attention was paid to abuse of elderly parents in the family.

ABUSE OF ELDERLY PARENTS

Probably in terms of numbers, abuse of parents occurs less in American families than all other forms of violence, but in terms of pain, fear, help-lessness, and destructiveness of the lives of all involved, it is a serious social problem. Abuse of parents by their adolescent offspring (Warren 1979) is not the issue addressed here. There are important differences in abuse of parents who are in their mid-years by adolescent children and abuse of aging parents by their middle-aged offspring or grandchildren. The etiology, alternative measures, and prevention are different in abuse of elderly parents, except in cases where the middle-aged parents are physically disabled or incapacitated. In this context, the terms *elderly* and *aged* arbitrarily refer to persons 65 years old or older because 65 is a "mile-stone" year, institutionally recognized as the year when attainment of that age signifies retirement for some, benefits for others, and being a mem-ber of a specific life stage. Social scientists now classify people 65 and over as the *young old* until age 75, after which people are classified as the *old old*.

Who Are the People at Risk?

At a family violence conference, psychologist Adacir H. Oliveira (1981a) offered a "profile" of elderly persons most likely to be abuse victims: women between the ages of 75 to 85, middle- to lower middle-class, Prot-estant, and suffering some form of physical and/or mental impairment. Some vignettes are:

> A 67-year-old woman, widowed for eight years, was regularly beaten by her 35-year-old unmarried son. After she transferred her little money and property to him, he quit working and they subsisted on her small Social Security and SSI income. She did some babysitting to supplement the income. (Gentry and Nel-son 1980, 75)

> Because of a stroke, Mrs. S was no longer able to manage living alone in her own home. Her children decided that she should live with her oldest daughter and husband. The daughter, who had been quite active in church and community activities, found she was unable to leave her mother alone. Mrs. S was often in conflict with her daughter and son-in-law about the care which she felt she needed or did not need. She expressed definite ideas about how the daughter's home should be man-aged. During these times of stress and emotional and psycho-logical upheaval, the daughter would lash out physically and

verbally at the mother. Following such episodes, there was a tendency for the daughter to misuse medication, both to calm herself and to manage her mother. (Gentry and Nelson 1980, 76)

People who suffer physical or mental disabilities, sometimes called the "frail elderly" (Cazenave 1981), which put them in powerless, dependent positions, are more likely to be abused than those who are able to maintain independence. They are subject to the same kinds of physical and psychological abuse and neglect, including sexual abuse, as children and wives, but in addition, they are also susceptible to financial manipulation and abuse.

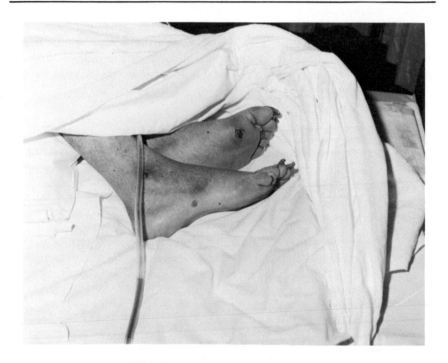

One of the most common forms of abuse of elderly parents is neglect, and this police file photograph shows an elderly man's feet, after he was rescued from his home where he received little or no care. His toenails are clawlike, as a result of not having been trimmed in a long time, and there are bedsores on his feet. This elderly parent was not physically beaten, but he was ignored and allowed to survive in filth and lack of care.

Source: Crimes Against the Elderly Unit, Santa Ana Police Department, Santa Ana, California.

Social indicators show there will be more parents "at risk" for abuse in the future. The growth of the percentage of older people in this population occurred rapidly in this century and promises to continue in the next. There are more than 24 million Americans over the age of 65; in 1978 there were 9.8 million males and 14.3 females, or a ratio of seven men to every ten women (U.S. Bureau of the Census 1979). In the year 1900, only 3 percent of the population had reached or exceeded age 65 (Schaie 1980, 4), and by 1978 they constituted 11 percent. Since the beginning of this century, the total population of the United States has increased by 300 percent, while the population of persons 65 and over has increased by almost 800 percent (U.S. Bureau of the Census 1979, 2). By the year 2000, persons aged 65 and over will probably constitute 15 percent of the population (Butler 1982, 407).

As noted above, the majority of the aged are women, and their proportion increases along the age scale. Females constitute 61 percent of those over 75 (Schaie 1982, 5), and in addition, their numbers are growing faster over time than men's. Between 1970 and 1978, their numbers increased by 22 percent, compared to a 16 percent increase in the number of men (U.S. Bureau of the Census 1979, 2). The large majority of elderly parents are widows for two basic reasons: they live an average of eight years longer than men, and they tend to marry men older than themselves. In addition, men who become widowed (or divorced) have higher remarriage rates than women. The remarriage rate for males 65 and over is seven times that of females the same age; most elderly men (77 percent) live with their spouses, whereas only 36 percent of elderly women live with husbands. Overall, the majority (63 percent) of older Americans live in families, 6 percent are institutionalized, and 30 percent live alone (U.S. Bureau of the Census 1979).

The elderly in this country are disproportionately represented among the poor; 15 percent were below the poverty level in 1978. However, as activist Tish Sommers stated at the White House Conference on Aging, "The severity of the economic circumstances of aging women has been masked by including them in the broader category of the aging" (1982, 9). In 1980 the median income for American women aged 65 and over was only $176 above the official poverty level for individuals; thus Sommers (1982, 9) concludes: "This means that nearly half of all women over the age of 65 are currently living on income less than the poverty level." Elderly women are more likely to be poor because only 20 percent collect private or government pensions; they are more likely to live alone; and when they collect Social Security based on their own earnings, payments are substantially less than those based on earnings of men. As the U.S. Bureau of the Census (1979, 33) reports: "About 31 percent of families with Social Security income only, and 49 percent of those with Social Security and Supplemental Security incomes were below the poverty level in 1977." Since 1977, the situation of women in general, and older or disadvantaged women in particular, has grown considerably worse.

The issue of poverty is important in identifying the group at greatest risk: The majority of abused elderly parents are females, largely because there are more of them and because of their greater economic dependency. Even if an elderly parent is in relatively good health, financial problems may cause them to share housing with their children for mutual economic advantages. Although only 26 percent of elderly persons are limited in their activities because of health reasons, and even fewer (16 percent) are unable to carry on major activities of daily living, 81 percent of persons over 65 have one or more chronic diseases or conditions (Schaie 1982, 5). Health and economics are interrelated because those with greater financial resources are able to maintain good health longer, and to obtain better medical care when ill than those with limited resources. The largest expenditures for medical care occur in the last few years of life, and sometimes chronic or acute illnesses deplete resources and lifetime savings very quickly. When older parents live with children and become physically or mentally handicapped, the difference between abuse and good care can depend on the ability to hire professionals or sitters, or to put them in good nursing homes, to relieve their caretakers' burden of responsibility.

By the time elderly parents require assistance, the children they call upon are often in their forties. This sort of role reversal of the parent-child background is stressful and demanding, and at the same time, the middle-aged caretakers still have their own teen-aged children going through their own growing-up crises, who need financial help to obtain an education and become economically self-sufficient. As life expectancy has increased since the turn of the century, the numbers of the "old old" have increased considerably, and it is becoming common to find that caretakers of elderly parents are most often their daughters and daughters-in-law (78 percent of caretakers of the elderly are women), who are themselves in the "young old" category, from 55 to over 70 years old. As three-generation families are becoming more numerous, four-generation families are also increasing. It soon may not be unusual for 70-year-old "children" to be caring for their frail 90-year-old parents (Douglass 1983, 396). As Suzanne Steinmetz (1981, 6) notes:

> This is the century not only of old age, but of multigenerational families, often composed of several generations of near elderly, elderly, and frail elderly women. About half of all those

over 65 who have living children are members of a four-generation family.

Stress is almost certain to be present in multigenerational families, particularly when the elder family member is incontinent or otherwise physically or mentally incapacitated (Johnson 1979; Mellor and Getzel 1980). With more people surviving to old age, the ranks of the old old increasing, and with severe shortages of good, and affordable, nursing homes, prospects are great that abuse of elderly parents will increase and become a major social problem in the coming decades.

The History of Concern
for Parents Abused by Families

Little was written about aged victims of violence until very recently.[8] Like the "discovery" of child abuse in the 1960s and the "discovery" of wife beating in the 1970s, the 1980s appears to be the decade for the "discovery" of parent abuse. Elaine Brody and Stanley Brody (1974) predicted that the 1980s would be the *Decade of Decision for the Elderly,* noting that advocates for the aged must address two fronts: more and improved institutional and community care. One of the earliest articles in the United States about the problem dubbed "granny bashing" by the British (Freeman 1979) was addressed to physicians (Kelly 1975).

With regard to abuse of the elderly, 1977 was a landmark year. Prior to that time, no scientific research had been conducted on elder abuse (Douglass 1981). After 1977 public, legislative, and professional interest and concern rapidly grew. Descriptive reports began appearing (Rathbone-McCuan 1980; Steinmetz 1978c); the media's attention "outpaced the conducting and dissemination of scholarly research" (Pedrick-Cornell and Gelles 1982, 458); and congressional committees "held a series of public hearings which were actually concurrent with pioneering research into the existence of domestic neglect and abuse of the elderly" (Douglass 1983, 395). A few research reports reached publication (Block and Sinnott 1979; Douglass et al. 1980; Lau and Kosberg 1979; O'Malley et al. 1979), followed by a vast proliferation of publications discussing these studies (King 1983; Milt 1982; National Paralegal Institute 1981; U.S. Department of Health and Human Services 1980). Probably the first national multidisciplinary conference focusing on elder abuse was held in Tennessee in 1980, and 12 articles on the topic were subsequently published (Holden and Carey 1981).

Suzanne Steinmetz's early article (1978c), helped sensitize people to the abused elder problem, showed the need for systematic research, and suggested "hypotheses for subsequent research to test and explore" (Douglas 1983, 396). In that brief article, she says:

> [T]he elderly, since they are perceived to be a nonproductive component of society, have not stirred the public conscience to take up their protection from abusive children as a cause. . . . [S]ociety has largely ignored this phenomenon. . . . The aged, however, are at the end of their economically productive life, which is the basis on which our culture values individuals and provides them with deference, status, respect, and rewards. Given the cost of providing humane, alternative care for the elderly, especially when subjected to cost-benefit analysis and compared in priority with other social service needs, selective inattention may be politically expedient. (Steinmetz 1978c, 55)

Some segments of society did not continue to ignore the problems of elderly parents abused by their children. Research findings and reports from professionals are now available, and they are examined next.

What Has Been Learned about Parent Abuse

When we think of parent abuse, the image comes to mind of direct commission of violence against the elderly, savage and cruel acts, like the most common assumptions of child abuse. Some cases of brutality are used as illustrations in the literature on parent abuse (Kelly 1975; Milt 1982; Rathbone-McCuan 1980), but evidence shows these may be relatively rare.

According to one expert who has spent years working with the elderly, the type of physical abuse that attracts the attention of neighbors and police occurs in only 19 percent of all cases (Oliveira 1981a). Oliveira maintains that the major portion of abuse of the elderly is much more insidious. They are abused by caretakers, physicians, and practitioners in homes and institutions through overmedication, having their civil rights taken away, and through virtual imprisonment. Oliveira states that 50 percent of the victimization of the elderly is psychological abuse: verbal threats, calling names, and so forth. They also suffer economic abuse: stealing their assets, forging their names on wills, and robbing them of legal rights (1981a). Abuse frequently takes the form of neglect: withholding medicine, water, food, or services to clean them, their clothing, or their beds. Other times they are abused by deliberate overmedication or by being locked in their rooms. According to Oliveira:

> Families grudgingly accept the burden of keeping elderly rela-

tives in their homes because of lack of alternatives, but they resent the intrusion into their lives. Children are inadequately prepared to make changes in their lives and personal sacrifices. When children are told, "we *must* take grandma in and you *must* give up your bedroom and move in with your sister/brother," the stage is set for resentment and overt or covert hostility. Some children react by playing "tricks," such as leaving their toys/possessions around for the oldsters to trip over; teenagers may refuse to vacate the bathroom for anxious grandparents.

Because of physiological changes, old people must use the bathroom more frequently, often causing several trips at night, and they also require less sleep. Frequently, since they are excluded from family activities, they retire early and awaken at three or four in the morning, only to disturb the rest of the family by rattling utensils in the kitchen, getting their own breakfasts. This the "Pots and Pans Syndrome." It is interpreted by the others as a sure sign of disorientation and the onset of senility, and soon they are presented to physicians or mental health workers who quickly diagnose them as "confused" or "disturbed," whereupon they are prescribed unneeded medication. We *hook* the elderly into abusing drugs! When they fight back, they are seen as "difficult" and medication is increased. (Oliveira 1981a)

In a strong indictment of our entire social system and of professionals in particular,[9] Oliveira (1981a, 1981b) says that we take away the elderly's freedom, their rights, and their ability to function by unnecessary medication, making them very dependent, until finally we put them in nursing homes for further neglect and abuse. Oliveira notes that all Americans abuse the elderly by having negative attitudes: 63 percent of all jokes about them have negative implications; TV commercials depicting them are insulting; and we deprive them of opportunities for growth and fulfillment.

How well do Oliveira's observations match research findings? In view of the fact that there have been so few systematic studies, it might seem that answers could be simple and straightforward. Unfortunately, that is not the case. In their critique of research on elder abuse, Claire Pedrick-Cornell and Richard Gelles (1982, 459) begin by noting the lack of consensus on definitions used in the studies, saying: "The variety of definitions of elder abuse in current studies makes the task of comparing the results of the research impossible." For example, one study uses a narrow definition of physical abuse only (Rathbone-McCuan 1980) while another attempts to distinguish between neglect and abuse and between passive and active neglect (Douglass et al. 1980). To see how difficult this can be, consider the following acts that were noted by Oliveira above: withholding water, food, or medication from a nonambulatory parent—when are these abusive and when are they neglectful? What about being slow to change their clothing or beds when they are incontinent—is that abuse or neglect? Stealing parents' homes and savings is abusive, but this is included in some studies and not included in others.

One result of the lack of concise and common definitions in studies of elder abuse is that estimates of the extent of the problem range widely: from 500,000 to 2.5 million cases per year (King 1983). For their estimates, some writers extrapolate data from the Straus et al. (1980) study and apply them to population data (cf. *U.S. News and World Report* 1979). In reference to this, Pedrick-Cornell and Gelles say that an estimate attributed to Gelles "has no more empirical standing than a guess . . ." (1982, fn. 3). One review of the major studies of elder abuse notes another serious problem, their methodologies: They all employ small and/or nonrepresentative samples with no control groups (National Paralegal Institute 1981, 14). As a result, their findings are not generalizable to the abused elderly population and further, "Due to their exploratory nature, these studies are inappropriate for generating a national incidence statistic" (Pedrick-Cornell and Gelles 1982, 461).

It is important to keep those limitations in mind when findings are outlined, but also to note that the Sengstock and Liang (1983) study obtained data directly from victims and did use a control group. Table 10–1 is an overview sketch of four studies of elder abuse and is provided as a heuristic device (Block and Sinnott 1979; Lau and Kosberg 1979; O'Malley et al. 1979; Sengstock and Liang 1982). Some of these studies yield data that are more easily quantified than others. For example, the O'Malley et al. (1979) study focused on agencies encountering abuse, action taken or not taken, and victim cooperation or lack of it (U.S. Department of Health and Human Services 1980). The table shows that 41 percent of abuses reported were physical, but the National Paralegal Institute report (1981, 3) indicates that "less frequently reported" abuses were "verbal harassment, malnutrition, financial mismanagement, unreasonable confinement, over-sedation and sexual abuse," which could be classified into several categories.

The study by Richard Douglass and his colleagues (1980) yields a wealth of information, but the literature contains no data that could be usefully employed here. The major focus of that study was on the types of abuse that professionals believe occur most often against elderly persons, and the reasons for its occurrence. Douglass (1983) explains that abuse was

Table 10–1. An Overview of Findings Reported from Four Studies of Elder Abuse

	University of Maryland/ Block & Sinnot	Ohio/Lau & Kosberg	Boston Legal Research & Services/ O'Malley et al.	Wayne State University/ Sengstock & Liang
	N = 26 cases	N = 39 cases	N = 183 professionals	N = 20 cases
Abuses identified:				
Psychological abuse	46–58%	51%		58%
Physical abuse:				
Direct	15%	28%	41%[a]	
Indirect	19–38%	49%		20%
Material/financial abuse	12–46%	31%		55%
Violation of their rights		18%		
Demographic features:				
Victim's age	84	over 75	36% over 80	
Victim's sex	81% female	77% female	80% female	
Victim's race	88% white	75% white		
Social class	58% middle			
Abuser's age	53% from 40–50			
Abuser's relationship	42% their children	Relatives	44% sons & husbands[b]	50% their children
Abuser's sex	58% female	"More" female	56% female	

[a]May include both direct and indirect abuse (which refers to neglect).
[b]Largest combined categories.

367

categorized into "verbal/emotional or physical," and neglect into "passive or active," with operational definitions provided. For example, passive neglect was defined as: "Elderly dependent is ignored, left alone, or not supplied with essential foods, clothing, medications because of ineptness or inability of the caregiver," whereas active neglect involved intentional deprivation (Douglass 1983, 398). Cases reported by 228 professionals show that:

> Passive neglect was considered by the sample to occur more often than active neglect. Active neglect occurred less frequently than emotional or verbal abuse, and physical abuse was generally considered to be a rare event among the respondents in this sample. (Douglass 1983, 399)

Since over half the respondents encountered passive neglect and little or no active neglect (Douglass 1983, 400), this seems to indicate that the major problem in maltreatment of the elderly is the ineptness or inability of the caregiver to provide proper care. Less verbal/emotional abuse was encountered, which differs from findings of most other studies, and observations made by Oliveira (1981a). Perhaps this can be explained by the fact that Sengstock and Liang (1983) and Oliveira obtained their data directly from elderly victims, rather than from professionals who relied on written records or memories of patients.

An underlying assumption of many practitioners is the familiar "cycle of violence" which suggests that abused elders are parents who formerly abused their children who are now abusing them. This may be another case of victim blaming, if untrue. In searching for causes, one study suggests the hypothesis, "A child who is abused or witnesses abuse grows up to be an abusive adult" (Douglas 1981, 7). Of their nine categories of professionals questioned, police officers were most likely to subscribe to this idea, while lawyers and aging service workers were least likely (Douglass 1981, 8). In their critique of the current research, Pedrick-Cornell and Gelles state:

> Despite the consistency of factors reportedly associated with elderly abuse in the variety of articles and reports written on this subject, it is clear that the support for these claims is intuitive, speculative, and/or based only on findings from studies of other forms of family violence. *There is almost no empirical evidence in the literature which supports the claims made for such associations.* (1982, 462)

Even the titles given to the problem of abuse of elderly parents: *the battered parent syndrome, the battered elder syndrome,* and so forth, have been questioned by some writers as misnomers, since being battered indicates the intentional infliction of physical harm (Katz 1979–80). However, emotion-arousing terms were used earlier in the *battered baby syndrome,* and later *battered wives,* both of which successfully instigated agency, community, and legal action. The same tactic seems to have been successful in arousing concern for another relatively helpless segment of the population, the aged.

Responses to the Parent Abuse Problem

Direct physical abuse occurs less than psychological abuse, but it is the kind most frequently seen by police officers who are seldom called by the victims themselves, but rather neighbors distressed by screams and sounds of violence. These obvious cases, whether committed by spouses, offspring, or other caretakers, are extremely frustrating to police. In the short time since abuse of the elderly became recognized as a serious social problem, 17 states enacted mandatory reporting laws to protect vulnerable elders from abuse, neglect, and exploitation (King 1983, 15; Salend et al. 1981).[10]

As in wife abuse and in child maltreatment before it, an early response to the newly identified problem of elderly parent abuse was the enactment of laws to protect the rights of helpless victims. Connecticut established a Department of Aging to investigate complaints of abuse of anyone over 60 years of age, and in the first three years after the mandatory reporting law went into effect, 3,380 cases were reported (King 1983). Most complaints involved neglect (74 percent); 15 percent were for physical abuse; 10 percent for exploitation; and 3 percent for abandonment. Law professor Katheryn Katz (1979–80) warns that some laws are too quickly drafted as solutions to problems about which there is very little knowledge. Katz says, "a too hasty response to elder abuse, such as reporting statutes, is particularly dangerous due to the perilous consequences of coercive intervention" (1979–80, 721).

Besides legislation, what other measures are being taken, or could be taken to protect the well-being of elderly parents? Most abuse is perpetrated by middle-aged or older persons on their very old and infirm parents or spouses. The majority of cases do not appear to involve deliberate, premeditated violent acts, but instead consists of psychological abuse and neglect from caretakers who are under extreme stress, frustration, or exhaustion from their burden of responsibility, as in the following cases:

> Mrs. M, age 83, had managed quite well, together with her husband. When he died, she became depressed and paranoid, refused to leave her apartment, and became too confused to take care of her household and her personal needs. A divorced

daughter, Elsie, age 63 lived nearby and came over after work every evening to do the cooking and cleaning. When Mrs. M was quiet and passive, Elsie, who was sickly and overworked, was able to cope. But there were times when the mother became hostile and abusive, and Elsie had to flee. Instead of coming every night, she cut her visits to two a week and then to one a week, bringing in some groceries and some food she had cooked. One evening Elsie telephoned and got no answer. She rushed over and found her mother on the floor, moaning in pain, unable to move. Mrs. M had fallen and broken several ribs. The hospital social worker made this entry in the record: "Mrs. M's body was emaciated. It was unclean and covered with sores. Her toenails had lengthened into long, horny claw-like growths which were curved around her toes." (Milt 1982, 7–8)

One respondent, a 68-year-old woman, blames her divorce on having to care for her demanding, selfish 82-year-old mother. She notes, "That was one of the contributing factors, my husband just had it up to here. One day he left." This caregiver later notes that her mother won't offer to contribute to household costs: "I'm making a woman's salary and keeping a big house. It's an obligation which I think she should partly assume. She doesn't feel that way. I'm her daughter, she gave me life, she provided for me when I was young and couldn't do for myself. This obligation is now on my shoulders." (Steinmetz 1981, 8)

What would *you* do? We do not know, until we find ourselves in situations that require more of us than we feel we are able to give. While it may be difficult and demanding to be a 24-hour-a-day, seven-day-a-week caretaker of young children, the burden of responsibility is much greater when tending an old parent. In childcare there is promise that the children will mature and gradually assume more responsibility for themselves; relief from care of physically and/or mentally infirm parents may not come until they die. Lifting a baby of 20 pounds and lifting a parent of 110 pounds or more are considerably different, and so is changing the diapers of a baby and the clothing of an incontinent adult. Babies may cry unreasonably, but Steinmetz's (1981, 9) study of the caretakers of elders shows that the favorite tactics used by the elderly to control their adult children were screaming and yelling and pouting or withdrawal. What then can be done to prevent abuse of elderly parents?

In a society that cares about all its citizens, there are many measures that could be enacted besides protective legislation. There could be recognition of the valuable social service rendered by in-home caretakers of the elderly, and some of the money saved by noninstitutional care could be used to provide subsidies to caretakers. Social services could be increased to provide frequent home visits, homemaker services, sitting services, community recreation, social events, transportation to respite care, and hot lines. Unlike many other industrialized nations, our government does not provide much in subsidized housing for the elderly who prefer to live independently but who would benefit from communal living; most group housing here is ventured by private, nonprofit organizations. To prevent parent abuse, this nation can begin by providing for the elderly and their overburdened caretakers. Their numbers promise to increase greatly in the future.

SUMMARY

Although much less research has been done on the three major topics addressed in this chapter, interest is growing and empirical findings from some exploratory studies are beginning to appear in the literature. The chapter focused on violence by children, abuse of adolescents, and abuse of elderly parents. These phenomena share some features in common with other types of family violence but there are also substantive differences, and it is obvious that much more scientific research is necessary before there is a possibility of clear understanding of the interpersonal dynamics involved, their etiology, and appropriate prevention and intervention methods.

Most people tend to ignore everyday violence by children, somehow assuming that it is *natural* for children to hit, punch, and kick each other, and that as they mature, they will become less and less violent. Most of the approval centers on little boys who are "scrappy" and who are ready to fight in response to insults or simply to get what they want. Since cultural approval of violence is directed at males, most of the research on how children learn to be violent has focused on samples of boys and their parents. Not surprisingly, research comparing violent with nonviolent children has found significant differences in parental values and attitudes toward each other and their sons' aggressiveness. Parents, particularly fathers, who physically punish, ridicule, and demean their sons are more likely to produce aggressive sons who are hostile toward them, and yet identify with them as their role models.

Criminal statistics show that juveniles proportionately commit more violent crimes than adults, and their arrests rates for violent crimes almost doubled in a nine-year period, even though many records are diverted into the juvenile justice system. Adolescents are also violent in the family, as more acts of violence were recorded in one year between siblings than any other combination of victim/aggressor acts reported by parents. Girls are less violent, but if they have one or more brothers, higher rates of violence are likely. Boys with violent fathers may model their behavior after their same-sex role model. Sometimes violent children attack and kill persons outside the home, or commit parricide, often in response to prior parental abuse.

When adolescents are abused, sometimes it comes from siblings close to their own ages, but it may also be perpetrated by substantially older siblings. Empirical research is lacking in this area, but there are impressionistic reports and some case histories that show it occurs, frequently taking the form of sexual abuse. When adolescents are abused by parents, it sometimes is a *continuation* or escalation of earlier parental abuse or "punishment." In other cases, the abuse *begins* at adolescence, just when youngsters are trying to attain autonomy from parental authority and parents, caught in their own mid-life turmoil, are trying to maintain control and authority over their previously less rebellious children. When discipline becomes abuse, adolescents are unlikely to turn to others outside the family, but when they so, they are often seen as *troublemakers* or children who "got what they deserved." They may become hypervigilant, withdraw, or run away from home.

Adolescents who run away and are found are likely to be sent back to their parents without full investigation of the kind of family they tried to escape. If they run away repeatedly and fall into the hands of the authorities, they will enter the juvenile justice system, only to learn more and "better" ways of delinquency. About half of all runaways are now believed to have left abusive home situations, yet if they avoid the juvenile justice system, they are most likely to do so by entering the world of prostitution and/or child pornography. Some young children are even sold into prostitution and pornography by their own parents.

Elderly persons are abused by a society that considers them worthless because they are no longer capable of economic productivity. Parents who are abused by their families are most likely to be dependent women over the age of 75 who are suffering physical and/or mental impairments. Projections are that the proportion of the population who live past 65 will increase greatly, but more importantly, the percentage who live into very old age, when infirmities are more pronounced, will increase. Old people, especially old women, are more likely to be poor, and thus unable to maintain good health and health services, or to deplete their resources in the last few years of life. Having few economic reserves, they are more likely to require services from their kin, causing their caretakers stress from responsibilities.

Very little research has been done on parent abuse, but now a few studies, while suffering from definitional and methodology problems, provide some insight into this problem. The major type of abuse suffered by the elderly seem to be psychological abuse or physical neglect, which may be due primarily to caretakers' inability to provide the services necessary for good health maintenance. Deliberate physical abuse appears to occur in only about 15 to 19 percent of all cases, but material/financial abuse occurs more frequently.

There are many ways that abuse and neglect of elderly parents can be prevented, if enough people become concerned and active. Caretaking services should be recognized for the important contribution they make to society and caretakers can be subsidized both financially and with support systems. Community services are essential, and alternative living arrangements for the noninstitutionalized elderly could be made more available by the government.

In the next chapter, the topic of sexual abuse in the family is addressed. It is an issue that has some commonalities with other types of family violence, yet is different in a number of important ways.

NOTES

1. The "example of deviance," used as an important factor in the parenting of aggressive boys, refers to *parental* deviance, according to McCord et al. (1970). *Deviance* is used to denote several different behaviors: "criminality, alcoholism, psychoses, desertion, sexual promiscuity, etc." (1970, 57). Under "deviant behavior" the authors list aggression, "escapism," an eccentric role in the family, being "relatively uninhibited," and irresponsible. Unfortunately, the sex of the parent is not clearly distinguished in descriptions of measures and tests. In addition, "aggressive" fathers were found not to be statistically associated with aggressive sons but apparently, some measures of aggression are also included with measures of "deviant" behavior. Finally, "deviance" was more characteristic of fathers of the middle group, which the authors called "assertive" (52 percent of the cases), than in the "aggressive" cases (48 percent) (McCord et al. 1970, 56–57).

2. During the same time period, adults age 18 or over arrested for violent crimes increased by 65 percent (Uniform Crime Reports 1977, 175).

3. The author visited shelters for battered women and their children across the United States and in five countries and never saw the destruction of facilities anywhere like Chiswick, in London. Maintained at below-poverty level budgets, most shelters are located in dilapidated buildings with substandard furniture and equipment, for example, plumbing. During a 1977 visit to Chiswick, the author observed the 16-year-old son of a woman who consented to be interviewed in depth. This young man was accused by staff of beating up his older sister and was generally disliked and feared by other residents. During the interview, he decided he wanted to go "out on the town," so he dressed up and constantly interrupted the interview, demanding spending money for his evening. He pressed, argued, and repeated his demands, becoming more hostile and determined as his mother tried to explain that she had to save her funds for food. Finally, the mother

acquiesced to her son's demands and gave him some money. It would not have been surprising if this boy had used his fists on his mother; the threat of violence was obvious.

4. Shelters usually involve communal living where too many women are crowded together in sleeping and living quarters. Almost always filled to capacity (and often beyond), there may be two or more mothers and their children sharing the same room.

5. Sometimes parents abuse a child even after that child has reached adulthood. One such example is a father who was arguing with his 23-year-old son, and when the son said "Don't you hit me, or I'll hit you back, dad," the father went to the bedroom, got a revolver, and shot his son to death (*Los Angeles Times* 1983c).

6. The effects of rape can be even more devastating to adolescent victims of rape than to adult victims. Although there are similarities, one of the differences is the potential for conflict between the needs of the child and the needs of the parents (Otey 1983). Emeline Otey notes one study that showed that only 50 percent of the victims' parents expressed fear for their safety, and most of these were parents whose child had also suffered physical injuries. Otey (1983, 8) says, "Forty-one percent of the parents blamed their child directly for the rape, and this was especially true if family conflict preceded the assault."

7. The runaways' toll-free hotline numbers are 1-800-232-6946; or in Texas they can call 1-800-392-3352, according to columnist Abigail Van Buren (1983). If runaway children call these numbers, operators will take messages without lectures, recrimination or tracing, and will call their parents to transmit messages. They will also ask the caller if they need anything, and be told where they can get it free.

8. Some of the writers who note abuse of elderly parents recognized the seriousness of the problem, despite the lack of sound empirical studies for documentation (Freeman 1979; Hendricks and Hendricks 1977; Kelly 1975; Krasnow and Fleshner 1979; Lau and Kosberg 1979; Rathbone-McCuan 1980; Renvoize 1978; Steinmetz 1978c; Steuer and Austin 1980; *U.S. News and World Report* 1979; Wiley 1980).

9. Odacir Oliveira's (1981a, 1981b) criticisms of professionals include the following: psychotherapists do not want to work with the elderly, they selectively pick patients; clinicians in particular neglect the elderly because they view them as a "dying cause;" and medical doctors, nurses, and social workers have negative attitudes toward them.

10. States that have enacted elder abuse mandatory reporting laws include: Alabama, Arkansas, Connecticut, Florida, Kentucky, Minnesota, Maryland, Nebraska, New Hampshire, North Carolina, Oklahoma, South Carolina, Tennessee, Texas, Utah, Vermont, and Virginia (King 1983, 15). California also has passed a mandatory reporting law.

PART VI

Sexual Abuse in the Family:
The Power Game

11

Sexual Abuse of Children in the Family

Many people believe that sexual abuse means forcible vaginal or anal penetration of a victim who verbally and/or physically resists unwanted acts. That type of sexual assault is least likely to occur, especially in the case of child victims, who are most often coerced, seduced, or intimidated into cooperating, or at least not offering any resistance. In addition, the majority of child victims are not subjected to vaginal or anal penetration. Adult victims such as wives are more likely to experience full sexual intercourse, but they may offer little or no resistance due to fear or their knowledge of its futility. Sexual abuse of children and women in the family share many similarities, but there are also important differences. The major similarity is the powerlessness of the victims to protect themselves from unwanted behavior, to avoid their abusers, or to stop the abuse. Other similarities may become obvious, but because of important distinctions between sexual abuse of children and adults, they are addressed separately in this section of the book on sexual abuse in the family. This chapter focuses on incest and sexual abuse of children in the family, and a movement advocating sex between adults and children, dubbed the *pro-incest lobby*. The next chapter concerns marital rape and pornography's relationship to both incest and wife rape.

INCEST: THE INVISIBLE CRIME

As noted earlier, due to underreporting and problems in research design and methodology, "the true incidence of child sexual abuse can only be approximated" (Maney 1983, 7). Ann Maney (1983), the head of the National Center for the Prevention and Control of Rape, estimates that about 85,000 children under the age of 18 are sexually exploited each year by parents, guardians, or caretakers. The figure becomes much larger when sexual abuse outside the family is included. "If the one to two ratio of familial to extrafamilial experiences that emerges in retrospective studies also were applied, approximately 240,000 children are victims of sexual abuse each year" (Maney 1983, 7). But the problems plaguing research on sexual abuse in the family are compounded by the lack of a common definition.

Trying to Distinguish between Sexual Abuse and "Normal" Family Sexuality

Defining just what constitutes sexual abuse is not easily resolved. Child psychologist Alvin Rosenfeld (1977) notes that there is a continuum of sexuality in the family from ranging incest and sexual abuse at one end, and affection, tenderness, and hygienic genital contact at the other. Activities such as breast feeding and genital contact during diaper changes and bathing are implicitly sexual and sometimes arouse in children an emotional response of a sexual nature, but they are seen by adults, who are not consciously aware of their implicit sexuality, as necessary and healthy activities (Rosenfeld 1977, 231). Hugging, kissing, and other close physical contact, such as cuddling of children by their parents, are also sexual, according to Rosenfeld, but such warm and tender acts are nurturant and growth promoting (1977, 231). Probably it is becoming more evident why it is so difficult to formulate a clear and concise definition of sexual abuse for researchers to measure. When the above acts are viewed by adults as nonsexual displays of tenderness and caring, they may be defined as *normal*. But when those same acts are consciously viewed by adults as providing sexual pleasure or stimulation, they have crossed that invisible line on the continuum and become *sexual abuse* (Summit and Kryso, 1978).

Much of Rosenfeld's focus is on sexual stimulation of the *child,* rather than the *adult.* However, overstimulation on the part of a child is hardly likely to lead to his or her becoming a victim of sexual abuse. The crux of the matter lies in the sexual stimulation of the adult and what he or she does or does not do about it.[1] Still, Rosenfeld (1977, 233) warns against any attempt by parents to satisfy their adult, genital-sexual needs through their children. This corresponds with the first of two questions mentioned in Chapter 2 that parents can ask themselves to determine if their behavior is appropriate: *Am I doing this for my own sexual satisfaction? Is this something I would not want anyone else to know about?*

For definitional purposes, the terms *sexual abuse* and *incest* are synonymous and are used interchangeably here, except when perpetrators are not related through blood, marriage, or quasi-marital status in a child's

One mother who physically abused her child said, "Children are abused because they're *safe* to abuse." When it comes to sexual abuse of children, no children are *safer* to abuse than one's own, because they are very trusting, and because they are so easily coerced into doing what an adult they love convinces them it is alright to do. In addition, because they are often frightened into believing that if they betray their "secret" their family will be destroyed, they are easily convinced that they must "never tell anyone."

Source: Nancy Dombeck, photographer.

family. Incest is sexual abuse, but not all sexual abuse is incest, thus when no such familial relationships exist, the concept "sexual abuse" alone applies.[2] The conceptualization used here builds upon the definition for incest offered by sociologist David Finkelhor (1979a, 84), which includes "sexual contact between family members, including not just intercourse but also mutual masturbation, hand-genital or oral-genital contact, sexual fondling, exhibition, and even sexual propositioning." Other forms of sexual activity that Finkelhor does not include can and do cause considerable trauma to some victims, such as "peeping-tomism," threatened or attempted assault without physical contact, promotion or permission of prostitution, or forcing children to display themselves for the amusement or stimulation of adult relatives and their friends. These abusive behaviors are included in the writer's conceptualization of sexual abuse of children. In fact, *any* unwanted touching of a child's body can constitute a violation of a child's rights if there is no hygienic or safety factor involved.

Some may insist that acts should be designated abusive only when there is resultant trauma for victims, but that begs the question of adults' responsibility for their behavior and throws the responsibility onto victims for their reaction to adults' behavior. Later in this chapter there is a discussion of the victimization of children through adults' inappropriate sexual behavior, but for now it should be noted that victims' reactions are extremely difficult to determine. Some have negative consequences, short-term or long-term, directly connected to the sexual abuse, but many others have problems that cannot be definitively determined to be consequences of childhood sexual abuse. For example, one high school girl suffered from extremely low self-esteem, seemed ashamed of her normally developed body, and had an obsessive, frantic desire for privacy so that gym and swimming classes were such agony for her that she became stigmatized among her peers as *odd*.

While there were undoubtedly many other variables that contributed to her psychological distress, her behavior seemed to be directly related to her childhood history. As a little girl, her mother took the child along when she went to bars, exhibiting her to male patrons. The mother frequently insisted that the little girl perform songs and dances for them. The prostitute-mother would then bring her "trick" and her little girl to their one-bedroom home, where the child again had to perform for their benefit as they began their sexual activities. Whether or not the child was clothed or naked during the home performances remained hidden in the girl's memory, but even had she been fully clothed, the shame and humiliation could be the same. Most adult women can relate to the child's feelings of degradation when they recall men they have encountered whose eyes seem to literally strip them naked.

Child Victims of Sexual Abuse in the Family

> When Rod was very young, his stepfather broke several of his ribs and both his arms during one of his regular beatings. At the age of seven, two relatives sexually abused him. At the ripe age of nine, he ran away from home for the rodeos and ranches of the West Coast. He never came back. He is Rod McKuen, nationally acclaimed poet and composer. At [a national conference] . . . McKuen revealed that he is one of millions of people who are sexually abused as children. He told the public that the sexual abuse still haunts him today. "My arms and ribs are fine," he explained, "but the emotional scars from the sexual abuse have never gone away and I expect they never will." (Dunwoody 1982, 1)

It takes particular courage for anyone (and probably more for a public figure) to reveal the double degradation of physical and sexual abuse as a child. Yet it seems that one of the most powerful methods for overcoming the fear, pain, and trauma is by exposing the awful *secret* that so many people live with for years. Some choose to reveal their identities, while others remain anonymous or use fictitious names, as in the accounts provided by Kee MacFarlane and her colleagues (1980, 97–121) who assert that it seems only right that the insights and experiences of a few victims be included to help professionals gain a more intimate understanding of the reactions of people who were sexually exploited by family members. MacFarlane et al. state, "Much of their writing is unembellished, raw with emotion, and may make the reader uncomfortable. This is, perhaps, as it should be, since the problem of incest cannot be dealt with effectively from a remote, theoretical vantage point" (1980, 97). For these reasons, some victims' accounts are included here.

Claudia Wayne and Laureen France ask "Who Will Speak for the Children?" (1980) and note that most of the literature on child sexual assault until very recently focused on sexual crimes by persons outside the family. Children are warned about strangers lurking in dark corners of the playground, the "dirty old man in the trench coat" who bribes children with candy, or the stranger who drives up in a van with the intention of snatching children away. However, "Informing girls of the potential for sexual abuse by their fathers, uncles, grandfathers or older brothers is a neglected responsibility" (Wayne and France 1980, 28). Many people do not like to read the accounts of victims of incest, because they prefer to believe that the crime is "so repugnant that only society's most perverse members can be considered suspect" (Wayne and France 1980, 28), and if it did not happen to themselves, there is something *different* about incest victims that somehow sets them apart. As Wayne and France correctly state, "Even if some of us escaped sexual victimization by our fathers, it is, like rape, not because we made a choice to avoid victimization, but rather because the men who were our fathers or guardians chose not to abuse their power" (1980, 28).

Fathers and Mothers of Victims

The following quotation is from a letter written by an incest victim to her father. Now an adult professional working with other victims of sexual abuse, the writer remains anonymous.

Dear Dad . . .

Please read this letter with an open heart, it is written from my heart and is not meant to hurt or attack you.

I need to tell you how I felt the seven years you sexually assaulted me. It is very hard for me to write this, my whole body is trembling with fear and anger.

Fear is what I remember as I think of being six years old. Oh God why . . . I remember the first time you raped me. You took me on a business trip with you, I was so excited, just me and my Daddy and getting to stay in a motel and eating out in restaurants with you.

It wasn't until that evening that my childhood crumbled. I remember you taking my clothes off and how trusting I was; even as you told me that what you were going to do was something wonderful, and that all little girls love it. Then came the tearing pain. I remember you covering my mouth to stifle my screams and the whole time telling me next time it won't hurt so much. I prayed . . . . God please don't let him do this to me again. But God didn't hear my prayers and I prayed for his mercy every day for seven years. I remember when you finished, I was still crying, and to this day I remember the pain I felt that night. You then asked me if I loved my mommy and I said yes. You asked if I loved my sisters and brothers and I said yes. That's when you told me if I told anyone of what you did to me you would put mom and everyone else against a wall and shoot them one by one and it would be my fault because I didn't keep your secret. I kept the secret and you found other ways to make sure I didn't tell as I got older. . . . For the next two years I only remember feeling confused and terrified of being alone with you and wondering when it would happen again.

Then I turned eight, I felt a hundred and I wished I was dead. I remember thinking I couldn't experience anything else that could make me feel more hurt than I already felt in my heart. Until the night you decided to force me to have oral sex with you. I remember you pinning my head down and the gagging and choking (it seemed as though you pinned me for an eternity) and how much I wanted to throw up. But even more important, I remember not being able to eat without choking and gagging because of flashbacks. For years Dad I couldn't stand to have anyone touch the back of my neck because of the tremendous force you used on me then and in the following years. Then came the night you fed me booze and I remember crying and feeling sick from the liquor and the fear of knowing something awful was going to happen. Then my fear became a reality and you forced anal sex. I remember screaming out in pain and you hitting me and telling me to shut up. I thought I was ripping apart and my only thoughts were prayers to God as I remembered the pain I had felt at age six and asked God when it would end. . . . (Response 1980, 3)

This letter describing a victim's experiences is not presented here as "typical," because in many ways her case is unique, although all victims' experiences are unique to them and their life circumstances. It differs from the bulk of the research on incest because there was overt force and violence and included vaginal intercourse, fellatio, and sodomy. These abuses occur in a minority of cases, but as Wayne and France note, "The type of activity itself is not as important as the manner and atmosphere in which it is conducted" (1980, 29). Many case histories reveal actual rape (Middleton 1978), but the more extreme sexual behaviors usually do not occur on the first occasion; they begin with touching, stroking, and/or fondling the genitals (while victims are being told "daddy loves you"). Sometimes it is much later, after various forms of masturbation, that the activities may develop into penile insertion. Herman and Hirschman (1980, 69) interviewed 15 victims in depth and note that their histories of incest contain similarities:

The majority . . . were oldest or only daughters and were between the ages of six and nine when they were first approached sexually by their fathers or male guardians. . . . The youngest girl was four years old; the oldest fourteen. The sex-

ual contact usually took place repeatedly. In most cases the incestuous relationship lasted three years or more. Physical force
was not used, and intercourse was rarely attempted with girls
who had not reached puberty; the sexual contact was limited
to masturbation and fondling.

It should be noted, however, that incest is not *limited* to oldest daughters
only, since evidence abounds that whenever there are younger daughters
in the family, the father begins his advances on the next child around the
time when the older victim reaches the age, or a point in her life, when
she is about to break out of the relationship. Some multiple incestuous
relationships occur simultaneously (Armstrong 1979; MacFarlane et al.
1980), as in one case to reach the California courts in which two daughters
and one son testified against their father. Others occur in tandem, as one
case cited by Middleton (1978, 8) in Northern Ireland, where one man had
incestuous relationships with his three daughters and five
granddaughters.

Returning to the letter cited earlier, the similarities the case shares with
many others are: betrayal of trust; coercion and threats to the child to
cooperated and maintain a "secret"; giving her the responsibility of protecting other family members (or maintaining the family unit, for instance,
"if you tell, they'll send me to jail . . . or I'll leave home . . . and then what
will you and mommy do?"); the child's reaction of fear and dread of future
assaults on her body—her emotional pain; and her concern not to hurt
the man who so badly hurt her when she was a defenseless child. Children must deal with conflicting emotions of both love and hatred, which
compounds their trauma. As a 15-year-old victim wrote to her father, "I
also want you to know how much I love you. I love you only because
you're my father, but I *hate* you for what you have done to me and are
doing to yourself" (MacFarlane et al. 1980, 114).

There is one feature of incest that is not always discussed in the literature: There may be a certain amount of *pleasure* experienced by victims.
When this happens, it adds to and intensifies the trauma victims suffer
later. Pleasure may stem from the unusual amount of attention paid to
children who were previously ignored, or whose mothers are temporarily
absent or incapacitated, such as the anonymous victim who writes: ". . .
it started when I was five. My mother had a nervous breakdown after my
youngest sister was born. I have four sisters, two older and two younger.
We were all plagued with sexual abuse by my father, except for my second
youngest sister" (MacFarlane et al. 1980, 109). Another victim writes about
her mother's attempted suicide, after which she was left alone with her
father who started to be friendly, warm, and touching, and began calling

her "Daddy's girl" (Myers 1980, 102). The change in personality and his treatment toward her, during her period of loss for a mother who had "abandoned" her, was at first welcomed by the child. The victim writes to her mother: "He was so nice. . . . He wasn't mean to me; he didn't scare me. He said he needed me. . . . I was so alone; I wanted to be close to someone. Mostly, I wanted you to come back" (Myers 1980, 102).

The "special" relationship may give pleasure in other ways. One aspect of some incestuous relationships almost never mentioned in the literature is an *involuntary physical response* of the victims' bodies to sexual stimulation (Samuels 1977). Gentle caressing and fondling can cause their bodies to react in ways that strangely feel good whether they want this response or not. At the same time, they hate themselves (and their bodies) for feeling pleasure under the circumstances. In essence, their bodies betray them, and they are left with extremely confusing psychosexual feelings (Samuels 1977). Other writers note another aspect of incest—the enhanced *power* victims may feel—especially when they are adolescents:

> The child often enjoys some aspects of the incest relationship, and with reason. In the initial stages of the relationship, the physical closeness and touching may feel good. The power that usually accompanies the relationship can be intoxicating. The child is often accorded adult-like status; she has control over a powerful secret; and she is often the recipient of special gifts and privileges. (Stern and Meyer 1980, 84)

Mothers of victims are not only frequently absent or incapacitated, they often are also victims of their husbands' domination or physical abuse. When fathers who beat and rape their wives begin to lavish affection on their daughters, the girls not only know by example that it is useless to resist, but they also may interpret this behavior as demonstrating their mothers' "unworthiness" and their own "superiority," and thus react accordingly (Pagelow 1982a). Like their battered mothers, they cannot escape or resist the powerful male in their families and sometimes sexual favors are traded for privileges or possessions. As one anonymous victim states: "It was the only way he would buy us a doll or shoes, and later, give us our allowance each week" (MacFarlane 1980, 109). One common finding in the research is that many incest victims maintain warm feelings toward their fathers; "Many described them in much more favorable terms than their mothers" (Herman and Hirschman 1980, 70). Some comments about their mothers made by victims include:

> She was nothing but a floor mat. She sold out herself and her self-respect. She was a love slave to my father. . . . She's always

> picking on me. She's so cold. . . . I really don't like my mom. I guess I am bitter. She's very selfish. She did a lousy job of bringing me up. (Herman and Hirschman 1980, 70)

By contrast, the following are comments made about their fathers:

> A handsome devil. . . . Good with kids. An honest, decent guy. . . . He was my confidant. . . . My savior. . . . He was a sweet, decent man. My mother ruined him. . . . I was in love with my father. He called me his special girlfriend. . . . I was very attracted to my father, and that just compounded the guilt. . . . I was scared of him, but basically I liked him. (Herman and Hirschman 1980, 70–71)

Victims also described their fathers as "blatantly authoritarian" men who held power in the family as well as status in the community, and their attachment included satisfaction from being *daddy's special girl*, often when they were special to no once else. In psychiatrist Judith Herman and clinical psychologist Lisa Hirschman's sample, all the mothers were houseworkers, and their fathers' occupations ranged from college administrator, police and army officer, engineer, manager, to skilled laborer. When the fathers had low social status, their daughters were likely to pity them and to blame their mothers: "The daughters seemed much more willing to forgive their fathers' failings and weaknesses than to forgive their mothers or themselves" (Herman and Hirschman 1980, 70). These women sometimes expressed disappointment in their fathers, even contempt, but they felt a stronger sense of betrayal against their mothers. According to Herman and Hirschman:

> Having abandoned the hope of pleasing their mothers, they seemed relieved to have found some way of pleasing their fathers and gaining their attention. . . . The father's sexual approach is clearly an abuse of power and authority, and the daughter almost always understands it as such. But . . . it occurs in the context of a caring relationship. The victim feels overwhelmed by her father's superior power and unable to resist him; she may feel disgust, loathing, and shame. But at the same time she often feels that this is the only kind of love she can get, and prefers it to no love at all. The daughter is not raped, but seduced. (1980, 71)

Many victims not only sense that they have an extraordinary power in the family as keepers of their fathers' "secret," but they feel an enormous sense of responsibility for keeping the family together. They often become surrogate wives and mothers to other family members as their fathers turn to their daughters for services, both sexual and domestic, that they formerly expected of their wives. Herman and Hirschman found that "Over half the mothers were partially incapacitated by physical or mental illness or alcoholism and either assumed an invalid role within the home or were periodically absent because of hospitalization" (1980, 70). As is commonly found, in one family where the father was an alcoholic, the mother went to work to support the family and the burden of "replacing" her mother's role fell on the oldest daughter.

> The father does not assume the wife's maternal role when she is incapacitated [or absent]. He feels that his first right is to continue to receive the services which his wife formerly provided, sometimes including sexual services. He feels only secondarily responsible for giving care to his children. (Herman and Hirschman 1980, 71)

Daughters, feeling estranged from their mothers, cannot understand why they have "abandoned" them, and harbor a keen sense of betrayal. Although the majority of victims admit they hinted or left "clues" they expected their mothers would understand, they did not actually *tell* them of the sexual activities. They, and others, believe that it should be impossible for incest to occur repeatedly in a household without a mother suspecting. They overlook the human tendency to avoid pain, even thoughts that are painful. Some ideas are so abhorrent they cannot be given conscious credibility.[3] A woman may note that her husband is engaging in suggestive "horseplay," tends to kiss his daughter/stepdaughter on the lips, or insists on what seems to be excessive displays of physical affection with their pre-pubescent daughter, but she brushes aside disquieting thoughts that she decides are *dirty,* convincing herself that what she sees is normal and healthy father/daughter love.[4]

However, their daughters join in society's expectation that the primary role of a mother is to protect her children against harm, and when the mother *fails* in that role (whether it is or is not beyond her capacity to fulfill), *the mother is to blame.* Blaming mothers for whatever harm befalls their children is endemic to this culture (Pogrebin 1974). As mentioned earlier, one former child protective service worker noted her own intense feelings of disgust for mothers whenever she encountered a case of maternal child abuse or neglect, or parental sexual abuse (Pagelow 1982c). She finally realized these reactions were due to her belief that "Mothers are the people we expect to be always endowed with love, warmth, and kindness—always there when we want or need them." Any mother was guilty whose child suffered harm because she did not *protect* her child, as mothers are supposed to do. "No matter who actually harms the child, mother has failed in her duty to create a safe environment for her young"

(Martin 1981, 3). This reaction to "unfit mothers" (Mahan 1982) is close to some other ideas on mothers' roles, which include:

> The mother, of course, is not usually a participant in father-daughter incest in the sense of joining in the overt sexual activities. . . . In incestuous families, the mother has often been perceived as the family member who "sets up" the father and daughter for the incest relationship, usually by withdrawing from her sexual role in the marriage and ignoring the special relationship that may then develop. . . . Even when the mother has played no demonstrable role in setting the stage for incest, she is thought to be partially responsible for the inception and continuance of the incestuous relationship through her failure to take any action that would prevent or terminate it. (Meiselman 1978, 111–12)

Psychologist Karin Meiselman later repeats the idea of maternal blame: that the mother who does not "restrain" the father from incest has failed in her maternal role to protect her child. One child victim whose mother had died said: "I know it sounds stupid to you, but I couldn't help it. I loved her so much, and then she died and left me alone with *him!* I hated her for doing that to me."

A substantial amount of research shows associations between sexual abuse of children and mothers who are absent, sick, powerless, or alienated from their children (Russell 1983, 207). Judith Herman contends that "mothers who are strong, healthy, and competent do not tolerate incest" (1981, 47). She admits that some mothers occasionally collude in incest, but when they do, it usually is a demonstration of their own powerlessness (1981, 49). Herman reviews the research showing the significantly greater probability that girls are sexually victimized when there is even a residential separation between mothers and daughters at any time before they reach 16 (in Finkelhor's study 1979a, victimization was three times as likely), and Herman concludes that "only a strong alliance with a healthy mother offers a girl a modicum of protection from sexual abuse" (1981, 48). Russell summarizes:

> Rather than facing the fact that daughters are vulnerable to sexual abuse when they do not have a strong mother to protect them from their own fathers and other male relatives, it has been easier to blame the mothers. But mothers should not have to protect their children from the children's fathers. (1983, 209)

Not all reports condemn the mother. One study found sexual abusers to be authoritarian fathers who often engaged in other forms of child abuse and wife bea*   *   writers argue against an "unconsciously *   *   instead propose that the *traditional sub* *   ır of abuse from their husbands contribute ...*   *o report the abuse.[5] A *conscious fear* of being beaten by ו...*   *   , compared to *unconscious consent,* seems to be a more powerful explanation of a mother's inability to act to protect her child (Pagelow 1982c). Battered wives are unable to protect themselves from abuse, much less their children, as the son of a battered woman recalled:

> As long as I can remember, I've hated my father; my feelings for my mother were a mixture of contempt and pity. I always thought I hated him because of his cruel beatings and how he was always "putting me down." An authoritarian, military man, he ran our house and everyone in it with an iron fist; I had plenty enough to hate him for. It wasn't until I was reading those first person accounts from incest victims [in MacFarlane it al. 1980] that I suddenly realized, "My god! that's me . . . that's what happened to me. That stinking bastard had sexually used me, as well as beating the hell out of me!" No wonder I hated him so much, but what he did to me was so awful, I guess I just buried it deep down inside me, trying to forget.

Mothers also need to protect their children from their boyfriends, their children's stepfathers and grandfathers, and other male relatives.

> My mother was pretty much a mess after she and my dad divorced, until she married my stepfather and then she was happy again. I was glad for her. Then he molested me one time when she wasn't home. I was crushed, but I couldn't bear to spoil it for her, so I made up some excuse (I can't even remember what it was, now) and moved out. I went to live with my grandparents, and can you believe it? My grandfather started in on me! When that happened, I thought I'd die (and hoped I would) because I was convinced that it had to be something about *me* that made two men I had trusted abuse me that way. What could I do? Where could a little kid go? All I could do was stay there and take it, hating myself, until I was old enough to move out on my own. Later, my grandmother had a stroke and was put into a nursing home. My grandfather came every single day, tenderly feeding and caring for her, showing such love and devotion that the nurses used to rave about him, even telling me how lucky I was to have such a wonderful man for a grandfather! I think that made my pain all the worse, that oth-

ers thought he was so wonderful while I knew the awful things he did to me. But I could never tell anybody. He knew his secret was safe with me.

These statements came from two apparently well-adjusted and adequately functioning young adults. The first was spoken by a male police officer with an unblemished record of several years' service; the second came from a successful female computer programmer. Neither of them was able to obtain effective professional assistance. The man's female therapist became emotional when he tried to discuss his incestuous past, avoided it, and focused only on his current problems. The woman's male psychiatrist insisted on drug therapy to control her symptoms of deep depression and anxiety. Unable to locate therapists who were capable of and/or willing to provide the help they needed, both victims continued their struggles to deal with their unhappy pasts.

Sexual Abusers and Their Victims

When writers discuss incest or sexual abuse, they usually refer to female victims and male perpetrators. As Herman and Hirschman write, "A constant finding in all existing surveys is the overwhelming predominance of father/daughter incest" (1980, 65). Most reports contain statistics that show between 92 and 95 percent of the victims are female and 97 to 99 percent of the offenders are male (Berliner 1977; Burgess et al. 1977; Giarretto 1976; Maisch 1972; Weinberg 1955). Caroline Swift (1977) is probably correct when she insists that many more cases of sexual abuse of boys actually occur than are reported or found in research samples, mainly because of the double stigma of incest and homosexual contact. Swift conducted a survey among clinicians at a mental health center and explains her findings in these terms:

> The data from this survey confirm two consistent findings in the literature on sexual child abuse: the abusers are almost always male, and in over half of the cases they are related to the child, usually the father. The survey also supports a conclusion at odds with popular consensus: young males are at substantial risk for sexual victimization. The survey showed young males constituted 33 percent of the child caseload reporting sexual abuse, 19 percent of the adult caseload reporting sexual abuse as children, and 16 percent of the victims of self-confessed abusers seen in treatment at the mental health center. (1977, 325)

David Finkelhor's survey (1979a) found that males were victimized by sexual abuse at a one to two ratio for females, which is similar to estimates from police agencies (Maney 1983). On the other hand, Ann Maney (1983, 8) notes that estimates from social service and medical agencies place the rate for boys at one-tenth the rate for girls, the same ratio estimated by Vincent DeFrancis (1969). In any case, it seems clear that many more boys are victims of sexual abuse than official statistics indicate. Finkelhor found important differences in the sexual victimization of boys and girls: boys are much more likely to be assaulted by unrelated persons; they are older when the assault/s occur; there is a greater likelihood of violence occurring with the sexual abuse; and they are likely to be one of several victims of the abusers.

Girls in Finkelhor's sample were much more likely than boys to have encountered a sexual experience under the age of 12 with an adult (11.3 percent versus 4.1 percent, respectively) (1979a, 55–56). Boys' sexual partners were generally younger, and since negative evaluation of the incidents increased with age disparity, boys reported fewer negative reactions; when boys' partners were adolescents, they were "evaluated fairly positively" (Finkelhor 1979a, 81). Boys and girls were equally likely to report coercion and force in initiating the encounters, which suggests that boys are generally not more consenting than girls. Reactions differed, however, Finkelhor says:

> In their overall evaluation, girls rate their experiences more negatively than do boys: 66 percent compared to 38 percent. Boys report feeling more interest and pleasure at the time, and girls remember more fear and shock. This finding certainly confirms the impression that the experiences were more traumatic for the girls, but it does not mean that the boys' experiences were never traumatic. Indeed, some were extremely so. . . . (1979a, 70)

The law enforcement officer cited earlier was one male victim whose early incest experiences with his father were extremely traumatic. Obviously, more and larger studies must be done on sexual abuse of boys. Finkelhor's volunteer sample of students contained only half as many males as females, and because only 23 men reported victimization by older persons (8.6 percent of 266 male respondents), the experiences of those few men cannot be generalized to the population. Nevertheless they provide useful information.

Most of the victimization of boys by adults (83 percent) took place outside the family with acquaintances or strangers, and none of them reported incest with a father, stepfather, or mother (Finkelhor 1979a, 58, 87). It seems that little boys need instruction on how to avoid *pedophiles* (men with a sexual fixation on pre-pubescent children) outside the home, and little girls need to be warned about older males in their homes. Of the girls abused by adults, almost half (43 percent) of their abusers were family members (1979a, 58). Most frequently the abusers were brothers and stepbrothers (39 percent) and male cousins (26 percent) for the 151 female students in Finkelhor's sample who reported incestuous assaults. Fathers and stepfathers[6] were perpetrators in only 4 percent of the cases, which amounts to over 1 percent of the total sample. Finkelhor points out that this is compatible with other surveys such as John Cagnon's (1965) and Morton Hunt's (1974). Data from the Child Sexual Abuse Training Program (CSATP), however, show that children "were most frequently molested by a natural parent (30.6%) or a stepparent (33.3%)" (California Department of Social Services 1980, 12).[7]

Diana Russell (1983) also found a higher rate for father/daughter incest in her randomly selected sample. Russell's survey revealed that, even using a narrow definition of incest, 149 women (16 percent) reported at least one incident of incest when they were under the age of 17, and the two largest categories of abusers were father-figures and uncles (1983, 170). Russell compares the two studies and says: "24 percent of the perpetrators of intrafamilial sexual abuse in our San Francisco survey were fathers (including step-fathers) and 26 percent were uncles as compared with only 4 percent fathers and 9 percent uncles in Finkelhor's sample" (1983, 169). Russell also screened out consensual sexual contact or propositions between peers, and as a result, 61 percent of the incidents reported were cross-generational (younger victims and older abusers). Brothers were perpetrators in only 14 percent of the cases, compared to Finkelhor's 39 percent. Russell (1983, 170) suggests:

> The differences in the findings of Finkelhor and Russell may also have occurred because women may be less likely to disclose the most taboo experiences of father-daughter incest on a self-administered questionnaire completed in a classroom situation, as was required by Finkelhor's methodology, than in a face-to-face interview with well trained interviewers who have had an opportunity to try to build good rapport with the respondent. . . . [B]ecause Russell's findings are based on a random sample of women and not limited to a college student population, the distribution of types of offenders that she reports likely has significantly greater validity than Finkelhor's or data from any other study available at this time.

The large majority of victims of sexual abuse who are reported to authorities or seek help are females, and both Finkelhor's and Russell's data show that about one out of every five girls is victimized by nonrelatives.

Russell's data reveal that about one out of every six girls (17 percent) are victims of incest before they reach the age of 18; Finkelhor's much higher proportion (28 percent) of incest victims may, as Russell suggests, be an overstatement of consensual sexual contact between peers and an understatement of father/daughter incest. Obviously, many little girls are not safe in their homes from predatory adult males who abuse their power and positions of trust and responsibility. What causes these men to commit sexual assault?

Theories of Incest

There are a number of theories, beginning with Freud (1962) who implied that all adults have a potential for being sexually stimulated by children, but because of socialization and cultural taboos, most repress it to some degree. Paul Gebhard and his colleagues (1965) explain that asexual physical contact may involuntarily become sexual, but usually these urges are not acted upon except when restraints become weakened by other forces, such as intoxication, hunger for affection, or stress. As Russell (1983) points out, these scientists fail to explain why women rarely act upon such urges, yet may have stress, need for affection, or be intoxicated. Instead, Gebhard et al. (1965, 10) contend that "The average female has a much weaker 'sex drive' than the average male"; however, Russell (1983, 177) notes that they make no attempt to substantiate that claim.

David Finkelhor (1981c) has produced a *Four Preconditions Model* that can be applied to explain both intra- and extrafamilial sexual abuse, suggesting a logical sequence that occurs thus:

1. Only some individuals have sexual feelings about children: Some do not act on them; Some do act on them →
2. Of those who act on them: Some fail to overcome internal inhibitions; Some overcome internal inhibitions →
3. Of those who overcome internal inhibitions: Some fail to overcome external inhibitions; Some overcome external inhibitions →
4. Of those who overcome external inhibitions: Some meet resistance by the child they do not overcome; Some overcome resistance by the child → sexual abuse occurs.

Finkelhor also theorizes on why the vast majority of sexual abusers of children are men. He finds a partial explanation in the differences in male/female socialization, making men more likely to have sexual feelings for children because men are: not as well socialized to distinguish between sexual and nonsexual forms of affection; socialized to become more easily aroused by sexual activities and fantasies divorced from the context of the relationships in which they occur; socialized to partners who are smaller, younger and less powerful than themselves—more childlike—whereas the opposite is true for women (Finkelhor 1981c, 4–5).

Finkelhor also believes that certain factors besides socialization predispose some men to have sexual feelings toward children. Among these are child pornography (almost all of which is consumed by men) and the sexualization of children in the media and advertising (1981c, 5).

Psychiatrist Roland Summit and psychiatric social worker JoAnn Kryso devised a typology of parent/child sexuality that ranges from *Incidental Sexual Contact* (controlled or repressed vague erotic interest) to *Perverse Incest* ("kinky, unfettered lechery" that is "more bizarre . . . and destructive") at the extreme end (1978, 240–47). Some other types are: *Misogynous* (who fear and hate women); *Imperious* (who set themselves up as emperors in their households); *Pedophilic* (who have an erotic fascination with innocent and nonjudgmental young children of either sex with whom they act out their fantasies nonviolently); and the *Child Rapist* (who only feels sexually adequate by frightening and overpowering his victims) (Summit and Kryso 1978).

The vast majority of incest cases are the type called *True Endogamous,* which develop without deliberate premeditation by "individuals who are not notably implusive and who may appear quite well adjusted and well functioning within other areas of their lives" (Summit and Kryso 1978, 242). These are the kinds of cases that made up the middle class clinical sample studied by Henry Giarretto (1976) at the Child Sexual Abuse Treatment Program (CSATP) in California.

Feminist writers tend to reject emphasis on individual factors based on sexual feelings and social psychological concepts, such as those proposed by Finkelhor (1981c) and Summit and Kryso (1978), and insist that patriarchal society sets into motion all types of abuses in the home:

> Feminists . . . argue that it is the power and position of men that is the source of rape, woman abuse and child sexual assault in the family. The still dominant view of the family holds that within his own home, a man has the right to do as he pleases. The decisions he makes regarding his property, his house, his wife, and children, are his concern and any input from society is seen as an illegitimate intrusion. Men often regard their children as extensions of themselves, not as individuals with feelings, needs and rights of their own. (Wayne and France 1980, 30)

Psychiatrist and researcher Judith Herman seems to agree and offers a more social-structural theory than many others:

> Male supremacy invest fathers with immense powers over their children, especially their daughters. The sexual division of labor, in which women nurture children and men do not, produces fathers who are predisposed to use their powers exploitatively. The rearing of children by subordinate women ensures the reproduction in each generation of the psychology of male supremacy. It produces sexually aggressive men with little capacity to nurture, nurturant women with undeveloped sexual capacities, and children of both sexes who stand in awe of the power of the father. . . . The greater the domination of the father, and the more the caretaking is relegated to the mother, the greater the likelihood of father-daughter incest. (Herman 1981, 62–63)

Russell (1983, 206) is inclined to agree with the thrust of Herman's thesis, which calls for greater involvement by fathers in child caretaking, but she believes there would have to be a concomitant change from male socialization in the present-day "masculinity and virility mystiques" before children would be safe from predatory males in the family.

These writers may be at the forefront of a new feminist analysis of incest, as were those who disputed traditionalist views of rape as a *sexual* act, now viewed by most professionals as a violent, aggressive act against victims wherein *sex is merely the weapon of assault*. Many others tend to focus on sex drives and sexual aspects of the assaults on children, which diverts attention from the major issue of abuse of power and trust. If their needs are for sex rather than power, what prevents these men from obtaining sexual services from adults—whether casual "pick-ups" for free, prostitutes for a price, or in the form of self-masturbation—instead of using children?

"Sexual abuse is the most concealed, most distressing, and most controversial form of child abuse" (Summit and Kryso 1978, 250). It is an extremely complex phenomenon, committed by a wide variety of people with differing motives and methods in different settings and circumstances. Many children are sexually assaulted both inside and outside their homes. Russell found that 357 of 930 women (38 percent) admitted to at least one experience before the age of 18 of incest and/or other sexual abuse. When Russell's broader definition of sexual abuse was used, which includes noncontact experience, such as exhibitionism, advances not acted upon, and so forth, 504 women, or 54 percent of the sample, had at least one such experience (1983, 169)! Clearly, young girls are vulnerable to at least one unsolicited and unwanted sexual experience before they reach their eighteenth birthday, and many concerned adults want to reduce the odds through recognition and intervention.

Recognition and Intervention in Incest

Child Victims

There are very few ways that persons outside their immediate family or the medical profession are able to identify sexually abused children unless they accidentally or purposely reveal their secret. Some children admit abuse only after gentle questioning by sensitive adults who encourage children to express their feelings openly. Detection depends almost entirely on the ability of adults to consider the possibility that an incestuous situation might exist (Sgroi 1975). Because most professionals do not recognize symptoms, the vast majority of cases are not discovered or reported to authorities. Indicators of possible incest are somewhat different from those presented in Chapter 6 for child maltreatment. Initiation may begin at any age, but the average age for girls is about nine years. Combinations of the following factors may indicate victimization or potential victimization.

Factors Indicating a Child May Be the Victim of Sexual Abuse

Inappropriate clothing: dresses too young or too old for her age; wears makeup or jewelry at a young age.

School attendance: habitually truant or late for school, or arrives at school early and remains late. Often tired and may fall asleep in class.

Physical contact: displays provocative behavior with males or jumps away from contact.

Sudden changes in conduct: nervousness, withdraws from close friendships, refuses to join in group activities, becomes a "loner," does not participate in after-school activities but leaves immediately. Little children may become intrigued with their own or others' anatomy or begin using inappropriate sexual terms.

Physical Trauma: may show unexplained signs or soreness or pain, such as when walking; frequent trips to the lavatory, minor physical complaints. Little children may cry or protest being bathed or touched; nightmares; have soreness around the mouth or genitals.

Scholastic changes: an unexplained drop, or a great improvement[8] in grades.

Social isolation: family has few friends; is inhospitable to outsiders.

Dating: a teen-aged girl with an overprotective male guardian who refuses to let her date boys, sets unreasonable restrictions, or acts like a jealous suitor when she does date.

Motherless home: mother is absent, ill, or incapacitated; if there is no healthy adult female resident and a young girl is responsible for housekeeping, caring for other siblings, and providing services for her male guardian, these services may include the sexual kind, *especially* if the father is a social isolate who has no intimate adult relationships.

Substitute father: stepfather, mother's boy friend, or adult male relatives live in the same household.

Mother is a battered wife: the chances of abuse greatly increase.

Sexual abuse of children is a crime that must be reported to officials by certain professionals who come in contact with or work closely with children, but reporting rates are lower than other forms of child maltreatment. Only 6 percent of the incidents were reported to authorities in John Cagnon's (1975) study of college-aged females. Sexual activity between adults and minor children is a crime in every state, although definitions of activities deemed criminal and the ages of victims vary widely. For example, most states punish sexual intercourse whether or not it was consenting or by force, but sexual contact involving oral or anal intercourse cannot be prosecuted under the incest laws in most states (Russell 1983, 154). Most sexual assault does not involve battery; thus physical findings are not often evident.

The presence of venereal disease in any prepubertal child is generally a reliable indicator of sexual exploitation (McNeese and Hebeler 1977; Sgroi 1977). Pediatricians Margaret McNeese and Joan Hebeler (1977, 17, 24) offer sound advice to medical professionals on how to conduct a gentle yet thorough physical examination of any child suspected of having been abused. They outline steps that should be taken when obtaining a history from a child, and note that little children usually answer honestly, but because school-aged children or adolescents may feel guilty or try to protect their parents, their honesty is less reliable. Lucy Berliner and Doris Stevens (1980) also provide valuable advice on the manner and setting of questioning children, and they agree that preschool-aged children, while they can present problems because of stubbornness or short attention spans, will usually be truthful. They say: "Although fantasy becomes an important element in the repertoire of preschoolers, they can usually distinguish fact from fantasy. When lying occurs, it is usually the child's attempt to make something look better or to escape a problem situation" (1980, 47). Children aged 6 through 11 may lie because of fear of retribution or to protect their abusers, but "Although they may become sullen, insolent, and taciturn with adults, they seldom lie about major issues" (Berliner and Stevens 1980, 48). In sum, children are unlikely to make false accusations or exaggerations; when they do lie, it is by minimizing or denying what adults in positions of authority did to them.

Sometimes victims attempt to tell adults what is happening between them and an adult male, but their comments are ignored or brushed aside as "imagination," or they produce reactions of shock and/or revulsion so the children quickly sense danger and refuse to continue or dismiss what they had just said. Experts warn that the initial reaction of the "confidant" is crucial; expressions on their own faces can stifle a child's attempt to reveal her or his secret. McNeese and Hebeler advise approaching the child in a calm, nonthreatening manner:

> [I]f the adult becomes angry or embarrassed, the child may feel guilty and responsible for his own injuries. Evidence of sexual abuse in particular confronts the adult with a strong taboo and may evoke in the interviewer deep anger, confusion, or disgust. These reactions must be controlled because they will interfere with subsequent evaluation of the child. (1977, 17)

When the interviewer is a member of the child's family, there may be even greater difficulty in preserving a calm, nonjudgmental facade because of overwhelming feelings of anger and disgust. On the other hand, family members may react by blaming the victim. When a child is discovered to be a victim of sexual assault, responses by their families and the community often differ, depending on whether the abuser is a stranger or a close family member. In their brief article, Kee MacFarlane, Linda Jenstrom, and Barbara McComb Jones say that when the perpetrator is *not related*, families are much more likely to offer support, love, and concern: "Usually, the family's efforts are directed toward child protection and reassurance" (MacFarlane et al. 1980, 123). However, if the child happens to be an adolescent raped by a stranger, research has shown that families are not *always* supportive. One study found that only 50 percent of the parents of raped teen-agers worried for their child's safety; 41 percent blamed their child; and only 20 percent were consistently supportive and understanding (Otey 1983). For the most part, families of small children are unlikely to blame the victim *except* when the perpetrator is a family member, particularly if he is a father-figure:

> Because such cases are often brought to the attention of authorities through the actions of the child rather than at the instigation of the parents, the child may be perceived by other family members as a betrayer. Consequently, the primary family reaction may be one of rejection toward the child and protection of the offender. (MacFarlane et at. 1980, 124)

To compound matters, the children frequently have extremely ambivalent feelings, since they have been impressed with the notion that if anything ever "happens," it will be *their fault,* and they must deal with the authority of intervening professionals, often alone and without any family support system. As MacFarlane and her colleagues state, "It is important to remember that most maltreated children want the abuse, not their families, to end" (1980, 124). Discovery of father/daughter incest has a devastating impact on every member of the family, which often results in father, mother, and siblings solidifying into a force opposing the victims. *The victim now becomes the accused.*

The tendency to blame victims of incest is similar to the way victims of rape and battered wives have been blamed for their own victimization. Children have been accused of inciting men into pedophilia (cf. Virkkunen 1975); little girls, even babies, have been accused of "seducing" fathers and stepfathers, as for example, in a 1982 case a judge granted probation to a man convicted of rape with the explanation that the victim was a "very provocative young lady." The victim was a *five-year-old* girl. Some professionals, such as psychiatrists, still receive training with textbooks that give the impression that an incestuous father is a helpless victim of his wife and daughter (Meiselman 1978, 162).[9]

Some of the most blatant victim blaming occurs in the legal setting, where defense attorneys traditionally present helpless clients, driven by uncontrollable sexual urges, who were charmed and seduced by little *Lolitas.* Defense attorneys attempt to destroy their credibility: victims are frequently presented as unable to distinguish fact from fantasy ("You play with your dolls and pretend you are their mommy, don't you?"); or at the more malignant extreme, portraying them as pathological liars or spiteful troublemakers and revenge seekers (Samuels 1977). As Berliner and Stevens note, "If child molesters are prosecuted, child victims must undergo the same processes as those imposed on adult victims, without benefit of special procedures or protection" (1980, 47). As in rape, the case belongs to the state and the victim is merely the witness to the crime; "If a child is *witness* to a crime committed by an adult, that child is drawn into the adult criminal justice system, where there is usually little allowance made for his or her more limited abilities" (Berliner and Stevens 1980, 47). Protections provided suspected juvenile *offenders* are not provided juvenile *witnesses*. The trauma inflicted on these children is described in detail by Berliner and Stevens and in various other sources. Many people believe the criminal justice process is even more traumatic for the victims than the actual abuse itself. However, changes are occurring as cooperation and communication between scientists and the legal system has increased. In 1981 the American Bar Association published two reports, *Sexual Abuse and the Law* by Berliner and her colleagues, and *Innovations in the Prosecution of Child Sexual Abuse Cases* (Bulkley 1981).[10]

While necessary improvements are being made to help protect victims from additional trauma, Lucy Berliner at Seattle's Sexual Assault Center (SAC) at Harborview Medical Center, does not believe in diversion from the criminal justice system, for the ultimate benefit of both the victim and the abuser. Dunwoody (1982, 13) cites Berliner's statements at a victimization conference:

> "When the conditions are right, testifying in court can be therapeutic for a child." Berliner told conference participants that it "can do worlds of good for a child to have adults in positions of authority take her story seriously." Berliner added that "some kids I've worked with have gotten very angry because their abusers plead guilty—they wanted their day in court."

Jim Mead, another expert on incest who works with both victims and the criminal justice system, says: "If a case is carefully prepared, the vast majority of abusers will plead guilty, rather than go to trial, especially when we videotape his child's pre-trial interview. Since he and his attorney are entitled to preview this testimony, he watches and listens to his child tell what he did to her and he usually breaks down at that point" (1982).[11]

At the beginning stages of the investigation when a case is reported, child victims almost always are removed from their homes and placed in temporary protective custody, which usually adds to the child's trauma and confusion. Whenever their safety is reasonably assured, these children should be returned to their home as quickly as possible; "if a member of the family must be removed from the home for any lengthy period of time in order to ensure that the abuse is stopped, it is usually in the child's best interests that the offending adult be the one to go" (MacFarlane et al. 1980, 124).[12]

Almost all professionals believe that victims need individual, group therapy, mother/daughter therapy, and in cases where there is a possibility of reunification of the family, family therapy. Counselors must help victims overcome feelings of guilt, fear, depression, and low self-esteem (Sgroi 1982). Primarily, they need to recover from feelings of shame and "differentness" and to know that they are not responsible for what happened to them. They must be given an opportunity and even encouraged to express their anger, something that is denied girls in their socialization process. Little children need help in expressing their feelings about their experiences, and this help comes in the form of stories, dolls, and art therapy. Children who are otherwise unable to express their emotions use colors, designs, and motion to release feelings and conflict and to grow emotionally (Stember 1980).

Victims as Adults

There are a multitude of books, articles, and reports debating effects of child sexual abuse on victims as children and in adulthood. Some contend that effects depend largely upon factors such as the child's age, relationship of victim and offender, type and duration of the assault, and so forth (Courtois 1979; DeVine 1980b), and that effects range from practically no trauma to severe, lifelong psychosexual damages. With Kee MacFarlane's help, one victim wrote an article titled "Incest: If you Think the Word Is Ugly, Take a Look at its Effects" (Myers 1980). When there are no obvious problems resulting directly from the experiences of child victims, professional can assume only that short-term trauma is minimal, but they cannot determine long-term effects. Some victims seem to cope very well, with the exception of occasional "flash backs," nightmares, and so forth. Others may have symptoms such as "Severe reactions that include acute depression, suicide attempts, learning problems, sleep disturbances, regressive behavior, low self-esteem, and lack of trust" (Dunwoody 1982, 2). These symptoms are mentioned frequently in the literature. Other results are more indirect, such as when children run away from home and begin a life of prostitution (West 1980) or misuse alcohol and other drugs. Possible effects may not be discovered for years.

Recently, Frank Putnam, a staff psychiatrist at the National Institute of Mental Health, speaking at a national conference on sexual victimization, noted that "virtually all his subjects who have multiple personalities were sexually abused over a period of time as children" (Whitman 1982, 3). Putnam reviewed the literature on cases of patients with multipersonality disorders (MPD) and found that 60 percent of them were also sexually abused as children. He emphasized that not all sexually abused children develop MPD, but those who were victimized had developed a method to dissociate themselves from their bodies during the assaults, thereby escaping the pain so that it seemed to be happening to someone else

(Whitman 1982). What began as a protective reaction to an unbearable situation becomes dysfunctional for adults no longer needing protection from reality.[13]

.However, if the recent research is correct, and about one out of every four to six girls is sexually abused by relatives or nonrelatives (Finkelhor 1979a; Russell 1983), then obviously many women are functioning adequately in our society who were child victims. At the same time, many of those otherwise well-adjusted and adequately functioning women may be privately dealing with bouts of deep depression, lack of self-esteem, inability to trust, and psychosexual problems. Eventually, some of them search for professional help.

Two experts emphatically state that female victims of incest must choose their therapists carefully, but male therapists are generally less suitable than female therapists since:

> We believe that the male therapist may have great difficulty in validating the victim's experience and responding emphatically to her suffering. Consciously or not, the male therapist will tend to identify with the father's position and therefore will tend to deny or excuse his behavior and project blame onto the victim. (Herman and Hirschman 1980, 73)

Psychiatrist Herman and psychologist Hirschman also point out that a female therapist tends to identify with the victim, thus limiting her effectiveness. Both the male and female therapists encountered by the victims cited earlier would not confront the basic problem their patients were attempting to resolve. Herman and Hirschman find that many therapists avoid full and detailed explorations of incestuous relationships (1980, 73).

After former victims have located skilled counselors, the next step in the process of recovery is group therapy, where the women[14] have an opportunity to reveal their secret face to face with others who have been part of a similar conspiracy. Individual therapy is not sufficient for many. Groups provide a safe environment in which former victims share their experiences. Some groups are provided by psychology departments on college campuses (Tsai and Wagner 1977), others are organized by incest survivors themselves (Duty 1983),[15] and some are an extension of consciousness raising by feminist groups. Probably the best known of these self-help groups is Daughters United, which was developed at CSATP after the Parents United group began in 1972 (Giarretto 1976). Originally planned for teen-aged girls at the program in Santa Clara County, California, the groups were expanded to Daughters and Sons United, and chapters were developed throughout the state (California Department of Social Services 1980). These groups help former victims rid themselves of guilt and increase their self-esteem. There are 500 Parents Anonymous chapters throughout the United States that invite people with sexual abuse problems (Summit and Kryso 1978, 249).

Herman and Hirschman (1980, 74) suggest an even more daring next step: "Incest will begin to lose its devastating magic power when women begin to speak out about it publicly and realize how common it is." Voices are beginning to be heard from incest victims, and it is possible they will get louder as more join in. As Terry Davidson broke the "family secret" of her minister-father's wife beating (1978), other writers like Louise Armstrong (1979) and Susan Forward (Forward and Buck 1978) broke the taboo of writing about their own fathers' incestuous advances. Armstrong insists the acts are not taboo—how can they be, since they occur so often?—but that talking about them is taboo. It is significant that books on incest use titles such as *The Best Kept Secret* (Rush 1980a), and *The Conspiracy of Silence* (Butler 1979). Laurie McLaughlin (1982) first gave a speech, then published it, asking:

> Is it any wonder that Incest Victims, Incest Survivors do not speak out? Everything we see tells us society supports our sexual assault and that our families and the men in our lives have the right, the power, to do with us as they wish. (1982, 15).

Others write their experiences anonymously or use pseudonyms, but whether or not they identify themselves, the very act of disclosure seems to be theraputic for them. One woman went beyond merely talking about her experiences with her adoptive father, whose abuse began with fondling at age 11 and escalated into intercourse, until he divorced her mother when she was 15. Lorey Newlander sued her stepfather for "infliction of emotional distress and assault and battery" (Oliver 1983). As more and more former victims reveal their dreaded "secret" to the public it may have a twofold effect—therapy plus prevention—because how many men would make that first sexual approach that is always accompanied by the warning, "Don't you *ever* tell anybody!" What if a man knew with certainty that *some day* his powerless child would broadcast to everyone the things he did in private? Would he *dare* to do it?

Perpetrators

Borrowing from a number of studies on sexual abuse (including, but not limited to, DeFrancis 1969; Julian and Mohr 1979; Summit and Kryso 1978), perpetrators of incest have the following general characteristics.

Commonly Noted Features and Background Factors of Incest Perpetrators

Males: between the ages of 35 and 39, usually living in intact families, but the ratio is high if they are the only parent present.

Ethnicity: mostly caucasian in terms of numbers, but minority groups except blacks, are overrepresented.

Large family: in one year, 36 percent had four or more children, compared to 6 percent of families in the United States that size.

Employment: 80 percent employed; professional, technical, and higher skilled laborers.

Education: at least three out of four have some high school or above.

Family features: family discord and/or alcoholism.

Personality features: rigid, patriarchal, and religious; possessive and domineering with extremely dependent wives.

Other: 80 percent have no previous court record.

There is a continuing and not easily resolved debate centering on what should be done to or for incest perpetrators. On the one side are those who argue that crimes, whether they occur inside or outside the home, are still crimes and should be punished according to the law. These people believe that protecting offenders from legal punishment indicates to them that what they did was not really criminal; thus they continue their sexual assaults, perhaps with different victims and being more careful than before about getting caught. On the other side are those who insist that the legal system merely punishes perpetrators by incarceration for a certain length of time, after which they are released, only to return to their old ways; they also fear the "destruction of the family." These people feel that, since the accused are usually men who have never been found guilty of other crimes, they are not "common criminals," but rather people who need professional help. The trend seems to be going increasingly in a therapeutic direction, such as the model guiding the Child Sexual Abuse Treatment Program (CSATP) in California.

The CSATP director, Henry Giarretto (1976, 3) says that "The therapeutic approach would follow a 'growth' model predicated on Humanistic Psychology." CSATP treats the family primarily as a *system,* advocating diversion from the criminal justice system; personal growth (rehabilitation) for the offender; therapy for all family members individually, with each other, and in groups; and marital counseling for families that want to be reunited (National Center on Child Abuse and Neglect 1978c). The program has generally been acclaimed as successful, largely because of the increasing rate of self-referrals by victims, offenders and families rather than agencies, and low recidivism rates (California Department of Social Services 1980; Giarretto 1976). On the latter point, the state report (CDSS 1980, 16) notes that these are self-monitored rates of recidivism, and that some cases dropped out before completing treatment but there was no follow-up.[16]

The CDSS (1980, 17) report noted the cost-effectiveness of the CSATP, compared to incarceration for offenders and the reunification of families that might otherwise have broken apart, thereby saving taxpayers the costs of incarceration, possible financial aid to the nonoffending parents, and/or the placement of victims/siblings in foster homes. The report states:

> Although the offender may initially be incarcerated for a brief period of time, he is usually released on his own recognizance . . . which allows the offender to continue his employment and therefore the financial support of his family." (CDSS 1980, 17)

In response to this kind of evaluation, some who oppose "decriminalization" of crimes committed in the home are likely to say that humanitarian psychology serves an economic purpose. For example, Louise Armstrong (1983, 2–3) talks about assigning crimes in the home to the "therapeutic state" rather than the legal state, saying:

> [W]hen I speak of crimes in the home, I am speaking of serious (and most often-repeated) behavior which would be criminal if directed toward a stranger. . . . The criminal justice system was declared "inappropriate." The enlightened response was treatment; treatment for the whole family, which was "dysfunctional." The goal of the treatment was to keep the abusive family intact.

On the other hand, even when they do enter the system as criminals, the chances are slim that fathers will be incarcerated, except possibly for a very short length of time. A California organization, Concerned Citizens for Stronger Legislation Against Child Molesters (SLAM), contends that very few convicted molesters are sent to prison (McLellan 1981); the majority of these are unrelated to their victims. Out of only 396 convictions in California in 1979, 26 percent went to state hospitals for an average of 18 months, and 14 percent went to prison for an average 41 months; the balance received probation. Some people get longer sentences for kiting checks.

Some experts believe that the criminal justice system has an important role in child sexual abuse; Berliner and Stevens (1980, 47) insist: "It has been our experience that child molesting is often a compulsive behavior; therefore, if the offender is not prosecuted for his crime, a series of children will undoubtedly be exposed to his abuse." Herman and Hirschman (1980, 74) say: "Offenders should be isolated and reeducated." Still, the legal system has traditionally been reluctant to proceed against fathers, and in states where reports are received by social service agencies, they usually limit their intervention to investigating and removing the child from the home (Response 1979a). The move has been toward treatment to encourage families to report incest, but the Sexual Assault Center (SAC) in Seattle, Washington, provides treatment in conjunction with the legal system. One report states:

> Lucy Berliner, social worker at the SAC, believes that incest is a form of sexual abuse that has been singled out for lenient treatment by the legal system. "Just because perpetrators are related to their victims," says Berliner, "does not mean that they should be treated differently from other sexual offenders." Berliner believes that the justice system should intervene in incestuous relationships because it is crucial for the victim to understand that she is not at fault and not responsible for the abuser's behavior. Also, most incestuous fathers . . . will deny their actions and refuse treatment unless they are under the threat of civil or criminal prosecution. (Response 1979a, 1)

Berliner is one of the pioneers in the field who has worked to educate communities, law enforcement officials, lawyers, and prosecutors in proper techniques for interviewing children and helping them through the system. Using her methods, 73 percent of the cases avoided trial because the defendant pleaded guilty, and of those who went to trial, 90 percent resulted in convictions (Response 1979). CSATP also works closely with the law, receiving some cases from the authorities, and reporting self-referrals to authorities (as demanded by California law), but not everyone agrees with CSATP's stated goal of reuniting the family. There are other programs developing around the country, one of which is in Dallas, Texas, but "the legal system is still more inclined to jail the offender than force him to enter therapy" (Response 1979, 2). The possibility of using the full force of the law against offenders who refuse to admit their guilt now promises to inflict less trauma on victims and nonoffending parents than it has traditionally, and Texas law permits videotaped interrogation of the child to be used in court. Due to the work of children's advocates like Lucy Berliner and others, the system is much more sensitive now toward victims and tries to protect them from additional trauma.

Not all offenders are appropriate clients for therapy, according to Summit and Kryso (1978), who indicated that those they categorize as "true endogamous" are the most common and amenable to treatment. However, these are at the lower end of the spectrum, and cases become less manageable so that:

> At some point in the spectrum, voluntary outpatient treatment programs must be replaced by mandatory, specialized institutional programs. . . . [I]t must be recognized also that some individuals will be refractory to any known treatment, and that institutionalization may serve a purely protective function. (Summit and Kryso 1978, 249)

For offenders undergoing treatment, Summit and Kryso believe the *threat* of punishment is important, otherwise the men tend to drop out. These experts applaud self-help programs for adult and child participants by saying: "Alcoholics Anonymous, Parents Anonymous, and Giarretto's Parents United and Daughters United groups have demonstrated the unique effectiveness of a united peer group in building identity and self-esteem in the face of majority censure" (1978, 249).

One man who led a counseling group, Rich Snowdon, wrote: "Working With Incest Offenders: Excuses, Excuses, Excuses" (1982). He found the men were "ordinary guys" who portrayed themselves as the true victims, and shifted the responsibility to their wives and children. Like wife beaters, they attempted to deny, project, or minimize the blame. Some insisted that they were *educating* their children in sex, or that their children wanted *loving*, so they gave it to them. Some comments from these fathers include: "My child's body is as much mine as it is hers." "I pick on children because they're safer, that's all. They don't talk back to you like women." "She's *my* girl, so that gives me the right to do anything with her I want to. So stick your nose out of it; *my* family is *my* business." Snowdon does not believe these men were helpless victims of society, their wives, or their children; they were *ordinary men* who "used nothing more than the power any ordinary father has" (1982, 62).

Prevention

Men abuse children because they are *safe* to abuse.

A variety of sources offer suggestions for the prevention of sexual abuse of children, many aimed at molestation outside the family, but some are applicable to family members. At the societal level, Herman and Hirschman (1980, 74) believe that incest will cease only when male supremacy ends, but that the power imbalance could be lessened by providing social support and services that most mothers do not have now. Rosenfeld

(1977) offers a list devised to illustrated boundaries of acceptable parent/child sexual behavior. Almost everyone agrees that children need to learn

Children can be taught they have a right to say "No!" to someone, even a trusted relative or person in an authority position. This book by Jill Haddad and Lloyd Martin presents an alternative to children who are so easily influenced by adults into "keeping secrets." The slogan of M. H. Cap and Company is "An Informed Child is a Protected Child," and they have designed a program that consists of educational cassette tapes and instructional self-help for parents and teachers. Most experts in the child sexual abuse field believe that the best way to prevent this crime is through education.

Source: M. H. Cap and Company.

about sex from their parents, but few parents seem to handle this important task adequately. Some adults never come to terms with their own views on sex and sexuality, and reveal their discomfort by being embarrassed or trying to avoid the subject. Communication is often strained or nonexistant. Yet these parents are often the ones who are adamantly opposed to sex education in schools. In her report on the National Conference on the Sexual Victimization of Children, Ellen Dunwoody (1982) notes that the single most effective tool in preventing sexual abuse is sex education, according to most professionals who work with child victims. These people say that children should learn appropriate sexual behavior and be able to openly discuss sexual matters. Nicholas Groth, who has worked extensively with sex offenders, reported that "these men say that the best way for a parent to protect a child is to teach the child about sex" (Dunwoody 1982, 4). Citing another conference speaker, Sol Gordon of the Institute for Family Research and Education, Dunwoody (1982, 14) writes:

> "Silence is the essence of the abuser's power. Take away the silence and you make him powerless." Gordon emphasized that although sex education can help prevent the molestation of children, it is still strongly opposed in many communities. "Less than 10 percent of our children get any kind of sex education," he stated, "and much of this isn't even sex education. It's about the body. How can we talk about incest when we can't even talk about sex?"

MacFarlane et al. (1980, 123–26) offer several suggestions which include parents educating themselves so they can transmit a consistent and healthy code of sexual conduct. They need to provide basic sex education so that children can distinguish what constitutes appropriate adult/child physical interaction.[17] Because emphasis is put on respect and obedience to their elders, children need to learn to differentitate among adults, to know there are limits to their compliance, and that not all adults are worthy of their trust. Children must be taught "that their bodies are their own and that they have the right to exercise control over them. It is of utmost importance that children be taught that they have the right to say no to anyone in matters of sexuality" (MacFarlane et al. 1980, 125).

The permission to say "no" to adults seems to be the crux of the matter, because parents and society teach children they have no right to disobey adult authority figures. A former Los Angeles police detective, Lloyd Martin, who spent many years fighting sexual exploitation of children has co-authored a book titled, *What if . . . I Say No!* (Haddad and Martin 1981) and designed a program to be presented to elementary school children.

The book emphasizes two major points: *say no* and *tell someone*. The other points are that *anyone* could be a molester[18] and that children have a *right* to their own bodies. This is a difficult point to present to parents, who often hug when their children squirm away or insist on kisses their child is unwilling to give. This presents the next point: What about children's rights?

THE "PRO-INCEST LOBBY"

Flying under the colors of the "children's liberation movement," there is a group in the United States that is actively lobbying for the legalization of sex between adults and children. The slogan of the Rene Guyon Society is *sex before eight or else it's too late*. Summit and Kryso (1978, 242) say: "the group advocates sexual rights for children, including abolition of laws restricting incest and sexual abuse. The Guyon Society claims a membership of '2000 parents and psychiatrists.'"[19] Judianne Densen-Gerber (1980) also refers to this organization, which she says is composed of American sympathizers to the International Pedophilic Information Exchange that held its first meeting in May 1977 in Wales. The society, says Densen-Gerber, "claims to have 5000 members who have filed an affadavit that they have each deflowered a child under eight (male or female)" (1980, 78). According to Jim Ohr (1983), a sheriff's department investigator, for a man to be admitted to one of their "meetings," he must bring a child with him who is given to the group for sex purposes. Guyon has appeared on television shows, eloquently claiming that his organization is interested in children's rights to enjoy sex.

Benjamin DeMott (1980, 12) dubbed this active political movement the *pro-incest lobby*, outlining their arguments for easing the incest taboo: a prohibition is absurd because it is so prevalent; reactions from discovery and intervention are more harmful than incest itself; and seductive behavior by parents is more destructive than incestuous acts. An insidious facet is the inclusion of some factual statements along with rhetoric, thus persons who are confused and uncertain about appropriated adult/child sexuality may become convinced that societal norms are "old-fashioned," and adopt the new wave of "liberal" sex ideology, especially if they were raised in rigid, sexually repressed households. For intellectual appeal, the arguments come "wrapped in the pieties of feminism (children, like women, have the right to control their own bodies) and the children's rights movement . . ." (Leo 1981, 69).

One criminology journal carried two articles in which both writers agreed on decriminalization of adult/child sex, but for different reasons.

Edward Brongersma, former member of the Dutch Parliament, talks about "mutually consenting relations," saying that punishment should not occur when acts are through "love, tenderness or affection" (1980, 30). The writer of the commentary that follows notes that "passive acquiescence" is not necessarily informed consent but still agrees on decriminalization because "the trauma of the criminal process is worse for the child" (West 1980, 33).

Ellen Dunwoody says, "The apologists for incest cast themselves in the unlikely role of protectors of the family" (1982, 2). John Leo (1981, 69) outlines the ideas of the proponents of sex between adults and children:

> According to the argument, children are sexual beings who need to develop skills early in life. . . . Wardell Pomeroy, co-author of the original Kinsey reports, says incest "can sometimes be beneficial" to children. Dutch Psychologist Frits Bernard . . . says adult-child sex is basically innocent and adds that the children he has studied "are not more neurotic than the average Dutchman." . . . Sociologist Floyd Martinson . . . thinks adults involved in affectionate sexual relationships with tots should not go to jail. "Intimate relations are important and precious," he feels. "I'd like to see as few restrictions placed on them as possible." . . . [A San Diego sex group] welcomes the new writing: "We believe children should begin sex at birth. It causes a lot of problems not to practice incest."

Leo (1981) includes names and quotations from other proponents of "children's sexual liberation" including: Mary S. Calderone, head of the Sex Information and Education Council of the United States (SIECUS), sexologist John Money of Johns Hopkins, anthropologist Richard Currier, family therapist Larry Constantine, Norwegian psychologist Thore Langfeldt, and psychologist Douglas Powell of the Harvard Health Service. Among the few opponents Leo cites are columnist Nancy Walker, child psychiatrist Leon Eisenberg, psychotherapist Sam Janus, and psychiatrist Edward Ritvo, who largely base their arguments on consequent harm for the child, rather than the benefits the others claim.

DeMott argues that research on which claims of beneficial results for children are based are scientifically suspect and conceptually flawed (1980), but Judith Herman (1981, 27) dismantles the idea that adult/child sex is consensual because of the power differential, stating:

> Because a child is powerless in relation to an adult, she is not free to refuse a sexual advance. Therefore, any sexual relationship between the two must necessarily take on some of the

coercive characteristics of a rape, even if, as is usually the case, the adult uses positive enticements rather than force to establish the relationship. (1981, 27)

David Finkelhor, in a brief but insightful article, similarly refutes the notion of consent in adult/child sex, saying, "the child not only cannot freely give consent, the child also cannot give *informed* consent" (1979b, 696). He examines other issues in the adult/child sex debate, but focuses on the inherently unequal balance of power and says:

The crucial difference in adult-child sex is the combination of children's lack of knowledge *and* lack of power. Children in relationships with adults are both uninformed and unable freely to say no. . . . This paper has argued that a stronger ethical argument exists against such behavior, involving children's incapacity to give true consent to sex with an adult. (Finkelhor 1979b, 696–97).

The debate may rage on about appropriate and inappropriate sexual behavior for children and whether or not it is harmful for children to be sexually stimulated at very young ages, but it seems that it will not be resolved until adults educate themselves about healthy sex. In the meantime, the "pro-incest lobby" demands careful watching by those who are concerned about preventing sexual abuse of children. Organized by affluent pedophiles, and dignified by the support of some high-ranking professionals, their basic purpose is to protect themselves against criminal charges of statutory rape of youngsters. Their campaign will be joined by some parents who see themselves as "enlightened," as well as some who actively engage in incest, or might consider it if it were not illegal. Most current state statutes protect minors up to the ages of 14 to 18, but one state, North Carolina, only prohibits intercourse with minors up to the age of 12 (Russell 1983, 153). Increasing pressure will be put on legislators to reduce years of protection until, if the "pro-incest lobby" is successful, the concept of statutory rape will be erased from law.

SUMMARY

This, the first of two chapters on sexual abuse in the family, focused on incest: the sexual abuse of children by adult relatives and caretakers. Cases of sexual abuse of children perpetrated by persons *outside* the family are reported at a ratio of about two to one by family members, but there are many more cases of incest that occur yet remain unreported and/or undetected. Most cases of incest are committed through coercion, seduction, or intimidation of a child by an adult s/he loves and trusts. Incestuous relationships generally begin with caressing and stroking, and sometimes fondling of the genitals. In some cases, overt force and violence does occur, as well as full sexual intercourse, but these cases are reported less frequently. One problem is defining exactly what constitutes sexual abuse, but when conceptualized as a continuum of sexual contacts that range from necessary and healthy behaviors at one end, it is easier to determine when they become exploitative. Any adult can differentiate by simply asking: "Am I doing this mainly for my own pleasure without regard for the child, and, is this something that must be kept secret?" Secrecy is a key word in incest.

When incestuous relationships occur, victims often derive short-term benefits from them which cause guilt and confusing feelings of love-hate toward the perpetrators. Relationships with their parents reveal that they often look at their fathers with mixed feelings of betrayal and pity, but they are less forgiving of themselves and their mothers, whom they often blame for not protecting them against their fathers. Some reasons for this are suggested. Incest perpetrators are most frequently father-figures and uncles. Both boys and girls are molested by family members, but girls are assaulted more frequently by family members, when they are younger, and by older men. Girls suffer more fear and shock. About one out of every six females is a victim of incest committed by a male caretaker before she reaches age 18.

Theories on incest tend to focus on sex drives and sexual motives that may or may not be repressed, but these theories usually fail to explain why women are so rarely implicated in incest. David Finkelhor (1981c) offers some social psychological factors that cause men to have sexual feelings for children. Feminist writers and researchers propose a social structural theory that focuses on patriarchal society and family relationships, wherein power vested in men and fathers contributes to abuses of women and children.

Recognition and intervention is divided into three parts. The first, on child victims, lists some factors that may indicate either incest occurring or potential, but it is particularly difficult for outsiders to recognize. Indicators may be present, but because observers subscribe to stereotypic notions of the "incestuous family," they fail to recognize them or respond inappropriately. Children are not likely to make false accusations, but when they do lie, it is usually to *protect* their abusers. Advice is available on how to interrogate and help child victims when incest is revealed. Many victims are blamed for their own victimization by their families and by society, especially if they become courtroom witnesses against the perpetrators. Children need professional assistance to overcome trauma associated both with the incest and additional problems arising from its revelation.

Many victims repressed their feelings of betrayal and reach adulthood without dealing with them. They sometimes begin to experience some long-term effects and need to carefully select a professional for individual and group therapy. A self-help group can enable them to continue their growth. Some experts recommend an important next step that a few have begun: to publicly disclose what happened to them. When they reach this point, the victims are no longer accepting the guilt, but they know that they were betrayed. In doing so, they help themselves as well as other victims and potential victims by exposing the "secret."

Because incest crosses all socioeconomic and ethnic lines, there are very few distinguishing characteristics of perpetrators: They are "ordinary guys" (Snowdon 1982). A "profile," or common characteristics of sexual abusers, based on reported cases, indicates a white male, between 35 and 39 years old, employed, middle class, with no court record. The abuser is a stern and religious man who would not allow his wife to work outside the home, and is devoted to his family with few close outside contacts. Experts are divided on whether incestuous fathers should be treated like anyone else in the criminal justice system, or whether to offer him treatment. The trend is toward diversion: compulsory therapy, treating the entire family, and reuniting them whenever possible.

A number of ideas have been offered on how incest can be prevented. Most of them involve *education:* better sex education (for parents as well as children) and training children to know their rights. One of these rights is to say "no" to adults when they do not want physical contact, and another is the right to their own bodies. Children need to be taught that *some* adults move beyond the bounds of respect and authority, and they need not comply in those cases.

Finally, the *pro-incest lobby* was discussed. Led by some articulate, affluent pedophiles who offer arguments couched in terms pleasing to intellectuals and "liberals," their organizations are actively engaged in influencing legislators to repeal statutory rape laws. Countering arguments are that there is an inherent imbalance of power in adult/child relationships that cannot be ignored, plus the fact that children are ignorant of sexuality and thus cannot give informed consent.

The next chapter examines the question of sex without consent between married people, or marital rape. Finally, the relationship of pornography to sexual assault of women and children is examined.

NOTES

1. On the other hand, Rosenfeld correctly notes that "normal" family sexuality varies by cultural background and that behavior must be modified to correspond with the

child's level of development (1977, 232).

2. The focus here is on sexual abuse of children in the family, or specifically, incest. This is to be distinguished from sexual abuse by strangers or persons who are outside the family, or at least not in a position of responsibility in the home. Pedophilia, the sexual fixation of some men on pre-pubescent children, is a phenomenon outside the parameters of interest here. As in rape, there are similarities, but there are also important differences, and this chapter focuses only on persons in positions of trust and affection within the family circle.

3. For example, when one spouse is carrying on an affair with someone else, frequently all their close friends and relatives are aware of it, with the exception of the other spouse. Others note what seems obvious: the covert touching, exchanged glances, and special courtesies that may be conducted in the presence of the unknowing spouse; people outside the triad cannot understand how these signs could be overlooked. The common saying is that the injured spouse is "always the last one to know," and for good reason. After the secret affair is revealed, he or she may mentally review the past and recall the signals that are now explained and agonize that "I should have known . . . the signs were all there . . . but I was too blind to see." The old saying, "Love is blind," means that people see that which they *wish* to see and tend to ignore or explain away that which is too painful. Florence Rush (1980a) ponders this feature of human relations, recalling how her accusations of molestation by a trusted friend of the family went ignored. Why, she wondered, was it easier for her parents to believe that she was a child who was "afraid of dentists" than to believe that their dentist friend had molested her?

4. It seems strange that whereas so many professionals have studied incest offenders, trying to determine what their motives or reasoning may be when they commit their crimes against children or theorizing what goes on in their minds, so little attention has been paid to the thought processes or cognitions of mothers who failed to recognize ongoing incestuous relationships in their own homes.

5. Many writers ignore strong evidence in some cases that the mothers could not protect themselves, any more than they could their youngsters. Middleton (1978) tells of one father whose rape of his daughters finally led to the children turning on him and murdering him. The wife was as fearful of him as the children; she had been constantly beaten and terrorized, and eventually was institutionalized. A more recent case involves an aerospace engineer who had beaten and raped his wife and children over a long time period (Maxwell and Perlman 1981). The wife and 15 children who lived in the same household might never have reported the abuse because they feared for their lives, except that he was arrested and detained on a burglary charge. Once he was in jail and they knew they were safe from retaliation, the wife and six oldest children (including two boys) told police about their lives of fear, sexual and physical violence, and complete domination. Called a "reign of terror" by police, the defendant's attorney asked for a psychiatric examination to set the stage for a defense plea of "not guilty by reason of insanity" (*Los Angeles Times* 1981). Ultimately, he stood trial; his wife, two daughters, and a son all testified against him; he was found guilty and sentenced to a 27-year prison term. All the children were removed from the household and placed in protective custody as soon as the incest was revealed in November 1981. The man's wife and mother of nine of the children was never charged with any crime (conversely, she assisted in obtaining a conviction), but her children are scattered in various institutions and foster homes, and she has not been able to secure their return to her care despite her efforts for two years. It seems that unofficially, this woman has been *found guilty* of child endangering, without legal charges, trial, or conviction.

6. Although only 4 percent of Finkelhor's female incest victims were assaulted by father-figures, he not only notes that this represents approximately three-quarters of a

million adult women in the population who have had this experience, but he also comments on the fact that two of the seven cases were with stepfathers (which amounts to 29 percent of the father/daughter category). Only 5 percent of his sample had stepfathers, which means they were greatly overrepresented and that girls with stepfathers are at greater risk of incest than girls living with their biological fathers. Finkelhor (1979a, 88) states: "this figure does confirm the widespread impression that incest with stepfathers is a particularly common form of father-daughter incest."

7. It should be noted that the California Department of Social Services (1980) report, while using the terms "parent" and "stepparent" is basically referring to male abusers, since 98 percent of the client perpetrators were male; "children" basically refers to females, since 94 percent of the child victims and 92 percent of adults molested as children were female. One hundred percent of the non-offending parents were also female. In other words, the most frequent abuser of girls was stepfathers and the next most frequent was biological fathers.

8. In combination with other changes after the onset of incest, a young girl who feels so different from others and fears others will notice her differentness, often withdraws from social activities and friendships. Thus, even more isolated than before, they sometimes occupy themselves by studying and gaining a sense of achievement by improved school grades.

9. According to some people in the New Right, victims of incest are not victims at all, because as Bonnie Sloan (1982, 5) says:

> Victims of incest will be interested to hear that, since incest is a "voluntary act" on the woman's part, abortion is not a proper remedy. This bit of creative semantics is brought to you by the *Conservative Digest,* explaining in their March 1981 issue that "if it (incest) were not voluntary, it would be rape."

10. Some sources that are available to professionals interested in helping child victims and their families reduce trauma after sexual abuse has been disclosed include the following:

Child Sexual Abuse and the Law by Lucy Berliner and associates 1981, 198 pages, $8.50; order from the American Bar Association, NCRC-CAP, 1800 M Street NW, Suite S-200, Washington, DC 20036.

Children Need Protection by the Carver County Program for Victims of Sexual Assault, 401 E. 4th Street, Chaska, MN 55318, 1980, 16 pages, $1.50.

The Child Advocacy Handbook by Happy Craven Fernandez, 1980, 165 pages, $6.95; order from the Pilgrim Press, 132 West 31st Street, New York, NY 10001.

Civil Sexual Assault Judgments and Settlements: A Summary of Cases by the Institute for the Study of Sexual Assault, 403 Ashbury Street, San Francisco, CA 94117, 1983, $35.00. This is a compendium of cases developed for attorneys that will be updated twice a year.

Directory of Services for Families Experiencing Incest by the Minnesota Department of Public Welfare, Child Sexual Abuse Treatment Project, 1981, 130 pages, $4.50 (includes shipping and handling). Specify code #1-6 when ordering from the Minnesota State Documents Center, 117 University Avenue, St. Paul, MN 55155.

Intrafamily Child Sexual Abuse Cases by the National Legal Resource Center for Child Advocacy and Protection, American Bar Association (same address as above), 1982, 57 pages, $5.00.

Sexual Violence: A Resource Manual for Clergy and Church Groups edited by Dottie Bellinger, director, Sexual Assault Crisis Aid, 14 Exchange Building, Winona, MN 55987, 1983, 74 pages, $7.00 prepaid only.

11. Although the California legislature has consistently rejected bills that would allow a videotaped interview with a sexually assaulted child to substitute for a child's court-

room testimony (Texas has passed such a law and several other states are working on one), tapes can be made and can be effective in persuading the defendant to plea bargain and plead guilty to a lesser crime to avoid trial. The main issue is in careful preparation of a case. Mead (1982) says that the vast majority of incest cases never go to trail. Most states now allow children to testify with the help of sexually explicit dolls to demonstrate what happened to them. Mead's organization, For Kids Sake, uses dolls made in both black and white by Analeka Industries, P.O. Box 141, West Linn, OR 97068 (telephone 503/655-3596). Other improvements in the California criminal justice system include the fact that child witnesses can be provided an advocate to help her or him through the system; and qualified expert witnesses can now testify their opinions about the case on the child's behalf.

12. Unfortunately, that is not the way it usually works. During a private discussion, one judge mentioned his aversion to incest cases where:

> The child is punished even more. Both parents turn against her and her siblings blame her for all their troubles. The child is removed (usually against her will) from her home and kept from her family in strange surroundings, like a prisoner. Her father, in the meantime, continues on his job in order to support the family. She must be the "bad" one, because she gets punished . . . no wonder some try to change their testimony. They can't win!

13. Another expert working on the multiple personality problem is clinical psychologist Susan Kuhner, who established the Kuhner Institute in 1980, as a research, education, and referral service. All of Kuhner's MPD patients were victims of sexual abuse. The Kuhner Institute for Multiple Personalities and Other Incest Survivors is located at 6736 Laurel Canyon Boulevard, Suite 221, North Hollywood, CA 91606 (telephone 213/851-9484).

14. Unfortunately, despite the use of the term "Daughters and Sons United" in the CSATP self-help group title, male victims of incest have difficulty finding suitable groups to join. Since the vast majority of identified victims are female, most groups are all-female, and comparable groups of all-male victims are almost nonexistant.

15. One self-help group organized by former incest victims is called "Victims of Incest Can Emerge" (VOICE); members are lobbying for stricter legislation on incest and sexual abuse and trying to forge links with other similar groups around the United States (Duty 1983). For information, contact: VOICE, Inc., P.O. Box 3724, Grand Junction, CO 81502 (telephone 303/243-3552). Another such self-help group is called "Incest Survivors Anonymous" and meets twice weekly. For information, send a stamped, self-addressed envelope to Incest Survivors Anonymous, P.O. Box 5613, Long Beach, CA 90805-0613 (Duty 1983, 2).

16. The evaluation report by the California Department of Social Services was not entirely complementary of the CSATP; criticisms in the form of recommendations were made, such as the need for a follow-up on clients who "dropped out" of the program without completing treatment, and that more emphasis and effort be expended on data collection and record keeping since, "The research and evaluations conducted on this program were curtailed by poor record keeping" (1980, 17–18). In addition, it should be noted that since 74 percent of cases in 1978–79 were intrafamilial self-referral, the low recidivism may be biased in a positive direction in that these families recognized they were dysfunctional and reached out for help (similar to the suggestion made earlier that battering husbands who were studied may be the "cream of the crop" of wife beaters).

17. Some materials that are available to help instruct parents, professionals, and little children to prevent child sexual abuse include the following for children's instruction:

What if . . . I Say No!, by Jill Haddad and Lloyd Martin, 1981, 26 pages, a coloring book, $3.50 for a single copy at M. H. Cap and Co., P.O. Box 3584, Bakersfield, CA 93385 (discounts on multi-copy orders).

The Red Flag Green Flag Sexual Abuse Prevention Program has also produced a coloring book, primarily at the third and fourth grade level, *Red Flag Green Flag,* for $4.00. Order from the Rape Abuse and Crisis Center, P.O. Box 1655, Fargo, ND 58107. There is also a program guide available for $12.00, and one-hour education videotapes that demonstrate classroom use of the coloring books for $125 (half inch), $150 (three-quarter inch).

Child Sexual Abuse Prevention Project: An Education Program for Children, by Cordelia Kent, 1979, 120 pages, $8.00. Helps children distinguish between caring and exploitative touch; was pilot-tested for two years in public schools. Order: Hennepin County Attorney's Office, Child Sexual Abuse Prevention Project, C-2100 Government Center, Minneapolis, MN 55487.

"Speak Up, Say No!"—film strip (preschool to Grade 3). *For Pete's Sake, Tell!*—filmstrip (Grades 3 to 6). Both available from Krause House, P.O. Box 880, Oregon City, OR 97045.

Carla Goes to Court, 1983, a book published by Jo Beaudry and Lynn Ketchum of the Victim/Witness Services program in Milwaukee County, Wisconsin. Tells realistic story about an 8-year-old girl witness to a burglary; traces progress through the criminal justice system. Illustrated with photographs in courthouse and district attorney's office. Available from: Human Sciences Press, New York.

For adults:

Protective Parenting: The Art of Teaching Children About Sexual Abuse, by the Minnesota Criminal Justice Program, 1982, 10 pages, single copies free (send 20 cent stamp). Order: Minnesota Criminal Justice Program, 480 Cedar, St. Paul, MN 55155. For prices on multiple copies, write Minnesota State Documents, 117 University, St. Paul, MN 55155.

We Have a Secret, by Lloyd Martin and Jill Haddad, hard bound edition, $12.50 (includes postage). For parents and professionals. Order: M. H. Cap and Co., P.O. Box 3584, Bakersfield, CA 93385.

Handbook of Clinical Intervention in Child Sexual Abuse, by Suzanne Sgroi, 1982, 398 pages, $15.95 softcover. Order: Lexington Books, D. C. Heath and Company, Lexington, MA. Recommended for professionals, but also of interest to general readers and/or parents.

18. The profusely illustrated book by Haddad and Martin (1981, 14) contains a page of faces for children to color under the heading "Who *could* be a child molester?" The male faces of those who "could be" are captioned "a religious person, a stranger, a coach, a policemen, a doctor;" plus a female "teacher;" and "mom or dad could be." The book specifically asks "what if" approaches are made by "dad's best friend," Sunday school teacher, babysitter, and aunts and uncles. It was, in fact, Martin's insistence that people realize that *anyone* can sexually assault children, including people in positions of trust, responsibility, and importance such as members of the clergy and organizations like the Boy Scouts and Big Brothers that embarrassed the police department. As a result, Martin was transferred out of the Juvenile Division's Sexually Exploited Child Unit, which he had worked for years to develop, and he subsequently retired on a disability pension. Martin and Haddad established a nonprofit organization: The Foundation for America's Sexually Exploited Children, Inc., P.O. Box 5835, Hacienda Heights, CA 91745 (telephone 213/633-5524 or 213/961-2796).

19. Summit and Kryso (1978, 251) reference this quotation to a pamphlet by the Rene Guyon Society, addressed to California legislators, and say it was "privately published: 324 So. First Street, Alhambra, CA 91802."

12

Marital Rape

As noted in the preceding chapter, sexual abuse of children and adults in the family share some commonalities, one of which is helplessness of the victims and their inability to prevent, avoid, or escape sexual exploitation by more powerful persons. Another similarity is that the sexual assault is committed by close family members, people they have loved and trusted. Whereas the child victim of sexual assault by a stranger is more likely to receive love, concern, and family support because of her ordeal than when she accuses an adult in her own family, the reaction to complaints by a wife of rape are likely to follow the same pattern. A woman raped by an acquaintance or stranger is much more likely to receive sympathy, concern, and assistance from her family and the community. The concept *rape* is defined here as unwanted sexual contact accomplished by force, intimidation, or coercion that results in vaginal, anal, or oral sexual intercourse or penetration of a woman's body with a penis and/or object/s. Research shows that the closer the prior association of rapist and victim, the more violent the assault tends to be (Black 1979; Queen's Bench Foundation 1979; Landau 1976; Russell 1975).

Characteristics of the *rape crisis syndrome* are now familiar to most professionals who come in contact with victims; thus their responses can be more appropriate and effective than before (Bard and Ellison 1974). The symptoms include humiliation, shame, disjointedness, anger, inability to concentrate or express oneself, or withdrawal. Until the mid-1970s in the United States, no woman raped by her husband could be classified a "rape victim" under the law, but the trauma suffered by these victims are at least as severe as those raped by strangers. The husband who violates his wife's body against her will is also her socially designated "protector," with whom she shares intimate sexual relations. He took an oath before witnesses to "love, honor, and cherish" her and, frequently, he is the father of her children.

> Perhaps the best known instance of marital rape occurs in the film "Gone With The Wind," when Rhett Butler, angered by his wife's rejection of him, sweeps the wildly protesting Scarlett into his arms and carries her up the stairs to their bedroom. In the next scene, the following morning, Scarlett stretches lazily amid the rumpled sheets, a look of contentment on her face. Clearly, we are to believe that the night of tempestuous romance has unlocked Scarlett's true passion for her husband.

> This scene romantically portrays one of the most pernicious myths about forced sex—that women enjoy it—and suggests that it is all right for a man to force his wife to have sex with him. These beliefs mask the brutality, anger, humiliation, and sense of betrayal that characterize real incidents of marital rape. (Mettger 1982c)

A society's norms and values are often reflected in its most popular plays and fiction. The now-classic *Gone With The Wind* is one of the biggest box-office movie attractions of all time, and one of its most unforgettable scenes occurs when Rhett determinedly advances upward on that graceful open staircase. Viewers know that impetuous, strong-willed Scarlett is going to "get what's coming to her!" and audiences cheer Rhett's masculinity. For even more years audiences cheered when Shakespeare's Kate was tamed by Petruchio in *The Taming of The Shrew*. Kate was a strong-willed woman who refused to obey her husband's commands; her spirit had to be broken so that she would make a properly dutiful wife. Petruchio accomplished this by *isolating and starving* Kate. A wife's duty was to obey her husband, and her body belonged to him.

THE HISTORICAL BACKGROUND
OF SPOUSAL IMMUNITY[1]

Traditional marriage vows call for a wife's promise to "love, honor, and obey," and the legal contract insures the husband's rights to sexual intimacy so that if a husband desires sex with his wife she has an obligation to cooperate. In most countries of the world and most states in the United States, women still cannot refuse their husbands sexual access to their bodies. Charlotte Mitra says:

Rape is an act of violence which subjects the victim to physical and emotional humiliation besides pain, fear, and not infrequently serious injury. It is recognized by the law as a crime, one of the most serious known. This same act however, if perpetrated within the marriage, is no offence and carries no sanctions; it is merely the exercise of the husband's right in pursuance of the marriage contract. (1979, 558).

A number of feminist scholars insist that rape laws were instituted to protect male privilege (Brownmiller 1976; Freeman 1981; Kurman 1980; LeGrand 1973; Mitra 1979; Russell 1975). Carol Smart (1977, 78) says, "The severe penalty for rape . . . was a punishment for the defilement of another man's property rather than a form of protection for women or a recognition of women's rights over their own bodies." If rape laws were for the protection of women, it would make no sense to make an exception for a man who rapes his wife (LeGrand 1973): "Rape is rape no matter who is the perpetrator of the crime" (Martin 1979b). But if rape laws are to protect men's property from *other* men, then they would exclude property owners with a clause defining rape as "forced sexual intercourse with a female *not the wife* of the perpetrator." They do contain such a clause. Zak Mettger says, "the law in most states protects a man from prosecution for the rape of his wife. The marital 'right' to rape one's wife is expressed in state criminal statutes . . ." (1982c, 1). What is the legal basis for this marital exemption?

The British Common Law precedent is traced to the seventeenth century Chief Justice Sir Matthew Hale. Sociologist Gilbert Geis states:

[T]he major figure in shaping this law was Sir Matthew Hale, whose dictum on the subject occupies but four lines in his encyclopedic *Historia Placitorum Coronae*, published posthumously in 1736. They read: "But the husband cannot be guilty of rape committed by himself upon his lawful wife, for by their mutual matrimonial consent and contract the wife hath given up herself in this kind unto the husband which she cannot retract." (1980, 1–2)

Geis contends that Hale was viciously misogynistic,[2] but his attitudes toward women were not singularly responsible for the spousal rape exemption, they were supported by the more general views about women's place in marriage. Another British jurist, Blackstone, had set forth the principle of matrimonial unity: in marriage, the man and woman become one (therefore how could a man rape his own body?); and there was also the principle that wives are the property of their husbands. Under common law, a wife could not refuse to have sex with her husband. An example from the relatively recent past is that by law, Winston Churchill's mother, Jennie Jerome, could not refuse to have sexual intercourse with his father, even though Lord Randolph Churchill had syphilis (Martin 1969).

Hale's brief statement and the doctrine it established, *irrevocable consent,* have no legal basis, according to legal scholars (Mettger 1982c). Although Hale offered no citations to support the rule, it was accepted because it "was congruent also with views prevailing in the social system of the time about women, about sexual assault, and about marriage" (Geis 1980, 3). Despite its flaws, it became part of American common law and "eventually was incorporated, either implicitly or explicitly, into state and federal criminal law as a 'marital exemption' which grants a husband immunity from prosecution for raping his wife" (Mettger 1982c, 2). Geis says there was "an unquestioning acceptance of the Hale dictum" in American case-law (1978a, 292).

"Baby, You Belong to Me!" or Does She?

Changes have occurred in rape laws since the 1970s, spearheaded by feminists who were joined by "law and order" groups (Russell 1982); "Conservatives support changes in evidentiary requirements for rape because they desire to see more criminals more readily convicted . . ." (Geis 1978a, 293). But conservative legislators balk at any attempt to eliminate the marital exemption clause, as expressed in these quotations cited by Joanne Schulman (1980):

> "[T]he Bible doesn't give the state permission anywhere in that Book for the state to be in your bedroom, and that is just exactly what this bill has gone to. It's meddling in your bedroom; the State of Florida, as an entity, deciding what you can do and what you can't do." (Rep. John Mica, May 29, 1980)

> "But if you can't rape your wife, who can you rape?"(California State Senator Bob Wilson, addressing a group of women lobbyists, spring 1979)

Only three states, New Jersey, Oregon, and Nebraska, had completely abolished the marital rape exemption in 1980, and it was partially stricken by five other states (Russell 1982); but by 1982 two more states, Massachusetts and Florida, had followed suit and two others joined the partial exemption[3] states. In the meantime, 13 other states *expanded* the marital privilege to include cohabiting couples (Mettger 1982c). Federal law was modernized to allow rape charges by a wife if there was a "violent" component (Geis 1980), but a proposal that would make marital rape a crime evoked this response:

> The Senate Judiciary Committee placed the provision in the bill over the strong objections of Committee member Jeremiah Denton (R-AL) and the Moral Majority, which feels it is "too hard on husbands accused of raping their wives," according to a *New York Times* article last November. Denton . . . told his fellow committee members that while he considers sexual abuse in marriage a "hideous crime," he does not believe a husband guilty of "a little coercion" should be placed in the same category as a criminal rapist. "Dammit," he declared, "when you get married you kind of expect to get a little sex." (Mettger 1982c, 2, 13)

Arguments against striking the exemption include claims that it would be difficult to enforce; it would undermine the family; victims are sufficiently provided redress under current laws; and it would lead to a virtual flood of complaints by vindictive wives. This has *not* happened in the states that have changed their laws. Oregon dropped the exemption in 1977 without such a deluge, although one, the Rideout case, did generate extensive publicity. The first trial in American history in which a man had been charged, indicted, and tried for raping his nonstranged wife opened on December 19, 1978, in Salem, Oregon. John Rideout was acquitted of raping his wife, Greta[4] (Footlick 1979; Fox 1979; *NOVA Newsletter* 1979). The first spousal rape conviction took place in Salem, Massachusetts, on September 21, 1979. In this case, Carmelina Chretien had filed for divorce in 1978 although the divorce was not yet final, and the couple had been living apart when James Chretien broke into her home (Response 1979b, 4; Time 1979a). Most cases that have been prosecuted have involved extreme violence or torture along with the rape.

Not all countries follow the Anglo-Saxon tradition. Poland has allowed husbands to be prosecuted for rape since 1932 (before the Communist takeover), as well as other Communist-bloc countries: the Soviet Union and Czechoslovakia (Geis 1980). Israel, Sweden, Norway, and Denmark also have no marital exemption. Sweden's law has stood since 1965 without doing any of the mischief opponents claim such laws will generate (Geis 1980, 6).

Why is it so important to so many people that the marital exemption by stricken from rape laws? The author attempted to answer this by noting: "As long as husbands can rape wives with impunity from the law—women do not own their own bodies" (Pagelow 1977, 24). Striking the marital *privilege to rape* will be a signal to some possessive and violent men that their wives are *not* their property; that their wives are full citizens under the law; and that men are responsible before the law for their private actions.

Del Martin (1979b), in her testimony before lawmakers considering a spousal rape bill said, "In effect existing law legalizes and condones rape in marriage." Society's values are expressed in its laws, according to Sherry Chase (1982, 22), who says: "It is no small oversight that four-fifths of this country's states have sexual assault laws which fail to criminalize rape when the man's victim is his wife. A state that fails to act in this regard gives its consent." Still, the nationwide organizing and lobbying to get the marital exemption eliminated from rape laws have helped educate the public that: "rape is not a husband's marital right; . . . women *are* raped by their husbands; that rape is a violent rather than sexual act; that it is an

It is apparent that many men still believe that their wives' bodies belong to them, and some states continue to support those ancient ideas by defining rape as "unwanted sexual intercourse with a woman not the wife of the accused" or "the forcible penetration of the body of a woman, not the wife of the perpetrator." Early marriage laws established the status of wife as property of the husband, and the fact that only recently have some states rewritten their rape laws to strike out the spousal exemption provides evidence that old ideas yield very slowly to change.

Source: Family Docudrama Series by Eileen Cowin, photographer. © Eileen Cowin. Reprinted with permission.

abhorrent act for which the state will take severe punitive measures" (Chase 1982, 21).

Extent of the Problem

Most people accept the stereotype that wife rape occurs infrequently, and then only among the lower classes by drunken, perverted husbands. Diana E. H. Russell's (1982) rigorously designed study obtained a representative sample of women who were personally interviewed in depth to determine how many had been sexually abused by strangers, family members, and husbands. Russell says:

> The study . . . is the only study of wife rape in the United States to be based on interviews with a random sample of women. *Fourteen percent (14%) of the 930 women interviewed who had ever been married had been raped by a husband or ex-husband.* . . . [I]t suggests that at least one woman out of every seven who has ever been married has been raped by a husband at least once, and sometimes many times over many years. (1982, 1–2)

Some writers speculated that more women are raped each year by husbands than by all other types of assailants, but Russell notes that answers to that depend on the way comparisons are made. When (completed) rape and attempted rape are combined, "acquaintances become the most prevalent type of rapists" (1982, 64). However, Russell points out that not all the women in her sample had been married, therefore they were not "at risk" for marital rape, but:

> If rape and attempted rape by husbands and ex-husbands were calculated as a percentage of women who had ever been married rather than as a percentage of the whole sample, then the 12 percent figure would still place rape and attempted rape by husbands right after rape and attempted rape by acquaintances. (Russell 1982, 65)

Some respondents reported single incidents while others reported multiple assaults. By using the midpoint of the number of assaults reported by each woman for each type of assailant, the *number* of incidents of rape and attempted rape is by far the highest for husbands and ex-husbands of all types of assailants (979 total number of incidents, compared to 237 incidents by acquaintances and 344 by lovers or ex-lovers) (Russell 1982, 67). Narrowing analysis to *completed* rapes only (leaving out attempted rapes), women reported more rapes by husbands and ex-husbands (almost twice as many as rapes by acquaintances), the highest number of incidents of rape, and the highest percentage of all categories (Russell 1982, 65).

It is obvious from reviewing Russell's reports (1980a, 1982) that the 14 percent of ever-married women in her representative sample is an *under-estimate* of marital rape in this country. Despite optimal interview conditions, "More women appear to have been willing to disclose violence in marriage than forced sex" (Russell 1982, 38). Some said enough to indicate they had been raped by their husbands, but refused to answer any more questions. Russell (1982, 39) comments, "it seems that honest disclosure of unwanted sexual experiences in marriage was more difficult for many women than disclosure of sexual abuse by all other categories of people, including victims of incestuous abuse."

Until Russell's study, empirical evidence of wife rape was obtained mostly through studies of women battering, but there are a few exceptions. For example, Julie Doron (1981, 4) ran a newspaper survey, asking readers to supply information on various forms of family violence, and about 7 percent said they had experienced violence or the threat of violence by spouses to force them to have sexual intercourse. Richard Gelles examined data from the 80 families he studied for family violence, and found four women who "felt they were coerced or forced into having sex" (1977, 345). Gelles says he "did not find an instance of a woman being violently forced into having sex," but one of the four women tells that her husband liked to "strike out and hit a lot," and "sometimes he took a shotgun to me" (1977, 345).

David Finkelhor and Kersti Yllo (1983) narrowed their study to marital rape, obtaining their sample through a variety of methods, but the majority of respondents were clients at a family planning clinic in New England. The women were asked, "Has your current partner (or a previous partner) ever used force or threat of force to try to have sex with you?" (Finkelhor and Yllo 1983, 122). Fifty women had consented to in-depth interviews when Yllo (1981) wrote her report. The research conducted by Finkelhor and Yllo was a singular attempt to focus on sexual assaults by husbands, and despite its methodological limitations due to sampling, it provides important data.

Russell (1980a, 9) has raised a question about marital rape, challenging the notion that it is just another form of abuse suffered by battered wives:

> [A]lthough ongoing intimate heterosexual relationships that are violent often involve both rape and beating, it is also important to recognize that the issues of wife rape and wife beating can be quite separate in many marriages, and that wife rape is not merely one more abuse suffered by the already battered woman. (1982, 21)

Tentative answers were provided by Finkelhor and Yllo (1983). Some men batter their wives but do not rape them; some rape them but do not batter them; and others do both. Yllo (1981) categorized husband rapists into three types: battering, nonbattering, and obsessive. The battering type is most common, in which the husband uses sex to humiliate and degrade his wife and to dominate her in a generally abusive relationship. Less frequent is rape in a nonviolent context, and these occur when husbands are attempting to gain a sense of control over the couple's type and frequency of intercourse. Least common are obsessive rapes, but they include sexual sadism, frequently involving anal intercourse. As Mettger (1982c, 14) says, "many men apparently consider anal sex 'the quintessential sexual act' by which to humiliate a woman."

Other empirical evidence of marital rape comes from studies of woman battering (Bowker 1983a, 1983b; Dobash and Dobash 1979; Frieze 1980; Pagelow 1980, 1981a; Shields and Hanneke 1983; Walker 1979). Lee H. Bowker (1983b) attempted to answer the question raised by Russell (1980a, 1982): Are rape and battering distinct phenomena, or is marital rape the extreme end of a continuum of violence against wives? In-depth interviews with 146 victims of marital violence revealed that 23 percent had experienced marital rape, whereas the others did not. Differences between the sexually violent and the nonsexually violent couples were the wives' higher marital dissatisfaction and the couples' value dissimilarities, but "it is not possible to specify the direction of the causal influence" (Bowker 1983b, 351). Raped wives were also more likely to divorce their husbands. On the basis of his data, Bowker concludes the following: "there is no distinct syndrome that differentiates raping marriages from nonsexual battering marriages"; helping professionals might anticipate that marital rape is a factor in the lives of some couples; "raped wives may need even more extensive support services than other battered wives"; and marital rape may damage marriages so extensively that its occurrence signifies the termination of the relationships (1983b, 351–52).

Nancy Shields and Christine Hanneke (1983) also investigated to see if marital rape is a distinct phenomenon or not. They believe that an important factor is whether or not victims perceive the act of rape as different from nonsexual acts of violence: Recognizing the violence as rape could be viewed as the "ultimate attack" (Shields and Hanneke 1983, 134). Marital rape may be more stressful than nonsexual battering because of victims' contradictory ideas about their sexual rights and obligations in marriage. On the other hand, the idea of living with a rapist may be too painful, so victims may redefine sexual aggression in nonsexual terms, as being part of the overall violence. Shields and Hanneke's sample of 92 wives of violent men, obtained through a variety of sources, reported that when they excluded the few wives whose husbands were violent only outside the family, *"46 percent of the women had experienced marital rape"* (1983, 136).

The Shields and Hanneke sample consisted of women who were raped and battered, and others who experienced nonsexual violence, but they had no comparison group of women who experienced sexual violence *alone*. When marital rape occurs in violent marriages, it seems to have a more profound negative effect on the victims' self-esteem, their attitudes toward men, and sex with their husbands (Shields and Hanneke 1983, 140). A combination of sexual and nonsexual violence seems to be at the highest level on a continuum of wife abuse, because these victims *"experienced more severe forms of nonsexual violence and stronger reactions"* (Shields and Hanneke 1983, 136). Wife rape, like rape of women not the rapists' wives, appears to be mainly an act of violence and aggression in which sex is a method used to humiliate and hurt.

The major problem in determining the extent of marital rape is in the subjective viewpoints of respondents: Many women are reluctant to describe any unwanted sexual experience with a husband or ex-husband as rape. Objectively, what occurred to them may fit any of a number of definitions of rape. Researchers may couch their questions in less threatening terms, such as "unwanted sexual experiences" (cf. Russell 1982), or "forced sex" (cf. Finkelhor and Yllo 1983, 121), rather than using the emotion-laden term "rape."

One question asked by psychologist Irene Frieze was more direct, as she explains: "After questions about violence in the marriage, the women were asked if their husbands had ever pressured them to have sexual relations and if their husbands had ever raped them" (1980, 10). Thirty-four percent of Frieze's self-selected sample of 137 battered women admitted they had been raped (1980, 15). Frieze had attempted to solicit a matched control group of 137 women for comparison purposes. However, after completing interviews, she found that 48 (35 percent) of the "controls" had also been physically assaulted by their husbands, so she designated them the "Battered-Control" group, and the balance were "Nonbattered-Controls" (Frieze 1980, 10). On the rape question, 6 percent of the battered-controls and only 1 percent of the nonbattered-controls said yes. In response to a less threatening question, "Sex is unpleasant because he forces you to have sex," 43 percent of the battered women, 13 percent of the battered-controls, and 2 percent of the nonbattered-controls agreed with the item. To an even less direct question, "He pressures you to have sex," the percentages of women who agreed were 73 percent, 60 percent, and 37 percent, respectively (Frieze 1980, Table 9).

Evidence has been growing in recent years that a great many wives are subjected to unwanted sexual contact through force, intimidation, or coercion. However, when she testified on a bill opposing the marital exemption, Del Martin (1979b) had few statistics or empirical studies available to support her argument. Martin had to rely on observations and a few cases, such as two quadriplegics, paralyzed for the rest of their lives because of marital rape:

> One wife whose refusal to have sex with her husband resulted in a karate chop that broke her neck and caused permanent injury. In the other instance the wife was beaten habitually and often forced to have sex with her husband in front of the children. (1979b, 4)

Martin cited findings from Lenore Walker's study (1979) and some preliminary findings from the Pagelow (1981a) study of woman battering.[5] The author's investigation was not designed to see if rape in marriage is a distinct phenomenon; marital rape was assumed to be one of many forms of violent attacks upon wives. It is unknown if any of these women went to shelters to escape marital rape alone, but the subject was introduced by many wives during interviews, and the survey instrument yielded data in response to an item that asked, "Were you ever sexually assaulted by him? (Forcible rape *is* an assault)" (Pagelow 1981a, 257). The question was posed in that way to first introduce the less threatening term "sexual assault," but use of the word "rape" was to insure that respondents filling out the self-administered questionnaires would have no doubts about the meaning of the question. If the answer was yes, the next question asked "about how often?"

Over one-third (37 percent), or 119 women out of the 325 who responded to this item, replied yes (it should be noted that 25 women did not answer the question). Out of the 119 women who admitted that the men who battered them had sexually assaulted them, 110 filled in the blank space, telling how many times it had occurred. Their responses are shown on Table 12–1.

Table 12–1. Number of Spousal Rapes of Survey Women

Response Category	N	Percent
Once	29	26.4
2 to 5 times	45	40.9
Many (more than 5 times)	26	23.6
Sex always on demand	10	9.1
Total	110	100.0

Source: Pagelow 1980, 5.

The table shows that almost three out of four of these women had been raped more than once; and 10 percent of them indicated that sex was always on demand; thus they felt they had no choice but to submit. Many responses were very specific, some noting 7, 13, or 17 times. In one case the woman wrote: "6 times, but the last time was the one that *did it! No more!*" Eighty percent of the women in the survey sample were married to their rapists and a marriage contract means that in the majority of states their abusers could not be arrested on rape charges and, regardless of severity of injuries from the rape or battery, they would not be prosecuted.

Many wives do not associate sexual assault with rape, regardless of whether it is accomplished with force, threat of force, or their own fears. As Russell noted, many women who were not included in her marital rape category "saw it as their 'duty' to submit to sexual intercourse with their husbands, even when they had no desire for sex or were repulsed by the idea" (1982, 58). During interviews and discussion, many of the women who indicated on the Pagelow questionnaire they had *not* been raped explained that they submitted to sexual demands in order to prevent beatings, not because they wanted sex. The subject of anal sex was mentioned several times, followed by comments like "disgusting," "painful," "unnatural," "horrible," and while some mentioned fighting to repel advances, no one mentioned rape or attempted rape. Most submitted to sex due to threats or their own fears, but one woman said she used sex to defuse a potential beating: When she saw signs of impending violence, she would quickly suggest intercourse, and if her spouse cooperated, a beating was avoided for the time being. Others who *denied* they had been raped wrote statements on the questionnaire like the following:

> No, not exactly—it wasn't part of the assault. This was our general sex life.

> I was married to a powerful politician who liked kinky sex—he forced me to masturbate while he watched.

> On a few occasions I felt afraid of a beating if I refused him.

> I gave in before it reached the rape stage.

> If he beat me at other times when I was trying to please him, I knew better than to refuse sex. (Pagelow 1980, 5)

The question of consent simply does not occur to many wives. Fear and coercion are obvious in many cases, such as one wife who said to Dobash and Dobash, "I didn't refuse him—I was too scared to refuse him . . ." (1979, 14). Another woman, married to a police officer, said she submitted to sex against her will, but did not define this as rape. She said she was terrified of having sex with her husband because:

> [H]e beat me only during intercourse. He would start choking me once he mounted me; sometimes he choked me so long I passed out. When I'd come to, he was finished. One time I know he almost killed me because my neck was terribly bruised afterward. (Pagelow 1980, 5)

During an interview, one older woman reflected society's dictum that it is the wife's responsibility to take care of her husband's needs, sexual or otherwise. She seemed to assume some of the blame for her unhappy marriage because of her inability to respond sexually to her husband. She said:

> I guess some of our problems came from the fact that I never knew much about sex, and I never enjoyed having him touch me that way. Maybe some of it came from the fact that the first time I ever had sex was when he raped me—I was so ignorant! It hurt and I hated him, and then when I got pregnant and had to be his "wife," I never could learn to feel good when he touched me.

After responding to the survey instrument, another woman asked for a personal interview. She began her account by saying:

> Perhaps our problem was due to the fact that my husband had studied for the priesthood and then quit the seminary—I don't know. At first, sex with him was great! We lived together for three years and it was fine. Then we took a trip to Las Vegas and got married. That night we attended a show where they had a contest, inviting the women in the audience to get up on the stage and do a strip act. My husband wanted *me* to get up there but I refused. We went back to our hotel but he was sulking; he left me on our wedding night and stayed out all night. After that, our sex life was awful: he either beat me first and then raped me or he would make me dress up in those terrible clothes like garter-belts and trashy things so he could make himself believe I was a whore so he could fuck me. He had to pretend I was a whore so he could hate me before he could have sex! I think I began hating him from our wedding night on.

This is one of many cases that confirms Lenore Walker's statement, "Good sex often turns into assaultive behavior after awhile . . ." (1979,

112). Other survey items asked about the frequency and quality of sexual intercourse between them and their spouses. Of the women responding to the frequency question, 181 women (59 percent) indicated that sexual relations occurred either often or very, very often, yet only 70 (23 percent) rated sex as extremely satisfying. The balance said their sex life was either about average or extremely unsatisfying. There was an open-ended question asking why they were unsatisfied, and 50 women said they did not want sex because it was forced, or their husbands were rough and/or brutal. Again, these data support Walker's conclusions when she says:

> The violence and brutality in the sexual relationship between assaultive couples seem to escalate with time. As marital rape becomes more frequent, loving, tender sex becomes more rare. When brutality is at its height in other areas of the marriage, it seems as if more coercive techniques need to be used in order for sex to happen at all. Almost all of the women in this sample report being sexually abused by their men. The concept of marital rape is not acceptable under the law in most states, although most married women could describe instances where it occurred. Most men feel that their wives' sexual availability is guaranteed by the marriage license. (1979, 126)

Walker adds that it is the same whether the couples are married to each other or not. One feature of the Pagelow data is that so many women recognized forced sexual relations with their spouses as rape, since at the time the study was conducted, the law did not acknowledge marital rape, and no legal charges could have been lodged. Others who submitted to sexual intercourse against their will out of fear of attack did not recognize that this is also classified as rape. As Gelles (1977, 339) states, "the concept of 'marital rape' is one which does not exist legally." Laws are slowly changing,[6] as noted earlier in this chapter, and will continue to change as more and more wives realize that they have rights to their own bodies, and that the marriage vows do not include an oath to submit to sexual contact whenever and however their husbands demand it.

Causes and Consequences of Marital Rape

What would cause a man to rape a woman who is his wife and (frequently) the mother of his children? The answer to that question may be indistinguishable from one asking "what would cause a man to rape *any* woman?" Zak Mettger's analysis of research reports leads to a conclusion that "marital rape, like stranger rape, is not an act of sexual desire but an expression of power and hostility" (1982c, 13). Russell (1982, 357) sees male sexual aggression both inside and outside marriage as an issue that stems from two very serious (predominantly male) problems: male violence and predatory male sexuality. Males constitute 90 percent of the perpetrators of violent crimes, and:

> Wife rape is equally a manifestation of a male sexuality which is orientated to conquest and domination, and to providing masculinity; masculinity unfortunately is defined in terms of power, superiority, competitiveness, control, and aggression. A "real man" is supposed to get what he wants, when he wants, particularly with his wife, and even more particularly, in his sexual relations with her. (Russell 1982, 357)

Russell also believes that rape laws exempting husbands from prosecution *promote* marital rape. She explains: "as the laws now stand in most states, men are taught that they can rape their wives, and women are taught that they have no right to say 'no'" (1982, 358). One researcher who has studied rapists, A. Nicholas Groth, concludes that men rape their wives to: assert power and strength, punish and degrade, prove their virility, overcome their feelings of being unloved, and set their world in order (1979, 178–79).

There is another feature of wife rape that may be equally important as it is in incest: that it is *safe* for a man to rape his wife. Psychologist Neil Malamuth has conducted a number of studies with colleagues on men's *proclivity* to rape, defined as "according to the *relative* likelihood for men to rape under various conditions . . ." (1981, 139). These studies found that *not being caught* increased college male's willingness to rape, which again increased (to 51 percent) if they were assured of *no punishment*. The significance of these findings relative to wife rape cannot be overlooked. About a third to half of all males tested indicate some interest in committing rape if they can get away with it, and there could be be no safer targets than their wives.[7]

Despite a dearth of research on marital rape, effects on victims found in various reports are remarkably consistent: Trauma is severe and long-lasting. Shields and Hanneke (1983) compared reactions of victims who were nonsexually assaulted to victims who suffered both sexual and nonsexual abuse, and found significant differences. One test found that "the more often the woman had been raped, the lower was her self-esteem, the more negative were her attitudes toward her own marriage, the more psychosomatic reactions she experienced, and the more likely she was to have attempted suicide" (Shields and Hanneke 1983, 140–41). Moreover, they found that the incidence of reactions "increase significantly during victimization and *continues to increase even after the relationship has ended"* (1983, 144, emphasis added). Bowker (1983b) found more negative attitudes toward their own marriages, and a greater likelihood for divorce among wives who suffered both types of assaults. Russell (1982, 59) found that two raped wives had been so upset at the abuse that they had attempted suicide, and several other women were afraid of being killed by their husbands, indicating long-term fears. Russell (1982, 359) points out that abundant evidence was presented showing:

> [T]he consequences of wife rape are often very severe, and that wife rape is not infrequently accompanied by life-threatening violence. In fact, wife rape appears to be the most traumatic form of rape by intimates, and many factors cause wife rape often to be more traumatic than rape by strangers and other non-intimates; for example, the sense of betrayal, the disillusionment, the fact that it frequently contaminates the entire marriage, and the additional fact that wife rape is often repeated, sometimes for years on end.

Most studies found that only a small minority of wives who had been raped were raped only once (Finkelhor and Yllo 1983; Pagelow 1980; Shields and Hanneke 1983). Also noting the betrayal of trust, the violence, and that most people believe that rape by a stranger is far more traumatic because they focus on sexual aspects of rape, Finkelhor and Yllo contend:

> It touches a woman's basic confidence in forming relationships and trusting intimates. It can leave a woman feeling much more powerless and isolated than if she were raped by a stranger. Moreover, a woman raped by her husband has to live with her rapist, not just a frightening memory of a stranger's attack. . . . Most of the women we interviewed were raped on multiple occasions. (1983, 126–27)

In the category of husbands they termed obsessive rapists, Finkelhor and Yllo note that these men were heavily involved in pornography (1983, 124). The next section examines some of the literature on pornography to see what kind of a relationship it may have to sexual violence in the family.

PORNOGRAPHY

Obsessive rapists were numerically few in Finkelhor and Yllo's study, but their behavior was bizarre and possibly life threatening. Not only were they involved in pornography, but they also "tried to get their wives to participate in making or imitating it" (1983, 124). Yllo (1981) says that sexual sadism occurred in these types of rape. In-depth interviews in the Page-low study revealed that many of the women who spoke of marital rape or sexual abuse of their children also had husbands who seemed obsessed with pornography. Two cases stand out, because they appear to have a direct connection.

One battered wife went looking for her husband on their farm and found a closed room in the barn. This is how she described her discovery:

> I was shocked, I didn't know what to make of it. It was a room with all kinds of big pictures on the walls, and crazy pieces of equipment, like whips and such. It wasn't like the rest of the barn—this was kind of like a shrine, or a temple, or something, you know? I don't remember if there were candles or not, but it had that feeling. I stood there stupefied, and when the shock got less, I started looking at those pictures. They were all—like women being bound up, whipped—with metal and chains and things, and some had men doing things to them. All of a sudden, I remembered that *he* [her husband] had tried to do some of those things to me, or tried to get me to do! There was a big dog in one, too! He must of been coming to this place to get psyched up before raping me. Then I *knew* I had to get away from him!

Another woman found a secret hiding place in their bathroom containing many books and magazines and was shocked at their contents; however, her husband discovered her there and beat her more violently than ever before. She took her four-year-old daughter to a shelter only after learning that her husband had sexually molested the child, and was convinced that the "dirty pictures" were the cause. Is there a connection, or is it circumstantial?

Defining Terms: Is Erotica—Pornography?

It is important to first clarify terms used in this discussion of pornography, because of the wide variation in what people subjectively define as "porn" or "dirty." The definition adopted here is from Russell's article on pornography and violence (1980b, 218), which reads: "By *pornography,* I mean *explicit representations of sexual behavior, verbal or pictorial, that have as a distinguishing characteristic the degrading or demeaning portrayal of human beings, especially women,*" and, it should be added, *children.* As Russell and others have noted (Bart and Jozsa 1980; Diamond 1980), many people fail to distinguish between pornography and other concepts like *erotica* and *explicit sexual materials,* and use all three interchangeably. Erotica intends to sexually excite and may be sexually explicit, but it tends to be more subtle and/or artistic and, most importantly, it is *not* degrading or demeaning. Sexually explicit contents are found in sex education materials, but they are designed to educate, not excite readers (although some may become stimulated), and unless they are sexist, they are not degrading or demeaning. If they are sexist, according to Russell (1980b, 219), they meet her definition of pornography. Unfortunately, not all researchers or politicians have been as explicit in their definitions. Another important point is that not all pornography is found in "sex shops" or hard-core pornographic materials—much of it surrounds all of us—it is pervasive in advertising, entertainment, popular songs and books, and language. It is so common that most people do not recognize it.

What Do the Experts Say?

Professor of political science Irene Diamond (1980) notes contradictory conclusions drawn by two large government-sponsored commissions, both staffed by some of the leading scientists of their time. In 1969 the President's Commission on the Causes and Prevention of Violence concluded that media violence can induce people to aggressive behavior. The following year, 1970, the President's Commission on Obscenity and Pornography, composed of 17 men and 2 women, published its report and the conclusion that exposure to pornography does not promote antisocial behavior. The commission concluded that at worst, pornography is harmless and, at best, it provides for better and increased openness in marital communication. The commission's findings have been widely hailed ever since as scientific evidence of the harmlessness of pornography (Diamond, 1980).[8]

The major focus of the commission was to determine if pornography had any ill effects on society in general, whereas our interest is in its possible effects on family life: Specifically, does pornography promote sexual abuse of wives and children in the family? However, the questions are, like the issue of rape in society and wife rape, almost inseparable. If pornography does *not* promote antiwoman attitudes, objectify females to male consumers, portray childlike innocence as "sexy," nor stimulate sexual violence in society, then it *cannot* have such effects on men *in their families.*

The research upon which the commission based its conclusions has been criticized as severely flawed, biased, and lacking many elements essential for rigorous scientific research (Bart and Jozsa 1980; Diamond 1980; Russell 1980b).[9] A common complaint is researchers' lack of conceptual clarity as noted above; the report did not use the term pornography, because commissioners felt this would indicate "subjective disapproval of the materials in question," using instead, "explicit sexual materials" (Diamond 1980, 193). Criticisms include: some findings showing negative effects were excluded; the "sex offender" groups studied contained a minority of rapists; no controlled laboratory studies were done with children and some done with adults had no control groups; biased sample selection, and so forth. It should be noted that the studies were done during a political atmosphere of sexual liberation; Irene Diamond (1980, 193) says the commission was a product of its time and "reflected both the best and worst of the liberal ideology." The current definition of obscenity was enunciated in 1973 by the Supreme Court in its decision on *Miller* versus *California*; the justices threw the decision of what is or is not obscene to "community standards" (Kaminer 1980, 243).

The theory tested in many of the commission's studies was the *catharsis* model which, when applied to pornography, "assumes that the more you see the less you do" (Bart and Jozsa 1980, 205). Assumptions at that time were that, with a flood of pornography on the market, it would serve as a *safety valve* and ultimately consumers would reach satiation. Men would not have to rape, because they could watch a woman being raped and vicariously achieve satisfaction and catharsis. However, Pauline Bart and Margaret Jozsa comment:

> [N]ew research has shown that the barriers have been pushed back each time former taboos became acceptable. Today we are faced with sadomasochism, incest, and violence in pornography rather than "mere" objectification such as is found in much of the milder pornography of the late sixties and early seventies. (1980, 208)

In addition, as the availability of pornographic materials has increased, so have violent crimes, including rape and femicide. Of the hundreds (perhaps thousands) of publications available, the three leading magazines sell in the millions. According to Russell (1982, 120), *Playboy, Penthouse,* and *Hustler* have "circulations of 5.7 million, 4.7 million, and 1.6 million, respectively," but circulation rates are tripled to determine *total* readership. Not all pornography may be blatantly violent, but as psychoanalyst Robert Stoller says, "An essential dynamic in pornography is hostility" (1975, 88). And Seymour Feshbach and Neil Malamuth state, "one exposure to violence in pornography can significantly influence erotic reactions to the portrayal of rape" (1978, 116). Malamuth (1981, 139) believes that many men possess a proclivity to rape, and although Russell's review of the research agrees, she adds that the inhibitors to rape are: one, *social control*—the possibility of being caught; two, *social norms*—socially unacceptable behavior; and three, *conscience*—viewing it as immoral and brutal (1980b, 233).

Contents of 428 "adults only" paperbacks published between 1968 and 1974 were analyzed by Don Smith, who found 4,588 sex episodes in them, 20 percent involving completed rape (cited in Bart and Jozsa 1980). Smith's review found that: the number of rapes increased in each year's publications; 6 percent involved incest; the victims' fear and terror transformed into orgasmic passion; and less than 3 percent had negative consequences while some were rewarded. Using Russell's three major inhibitors to rape, it can be seen that these kinds of portrayals serve to reduce inhibitions: *social control*—rapists do not get caught; *social norms*—normal men rape, thus it is socially acceptable; and *conscience*—women really enjoy being raped. The new research shows clearly that exposure to violent pornography increases men's proclivity to rape, but it increases even more when they believe they will not be caught or punished (Malamuth 1981). Where can rape, sadism, and incest be committed with an almost guaranteed probability of not being caught or punished? In a man's own home!

Wives Victimized by Pornography

Correctly, Russell cautions that finding an association between marital rape and pornography does not justify a conclusion that rape is *caused* by a husband's exposure to pornography, but she believes that "at minimum, it *does* have some effect" (1982, 85). Undoubtedly, many men would rape their wives, with or without the encouragement of pornography, and many other men are consumers of pornography without raping. The question is, how many men—who might not otherwise be inclined to rape—accept messages from pornographic material that women *like* to be dominated and raped, and when they feel that their old methods have not worked in the past, why not try something new? For example, in one of the few trials of a man accused of raping his wife, a newspaper item gives a prosecutor's account of the crime:

> The alleged assault, Novick said, occurred after months of intermittent and ultimately fruitless marriage counseling for what Mrs. Beglin felt was a lack of communication. . . . On the day of the alleged attack, she began looking for an apartment and told Beglin she was moving out, the prosecutor said. That night, Novick said, Mrs. Beglin was watching the Miss American beauty pageant on a television in a bedroom while Beglin was watching an X-rated movie in the family room. Beglin allegedly entered the bedroom, threw her on the bed and bound her. Beglin also ripped off her clothing and began taking nude

photos of her, Novick said. He then sexually assaulted her. . . . (Brown 1981, 6)

As noted earlier, many women in the Pagelow study mentioned that their husbands tried to get them to perform sexual acts they found objectionable; some associated these requests with pornography, others did not. An example is the wife whose husband wanted her to perform in an amateur strip contest; she made no reference to pornography *per se*. Still, their sex life deteriorated after her husband required her to wear garter belts and costumes that he brought home (some men see these items as provocative and develop a fetish for them). Many wives are totally unaware of their husbands' consumption of pornography. Millions of dollars are spent each year in "sex shops" that pander directly to consumers, and there is a growing mail order business which send materials to offices or post office boxes.[10] Many rapists are discovered by police to have pornographic materials in their possession. Commander James Bannon of the Detroit Police Department is cited by Diamond (1980, 201) as saying: "often we find that the man is trying to enact a scene in some pornographic pictures."

Once more, the leading expert on the topic of pornography and wife rape is Diana E. H. Russell, who asked respondents in her representative sample of women over 18 a direct question, *"Have you ever been upset by anyone trying to get you to do what they'd seen in pornographic pictures, movies or books?"* (1982, 84). Out of the total sample of 930, 93 women (10 percent) answered yes, but of the victims of wife rape, 24 percent said yes. Activities that the wives directly connected to their husbands' interest in pornography (books, magazines, movies, and so forth) included: sadomasochism (being tied or beaten), group sex, inserting objects (including champagne) in their vaginas, anal intercourse,[11] and oral intercourse (1982, 84–85). Of the women not married to their lovers, the activities proposed (and often acquiesced to) included (besides the above): *urolagnia* (urination in the mouth) and *bestiality* (intercourse with animals). One woman is quoted as saying:

My old man and I went to a show that had lots of tying up and anal intercourse. We came home and proceeded to make love. He went out and got two belts. He tied my feet together with one, and with the other he kinda beat me. I was in the spirit, I went along with it. But when he tried to penetrate me anally, I couldn't take it, it was too painful. I managed to convey to him verbally to quit it. He did stop, but not soon enough to suit me. (Russell 1980b, 226–27)

It seems clear that there is an association between pornography and sexual abuse of women, including wife rape, but there is no way to determine if there is a *causal* connection. Malamuth (1981) believes "average men" have a proclivity to rape under certain circumstances. In his laboratory experiments, Malamuth has used written scenarios of rape scenes, or shown R-rated films which imply that women welcome violence and rape is justified. The scenarios depict rape after rejection by a casual date, and 51 percent of male college students indicate they might be willing to rape in those circumstances. What about men who believe their wives have rejected them? Russell (1980b, 224) queries, "one wonders how much the percentage might increase if the story were about a man who forced intercourse on his wife after she had declined his sexual advances for over a week." On the other hand, what about the man whose wife is ill, absent from home, incapacitated, or too terrorized to fulfill fantasies of conquest?

Children Victimized by Pornography

Children are victims of the multibillion dollar pornography industry in three major ways: one, by its encouragement of adult consumers to view children as desirable and acceptable sex objects; two, by being used and abused as models; and three, through being "educated" into exploitative sexuality.

Addressing the latter point first, many parents who consider themselves progressive, modern, and sexually liberated see no harm in exposing their children to X- and R-rated films on home television, or leaving explicit materials around where the children will find them. Roland Summit and JoAnn Kryso identified one sexual abuse case they categorized as *Ideological Sexual Contact,* in which parents are naive about the consequences for the child:

> A mother in a parent-education class expressed concern when she encountered her five-year-old son attempting intercourse with his female playmate. A few questions from the instructor illustrated that the boy and his friend were stimulated by their habitual perusal of "Penthouse" magazine, which the parents felt should not be hidden away. . . . (1978, 241)

Florence Rush mentions a case from police files of an attempted rape by a 15-year-old boy of a 9-year-old girl. When caught, the boy admitted that he had done it before, and "He said his father kept pornographic pictures in his top dresser drawer and that each time he pored over them the urge would come over him" (Neil Gallagher, cited in Rush 1980b, 77).

Children may not try to imitate what they see, but they are not likely to forget it, either. Neil Malamuth, who teaches courses on the link between media portrayals of women and violence against women, talked about his youth to a newspaper reporter who relates: "Raised in a liberal environment where *Playboy* and *Penthouse* magazines were displayed freely in the house, 'I always though of pornography as something relatively positive,' he said" (Japenga 1984, 1). On the basis of his many studies, Malamuth concludes that humanistic sexually explicit material is harmless, but certain types of violent pornography encourages attitudes of violence against women (Japenga 1984). Another expert, A. Nicholas Groth, spoke at a conference on rape and child sexual abuse and pointed out that sadistic rapes are committed by men who fantasize that their victims will enjoy the rape and return for more, and these are the kinds that are publicized in the news and magazines. Magazines like *True Detective*, according to Groth, are "too readily available to impressionable adolescents" (Myers 1983, 16). The prevalence and approval of violence in this culture was discussed in detail in Chapter 4 so it is not repeated here, but pornography contains both sex and violence, a fusion that Seymour Feshbach (1980) has termed a "dangerous alchemy."

Another serious danger to children from pornography is their being portrayed as desirable and acceptable sex objects. These portrayals are not only found in sex shops or in hard-core printed materials, they are also found in magazines like *Bazaar*, which run an advertisement in December 1983 for Chanel No. 5 perfume. A full-page color illustration contains a close-up photograph of an approximately three- to four-year-old girl, wearing obviously adult eye and lip makeup and nothing else. Her blond curls flow around her head and down the length of her arm, her head is tilted, and she wears a provocative expression. Her bare torso is shown to just below her nipple.[12]

Men's fashion magazines carried an advertisement of Fabio Inghirami Italian shirts: A blond haired adult male models a shirt, standing with his fists clenched on both hips in a masculine pose with an expression of readiness on his face. Just behind the man's bent arm stands a full figure of a little girl of about three years, with long, blonde hair and a serious expression on her face; she appears to also have her hands on her hips. All parts of her body that are visible from behind the man's arm are nude. Why is the child in that picture? Why is she nude?[13]

The author of a book on child sexual abuse and former social worker, Florence Rush, also wrote on child pornography (1980a, 1980b). Rush strongly condemns the Commission on Obscenity and Pornography for its refusal to consider pedophilia as a problem connected with pornography, and the report's claim that children were almost never used in pornography (1980b, 79). She believes that men are sexually attracted to and prefer childlike helplessness and says, "Today our society either makes the child look like a woman or the woman look like a child" (Rush 1980b, 71). Rush (1980b, 79) contends:

> I never even found it necessary to browse in Forty-second Street sex shops for my research. From San Francisco to New York, in every airport, train, and bus station, the most respectable bookstores and newsstands carry such titles as *Uncle Jack and Little Paula, The Child Psychiatrist, Lust for Little Girls, Adults Balling Children,* ad nauseam. With little difficulty one can easily obtain *Lollitots,* which introduces Patti, "the most exotic ten-year-old you'll ever meet," or *Little Girls,* which offers pictures of ten- and twelve-year-olds in intercourse with adult males. For forty-five dollars one can purchase a film in living color and see a nine-year-old getting fucked by two Arab boys, then by an adult.

Adults often use legally purchased books and films to break down children's inhibitions against participating in pornographic modeling or sexual activities with adults for prostitution. Sheriff's investigator Jim Ohr (1983) says that a relatively expensive "sex education" book, *Show Me!* which is profusely illustrated with explicit photographs of naked adult men and women, boys and girls, separately and together, is one such favorite; but there has also been a sharp upswing in videotapes lately. During a lecture, Ohr displayed confiscated copies of magazines illegal in California, showing children engaging in various sex acts with each other and with adults. Included was urolagnia (adults urinating into children's mouth's); Ohr says there is a large pedophile organization called the *Golden Rain Society,* made up of mostly upper middle-class males. "Child pornography is very big business," says Laura Lederer in her introduction to Rush's article, and she continues:

> [C]hild models are not difficult to recruit: Many magazine publishers and film producers use their own children; others advertise to parents. A recent advertisement in Al Goldstein's magazine *Screw* offered $200 for young girl-child models. . . . A writer who followed up the ad reports: "Some parents appeared in the movie with their children; others merely allowed their children to have sex. One little girl, age 11, who ran crying from the bedroom after being told to have sex with a man of 40 protested, 'Mommy, I can't do it.' 'You have to do it,' her mother answered. 'We need the money.' And of course the little girl did." (Robert Anson, cited in Lederer 1980, 71)

Judianne Densen-Gerber (1980) agrees that producers of "kiddie porn" or "chicken porn" have no difficulty obtaining youngsters: They use their own, buy the children of others, or pick up runaways. Densen-Gerber says that in 1977, at least 264 different sex magazines featuring children were produced in American each month, selling for an average $7.00 each at bookstores across the country (1980, 79). About New York's Times Square adult book stores, she says:

> Also available is a film depicting female children violently de-flowered on their communion day at the feet of a "freshly cru-cified" priest replacing Jesus on the cross. Another film shows an alleged father engaged in urolagnia with his four-year-old daughter. Of sixty-four films previewed, nineteen showed chil-dren, and an additional sixteen involved incest. (Densen-Ger-ber 1980, 79)

It seems clear that children are victimized by pornography in many ways: One of the most important is that they are *set up* for sexual assault by family members as well as persons outside the home. Children directly involved in the industry itself are sexually exploited and abused for the profit and pleasure of others, including their own parents. And by viewing pornographic materials when they are young, impressionable, and sex-ually ignorant, they are given messages that sexual activities are exploita-tive and violent, and that it is "normal" for men to be aggressive predators and women to be willing victims. What can or should be done about pornography?

Protection from Pornography

Once they recognize pornography's pernicious effects on the lives of all citizens, but especially young children, some people react immediately with demands for censorship. Others want new regulations and stricter enforcement of current laws. Still others believe that there are ways that are more effective in the American free-enterprise system. The issues can-not be discussed in their entirety here, but a combination of the latter two is most likely to receive popular support. The moment censorship is men-tioned in the United States, most citizens are likely to cite the First Amend-ment and its guarantee of free speech. However, other countries have decided, on the basis of the evidence, to censor. For example, the Board of Censorship in England cut four minutes of Charles Bronson's film, *Death Wish II*, which shows a maid being raped at knifepoint (Japenga 1984). Ann Japenga says that Neil Malamuth's research was also instru-mental in censorship of films in New Zealand, but the researcher is quoted as saying, "'In some ways it (the censorship) was gratifying,' Malamuth said, 'but the whole issue of censorship raises questions for me'" (1984, 1).

These are serious questions that are not easily answered. If liberals were to adopt such a position, it would "throw them into bed" with conservatives, who staunchly advocate censorship of books and any materials that are counter to their viewpoint. Conservatives oppose sex education and support what liberals call "repressive" sexuality, and "pornography's depictions of sexual relations represent the flip side of repressive morality" (Ratterman 1982, 47). Feminists, who view themselves as civil rights advocates, are divided on the issue. Andrea Dworkin (1980) and Susan Brownmiller (1980) take a pro-censorship viewpoint. Brownmiller quotes Chief Justice Warren Burger's comment on the 1973 *Miller* versus *California* case:

> To equate the free and robust exchange of ideas and political debate with commercial exploitation of obscene material demeans the grand conception of the First Amendment and its high purposes in the historic struggle for freedom. It is a misuse of the great guarantees of free speech and free press. (Justice Burger, cited in Brownmiller 1980, 253)

Dissenting Justice William O. Douglas claimed that no one is compelled to look at objectionable material, but Brownmiller (1980, 254) says that looking is unavoidable—at newsstands, on billboards, and in the media—we involuntarily see women's bodies dehumanized, chopped-up, and packaged like pieces of meat at the market.

Attorney Robin Yeamans (1980, 249) argues that the legal battle to censor pornography must be based on the "intimate connection between violence and pornography," and that pornography contains an implicit (rather than explicit) effect of soliciting men to commit crimes of violence. The United States already has laws restricting free speech (such as libel and certain advertising) and, "Speech soliciting people to commit crimes is not permitted" (Yeamans 1980, 250). Decisions are determined in large part by the political climate, and to support her stance Yeamans cites the 1896 and the 1954 decisions on a "separate but equal" education for blacks. As she correctly notes, in 1954 the Supreme Court "did not require *evidence* that segregation hurts. They just said segregation is *inherently* unequal" (Yeamans 1980, 250).

Most prefer to avoid asking for government control. One feminist asks, "The Right is all for banning ideas. Does anyone really believe that we could safely stop at violent pornography once we let the government start banning?" (Lippitt 1980, 4). Another asks, "Can this tool be used against us?" (Hunter 1980). Attorney Wendy Kaminer discusses the pros and cons of censorship of pornography and explains that "Only the government, by definition, can violate a First Amendment right" (1980, 242). She urges instead that people opposed to pornography coalesce into an *antidefamation movement*, educate the public, raise peoples' consciousness, and develop private strategies, saying "we cannot ask the government to speak for us" (Kaminer 1980, 247). Feminists generally favor organizing pressure groups for protests, demonstrations, boycotts, and letter-writing campaigns. Law professor Edward Shaughnessy (1980) says that pornography can be controlled by treating it as a *public nuisance*. Jurists who now must decide on the vague concept *obscenity* not meeting "community standards" would likely have far less trouble defining pornography that the public is unwillingly exposed to as a nuisance.

Columnist Ellen Goodman (1984) discusses an ordinance that may become law in Minneapolis. Authored by law professor Catherine MacKinnon and Andrea Dworkin, the bill attacks pornography on the basis of sex discrimination, saying that it creates and maintains inequality of the sexes and that all women are injured by pornography. Goodman's thoughtful argument concludes that even though the bill was carefully written to avoid problems of banning and prior restraint, its claims are too broad and "it seems destined to lead to censorship." But note how Goodman begins her article:

> Just a couple of months before the pool-table gang rape in New Bedford, Mass., Hustler magazine printed a photo feature that reads like a blueprint for the actual crime. There was a difference between Hustler and real life. In Hustler the woman enjoyed it. In real life the woman charged rape. There is no evidence that the four men charged with this crime had actually read the magazine. Nor is there evidence that the spectators who yelled encouragement for two hours had held previous ringside seats at pornographic events. But there is a growing sense that the violent pornography being peddled in this country helps to create an atmosphere in which such events occur. (1984, 11)

Public opinion polls in 1980 reveal that 54 percent of Americans believe that pornographic materials lead people to commit rape (Flanagan and McLeod 1983).

Regarding child pornography, Judianne Densen-Gerber, attorney and physician who founded Oddessy Institute in New York City, demands some new laws and enforcement of existing ones (1980, 77–81). She notes that one convicted major wholesaler of pornographic materials could have been sentenced to seven years but instead got six months' time, served on weekends. Laws are inconsistent and they usually focus on distribution of obscene *materials*. "In early 1977, only six states . . . specifically prohibited the *participation* of minors in an obscene performance that could be harmful to them" (Densen-Gerber 1980, 80). In abbreviated form, Densen-Gerber's recommendations include:

> Amend child abuse and neglect statutes to include commercial sexual exploitation and prescribe harsh penalties for offenders.
>
> Amend civil codes for licensing of all children in commercial modeling with carefully worded proscriptions and substantial sanctions against the use of children in sexually explicit activities.
>
> Extend criminal liability to include promoters and distributors of child pornography.
>
> Develop intervention and treatment programs for victimized children.

There are no easy answers, and the issues are complex. On the one hand, there is danger in ignoring the trend toward the increasingly violent and sexually explicit, and the phenomenal growth of child pornography. On the other hand, there is freedom of speech and a multibillion dollar industry that will fight every inch of the way against control. Kaminer states, "The Women's Movement is a civil rights movement, and we should appreciate the importance of individual freedom of choice and the danger of turning popular sentiment into law in areas affecting individual privacy" (1980, 247).

But what about children, who have no individual freedom of choice? People who choose freedom of choice over censorship and do not use the courts to control pornography may not notice the activities of peodophile organizations that are working very hard to change laws in their favor, by removing restrictions on sex with minors. Laws setting the age of consent at higher levels have only existed for a relatively short time, and Rush reminds readers:

> In 1962 the American Law Institute recommended that the legal age of consent to sex . . . be uniformly dropped to age ten. And until recently, the legal age of consent in the state of Delaware was seven; if a man of forty had sex with a child of seven or over, he did so legally. (1980b, 72)

Complacent citizens may unwittingly allow pedophiles to use the law to their benefit. While their rhetoric claims they favor the rights of children to enjoy sex, the fact is that their interest is in their being able to enjoy sex with children, legally. The solution is probably to avoid censorship whenever possible; change laws where necessary; enforce laws already in effect; exert pressure on the media; and work very hard to educate and sensitize people to the serious problems inflicted upon society by pornography run wild and constantly looking for more shocking, titillating, and profitable scenarios to offer to a sexually repressed and ignorant society. Children well educated in sex and sexuality are unlikely customers for pornography as future adults.

SUMMARY

This chapter competed Part VII of the book dealing with sexual abuse in the family. Sharing many common features, incest and the pro-incest lobby was discussed in Chapter 11, and this chapter concentrated on marital rape and the association between pornography and sexual abuse in the family. Relatively little research has been done on marital rape. An important reason for this is because until very recently a spouse was immune from criminal charges of rape; therefore, in a legal sense at least, marital rape did not exist. In most states today a husband cannot be charged with rape; in some states there are partial exemptions and, in others, rape can only be charged when one spouse has filed for divorce and husband and wife are living separately.

The first section covered the history of the marital exemption, which came to the United States from English Common Law, traced back to a dictum of Chief Justice Hale, who made his pronouncement without citing legal precedent. His ideas were readily accepted because they reflected legal scholars' ideas of marriage, as stated earlier by Blackstone, who decreed that in marriage the two became one, and that one was the husband. A husband owned his wife's body as he owned his own; therefore he could not rape himself.

The marital rape exemption was challenged and laws began to be amended in various states in the mid-1970s. Most opponents voiced the belief that to change from tradition would introduce laws that are difficult to enforce and would undermine the family, that wives were sufficiently protected under the assault and battery laws, and that the courts would be flooded with frivolous complaints from vengeful wives. Evidence from the few states that have eliminated spousal exemption and other countries that do not protect husbands do *not* bear out these claims. Relatively few cases have come to court and they usually involved very unstable marriages, couples separated or with divorce decrees pending, and involving extreme violence, torture, and/or kidnapping. Proponents of new laws striking the marital exemption believe the major benefit is in their symbolic worth: They signify that husbands do *not* own their wives' bodies and that *rape is rape*, regardless of who the perpetrator may be and regardless of the relationship between rapist and victim.

Determining the extent of the problem of marital rape is impossible, because many wives still see sexual intercourse as a duty, and even if sex is forced on them, they do not define it as rape. They may submit to sexual activities even when they do not want them out of fear, coercion, or threat of physical harm. The only study of rape employing a representative sample (Russell 1982) found that 14 percent of the women who had ever been married admitted they had been raped by a husband or ex-husband; this generalizes to one out of every seven married women. Studies of battered women found high rates of marital rape, ranging from 23 percent (Bowker 1983a) to 46 percent (Shields and Hanneke 1983). Most raped wives were raped more than once. Some men force sex on their wives but do not beat them, but because the rates among battered wives are so high, it indicates that wife beaters use forced sex in addition to other forms of physical assault.

Why men rape their wives seems to be inseparable from the question of why men rape outside of marriage: Marital rape occurs because of male sexual aggression that has less to do with sexual desire and more to do with power and hostility. Russell (1982) believes that rape stems from male violence and predatory male sexuality, and Malamuth (1981) believes that the average man may rape when he believes that he will not get caught or punished for his crime. Married men can hardly find better targets on whom to express power and hostility without fear of punishment. Raped wives suffer trauma similar to that of women raped outside the home, only as Finkelhor and Yllo (1983) note, they must continue to live with their rapists. As in other rapes, some effects are short term and others last long after the relationships cease.

The Commission on Obscenity and Pornography submitted its report in 1970, and its findings, coming during a period of sexual liberation, were widely accepted as proof that pornography is harmless or even beneficial. The report, and the studies upon which it was based, has come under intense criticism. The report marked the beginning of the growth of a multibillion dollar industry that has become increasingly more violent and explicit. As barriers were removed, there followed a phenomenal growth in child pornography.

Many husbands attempt to act out their sexual fantasies portrayed in pornography with their wives. Some wives are unaware of their husbands' interest in pornography, but Russell's study (1982) found that 24 percent of the raped wives directly associated their husbands' demands to their involvement in pornography. Children are victimized by pornography in three basic ways: by being portrayed as desirable and acceptable sex objects, by serving as models in the industry, and by learning inappropriate sexuality. Parents may inadvertently introduce their children into exploitative sex by exposing them to materials that teach unintended lessons. The sexualization of little children is not restricted to sex shops and hardcore materials; it is pervasive in high-fashion advertising. As Rush says, "our society makes the child look like a woman or the woman look like a child" (1980b, 71). Children are used and abused by pornography and by their parents.

How can concerned citizens protect themselves from pornography? Some of the best minds of this century have grappled with the question of protection from pornography, but no one seems to have found *the* answer yet. Some opt for outright control through censorship. Others demand more specific laws and stronger enforcement of present laws. A few want to try to control pornography by making it a less lucrative industry. Like so many others discussed in this book, the issue of pornography is complex and will not yield to simple solutions. As long as there is a purchasing public that wants to buy pornography's products, they will be made available, whether they are legal or not. If there are no profits, pornographers will go out of business. The question is, how can consumers be dissuaded from purchasing?

NOTES

1. The terms *spousal immunity* and *marital exemption* are commonly used to refer to the fact that these laws are not gender-specific—to convey the notion that they do not discriminate on the basis of sex. It implies that wives are equally immune from prosecution for raping their husbands, since the marriage contract binds both to sexual intimacy. Thus, in a legal sense, both husband and wives have a "duty" to have sexual relations with each other; the reality is that wives are much more likely to be forced to submit (Gillespie 1971). The terms *marital rape* and *spousal rape* are commonly used for political purposes to infer that new legislation would not only protect wives, but would allow husbands to charge their wives with rape (Russell 1982, 9). As used herein, the spouse who is immune from prosecution and the spouse who rapes refers to the husband; marital and spousal rape refers to wives raped by husbands.

2. According to Geis, Hale's writings about rape were hostile to the interests of the female victim of rape. Hale was the originator of the doctrine that rape is an easy charge to make but a difficult one to rebut, which became cautionary instructions that judges traditionally have given to juries; and he was instrumental in overriding empirical evidence and convinced a jury to convict two women to hang for witchcraft (1978a, 1978b).

3. Partial exemption refers to any deviations from the general rape laws, specifying different conditions from those that would merit prosecution if perpetrated by strangers. For example, in California, the Mori Bill, AB546, was hotly debated and subjected to amendments, but was finally passed and received Governor Jerry Brown's signature on September 22, 1979, becoming effective on January 1, 1980. Unlike stranger-rapes, special provisions in the spouse rape law included a time limitation for filing charges (30 days); defendants found guilty would not be required to register with their local police depart-

ments as convicted sex offenders; and the following special circumstances do not apply to husbands: when the victim is under the influence of "any intoxicating, narcotic, or anesthetic substance administered by or with the privity of the accused" or "where a person is at the time unconscious of the nature of the act, and this is known to the accused." A "lunacy" provision also applies in nonmarital rape but is not included in marital circumstances. Thus, a wife who is most defenseless to sexual attack—someone with diminished capacity to resist or refuse—is not protected by the new law. In addition, there is a built-in avenue of defense for husbands who rape drugged or intoxicated wives (or who claim their wives were drunk at the time).

4. The Rideout case attracted extensive media publicity, and shortly afterward the story that the Rideouts had reconciled also hit the headlines. As the NOVA Newsletter (1979) stated, the reconciliation called into question the credibility of the plaintiff and raised a considerable amount of criticism, some calling it a travesty and a sham. However, Laura X, who followed the case intently, noted that after her defeat in court, Greta believed she had few options except to reunite with her husband, but the abuse became so severe that she had to run away, and was still in hiding two years later. However, this development was not reported by the media. Laura X established the Women's History Research Center, which is also a clearinghouse on a marital rape. The center is located at 2325 Oak Street, Berkeley, California 94708 (telephone 415/548-1770).

5. Much of the material on the writer's study in this section on marital rape is from an earlier paper on the relationship between the law and violence against women in the home (Pagelow 1980).

6. For a review of "State-by-State Information on Marital Rape Exemption Laws," see Appendix II in Russell's book *Rape in Marriage* (1982). For most recent changes or to subscribe to their newsletter, contact the National Center on Women and Family Law, 799 Broadway, Room #402, New York, NY 10003 (telephone 212/674-8200). For insight into cases of marital rape that have been brought to court since some laws have been changed, see also Russell's book, Appendix I (1982, 362–74).

7. Some men may even practice their rape skills at home. Finkelhor and Yllo (1983, 124–25) present a case history of an "obsessive" wife-rapist whose wife found a file card on which her husband recorded the various types of attacks, their dates, and a ranking of how much he enjoyed each.

8. One member of the President's Commission on Obscenity and Pornography, sociologist Marvin Wolfgang (Time 1979b) appears to have changed his position on the effects of pornography; he indicated publicly that evidence suggests that exposure to the portrayal of violence encourages the use of physical aggression.

9. For an excellent overview and critiques of the studies upon which the President's Commission on Obscenity and Pornography based its conclusions, see *Take Back the Night: Women on Pornography* (1980), edited by Laura Lederer. Articles by Irene Diamond, Pauline B. Bart and Margaret Jozsa, and Diana E. H. Russell specifically address the report.

10. It would be advisable for anyone reading this material to make the effort to go personally to "sex shops" and view the array of merchandise on display there. Groups are best, and a guided tour is even better. All larger cities have at least one area of town with a section containing these places of business. In many cities, tours are conducted by groups. On the East Coast, contact Women Against Pornography, 358 W. 47th Street, New York, NY 10036 (telephone 212/307-5055). On the West Coast, contact Women Against Violence in Pornography and Media, P.O. Box 14635, San Francisco, CA 94114 (telephone 415/552-2709), or Women Against Violence against Women, 543 N. Fairfax Avenue, Los Angeles, CA 90036 (telephone 213/658-8350). These people will tell you how you may contact a group in your area.

11. The author is not an expert on pornography, having viewed very little of the massive amounts available, but the subject of anal intercourse is frequently mentioned in the scientific literature. Since studies have been done on almost every conceivable subject, including masturbation, barriers may have been penetrated sufficiently so that, in light of pornography's seeming fixation on anal intercourse, perhaps the time is right to conduct an investigation of women's response to it. A review of hard-core pornography like *Hustler*, which concentrates heavily on anal intercourse and feces, indicates that some men seem to feel that this type of activity is the ultimate in sexual pleasure. What do most women feel about it? Do any women achieve sexual satisfaction in anal intercourse (in light of what we know about sexual stimulation of women)?

12. It should be pointed out that *nothing* in expensive advertisement is left to chance. Everything in the finished product is carefully and meticulously planned in advance, and symbolism is extensive. Including that child's nipple just at the very bottom of the borderless ad was no oversight. One writer who tells about his experiences when working in a "porno factory" says that his guidelines were to emphasize the innocence of children and "emphasize hairlessness—tiny privates, lack of tits" (Sproat 1974).

13. Another full-page advertisement is very suggestive. It is in the first page of the hotel/motel guest books that are left in each room. In the Los Angeles area, hotel guests in 1983 saw an advertisement from a Beverly Hills men's shop, Bijan, containing six different photographs. One is a nude torso of a reclining adult female, one man's shoe perched atop the knee of her bent right leg, the other shoe leaning against her left leg, close to her crotch. Another picture is of a smiling adult male fully dressed in a white suit, surrounded by four little children, clothed only in what looks like pink towels tied around their midriffs. Another shows the same smiling, white-suited man perched in a convertible Rolls Royce, with three white-garmented smiling nuns immediately behind him. Finally, another picture is an extreme close-up of a furry animal, possibly a puppy, sleeping on satin cloth. Interpretation of the symbolism is best left to readers.

PART VII

The Violent Family—
Present and Future

13

The Family in Turmoil and Pain:
Is it Hopeless?

It has probably been difficult for most people to read this book because of the sensitive and discomforting topics it discussed and because of some strong emotions it aroused. Emotions may have ranged from pity for victims, anger at abusers, horror at some acts that are committed, to outrage that more is not done to prevent abuses in the family. The chapter title asks, is it hopeless? If the author believed that it is, this book would not have been written. An underlying hope is that readers, armed with new knowledge, will find and use a variety of ways to prevent some violence among family members and in society, and to help victims of past abuses. There are many more victims of family violence that never reveal what is happening, or did happen to them, than are reported or come to the attention of persons in the helping professions. By now readers may have greater sensitivity to subtle "signals" and be able to respond in more effective and appropriate ways.

This chapter is divided into three major sections: intervention strategies; long-range prevention strategies; and suggestions on what individuals can do to reduce societal and intrafamilial violence. It is hoped that readers will develop their own ideas and methods for reducing violence beyond those contained here. As noted in the beginning of this book: people create a society, and therefore people can change it.

INTERVENTION STRATEGIES

This book began by addressing the issue of family privacy and the reluctance of outsiders, including the state, to intervene in family affairs. Some feel that the state has gone too far and frequently acts inappropriately, while others call for more intervention to protect the rights of helpless individuals in the family. Generally, people who object to excessive government intervention complain about charges of child neglect because of subjective biases of the labelers and their inability to understand cultural, ethnic, and social class differences. Persons who call for even more intervention are in the majority: Far more writers accept the idea that it is not only proper for the state and its institutions to intervene, but that it is an almost inescapable necessity. Their major differences concern how, when, where, and by whom such intervention should be conducted.

It seems clear that the family cannot be considered impregnable to outside intervention, and the ideas of the "sacredness" of the family and "a man's home is his castle" are archaic notions originally established to protect the privacy of the most powerful family members. The family is an institution that performs a vital function for any society, but laws that govern social interaction in the larger society should also apply within the family. American citizens have a constitutional right of life, liberty, and the pursuit of happiness, and protection from those who would deny them these rights. Within the family, more powerful members frequently abuse the rights of the less powerful and the state has a moral, legal, and ethical obligation to stop such abuses not only for individuals but for the benefit of society as a whole.

Writers who recommend intervention techniques[1] generally approach a specific type of abuse. Below are some suggestions by social scientists according to the categories of abuse they address.

Child Abuse and Neglect

Intervention strategies suggested for preventing, identifying, and treating child abuse and neglect are far-ranging, and their modalities are presented in detail in many government, commercial, and scientific books, articles, and pamphlets which are available to readers. Exactly how the various approaches are conducted are beyond the scope of this book. Only a few writers develop a single strategy; most offer several models of intervention.

There are mandatory reporting laws in all states, but investigating suspicions is the responsibility of various professionals. If investigation indicates imminent danger to a child's life or health, the child is removed from the home and placed in protective custody. When that happens, most interest centers on the child's welfare; very little is done for or with perpetrators, except for punishment in extreme cases. Unfortunately, when the child is returned home, nothing has changed and maltreatment is likely to recur. More effort should be directed toward abusive families, whether or not a maltreated child is in their care, both to protect the child's siblings, and to adequately strengthen the family for reunification, which is the official goal of most agencies. Multidisciplinary teams are highly recommended by many specialists, to work with victims and their families, whether in hospitals, the community, or particular agencies. Child abuse registries are established in many areas, and efforts are being made for communication and coordination between various agencies. Paraprofessionals are effective in direct services to victims when they are in foster homes or day-care programs.

Education is highly recommended, both awareness training for school personnel for identification purposes and parenting training for everyone, but especially for parents of maltreated children. Home visits by social workers and nurses should be increased, and paraprofessionals can fill the role of parent-aides, who offer "on-the-job training" to suspected or convicted abusers. The self-help group, Parents Anonymous, has proved highly effective in educating parents who have maltreated their children or fear they will.

Because they view the "state of the art" of theory development, theory testing, and research methods as relatively primitive, some authors are highly critical of most intervention strategies employed to date and call for more and better research, as summarized in this statement:

> Clinical approaches to child abuse remain constrained by an inadequate foundation of theory and knowledge. Advances in research are not yet assembled into a set of useful guideposts for practice and policy. Well-conceived, controlled, and longitudinal studies hold great promise for prevention and treatment of child abuse. (Newberger and Newberger 1981, 13)

Researchers also express concern that most intervention models focus on the individual level, which are hardly more than "band-aids" to attend to gaping wounds, when truly effective intervention methods must be applied at the societal level. Others are concerned that improperly informed social policy does more harm than good, particularly for children, for example:

> When abuse is conceptualized as an illness, policy is shaped accordingly. One component of this policy is the removing of children who are abused from their parents. Although this type of intervention effectively prevents further abuse, associated with it are negative side effects. . . . Because of the harmful consequences that the illness model poses, I would recommend that it be set aside and that participants be cautioned about the validity and reliability of current child abuse re-

search. . . . More research is necessary into the causes of child abuse. (Turbett 1979, 211–12)

In the early years, intervention focused entirely on individuals: victims and their abusers. As more studies were done, despite their limitations, it became obvious that child-abusing families are multiproblem and highly dysfunctional, and intervention programs now usually take a wider approach. Individual psychotherapy is still widely used, however, but some within the profession suggest that therapists may exacerbate the situation, since most are disinclined to focus on external realities. One psychiatrist claims: "psychiatric intervention may only serve to fix that blame within him [the patient]. Being a patient implies that there is a defect within the person which can be repaired by a professional" (Dumont 1977, 32).

Another ongoing debate revolves around when, and for how long, maltreated children should be placed in foster or group homes. Despite different viewpoints, change is occurring because intervention programs are increasingly adopting the multidisciplinary team approach. This is the most effective way of dealing with the complicated problem of child maltreatment.

Spouse Abuse

There are many recommendations for intervention on behalf of wife victims. One of the most commonly recommended and effective is the establishment and maintenance of shelters for battered women and their children so they have a safe haven in which to: avoid the violence, assess their past and plan their future, and contact community services to explore their options. Experts believe that victims need outside assistance in stopping the abuse, and since direct confrontation can accelerate it, battered wives need safety while they decide what to do to prevent further violence. Shelters offer many other benefits to battered wives besides protection. Depending on the particular shelter, it may provide assertion and/or parenting training; pre-employment, psychological, and legal counseling; assistance in locating housing and obtaining public assistance; and self-help groups. Shelters also provide counseling and services for children who accompany their mothers.

Writers often focus on what practitioners in their specific professional fields, such as social workers and nurses, can do to identify and help battered women. Lawyers and criminal justice officials recommend legal remedies: new and improved laws or more stringent enforcement of existing laws. Some psychiatrists advise psychotherapy for victims, an idea that is denounced by others who believe abusers are the ones needing treatment. Some say intervention strategies that focus on merely the physical assaults or psychopathology may actually exacerbate the problem to "virtually insure [that] women will be abused in systematic and arbitrary ways" (Stark et al. 1979, 461).

Proposals for intervention with men who batter are less common, but a few models for batterers include assertion training, helping men learn to deal with their feelings, and improve communications. Most groups offering programs for violent men coordinate services with battered women's groups; a few organizations have programs for both husbands and wives. Less emphasis is put on reunification because most experts believe victims should exercise their own choice, after being introduced to options. People working with battering men usually focus on helping them deal with their problems so they will be nonviolent in their future (or when mutually desired, their current) relationships.

An ongoing debate revolves around whether or not to impose mandatory reporting and if battery cases should be prosecuted even without cooperation from victims.

Sexual Abuse of Children

Intervention techniques in cases of sexual abuse of children usually include counseling, psychotherapy or treatment programs for victims, abuser and the entire family, generally following the CSATP model in San Jose, California. The underlying goal of CSATP is reunification of the family whenever possible, and it relies on diversion from the criminal justice system to provide incentives and pressure for those who sexually abuse children. This program developed self-help groups, Parents United and Daughters United, similar to Parents Anonymous and Alcoholics Anonymous.

Other programs, such as SAC at Harborview Medical Center in Seattle, Washington, focus primarily on victims. Most experts believe that offenders require legal intervention and others point out that not all sexual offenders are amenable to psychotherapy. Those who oppose using the full force of the law refer to further trauma inflicted on victims; however, others note that proportionately few cases reach the courtroom, if they are handled properly. A few cases necessarily go to court, but there are many ways the process can be modified to prevent further trauma to young victims. Some changes have been instituted and improvements are likely to continue.

Some writers focus on detection and substantiation of evidence, explaining how physicians should conduct necessary medical examinations in ways to reduce fear, pain, and trauma for victims. Others have the same goal when they explain the best methods for both professionals and nonprofessionals to use in interviewing children. Advice ranges from basic ideas (like being sure not to react emotionally to what the child says, even by facial expressions) to optimal settings for interviews.

An ongoing debate revolves around whether or not perpetrators should be treated the same as any other offenders, or be diverted from the criminal justice process into treatment programs. Another debate related to sexual abuse concerns whether or not society should be protected from pornography through government censorship or through other methods.

Other Types of Family Violence

The majority of the literature on family violence focuses on the three major types just discussed; therefore most recommendations for intervention come from those sources. Intervention strategies are less frequently mentioned regarding abuse of adolescents or abuse of the elderly, but there are some ideas that should be considered.

Studies of maltreated adolescents suggest that children over the age of 11 are much less likely to evoke sympathy or concern by observers because they often interpret abusive behavior as provoked and justified, thus blaming the victims. Even when there are obvious indicators of ongoing abuse, observers tend to discount them because their ideas of child abuse involve stereotypes of battered babies and lower-class families. Children who get in trouble at school or with authorities are frequently victims of past or current parental maltreatment, but too often investigation focuses solely on the individual child and not his or her environment. Runaway adolescents are likely to be victims of maltreatment in the home, but official response has been to return them to their caretakers without investigation, where the abuse continues or the children run away again. Some fall into the juvenile justice system, are labeled delinquent, and are institutionalized. Of all the millions of children who run away, only a few can be sheltered in community-based halfway houses, such as Covenant House in New York City. Laws regarding youths, such as labor laws, often restrict the efforts of these programs to help the children become independent and self-sufficient. Lacking alternatives, many of them drift into prostitution and/or the pornography industry.

Intervention for these victims requires some changes in juvenile laws, many more shelters for young runaways (or throwaways), and sufficient funding for shelters to continue and expand their services to youngsters. The major debate regarding abused adolescents revolves around how they can be protected from exploitation in prostitution and pornography.

Relatively few writers refer to intervention techniques for abused elders, probably because this issue has only recently been recognized and researched. Professionals are likely to insist that the best way to intervene is by removing the abused elderly from their homes, without taking into consideration that this can be a life-threatening shock to an old person. One reason maltreated elders are unwilling to report to authorities is because they fear losing the home they have; the cost of stopping abuse is too high. But professionals may perceive them to be in imminent danger to life and health, and have them institutionalized without their consent. Many people accept stereotypes about old persons, treat them like children, and discount whatever they say because they are "senile." Professionals who wish to assist elders must begin to recognize symptoms of abuse, accept elderly people's capabilities as well as their limitations, and allow abused elders to participate in decision making about what can or should be done for them. In his book advocating children's rights, John Holt (1974, 78) warned about "helpers": "The Helping Hand Strikes Again!" Similarly, well-intentioned people can literally "kill them (old people) with kindness." Some states have passed laws specifying mandatory reporting of suspected abuse of the elderly.

Progress is being made but scientifically sound empirical research is needed to guide intervention. A review of the child abuse literature brought this response:

> [W]e must mandate that one of . . . [our] priorities be that of a valid search for knowledge in this area. The funneling of money into programs built upon a less than secure base, largely as a result of the lack of solid empirical knowledge, is truly wasted and may even border upon damaging due to its false promises. The time has come to recognize the false promises made by the child maltreatment "literature" and move forward to build a body of knowledge which can survive rigorous scientific scrutiny. (Bolton et al. 1981, 538)

We must learn from past mistakes. "Tinkering" with the social system without knowledge compounds problems. Much more, and better empirical research is needed on the long-range effects of family violence. We need to know when and how to intervene in violent families, and follow up on that intervention. It is obvious that not all experts define appropriate intervention in the same terms, which is to be expected, since they approach their topics with different theoretical assumptions, definitions, methods of study, and professional backgrounds. As David Finkelhor (1981a, 18) notes, "there has been a substantial degree of specialization by discipline," but the field now seems to be moving gradually in the direction of *interdisciplinary* study.

Some programs and policies that were instituted originally to help are also accused of exacerbating some problems and causing others, such as efforts to control juvenile delinquency.

The Juvenile Justice System

Some writers see strong connections between dysfunctional families, a misguided and inefficient system of programs and policies, and juvenile delinquency because of the way the system now operates. They insist that our society sanctions child abuse and that current programs for child abuse and neglect contribute to juvenile delinquency. Going a step further, Adrienne Haeuser and her colleagues see our "solutions" as partially *causing* juvenile delinquency (1981, 22). Nevertheless, professor of social work Vincent Faherty (1981) suggests that sufficient improvement can be made without changing the entire system. Faherty calls for an even closer institutional association between child maltreatment and delinquency.

Faherty believes our approach and solutions have been all wrong; in fact, he says we "muddle through" human problems. He sees these issues as interlocking manifestations of dysfunctional families that have been politically separated into two very different government institutions: child abuse/neglect coming under the aegis of the Department of Health and Human Services (now HHS, then DHEW), and juvenile delinquency under the Department of Justice's (DOJ) Law Enforcement Assistance Administration (LEAA). In the former, victims must be protected, whereas in the latter the public must be protected from the perpetrators. Faherty sees these issues as interrelated, but the approaches taken by the two agencies to which they are assigned are vastly different. He believes no progress will be made until we recognize both as part of the same continuum and set up an alternative policy, saying:

> The consequences are equally dichotomized. The emphasis in the child abuse law is on protection, identification and treatment under the Department of Health, Education, and Welfare; while the emphasis in the Juvenile Delinquency act is on control and retribution within The Law Enforcement Assistance Administration. (Faherty 1981, 30)

The divergence is clear: in one the child is the victim, in the other the child is the perpetrator; one is to help, the other to punish. According to Faherty, "what becomes apparent is that the two national policies—The Child Abuse Prevention and Treatment Act and The Juvenile Justice and Delinquency Prevention Act—are dealing with the same issue: the emotional and physical health of children" (1981, 28). Faherty proposes "to establish and institutionalize a national policy on personal social services" (1981, 31) to unite children and families into one governmental unit for the creation of improved social policies. In view of Faherty's social work background, presumably this unit would be housed in HHS, rather than in the DOJ.

Other writers support the idea of a continuum and urge consolidation, but not in HHS. Charles Smith and his colleagues (1980) also propose merging agencies and services. They conducted their review and wrote their report with funding by LEAA, and first author Smith is the director of the National Juvenile Justice System Assessment Center. The Smith et al. report recommends that the juvenile justice system expand its scope of concern beyond abuse, neglect, and juvenile delinquency, and include a concern for families in crisis and their neighborhoods (1980, 150). The authors suggest centralizing research and statistical information and say, "This effort would require one Federal agency taking the responsibility for coordinating with other government agencies" (Smith et al. 1980, 150).

One set of arguments shows that society expects maltreated children to become delinquents, and that by not distinguishing between children who are victims and those who are perpetrators, victimized children are more likely to be further stigmatized and punished. Others claim that child abuse and delinquency are interrelated problems on the same continuum. However, one side calls for a consolidation of intervention services within a government agency for human services, while the other side would place them in a criminal justice agency.

Recognizing the intense political "turf wars" waged by various government agencies (Faherty admits to "boundary maintenance"), it is unlikely that either of these camps (HHS or DOJ) would willingly relinquish control over the massive bureaucracies that have been set up in each to deal with children who *have* problems (abused, neglected), or children who *are* problems (status offenders, delinquents). The question may resolve itself by the course of events in the present political climate: the National Center on Child Abuse and Neglect (NCCAN), housed in HHS, faces extreme reductions, LEAA has been dismantled, and all that will remain is the powerful Department of Justice.

Maltreated children who come in contact with the juvenile justice system are a classic example of "victim blaming"; they are the victims, but for this they are *punished*. Charles Smith and his co-authors state:

> Officials of the juvenile justice system . . . take the pragmatic approach of filing status offense petitions against abused and neglected children and youth, *rather than filing complaints against their parents* since the latter are more difficult and costly to prove. . . . To be a victim of abuse and neglect at home, and then to become a victim of institutional abuse and neglect, is a clear case of double jeopardy. Some indication of the impact the system has upon these children is revealed by the fact that neglected youth who were labeled as status of-

fenders tend to have a higher recidivism rate than the nonne-
glected offenders. (1980, 144, emphasis added)

Reports show a somewhat stronger likelihood that maltreated children,
more than nonmaltreated children, again become publicly labeled, this
time as delinquents or deviants when they reach adolescence or later.
There is little evidence that abusive parents and victims receive even
short-term remedial intervention, although there is a need for long-term
assistance. But what kinds, and who should administer it?

It almost seems strange that research has not found an even stronger
association between reported child abuse/neglect and juvenile delinquency, considering what happens to so many of these children once
they enter the system. Adrienne Haeuser and her colleagues may be correct when they say: "The authors believe these policies and programs for
child abuse/ neglect contribute to the juvenile delinquency problem."
They conclude by suggesting that, "It may be necessary to adopt an anti-
child welfare posture" (Haeuser et al. 1981, 22), an idea that may have
merit.

There is a continuing debate about the kinds of social engineering that
has been done or should be done. Some argue that the state and its
agents of social control have done more to harm children and their families than help: by imposing high demands, limited resources punitive social policy, and reduced parental control. Many call for a complete institutional restructuring to ameliorate systematic injustices that spawn
problematic families.

We have already gathered enough information to enable us to analyze
what we have learned about child maltreatment, the social policies that
have been developed to deal with it (including what seems to work and
what has serious flaws), and all this should help us draw blueprints for
restructuring our institutions. What has been proposed to prevent family
violence?

LONG-RANGE PREVENTION STRATEGIES: REORDERING PRIORITIES

It is difficult to discuss long-range prevention according to specific categories of family violence, because most proposed strategies are on a more
global scale. Families are a unit in the social system, therefore any changes
on the structural and institutional level affect family living. Alterations in
the social system could prevent several types of abuse simultaneously.
Families in which violence occurs are usually multiproblem families. For

example, child victims of incest may also be beaten or neglected, or have mothers who are battered. Prevention requires extensive changes.

Inequality: Economic and Sexual

An economic system that is unable to accommodate all willing workers and has large segments of the population living whole lifetimes in financial insecurity or poverty while a tiny minority lives in opulence and splendor must be considered a strong contributor to family violence. In addition, women's subordinate status in society and the family also contributes. Recommendations for violence prevention by reducing poverty are discussed first.

Economic Inequality

There is insufficient proof that poor families are more prone to violence, but economic insecurity or inadequacy can contribute to violent behavior due to *lack of alternatives*. For example, there are few escape routes for welfare mothers living in substandard housing, compared to those available to affluent mothers. Incontinent elderly parents can be cleaned and changed by paid professionals, but this can be too expensive for people on moderate or low incomes.

Some writers strongly contend that social inequality is embedded in the political and economic structure of our society and this is what defines and limits the futures of people, regardless of individual traits. Richard De Lone insists that "no amount of individual 'help,' whether delivered by schools, judges, or social workers, can make changes that are needed. It is the original inequality of social class that must be changed." (De Lone 1979, 112). People who are disadvantaged at the very beginning of life are unlikely to overcome early handicaps throughout their lives.

What can be done about poverty? As some have noted, Americans pay homage to the ideals of freedom, equality, democracy, and justice, yet when we learn that large segments of the population lack the freedom to make important life choices due to economic inequalities that have remained constant for years, we refuse to do the massive restructuring necessary to effect real change. The *here and now* realities of families are ignored: Families are isolated, torn apart by problems over which they have no control, and dysfunctional due to an economic/political system that gives them responsibility for socializing future generations without adequate financial and social support. The Puritan ethic of individualism and competition still clouds our judgment of interpersonal and social relations: Those who do not succeed financially and socially are viewed as "sinners"—they are "losers" because of personal deficiencies. A report from the Carnegie Council on Children explains:

> In the late nineteenth century, the popular minister Henry Ward Beecher stated very bluntly a conviction still held (although in other terms) by many Americans: "No man in this country suffers from poverty unless it be more than his own fault—unless it be his sin." . . . The excluded are now described as "deprived"—culturally, familially, and cognitively. It is not exactly their fault; they are "disadvantaged" or perhaps even "sick." . . . Above all, the problem lies in the families of these children. . . What unites all these explanations of exclusion is a tacit agreement that there is something wrong with the excluded children and parents. . . . [I]t is taken for granted that the immediate cause for being at the bottom lies in the characteristics of those who live there. (Keniston 1977, 38)

Kenneth Keniston says, "Rather than try to modify directly the distribution of economic rewards and social standings, we have concentrated on uplifting the next generation." (1979, xiii) If we condone poverty, we condone violence. To approach the American ideal of equality, there are a number of ways that wealth can be redistributed through income maintenance plans. A negative income tax or an income floor could lift one out of every four children that now lives in poverty into a decent standard of living, an idea that has been proposed by many professionals, but always ignored by policymakers. We need to guarantee equality of opportunity for all citizens so that the countless hordes of children who now grow up in poverty without hope of bettering themselves beyond the fruitless struggles of their parents, will some day have hope. Is it possible? Even before the massive increases in military spending, all it would have required was less than 2 percent of our gross national product in 1976 to eliminate poverty (U.S. Bureau of the Census, 1978). Now it is substantially less, but then the $16.7 billion a year was only one-fifth of the military budget, or a little more than what Americans spend yearly for tobacco products.

At the Children's Hospital Medical Center in Boston, Eli Newberger is the author of many critiques of the "helping" services, child "protective" services, and our welfare system. In one article, he notes a book containing a "brilliant chapter called 'Tireless Tinkering with Dependent Families,' [that] makes it plain that Welfare Departments mess around with some aspects of poverty but have an investment in maintaining it." (Newberger 1979, 17) In the same vein, researcher David Gil does not call for short-term intervention methods for abused and neglected children. Gil's recommendations call for changing the entire social system which now, through below-poverty levels of income maintenance by AFDC, "virtually condemns millions of children to conditions of existence under which physical, social, emotional, and intellectual development are likely to be severely handicapped" (1975, 348). He contends:

> Similarly destructive versions of legally sanctioned abuse on the institutional level are experienced by several hundred thousands of children living in foster care, in training and correctional institutions, and in institutions for children defined as mentally retarded. That these settings of substitute child care usually fail to assure optimum development for the children entrusted to them has been amply demonstrated. . . . (Gil 1975, 349)

Psychiatrist Matthew Dumont (1977) writes a strong indictment of our social and economic system that treats human labor as a commodity and ignores the physical and mental health dangers to citizens caught up in internalized messages of individualism and competition. The factor that Dumont points to as causing the most damaging effects on the family is unemployment, with its attendant "noxious effects" such as mental illness, sexual impotence, crime, child abuse, alcoholism, suicide, and divorce.

All the problems that economic inequality cause families are compounded greatly for minority group families or families headed by women, and although economic restructuring would assist most poor families, there remain distinctive problems of inequality due to women's status in society and the family.

Inequality Based on Sex

Whether their focus is on wife battering, marital rape, incest, child abuse and neglect, or parent abuse, many writers note economic disadvantages faced by women in society that contribute to each type of violence. Women frequently remain in abusive relationships with men who rape, batter them or their children, or sexually abuse their children, because they know they could not survive economically. Old age poses serious problems for women. Their longer life spans and lower lifetime earnings put many of them at an economic disadvantage and often dependent on other older women (their daughters or sisters) so females are more likely to be both abusers of the elderly *and* the abused elderly themselves. Other factors besides economics contribute to inequality based on sex: One is the division of labor in the family, where the major responsibility of caretaking (of children and elders) is placed on females. Another is the unequal power relationship inherent in traditional marriages. Inequality in parenting responsibilities is addressed first.

David Gil studied child abuse and wrote extensively on his findings and made suggestions that generally were ignored. His major recommendation would require a massive restructuring of society, but he also called for a reduction of the stresses on family life:

> . . . especially on mothers who carry major responsibility for the child-rearing function. Such stresses are known to precipitate incidents of physical abuse of children. . . . Family counseling, homemaker and housekeeping services, mothers' helpers and baby-sitting service, family and group day-care facilities for preschool and school age children are all examples of such services. . . . Nor should such services be structured as emergency services; they should be for normal situations, in order to prevent emergencies. No mother should be expected to care for her children around the clock, 365 days a year. Substitute care mechanisms should be routinely available to offer mothers opportunities for carefree rest and recreation. (Gil 1970, 118)

These suggestions are similar to the ones submitted by the author to a state commission on violence prevention more than a decade later. People in decision-making positions are unlikely to heed or advocate our recommendations unless they receive popular support. The social system places the burden of socializing new generations of citizens almost completely onto individual parents, especially mothers. Sociologist Jessie Bernard notes the unequal burden of child-rearing placed on women and agrees that Gil's demands for restructuring society and the institution of motherhood are "clearly imperative." Bernard (1975, 88) states:

> We have here a genuine blue-print for at least a partial re-institutionalizing of motherhood in our society. There remains one major defect: it assumes that mothers still "carry major responsibility for the child-rearing function." Not, however, a defect any sensible person would cavil with at the present time.

That "major defect" must be addressed. As motherhood is currently structured in the United States, it becomes an awesome private responsibility. The task of parenting the young to become productive members of society receives no societal reward and only token recognition, but carries severe penalties if mishandled. The modern family is unlike earlier models where family units worked together for sustenance. Some factors that contribute to maternal child abuse and neglect were noted earlier: the isolation of the modern nuclear family; the much greater responsibility assigned to mothers for the care, nourishment, and behavior of children; and the greater percentage of time mothers spend with children. As the institutions of the family and motherhood have changed over time to evolve into the current structures, they will continue to change.

It is no longer necessary nor inevitable that most women become mothers; pronatal social pressures could be reduced so that it is just as normative to have child-free families as child-rearing families. The most important factor in making informed decisions about whether or not to have children is education. For one of the most important jobs in the world, mothers now receive almost no training, carry out their tasks in private, and receive little or no outside assistance. All other important careers require years of preparation and training, even apprenticeships. Unlike other careers, if a woman takes on the role of mother and finds she is dissatisfied or unsuited, there is no way of resigning with dignity to switch to another field of work.[2] This equally applies to fathers, who are also inadequately prepared for parenthood, and who cannot resign with dignity from a role for which they may not be suited.

Producing changes requires a blueprint for action and massive citizen pressure for new social policy. For the purpose of opening debate and exploring new ideas, consider the following futuristic scenarios.

Informed Choice. To prepare young people to make such important decisions and to extend the responsibilities of parenthood to fathers, family living classes become part of the regular school curricula beginning at the elementary level and progressing through high school. This training includes sex education, birth control methods, and parenting. The parenting classes teach *equal* and *nonviolent* parenting, training men in nurturance, and both men and women in disciplinary techniques that avoid the use of physical punishment. Corporal punishment of children is outlawed, in the family as well as in schools and other institutions.

People are required by law to pass accredited courses before being issued marriage licenses or becoming parents (medical services require it). Giving birth is a matter of informed choice, selected by some because they understand the responsibilities and willingly accept them. For those who elect not to have children, or for spacing desired births, safe and effective contraceptives and abortions are freely available. People who have children and find they are unsuited for parenthood are provided ways of relinquishing them without stigma, and the children are placed with parents who want them.

If these ideas were translated into social policy, no children would be forced to live with parents too ignorant to give them proper care or training, nor with parents who do not want them and therefore cannot give them love. Men would be brought back into the family as fathers, equally responsible for nurturance and caregiving. What would a futuristic scenario about caretakers of both the young and the elderly portray? Consider the following.

Social Recognition and Support for the Task of Caretaking. Under this system, parents not only receive appropriate recognition and honors but also economic rewards in the forms of guaranteed health care for the entire family, income maintenance, decent housing, retirement benefits, paid vacations, and so forth. Caretakers of the elderly receive income maintenance and guaranteed health care for themselves and their charges. Professional and paraprofessional assistance is available to all caretakers in the forms of guidance counselors, visiting home nurses, hot lines, respite stations, quality day-care centers for youngsters and mobile elders and baby-sitting and homemaking services. Families with dependents (children or the aged) are incorporated into community networks with social services and other caretaking families to provide modern "extended kin" systems, and neighborhood schools are open past classroom hours for community events for all families: social, recreational, artistic, theatrical, and general community projects.

If these ideas became social policy, the privatization and isolation of current caretaking practices would be eliminated, the dependent young and old would not be subjected to abuse and neglect, and the social system would carry a more equitable share of the burden of responsibility.

These scenarios (albeit utopian) are an attempt to provide a holistic, rather than the usual piecemeal, approach to the prevention of child and elder maltreatment. *Prevention* today largely consists of identification, treatment, and sometimes attempts to prediction. Admittedly, a radical approach requires a massive restructuring of priorities and the entire social system, which is unlikely to occur without strong popular demand. Nevertheless, people build societies, therefore people can also change them. As popular ideas about children, childhood, and parenting have evolved through the centuries, they can continue to improve. The family and motherhood are institutionalized now in *the worst possible way* so that it has destructive effects on women and children (Bernard 1975), and thus ultimately on all people.

Despite the obviously high financial cost of reorganizing society as just implied, some features are appealingly cost-effective, such as assistance to caretakers of the elderly in their homes. It costs far more to institutionalize the elderly than some services that are now provided at low cost, such as community-based Meals on Wheels, which brings hot, nourishing meals to persons confined to their homes, or provides them in community centers. A prototype for the community network system has been established in the Neighborhood Watch concept, which not only results in fewer household burglaries, but has opened up lines of communication between neighbors. In some areas it has already expanded to include other helpful neighborly interaction.

Many of Robert Kahn's (1982) 12 suggestions are useful for preventing family abuse of the elderly, although his focus is on servicing the future mental health care needs of this growing population. For example, he calls for intervention that is least disruptive of their usual functioning, saying:

> Thus, it would be more sensible to provide care in the home or day-care center than in the hospital; the storefront rather than in the clinic; in the neighborhood rather than downtown; for brief rather than for long periods; with neighborhood personnel rather than with explicit medical or social agency professionals. (Kahn 1982, 400)

Kahn calls for continuity of care (personnel, agencies, and institutions to be integrated), and for providing supportive help to the family, such as "holiday relief" where the old person may be hospitalized for a week or two so caretakers can take a vacation. Even more "radical" is Kahn's suggestion that nonprofessionals be used as outreach workers for liaison to professionals who serve as consultants. These workers would preferably come from the same background, neighborhood, and general age group as their elderly clients, serving as friendly confidantes. Kahn advises helpers to allow old persons a sense of control saying, "The very act of being helped can have the paradoxical effect of increasing the impairment because of the infantilization. . ." (1982, 401). One excellent suggestion is this: "'potential service' may be as useful as any form of actual help. The basis of this concept is to guarantee that service will be available when needed"; yet Kahn states: "The new approaches may have the multiple virtues of not only being more effective than many conventional practices but also far more economical and efficient in the use of our resources" (1982, 401, 402). Better may even be cheaper!

In health care, the United States spends billions of dollars for curing diseases and little on preventative medicine; so too do we mostly concern ourselves with family violence after it occurs, not with prevention. We already spend billions of dollars in medical services, lost employment time, caretaking and penal institutions, and the criminal justice system, attending to fractured lives after family violence occurs. Futurists build scenarios for study—perhaps it is time for us to suggest new goals for building societies of the future. No goal can ever be attained if it is not established in the first place, so why not at least consider these ideas as a starting point?

The second way in which inequality based on sex promotes family violence is the unequal distribution of power in the traditional family. As long as society's patriarchal institutions support male legal, economic, political, and marital power, there will be conflict and violence in the home.

Men were pulled out of the family by capitalism and a marketplace ideology that promoted masculine ideals of aggression, competitiveness, control, domination, and impersonal sex. Males and females are socialized into antithetical modes of behavior; the extremes of each are dysfunctional to both sexes. Family violence can be reduced by changing gender role socialization for both sexes (being *macho* could come to be viewed as ridiculous and helpless femininity as silly), and with concomitant changes in the social system, there will be less power imbalance in the family and far fewer abuses.

There are indicators of some potential changes that will reduce the economic inequality women now suffer which handicap them in their family relations. One is a proposal to establish equal shares in social security accounts in one-income families, so that when one person stays out of the labor market to be a full-time parent, she (or he) is not penalized by losing social security benefits in old age. Social security laws now severely penalize women who are full-time homemakers and mothers.

Another indicator of change is the number of bills now before Congress, proposing different methods of collecting child-support payments from defaulting parents (Nakamoto et al. 1983). One bill proposes that all court orders for child support be sent automatically to employers for payroll deductions; there would be no stigma because it would occur in every case. Self-employed parents are not covered, but other bills call for state and federal tax interceptions of refund checks for default payments. These proposals have bipartisan support because they would provide for women and children who need the income and take many families off AFDC, saving taxpayers billions of dollars now spent on children not supported by their biological parents.

Change is inevitable. The question is, what kinds of changes will occur?

Recommendations

This nation spends billions of dollars on technology and scientific discovery but neglects the *quality* of life, which has deteriorated as advances were made elsewhere. Our priorities must be re-evaluated. If it is quality of life we want, broad and deep changes must be made in the fabric of our social structure. We must begin *somewhere* or resign ourselves to the "inevitability" of violence. The place and time to begin is here and now.

The following are the social, economic, legal, and individual changes needed to control violent crime and prevent violence in the future. They may appear utopian, radical, or totally impossible, but there are no illusions that they will be swiftly adopted. Regardless, if we are really serious about the elimination of violence in our society—if we are truly determined to make our society a civilized one in which the vast majority of people can live their lives without terror and violence in the home and beyond—then these measures should be given serious consideration. The majority of these recommendations have been gathered from a wide range of respected and informed sources; some are original to the author; but many persons have contributed to the thoughts expressed here, and although their contributions cannot be acknowledged on an individual basis, their insight and inspiration are greatly appreciated.[3] The list of recommendations begins with items for abolition, restriction, or reduction; the next section outlines laws, services, or programs to be instituted.

Recommended to be Abolished,
Restricted, or Reduced

Corporal punishment of children by any and all adult care-takers: in the home, schools, or other institutions.

Capital punishment—institute life sentences that cannot be reduced.

Extremely violent sports; promote nonviolent recreation and sports.

Child pornography and any pornography that features violence.

Violent toys.

Violence in the media: comics, cartoons, magazines, movies, advertising, and television.

Racist, sexist, and ageist images in the media.

Recommended to be Adopted

Gun control laws.

Laws requiring sexual equality to reduce the sexist structure of society and its institutions, including the family. Equal pay for work of equal value. Spouses share equally in all retirement plans; if divorce occurs the benefits are prorated.

Children's Bill of Rights, including providing an advocate for court. The rules governing victim/witnesses need to be overhauled to protect child victims of crime from courtroom trauma. Recommendations include videotaping testimony to be admitted as evidence in court in lieu of testimony in person; small children allowed to testify using genital-specific dolls and drawings. If the child must appear in court, the courtroom should be closed as is provided in juvenile court hearings.

Elimination of poverty through a guaranteed decent annual income for all (negative income maintenance).

Elimination of inequality by opening up opportunities for all, including higher educational opportunities.

Guaranteed health care for all: medical, dental, optometry services, neighborhood based, with emphasis on maintenance of good health and preventative medicine. Free contraceptives, and abortion on demand.

Dependable and sufficient financial support for shelters for battered women and their children at least on a par with correctional institutions, in view of the many services they provide for the community and clients that are not available elsewhere.

Dependable and sufficient financial support for shelters and advocacy services for adolescent runaways.

Decent housing for the low-income, handicapped, and aged.

Good, inexpensive public transportation, including specially equipped vans for the handicapped and aged.

Community service centers for homemaker and housekeeping services, mothers' helpers, baby sitters.

Meals on Wheels providing nourishing, balanced diets to the aged, infirm, and handicapped. Transportation to bring these people to community centers on a regular basis for socializing, entertainment, training, counseling, and so forth.

Agencies that accept unwanted children without attaching blame or stigma to parents; people unable to cope with responsibilities of parenthood should be provided a means to abdicate with dignity.

Training, proper compensation, support services, and public recognition to foster parents for community services, to attract and keep high-quality homes; the same for caretakers of elderly relatives.

Cooperation, communication, and networking between community social services so that clients with multiple problems get appropriate assistance, including follow-up. Diversion programs for troubled youth and trained team-leaders in problem neighborhoods, with recreational programs including sports, art, theatre, and community projects.

Children charged with status offenses should not be institutionalized in security facilities; all communities should provide counseling, assistance, and good foster homes or provide nonpunitive residential shelters with guidance and advocacy. Children in security facilities should be segregated by type of crime, for example, property versus violent crimes. Reduced caseloads for juvenile probation officers.

Families identified as having been abusive to children or parents should receive intensive intervention services such as mandated in the Child Protective Services Act, but they should also include educational and follow-up services with the same social worker involved throughout on a person-to-person (not telephone) basis for continuity. Reduced caseloads for social workers and more visiting nurses are needed.

Quality child care for preschoolers, charged on a sliding scale, free to low-income parents. Provided in neighborhood schools during the regular school day, and after hours, Saturdays, and school holidays for both preschool and school-aged children to reduce the number of "latch key kids."

Hot lines in every community, with a list of "family helpers" who make home visits to give "on-the-job training" to parents in need, and assist with care for the elderly. Helpers stay for a few hours or days to provide respite for caretakers of the elderly.

Drop-off centers where all parents (not just those already in the mental health system) may leave youngsters for brief "time-out" periods (a few hours or up to two days) when needed; charged on a sliding scale.

Elementary schools available as community centers for neighborhood gatherings where people can meet, develop a sense of community, and act collectively to protect their children, their neighbors, and themselves from violence.

Elementary and high schools used after school hours for neighborhood social and cultural events to attract and involve all members of the community.

Nonsexist education and texts at all levels; eliminate sex role stereotypes remove violence and aggression from "masculinity," encourage girls to be self-reliant.

Family life classes beginning at the elementary school level and progressing through high school. Includes sex education and birth control methods, parenting, interpersonal relations, and assertion training. Children are trained to feel free to reject unwanted physical contact by elders and to reveal any abuse that occurs in the home.

Academic courses on family violence required for credentials in the helping professions, legal, and criminal justice fields. These are needed for identification, effective intervention, and prevention.

Effective parenting classes free at local schools in evenings and on weekends; mandatory certification for obtaining marriage licenses.

Same classes as above for persons already parents, strongly urged or demanded by all persons in medical professions, counselors, and members of the clergy.

Training classes, including a support system, for persons caring for the elderly in their homes.

At first glance, these ideas may seem too broad and all-inclusive. Some will gasp at the financial costs of instituting programs and services like these. However, we are currently paying extremely high bills for social ills that were not addressed years ago. What is needed is a *preventative* program that will pay a return that far outweighs its expenses. There will be savings in lives, property, *and* money. The quality of life for all citizens will be improved. If we knew that allocating half the funds now budgeted to maintain the prison system would reduce the inmate population by half if spent on these social changes, we would probably feel that this is a good exchange. In addition, there are the days lost from work and school, the need for mental health and medical services, the crippling and sometimes fatal effects of violence occurring on a daily basis in millions of homes—the costs for all this is beyond estimation!

Many of the recommendations would not be as expensive as they seem to be at first glance. For example, schools are underutilized now. Many school yards are locked up immediately after students are released. These are public buildings within communities that could service the entire community better. Many people are willing to volunteer services for good programs, to work part-time or work for minimal wages, in order to be able to contribute to the common good. This is particularly true of retired persons or mothers with small children.

For those who fear state intervention and insist that the privacy of the family should not be invaded, here are some words from others who take a stance similar to the author's and advocate many social changes compatible with those listed above.

> One function of these educational programs would be to help change these norms. The response of "none of your business," which some privacy advocates feel is used too infrequently, should give way to the recognition that child rearing is the business of the community. . . . The community's contribution is through the medium of education and the provision of concrete support mechanisms for the assistance of individuals in their critical social role as parents. . . . Hopefully, the benefactors of these joint contributions will be the community, the family, and, most important, the child. (Feshbach and Feshbach 1978, 176)

Seymour Feshbach and Norma Feshbach were, of course, concentrating on benefits to children. The same is true of David Gil when he called for massive changes in our values, institutions, and human relations; he says:

> Whatever one's attitude may be toward these fundamental political issues, one needs to recognize and face the dilemmas implicit in them and, hence in primary prevention of child abuse. If one's priority is to prevent all child abuse, one must be ready to part with its many causes, even when one is attached to some of them, such as the apparent blessings, advantages, and privileges of inequality. If, on the other hand, one is reluctant to give up all aspects of the causal context of child abuse, one must be content to continue living with this social problem. In that latter case, one ought to stop talking about primary prevention and face the fact that all one may be ready for is some measure of amelioration. (Gil 1975, 355–56)

Gil is speaking of child abuse, but his ideas apply to all types of family violence. The big question is: *are we serious,* or are we *just talking?*

MAKING A START:
WHAT INDIVIDUALS CAN DO

The title of this last section might be more accurately stated in terms of preventing violence in society and the family, because the two are so intimately related. Behaviors in the privacy of the home among family members are reflections of the world outside the front door. Families in Japan, Iran, and the United States display courtesy in different ways and have greatly differing rituals, dietary habits, clothing, furniture, and customs, but each reflects the culture in which they live. No family lives in total isolation from the environment; therefore, if people want to reduce or prevent family violence, they must also attempt to reduce cultural violence.

Perhaps readers already have formed some notions on how they can become involved in reducing violence. Here are a few suggestions that are not all-inclusive, they are merely presented in the hope of stirring ideas that can lead to action. These ideas are specifically for parents or those who are in frequent contact with children, but, of course, they are in addition to taking parent education classes and using nonviolent types of discipline.

> Focus on the "good" behavior rather than the "bad," and make the child proud for settling disputes nonviolently; encourage imaginative play and discourage violent play. *Listen* to children. *Be courteous* to children.

> Be careful to avoid sex-role stereotypes when interacting with children; they are sensitive to subtle messages of expectations, so even if you do not praise a boy for being a "tough guy," or tell a girl she is too "weak" to do something, you may still see the self-fulfilling prophesy.

> Watch television programs aimed at children and decide what you feel is appropriate for yours; you may have to be creative to think up activities to which they can be diverted. If there is a worthwhile program that has violent episodes, watch it with your child and discuss it later.

> Do not provide your child with violent toys or games, including video games; be very selective and choose ones that require skill or creativity, or are educational (children do enjoy learning). There are such toys on the market, but you may have to look at the back of the shelf.

> Check your child's school books for sexist, racist, or age-ist

stories or images; if you find some objectionable material, discuss it with your child. You may want to call it to the attention of your school principal who may have been unaware of it. (This is not to imply that anyone should go on a book-crusade; some people are just not sensitized to covert messages.)

For all adults, but especially for parents, it is important to watch our own language. Comedian Henry Gibson (1982) pointed that out when he wrote suggestions for Americans who desire world peace: Begin with our own violent, belligerent language. One of our cultural artifacts is extremely violent slang expressions (sporting events bring out some of the worst, but our colloquialisms for sexual intercourse are also very violent).

Another suggestion is for people to volunteer their services to one of the many agencies that help families, such as community centers for the aged, or the victims of violence. Most community-based, nonprofit organizations are underfunded and desperately need volunteers. People gain as much (or more) as they give when they become involved in this kind of activity. Despite sounding trite, being a good neighbor is a way of preventing violence. For example, one can offer to stay and give someone relief from the caretaking of an elderly person. Hearing a child's incessant screaming can indicate two possibilities: the child is being abused or the child is a "screamer" and the parent is extremely frustrated. Volunteering in a neighborly way to baby-sit for a short time may or may not dispel suspicions of abuse but it may serve to *prevent* its occurrence by relieving a parent of unbearable stress. Unmanageable children are frequently less so when attended by strangers than by parents, and lasting help may be given by recommending a hot-line number or a parenting class to the distraught mother or father.

Finally, there are ways of preventing violence that are not as direct and may not give an immediate sense of accomplishment, but nevertheless *are* effective. These are by writing letters to, protesting, and boycotting advertisers or merchants who offend. This method is effective, whether done as an individual or by joining in a group effort. If we are serious about wanting a less violent environment inside and outside the home, then it is about time that we open our eyes to the messages of cultural approval of violence. The next step is to decide how much violence and symbols of violence we want to protect ourselves and our families from, and then begin to work individually and collectively to reduce it. As long as violence is financially profitable for some, they will fight hard to protect their profits. One writer discussed sex stereotypes in advertising and referred to the response heard so frequently by groups that protest insulting and dangerous images in the media; Billie Wahlstrom (1981, 40) says:

> Too often advertisers comment that they are only using images that the American public wants to see. In some cases one wonders how that can be totally true when the public has not ever had the opportunity to see alternatives. Even if it is true, however, that does not absolve advertisers of their ethical responsibility to American viewers and readers.

Wahlstrom noted that textbook publishers had given the same arguments when accused of the invisibility of minorities in business or government roles in books they supplied to schools. After being pressured, the publishers became convinced they had some responsibility for "making the world better and not just reflecting it as they thought it to be." The ethical argument needs to be brought home to advertisers because: "They create ads that sell us things, whether or not we want them" (Wahlstrom 1981, 40). If enough of us got upset at what we see all around us, we could create enough pressure to convince the media, and the advertisers who use it, to "sell" all of us a less violent society. What is currently *legal* may not be *ethical*; this is the topic of a collection of excellent articles under the title, *The Ethical Eye: Examining Media Responsibility* (Interface 1981).

When anyone is offended by a television commercial or program, an advertisement, or a product, there are sponsors and merchants who can be contacted and advised of the disapproval. If there is no response, or an unsatisfactory response to complaints, they can be advised that they have lost a customer, for example, of a product, television station viewer, and so forth. This is the time-honored way of expressing power in a free-market economy. If potential customers are lost and products do not sell, they are taken off the market. Marketing directors and other decision makers are sensitive to complaints. They know that for every complaint they receive there are many more dissatisfied people who do not bother to complain. They can be reminded that the writer has family and a network of friends and associates who are also upset. These are the methods that have been used by organizations who protest violent and child pornography; sometimes they stage public demonstrations to register their disapproval. They have frequently been successful, but not always.

Another way to become involved in reducing violence is through organizing or joining political pressure groups to lobby for legislation, such as on the child care issue, or for better social services (or housing) for the elderly. People can become informed about pending legislation and register their approval/disapproval of bills by writing letters, sending telegrams, or telephoning legislators' offices. They can go even further, and suggest needed legislation, such as by proposing that family living classes become part of the regular school curricula. Legislators do *not* ignore communications from their constituents, contrary to popular belief. Unfortunately, the pressure applied to legislators is frequently funded by special-interest groups that wage well-organized campaigns that give the impression of popular support.

There is no need to despair about the future of the family, as long as citizens are not apathetic. This brings to mind the movie, *Network*, in which a despairing man yells out the window, "I'm mad as hell, and I'm not gonna take it any more!" Many people do not like what they see, and they are not going to "take it any more!" *Family violence can be prevented.*

NOTES

1. Most of the following comments on intervention and prevention are derived from writers mentioned earlier in the book, and they are not individually cited here since this is an holistic overview of the recommendations made by many professionals. In some cases, ideas or comments may be originally to the writer. However, when direct quotations or new material not previously mentioned is used here, it is appropriately cited.

2. It has always seemed ironic that women who attempt to assume the motherhood role but fail through abuse or neglect are stigmatized and punished under the law when maltreatment is disclosed. On the other hand, when women believe they are unable to adequately care for their babies and abandon them, they are also stigmatized and punished under the law when they are located. There is never a public outcry over the expenditure of funds to track down and prosecute abandoning mothers (who may have saved their babies from a far worse fate), but there is extreme public disapproval over expenditure of funds to support mothers and their children, particularly during political campaigns.

3. As mentioned in the text, individual acknowledgments cannot be listed, because there are so many who contributed in different ways to the ideas expressed here. However, there are a few that need be mentioned, because the writer found in their works the joy of knowing that others share in many ways her own viewpoint—"kindred spirits," so to speak. Although they are not responsible for the recommendations made here, the author gratefully acknowledges inspiration received from the works of David Gil, Robert L. Kahn, Eli H. Newberger, Diana E. H. Russell, and Jim Mead, the executive director of For Kids Sake. Besides maintaining an extensive research library, counseling abusive parents, and conducting parenting classes, For Kids Sake, a nonprofit organization is now publishing 22 pamphlets to help guide parents. The pamphlets available at this writing are: *Crying, and Crying, and Crying* . . . (for parents of babies who cry excessively), *If Your Child Is Molested, Prevent Burns to Kids,* and *Child Sexual Abuse: Who? What? and Why?* They sell for $7.50 per hundred copies. Other publications by For Kids Sake are: *An Educator's Handbook on Prevention and Recognition: Child Abuse and Neglect,* by Charles E. Campbell and James Mead, which costs $5.95, and *A Manual for Nursing Personnel: Child Abuse and Neglect,* by Jim Mead, Charles Campbell, and Eulajean Sanson, which costs $9.95 (plus tax for California residents). They may be obtained from: For Kids Sake, P.O. Box 471, Brea, CA 92621 (telephone 714/529–8358).

Appendix:
Annotated Parenting
Bibliography

Compiled by Eulajean Sanson
For Kids Sake, Brea, California

For Professionals:

Adler, Alfred. *Understanding Human Nature,* Fawcett Premier Books, 1954.

> Adler's Individual Psychology briefly stated is: all people are equal. Even though children are mentally and physically inferior to adults, they have certain inalienable rights that cannot be denied them. Adults and children are in a cooperative social relationship, and they each have responsibilities and duties. The first major responsibility of an individual is to cooperate in the attainment of the group's goal; specifically in modern human society, to the goals of the family.

The STEP Program in Book Form:

Dinkmeyer, Don, and Gary McKay. *Raising a Responsible Child: Practical Steps to Successful Family Relationships.* Simon and Schuster, 1973.

> Children are no longer willing to acquiesce to total parental control. Authoritarian techniques are no longer effective. But neither are the permissive approaches that fail to set limits or to guide, that permit chaos, and that shield the child from the unpleasant but realistic consequences of life. Dinkmeyer and McKay explore democratic motivators for parents who are ac-

tively seeking to establish or reestablish ties with their children. The authors' methods benefit the parent as well as the child and create a healthy environment for the child's growth.

Dinkmeyer, Don, and Rudolf Dreikurs. *Encouraging Children to Learn.* Hawthorn Books, 1963.

For educators and parents on effectively motivating children to achieve their full potential in the classroom. If children are not encouraged to develop their potential, there is great risk that they will establish a lifelong pattern of underachievement and frustration. This book is aimed at enabling teachers and parents to understand and use techniques of encouragement so that students in school will take full advantage of learning opportunities.

Dreikurs, Rudolf, Raymond Corsini, Raymond Lowe, and Manford Sonstegard. *Adlerian Family Counseling: A Manual for Counseling Centers.* University Press, University of Oregon, 1959.

A psychiatrist, clinical psychologist, school counselor, and an educational psychologist talk about their extensive experience in Adlerian family counseling. Extensive case examples are offered.

For Counselors:

Dreikurs, Rudolf. *Fundamentals of Adlerian Psychology.* Alfred Adler Institute, Chicago, 1953.

The basics of Adlerian psychology as used in Dreikurs's writings.

Dreikurs, Rudolf. *The Challenge of Parenthood.* Hawthorn Books, 1958.

Practical advice on specific situations—from temper tantrums to classroom difficulties—and also a basic attitude of mind and heart toward children and child training.

Dreikurs, Rudolf, and Loren Grey. *A Parent's Guide to Child Discipline.* Hawthorn Books, 1970.

An easy to understand guide that explains to parents why their children misbehave and shows how to deal with behavior problems based on logical consequences. Practical solutions for psychological and physical problems, numerous case histories, and step-by-step directions for children from birth to 21.

Dreikurs, Rudolf, and Loren Grey. *A New Approach to Discipline: Logical Consequences*. Hawthorn Books, 1968.

> The harsh discipline accorded children by some parents and teachers tends to debase rather than prepare them for the demands of adult life. Discipline arranged by an adult must have a logical relationship to the child's action. *Logical Consequences* removes sudden, unreasonable anger, brings about an intrinsic relationship with the child's acts, and looks toward the future instead of the past.

This is a MUST for Parents—
Examples of How to Use STEP Methods:

Dreikurs, Rudolf, with Vicki Soltz. *Children: The Challenge*. Hawthorn Books, 1964.

> This book is designed to meet the needs of all parents—to enable those who can deal with their children to formulate a consistent philosophical approach as well as to point the way toward tested solutions for those parents who are somewhat less effective.
>
> *Recommended:* The following workbook is structured to give a step-by-step, systematic approach for applying the principles found in the book *Children: The Challenge:* Zuckerman, Lawrence, Valerie Zuckerman, Rebecca Costa, and Michael T. Yura. *A Parent's Guide to Children: The Challenge*. Hawthorn Books, 1978.

Dreikurs, Rudolf, and Pearl Cassel. *Discipline Without Tears,* featuring the *Discipline Without Tears Workbook* by David Kehoe. Hawthorn Books, 1972.

> Details how the sensitivity of the teacher can be used to detect, diagnose, and correct typical classroom behavior problems.

Dreikurs, Rudolf. *Coping with Children's Misbehavior: A Parent's Guide*. Hawthorn Books, 1972.

> Investigates the reasons behind children's misbehavior, explaining that once the child's motivations are understood, the parent can learn to deal effectively with the causes of misconduct. Every type of misbehavior and many major behavioral problems are thoroughly analyzed, and specific, practical advice is provided.

Dreikurs, Rudolf. *The Challenge of Child Training: A Parent's Guide*. Hawthorn Books, 1972.

> Provides practical advice on specific situations—from weaning to classroom difficulties. The author explores the reasons behind children's behavior, discusses the most common mistakes in child training, and describes the most effective methods of training. Based on the book *The Challenge of Parenthood*.

Eimers, Robert, and Robert Aitchison. *Effective Parents/Responsible Children: A Guide to Confident Parenting*. McGraw-Hill, 1977.

> Offers effective techniques that parents can apply in a wide variety of situations. The authors present a detailed description of exactly when and how to use specific parenting skills, such as effective praising, effective ignoring, mild social punishment, how to set up special incentive systems, and "time out" periods for misbehavior. In addition to helping parents deal with routine misbehavior, the authors discuss in depth four groups of children who present special problems.

Hauck, Paul A. *The Rational Management of Children*. Libra, 1972.

> This book attempts to bring the principles of Rational-Emotive Psychotherapy to the assistance of the adult world in its task of raising sound and undisturbed children. According to Rational-Emotive Therapy (RET), all misbehaviors are clearly the product of stupidity, ignorance, or disturbance. Prevent mental retardation; inform, educate, and train the ignorant; teach rational thinking to the disturbed.

For Counselors:

Helfer, Ray E. *Childhood Comes First: A Crash Course in Childhood for Adults*. Order book directly from Ray E. Helfer, Box 1781, East Lansing, Mich. 48823.

> Lack of positive parenting models and other traumatic childhood deprivations often contribute to the cycle of abuse and neglect. This book is "dedicated to those adults who were unable to learn basic interpersonal skills when they were children." The book was developed with the conviction that learning and improving upon the skills of relating to oneself and others, especially one's children, are both critical and possible,

even though this training begins late in life, rather than early in childhood.

Ilg, Frances L., and Louise Bates Ames. *The Gesell Institute's Child Behavior from Birth to Ten*. Perennial Library, Harper & Row, 1955.

> All parents feel at one time or another the need for a realistic guide to help them cope with the problems that arise daily with the growing child. The authors provide specific ages on: eating behavior, sleeping and dreams, elimination, tension outlets, fears, walking and talking, sexual development, mother-child relationships, father-child relationships, sibling relationships, comics, television and movies, school, intelligence, social behavior, ethical sense, and discipline.

Leman, Kevin. *Parenthood Without Hassles * Well Almost*, Harvest House, 1979.

> The aim of this book is not to teach parents how to parent, but to teach parents how to better understand themselves and their children. The author presents concrete situations that people can relate to their family's growth, maturity, and harmony.

Recommended:

Losoncy, Lewis E. *Turning People On: How to Be an Encouraging Person.* Prentice-Hall, 1977.

> The author has systematically introduced the reader to the process of discouragement, clarifying the behaviors and attitudes that constrict human growth. The art of encouragement section presents the fundamentals of encouragement in a programed, instructional format.

Nicholson, Luree, and Laura Torbet. *How to Fight Fair With Your Kids . . . and Win*. Harcourt Brace Jovanovich, 1980.

> This book offers both the parents and the children practical lessons in the art and uses of "Fair Fighting." Fair Fighting respects the sensitivies of its participants and is conducted only with their consent. It is governed by rules that are simple to learn and enjoyable to practice. By using the Fair Fight System, time otherwise wasted in fruitless bickering, nagging, silent rages, or unpredictable explosions of anger is transformed into experiences of real family sharing and trust.

The author of *How to Fight Fair With Your Kids* used the theories from the following book to develop her Family Fair Fight System: Bach, George R., and Herb Goldberg. *Creative Aggression: The Art of Assertive Living.* Avon Books, 1973.

Patterson, Gerald R. *Living With Children: New Methods for Parents and Teachers.* Research Press, 1979.

This book was written for parents who are not great readers of books. Some parents like to have their ideas laid out in a straightforward manner. This volume was written for them. The book is intended to assist parents of normal and problem children to deal with the situations that come up in any family. Social learning theories underline the fact that people teach people. Section 1 of this book will help the reader to understand how that works. Sections 2, 3, and 4 will provide specific instructions on what to do about it.

Patterson, Gerald R. *Families: Applications of Social Learning to Family Life.* Research Press, 1979.

The author describes the practical application of social learning principles to problems with which we are all familiar. The general process by which people change is the prime focus of this book. Section 1 outlines a social learning explanation of how parents and children go about the normal process of changing each other. Practical procedures necessary for changing behavior are detailed in Section 2. In Section 3 the procedures are applied in changing the behavior of both the older and the very young members of the normal family. Section 4 describes the details of how to work with the preadolescent who steals or is very aggressive.

Wood, Paul, and Bernard Schwartz. *How to Get Your Children to Do What You Want Them to Do.* Prentice-Hall, 1977.

This is not a total or comprehensive child-rearing book. It focuses specifically on the "hows and whys" of problem behaviors. The approach here is a positive one. What the authors do is help parents better understand what it is they are doing when they are effective, so that they can extend that approach to the situations that are causing them difficulties. The book does not advise or tell parents what kinds of things they should or should not try to get their kids to do.

For Counselors:

Arnold, L. Eugene (ed.). *Helping Parents Help Their Children.* Brunner/ Mazel, New York, 1978.

> A practitioner's guide. The book treats parent guidance in five dimensions: (1) General principles are first explicated; (2) The insights of various schools of clinical thought and their special contributions to effective parent guidance are elucidated by experts of those schools; (3) The special considerations pertaining to guidance of parents whose children suffer various types of problems are dealt with in appropriately titled chapters; (4) Special considerations in guiding special kinds of parents are discussed; (5) A description of parent guidance by professionals who are not ordinarily considered mental health specialists but who are often called on by parents for advice and counsel.

Bank, Stephen P., and Michael D. Kahn. *The Sibling Bond.* Basic Books, 1982.

> This book is based on a decade of research and clinical evidence. The many portraits of brothers and sisters in childhood, adolescence, and adulthood provide a profound understanding of these complex and enduring relationships. The influence of childhood intimacy, parental behavior, family turmoil, birth order, and gender are all examined.

Recommended:

Corsini, Raymond J., and Genevieve Painter. *The Practical Parent: ABCs of Child Discipline.* Harper & Row, 1975.

> This book is for normal parents with normal children with normal problems. Based on the psychological theories of Alfred Adler, this book gives parents who are having difficulty handling their children both general and specific advice on how to deal with uncooperative behavior, picky eating, thumb sucking, bickering, resisting bedtime—problems not difficult enough to call in professionals for, yet difficult to live with.

Curran, Dolores. *Traits of a Healthy Family.* Winston Press, 1983.

> Most books tell readers what is wrong with families. Here is one that proclaims what is right—and shows families how to

build on their strengths to produce even healthier families. The author sent out questionnaires to 500 family professionals and received 551 back! The top 15 traits chosen by these professionals are what the book discusses.

Davitz, Lois, and Joel Davitz. *How to Live Almost Happily with a Teenager.* Winston Press, 1982.

Using their own childrearing problems as examples, the authors advocate the technique of "rational parenting," in which parents try to develop a good relationship with their teenagers based on honesty, trust, and respect. Rather than placing all the blame for conflicts on the adolescent, the book appeals to the parent to understand the adolescent's point of view, calling for cooperation, compromise, and an open, nonjudgmental dialogue.

Highly Recommended:

Dinkmeyer, Don, and Lewis E. Losoncy. *The Encouragement Book: Becoming a Positive Person.* Prentice-Hall, 1980.

This book takes you through a series of simple, easy-to-do exercises that will bring out the encouraging person in you. It shows how to: evaluate your present ability to encourage others; sharpen your perceptive powers and identify individual assets and strengths in other people; turn stubbornness and excitability into determination and enthusiasm; use humor as a powerful antidote, to self-defeating behavior and an effective tool in problem solving; and zero in on what others are really feeling by learning the dynamics of body language.

This Book is Used in
For Kids Sake Group Programs:

Faber, Adele, and Elaine Mazlish. *How to Talk So Kids Will Listen and Listen So Kids Will Talk.* Rawson, Wade, New York, 1980.

Each chapter of this book is filled with dialogues, role-playing exercises, and lively cartoons that show at a glance the contrast between helpful methods of communication. The book is a practical book. It addresses itself to everyday problems that parents have to cope with such as anger, neglected household chores, fighting between kids, defiance, misbehavior, and so forth.

PARENT GROUP PROGRAMS

STEP (Systematic Training for Effective Parenting). Developed by Don Dinkmeyer and Gary McKay. Order from: American Guidance Service, Publishers' Building, Circle Pines, Minn. 55014.

Topics include how to promote self-esteem, understanding, and mutual respect; and the use of reflective listening, encouragement, "I" messages, and family meetings. Recorded dramatizations, thought-provoking discussion questions, carefully organized role-playing activities, at-home exercises, and readings help demystify parent-child relations. The group meetings are usually held for two to three hours for eight or nine consecutive weeks.

The complete STEP program includes: Leader's Manual; five instructional cassette tapes; full-color Parent's Handbook; ten full-color 19- × 30-inch charts summarizing the major principles of the STEP sessions; six discussion guide cards focusing on rules and objectives for productive group discussions; nine 15- × 19-inch posters on spiral-bound easel illustrating skills presented in each session; Announcement Poster; Invitational Brochures; lightweight 20- × 16- × 1-inch carrying case to store and tote materials.

The components are available separately or as a complete package.

STEP/Teen (Systematic Training for Effective Parenting of Teens). Developed by Don Dinkmeyer and Gary McKay. Order from: American Guidance Service, Publishers' Building, Circle Pines, Minn. 55014.

Topics include ways to build positive parent-teen relationships; the seven goals of teen misbehavior, the importance of lifestyle, emotions of both teens and parents, encouragement (the key to self-esteem), effective listening skills, expressing feelings and exploring alternatives, natural and logical consequences as a means for building responsibility in teenagers, selecting the appropriate approach to a variety of discipline challenges, ways to establish regular family meetings, and unique challenges faced by single parents, divorced parents, and stepparents, plus approaches to especially troubling teen problems.

The format is similar to STEP with all components available separately or as a complete package.

STET (Systematic Training for Effective Teaching). Developed by Don Dinkmeyer, Gary D. McKay, and Don Dinkmeyer, Jr. Order from: American Guidance Service, Publishers' Building, Circle Pines, Minn. 55014.

How to Talk So Kids Will Listen. Adele Faber and Elaine Mazlish. Order from: Negotiation Institute, 230 Park Avenue, New York, NY 10169.

> A group workshop kit. The workshop is a completely self-contained, seven-session, multimedia parenting course, designed to be used by a group of six to twelve parents. You may organize a group either on your own or through a local community organization. The central goal is to help communicate more effectively with children. The course does not offer a script or preprogrammed responses for dealing with children. In each workshop, you will be introduced to skills that will help you to: teach your child to understand, identify, and communicate his or her feelings, encourage your child's willing cooperation, discipline without hurting or alienating, help you child develop a positive and realistic self-image, and foster a family atmosphere of love and respect. This group is all role playing.
>
> Order as a kit or portions as needed.

New in 1984:

Responsive Parenting (A Group-Support Program), by Saf Lerman. Order from: American Guidance Service, Publishers' Building, Circle Pines, Minn. 55014.

> A comprehensive, issue-oriented group discussion program geared to parents of babies, toddlers, and young children. The program provides parents with choices in methods of discipline and communication and provides opportunities for parents to clarify their own needs and feelings around a broad range of issues.
>
> The program addresses: children's fears and feelings; helping children understand death; positive approaches to discipline; helping children adjust to a new baby; talking with children and teenagers about sex; children's feelings about divorce; parents' own childhoods; family sculptures; ages and stages; sibling fighting and jealousy; building children's self-esteem; family relationships; encouraging independence; teaching cooperation and responsibility.
>
> Parenting kit consists of one set of nine illustrated booklets, one leader's manual, ten charts, sample certification of partici-

pation, announcement poster, invitational fliers, news release, and carrying case. All components are available separately or as a complete package.

Small Wonder! by Merle B. Karnes. Order from: American Guidance Service, Publishers' Building, Circle Pines, Minn. 55014.

A two-part program that encourages the emotional, physical, and intellectual growth of babies and toddlers—with special emphasis on language development. Level 1: birth to 18 months, remedially tage three; Level 2: 18 to 36 months, remedially to age five.

Level 1 stresses the interaction between babies and caregivers on an individual basis. Babies learn to trust, to understand and say simple words, and to strengthen muscle coordination as they participate in the activities provided on the activity cards.

Materials consist of User's Guide, Activity Cards, Look Book and Picture Cards, My First 18 Months (a diary), Caper the Caterpillar (puppet), and Picture Card Stories and Ideas.

Level 2, for toddlers, stimulates toddlers' special readiness to speak, socialize, and begin performing independently. Skills in problem solving, understanding abstract concepts, toileting, and cooperation are introduced. Group games, outdoor play, and simple action songs make this level ideal for use in day care and nursery settings as well as in private homes.

Materials are User's Guide, Activity Cards, Look Book, Progress Chart, Sound Sheet, Picture Card Stories and Ideas, and Flutter the Butterfly (puppet).

Each level comes in a handy storage box. All components are available separately or as a complete package.

References

Abrams, Susan

1978   "The battered husband." *Seven Days,* p. 20.

Adelson, Lester

1973   "The battering child." *Criminologist* 8(27): 26–33.

Adler, Emily Stier

1977   "The underside of married life: Power, influence, and violence."
        Paper presented at the annual meeting of the American Sociolog-
        ical Association, Chicago.
1981   "The underside of married life: Power, influence, and violence."
        In Lee H. Bowker (ed.), *Women and Crime in America,* pp. 300–
        19. New York: Macmillan.

Ainsworth, Mary D. Salter

1980   "Attachment and child abuse." In George Gerbner, Catherine J.
        Ross, and Edward Zigler (eds.), *Child Abuse: An Agenda for Ac-
        tion,* pp. 35–47. New York: Oxford University Press.

Akers, Ronald L.

1973   *Deviant Behavior.* Belmont, Calif.: Wadsworth.

Alexander, F., and H. Ross

1961   *The Impact of Freudian Psychiatry.* Chicago: University of Chi-
        cago Press.

Alfaro, Jose D., Project Director

1978   *Summary Report on the Relationship Between Child Abuse and
        Neglect and Later Socially Deviant Behavior.* New York State Se-
        lect Committee on Child Abuse.

Allen, Hugh D., Edward J. Kosciolek, Robert W. ten Bensel, and Richard
B. Raile

1969   "The battered child syndrome." *Pediatrics* (January): 155–56.

Alvy, K. T.

1975   "Preventing child abuse." *American Psychologist* 30:921–28.

American Humane Association

1980   *National Analysis of Official Child Neglect and Abuse Reporting (1978).* Department of Health and Human Services. Washington, D.C.: Government Printing Office. Pub. No. (OHDS)80-30271.
1981   *National Analysis of Official Child Neglect and Abuse Reporting (1980).* Denver: American Humane Association.
1983   *National Analysis of Official Child Neglect and Abuse Reporting (1981).* Denver: American Humane Association.

Amsterdam, Beulah, Mary Brill, Noa Weiselberg Bell, and Dan Edwards

1979   "Coping with abuse: Adolescents' views." *Victimology* 4(4): 278–84.

Andelin, Helen

1975   *Fascinating Womanhood.* New York: Bantam.

Ardrey, Robert

1966   *The Territorial Imperative: A Personal Inquiry Into the Animal Origins of Property and Nations.* New York: Dell.

Aries, Phillippe

1962   *Centuries of Childhood.* New York: Knopf.

Armstrong, Louise

1979   *Kiss Daddy Goodnight: A Speak-Out on Incest.* New York: Pocket Books.
1983   *The Home Front: Notes From the Family War Zone.* New York: McGraw-Hill.

Bach-y-rita, George, and Arthur Veno

1974   "Habitual violence: A profile of 62 men." *American Journal of Psychiatry* 131(9): 1015–17.

Bacon, Gertrude M.

1977   "Parents anonymous." *Victimology* 2(2): 331–36.

Bakan, David

1971   *Slaughter of the Innocents: A Study of the Battered Child Phenomenon.* San Francisco: Jossey-Bass.

Baker, C. D.

1978   "Comment: Preying on playgrounds—The sexploitation of children in pornography and prostitution." *Pepperdine Law Review* 5(3): 809–46.

Bandura, Albert

1973   *Aggression: A Social Learning Analysis.* Englewood Cliffs, N.J.: Prentice-Hall.

Bandura, Albert, and S. Ross

1961   "Transmission of aggression through imitation of aggressive models." *Journal of Abnormal Psychology* 63:575–82.

Bandura, Albert, and Richard H. Walters

1973   *Social Learning and Personality Development.* New York: Holt, Rinehart and Winston.
1970a   "Adolescent aggression." In Edwin Megargee and Jack Hokanson (eds), *Dynamics of Aggression,* pp. 89–100. New York: Harper & Row.
1970b   "Reinforcement patterns and social behavior: Aggression." In Edwin Megargee and Jack Hokanson (eds.), *Dynamics of Aggression,* pp. 33–38. New York: Harper & Row.

Bannon, James

1975   "Law enforcement problems with intra-family violence." Paper presented at the annual meeting of the American Bar Association, Montreal, Canada.
1977   "Presentation on police difficulties with female battering cases." Paper prepared for presentation before the U.S. Civil Rights Commission, Connecticut Advisory Committee, September.

Bard, Morton

1969   "Family intervention police teams as a community mental health resource." *Journal of Criminal Law, Criminology, and Police Science* 60(2): 247–50.
1970   *Training Police as Specialists in Family Crisis Intervention.* Department of Justice. Washington, D.C.: Government Printing Office.

Bard, Morton, and Katherine Ellison

1974   "Crisis intervention and investigation of forcible rape." In Lisa Brodyaga, M. Gates, S. Singer, M. Tucker, and R. White (eds.), *Rape and Its Victims: A Report for Citizens, Health Facilities, and*

Criminal Justice Agencies, pp. 165–71. Washington, D.C.: Department of Justice.

Bard, Morton, and Joseph Zacker

1971   "The prevention of family violence: Dilemmas of community intervention." *Journal of Marriage and the Family* 33(November): 677–82.
1974   "Assaultiveness and alcohol use in family disputes: Police perceptions." *Criminology* 12(3): 281–92.
1976   "How police handle explosive squabbles." *Psychology Today* (November): 71–74, 113.

Barnett, Ellen R., Carla B. Pittman, Cynthia K. Ragan, and Marsha K. Salus

1980   *Family Violence: Intervention Strategies.* Department of Health and Human Services. Washington, D.C.: Government Printing Office. Pub. No. (OHDS)80-30258.

Bart, Pauline B., and Margaret Jozsa

1980   "Dirty books, dirty films, and dirty data." In Laura Lederer (ed.), *Take Back the Night: Women on Pornography,* pp. 204–17. New York: William Morrow.

Bates, Vernon, assisted by Dyan Oldenberg

1980   "Domestic violence and the law." Paper presented at the annual meeting of the Pacific Sociological Association, San Francisco.

Beck, Mildred B.

1970   "Abortion: The mental health consequences of unwantedness." *Seminars in Psychiatry* 2(3): 263–74.

Becker, Howard S.

1966   *Outsiders.* New York: Free Press.

Behling, Daniel W.

1979   "Alcohol abuse as encountered in 51 instances of reported child abuse." *Clinical Pediatrics* 18(2): 87–91.

Bellucci, M. T.

1972   "Group treatment of mothers in child protection cases." *Child Welfare* 51(2): 110–16.

Bender, Laurette, and F. J. Curran

1974   "Children and adolescents who kill." *Journal of Criminal Psycho-*

pathology 1:267.

Bennie, E., and A. Sclare

1969   "The battered child syndrome." *American Journal of Psychiatry* 125(7): 147–51.

Berdie, Jane, Michael Baizerman, and Ira S. Lourie

1977   "Violence towards youth: Themes from a workshop." *Children Today* 6(2): 7–10, 35.

Berger, Lawrence R.

1978   "Abortions in America: The effects of restrictive funding." *New England Journal of Medicine* 298(6): 1474–77.

Berger, Peter

1963   *Invitation to Sociology: A Humanistic Perspective.* Garden City, N.Y.: Doubleday Anchor.

Berk, Richard A., Sarah Fenstermaker Berk, Donileen R. Loseke, and David Rauma

1981   "Mutual combat and other family violence myths." Paper presented at the National Conference for Family Violence Researchers, Durham, N.H.

Berkowitz, L.

1965   "The concept of aggressive drive: Some additional considerations." In L. Berkowitz (ed.), *Advances in Experimental Social Psychology,* pp. 301–29. Vol. 2. New York: Academic Press.

Berliner, Lucy

1977   "Child abuse: What happens next?" *Victimology* 2(2): 327–31.

Berliner, Lucy, and Doris Stevens

1980   "Advocating for sexually abused children in the criminal justice system." In Kee MacFarlane, Barbara McComb Jones, and Linda L. Jenstrom (eds.), *Sexual Abuse of Children: Selected Readings,* pp. 47–50. Department of Health, Education, and Welfare. Washington, D.C.: Government Printing Office.

Bernard, Jessie

1975   *The Future of Motherhood.* New York: Penguin Books.
1982   *The Future of Marriage.* 2nd ed. New Haven: Yale University Press.

Besharov, Douglas J.

1978   "The legal aspects of reporting known and suspected child abuse and neglect." *Villanova Law Review* 23(3): 458–520.

Billings, Andrew G., Marc Kessler, Christopher A. Gomberg, and Sheldon Weiner

1979   "Marital conflict resolution of alcoholic and nonalcoholic couples during drinking and nondrinking sessions." *Journal of Studies on Alcohol* 40(3): 183–95.

Bird, Carolyn

1979   *The Two-Paycheck Marriage.* New York: Rawson, Wade.

Black, Claudia

1979   "Children of alcoholics." *Alcohol Health and Research World* 4(1): 23–27.

Blalock, Hubert M., Jr.

1969   *Theory Construction.* Englewood Cliffs, N.J.: Prentice-Hall.

Blau, Francine D.

1979   "Women in the labor force: An overview." In Jo Freeman (ed.), *Women: A Feminist Perspective,* pp. 265–89. 2nd ed. Palo Alto: Mayfield.

Block, Irving

1976   *Gun Control: One Way to Save Lives.* Pamphlet No. 536. New York: Public Affairs Pamphlets.

Block, Marilyn R., and Jan D. Sinnott (eds.)

1979   *The Battered Elder Syndrome: An Exploratory Study.* Division of Human and Community Resources. College Park: University of Maryland.

Blumberg, Myrna

1964   "When parents hit out." *Twentieth Century* 173(Winter): 39–44.

Bokemeier, Janet, and Pamela Monroe

1983   "Continued reliance on one respondent in family decision-making studies: A content analysis." *Journal of Marriage and the Family* 45(3): 645–52.

Bolton, F. G., Jr.

1981   "Failed attachment: A hidden predictor of maltreatment in the adolescent parent." Paper presented at the National Conference for Family Violence Researchers, Durham, N.H.

Bolton, F. G., Jr., Roy H. Laner, Dorothy S. Gai, and Sandra P. Kane

1981   "The 'study' of child maltreatment: When is research . . . research?" *Journal of Family Issues* 2(4): 531–41.

Bolton, F. G., Jr., J. W. Reich, and S. E. Gutierres

1977   "Delinquency patterns in maltreated children and siblings." Phoenix, Ariz.: Community Development for Abuse and Neglect.

Bordin-Sandler, Suzanne

1976   "If you don't stop hitting your sister, I'm going to beat your brains in." *Journal of Clinical Child Psychology* 5(1): 27–30.

Borland, Marie (ed.)

1976   *Violence in the Family.* Atlantic Highlands: Manchester University Press.

Bosma, William G. A.

1975   "Alcoholism and teenagers." *Maryland State Medical Journal* 24(6): 62–68.

Bowker, Lee H.

1978   *Women, Crime, and the Criminal Justice System.* Lexington, Mass.: D. C. Heath.
1981   *Women and Crime in America,* (ed.). New York: Macmillan.
1983a   *Beating Wife-Beating.* Lexington, Mass.: Lexington Books.
1983b   "Marital rape: A distinct syndrome?" *Social Casework: The Journal of Contemporary Social Work* (June): 347–52.

Bowker, Lee H., and Kristine MacCallum

1981   "Marital values, interaction, and decision-making in violence-prone families." Paper presented at the annual meeting of the National Council on Family Relations, Milwaukee, Wis.

Boyer, Debra, and Jennifer James

1982   "Easy money: Adolescent involvement in prostitution." In Sue Davidson (ed.), *Justice for Young Women: Close-up on Critical Is-*

sues, pp. 73–97. Tucson: New Directions for Young Women.

Brandon, Sydney

1976   "Physical violence in the family: An overview." In Marie Borland (ed.), *Violence in the Family,* pp. 1–25. Atlantic Highlands: Manchester University Press.

Brenzel, Barbara

1982   "Domestication as reform: A study of the socialization of wayward girls, 1856–1905." In Sue Davidson (ed.), *Justice for Young Women: Close-up on Critical Issues,* pp. 27–50. Tucson: New Directions for Young Women.

Briggs, Robert R.

1979   "Overview." In *Child Abuse and Developmental Disabilities: Essays.* Department of Health, Education, and Welfare. Washington, D.C.: Government Printing Office. Pub. No. (OHDS) 79-30226.

Brody, Elaine M., and Stanley J. Brody

1974   "Decade of decision for the elderly." *Social Work* 19(5): 544–54.

Brongersma, Edward

1980   "The meaning of 'indecency' with respect to moral offences involving children." *British Journal of Criminology* 20(1): 20–33.

Brown, John A.

1981   "Some etiological factors and treatment considerations in child abuse." In Robert J. Hunner and Yvonne Elder Walker (eds.), *Exploring the Relationship Between Child Abuse and Delinquency,* pp. 34–42. Montclair, N.J.: Allanheld, Osmun.

Brownmiller, Susan

1976   *Against Our Will: Men, Women and Rape.* New York: Bantam.
1980   "Let's put pornography back in the closet." In Laura Lederer (ed.), *Take Back the Night: Women on Pornography,* pp. 252–55. New York: William Morrow.

Bulkley, Josephine (ed.)

1981   *Innovations in the Prosecution of Child Sexual Abuse Cases.* Washington, D.C.: American Bar Association.

Bulkley, Josephine, and Howard A. Davidson

1980   *Child Sexual Abuse: Legal Issues and Approaches.* National Legal Resource Center for Child Advocacy and Protection. Washington, D.C.: American Bar Association, Young Lawyers Division.

Bullough, Vern L.

1974   *The Subordinate Sex: A History of Attitudes Toward Women.* New York: Penguin.

Burgess, Ann Wolbert, and Lynda Lytle Holmstrom

1975   "Sexual trauma of children and adolescents." *Nursing Clinics of North America* 10(3): 551–63.

Burgess, Ann W., Lynda L. Holmstrom, and Maureen P. McCausland

1977   "Child sexual assault by a family member: Decisions following disclosure." *Victimology* 2(2): 236–50.

Burt, Martha R.

1978   "Attitudes supportive of rape in American culture." *Research into Violent Behavior: Overview and Sexual Assaults.* Testimony submitted to the House of Representatives Committee on Science and Technology, Subcommittee on Domestic and International Scientific Planning, Analysis, and Cooperation. Washington, D.C.: Government Printing Office.

Butler, Robert N.

1982   "The gift of life." In K. Warner Schaie and James Geiwitz (eds.), *Adult Development and Aging,* pp. 407–20. Boston: Little, Brown.

Butler, Sandra

1979   *Conspiracy of Silence: The Trauma of Incest.* New York: Bantam.

Button, Alan

1973   "Some antecedents of felonious and delinquent behavior." *Journal of Clinical Child Psychology* 2(3): 35–37.

Byles, J. A.

1978   "Violence, alcohol problems and other problems in disintegrating families." *Journal of Studies in Alcohol* 39:551–53.

Caffey, J.

1957   "Some traumatic lesions in growing bones other than fractures and dislocations." *British Journal of Radiology* 23:225–38.

Calef, Victor

1972   "The hostility of parents to children: Some notes on infertility, child abuse, and abortion." *International Journal of Psychoanalytic Psychotherapy* 1(2): 76–96.

California Commission on Crime Control and Violence Prevention

1982   *An Ounce of Prevention: Toward an Understanding of the Causes of Violence*. Sacramento: Commission on Crime Control and Violence Prevention.

California Department of Justice

1978   *Child Abuse. The Problem of the Abused and Neglected Child*. Sacramento: California Department of Justice.
1982   *The Child Abuse Prevention Handbook*. Sacramento: California Department of Justice.

California Department of Social Services

1980   *The Hidden Tragedy: Incest*. A Report on the Santa Clara County Child Sexual Abuse Demonstration and Training Project. Sacramento: Report to the Legislature.

Calvert, Robert

1974   "Criminal and civil liability in husband-wife assaults." In Suzanne Steinmetz and Murray Straus (eds.), *Violence in the Family*, pp. 88–91. New York: Harper & Row.

Cantwell, Hendrika B.

1980   "Standards of child neglect." In *Selected Readings on Child Neglect*, pp. 11–33. Department of Health, Education, and Welfare, Office of Human Development Services. Washington D.C.: Government Printing Office. Pub. No. (OHDS) 80-30253.

Cate, Rodney M., June M. Henton, James Koval, F. Scott Christopher, and Sally Lloyd

1982   "Premarital abuse. A social psychological perspective." *Journal of Family Issues* 3(1): 79–90.

Cazenave, Noel A.

1981   "Stress management and coping alternatives for families of the frail elderly." Paper presented at the National Conference for Family Violence Researchers, Durham, N.H.

Chafetz, Morris E.

1979   "Children of alcoholics." *New York University Education Quarterly* 95(3): 23–29.

Chambers, Mary Jane

1980   "The murder of Robbie Wayne, age 6." *Reader's Digest,* November, pp. 215–51.

Chase, Naomi Feigelson

1976   *A Child is Being Beaten.* New York: McGraw-Hill.

Chase, Sherry

1982   "Outlawing marital rape: How we did it and why." *Aegis* (Summer): 21–26.

Chesney-Lind, Meda

1978   "Young women in the arms of the law," and "Chivalry reexamined: Women and the criminal justice system." In Lee H. Bowker, *Women, Crime, and the Criminal Justice System,* pp. 171–224. Lexington, Mass.: D. C. Heath.

1982   "From benign neglect to malign attention: A critical review of recent research on female delinquency." In Sue Davidson (ed.), *Justice for Young Women: Close-up on Critical Issues,* pp. 51–72. Tucson: New Directions for Young Women.

Chicago Daily News

1977   "Husband is more battered spouse." August 31, p. 3.

Chicago Sun Times

1978   "Some statistics in the battle of the sexes." February 5, p. N-3.

Childers, Carolyn

1982   "WAVAW fights sexist video games." *Women Against Violence Against Women: WAVAW Speaks* 10(December): 1–2.

Coalition on Women and the Budget

1983   "Inequality of sacrifice: The impact of the Reagan budget on women." March.

Cobbe, Frances Power

1878   "Wife-torture in England." *Contemporary Review* (April): 55–87.

Cohen, Sidney

1980   Public Hearing on "Nutritional and biochemical influences on aggressive and violent behavior," San Diego, December 4. Sacramento: California Commission on Crime Control and Violence Prevention.

Coleman, Karen Howes

1980   "Conjugal violence: What 33 men report." *Journal of Marital and Family Therapy* 6(2): 207–13.

Collins, John P.

1981   "The American juvenile justice system: A history of failure." In Ruth Crow and Ginny McCarthy (eds.), *Teenage Women in the Juvenile Justice System: Changing Values,* pp. 108–12. Tucson: New Directions for Young Women.

Conger, Rand D., Benjamin B. Lahey, and Stevens S. Smith

1981   "An intervention program for child abuse: Modifying maternal depression and behavior." Paper presented at the National Conference for Family Violence Researchers, Durham, N.H.

Cooley, Charles Horton

1902   *Human Nature and the Social Order.* New York: Scribner's.

Cork, Margaret R.

1969   *The Forgotten Children: A Study of Children with Alcoholic Parents.* Toronto: Alcoholism and Drug Addiction Research Foundation of Ontario, Canada.

Coser, Lewis A.

1964   *The Functions of Social Conflict.* Glencoe, Ill.: Free Press.

Court, Joan, and Anna Kerr

1971   "The battered child syndrome—A preventable disease?" *Nursing Times* (June): 695–97.

Courtois, Christine

1979   "The incest experience and its aftermath." *Victimology* 4(4): 337–47.

Crow, Ruth, and Ginny McCarthy (eds.)

1981   *Teenage Women in the Juvenile Justice System: Changing Values.*

Tucson: New Directions for Young Women.

Crozier, Jill, and Roger C. Katz

1979   "Social learning treatment of child abuse." *Journal of Behavior Therapy and Experimental Psychiatry* 3(September): 213–19.

Cuber, John, and Peggy Harroff

1965   *The Significant Americans: A Study of Sexual Behavior Among the Affluent.* New York: Appleton-Century-Crofts.

Curtis, George C.

1963   "Violence breeds violence—perhaps?" *American Journal of Psychiatry* 120:386–87.

Daily Pilot

1978   "Suspect Rifle." May 19, p. A-4.

David, Deborah S., and Robert Brannon (eds.)

1976   *The Forty-nine Percent Majority: The Male Sex Role.* Menlo Park, Calif.: Addison Wesley.

David, Lester, and Irene David

1980   "Violence in our schools." New York: Public Affairs Committee.

Davidson, Sue (ed.)

1982   *Justice for Young Women. Close-up on Critical Issues.* Tucson: National Female Advocacy Project, New Directions for Young Women.

Davidson, Terry

1977a   "Wife beating: It happens in the best of families." *Family Circle,* November 15, pp. 62, 68, 70, 72.
1977b   "Wifebeating: A recurring phenomenon throughout history." In Maria Roy (ed.), *Battered Women: A Psychosociological Study of Domestic Violence,* pp. 2–23. New York: Van Nostrand Reinhold.
1978   *Conjugal Crime: Understanding and Changing the Wifebeating Pattern.* New York: Hawthorn Books.

Davis, Elizabeth Gould

1971   *The First Sex.* New York: Penguin.

DeFrancis, Vincent

1969   *Protecting the Child Victim of Sex Crimes Committed by Adults.*

Denver: American Humane Association.

Delaney, Janice, Mary Jane Lupton, and Emily Toth

1976   *The Curse: A Cultural History of Menstruation.* New York: E. P. Dutton.

deLissovoy, Vladimir

1979   "Toward the definition of 'abuse provoking child.'" *Child Abuse and Neglect* 3:341–50.

de Lone, Richard H., for the Carnegie Council on Children

1979   *Small Futures: Children, Inequality, and the Limits of Liberal Reform.* New York: Harcourt Brace Jovanovich.

deMause, Lloyd

1975   "Our forebears made childhood a nightmare." *Psychology Today,* April, pp. 85–88.

DeMott, Benjamin

1980   "The pro-incest lobby." *Psychology Today,* March, p. 12.

Densen-Gerber, Judianne

1980   "Child prostitution and child pornography: Medical, legal, societal aspects of the commercial exploitation of children." In Kee MacFarlane, Barbara McComb Jones, and Linda L. Jenstrom (eds.), *Sexual Abuse of Children: Selected Readings,* pp. 77–81. Department of Health, Education, and Welfare. Washington D.C.: Government Printing Office. Pub. No. 78-30161.

DeVine, Raylene

1980a   "Incest: A review of the literature." In *Selected Readings on Child Neglect,* pp. 25–28. Department of Health, Education, and Welfare. Washington, D.C.: Government Printing Office. Pub. No. (OHDS) 79-30166.
1980b   "Sexual abuse of children: An overview of the problem." In Kee MacFarlane, Barbara McComb Jones, and Linda L. Jenstrom (eds.), *Sexual Abuse of Children: Selected Readings,* pp. 3–6. Department of Health, Education, and Welfare. Washington, D.C.: Government Printing Office. Pub. No. 78-30161.

Dewsbury, Anton R.

1975   "Family violence seen in general practice." *Royal Society of Health Journal* 95(6): 290–94.

Dexter, L. A.

1958   "A note on selective inattention in social science." *Social Problems* 6(Fall): 176–82.

Diamond, Irene

1980   "Pornography and repression: A reconsideration of 'who' and 'what.'" In Laura Lederer (ed.), *Take Back the Night: Women on Pornography,* pp. 187–203. New York: William Morrow.

Dickman, Irving R.

1981   *Teenage Pregnancy—What Can Be Done?* Public Affairs Pamphlet No. 594. New York: Public Affairs Committee.

Dietz, C. A., and J. L. Craft

1980   "Family dynamics of incest: A new perspective." *Social Casework* 61(10): 602–9.

Dinkmeyer, Don, and Gary D. McKay

1976   *Parent's Handbook.* Circle Pines, Minn.: American Guidance Service.

Dobash, R. Emerson, and Russell P. Dobash

1976   "The importance of historical and contemporary context in understanding marital violence." Paper presented at the annual meeting of the American Sociological Association, New York.

1978   "Wives: The 'appropriate' victims of marital violence." *Victimology* 2(3/4): 426–42.

1979   *Violence Against Wives: A Case Against the Patriarchy.* New York: Free Press.

1980   "A context specific approach to studying violence against wives." Paper prepared for the Sociological Review Monograph on Violence in the Family, April.

Dobash, Rebecca

N.D.   "Battered women: In defence of self defence." *Spare Rib,* pp. 52–54.

Doran, Julie Blackman

1981   "Multiple victimizations: Those who suffer more than once." Paper presented at the National Conference for Family Violence Researchers, Durham, N.H.

Douglass, Richard L.

1981   "The etiology of neglect and abuse of older persons." In David F. Holden and Peggie L. Carey (eds.), *Abuse of Older Persons,* pp. 3–15. Knoxville: University of Tennessee, School of Social Work.
1983   "Domestic neglect and abuse of the elderly: Implications for research and service." *Family Relations* 32(3): 395–402.

Douglass, Richard L., Tom Hickey, and Katherine Noel

1980   *A Study of Maltreatment of the Elderly and Other Vulnerable Adults.* Ann Arbor: University of Michigan.

Dumont, Matthew P.

1977   "Is mental health possible under our economic system?—No!" *Psychiatric Opinion* (May/June): 9, 11, 32–33, 44–45.

Duncan, Glen M., Shervert H. Frazier, Edward M. Litin, Adelaide M. Johnson, and Alfred J. Barron

1958   "Etiological factors in first-degree murders." *Journal of the American Medical Association* 168.

Dunwoody, Ellen

1982   "Sexual abuse of children: A serious, widespread problem." *Response* 5(4): 1–2, 13–14.

Durkheim, Emile

1964   *The Rules of Sociological Method.* 8th ed. Translated by Sarah A. Solovay and John H. Mueller and edited by George E. G. Catlin. New York: Free Press.
1966   *Suicide: A Study in Sociology.* Translated by John A. Spauling and George Simpson and edited by George Simpson. New York: Free Press.

Duty, Juana E.

1983   "Group helps victims of incest overcome the shame, trauma." *Los Angeles Times,* March 22, pp. V-1–2.

Dworkin, Andrea

1974   *Woman Hating.* New York: E. P. Dutton.
1980   "For men, freedom of speech; for women, silence please." In Laura Lederer (ed.), *Take Back the Night: Women on Pornography,* pp. 256–58. New York: William Morrow.

Easson, W. M., and R. M. Steinhilber

1961   "Murderous aggression by children and adolescents." *Archives of General Psychiatry* 4:1–10.

Ebert, Roger

1981   "Why movie audiences aren't safe anymore." *American Film,* March, pp. 54–56.

Edelman, Edmund D.

1983   "The best way to fight child abuse in L.A." *Los Angeles Times,* August 24:II–13.

Eisenberg, Alan D.

1979   "An overview of legal remedies for battered women." Pt. I. *Trial* 15(8): 28–31.

Eisenberg, Alan D., and Earl J. Seymour

1978   "Self-defense plea and battered women." *Trial* 14(7): 34–36, 41–42, 68.

1979   "An overview of legal remedies for battered women." Pt. II. *Trial* 15(10): 42–45, 60–69.

Eisenberg, Sue E., and Patricia L. Micklow

1974   *The Assaulted Wife: "Catch 22" Revisited.* Ann Arbor: University of Michigan Law School.

1977   "The assaulted wife: Catch 22 revisited." *Women's Rights Law Reporter* (March): 183–61.

Elbow, Margaret

1977   "Theoretical considerations of violent marriages." *Social Casework* 58(9): 515–26.

Elias, Veronica Diehl

1979   "The male image in the media: Some sociological notes on male roles in popular American films." Paper presented at the annual meeting of the Pacific Sociological Association, Anaheim, Calif.

Ellis, Robert H.

1981   "Making sense of child abuse: An interactive model and implications for treatment." Paper presented at the National Conference for Family Violence Researchers, Durham, N.H.

Elmer, Elizabeth

1977   "A follow-up study of traumatized children." *Pediatrics* 59(2): 273–79.

1979   "Child abuse and family stress." *Journal of Social Issues* 35(2): 60–71.

EMERGE

1982   From a fund-raising appeal dated September 10. EMERGE'S address is 25 Huntington Avenue, Room 324, Boston, Mass. 02116.

Epstein, David G.

1981   "False economy in child-abuse cases." *Los Angeles Times,* November 7, p. II-2.

Erlanger, Howard

1974   "Social class and corporal punishment in childrearing: A reassessment." *American Sociological Review* 39(February): 68–85.

Eskin, Marian, and Marjorie Kravitz

1980   *Child Abuse and Neglect: A Literature Review and Selected Bibliography.* Department of Justice, National Institute of Justice. Washington, D.C.: Government Printing Office.

Fabricant, Michael

1981   *Juvenile Injustice: Dilemmas of the Family Court System.* New York: Community Service Society.

Fagan, Jeffery A., Douglas K. Stewart, and Karen V. Hansen

1981   "Violent men or violent husbands? Background factors and situational correlates of severity and location of violence." Paper presented at the National Conference for Family Violence Researchers, Durham, N.H.

Faherty, Vincent

1981   "National policies on child abuse and delinquency: Convergence or divergence?" In Robert J. Hunner and Yvonne Elder Walker (eds.), *Exploring the Relationship Between Child Abuse and Delinquency,* pp. 25–33. Montclair, N.J.: Allanheld, Osmun.

Faulk, M.

1974   "Men who assault their wives." *Medicine, Science, and the Law* 14:180–83.

Feinman, Clarice

1980   *Women in the Criminal Justice System.* New York: Praeger.

Ferraro, Kathleen J.

1979   "Definitional problems in wife battering." Paper presented at the annual meeting of the Pacific Sociological Association, Anaheim, Calif.

Feshbach, Norma Deitch

1976   "Corporal punishment in the schools, a special case of child abuse." Paper presented at the annual meeting of the American Psychological Association, Washington, D.C.

1980a   "Corporal punishment in the schools: Some paradoxes, some facts, some possible directions." In George Gerbner, Catherine J. Ross, and Edward Zigler (eds.), *Child Abuse: An agenda for Action,* pp. 204–24. New York: Oxford University Press.

1980b   "Tomorrow is here today in Sweden." *Journal of Clinical Child Psychology* 9(2): 109–12.

Feshbach, Seymour

1980   "Mixing sex with violence—A dangerous alchemy." *New York Times,* August 3.

Feshbach, Seymour, and Norma Deitch Feshbach

1978   "Child advocacy and family privacy." *Journal of Social Issues* 34(2): 168–78.

Feshbach, Seymour, and Neil Malamuth

1978   "Sex and aggression: Proving the link." *Psychology Today* 7(6): 111–17, 122.

Field, Martha H., and Henry F. Field

1973   "Marital violence and the criminal process: Neither justice nor peace." *Social Service Review* 47(22): 221–40.

Fields, Marjory D.

1977   "Representing battered wives, or what to do until the police arrive." *Family Law Reporter* 3(22): 4025–29.

1978   "Does this vow include wife beating?" *Human Rights* 7(20): 40–45.

Fields, Marjory D., and Rioghan M. Kirchner

1978   "Battered women are still in need: A reply to Steinmetz." *Victi-*

mology 3(1–2): 216–22.

Finkelhor, David

1979a *Sexually Victimized Children.* New York: Free Press.
1979b "What's wrong with sex between adults and children? Ethics and the problem of sexual abuse." *American Journal of Orthopsychiatry* 49(4): 692–97.
1980 "Risk Factors in the sexual victimization of children." *Child Abuse and Neglect* (4): 265–73.
1981a "Common features of family abuse." Paper presented at the National Conference for Family Violence Researchers, Durham, N.H. This article has since been published: In David Finkelhor, Richard J. Gelles, Gerald T. Hotaling, and Murray A. Straus (eds.), *The Dark Side of Families,* pp. 17–18. Beverly Hills: Sage, 1983.
1981b "Sexual abuse: A sociological perspective." Paper presented at the National Conference for Family Violence Researchers, Durham, N.H. 1981c "Four preconditions of sexual abuse: A model." Unpublished paper.

Finkelhor, David, and Kersti Yllo

1983 "Rape in marriage: A sociological view." In David Finkelhor, Richard J. Gelles, Gerald T. Hotaling, and Murray A. Straus (eds.), *The Dark Side of Families,* pp. 119–30. Beverly Hills: Sage.

Fiora-Gormally, Nancy

1978 "Battered wives who kill. Double standard out of court, single standard in?" *Law and Human Behavior* 2(2): 133–65.

Fisher, Bruce, and Jane Berdie

1978 "Adolescent abuse and neglect: Issues of incidents, intervention, and service delivery." *Child Abuse and Neglect* 2(3): 173–92.

Flanagan, Timothy J., and Maureen McLeod (eds.)

1983 *Sourcebook of Criminal Justice Statistics—1982.* Department of Justice, Bureau of Justice Statistics. Washington, D.C.: Government Printing Office.

Flanagan, Timothy J., David J. van Alstyne, and Michael R. Gottfredson (eds.)

1982 *Sourcebook of Criminal Justice Statistics—1981.* Department of Justice, Bureau of Justice Statistics. Washington, D.C.: Government Printing Office.

Fleming, Jennifer Baker

1979   *Stopping Wife Abuse: A Guide to the Emotional, Psychological, and Legal Implications for the Abused Woman and Those Helping Her.* Garden City, N.Y.: Anchor Press.

Flynn, John, P. Anderson, B. Coleman, M. Finn, C. Moeller, H. Nodel, R. Novara, C. Turner, and H. Weiss

1975   *Spouse Assault: Its Dimensions and Characteristics in Kalamazoo County, Michigan.* Kalamazoo: Western Michigan University, School of Social Work.

Flynn, W. R.

1970   "Frontier justice: A contribution to the theory of child battery." *American Journal of Psychiatry* 127(3): 375–79.

Fojtik, Kathleen

1982   Interview in *SANEnews. SANEnews: A National Newsletter on Battered Women* 2(2): 7–8.

Fontana, Vincent J.

1964   *The Maltreated Child: The Maltreatment Syndrome in Children.* Springfield, Ill.: Charles C. Thomas.
1973   *Somewhere a Child Is Crying: Maltreatment—Causes and Prevention.* New York: Macmillan.
1976   *Child Abuse in the Name of Discipline.* New York: New York Foundling Hospital Center for Parent and Child Development.

Fontana, Vincent J., and Esther Robinson

1976   "A multidisciplinary approach to the treatment of child abuse." *Pediatrics* 57(5): 760–64.

Footlick, Jerrold K.

1979   "Beating the rape rap." *Newsweek,* January 8, p. 41.

Forward, Susan, and Craig Buck

1978   *Betrayal of innocence: Incest and its devastation.* New York: Penguin.

Fox, Catherine

1979   "With this ring I thee rape." *MacLeans Magazine,* January 8, p. 23.

Fox, R.

1968   "Treating the alcoholic's family." In R. J. Catanzaro (ed.), *Alcoholism*, pp. 105–15. Springfield, Ill.: Charles C. Thomas.

Frazer, James G.

1958   *The Golden Bough*. New York: Macmillan.

Frazier, S. H.

1974   *Murder—Single and Multiple*. Association for Research in Nervous and Mental Disease. Research Publications. 52:304–12.

Frederick, Robert E.

1979   "Domestic violence: A guide for police response." Harrisburg: Pennsylvania Coalition Against Domestic Violence.

Freeman, Michael D. A.

1979   *Violence in the Home*. Westmead, England: Saxon House.
1981   "'But if you can't rape your wife who(m) can you rape?': The marital rape re-examined." *Family Law Quarterly* 15(1): 1–29.

Freud, Sigmund

1962   *Three Essays on the Theory of Sexuality*. New York: Basic Books.

Friedman, Stanford B., and Carole W. Morse

1974   "Child abuse: A five-year follow-up of early case findings in the emergency department." *Pediatrics* 54(4): 404–10.

Friedrich, William M., and Jerry A. Boriskin

1976   "The role of the child in abuse: A Review of the literature." *American Journal of Orthopsychiatry* 46(4): 580–90.

Frieze, Irene Hanson

1979   "Perceptions of battered wives." In Irene Frieze, Daniel Bar-Tal, and John S. Carroll (eds.), *New Approaches to Social Problems*, pp. 79–108. San Francisco: Jossey-Bass.
1980   "Causes and consequences of marital rape." Paper presented at the annual meeting of the American Psychological Association, Montreal, Canada.

Frieze, Irene Hanson, and Jaime Knoble

1980   "The effects of alcohol on marital violence." Paper presented at the annual meeting of the American Psychological Association,

Montreal, Canada.

Fromson, Terry L.

1977   "The case for legal remedies for abused women." *New York University Review of Law and Social Change* 6(2): 135–74.

Fullwood, P. Catlin

1983   "Legislative alert." *Southern California Coalition on Battered Women* 8(4): 10.

Gagnon, John H.

1965   "Female child victims of sex offenses." *Social Problems* 13(2): 176–92.

Gaines, Richard, Alice Sandgrund, Arthur H. Green, and Ernest Power

1978   "Etiological factors in child maltreatment: A multivariate study of abusing, neglecting, and normal mothers." *Journal of Abnormal Psychology* 87(5): 531–40.

Ganley, Anne L.

1981   "Counseling programs for men who batter: Elements of effective programs." *Response* 4(8): 3–4.

Ganley, Anne L., and Lance Harris

1978   "Domestic violence: Issues in designing and implementing programs for male batterers." Paper presented at the annual meeting of the American Psychological Association, Toronto, Canada.

Garbarino, James

1976   "A preliminary study of some ecological correlates of child abuse: The impact of socioeconomic stress on mothers." *Child Development* 47(1): 178–85.
1980   "Meeting the needs of mistreated youths." *Social Work* 25(2): 122–26.

Garbarino, James, and Nancy Jacobson

1978   "Youth helping youth in cases of maltreatment of adolescents." *Child Welfare* 17(8): 505–10.

Gayford, Jasper

1975a   "Wife battering: A preliminary survey of 100 cases." *British Medical Journal* 1(January): 194–97.
1975b   "Research on battered wives." *Royal Society of Health Journal*

            95(6): 288–90.
1975c   "Battered wives." *Medicine, Science, and the Law* 15(5): 237–45.
1976   "Ten types of battered wives." *Welfare Officer* 25(1): 5–9.

Gebhard, Paul H., John H. Gagnon, Wardell B. Pomeroy, and Cornelia V. Christenson

1965   *Sex Offenders: An Analysis of Types.* New York: Harper & Row.

Geen, R. G., and L. Berkowitz

1966   "Name-mediated aggressive cue properties." *Journal of Personality* 34:456–65.
1967   "Some conditions facilitating the occurrence of aggression after the observation of violence." *Journal of Personality* 35:666–76.

Geis, Gilbert

1978a   "Rape-and-marriage: Law and law reform in England, the United States, and Sweden." *Adelaide Law Review* 6(2): 284–303.
1978b   "Lord Hale, witches, and rape." *British Journal of Law and Society* 5(Summer): 26–44.
1980   "Rape and marriage: Historical and cross-cultural considerations." Paper presented at the annual meeting of the American Sociological Association, New York.

Gelles, Richard J.

1973   "Child abuse as psychopathology: A sociological critique and re-formulation." *American Journal of Orthopsychiatry* 43(4): 611–21.
1974   "Child abuse as psychopathology: A sociological critique and re-formulation." In Suzanne Steinmetz and Murray Straus (eds.), *Violence in the Family*, pp. 190–204. New York: Harper & Row.
1975a   "The social construction of child abuse." *American Journal of Orthopsychiatry* 45(3): 363–71.
1975b   "Violence and pregnancy: A note on the extent of the problem and needed services." *Family Coordinator* (January): 81–86.
1976   "Abused wives: Why do they stay?" *Journal of Marriage and the Family* 38(4): 659–68.
1977   "Power, sex, and violence: The case of marital rape." *Family Coordinator* 26(October): 339–47.
1979   *Family Violence.* Beverly Hills: Sage.
1981   "An exchange/social control theory of intrafamily violence." Paper presented at the National Conference for Family Violence Researchers, Durham, N.H.

Gelles, Richard J., and Murray A. Straus

1979   "Violence in the American family." *Journal of Social Issues* 35(2): 15–39.

Gentry, Charles E., and Barbara D. Nelson

1980   "Developmental patterns for abuse programs: Application to the aging." In David F. Holden and Peggie L. Carey (eds.), *Abuse of Older Persons*, pp. 75–87. Knoxville: University of Tennessee, School of Social Work.

Gepfert, Ken

1979   "Mother shot to death in front of 2 children." *Los Angeles Times* May 24, pp. I-1, 12.

Gerbner, George, Catherine J. Ross, and Edward Zigler (eds.)

1980   *Child Abuse: An Agenda for Action.* New York: Oxford University Press.

Giarretto, Henry

1976   "The treatment of father daughter incest: A psycho-social approach." *Children Today* 34 (July-August): 2–5.

Gibson, Henry

1982   "But Americans can act in many ways." *Los Angeles Times* April 26, p. II-5.

Gil, David G.

1970   *Violence Against Children.* Cambridge, Mass.: Harvard University Press.
1971   "Violence against children." *Journal of Marriage and the Family* 33(4): 637–48.
1974   "A holistic perspective on child abuse and its prevention." *Journal of Sociology and Social Welfare* 2(2): 110–25.
1975   "Unraveling child abuse." *American Journal of Orthopsychiatry* 45(3): 346–56.

Gillespie, Dair L.

1971   "Who has the power? The marital struggle." *Journal of Marriage and the Family* 33(August): 445–58.

Giovannoni, Jeanne M.

1971   "Parental mistreatment: Perpetrators and victims." *Journal of Marriage and the Family* 33:649–57.

Giovannoni, Jeanne M., and Rosina M. Becerra

1979   *Defining Child Abuse.* New York: Free Press.

Giovannoni, Jeanne M., and Andrew Billingsley

1970   "Child neglect among the poor: A study of parental adequacy in families of three ethnic groups." *Child Welfare* 49(4): 196–204.

Glasser, Paul, and Charles Garvin

1981   "A framework for family analysis relevant to child abuse, neglect and juvenile delinquency." In Robert J. Hunner and Yvonne Elder Walker (eds.), *Exploring the Relationship Between Child Abuse and Delinquency,* pp. 100–14. Montclair, N.J.: Allanheld, Osmun.

Glenn, Norval D., and Sara McLanahan

1982   "Children and marital happiness: A further specification of the relationship." *Journal of Marriage and the Family* 44(1): 63–72.

Glick, Paul C., and Graham B. Spanier

1980   "Married and unmarried cohabitation in the United States." *Journal of Marriage and the Family* 42(1)19–30.

Goffman, Erving

1963   *Stigma.* Englewood Cliffs, N.J.: Prentice-Hall.

Goldwater, Gary

1980   Personal letter, December 29.

Gomes-Schwartz, Beverly

1981   "A model for assessing factors contributing to trauma in child sexual abuse." Paper presented at the National Conference for Family Violence Researchers, Durham, N.H.

Goode, William J.

1964   *The Family.* Englewood Cliffs, N.J.: Prentice-Hall.
1969   "Violence between intimates." In Donald J. Mulvihill and Melvin M. Tumin (eds.), *Crime of Violence,* pp. 941–77. Washington, D.C.: Government Printing Office.
1971   "Force and violence in the family." *Journal of Marriage and the Family* 33(November): 624–35.

Goodman, Ellen

1984   "Pornography—Free speech conflict is unresolved." *Los Angeles*

Times, January 17, pp. II-11.

Goodwin, J., M. Simms, and R. Bergman

1979   "Hysterical seizures: A sequel to incest." *American Journal of Orthopsychiatry* 49(4): 698–703.

Green, Arthur H.

1976   "A psychodynamic approach to the study and treatment of child abusing parents." *Journal of American Academy of Child Psychiatry* 15(Summer): 414–29.

Greenberg, Nahman H.

1979   "The epidemiology of childhood sexual abuse." *Pediatric Annals* 8(5): 289–98.

Greenwood, Marion

1980   "The double victimization of children who are victims of domestic violence." Paper presented at the annual meeting of the Law and Society Association, Madison, Wis.

Griffin, Susan

1975   "Rape: The all-American crime." In Leroy G. Schultz (ed.), *Rape Victimology,* pp. 375–95. Springfield, Ill.: Charles C. Thomas.

Gross, M.

1979   "Incestuous rape: A cause for hysterical seizures in four adolescent girls." *American Journal of Orthopsychiatry* 49(4): 704–8.

Grossman, Beth

1977   "Children's 'Ideal Self'—Which sex?" Paper presented at the annual meeting of the American Psychological Association, San Francisco.

Groth, A. Nicholas, with H. Jean Birnbaum

1979   *Men Who Rape: Psychology of the Offender.* New York: Plenum.

Guttmacher Institute, Alan

1979   *Abortions and the Poor: Private Morality, Public Responsibility.* New York: Alan Guttmacher Institute.
1981   *Teenage Pregnancy: The Problem That Hasn't Gone Away.* New York: Alan Guttmacher Institute.

Haddad, Jill, and Lloyd H. Martin

1981   *What if . . . I Say No?* Bakersfield: M. H. Cap.

Haeuser, Adrienne A., Janet Stenlund, and Laura Daniel

1981   "Policy and program implications in the child delinquency corre-
        lation." In Robert J. Hunner and Yvonne Elder Walker (eds.), *Ex-
        ploring the Relationship Between Child Abuse and Delinquency,*
        pp. 11–24. Montclair, N.J.: Allanheld, Osmun.

Hafen, Brent Q., with Molly J. Brog

1983   *Alcohol.* 2nd ed. New York: West.

Haggerty, Robert J.

1964   "Discussion on the child's role in battered child syndrome." Ab-
        stract in *Society for Pediatric Research* 64(6): 1079–81.

Hamlin, D. E., D. B. Hurwitz, and G. Spieker

1979   "Perspective." *Alcohol Health and Research World* 4(1): 17–22.

Hampton, Marilynne Brandon

1979   "Reducing victim/witness intimidation in domestic violence
        crimes." Testimony for the American Bar Association Section of
        Criminal Justice Committee on Victims Hearings on Victim/Wit-
        ness Intimidation, Washington, D.C.
1982   "The politics of domestic violence." Unpublished paper.

Hanneke, Christine R., and Nancy M. Shields

1981   "Patterns of family and non-family violence: An approach to the
        study of violent husbands." Paper presented at the National Con-
        ference for Family Violence Researchers, Durham, N.H.

Hays, H. R.

1964   *The Dangerous Sex: The Myth of Feminine Evil.* New York: G. P.
        Putnam's Sons.

Helfer, Ray E., and C. Henry Kempe (eds.)

1968   *The Battered Child.* Chicago: University of Chicago Press.
1974   *The Battered Child.* 2nd ed. Chicago: University of Chicago Press.
1976   *Child Abuse and Neglect: The Family and the Community.* Cam-
        bridge, Mass.: Ballinger.

Hendricks, Jon, and D. Davis Hendricks

1977   *Aging in Mass Society, Myths and Realities.* Cambridge, Mass.: Winthrop.

Henshaw, Stanley K., and Kevin O'Reilly

1983   "Characteristics of abortion patients in the United States, 1979 and 1980." *Family Planning Perspectives* 15(1): 5–16.

Henton, June, Rodney Cate, James Koval, Sally Lloyd, and Scott Christopher

1983   "Romance and violence in dating relationships." Unpublished paper.

Herman, Judith

1981   *Father-Daughter Incest.* Cambridge, Mass.: Harvard University Press.

Herman, Judith, and Lisa Hirschman

1980   "Father-Daughter incest." In Kee MacFarlane, Linda L. Jenstrom, and Barbara McComb Jones (eds.), *Sexual Abuse of Children: Selected Readings,* pp. 65–77. Department of Health, Education, and Welfare. Washington, D.C.: Government Printing Office. Pub. No. (OHDS) 78-30161.

Herrenkohl, Ellen C., and Roy C. Herrenkohl

1981   "Explanations of child maltreatment: A preliminary appraisal." Paper presented at the National Conference for Family Violence Researchers, Durham, N.H.

Herrenkohl, Roy C., Ellen C. Herrenkohl, and Lori J. Toedter

1981   "Perspectives on the intergenerational transmission of abuse." Paper presented at the National Conference for Family Violence Researchers, Durham, N.H.

Herzberger, Sharon D.

1981   "A social cognitive approach to the cross-generational transmission of abuse." Paper presented at the National Conference for Family Violence Researchers, Durham, N.H.

Hilberman, Elaine

1980   "Overview: The 'Wife-beater's wife' reconsidered." *American Journal of Psychiatry* 137(11): 1336–47.

Hilberman, Elaine, and Kit Munson

1978   "Sixty battered women." *Victimology* 2(3/4): 460–70.

Hilgard, Ernest R., and Gordon H. Bower

1966   *Theories of Learning.* 3d ed. New York: Meredith.

Hill, Winfred F.

1971   *Learning: A Survey of Psychological Interpretations.* Scranton, Pa.: Chandler.

Hindelang, Michael J., Michael R. Gottfredson, and Timothy J. Flanagan (eds.)

1981   *Sourcebook of Criminal Justice Statistics—1980.* Department of Justice, Bureau of Justice Statistics. Washington, D.C.: Government Printing Office.

Hindman, Margaret H.

1977   "Child abuse and neglect: The alcohol connection." *Alcohol Health and Research World* 1(3): 2–7.
1979   "Family violence." *Alcohol Health and Research World* 4(1): 2–10.

Hoffman, Lois Wladis, and Jean Denby Manis

1979   "The value of children in the United States: A new approach to the study of fertility." *Journal of Marriage and the Family* 41(3): 583–96.

Hogbin, Ian

1970   *The Island of Menstruating Men: Religion in Wogebo, New Guinea.* Scranton, Pa.: Chandler.

Holden, David F., and Peggie L. Carey (eds.)

1981   *Abuse of Older Persons.* Knoxville: University of Tennessee, School of Social Work.

Holt, John

1974   *Escape From Childhood. The Needs and Rights of Children.* New York: Ballantine Books.

Huffman, Starr

1975   "Some observations on weekend foster home visitation as a step out of the institution." *Child Welfare* 54(5): 351–53.

Human Relations

1981   "TV and families: The plug-in drug?? Part III." *Human Relations* 6(8), University of California, Cooperative Extension.

Hunner, Robert J., and Yvonne Elder Walker (eds.)

1981   *Exploring the Relationship Between Child Abuse and Delinquency.* Montclair, N.J.: Allanheld, Osmun.

Hunt, Morton

1970   *Parents and Children in History: The Psychology of Family life in Early Modern France.* New York: Basic Books.
1974   *Sexual Behavior in the 1970's.* Chicago: Playboy Press.

Hunter, Ann

1980   "Legal strategies for fighting pornography." *Newspage* 5(4): 5–6.

Interface

1981   *The Ethical Eye: Examining Media Responsibility.* Vol. 2. Fullerton: California State University.

Jacobucci, Louis

1965   "Casework treatment of the neglectful mother." *Social Casework* 46(6): 221–26.

Jaffe, Natalie

1980   *Assaults on Women: Rape and Wife Beatings.* Public Affairs Pamphlet No. 579. New York: Public Affairs Committee.

James, Howard

1969   *Children in Trouble: A National Scandal.* Boston: Christian Science Publishing Society.

Japenga, Ann

1984   "Sex violence research: He takes a feminist approach." *Los Angeles Times,* January 6, pp. V-1, 16.

Jensen, Rita Henley

1978   "Battered wives: A survey." *Social Service Quarterly* 47(14): 142–46.

Johnson, Douglas G.

1979   "Abuse and neglect—not for children only!" *Journal of Geronto-*

logical Nursing 5(4): 11–13.

Johnson, John M.

1981   "Program enterprise and official cooperation in the battered women's shelter movement." *American Behavioral Scientist* 24(6): 827–42.

Jones, Ann

1980   *Women Who Kill.* New York: Fawcett Columbine.

Jordan, Nancy

1983   "AMI is 'playing around.'" *News Page: Women Against Violence in Pornography and Media* 7(4): 5.

Julian, Valerie, and Cynthia Mohr

1979   "Father-daughter incest: Profile of the offender." *Victimology* 4(4): 348–60.

Kadushin, Alfred

1974   *Child Welfare Services.* 2nd ed. New York: Macmillan.

Kadushin, Alfred, and Judith A. Martin

1981   *Child Abuse: An Interactional Event.* New York: Columbia University Press.

Kahn, Robert L.

1982   "The mental health system and the future aged." In K. Warner Schaie and James Geiwitz (eds.), *Adult Development and Aging,* pp. 393–403. Boston: Little, Brown.

Kaminer, Wendy

1980   "Pornography and the first amendment: Prior restraints and private action." In Laura Lederer (ed.), *Take Back the Night: Women on Pornography,* pp. 241–47. New York: William Morrow.

Kanowitz, Leo

1969   *Women and the Law: The Unfinished Revolution.* Albuquerque: University of New Mexico.

Katz, Katheryn D.

1979   "Elder abuse." *Journal of Family Law* 18(4): 695–722.

Kellermann, Joseph L.

1974   "Focus on the family." *Alcohol Health and Research World* (Fall):
        9–11.

Kelly, John

1975   "The battered parent." *Practical Psychology for Physicians* 2(9):
        65–67.

Kempe, C. Henry, and Ray E. Helfer (eds.)

1972   *Helping the Battered Child and His Family.* Philadelphia: J. B.
        Lippincott.

Kempe, C. Henry, F. N. Silverman, B. F. Steele, W. Droegemuller, and H.
K. Silver

1962   "The battered-child syndrome." *Journal of the American Medical
        Association* 181(1): 105–12.

Kempe, R., and C. Henry Kempe

1978   *Child Abuse.* Cambridge, Mass.: Harvard University Press.

Keniston, Kenneth, for the Carnegie Council on Children

1977   *All Our Children.* New York: Harcourt Brace Jovanovich.
1979   "Foreword." In Richard de Lone, *Small Futures,* pp. ix–xiv. New
        York: Harcourt Brace Jovanovich.

Kent, James T.

1973   *Follow-up Study of Abused Children.* Los Angeles: Los Angeles
        Children's Hospital, Division of Psychiatry.
1976   "A follow-up study of abused children." *Journal of Pediatric Psy-
        chology* (Spring): 25–31.

Kiersh, Edward

1980   "Can families survive incest?" *Corrections Magazine* 6(2): 31–38.

Kinard, E. Milling

1979   "The psychological consequences of abuse for the child." *Journal
        of Social Issues* 35(2): 82–100.

King, Charles H.

1975   "The ego and the integration of violence in homicidal youth."
        American Journal of Orthopsychiatry 45(1): 134–45.

King, Nancy

1983   "Exploitation and abuse of older family members: An overview of the problem." *Response* 6(2): 1–2, 13–15.

Kirchner, Rioghan M.

1977   "Pregnancy and violence." Unpublished paper.

Kitsuse, John I.

1967   "Societal reactions to deviant behavior: Problems in theory and method." In Howard S. Becker (ed.), *The Other Side*, pp. 87–102. New York: Free Press.

Klagsbrun, Micheline, and Donald I. Davis

1977   "Substance abuse and family interaction." *Journal of Family Process* 16(2): 149–74.

Klatt, Michael R.

1980   "Rape in marriage: The law in Texas and the need for reform." *Baylor Law Review* 32(1): 109–21.

Kleckner, James H.

1978   "Wife beaters and beaten wives: Co-conspirators in crimes of violence." *Psychology* 15(1): 54–56.

Klein, Dorie

1982   "Men who batter: The social causes of violence." Paper presented at the annual meeting of the Sociologists for Women in Society, San Francisco.

Koestler, Frances A.

1977   *Runaway Teenagers*. Public Affairs Pamphlet No. 552. New York: Public Affairs Committee.

Konopka, Gisela

1975   *Young Girls: A Portrait of Adolescence*. Englewood Cliffs, N.J.: Prentice-Hall.

Koop, C. Everett

1982   "Violence and Public Health." National Organization of Victim Assistance, *NOVA Newsletter* 6(10): 1–8.

Koval, James E., James J. Ponzetti Jr., and Rodney M. Cate

1982 "Programmatic intervention for men involved in conjugal violence." *Family Therapy* 9(2): 147–54.

Krasnow, E., and E. Fleshner

1979 "Parental abuse, another form of family violence. An identification of a specified need and a gap in the delivery of services." Paper presented at the annual meeting of the Gerontological Society, Washington, D.C.

Kremen, Eleanor

1976 "The 'discovery' of battered wives: Considerations for the development of a social service network." Paper presented at the annual meeting of the American Sociological Association, New York.

Kroth, Jerome A.

1978 *Evaluation of the Child Sexual Abuse Demonstration and Treatment Project.* California Department of Health. Sacramento: Office of Child Abuse Prevention.

Kuhl, Anna F.

1981 "A preliminary profile of abusing men." Paper presented at the Academy for Criminal Justice Sciences, Philadelphia.

Kurman, Wendy

1980 "Marital rape: A comparative study—Great Britain and California." Unpublished paper.

Landau, Simha F.

1976 "The rape offender's perception of his victim: Some cross-cultural findings." Paper presented at the Second International Symposium on Victimology, Boston.

Laner, Mary Riege

1982 "Courtship abuse and aggression: Contextual aspects." Paper presented at the Conference on Families and Close Relationships, Lubbock, Tex.

Laner, Mary Riege, and Jeanine Thompson

1982 "Abuse and aggression in courting couples." *Deviant Behavior* 3:229–44.

Lang, A. R., D. J. Goeckner, V. J. Adessor, and G. A. Marlatt

1975   "Effect of alcohol on aggression in male social drinkers." *Journal of Abnormal Psychology* 84:508–18.

Langer, T. S., J. C. Gersten, and J. G. Eisenberg

1976   "The epidemiology of mental disorder in children: Implications for community psychiatry." Paper presented at the Fourth International Symposium of the Kittay Scientific Foundations, New York.

Langer, William L.

1972   "Checks on population growth: 1750–1850." *Scientific American* 226:93–100.

Langley, Roger, and Richard C. Levy

1977   *Wife Beating: The Silent Crisis.* New York: E. P. Dutton.

Latina, Jane C., and Jeffrey L. Schembera

1976   "Volunteer homes for status offenders: An alternative to detention." *Federal Probation* 40(4): 45–49.

Lau, Elizabeth, and Jordan I. Kosberg

1979   "Abuse of the elderly by informal care providers." *Aging* 299–300 (September/October): 10–15.

Lederer, Laura (ed.)

1980   *Take Back the Night: Women on Pornography.* New York: William Morrow.

Leghorn, Lisa

1978   "Grass roots services for battered women: A model for long-term change." In *Battered Women: Issues of Public Policy,* pp. 138–42, 444–62. Washington, D.C.: Commission on Civil Rights.

LeGrand, Camille

1973   "Rape and rape laws: Sexism in society and law." *California Law Review* 61(919).

Lemert, Edwin M.

1972   *Human Deviance, Social Problems, and Social Control.* 2nd ed. Englewood Cliffs, N.J.: Prentice-Hall.

Leo, John

1981   "Cradle-to-grave intimacy." *Time,* September 7, p. 69.

Lerman, Lisa

1981a   "State legislation on domestic violence." *Response* 4(7): 1–18.
1981b   "Criminal prosecution of the wife beaters." *Response* 4(3): 1–19.

Lerman, Lisa G., and Franci Livingston

1983   "State legislation on domestic violence." *Response* 6(5).

Lerner, Melvin J.

1980   *The Belief in a Just World: A Fundamental Delusion.* New York:
        Plenum Press.

Levine, Milton I.

1976   "A pediatrician's view." *Pediatric Annals* 5(3): 6–9.

Lewin, Tamar

1979   "When victims kill." *National Law Journal* 2(7): 2–4, 11.

Lewis, Dorothy Otnow, and Shelley S. Shanok

1979   "A comparison of the medical histories of incarcerated delin-
        quent children and a matched sample of non-delinquent chil-
        dren." *Child Psychiatry and Human Development* 9(4): 210–14.

Lewis, Dorothy Otnow, Shelley S. Shanok, and David A. Balla

1979a   "Parental criminality and medical histories of delinquent chil-
        dren." *American Journal of Psychiatry* 136(3): 288–92.

Lewis, Dorothy Otnow, Shelley S. Shanok, Jonathan H. Pincus, and Gilbert H. Glaser

1979b   "Violent juvenile delinquents." *Journal of Child Psychiatry* 18(2):
        307–19.

Libbey, Patricia, and Rodger Bybee

1979   "The physical abuse of adolescents." *Journal of Social Issues*
        35(2): 101–26.

Libby, Roger W., and Murray A. Straus

1980   "Make love not war? Sexual meanings, and violence in a sample
        of university students." *Archives of Sexual Behavior* 9(2): 133–46.

Liddick, Betty

1978   "Women victims—Statistics to sales gimmicks." *Los Angeles Times,* February 16, pp. IV-1, 11–12.

Light, Richard J.

1973   "Abused and neglected children." *Harvard Educational Review* 13(4).
1974   "Abused and neglected children in America: A study of alternative policies." *Harvard Educational Review* 43:356–98.

Lion, John R.

1977   "Clinical aspects of wifebattering." In Maria Roy (ed.), *Battered Women,* pp. 126–36. New York: Van Nostrand Reinhold.

Lipner, Joanne D.

1979   "The use of community resources in work with abusive families." In *Child Abuse and Development Disabilities: Essays,* pp. 34–38. Department of Health, Education, and Welfare. Washington, D.C.: Government Printing Office. Pub. No. (OHDS)79-30226.

Lippitt, Jill

1980   "Choosing a strategy to fight pornography." *Newspage* 5(4): 4.

Lorenz, K.

1966   *On Aggression.* New York: Harcourt Brace.

Los Angeles Times

1978   "Who struck Jane . . . or John?" February 12, p. VIII-28.
1979   "Reporter to be arraigned in stabbing death of wife." May 28, pp. II-1, 6.
1981   "Insanity defense for defendant hinted: Psychiatric exam ordered in family abuse case." December 19, p. II-6.
1983a   "Boy guilty in slaying of his abusive father." February 20, p. I-5.
1983b   "Wyoming girl convicted of aiding brother in slaying father." March 12, p. I-23.
1983c   News item, November 24, I-2.

Loseke, Donileen R., and Sarah Fenstermaker Berk

1983   "The work of shelters: Battered women and initial calls for help." Forthcoming in *Victimology.*

Lourie, Ira S.

1977 "The phenomenon of the abused adolescent: A clinical study." *Victimology* 2(2): 268–76.

Loving, Nancy

1980 *Responding to Spouse Abuse and Wife Beating: A Guide for Police.* Washington, D.C.: Police Executive Research Forum.

Lubenow, Gerald C.

1983 "When kids kill their parents." *Newsweek,* June 27, pp. 35–36.

Lukianowicz, N.

1972 "Incest." *British Journal of Psychiatry* 120:301–13.

Lynch, Catherine G.

1977 "Women as victims—Rape, battering, incest and muggings—Victim advocacy and victims within the system." Paper presented at the annual meeting of the Sociologists for Women in Society section of the American Sociological Association, Chicago.

Lystad, Mary (ed.)

1974 *Violence at Home: An Annotated Bibliography.* Division of Special Mental Health Programs. Rockville, Md.: National Institute of Mental Health.

MacAndrew, Craig, and Robert Edgerton

1969 *Drunken Comportment: A Social Explanation.* Chicago: Aldine.

MacFarlane, Kee

1978 "Resource paper: Sexual abuse of children." In Jane Roberts Chapman and Margaret Gates (eds.), *The Victimization of Women,* pp. 81–109. Beverly Hills: Sage.

MacFarlane, Kee, and Leonard Lieber

1978 *Parents Anonymous: The Growth of An Idea.* Department of Health, Education, and Welfare. Washington, D.C.: Government Printing Office. Pub. No. (OHDS)78-30086.

MacFarlane, Kee, Barbara McComb Jones, and Linda L. Jenstrom (eds.)

1980 *Sexual Abuse of Children: Selected Readings.* Department of Health, Education, and Welfare. Washington, D.C.: Government Printing Office. Pub. No. 78-30161.

MacPherson, Myra

1977   "Battered wives and self-defense pleas." *Washington Post*, December 4, pp. A-1, 14.

Madden, Denis J., and John R. Lion (eds.)

1976   *Rage-Hate-Assault and Other Forms of Violence*. New York: Halsted.

Maden, Marc F., and David F. Wrench

1977   "Significant findings in child abuse research." *Victimology* 2(2): 196–24.

Mahan, Sue

1982   *Unfit Mothers*. Palo Alto: Research Associates.

Maisch, Herbert

1972   *Incest*. New York: Stein and Day.

Makepeace, James M.

1981   "Courtship violence among college students." *Family Relations* 30(1): 97–101.
1982   "Courtship violence on a low-risk campus." Paper presented at the annual meeting of the Pacific Sociological Association, San Diego.

Malamuth, Neil M.

1981   "Rape proclivity among males." *Journal of Social Issues* 37(4): 138–57.

Maney, Ann

1983   "Child sexual abuse: Incidence and prevalence." *Response* 6(6): 7–8.

Mar, Lily

1983   "Write back! fight back!" *News Page: Women Against Violence in Pornography and Media* 7(5): 3.

Marquardt, Jane A., and Cathie Cox

1979   "Violence against wives: Expected effects of Utah's spouse abuse act." *Journal of Contemporary Law* 5(Spring): 277–92.

Marsden, Dennis, and David Owens

1975   "Jekyll and Hyde marriages." *New Society* 8(May): 333–35.

Martin, Del

1976   *Battered Wives*. San Francisco: Glide.
1979a   "Foreword." In Jennifer Baker Fleming, *Stopping Wife Abuse: A Guide to the Emotional, Psychological, and Legal Implications for the Abused Woman and Those Helping Her*, pp. 9–13. Garden City, N.Y.: Anchor.
1979b   Presentation before the State of California Assembly Criminal Justice Committee Hearing on AB-546, April 23.
1982   "Introduction." In Ginny NiCarthy, *Getting Free: A Handbook for Women in Abusive Relationships*, pp. xvii–xix. Seattle: Seal Press.

Martin, Harold P., and Patricia Beezley

1977   "Behavioral observations of abused children." *Developmental Medicine and Child Neurology* 19(3): 373–87.

Martin, Harold P., Patricia Beezley, Esther F. Conway, and C. Henry Kempe

1974   "The development of abused children." *Advances in Pediatrics* 21:25–73.

Martin, Judith

1981   "Maternal and paternal abuse of children: Theoretical and research perspectives." Paper presented at the National Conference for Family Violence Researchers, Durham, N.H.

Martin, Ralph E.

1969   *Jennie: The Life of Lady Randolph Churchill*. New York: New American Library.

Martz, Hugo E.

1979   "Indiana's approach to child abuse and neglect: A frustration of family integrity." *Valparaiso University Law Review* 14(1): 69–121.

Masters, Robert E. L.

1964   "Misogyny and sexual conflict." In Robert E. L. Masters and Eduard Lea (eds.), *The Anti-Sex. The Belief in the Natural Inferiority of Women: Studies in Male Frustration and Sexual Conflict*, pp. 3–52. New York: Julian Press.

Masters, Robert E. L., and Eduard Lea (eds.)

1964   *The Anti-Sex. The Belief in the Natural Inferiority of Women: Stud-*

ies in Male Frustration and Sexual Conflict. New York: Julian Press.

Matza, David

1969   *Becoming Deviant.* Englewood Cliffs, N.J.: Prentice-Hall.

Maurer, Adah

1981   *Paddles Away: A Psychological Study of Physical Punishment in Schools.* Palo Alto: R & E Research Associates.

Maxwell, Evan, and Jeffrey Perlman

1981   "Wife tells of fear in household: Hearing held for husband charged with incest, assault." *Los Angeles Times,* December 9, pp. II-1, 8.

May, Margaret

1978   "Violence in the family: An historical perspective." In J. P. Martin (ed.), *Violence and the Family,* pp. 135–68. New York: John Wiley and Sons.

Mayer, Joseph, and Rebecca Black

1977   "Child abuse and neglect in families with an alcohol or opiate addicted parent." *Child Abuse and Neglect* 1:85–98.

Mayfield, D.

1976   "Alcoholism, alcohol, intoxication, and assaultive behavior." *Diseases of the Nervous System* 37:288–91.

McCaghy, C. H.

1968   "Drinking and deviance disavowal: The case of child molesters." *Social Problems* 16(1): 43–49.

McClelland, D. C., W. N. Davis, R. Kalin, and E. Wanner

1972   *The Drinking Man.* New York: Free Press.

McCord, William, Joan McCord, and Alan Howard

1970   "Familial correlates of aggression in nondelinquent male children." In Edwin Megargee and Jack Hokanson (eds.), *Dynamics of Aggression,* pp. 41–65. New York: Harper & Row.

McDermott, M. Joan

1979   *Criminal Victimization in Urban Schools.* Department of Justice, Law Enforcement Assistance Administration. Washington, D.C.:

Government Printing Office.

McLaughlin, Laurie

1982   "Child sexual assault is your issue." *Aegis* (Winter): 14–16.

McLellan, Dennis

1981   "SLAM gets tough with child molesters." *Los Angeles Times,* December 3, p. V-1.

McNeese, Margaret C., and Joan R. Hebeler

1977   "The abused child: A clinical approach to identification and management." *Clinical Symposia* 29(5).

Mead, Jim

1982   Personal conversation. October 22.

Mead, Margaret

1973   "Sex and temperament." In Alice S. Rossi (ed.), *The Feminist Papers,* pp. 658–71. New York: Bantam.

Meiselman, Karin

1978   *Incest.* San Francisco: Jossey-Bass.

Mellor, Joanna, and George S. Getzel

1980   "Stress and service needs of those who care for the aged." Paper presented at the annual meeting of the Gerontological Society, San Diego.

Mercer, Jane

1972   "Who is normal? Two perspectives on mild mental retardation." In E. Gartley Jaco (ed.), *Patients, Physicians and Illness,* pp. 67–86. New York: Free Press.

Merton, Robert K.

1968   *Social Theory and Social Structure.* 2nd ed. New York: Free Press.

Mettger, Zak

1982a   "Help for men who batter: An overview of issues and programs." *Response* 5(6): 1–2, 7–8, 23.
1982b   "More than a shoestring budget: Survival and growth for family violence programs." *Response* 5(3): 1–2, 15, 17–20.

1982c "A case of rape: Forced sex in marriage." *Response* 5(2): 1–2, 13–16.

Metzger, Mary

1976 "'What did you do to provoke him?' An analysis of 'The Battered Wife Syndrome.'" *Politics and Health Policy* (Spring): 1–24.

Meyers, Laura

1983 "Battered wives, dead husbands." In Arlene S. Skolnick and Jerome H. Skolnick (eds.), *Family in Transition,* pp. 345–52. 4th ed. Boston: Little, Brown.

Middleton, Audrey

1977 "A refuge in Belfast." Paper presented at the International Sociological Association Seminar on Sex Roles, Deviance, and Agents of Social Control, Dublin, Ireland.
1978 "When 'incest' is rape." *Fortnight* (January-February): 8–9.

Mill, John Stuart

1971 *On the Subjection of Women.* Greenwich, Conn.: Fawcett.

Miller, Dorothy, and George Challas

1981 "Abused children as adult parents: A twenty-five year longitudinal study." Paper presented at the National Conference for Family Violence Researchers, Durham, N.H.

Miller, S. M.

1974 "The making of a confused, middle-aged husband." In Joseph H. Pleck and Jack Sawyer (eds.), *Men and Masculinity,* pp. 44–52. Englewood Cliffs, N.J.: Prentice-Hall.

Mills, C. Wright

1956 *The Power Elite.* New York: Oxford University Press.

Milner, Joel S.

1981 "The child abuse potential inventory: Current status and uses." Unpublished paper.

Milowe, I. D., and R. S. Lourie

1964 "The child's role in the battered child syndrome." *Abstracts of the Society for Pediatric Research* 11079.*

Milt, Harry

1982   *Family Neglect and Abuse of the Aged: A Growing Concern.* Public Affairs Pamphlet No. 603. New York: Public Affairs Committee.

Minnesota Department of Corrections

1979   *Report to the Legislature.* St. Paul: Minnesota Department of Corrections.

Mitchell, Marilyn Hall

1978   "Does wife abuse justify homicide?" *Wayne Law Review* 24(5): 1705–31.

Mitra, Charlotte

1979   "'. . . for she has no right or power to refuse her consent.'" *Criminal Law Review* (September): 558–65.

Montagu, Ashley

1968   *The Natural Superiority of Women.* New York: Macmillan.
1973   *Man and Aggression.* New York: Oxford University Press.
1976   *The Nature of Human Aggression.* New York: Oxford University Press.

Morgan, P. A.

1981   "Leisure, alcohol, and domestic violence." In Van Clestichting, *Leisure in Crisis Time,* pp. 97–113. Antwerp: Foundation Van Cle.

Most, Bruce W.

1981   "New help (and hope) for wife abusers." *Family Weekly,* September 27, p. 8.

Mrazek, Patricia Beezley

1980   "Annotation, sexual abuse of children." *Journal of Child Psychology and Psychiatry* 21(1): 91–94.

Mulvihill, Donald J., and Melvin M. Tumin, Codirectors

1969   *Crimes of Violence.* Staff report submitted to the National Commission on the Causes and Prevention of Violence. Vols. 11, 12, and 13. Washington, D.C.: Government Printing Office.

Murphy, Patrick T.

1977   *Our Kindly Parent . . . The State: The Juvenile Justice System and How It Works.* New York: Penguin.

Myers, Barbara L., with Kee MacFarlane

1980 "Incest: If you think the word is ugly, take a look at its effects." In Kee MacFarlane, Barbara McComb Jones, and Linda L. Jenstrom (eds.), *Sexual Abuse of Children: Selected Readings,* pp. 98–101. Department of Health, Education, and Welfare. Washington, D.C.: Government Printing Office. Pub. No. 78-30161.

Myers, Virginia

1983 "Work shops on sexual assault." *Response* 6(3): 16.

Nagi, R.

1975 "Child abuse and neglect programs: A national overview." *Children Today* 4(May-June): 13–17.

Nakamoto, Lynn, Charlotte Owens-Wise, and Laurie Woods.

1983 "A review of some proposed measures for the improvement of child support delivery." National Center on Women and Family Law, *The Women's Advocate* 4(5): 1–3.

Nakashima, Ida I., and Gloria Zakus

1979 "Incestuous families." *Pediatric Annals* 8(5): 29–30, 32–33, 36–37, 40–42.

National Center on Child Abuse and Neglect

1975a *Child Abuse and Neglect: The Problem and Its Management.* Vol. 1. Department of Health, Education, and Welfare. Washington, D.C.: Government Printing Office. Pub. No. (OHD)75-30074.

1975b *The Roles and Responsibilities of Professionals.* Vol. 2. Department of Health, Education, and Welfare. Washington, D.C.: Government Printing Office. Pub. No. (OHD)75-30074.

1978a *Child Abuse, Neglect and the Family Within A Cultural Context: Special Issue.* Department of Health, Education, and Welfare. Washington, D.C.: Government Printing Office. Pub. No. (OHDS)78-30135.

1978b *Child Abuse and Neglect in Residential Institutions: Selected Readings on Prevention, Investigation, and Correction.* Department of Health, Education, and Welfare. Washington, D.C.: Government Printing Office. Pub. No. (OHDS)78-30160.

1978c *Child Sexual Abuse: Incest, Assault, and Sexual Exploitation.* Department of Health, Education, and Welfare. Washington, D.C.: Government Printing Office. Pub. No. (OHDS)79-30166.

1979   *Child Abuse and Development Disabilities: Essays.* Department of Health, Education, and Welfare. Washington, D.C.: Government Printing Office. Pub. No. (OHDS)79-30226.

1980a   *Wife Abuse: The Role of the Social Worker.* Department of Health, Education, and Welfare. Child Welfare Resource Information Exchange and the Office of Domestic Violence, April. Washington, D.C.: Government Printing Office.

1980b   *Selected Readings on Child Neglect.* Department of Health, Education, and Welfare. Washington, D.C.: Government Printing Office. Pub. No. (OHDS)80-30253.

1980c   *Child Abuse and Neglect: State Reporting Laws.* Department of Health, Education, and Welfare. Washington, D.C.: Government Printing Office. Pub. No. 9(OHDS)80-30265.

National Paralegal Institute

1981   *Elder Abuse and Neglect: A Guide for Practitioners and Policy Makers.* San Francisco: National Paralegal Institute.

Newberger, Eli H.

1973   "The myth of the battered child syndrome." *Current Medical Dialog* 40(April): 327–30.

1979   "The myth of the battered child syndrome." In Richard Bourne and Eli H. Newberger (eds.), *Critical Perspectives on Child Abuse,* pp. 15–18. Lexington, Mass.: D. C. Heath.

Newberger, Eli H., and Richard Bourne

1978   "The medicalization and legalization of child abuse." *American Journal of Orthopsychiatry* 38(4): 594–607.

Newberger, Eli H., and Carolyn Moore Newberger

1981   "A clinical view of research needs on child abuse." Paper presented at the National Conference for Family Violence Researchers, Durham, N.H.

Newberger, Eli H., R. B. Reed, J. H. Daniel, J. N. Hyde, and M. Kotelchuck

1977   "Pediatric social illness: Toward an etiologic classification." *Pediatrics* 60(1): 178–85.

News Page

1981   "Radical feminists tattoo 'Tattoo.'" *Women Against Violence in Pornography and Media* 5(11): 4.

1983   "Snuff in British Columbia." *Women Against Violence in Pornog-*

raphy and Media 7, no. 3 (April).

NiCarthy, Ginny

1982   *Getting Free. A Handbook for Women in Abusive Relationships.* Seattle: Seal Press.

1983a   "Addictive love and abuse: A course for teen-aged women." In Sue Davidson (ed.), *The Second Mile: Contemporary Approaches in Counseling Young Women,* pp. 115–59. Tuscon: New Directions for Young Women.

1983b   Personal communication. October 29.

NOVA Newsletter

1979   "First marital rape case bad news for victims." National Organization of Victim Assistance, *NOVA Newsletter* 11(1): 1–3.

Oberg, Shirley

1982   "'Honey, have we got a deal for you!' Selling the cops on arresting batterers." *Aegis* (Autumn): 4–7.

O'Brien, John E.

1971   "Violence in divorce prone families." *Journal of Marriage and the Family* (November): 692–98.

Ochberg, F. M.

1980   "Victims of terrorism" (editorial). *Journal of Clinical Psychiatry* 41:72–74.

O'Faolain, Julia, and Lauro Martines

1973   *Not in God's Image: Women in History from the Greeks to the Victorians.* New York: Harper & Row.

Ohr, Jim

1983   Lecture at California State University, Fullerton, April 26. Investigator Ohr is in the Sex Crimes/Child Abuse Detail of the Orange County Sheriffs Department.

Oliveira, Odacir H.

1981a   "Psychological and physical factors of abuse of older people." Excerpts from his speech at the Multidisciplinary Conference on Family Violence, June 11, Long Beach, Calif.

1981b   "Psychological abuse of the elderly." In David Holden and Peggie Carey (eds.), *Abuse of Older Persons,* pp. 115–22. Knoxville: University of Tennessee, School of Social Work.

Oliver, Myrna

1983   "ACLU joins woman's lawsuit over incest." *Los Angeles Times,*
        March 17, pp. II-1, 8.

O'Malley, Helen, Howard Segars, Rubin Perez, Victoria Mitchell, and
George M. Knuepfel

1979   *Elder Abuse in Massachusetts.* Boston: Legal Research for the
        Elderly.

O'Neill, James A., W. F. Meachem, P. P. Griffin, and J. L. Sawyers

1973   "Patterns of injury in the battered child syndrome." *Journal of
        Trauma* 13(4): 332–39.

O'Reilly, Jane

1983   "Wife beating: The silent crime." *Time Magazine,* September 5,
        pp. 23–24, 26.

Orford, Jim

1975   "Alcoholism and marriage: The argument against specialism."
        Journal of Studies in Alcohol 36:1537–63.

Orr, Margaret Terry

1982   "Sex education and contraceptive education in U.S. public high
        schools." *Family Planning Perspectives* 14(6): 304–13.

O'Toole, Richard J., Patrick Turbett, and Claire Nalepka

1981   "Theories of child abuse, professional knowledge, and diagnosis
        of child abuse." Paper presented at the National Conference for
        Family Violence Researchers, Durham, N.H.

Otey, Emeline

1983   "Adolescent victims of rape." *Response* 6(3): 7–8.

Owens, David J., and Murray A. Straus

1975   "Social structure of violence in childhood and approval of vio-
        lence as an adult." *Aggressive Behavior* 1:193–211.

Pagelow, Mildred Daley

1976   "Preliminary report on battered women." Paper presented at the
        Second International Symposium on Victimology, Boston.
1977   "Blaming the victim: Parallels in crimes against women—Rape
        and battering." Paper presented at the annual meeting of the So-

ciety for the Study of Social Problems, Chicago.

1978a "Social learning theory and sex roles: Violence begins in the home." Paper presented at the Ninth World Congress of Sociology, Uppsala, Sweden.

1978b "Secondary battering: Breaking the cycle of domestic violence." In *Hearings before the Subcommittee on Child and Human Development of the Committee on Human Resources,* pp. 484–520. U.S. Senate, 95th Cong., Los Angeles, March 4, and Washington, D.C., March 8. Washington, D.C.: Government Printing Office.

1979 "Personal and material resources of battered women." Paper presented at the annual meeting of the Pacific Sociological Association, Anaheim, Calif.

1980 "Does the law protect the rights of battered women? Some research notes." Paper presented at the annual meeting of the Law and Society Association and the ISA Research Committee on the Sociology of Law, Madison, Wis.

1981a *Woman-Battering: Victims and Their Experiences.* Beverly Hills: Sage.

1981b "Factors affecting women's decisions to leave violent relationships." *Journal of Family Issues* 2(4): 391–414.

1981c "Sex roles, power, and woman battering." In Lee H. Bowker (ed.), *Women and Crime in America,* pp. 239–76. New York: Macmillan.

1981d "Secondary battering and alternatives of female victims to spouse abuse." In Lee H. Bowker (ed.), *Women and Crime in America,* pp. 277–300. New York: Macmillan.

1982a "Children in violent families: Direct and indirect victims." In Shirley Hill and B. J. Barnes (eds.), *Young Children and Their Families,* pp. 47–72. Lexington, Mass.: D. C. Heath.

1982b "Child abuse and delinquency: Are there connections between childhood violence and later deviant behavior?" Paper presented at the Tenth World Congress of the International Sociological Association, Mexico City.

1982c "Mothers, maltreatment of children, and social policy." Paper presented at the Tenth World Congress of Sociology, Mexico City.

Parcell, Stanley R., and Eugene J. Kanin

1976 "Male sex aggression: A survey of victimized college women." Paper presented at the Second International Symposium on Victimology, Boston.

Parnas, Raymond I.

1967 "The police response to the domestic disturbance." *Wisconsin Law Review* (Fall): 914–60.

Pascoe, Delmer J.

1979   "Management of sexually abused children." *Pediatric Annals* 8(5): 44–45, 49–50, 52–53, 57–58.

Pedrick-Cornell, Claire, and Richard J. Gelles

1982   "Elder abuse: The status of current knowledge." *Family Relations* 31(3): 457–65.

Pfohl, Stephen J.

1977   "The 'discovery' of child abuse." *Social Problems* 24(3): 310–23.

Pfouts, Jane H., Janice H. Schopler, and H. Carl Henley, Jr.

1981   "Deviant behaviors of child victims and bystanders in violent families." In Robert J. Hunner and Yvonne Elder Walker (eds.), *Exploring the Relationship Between Child Abuse and Delinquency*, pp. 79–99. Montclair, N.J.: Allanheld, Osmun.

Piven, Frances Fox, and Richard A. Cloward

1971   *Regulating the Poor: The Functions of Public Welfare*. New York: Vintage.

Pizzey, Erin

1974   *Scream Quietly or the Neighbours Will Hear*. Short Hills: Ridley Enslow.

Platt, Anthony M.

1969   *The Child Savers: The Invention of Delinquency*. Chicago: University of Chicago Press.

Pleck, Elizabeth

1977   "Wife-beating in nineteenth century America." Unpublished paper.
1979   "Wife-beating in nineteenth century America." *Victimology* 4(1): 60–74.

Pleck, Elizabeth, Joseph H. Pleck, Marlyn Grossman, and Pauline B. Bart

1978   "The battered data syndrome: A comment on Steinmetz' article." *Victimology* 2(3/4): 680–83.

Pleck, Joseph H., and Jack Sawyer (eds.)

1974   *Men and Masculinity*. Englewood Cliffs, N.J.: Prentice-Hall.

Plumb, J. H.

1972 "Children, the victims of time." In J. H. Plumb (ed.), *In the Light of History,* pp. 153–65. London: Penguin.

Pogrebin, Letty Cottin

1974 "Do women make men violent?" *Ms. Magazine,* November pp. 49–50, 80–89.

Polansky, N. A., C. Hally, and N. F. Polansky

1977 "Definition of neglect." In N. A. Polansky, C. Hally, and N. F. Polansky (eds.), *Profile of Neglect: A Survey of the State of Knowledge,* pp. 3–7. Department of Health, Education, and Welfare. Washington, D.C.: Government Printing Office. Pub. No. (OHDS)77-02004.

Polier, Justine Wise

1941 *Everyone's Children, Nobody's Child.* New York: Charles Scribner's Sons.

Prelgovisk, Jacquelyn, Michael Mend, and Francine Lazara

1977 "The portrayal of feminine gender roles on daytime television commercials." Paper presented at the annual meeting of the Pacific Sociological Association, Sacramento, Calif.

Prescott, James W.

1975 "Abortion or the unwanted child: A choice for a humanistic society." *Humanist* 335(2): 11–15.

Queen's Bench Foundation

1976 *Rape: Prevention and Resistance.* San Francisco: Queen's Bench Foundation.

Quirk-Haas, Renee

1980 "Incest—A tragic family affair." *The Register* (Orange County, Calif.), February 18, p. D-1.

Radbill, Samuel X.

1974 "A history of child abuse and infanticide." In Ray E. Helfer and C. Henry Kempe (eds.), *The Battered Child,* pp. 3–21. 2nd ed. Chicago: University of Chicago Press.

Rathbone-McCuan, Eloise

1980   "Elderly victims of family violence and neglect." *Social Casework* 61(5): 296–304.

Ratterman, Debbie

1982   "Pornography: The spectrum of harm." *Aegis* (Autumn)36:42–48.

Rawlings, Stephen W.

1978   *Perspectives on American Husbands and Wives.* Department of Commerce, Bureau of the Census. Washington, D.C.: Government Printing Office.

1980   *Families Maintained by Female Householders, 1970–79.* Current Population Reports, Special Studies, Series P-23, No. 107. Department of Commerce, Bureau of the Census, Washington, D.C.: Government Printing Office.

The Register (Orange County, Calif.)

1982   "College teacher slain as students watch." April 13, p. A-3.

Reich, J. W.

1978   "Sexual abuse and escape-aggression incidence in juvenile delinquents." Arizona State University, Tempe. Washington, D.C.: Government Printing Office.

Renvoize, Jean

1978   *Web of Violence: A Study of Family Violence.* London: Routledge and Kegan Paul.

Response

1979a   "Using the law to help incestuous families." *Response* 2(5): 1–2.
1979b   "Husband convicted of raping wife." *Response* 3(3): 4. 1980 "Dear dad . . . " *Response* 3(9): 3.
1983   "Federal budget cuts jeopardize domestic violence programs: A national survey report." *Response* 6(3): 1–4, 12–15.

Rhoades, Philip W., and Sharon L. Parker

1981   *Connections between Youth Problems and Violence in the Home: Preliminary Report of New Research.* Belmont: Oregon Coalition Against Domestic and Sexual Violence.

Richardson, D. C., and J. L. Campbell

1980   "Alcohol and wife abuse: The effects of alcohol on attributions of blame for wife abuse." *Personality and Social Psychology Bulletin* 6:51–56.

Richette, Lisa Aversa

1969 *The Throwaway Children*. New York: Delta.
1981 "Infantilization of women in the juvenile justice system." In Ruth Crow and Ginny McCarthy (eds.), *Teenage Women in the Juvenile Justice System: Changing Values,* pp. 104–7. Tucson: New Directions for Young Women.

Ritter, B.

1979 "Adolescent runaway—A national problem." *USA Today* 107(2406): 24–28.

Rizley, Ross, and Dante Cicchetti

1981a "The role of adult psychopathology in child maltreatment and family violence: Preliminary findings from the Harvard University Child Maltreatment Project." Paper presented at the National Conference for Family Violence Researchers, Durham, N.H.
1981b "Theoretical and research issues in the longitudinal study of child abuse and neglect: The Harvard University Child Maltreatment Project." Paper presented at the National Conference for Family Violence Researchers, Durham, N.H.

Rohner, Evelyn C.

1981 "Consequences of parental rejection: A world wide study." Paper presented at the National Conference for Family Violence Researchers, Durham, N.H.

Rohner, Ronald P.

1981 "Parental acceptance-rejection theory: Main features and methodologies." Paper presented at the National Conference for Family Violence Researchers, Durham, N.H.

Rosen, Barbara

1979 "Interpersonal values among child-abusive women." *Psychological Reports* 45(3): 819–22.

Rosenbaum, Alan, and K. Daniel O'Leary

1981 "Marital violence: Characteristics of abusive couples." *Journal of Consulting and Clinical Psychology* 49(1): 63–71.

Rosenberg, Howard

1982   "Violence on TV: A shot in the dark." *Los Angeles Times,* October 20, pp. VI-1, 7.

Rosenfeld, Alvin A.

1977   "Sexual misuse and the family." *Victimology* 2(2): 226–35.

Rosenheim, Margaret K.

1978   "The child and the law." In Edith H. Grotberg (ed.), *200 Years of Children,* pp. 423–79. Department of Health, Education, and Welfare. Washington, D.C.: Government Printing Office. DHEW Pub. No. (OHD)77-30103.

Ross, Robert R.

1980   "Violence in, violence out: Child-abuse and self-mutilation in adolescent offenders." *Juvenile and Family Court Journal* (August): 33–44.

Rouse, Linda P.

1983a   "Models, self-esteem, and locus of control as factors contributing to spouse abuse." (To be published in *Victimology.*)
1983b   "You are not alone: A guide for battered women." (To be published by Learning Publications.)

Rouse, Linda, and Charlotte Coulston

1982   "Spouse abuse: Methods for collecting data from male assailants." Unpublished paper.

Roy, Maria (ed.)

1977   *Battered Women, A Psychosociological Study of Domestic Violence.* New York: Van Nostrand Reinhold.

Rush, Florence

1980a   *The Best Kept Secret: Sexual Abuse of Children.* New York: McGraw-Hill.
1980b   "Child pornography." In Laura Lederer (ed.), *Take Back the Night: Women on Pornography,* pp. 71–81. New York: William Morrow.

Russell, Diana E. H.

1975   *The Politics of Rape: The Victim's Perspective.* Briarcliff Manor, N.Y.: Stein and Day.
1980a   "The prevalence and impact of marital rape in San Francisco." Paper presented at the annual meeting of the American Sociological

Association, New York.

1980b   "Pornography and violence: What does the new research say?" In
         Laura Lederer (ed.), *Take Back the Night: Women on Pornogra-*
         phy, pp. 218–38. New York: William Morrow.

1981   "Preliminary report on some findings relating to the trauma and
         long term effects of intrafamily childhood sexual abuse." Paper
         presented at the National Conference for Family Violence Re-
         searchers, Durham, N.H.

1982   *Rape in Marriage.* New York: Macmillan.

1983   *Rape, Child Sexual Abuse, Sexual Harassment in the Workplace:*
         An Analysis of the Prevalence, Causes, and Recommended Solu-
         tions. Final Report for the California Commission on Crime Con-
         trol and Violence Prevention. To be published by Sage, 1984.

Russell, Diana E. H., and Nicole Van de Ven

1976   *Crimes Against Women: Proceedings of the International Tri-*
         bunal. Millbrae: Les Femmes.

Ryan, Desmond

1981   "Festering hatred for women makes a vile, bloody movie." *Inde-*
         pendent Press-Telegram, Long Beach, Calif., March 6.

Ryan, William

1971   *Blaming the Victim.* New York: Random House.

Sachs, Albie, and Joan Hoff Wilson

1978   *Sexism and the Law: Male Beliefs and Legal Bias.* New York: Free
         Press.

Safilios-Rothschild, Constantina

1978   Excerpts from her presentation at the Ninth World Congress of
         Sociology, Uppsala, Sweden.

Salend, Elyse, Maureen Satz, and Jon Pynoos

1981   "Mandatory reporting legislation for adult abuse." Paper pre-
         pared for presentation at the National Conference on Elder
         Abuse, UCLA/USC Long Term Care Gerontology Center.

Samuels, Fred

1977   "Incest: Not a private family matter." Paper presented at the an-
         nual meeting of Sociologists for Women in Society, American So-
         ciological Association, Chicago.

Sanchez-Dirks, Ruth

1979 "Reflections on family violence." *Alcohol Health and Research World* 4(1): 11–15.

Sanford, Linda Tschirhart

1980 *The Silent Children.* Garden City, N.Y.: Anchor Press.

San Gabriel Valley Tribune

1978 "Not only wives: Study shows husbands battered too." January 29, p. A-5.

Sarafino, Edward P.

1979 "An estimate of nationwide incidence of sexual offenses against children." *Child Welfare* 58(2): 127–34.

Saul, Leon J.

1972 "Personal and social psychopathology and the primary prevention of violence." *American Journal of Psychiatry* 128(12): 1578–81.

Sawhill, Isabel V.

1979 "Comments." In *Census Bureau Conference on Issues in Federal Statistical Needs Relating to Women,* pp. 20–22. Washington, D.C.: Government Printing Office.

Schaie, K. Warner

1982 "America's elderly in the coming decade." In K. Warner Schaie and James Geiwitz (eds.), *Adult Development and Aging,* pp. 3–11. Boston: Little, Brown.

Scheirell, Robert, and Irwin Rinder

1973 "Social networks and deviance: A study of lower class incest, wife beating, and nonsupport offenders." *Wisconsin Sociologist* 10:56–73.

Schneiger, Frank

1978 "Introduction." In *Child Abuse, Neglect and the Family Within a Cultural Context: Special Issue.* pp. 2–3. Department of Health, Education, and Welfare. Washington, D.C.: Government Printing Office. Pub. No. (OHDS)78-30135.

Schuckit, Marc

1980 Testimony at the public hearing on "Nutritional and biochemical influences on aggressive and violent behavior," sponsored by the California Commission on Crime Control and Violence Prevention, San Diego.

Schudson, Charles

1978 Telephone interview. July 20.

Schulder, Diane B.

1970 "Does the law oppress women?" In Robin Morgan (ed.), *Sisterhood is Powerful*, pp. 153–75. New York: Vintage.

Schulman, JoAnne

1980 "The marital rape exemption in the criminal law." *Clearinghouse Review* 13(6).

Schultz, Leroy G.

1960 "The wife assaulter." *Journal of Social Therapy* 6:103–12.

Schwartz, Martin D., and Molly Fitzgerald

1980 "Incest offenders and the law: A profile." Paper presented at the annual meeting of the American Society of Criminology, San Francisco.

Scott, Edward M.

1979 "Violence in America: Violent people and violent offenders." *International Journal of Offender Therapy and Comparative Criminology* 23(3): 197–209.

Scott, P. D.

1973 "Fatal battered baby cases." *Medicine, Science, and the Law* 13(3): 197–206.

1974 "Battered Wives." *British Journal of Psychiatry* 125(November): 433–41.

Scratton, Joan

1976 "Violence in the Family." In Denis J. Madden and John R. Lion, *Rage-Hate-Assault and Other Forms of Violence*, pp. 17–32. New York: Spectrum.

Seal, Marcia

1980 "Parents anonymous works." In *Child Abuse and Development Disabilities: Essays*, pp. 39–40. Department of Health, Education, and Welfare. Washington, D.C.: Government Printing Office.

Pub. No. (OHDS)79-30226.

Seligman, Martin P.

1975   *Helplessness: On Depression, Development, and Death.* San Francisco: W. H. Freeman.

Sendi, Ismail B., and Paul G. Blomgren

1975   "A comparative study of predictive criteria in the predisposition of homicidal adolescents." *American Journal of Psychiatry* 132(4): 423–27.

Sengstock, Mary Cay, and Jersey Liang

1983   "Identifying and characterizing elder abuse." *Human Relations* (August): 7.

Sergent, D. A.

1972   "The lethal situation: Translation of the urge to kill from parent to child." In J. Fawcett (ed.), *Dynamics of Violence,* pp. 105–14. Chicago: American Medical Association.

Service Delivery Assessment for the Office of the Inspector General

1980   *Domestic Violence.* Report for the Department of Health, Education, and Welfare.

Sgroi, Suzanne M.

1975   "Sexual molestation of children: The last frontier in child abuse." *Children Today* 4(3): 18–24, 44.
1977   "'Kids with clap:' Gonorrhea as an indicator of child sexual assault." *Victimology* 2(2): 251–67.
1982   *Handbook of Clinical Intervention in Child Sexual Abuse* (ed.). Lexington, Mass.: D. C. Heath.

Shainess, Natalie

1977   "Psychological aspects of wife-battering." In Maria Roy (ed.), *Battered Women,* pp. 111–19. New York: Van Nostrand Reinhold.

Shamroy, Jerilyn A.

1980   "A perspective on childhood sexual abuse." *Social Work* 25(2): 128–31.

Shapiro, Deborah

1979   *Parents and Protectors: A Study in Child Abuse and Neglect.* New York: Child Welfare League of America.

Shaughnessy, Edward J., with Diana Trebbi

1980   *A Standard for Miller: A Community Response to Pornography.* Lanham: University Press of America.

Shaw, David

1982   "Editors disagree. Crime news: How much is too much?" *Los Angeles Times,* August 11, pp. I-1, 15.

Shields, Nancy M., and Christine R. Hanneke

1983   "Battered wives' reactions to marital rape." In David Finkelhor, Richard J. Gelles, Gerald T. Hotaling, and Murray A. Straus (eds.), *The Dark Side of Families,* pp. 131–48. Beverly Hills: Sage.

Shwed, John A., and Murray A. Straus

1979   "The military environment and child abuse." Unpublished paper.

Silver, Larry B., Christina C. Dublin, and Reginald S. Lourie

1969a   "Child abuse syndrome: The 'grey areas' in establishing a diagnosis." *Pediatrics* 44(4): 594–600.
1969b   "Does violence breed violence? Contributions from a study of the child abuse syndrome." *American Journal of Psychiatry* 126(3): 152–55.

Simmel, Georg

1904   *Conflict and the Web of Group Affiliation.* Glencoe, Ill.: Free Press.

Simon, Rita J.

1981   "American Women and Crime." In Lee H. Bowker (ed.), *Women and Crime in America,* pp. 18–38. New York: Macmillan.

Sink, Frances

1981   "Defining sexual abuse: A research based guide for clinical decision making." Paper presented at the National Conference for Family Violence Researchers, Durham, N.H.

Sloane, Bonnie K.

1982   "In brief." *National NOW Times* 15(4): 5.

Smart, Carol

1977   *Women, Crime and Criminology: A Feminist Critique.* London: Routledge and Kegan Paul.

Smith, Charles P., David J. Berkman, and Warren M. Fraser

1980   *A Preliminary National Assessment of Child Abuse and Neglect and The Juvenile Justice System: The Shadows of Distress.* Reports of the National Juvenile Justice Assessment Centers. Department of Justice. Law Enforcement Assistance Administration. Washington, D.C.: Government Printing Office.

Smith, Peggy, Marvin Bohnstedt, and Kathleen Grove

1982   "Long-term correlates of child victimization: Consequences of intervention." Paper presented at the annual meeting of the Pacific Sociological Association, San Diego.

Smith, Selwyn M.

1975   *The Battered Child Syndrome.* London: Butterworths.

Smith, Selwyn M., and Ruth Hanson

1974   "134 battered children: A medical and psychological study." *British Medical Journal* (3): 666–70.
1975   "Interpersonal relationships and child-rearing practices in 214 parents of battered children." *British Journal of Psychiatry* (127): 513–25.

Smith, Selwyn M., Ruth Hanson, and Sheila Noble

1973   "Parents of battered babies: A controlled study." *British Medical Journal* (4): 388–91.

Snell, John, Richard Rosenwald, and Ames Robey

1964   "The wifebeaters wife." *Archives of General Psychiatry* 11(August): 107–12.

Snowden, Rich

1982   "Working with incest offenders: Excuses, excuses, excuses." *Aegis* 35(Summer): 56–63.

Solnit, Albert J.

1980   "Too much reporting, too little service: Roots and prevention of child abuse." In George Gerbner, Catherine J. Ross, and Edward Zigler (eds.), *Child Abuse, An Agenda for Action,* pp. 135–46. New York: Oxford University Press.

Sommers, Tish

1982   "Concerns of older women: Growing numbers, special needs."

California Commission on the Status of Women, *California Women,* March, pp. 9–12.

Spencer, Joyce

1978   "Father-daughter incest: A clinical view from the corrections field." *Child Welfare* 57(9): 581–90.

Spieker, Gisela

1978   "Family violence and alcohol abuse." Paper presented at the Twenty-fourth International Institute on Prevention and Treatment of Alcoholism, Zurich, Switzerland.

Sproat, Ron

1974   "Working day in a porno factory." *New York Magazine,* March 11.

Stankler, L.

1977   "Factitious skin lesions in a mother and two sons." *British Journal of Dermatology* 97(2): 217–19.

Stannard, Una

1977   *Mrs Man.* San Francisco: Germain.

Star, Barbara

1978   "Comparing battered and nonbattered women." *Victimology* 3(1–2): 32–42.
1980   "Patterns in family violence." *Social Casework* 61(6): 339–46.

Stark, Evan, and Anne Flitcraft

1981   "Therapeutic intervention as a situational determinant of the battering syndrome." Paper presented at the National Conference for Family Violence Researchers, Durham, N.H.

Stark, Evan, Anne Flitcraft, and William Frazier

1979   "Medicine and patriarchal violence: The social construction of a 'private' event." *International Journal of Health Services* 98(3): 461–91.

Stark, Rodney, and James McEvoy, III

1970   "Middle-class violence." *Psychology Today* (November): 52–54, 110–112.

Steele, Brandt F.

1974   "Child abuse: Its impact on society." Paper presented at the Fiftieth Anniversary Celebration of the James Whitcomb Riley Hospital for Children, Indianapolis, Ind.

1976   "Violence within the family." In Ray E. Helfer and C. Henry Kempe (eds.), *Child Abuse and Neglect,* pp. 3–23. Cambridge, Mass.: Ballinger.

Steele, Brandt, and Carl Pollock

1968   "A psychiatric study of parents who abuse infants and small children." In R. Helfer and C. H. Kempe (eds.), *The Battered Child,* pp. 103–48. Chicago: University of Chicago Press.

1974   "A psychiatric study of parents who abuse infants and small children." In R. Helfer and C. H. Kempe (eds.), *The Battered Child,* pp. 89–134. 2nd ed. Chicago: University of Chicago Press.

Steinglass, Peter

1976   "Experimenting with family treatment approaches to alcoholism, 1950–1975: A review." *Family Process* 15(1): 97–123.

Steinmetz, Suzanne

1977a   "Wifebeating, husbandbeating—A comparison of the use of physical violence between spouses to resolve marital fights." In Maria Roy (ed.), *Battered Women,* pp. 63–72. New York: Van Nostrand Reinhold.

1977b   *The Cycle of Violence: Assertive, Aggressive, and Abusive Family Interaction.* New York: Praeger.

1978a   "The battered husband syndrome." *Victimology* 2(3/4): 499–509.

1978b   "Reply to Pleck, Pleck, Grossman and Bart." *Victimology* 2(3/4): 683–84.

1978c   "Battered parents." *Society* 15(5): 54–55.

1980   "Women and violence: Victims and perpetrators." *American Journal of Psychotherapy* 34(3): 334–50.

1981   "Elder abuse." *Aging* 315–16, 6–10.

Steinmetz, Suzanne K., and Murray A. Straus (eds.)

1974   *Violence in the Family.* New York: Harper & Row.

Stember, Clara Jo

1980   "Art therapy: A new use in the diagnosis and treatment of sexually abused children." In Kee MacFarlane, Barbara McComb Jones, and Linda L. Jenstrom (eds.), *Sexual Abuse of Children: Selected Readings,* pp. 59–64. Department of Health, Education, and Welfare. Washington, D.C.: Government Printing Office. Pub. No. (OHDS)78-30161.

Stern, Leo

1979   "The high risk infant and battering." In *Child Abuse and Developmental Disabilities: Essays*, pp. 20–24. Department of Health, Education, and Welfare. Washington, D.C.: Government Printing Office. Pub. No. (OHDS)79-30266.

Stern, Maddi-Jane, and Linda C. Meyer

1980   "Family and couple interactional patterns in cases of father-daughter incest." In Kee MacFarlane, Barbara McComb Jones, and Linda L. Jenstrom (eds.), *Sexual Abuse of Children: Selected Readings*, pp. 83–86. Department of Health, Education, and Welfare. Washington, D.C.: Government Printing Office. Pub. No. (OHDS)78-30161.

Steuer, J., and E. Austin

1980   "Family abuse of the elderly." *Journal of the American Geriatric Society* 28:372–76.

Stibner, Inga-Britt

1981   "Experiences in working with maltreated children." Paper presented at a seminar on the Prevention of Child Abuse and Neglect sponsored by the Swedish Embassies in Ottawa and Washington and the Swedish Information Service, New York.

Stix, Harriet

1981   "Heading off parent-baby conflicts." *Los Angeles Times*, September 28, pp. V-1, 8.

Stoller, Robert

1975   *Perversion: The Erotic Form of Hatred*. New York: Pantheon.

Storch, Gerald

1978   "Claim of 12 million battered husbands takes a beating." *Miami Herald*, April 23, p. G-16.

Straus, Murray A.

1973   "A general systems theory approach to a theory of violence between family members." *Social Science Information* 12(3): 105–25.
1974   "Leveling, civility, and violence in the family." *Journal of Marriage and the Family* 36(February): 13–29.
1976a   "Measuring intrafamily conflict and violence: The CRT scales." Unpublished paper.

1976b "Sexual inequality, cultural norms, and wife-beating." In Emilio C. Viano (ed.), *Victims and Society,* pp. 543–59. Washington, D.C.: Visage Press.

1978 "Wife beating: How common and why?" *Victimology* 2(3/4): 443–58.

1979 "Family patterns and child abuse." *Child Abuse and Neglect* (3): 213–25.

1980a "Stress and physical child abuse." *Child Abuse and Neglect* 4(2): 75–88.

1980b "Social stress and marital violence in a national sample of American families." *Annals of the New York Academy of Sciences* (347): 229–50.

1981a "A reevaluation of the conflict tactics scale violence measures and some new measures." Paper presented at the National Conference for Family Violence Researchers, Durham, N.H.

1981b "Ordinary violence versus child abuse and wife beating: What do they have in common?" Paper presented at the National Conference for Family Violence Researchers, Durham, N.H. This article has since been published: In David Finkelhor, Richard J. Gelles, Gerald T. Hotaling, and Murray A. Straus (eds.), *The Dark Side of Families,* pp. 17–28. Beverly Hills: Sage, 1983.

Straus, Murray, Richard Gelles, and Suzanne Steinmetz

1980 *Behind Closed Doors: Violence in the American Family.* New York: Doubleday.

Sudia, Cecelia Elson

1978 "Historical trends in American family behavior: An essay." In Edith H. Grotberg (ed.), *200 Years of Children,* pp. 41–60. Department of Health, Education, and Welfare. Washington, D.C.: Government Printing Office. DHEW Pub. No. (OHD)77-30103.

Summit, Roland, and JoAnn Kryso

1978 "Sexual abuse of children: A clinical spectrum." *American Journal of Orthopsychiatry* 48(2): 237–51.

Sussman, Alan

1974 "Reporting child abuse: A review of the literature." *Family Law Quarterly* 8(Fall): 245–313.

Sutherland, Edwin H.

1939 *Principles of Criminology.* Philadelphia: J. B. Lippincott.

Sutton, Jo

1978   "Dealing with the problem of the problem of battered women." Unpublished paper.

Swartz, Mimi

1981   "The pass-along problems of parenting: Why does Melissa beat her baby? Because Melissa was once abused herself." *Glamour* (August): 245, 247, 325–27, 329.

Sweet, Jerry J., and Patricia A. Resnick

1979   "The maltreatment of children: A review of theories and research." *Journal of Social Issues* 35(2): 40–59.

Swift, Carolyn

1977   "Sexual victimization of children: An urban mental health center survey." *Victimology* (2): 322–27.

Symonds, M.

1975   "Victims of violence: Psychological effects and after-effects." *American Journal of Psychoanalysis* 355:19–26.

Szinovacz, Maximiliane E.

1983   "Using couple data as a methodological tool: The case of marital violence." *Journal of Marriage and the Family* 45(3): 633–44.

Takanishi, Ruby

1978   "Childhood as a social issue: Historical roots of contemporary child advocacy movements." *Journal of Social Issues* 34(2): 827.

ten Bensel, R. W.

1978   *Training Manual in Child Abuse and Neglect.* Minneapolis: Minnesota Systems Research.

ten Bensel, Robert W., and Jane Berdie

1976   "The neglect and abuse of children and youth: The scope of the problem and the school's role." *Journal of School Health* 46(8): 453–61.

Thomas, Ellen K.

1974   "Child neglect proceedings—A new focus." *Indiana Law Journal* 50(1): 60–81.

Thomas, William I., and Dorothy Swaine Thomas

1928   *The Child in America.* New York: Knopf.

Tierney, Kathleen J.

1982   "The battered women movement and the creation of the wife beating problem." *Social Problems* 29(3): 207–20.

Tierney, Kathleen J., and David L. Corwin

1981   "Exploring intra-familial child sexual abuse: A systems approach." Paper presented at the National Conference for Family Violence Researchers, Durham, N.H.

Tietze, Christopher

1978   "Teenage pregnancies: Looking ahead to 1984." *Family Planning Perspectives* 10(4): 205–7.

Time Magazine

1977   "A killing excuse. Expanding the limits of self defense." November 28, p. 108.
1978   "The battered husbands." March 20, p. 69.
1979a   "Wife rape: The first conviction." October 8, p. 80.
1979b   "Women's war on porn." August 27, p. 64.

Torres, Aida, and Jacqueline Darroch Forrest

1983   "The costs of contraception." *Family Planning Perspectives* 15(2): 70–72.

Truninger, Elizabeth

1971   "Marital violence: The legal solutions." *Hastings Law Journal* 23(1): 259–76.

Tsai, Mavis, and Nathaniel N. Wagner

1977   "Therapy groups for women sexually molested as children." A paper under editorial review.

Turbett, J. Patrick

1979   "Intervention strategies and conceptions of child abuse." *Children and Youth Services Review* 1(Summer): 205–13.

Turner, Jonathan H.

1974   *The Structure of Sociological Theory.* Homewood, Ill.: Dorsey.

Turner, Willie, M., and Lois A. West

1981   "Violence in military families." *Response* 4(5): 1–5.

Udry, J. Richard

1974   *The Social Context of Marriage*. 3d ed. New York: J. B. Lippincott.

Uniform Crime Reports for the United States

1977   *Crime in the United States 1975*. Department of Justice. Washington, D.C.: Government Printing Office.

1977   *Crime in the United States 1976*. Department of Justice. Washington, D.C.: Government Printing Office.

U.S. Bureau of the Census

1978   *Characteristics of the Population Below the Poverty Level: 1976.* Series P-60, No. 115. Department of Commerce. Washington, D.C.: Government Printing Office.

1979   *Social and Economic Characteristics of the Older Population: 1978.* Special Studies. Series P-23, No. 85. Department of Commerce. Washington, D.C.: Government Printing Office.

1980   Current Population Reports, Series P-60, No. 125. *Characteristics of the Population Below the Poverty Level: 1979.* Department of Commerce. Washington, D.C.: Government Printing Office.

1981   Current Population Reports, Series P-23, No. 112. *Child Support and Alimony: 1978.* Department of Commerce. Washington, D.C.: Government Printing Office.

1983   Current Population Reports, Series P-60, No. 138. *Characteristics of the Population Below the Poverty Level: 1981.* Department of Commerce. Washington, D.C.: Government Printing Office.

U.S. Commission on Civil Rights

1978   *Battered Women: Issues of Public Policy.* Washington, D.C.: Government Printing Office.

1982a   *The Federal Response to Domestic Violence.* Washington, D.C.: Government Printing Office.

1982b   *Under the Rule of Thumb. Battered Women and the Administration of Justice.* Washington, D.C.: Government Printing Office.

U.S. Department of Justice

1980   *Intimate Victims: A Study of Violence Among Friends and Relatives.* Bureau of Justice Statistics, Bulletin. Washington, D.C.: Government Printing Office.

1983   *Jail Inmates 1982.* Bureau of Justice Statistics, Bulletin. Washington, D.C.: Government Printing Office.

U.S. Department of Health and Human Services

1980   *Elder Abuse.* Office on Human Development Services. Washington, D.C.: Government Printing Office. DHHS Pub. No. (OHDS)81-20152.

U.S. Department of Labor

1982   *Labor Force Statistics Derived From the Current Population Survey: A Databook, Volume 1.* Bureau of Labor Statistics. Washington, D.C.: Government Printing Office.

U.S. News and World Report

1979   "Battered families: A growing nightmare." January 15, pp. 60–61.

Van Buren, Abigail

1983   "Phone call from runaway eases parents' heartache." *Los Angeles Times,* November 21, p. II-12.

Virkkunen, Matti

1975   "Victim-precipitated pedophillia offences." *British Journal of Criminology* 15(2): 175–80.

Vogue Magazine

1981   "What to wear with what in a season of change." August, pp. 253–61.

Voluntary Legal Services Program

1980   *The Legal Rights of Battered Women in California.* Voluntary Legal Services Program, State Bar of California, San Francisco.

Walker, Lenore E.

1978   "Battered women and learned helplessness." *Victimology* 2(3/4): 525–34.
1979   *The Battered Woman.* New York: Harper Colophon.
1981   "The battered women syndrome study: Results and discussion." Paper presented at the National Conference for Family Violence Researchers, Durham, N.H.
1983   "The battered woman syndrome study." In David Finkelhor, Richard J. Gelles, Gerald T. Hotaling, and Murray A. Straus (eds.), *The Dark Side of Families,* pp. 31–48. Beverly Hills: Sage.

Wardell, Laurie, Dair L. Gillespie, and Ann Leffler

1981   "Science and violence against wives." Unpublished paper.

Warren, Carol A. B.

1979   "Parent batterers: Adolescent violence and the family." Paper presented at the annual meeting of the Pacific Sociological Association, Anaheim, Calif.

Washburn, Carol, and Irene Hanson Frieze

1980   "Methodological issues in studying battered women." Paper presented at the annual Research Conference of the Association for Women in Psychology, Santa Monica, Calif.

Watkins, Carol R.

1982   *Victims, Aggressors and the Family Secret: An Exploration Into Family Violence.* St Paul: Minnesota Department of Public Welfare.

Wayne, Claudia, and Laureen France

1980   "Who will speak for the children? Child sexual assault in the family." *Aegis* (Summer/Autumn): 28–35.

Weber, Max

1964   *The Theory of Social and Economic Organization.* Translated by A. M. Henderson and Talcott Parsons. New York: Free Press.

Weinberg, S. K.

1955   *Incest Behavior.* New York: Citadel.

Weinstock, Edward, Christopher Tietze, Frederick S. Jaffe, and Joy G. Dryfoos.

1976   "Abortion need and services in the United States, 1974–1975." *Family Planning Perspectives* 8(2): 58–69.

Weitzman, Lenore

1981   *The Marriage Contract: Spouses, Lovers, and the Law.* New York: Free Press.

Wellins, Michael

1980   Excerpts from an interview, March 31. Wellins heads the Crisis Intervention Unit of the Police Department of Orange, Calif.

Welsh, Richard

1976   "Severe parental punishment and delinquency." *Journal of Clinical Child Psychology* (Spring).

1977   Welsh's reply to a letter to the editor regarding the above article. *Journal of Clinical Child Psychology* (Spring).

Wertheimer, B. M.

1979   "'Union is power': Sketches from women's labor history." In Jo Freeman (ed.), *Women: A Feminist Perspective,* 2nd ed, pp. 339–58. Palo Alto: Mayfield.

West, D. J.

1980   "A commentary." *British Journal of Criminology* 20(1): 32–34.

West, Lois A.

1980   "Sexually abused children and teen-aged prostitution." *Response* 3(9): 2.

Westin, A.

1970   *Privacy and Freedom.* New York: Atheneum.

Weston, J. T.

1974   "The pathology of child abuse." In R. Helfer and C. H. Kempe (eds.), *The Battered Child,* pp. 61–88. 2nd ed. Chicago: University of Chicago Press.

Wahlstrom, Billie

1981   "Sex stereotypes in advertising: Geritol days and aviance nights." *Interface* 2:39–40. Fullerton: California State University.

White, Kathleen, and Eli H. Newberger

1981   "Pediatric social illness: Classification and misclassification." Paper presented at the National Conference for Family Violence Researchers, Durham, N.H.

Whitman, Grace

1982   "Research links multipersonality disorders to child sexual abuse." *Response* 5(5): 3–4.

Wiley, D. B.

1980   "Elderly becoming the target of their own children's abuse." *The Bulletin* 17(January): 27–28.

Wilson, Elizabeth

1976   *The Existing Research into Battered Women.* Camden Women's Aid: National Women's Aid Federation.

Wilson, Clare, and Jim Orford

1978   "Children of alcoholics. Report of a preliminary study and comments on the literature." *Journal of Studies on Alcohol* 39(1): 121–42.

Wilson, C. A., G. Trammel, B. G. Greer, and G. Long

1977   *An Exploratory Study of The Relationship Between Child Abuse-Neglect and Alcohol-Drug Abuse.* Memphis: Tennessee State Department of Human and Social Services.

Wolfe, David A., John A. Fairbank, Jeffrey A. Kelly, and Drew Bradlyn

1981   "Child abusers' responses to stressful and non-stressful parent/child interactions." Paper presented at the National Conference for Family Violence Researchers, Durham, N.H.

Wolfe, Nancy

1979   "Victim provocation: The battered wife and legal definition of self defense." *Sociological Symposium* 25(Winter): 98–118.

Wolfgang, Marvin E.

1958   *Patterns in Criminal Homicide.* Philadelphia: University of Pennsylvania.
1967a   "A sociological analysis of criminal homicide." In Marvin Wolfgang (ed.), *Studies in Homicide,* pp. 15–28. New York: Harper & Row.
1967b   "Victim-precipitated criminal homicide." In Marvin Wolfgang (ed.), *Studies in Homicide,* pp. 72–87. New York: Harper & Row.

Wolfgang, Marvin E., and Franco Ferracuti

1982   *The Subculture of Violence: Towards an Integrated Theory in Criminology.* Beverly Hills: Sage.

Wolfgang, Marvin E., and R. B. Strohm

1957   "The relationship between alcohol and criminal homicide." *Quarterly Journal of Studies on Alcohol* 17:411–25.

Woods, Laurie

1978   "Litigation on behalf of battered women." *Women's Rights Law Reporter* 5(1): 7–33.

Wright, Janet M.

1982   *Chemical Dependency and Violence: Working With Dually Af-*

fected Families. Madison: University of Wisconsin Hospital and Clinics.

Wright, Janet M., and Judy Popham

1982 "Alcohol and battering: The double bind." *Aegis* 36(Autumn): 53–59.

Yeamans, Robin

1980 "A political-legal analysis of pornography." In Laura Lederer (ed.), *Take Back the Night: Women on Pornography,* pp. 248–51. New York: William Morrow.

Yllo, Kersti

1981 "Types of marital rape: Three case studies." Paper presented at the National Conference for Family Violence Researchers, Durham, N.H.

Yllo, Kersti, and Murray A. Straus

1981 "Interpersonal violence among married and cohabitating couples." *Family Relations* 30(3): 339–47.

Young, Leotyne

1964 *Wednesday's Child: A Study of Child Neglect and Abuse.* New York: McGraw-Hill.

Younger, Evelle J.

1978 *Handbook on Domestic Violence.* Office of the Attorney General. Sacramento: California Department of Justice.

Zalba, Serapio R.

1966 "The abused child: 1. A survey of the problem." *Social Worker* 11(4): 3–16.

Zellman, Gail L.

1982 "Public school programs for adolescent pregnancy and parenthood: An assessment." *Family Planning Perspectives* 14(1): 15–21.

Zelnick, Melvin, Young J. Kim, and John F. Kantner

1979 "Probabilities of intercourse and conception among U.S. teenage women, 1971 and 1976." *Family Planning Perspectives* 11(3): 177–207.

Zuckerman, Michael

1976   "Children's rights: The failure of 'reform.'" *Policy Analysis* 2:371–85.

Zuckerman, Steven

1979   "50 protest at L.A. magazine over ad they say encourages violence to women." *Los Angeles Times*, December 27, p. II-6.

Author Index

Subject Index

abortion, 176–78, 180, 199, 315, 469, 181 n. 5

abused abusers, 225–29, 253, 254

abused husbands. *See* battered husbands

abused wives/women. *See* battered women

abuse-proneness, 164, 209

Abusive Men Exploring New Directions (AMEND), 328, 329

accusers and accused, 164, 166, 171, 254

accidents, 50, 52, 138

adages: "A Man's Home is His Castle," 16, 456; "boys will be boys," 341; "Child abuse begins with the first slap," 206, 220; "I'm going to beat the devil out of you!" 154; "kids will be kids," 341; "monkey see, monkey do," 253; "spare the rod and spoil the child," 149, 204, 343

addictive love, 295, 298

adolescents (*see also* children), 48, 341–58, 460; cycle of violence, 228–44, 344; intervention, 460; juvenile delinquency, 49, 122, 228–44, 255, 460, 462–64; pornography, 356–57, 372, 440–41, 442–43, 460; pregnant/ pregnancy, 176–77, 193, 181 n. 6, 181 n. 7; prostitution, 356–57, 372, 460; runaways, 49, 352–58, 372, 460, 374 n. 7; sexual abuse/sexploitation, 351–53, 354–58, 398–99; teen-agers, 48, 176–78, 193; "throwaways," 356, 460; victims of parents, 75–76, 350–51, 353–56, 372; victims of siblings, 341–53, 372; violent, 21, 341–53

advertisements, 129–32, 394, 436, 441, 444, 449, 142 n. 10, 451 n. 13

AFDC. *See* Aid to Families with Dependent Children

aggression, by children, 341–51; age characteristics, 348–49; attitudes of children to parents, 344–46; criteria for comparison, 343–44; "example of deviance," 373 n. 1; family environment, 344–46; "masculine" aggressiveness, 344; non-aggressive boys, 343–44

Aid to Families with Dependent Children (AFDC), 177, 193, 207, 210, 466–67, 472

alcohol abuse/chemical dependency, 87–97, 103; child maltreatment, neglect, 90–91, 95; children, direct and indirect victims, 91; disavowal theory, 93; disinhibitory theory, 93; intergenerational, 90–91, 96, 104 n. 3; prevention and treatment, 88–89, 96; professional approaches to, 95; spouse abuse, 92, 294, 327; (some) statistics, 88–89, 91, 93–94; stress, 90, 200; time out, 93; violence, 88–90, 105 n. 3; wife abuse, 94–95, 104 n. 2, 105 n. 3; wife murder, 89

Alcoholics Anonymous, 407, 459, 298 n. 2

almshouses, 156–57

Altzheimer's disease, 108

AMEND. *See* Abusive Men Exploring New Directions

American Academy of Pediatrics, 161

American Dream, 102

American Federation of Labor, 208

American Lake Veterans' Hospital, 325, 329

American Psychological Association, 204

Amnesty International, 308

Anger Control Group, 338 n. 9

About the Author

Mildred Daley Pagelow is the author of a book on wife beating and many articles, reviews, and book chapters on a variety of topics: child abuse, delinquency, crime, spousal violence, single mothers, and variant lifestyles. She has written over 30 professional papers and given numerous workshops and talks on family violence before public and professional audiences in this country and abroad.

Dr. Pagelow has testified as an expert witness in courts of law, before congressional committees considering domestic violence legislation, and attended a White House meeting on family violence. She served as consultant to the California Commission on Crime Control and Violence Prevention, and findings from her extensive report were published in the commission's report, *Ounces of Prevention: Toward an Understanding of the Causes of Violence* (1982).

Dr. Pagelow received her doctorate in 1980 from the University of California, Riverside, and is currently teaching sociology and human development at California State University. Her courses include Family Violence, Women and Violence, Sociology of the Family, Human Development over the Life Span, and Marriage and Family Living.